A Quick Guide to Key Topics by Paragraph Number

THE
GREGG
REFERENCE
MANUAL

PART 3. REFERENCES

CONTENTS

DEDICATION

The eighth edition of *The Gregg Reference Manual*
is dedicated to the memory of Roy Poe—an outstanding
editor, publisher, author, educator, mentor, and friend.

Cover photo: © David Bishop/Phototake

Library of Congress Cataloging-in-Publication Data

Sabin, William A.
    The Gregg reference manual/William A. Sabin.—8th ed.
      p. cm.
    Includes index.
    ISBN 0-02-803287-X (hc)—ISBN 0-02-803286-1 (spiral trade)—ISBN
      0-02-803285-3 (spiral text)
     1. English language—Business English—Handbooks, manuals, etc.
  2. English language—Grammar—Handbooks, manuals, etc. 3. English
language—Transcription—Handbooks, manuals, etc. 4. Business
writing—Handbooks, manuals, etc. I. Title.
PE1479.B87S23   1995
808′.042—dc20   95-45701
                                           CIP

Glencoe/McGraw-Hill

A Division of The McGraw·Hill Companies

The Gregg Reference Manual, Eighth Edition

Imprint 1998
Copyright © 1996 by The McGraw-Hill Companies, Inc. All rights reserved. Copyright ©
1992, 1985, 1977, 1970, 1961, 1956 by The McGraw-Hill Companies, Inc. All rights
reserved. Copyright 1951 by The McGraw-Hill Companies, Inc. Printed in the United
States of America. Except as permitted under the United States Copyright Act of 1976,
no part of this publication may be reproduced or distributed in any form or by any
means, or stored in a database or retrieval system, without the prior written permission
of the publisher.

Send all inquiries to:
Glencoe/McGraw-Hill
936 Eastwind Drive
Westerville, Ohio 43081

ISBN 0-02-803287-X (hardcover text edition)

 6 7 8 9 0   003/043   02 01 00 99 98

THE
GREGG
REFERENCE
MANUAL

EIGHTH EDITION

WILLIAM A. SABIN

GLENCOE

McGraw-Hill

New York, New York
Columbus, Ohio
Woodland Hills, California
Peoria, Illinois

PREFACE

The Gregg Reference Manual is intended for anyone who writes, edits, or prepares final copy for distribution or publication. It presents the *basic rules* that apply in virtually every piece of writing, as well as the *fine points* that occur less often but cause no less trouble when they do. This manual offers an abundance of examples and computer-generated illustrations so that you can quickly find models on which to pattern a solution to the various problems you encounter in your communications—from e-mail messages to formal reports. It also provides the rationale underlying specific rules so that you can manipulate the principles of style with intelligence and taste.

FEATURES OF THE NEW EDITION. The eighth edition of *The Gregg Reference Manual* has been revised and enhanced in many ways to span the stylistic demands of business and academic writing.

1. The *basic rules* of grammar, usage, and style—those rules dealing with problems that will arise frequently in your work—have been highlighted in Sections 1–11 with a bold bar beneath certain rule numbers. If you want to reduce the number of things you need to look up, these basic rules are the ones you need to master.

2. The most significant changes in the eighth edition reflect the enormous impact that *computer technology* has had on the way written communications are created and produced.

   - The easy access to *word processing templates* (built-in formats for a variety of documents) greatly simplifies the way in which letters, memos, reports, and other documents may be prepared. Section 13 (dealing with letters and memos) and Section 14 (dealing with reports) provide sample templates along with guidelines showing how to modify these templates for more effective results. Section 13 also discusses the use of *macros* as an efficient way to repeat identical material in various documents (for example, the closing of the letters you write).
   - The eighth edition discusses the special features of word processing software that make it easier for you to create and format footnotes, endnotes, and tables (including a table of contents for a formal report). The manual also discusses the problems that may be created by these timesaving features. For example, Section 16 (on tables) provides a sequence of six illustrations (see ¶1601f) that shows how a table created with the table feature of WordPerfect 6 for Windows can be progressively modified to achieve more readable and more attractive results. Similarly, Section 15 (on notes) shows how you can modify the formats created by the footnote and endnote features of word processing software. Section 14 (on reports) shows how you can use the outline feature to generate a table of contents. Section 13 (on letters and memos) discusses the use of the date feature and the date code feature (¶1314c), the envelope feature (¶¶1388b, 1389g), the label feature (¶1397), and the use of a file name notation to permit quick access to documents stored on disk (¶1372).

- The dramatic increase in the use of e-mail has prompted a detailed discussion of how to create and format e-mail messages (see ¶¶1708–1711). These paragraphs also provide a list of abbreviations often used in e-mail messages. (If you do not know the meaning of ROTFL, turn to ¶1711g at once.)
- Word processing software has made various typeface characteristics readily available. As a result, ¶¶285–290 have been revised to reflect the ways in which you can use italics in place of underlining. Many format guidelines in Part 2 of the manual indicate where boldface type may be used in various documents. Moreover, ¶¶1357e and 1424g show how bullets (for example, ▪ and •) can serve as an attractive alternative to the use of numbers and letters in displayed lists. Finally, the eighth edition discusses the use of special character sets that offer ready access to symbols not provided on a typewriter keyboard. (See ¶¶413 and 1502f for examples.)
- Section 7 (on spelling) now discusses the use of electronic dictionaries and the need to expand them with your own list of frequently used words, expressions, and names. Both Section 7 and Section 12 discuss the use of spell checkers and alert readers to the dangers of relying excessively on this electronic tool to detect all spelling errors. (See ¶1202b for examples of the kinds of spelling mistakes no spell checker will catch.) In addition, Section 9 (on word division) discusses the use of automatic hyphenation and the use of a justified right margin.
- The discussion of editing and proofreading in Section 12 has been expanded to deal with a new phenomenon in many offices. Executives who used to have assistants produce the documents they had drafted or dictated increasingly have to handle these functions themselves. Accordingly, Section 12 now discusses how editing and proofreading have become an integral part of the overall writing process. Section 12 also provides an expanded discussion of editing and proofreading at the computer.
- Section 12 now includes notes on how to prepare alphabetized lists of names on a computer in accordance with the latest rules from ARMA (the Association of Records Managers and Administrators). (See ¶¶1209, 1210, 1213, and 1218.)

3. Many people today inhabit two worlds—the business world and the academic—either as full-time students who are also working or as full-time employees who are going to school to upgrade their skills or train for a new career or enrich their personal lives. Such people are bound to encounter different requirements, different formats, and different styles in whatever written work they produce. The eighth edition of *The Gregg Reference Manual* acknowledges this situation in a number of ways.

- Section 17 expands the existing coverage of résumés (¶¶1712–1713) by providing new guidelines and illustrations on how to write and format letters to apply for a job, follow up on a job interview, and accept a job. (See ¶¶1714–1717.)
- Sections 14 and 15 provide guidelines for academic reports, notes, and bibliographies wherever they differ from what is done in business writing. (See, for example, ¶¶1412–1414, 1508b, 1534c).
- New to this edition is the treatment of outlines, whether you use the outline feature of a word processing program to produce them or you format the outlines yourself. (See ¶¶1718–1723.)

4. The text and illustrations have been changed throughout the eighth edition to reflect the new words, phrases, and acronyms that are continually entering the language. (If you do not understand why certain high-level decisions were made in your organization, you may need to consult ¶522 for the acronym BOGSAT.) Computer technology is the major source of new words and phrases these days. The glossary of computer terms in Appendix B has been expanded and updated to include state-of-the-art terms such as *cyberspace, file transfer protocol* (an Internet term), *hypertext, motherboard, mouse elbow, newbie,* and *SYSOP.* The glossary also includes terms that reflect the wacky humor of computer users. If you do not know the meaning of *Easter egg, notwork, sneakernet,* or *smiley* [for example, :-)], turn at once to Appendix B.

5. Questions and suggestions from users of the previous edition have had a major impact on what has been added to the eighth edition.* For example:

   • How do you address a married couple when the wife does not wish to have her identity submerged in her husband's name? (See ¶1323d.)
   • When do you use such terms as *Hispanic, Latino,* and *Chicano?* (See the entry on ethnic references in Section 11.)
   • How do you construct a footnote or endnote for a quotation taken from a CD-ROM source? (See ¶1519.)
   • What is a *mailstop code* and where does it go in an inside address? (See ¶1338d.)

AN OVERVIEW OF THE ORGANIZATION OF THE EIGHTH EDITION. This edition of *The Gregg Reference Manual* consists of 18 sections and 2 appendixes, organized in three parts:

Part 1 (Sections 1–11) deals with grammar, usage, and the chief aspects of style—punctuation, capitalization, numbers, abbreviations, plurals and possessives, spelling, compound words, and word division.

Part 2 (Sections 12–18) deals with the techniques and procedures for creating and formatting all kinds of written communications–letters, memos, reports, manuscripts, tables, agendas, minutes, itineraries, fax cover sheets, e-mail, outlines, and résumés and other employment communications. It also provides detailed guidelines on forms of address.

Part 3 (Appendixes A and B) provides a glossary of grammatical terms and a glossary of computer terms.

OTHER COMPONENTS OF THE EIGHTH EDITION. Accompanying the eighth edition of *The Gregg Reference Manual* are the following components:

   • **Two sets of worksheets.** The availability of two sets of worksheets now affords more flexibility in meeting users' needs.

   Worksheets on Grammar, Usage, and Style. This all-new set of worksheets focuses on the basic rules presented in Sections 1–11. These worksheets have been

---

*Because of the immense value that readers' comments have in ensuring that each new edition is truly responsive to users' needs, I invite you to submit your questions and suggestions to me through the publisher's office in Westerville, Ohio. Please see the copyright page for the full address.

designed to build three critical skills. First, they will familiarize you with the potential problems that frequently occur in any material that you create or produce. Second, these worksheets will direct you to the appropriate rules in Sections 1–11 so that later on, when you encounter similar problems in your own work, you will know where to look. Third, they will sharpen your ability to apply the rules correctly under many different circumstances.

This set of worksheets begins with a diagnostic survey of your editing skills at the outset. Then, after you complete a series of twenty-one worksheets, you will encounter a parallel survey at the end that will show you how much your editing skills have improved. In most of the intervening worksheets, rule numbers are provided alongside the answer blanks so that you can quickly locate the answer you need to solve the problem at hand. At the end of each of these worksheets is an editing exercise that requires you to identify and correct the implanted errors on your own, without the help of rule numbers alongside. Interspersed within this sequence of worksheets are three editing surveys that will help you integrate all the things you have been learning in the preceding worksheets.

Comprehensive Worksheets. This set of worksheets has been designed to build the same three skills as the worksheets described above. However, this comprehensive set draws on material from the entire manual and not simply from Sections 1–11. Moreover, these worksheets deal with problems of formatting letters, memos, and other business documents. *Comprehensive Worksheets* begins with a diagnostic survey and then, after a series of thirty-one worksheets, concludes with a parallel survey that allows you to demonstrate how much your editing skills have increased. Interspersed within this sequence of worksheets are four editing surveys that will help you integrate all the things you have been learning up to that point.

- **Instructor's Guide to the Worksheets.** The *Instructor's Guide to the Worksheets for The Gregg Reference Manual* provides strategies showing how to make the best use of the two sets of worksheets. This guide also provides full-size keys to the *Worksheets on Grammar, Usage, and Style* and to the *Comprehensive Worksheets.*
- **Transparency Masters.** This new component provides over 120 transparency masters designed to reinforce the basic rules of grammar, usage, and style as well as models for formatting letters, memos, reports, and other documents.

As you make your own survey of the eighth edition of *The Gregg Reference Manual,* you will want to give special attention to the basic rules that deserve further study; these are the rules that you will encounter in everyday situations, the rules you need to have at your command. You will also want to develop a passing acquaintance with the fine points of style. It is sufficient simply to know that such rules exist. Then, when you need them, you will know where to find them. Finally, you will want to take note of special word lists, sentence patterns, and illustrations that could be useful to you later on. If you find out now what the manual provides, you will know what kind of help you can count on in the future. And what is more important, you will be able to find what you are looking for faster.

Acknowledgments
A book of this type cannot be put together without the help and support of many people. To my colleagues in Glencoe/McGraw-Hill, to my many good

friends in business and office education, and to the teachers and professional business training consultants who allowed me to observe their classes and their training programs, I want to express a deep feeling of gratitude. I also need to thank the countless teachers, administrators, students, and professionals who all helped me—by their questions and suggestions—to see what was missing from the seventh edition of *The Gregg Reference Manual* and how things could be made better in this new edition.

There is not enough space to acknowledge all of these people individually. However, I must single out a few people by name in order to thank them for their extraordinary help and support.

To Nina Watson, my gifted editor, for her masterful work on the manuscript and for her constant commitment to the highest standards of publishing.

To Price Voiles, my close friend and colleague in the Gregg Division for many years, for his indispensable help in revising Sections 12–17.

To those people who reviewed the seventh edition of *The Gregg Reference Manual,* for their helpful suggestions on how to make the eighth edition better:

Judy Diffley, Washburn University, Topeka, Kansas
Alice M. Fuller, Los Angeles Unified School District, Anaheim Hills, California
Linda Jacobson, Communication Consultants, Inc., East Northport, New York
Susan Jacobson, Air Products and Chemicals, Inc., Allentown, Pennsylvania
Donna Malloy, Air Products and Chemicals, Inc., Allentown, Pennsylvania
Barbara McGovern, WD Communications, Holmdel, New Jersey
Judy Sanchez, Leary Technical Center, Tampa, Florida

To those individuals who reviewed the eighth edition of *The Gregg Reference Manual,* for their helpful comments:

Janet Aubuchon, McDonnell-Douglas Corporation, St. Louis, Missouri
Mona J. Casady, Southwest Missouri State University, Springfield, Missouri
Elise Earl, Tulsa Junior College, Metro Campus, Tulsa, Oklahoma
Katie Forbish, Dominion Business School, Roanoke, Virginia
Christopher M. "Jay" Hopper, Pryor Resources, Shawnee Mission, Kansas
Margie Kinzley, Davenport College—Lansing Campus, Lansing, Michigan
Frank Moody, Tompkins/Cortland Community College, Dryden, New York
Marilyn Price, Kirkwood Community College, Cedar Rapids, Iowa
Ginny Richerson, Murray State University, Murray, Kentucky
Carol Rodriguez, Johnson County Community College, Overland Park, Kansas
Karen Schneiter, Rochester Community College, Rochester, Minnesota
Carolyn Schuler, State Farm Insurance, Bloomington, Illinois
Nelda Shelton, Tarrant County Junior College, Fort Worth, Texas
Janet Smith, Procter & Gamble Company, Cincinnati, Ohio
Thelma Spurgeon, Forsyth Technical Community College, Winston-Salem, North Carolina
JoAnn Witz, Bryant & Stratton Business Institute, Cicero, New York

To the people who gave me special assistance with computer terminology and formats:

Anne Block, Profound Consulting, Indianapolis, Indiana
Christopher Schaber, president, FSCreations, Inc., Cincinnati, Ohio
Nancy Stonick and David Dillingham, Worldwide Church of God, Pasadena, California

To those professional colleagues who have been especially generous with their help and support on the eighth edition—and in many cases on earlier editions as well:

Olive Collen, editorial consultant, Little Neck, New York

Marie Longyear Dunphy, McGraw-Hill author and former director of communications, McGraw-Hill, Woodstock, New York

Jane deLeeuw, editorial consultant, Montclair, New Jersey

Geraldine Fahey, director of information management and publishing systems, Warren, Gorham & Lamont, New York, New York

Beverley Funk, Glencoe author and former instructor, Everett Community College, Everett, Washington

Dr. Helen Green, Glencoe author and professor emerita of business education, Michigan State University, East Lansing, Michigan

Eva Lewis, editorial consultant, El Cajon, California

Russell Lewis, editorial consultant, El Cajon, California

Mary Madden, former supervisor of business and distributive education, New Orleans Public Schools, New Orleans, Louisiana

Gloria Mahoney, business training consultant, Hollywood, Florida

Ann Miller, business training consultant, WD Communications, Newark, Delaware

Sibyl Parker, publisher, technical, reference, and new media, McGraw-Hill, New York, New York

Dr. Robert Poland, professor emeritus of business and marketing education, Michigan State University, East Lansing, Michigan

Barry Richman, senior vice president, Knight-Ridder Information Inc., Mountain View, California

Arlene Ross, office administration curriculum coordinator, Heald Colleges, San Francisco, California

Linda Stern, editorial consultant, New York, New York

Dr. Jeffrey Stewart, Glencoe author and professor emeritus of education, Virginia Polytechnic Institute and State University, Blacksburg, Virginia

Merle Wood, Glencoe author and former supervisor, business education, Oakland Unified School District, Lafayette, California

Mark Yannone, CEO, Perfect Data, Peoria, Arizona

And to my family—to my mother, who gave me my first sense of what language could accomplish (and a good deal more); to Margaret, John, Kate, Chris, and Jim, from whom I have gained much wisdom; and ultimately to my wife Marie, who has made the journey worth the struggle—my thanks and my love.

William A. Sabin

HOW TO LOOK THINGS UP

Suppose you were writing to someone in another department:

> I understand you are doing a confidential study of the Bronson matter. May I please get an advance copy of your report [At this point you hesitate. Should this sentence end with a period or a question mark?]

This is the kind of problem that continually comes up in any type of written communication. How do you find a fast answer to such questions? In this manual there are several ways to proceed.

USE THE INDEX. The surest approach, perhaps, is to check the detailed index at the back of the manual (16 pages, with over 2000 entries). For example, any of the following entries will lead you to the right punctuation for the problem sentence above:

> Periods, **101–109**   Question marks, **110–118**   Request, punctuation
> . . .   . . .   of, **103**
> at end of requests, **103**   at end of requests, **103, 113**

In each entry the **boldface number** refers to the proper rule, ¶103. (If you look up ¶103, you will find that a question mark is the right punctuation for the sentence in question.)

In almost all of the index entries, references are made to specific rule numbers so that you can find what you are looking for fast. In a few cases, where a page reference will provide a more precise location (for example, when a rule runs on for several pages), a page number is given in lightface type. Suppose you were confronted with this problem:

> If you compare the performance records of Catano, Harris, and Williams, you won't find much difference (*between/among*) them.

The index will show the following entries:

> *among* (see *between*, 257–258)   **or**   *between–among*, 257–258

The rule beginning on page 257 indicates that *between* is correct in this situation.

USE A FAST-SKIM APPROACH. Many users of reference manuals have little patience with detailed indexes. They would rather open the book and skim through the pages until they find what they are looking for. If you prefer this approach, you will find several features of this manual especially helpful.

- The brief topical index on the inside front cover indicates the key paragraphs for each major topic.
- At the start of each section except the glossaries, you will find a detailed list of all the topics covered in that section. This list will help you quickly focus on the rule or rules that pertain to your problem. Suppose the following problem came up:

> The only point still at issue is whether or not new *Federal* [or is it *federal*?] legislation is required.

The index on the inside front cover indicates that ¶¶301–365 deal with the topic of capitalization. A fast skim of the outline preceding ¶301 will turn up the entry *Names of Government Bodies* (¶¶325–330). If you turn to that set of rules, you will find in ¶328 that *federal* is the proper form.

- Extensive cross-references have also been provided throughout the manual so that you can quickly locate related rules that could prove helpful. Some cross-references take this form: *See ¶324;* others may read *See also ¶324.* The form *See ¶324* indicates that ¶324 contains significant information that adds to or qualifies the rule you are currently reading; the word *See* suggests that you really ought to pursue the cross-reference before making a decision. The form *See also ¶324* carries a good deal less urgency. It indicates that you will find some additional examples in ¶324 and perhaps a restatement of the rule you are currently reading but nothing altogether new. In effect, *See also* suggests that you don't have to pursue the cross-reference if you don't want to—but it couldn't hurt.

PLAY THE NUMBERS. There is still a third way to find the answer to a specific problem—and this is an approach that will grow in appeal as you become familiar with the organization and the content of the manual. From a fast inspection of the rule numbers, you will observe that they all carry a section number as a prefix. Thus Section 3 (on capitalization) has a "300" series of rules—from 301 to 365; Section 4 (on number style) has a "400" series—from 401 to 470; and so on. Once you become familiar with the section numbers and the section titles, you can find your way around fairly quickly, without reference to either index, by using the section number tabs. For example, you are about to write the following sentence:

> *43* percent of the questionnaires have now been returned. [Or should it be
> "*Forty-three* percent of the questionnaires . . ."?]

If you know that matters of number style are treated in Section 4, you can quickly turn to the pages tabbed "4," where a fast skim of the outline of topics at the start of the section will lead you to the answer in ¶421. (*Forty-three percent* is the right answer in this instance.)

A familiarity with the section numbers and section titles can also save you time when you are using the index. If your index entry lists several different paragraph numbers, you can often anticipate what the paragraphs will deal with. For example, if you want to know whether to write *5 lb* or *5 lbs* on a purchase order, you might encounter the following entry in the index:

> Weights, **429–431, 535–538, 620**

If you know that Section 6 deals with plurals, you will try ¶620 first.

LOOK UP SPECIFIC WORDS. Many of the problems that arise deal with specific words. For this reason the index provides as many entries for such words as space will permit. For example, in the following sentence, should *therefore* be set off by commas or not?

> It is(,) *therefore*(,) essential that operations be curtailed.

A check of the index will show the following entry:

> *therefore,* **122, 138–142, 178**

A reading of the rules in ¶141 will indicate that no commas should be used in this sentence. If you ask the same question about another specific word and do not find it listed as a separate entry in the index, your best approach will be to check the index under "Comma" and investigate the most promising references or make a direct scan of the comma rules in Section 1 until you find the answer you are looking for.

If you are having difficulty with words that look alike and sound alike—*gibe* and *jibe* or *affect* and *effect*—turn directly to ¶719. For other troublesome words and phrases, consult Section 11.

ESSAYS

The six brief essays that follow deal with a number of points of style that cause great difficulty for those who work with words. Out of this consideration of specific problems, these essays attempt to draw broader conclusions about the nature of style and the art of tailoring one's use of language to fit the needs of each situation.

MASTERING NUMBER STYLE: ONE (OR 1?) APPROACH

A number of years ago, while making a presentation on the subject of style, I asked the audience to select the preferable form in each of the following pairs of examples:

$87,525	OR	eighty-seven thousand five hundred and twenty-five dollars
$4.8 trillion	OR	$4,800,000,000,000
4:30 p.m., January 19	OR	half after four o'clock, on the nineteenth of January

No one could see any use for the forms in the second column. Those in the first column were far easier to read and simpler to write and were clearly to be preferred in business writing. However, after some discussion, we tended to agree that Tiffany's had had the right idea in a recent ad, where beneath a picture of an elegant diamond necklace was the legend "Eighty-seven thousand five hundred and twenty-five dollars." Somehow, we felt, if they were going to charge that elegant a price, the least they could do was spell it out. Moreover, we tended to agree that a liberal in fiscal matters might readily dismiss the federal debt as "only $4.8 trillion," whereas a fiscal conservative who wanted to emphasize the enormity of the amount might well have written "The federal debt now stands at $4,800,000,000,000" and thereby have forced upon us a sense of the magnitude of the amount by making us calculate it for ourselves. Finally, we agreed that we would much rather be married at "half after four o'clock, on the nineteenth of January" than at "4:30 p.m., January 19."*

These, admittedly, are extreme examples of occasions on which an unusual number style could be justified, but they tend to throw light on the more customary style for expressing numbers and on the notion of style in general. At the

---

*One dissenter indicated that she simply wanted to get married and didn't much care how the invitations read.

very least, these examples suggest that style should not be thought of as a rigid set of rules but rather as a set of principles for adjusting one's means of expression to fit a particular set of circumstances. We express our style in clothes through a varied wardrobe that suits the needs not only of everyday situations but of formal and informal occasions as well. It is the impoverished person who meets every situation with the same set of clothes. By the same token, it is an impoverished writer who meets all situations with a rigid set of rules. The writer of the Tiffany ad, who chose words instead of figures to express an amount of money, in this instance had some true sense of how to vary style for best effect.

Manipulating principles of style for specific effect ought not to be a random, hit-or-miss exercise but should proceed from some coherent notion about style itself. In the case of numbers, an intelligent control of number style proceeds from an awareness of the difference in effect that results from using figures or words to express numbers.

Figures are big (like capital letters); when used in a sentence, they stand out clearly from the surrounding tissue of words. As a result, they are easier to grasp on first reading, and they are easier to locate for subsequent reference. Thus whenever quick comprehension and fast reference are important (and this is true of most business writing), figures are to be preferred to words.

But the very characteristics of figures that make them preferable to words can be disadvantageous in certain circumstances. Figures stand out so sharply against a background of words that they achieve a special prominence and obtain a special emphasis. Not all numbers warrant that kind of emphasis, however, and in such cases words are preferable to figures. Keep in mind, too, that figures have the conciseness and the informality of an abbreviation. Thus the more formal the occasion, the more likely one is to spell numbers out (as in the wedding announcement cited on page xv).

Given these basic differences between using figures and using words, it is quite clear why figures are preferred in ordinary business letters. These are typically straightforward communications that pass between business firms and their suppliers or their customers, containing frequent references to price quotations, quantities, shipping dates, credit terms, and the like. Frequently, these numbers represent data that has to be extracted from the letter and processed in some way: they may have to be checked against other numbers or included in some computation or simply transferred to another document. The advantage of figures to words in these ordinary cases is so clear that the point does not need to be argued.

But there is another kind of business writing in which the writer is not typically dealing with the workaday transactions of the business. It may be a special promotion campaign with an air of elegance and formality; it may be a carefully constructed letter with special stylistic objectives in mind; or it may be a special report which involves community relations and will have a wider distribution than the normal technical business report. This kind of writing tends to occur more often at the executive level, and it tends to occur in the more creative departments of a business (such as sales promotion, advertising, public relations, and customer relations). In this kind of writing, numbers don't occur very frequently; when they do, they are usually expressed in words.

$\mathbf{A}$s a response to the different needs posed by these two kinds of writing, there are two basic number styles in use today. Both use figures and words but in different proportions. The *figure style* uses figures for all numbers above 10, whether exact or approximate; the *word style* spells out all numbers up through 100 and all numbers above 100 that can be expressed in one or two words (such as *twenty-five hundred*).

As a practical matter, your immediate job may require you to use only the figure style. However, your next job may call for the use of the word style. And if you are working and going to school at the same time (as more and more people are these days), you will probably find yourself following one style for office work and another for your academic work. Under these circumstances, if you grasp the basic difference between using words and figures to express numbers, you will be better able to decide how to proceed in specific situations without having to consult a style manual each time. In any case, keep the following ideas in mind:

1. There are no absolute rights and wrongs in number style—only varying sets of stylistic conventions that people follow in one set of circumstances or another. There are, however, effective differences in using words or figures, and you should take these differences into account.
2. Before deciding on which number style to follow for a given piece of writing, first determine the basic objective of the material. If the material is intended to communicate information as simply and as briefly as possible, use the *figure style*. If the material is of a formal nature or aspires to a certain level of literary elegance, use the *word style*.
3. Having decided on a basic style, *be consistent in context*. When related numbers occur together in the same context and according to the rules some should go in figures and some should go in words, treat these related numbers all the same way.
4. Treat an approximate number exactly the same way you would treat an exact number. If you would write *50 orders,* then you should also write *about 50 orders.* (If the figure 50 looks too emphatic to you when used in an approximation, the chances are that you should be using the word style—and not just for approximate numbers but throughout.)
5. In areas where the style could go either way (for example, *the 4th of June* vs. *the fourth of June* or *9 o'clock* vs. *nine o'clock*), decide in accordance with your basic style. Thus if you are following the figure style, you will automatically choose *the 4th of June* and *9 o'clock.*
6. In expressions involving ages, periods of time, and measurements, use figures whenever these numbers have technical significance or serve as measurements or deserve special emphasis; otherwise, use words. (For example, *you receive these benefits at 65, the note will be due in 3 months, the parcel weighs over 2 pounds;* but *my father will be sixty-five next week, that happened three months ago, I hope to lose another two pounds this week.*)
7. Use figures in dates (*June 6*) and in expressions of money (*$6*), except for reasons of formality or special effect (as in the wedding announcement or the Tiffany ad). Also use figures with abbreviations and symbols and in percentages, proportions, ratios, and scores.
8. Use words for numbers at the beginning of a sentence, for most ordinals (*the third time, the twentieth anniversary*), and for fractions standing alone (*one-third of our sales*).

All manuals of style (including this one) include many more than eight rules. They give exceptions and fine points beyond those just summarized. Yet for all practical purposes these eight rules—and the philosophy that underlies them—will cover almost every common situation. Just remember that the conventions of number style were meant to be applied, not as an absolute set of dogmas, but as a flexible set of principles that help to fit the form to the occasion. When manipulated with intelligence and taste, these principles of style can enhance and support your broader purposes in writing.

A Fresh Look at Capitalization

The rules on capitalization give most people fits. First of all, there are a seemingly endless number of rules to master; second, the authorities themselves don't agree on the rules; and third, the actual practices of writers often don't agree with any of the contradictory recommendations of the authorities.

A frequent solution is to pretend that disagreements on capitalization style don't exist; instead, people are given one fixed set of rules to be applied under all circumstances. Yet all too many people never do remember the full complement of rules, and those they do remember they apply mechanically without comprehension. As a result, they never get to see that capitalization can be a powerful instrument of style if it is shrewdly and knowingly used.

To understand the basic function of capitalization, you should know that capitalization gives importance, emphasis, and distinction to everything it touches. That's why we capitalize the first word of every sentence—to signify emphatically that a new sentence has begun. That's why we capitalize proper nouns like *Marianne* and *California* and *April*—to indicate distinctively that these are the official names of particular people, places, or things. Moreover, when we take a word that normally occurs as a common noun and capitalize it, we are loading into that word the special significance that a proper noun possesses. The *fourth of July*, for example, is just another day in the year; when it signifies a national holiday, it becomes the *Fourth of July*. In exactly the same way, the *white house* that stands at 1600 Pennsylvania Avenue becomes the *White House* when we think of it, not as one of many white houses, but as the residence of the *President*, who is himself something special compared to the *president* of a business firm.

This process of giving special significance to a common noun and transforming it into a proper noun explains why we capitalize names coined from common nouns—for example, the *Windy City*, the *First Lady*, the *Sunflower State*, the *Stars and Stripes*, *Mother's Day*, and the *Industrial Revolution*. And it also explains why manufacturers who coin trade names try to register them whenever possible. As long as they can get legal protection for these names, they are entitled to capitalize them. The owners of such trade names as *Coke, Kleenex, Frisbee, Dacron, Levi's,* and *Xerox* are likely to take legal action against anyone who uses such words generically. They are determined to protect their rights zealously because they don't want to lose the distinctive forcefulness that a capitalized noun possesses. In this respect they demonstrate an understanding of the function of capitalization that few of us can compete with.

Once it becomes clear that capitalization is a process of loading special significance into words, it's easier to understand why capitalization practices vary so widely. Individual writers will assign importance to words from their own vantage points. The closer they are to the term in question, the more inclined they will be to capitalize it. Thus it is quite possible that what is important to me (and therefore worthy of capitalization) may not be important to you and thus will not be capitalized.

One could cite any number of examples to prove the point. A retail merchant will take out full-page ads so that he can exclaim in print about his *Year-End Clearance Sale.* The rest of us can respect his right to capitalize the phrase, but we are under no obligation to share his enthusiasm for what is, after all, just another *year-end clearance sale.* In legal agreements, as another example, it's customary to load such terms as *buyer* and *seller* with the significance of proper nouns and thus write, "The *Buyer* agrees to pay the *Seller . . .*"; in all other contexts, however, this kind of emphasis would not be warranted.

When it is understood that it is appropriate to capitalize a given term in some contexts but not necessarily in all contexts, a lot of the agony about capitalization disappears. Instead of trying to decide whether *Federal Government* or *federal government* is correct, you should recognize that both forms are valid and that depending on the context and the importance you want to attach to the term, one form will be more appropriate to your purpose than another. If you are a federal employee, you are very likely to write *Federal Government* under all circumstances, out of respect for the organization that employs you. If you are not a government employee, you are more likely to write *federal government* under ordinary circumstances. If, however, you are writing to someone connected with the federal government or you are writing a report or document in which the federal government is strongly personified, you will probably choose the capitalized form.

By the same token, you need not agonize over the proper way to treat terms like *advertising department, finance committee,* and *board of directors.* These are well-established generic terms as well as the official names of actual units within an organization. Thus you are likely to capitalize these terms if they refer to units within your own organization, because you would be expected to assign a good deal of importance to such things. But you wouldn't have to capitalize these terms when referring to someone else's organization unless for reasons of courtesy or flattery you wanted to indicate that you considered that organization important. (For example, "I would like to apply for a job as copywriter in your Advertising Department.") Moreover, when writing to outsiders, you should keep in mind whether or not they would assign the same importance you do to units within your organization. In an interoffice memo you would no doubt write, "David Walsh has been appointed to the Board of Directors"; in a news release intended for a general audience, you would more likely write, "David Walsh has been appointed to the board of directors of the Wilmington Corporation."

This switch in form from one context to another will appear surprising only to those who assume that one form is intrinsically right and the other intrinsically wrong. Actually, there are many more familiar instances of this kind of flexibility. We normally write the names of seasons in lowercase (for example, *spring*), but when the season is meant to be personified, we switch to uppercase (*Spring*). The words *earth, sun,* and *moon* are normally expressed in lowercase, but when these terms are used in the same context with proper names like *Mars* and *Venus,* they also become capitalized. Or we write that we are taking courses in *history* and *art,* but once these terms become part of the official names of courses, we write *History 101* and *Art 5C.*

Once you come to view capitalization as a flexible instrument of style, you should be able to cope more easily with ambiguous or conflicting rules. For example, one of the most troublesome rules concerns whether or not to capitalize titles when they follow a person's name or are used in place of the name. According to many authorities, only the titles of "high-ranking" officials and dignitaries should be capitalized when they follow or replace a person's name. But how high is high? Where does one draw the line? You can easily become confused at this point because the authorities as well as individual writers have drawn the line at various places. So it helps to understand that the answer to how high is high will depend on where you stand in relation to the person named. At the international level, a lot of us would be willing to bestow initial caps on the *Queen of England,* the *Pope,* the *Secretary General of the United Nations,* and people of similar eminence. At the national level in this country, many of us would agree on honoring with caps the *President,* the *Vice President,* Cabinet members (such as the *Attorney General* and the *Secretary of Defense*), the heads of federal agencies and bureaus (such as the *Director* or the *Commissioner*), but probably not lower-ranking officials in the national government. (However, if you worked in Washington and were closer to those lower-ranking people, you might very well draw the line so as to include at least some of them.) At the state level, we would probably all agree to honor the *Governor* and even the *Lieutenant Governor,* but most of us would probably refer to the *attorney general* of the state in lowercase (unless, of course, we worked for the state government or had dealings with the official in question, in which case we would write the *Attorney General*). Because most people who write style manuals are removed from the local levels of government, they rarely sanction the use of caps for the titles of local officials; but anyone who works for the local government or on the local newspaper or has direct dealings with these officials will assign to the titles of these officials a good deal more importance than the writers of style manuals typically do. Indeed, if I were writing to the mayor of my town or to someone in the mayor's office, I would refer to the *Mayor.* But if I discuss this official with you in writing, I would refer to the *mayor;* in this context it would be bestowing excessive importance on this person to capitalize the title.

What about titles of high-ranking officials in your own organization? They certainly are important to you, even if not to the outside world. Such titles are usually capped in formal minutes of a meeting or in formal documents (such as a company charter or a set of bylaws). In ordinary written communications, however, these titles are not—as a matter of taste—usually capitalized, for capitalization would confer an excessive importance on a person who is neither a public official nor a prominent dignitary. But those who insist on paying this gesture of respect and honor to their top executives have the right to do it if they want to. (And in some companies this gesture is demanded.)

In the final analysis, the important thing is for you to establish an appropriate capitalization style for a given context—and having established that style, to follow it consistently within that context, even though you might well adopt a different style in another context. Though others may disagree with your specific applications of the rules, no one can fault you if you have brought both sense and sensitivity to your use of capitalization.

THE COMMA TRAUMA

Consider the poor comma, a plodding workhorse in the fields of prose—exceedingly useful but like most workhorses overworked. Because it can do so many things, a number of writers dispense the comma to cure their ailing prose the way doctors dispense aspirin: according to this prescription, you take two at frequent intervals and hope the problem will go away. Other writers, having written, stand back to admire their handiwork as if it were a well-risen cake—and for the final touch they sprinkle commas down upon it like so much confectioner's sugar. And one writer I know, when pushed to desperation, will type several rows of commas at the bottom of her letter and urge you to insert them in the copy above wherever you think it appropriate.

It's too bad that commas induce a trauma in so many writers. Despite the seemingly endless set of rules that describe their varied powers, commas have only two basic functions: they either separate or set off. Separating requires only one comma; setting off requires two.

The separating functions of the comma, for the most part, are easy to spot and not hard to master. A separating comma is used:

1. To separate the two main clauses in a compound sentence when they are joined by *and, but, or,* or *nor.*
2. To separate three or more items in a series (*Tom, Dick, and Harry*)—unless all the items are joined by *and* or *or* (*Bob and Carol and Ted and Alice*).
3. To signify the omission of *and* between adjectives of equal rank (as in a *quiet, unassuming personality*).
4. To separate the digits of numbers into groups of thousands (*30,000*).

Writers get into trouble here mostly as a result of separating things that should not be separated—for example, a subject and a verb (*Bob, Carol, Ted, and Alice✓decided to see a movie*) or an adjective and a noun (*a quiet, unassuming✓ personality*). Yet this is not where the comma trauma begins to set in.

The real crunch comes with the commas that set off. These are the commas that set off words, phrases, or clauses that (1) provide additional but nonessential information or (2) are out of their normal order in the sentence or (3) manage, in one way or another, to disrupt the flow of the sentence from subject to verb to object or complement. What makes it so difficult for people to use these commas correctly is that they have a hard time analyzing the difference between an expression used as an essential element in one context and as a nonessential element in another.

Consider the following example. I would venture that most people have been taught to punctuate the sentence exactly as it is given here:

> It is, therefore, essential that we audit all accounts at once.

To be specific, they have probably been taught that *therefore* is always nonessential when it occurs within a sentence and that it must therefore always be set off by commas. What they probably have not been taught is that commas that set off (unlike commas that separate) usually signal the way a sentence should sound when spoken aloud. For example, if I were to read the foregoing sentence aloud the way it has been punctuated, I would pause slightly at the sign of the first comma and then let my voice drop on the word *therefore:*

IT IS, therefore, ESSENTIAL . . .

Now if this is the reading that is desired, then the use of commas around *therefore* is quite correct. Yet I would venture that most people would read the sentence this way:

It is THEREFORE essential . . .

letting the voice rise on *therefore* to give it the special emphasis it demands. If this is the desired reading, then commas would be altogether wrong in this sentence, for they would induce a "nonessential" inflection in the voice where none is wanted.

If people have been mechanically inserting commas around *therefore* and similar words where commas do not belong, it is because they have not been encouraged to listen to the way the sentences are supposed to sound. Certainly once you become aware of the differences in inflection and phrasing that accompany essential and nonessential elements, it becomes a lot easier for you to distinguish between them and to insert or omit commas accordingly. Given this kind of approach, sentences like the following pair are simple to cope with.

Please let me know *if I have remembered everything correctly.*

He said he would meet us at three, *if I remember correctly.*

Although it would be possible, by means of a structural analysis, to establish why the first *if* clause is essential and why the second is not, you would do well to be guided by the inflection implied in each sentence. In the first instance, the voice arcs as it bridges the gap between *Please let me know* and *if I have remembered everything correctly.* In the second instance, the inflectional arc embraces only the first part of the sentence, *He said he would meet us at three;* then comes a slight pause followed by the *if* clause, which is uttered in a much lower register, almost as if it were an afterthought.

As you gain confidence in your ability to detect the inflectional patterns characteristic of essential and nonessential expressions, you should have no difficulty in picking your way through a variety of constructions like these:

I must report, *nevertheless,* that his work is unsatisfactory.
I must *nevertheless* report that his work is unsatisfactory.

The location, *I must admit,* is quite attractive.
The location is one *I must admit* I find attractive.

There are, *of course,* other possible answers to the problem.
It is *of course* your prerogative to change your mind.

This awareness of inflectional patterns is especially helpful when it comes to coping with appositives, a frustrating area in which the use or omission of commas often seems illogical. When the appositive expression is truly nonessential, as in:

Ed Brown, *the president of Apex,* would like to meet you.

the customary pause and the characteristic drop in voice are there. And when the appositive expression is essential, as in phrases like *the year 1996* and *the term* "*recommend,*" you can hear the single inflectional arc that embraces each group of words in one closely knit unit. You can also hear the same continuous arc in the phrase *my wife Marie.* By all that is logical, the name *Marie* should be set off by commas because it is not needed to establish which of my wives I'm speaking about; unlike an Arabian sheik, I have only one wife. Yet according to today's standards, *my wife Marie* is considered good form. Although not essential to the meaning, the name *Marie* is treated as if it were essential because of what style manuals call "a very close relationship with the preceding words." Although it is difficult, if not impossible, to state in concrete terms what constitutes "a very close relationship," you can tell by the sound when it exists. There is a subtle but very real difference in the phrases *my sister Florence* and *my sister, Florence Stern.* When the full name is given, there tends to be a slight pause after *sister* and the voice tends to drop while uttering the full name. Yet it is not safe to conclude that adding the second name accounts for the difference in the inflection, for when one speaks of *the composer John Cage* or *the author John Fowles,* one hears the same inflectional pattern as in *my wife Marie* or *the year 1996.* So in the case of appositives, it is wise to be wary of simple generalizations and to listen attentively in each case to the way the expression ought to sound.

In stressing, as I have, the significance of inflection and phrasing as a guide to the use of commas, I do not mean to suggest that one can punctuate by sound alone and can safely ignore structure and meaning. What I am suggesting is that in a number of cases, such as those I have cited, an awareness of the sound of sentences can help you grasp relationships that might otherwise be obscure.

There are many other problems involving the comma that should be discussed here, but someone else (Ogden Nash, perhaps) will have to take over . . .

And now if you'll excuse me comma

I must lie down and have my trauma . . . ,

THE PLIGHT OF THE COMPOUND ADJECTIVE—OR, WHERE HAVE ALL THE HYPHENS GONE?

The hyphen, it grieves me to report, is in trouble. Indeed, unless concerted action is taken at once, the hyphen is likely to become as extinct as the apostrophe in *ladies aid*. The problem can be traced to two dangerous attitudes that are afoot these days. One is revolutionary in tone; its motto: "Compound adjectives, unite! You have nothing to lose but your hyphens." The other attitude reflects the view of the silent majority. These are the people who don't pretend to know how to cope with the "hyphen" mess; they just earnestly wish the whole problem would quickly disappear. It may now be too late to reverse the long-range trend. For the present, however, the hyphen exists—and anyone who expects to work with words at an acceptable level of proficiency needs to come to terms with the noble beast. Here, then, is a last-ditch effort to make sense out of an ever-changing and possibly fast-disappearing (but not-soon-to-be-forgotten) aspect of style.

As a general rule, the English language depends largely on word order to make the relationships between words clear. When word order alone is not sufficient to establish these relationships, we typically resort to punctuation. It is in this context that the hyphen has a service to offer. The function of the hyphen is to help the reader grasp clusters of words—or even parts of words—as a unit. When a word has to be divided at the end of a line, the hyphen signifies the connection between parts. Whenever two or more words function as a unit but cannot (for one reason or another) be written either as a solid word or as separate words, the hyphen clearly establishes the relationship between these words and prevents a lapse in comprehension.

If hyphens are typically required in compound adjectives, it is because there is something "abnormal" about the word order of such expressions. Other kinds of modifiers, by contrast, do not require hyphens. For example, if I write about "a *long, hard* winter," I am actually referring to a winter *that will be long and hard;* so I need a comma—not a hyphen—to establish the fact that *long* and *hard* modify *winter* independently. If I write about "a *long opening* paragraph," the word order makes it clear that *opening* modifies *paragraph* and that *long* modifies the two words together; so no punctuation is needed to establish the fact that I'm speaking about "*an opening paragraph that is long.*"

However, if I write about "a *long-term* loan," an entirely different relationship is established between the elements in the modifier. I am not speaking of a *loan* that is *long* and *term*, nor am I referring to a *term loan* that is *long*. I am speaking about a loan "that is to run for a *long term* of years." The words *long-term* (unlike *long, hard* or *long opening*) have an internal relationship all their own; it is only as an integral unit that these two words can modify a noun. Thus a hyphen is inserted to establish this fact clearly.

For a better understanding of the internal relationship that exists between the elements in a compound adjective, one has to go back to its origins. A compound adjective is actually a compressed version of an adjective phrase or clause. For example, if I describe a product as carrying "a *money-back* guarantee," I am actually talking about "a guarantee *to give you your money back if you are not satisfied with the product.*" Or if I refer to "a *take-charge* kind of guy," I am really speaking of "the kind of guy *who always takes charge of any situation he finds himself in.*" One can easily see from these examples why compound adjectives are so popular, for these expressions are usually a good deal crisper and livelier than the phrases or clauses they represent. These examples give further evidence of why a hyphen is needed. In each case we have zeroed in on a couple of words, we have wrenched them out of context and out of their normal order in a descriptive phrase or clause, and we have inserted them before a noun as if they were an ordinary adjective—a role these two words were never originally designed to play. Deprived of all the other words that would clearly establish the relationship between them, these elements require a hyphen to hold them together.

The two factors of compression and dislocation are all the justification one needs to hyphenate a compound adjective. However, there are often additional clues to the need for a hyphen. In the process of becoming a compound adjective, the individual words frequently undergo a change in form: "a contract for *two years*" becomes "a *two-year* contract"; a blonde with *blue eyes*" becomes "a *blue-eyed* blonde." Sometimes the words are put in inverted order: "lands *owned by the government*" becomes "*government-owned* lands." Sometimes the elements undergo a change both in form *and* in word order: "an employee *who works hard*" becomes "a *hard-working* employee"; "bonds *exempt from taxation*" becomes "*tax-exempt* bonds." The change in form or the inversion in word order is an additional signal that you are in the presence of a compound adjective and ought to hyphenate it.

If the compound adjective is so simple to understand in theory, why is it so difficult to handle in practice? A good deal of the problem can be traced to that neat but now-discredited rule, "Hyphenate compound adjectives when they precede the noun but not when they follow the noun." It was indeed a very neat rule but not a very precise one. Let's take it apart and see why.

It is quite true that compound adjectives should be hyphenated when they occur *before* a noun—for the most part. There's the catch—"for the most part." The exceptions seem to occur in such a random, hit-and-miss, now-and-then, flip-a-coin, make-it-up-as-you-go-along fashion that one begins to lose respect for the rule. Yet there is a very definite pattern to the exceptions. Keep in mind that the hyphen serves to hold a cluster of words together as a unit. If, through some other means, these words make themselves clearly recognizable as a unit, the hyphen is superfluous and can be omitted. There are at least three such situations where a hyphen is unnecessary: when the compound modifier is a proper name, when it is a well-recognized foreign expression, and when it is a well-established compound noun serving as a compound adjective. Let's look at some samples.

If I speak of "a *Madison Avenue* agency," the capital *M* and *A* virtually guarantee that the expression will be quickly grasped as a unit. And if I talk about "a *bona fide* contract," the reader will recognize this Latin expression as a unit without the help of a hyphen. By the same token, terms like *social security, life insurance,* and *high school* are so well established as compound nouns that when they are used as adjectives, we immediately grasp such expressions as a unit, without the support of any punctuation.

If no hyphen is needed in "*social security* benefits," one may well ask why a hyphen is required in "*short-term* benefits." After all, words like *short term* and *long range* are adjective-noun combinations that closely resemble *social security, life insurance,* and *high school.* Why hyphenate some and not others? The reason is this: Words like *short term, long range,* and *high level* don't have any standing as compound nouns in their own right; they do not represent a concept or an institution (as terms like *social security* and *life insurance* do). Therefore, these words require a hyphen to hold them together when they occur before a noun.

Once you grasp the difference between *social security* and *short-term* as compound adjectives, you can use these two expressions as touchstones in deciding how to handle other adjective-noun combinations. With a principle like this in hand, you don't have to engage in profound analysis to resolve the "hyphen problem." Consider a random list of examples such as these:

a *red letter* day	a *white collar* worker
a *civil service* test	a *real estate* agent
income tax refund	*word processing* software
long distance calls	*high level* decisions

The expressions *civil service, income tax, real estate,* and *word processing* all resemble *social security,* since they stand for well-known concepts or institutions; therefore, as compound adjectives they can all be written without hyphens. However, *red-letter, long-distance, white-collar,* and *high-level* are much more like *short-term* and should have a hyphen.

So much for compound adjectives before the noun. When they occur *after* the noun, according to the traditional rule, they should not be hyphenated. Yet this traditional formulation is somewhat misleading. If we aren't supposed to hyphenate a "compound adjective" when it follows a noun, it's for the simple reason that the words in question no longer function as a compound adjective—they are playing a normal role in a normal order. It's one thing to use hyphens in the expression "an *up-to-date* report," for a prepositional phrase doesn't normally belong before a noun. However, if I said "This report is *up to date,*" there would be no more justification for hyphenating here than there would be if I said "This report is *in good shape.*" Both expressions—*in good shape* and *up to date*—are prepositional phrases playing a normal role in the predicate.

However, if the expression still exhibits an abnormal form or inverted word order in the predicate, it is still a compound adjective—and it must still be hyphenated. For example, whether I speak of "*tax-exempt* items" or say "these items are *tax-exempt,*" the hyphen must be inserted because regardless of where it appears—*before* or *after* the noun—the expression is a compressed version of the phrase "exempt from taxation."

There are at least four kinds of compound adjectives that must always be hyphenated *after* as well as *before* the noun (because of inverted word order or change of form). These compound adjectives consist of the following patterns:

noun + adjective (*duty-free*)

noun + participle (*interest-bearing*)

adjective + participle (*soft-spoken*)

adjective + noun + *ed* (*old-fashioned*)

Once you learn to recognize these four patterns, you can safely assume that any compound adjective that fits one of these patterns must always be hyphenated, no matter where it falls in a sentence.*

It does no good to pretend that compound adjectives are an easy thing to master. They aren't. And for that very reason people who have to cope with these expressions need more guidance than they get from a simple "hyphenate before but not after" kind of rule. In the final analysis, what becomes of the hyphen over the long run is of little consequence. What does matter is that we express ourselves with precision, verve, and grace. If the hyphen can help us toward that end, why not make use of it?

---

*There is only one worm in this rosy apple: some of the words that fit these patterns are now acceptably spelled as one word. For example:

Normal Pattern	Exception
water-repellent	waterproof
time-consuming	timesaving
half-baked	halfhearted
clear-sighted	clearheaded

THE SEMICOLON; AND OTHER MYTHS

In certain circles that I move in, the fastest way I know to start a quarrel is to attack the semicolon. If I knocked my friends' politics or sneered at their religious beliefs, they would simply smile. But attack their views on the semicolon and they reach for a breadknife. Why this particular mark of punctuation should excite such intense passion escapes me. The semicolon has always been a neurotic creature, continually undergoing an identity crisis. After all, it is half comma and half period, and from its name you would think it is half a colon. It is hardly any wonder, then, that a lot of people are half crazy trying to determine who the semicolon really is and what its mission in life is supposed to be.

In the course of this brief essay, I am going to explore three myths that have grown up over the years about the semicolon and about some other marks of punctuation.

Myth No. 1: If either clause in a compound sentence contains an internal comma, use a semicolon (not a comma) before the coordinating conjunction that connects the clauses. According to this line of reasoning, it is all right to use a comma in a compound sentence like this:

> The regional meeting in Salem has been canceled, but all other meetings will go on as scheduled.

However, if I use commas for a lesser purpose within either clause (for example, by inserting *Oregon* after *Salem* and setting if off with commas), then the comma before the conjunction must be upgraded to a semicolon.

> The regional meeting in Salem, Oregon, has been canceled; but all other meetings will go on as scheduled.

It is harsh, I concede, to dismiss this rule as a myth when it has been taught for years in various classes and various texts. But the unhappy fact is that outside those classes and those texts, almost no one punctuates that way anymore. The trouble with using a semicolon in such sentences is that it creates a break that is too strong for the occasion. It closes down the action of the sentence at a point where the writer would like it to keep on going. So contemporary writers see nothing wrong with using commas simultaneously to separate clauses and to perform lesser functions within the clauses—unless, of course, total confusion or misreading is likely to result. But in most cases it doesn't. In the following sentence, commas are used both *within* clauses and *between* clauses without any loss of clarity and also without any loss of verbal momentum.

> On March 14, 1997, I wrote to your credit manager, Mr. Lopez, but I have not yet heard from him.

This simultaneous use of commas within and between clauses may look offensive to anyone accustomed to the traditional rule. The fact remains that we have been using commas for both purposes in *complex* sentences all along, and it has never occasioned any comment.

> Although I wrote to your credit manager, Mr. Lopez, on March 14, 1997, I have not yet heard from him.

It should be clearly understood that the use of a semicolon before the conjunction in a compound sentence is not wrong. If you want a strong break at that point, the semicolon can and should be used. But you ought to know that the reason for using it is the special effect it creates—and not the presence of internal commas. For example:

> I have tried again and again to explain to George why the transaction had to be kept secret from him; but he won't believe me.

Myth No. 2: Always use a semicolon before an enumeration or an explanation introduced by *for example, namely,* or *that is.* In many cases this rule is quite true, but in other cases either a colon or a comma is better suited to the occasion. Let's look at some examples.

> There are several things you could do to save your business (?) namely, try to get a loan from the bank, find yourself a partner with good business judgment, or pray that your competitor goes out of business before you do.

If you put a semicolon before *namely*, you will close the action down just when the sentence is starting to get somewhere. Because the first part of the sentence creates an air of anticipation, because it implicitly promises to reveal several ways of saving the business, you need not a mark that closes the action down but one that supports the air of anticipation. Enter the colon.

The colon is one of the underrated stars in the firmament of punctuation. It would be more widely used, perhaps, if its sound effects were better understood. The colon is the mark of anticipation. It is a blare of trumpets before the grand entrance; it is the roll of drums before the dive off the 100-foot tower. It marks the end of the buildup and gets you ready for "the real thing." Thus:

> There are several things you can do to save your business: namely, try to get a loan . . .

Consider this example, however:

> Always express numbers in figures when they are accompanied by abbreviations; for example, *4 p.m., 8 ft.*

The first part of this sample sentence expresses a self-contained thought. If the sentence ended right there, the reader would not be left up in the air. The examples that follow are unexpected, unanticipated, added on almost as an afterthought. We're glad to have them, but they aren't anything we were counting on. The semicolon here is quite appropriate; it momentarily closes down the action of the sentence after the main point is expressed.

In other situations a comma may be the best mark to use before *namely, for example,* or *that is.* Consider this sentence as an example:

> Do not use quotation marks to enclose an *indirect quotation*, that is, a restatement of a person's exact words.

In this case, a semicolon would be inappropriate before *that is* because it would close off the action just as we were about to get a definition of a term within the main clause. Moreover, a colon would be inappropriate because it would imply that the sentence up to that point was a buildup for what follows—and that is not true in this case. Here all that is needed is a simple comma to preserve the close relationship between the term *indirect quotation* and the explanatory expression that follows it.

Myth No. 3: When a polite request is phrased as a question, end it with a period. This is another statement that does not, unfortunately, always hold true. In fact, once a period is used at the end of some requests, they no longer sound very polite. I once posted the following note in my home: "Will you please close the door." My children knew that was not really a polite request but a firm parental command. When they chose to ignore it, I amended the sign to read, "Will you please close the door!" (I was relying on the exclamation point to carry the full force of my exasperation.) That approach failed too, so I tried a new tack in diplomacy, amending the sign once again: "Will you please close the door?" My children now knew they had broken my spirit. They now sensed in the sign a pleading note, a petitioning tone, the begging of a favor. They also knew that now I was asking them a real yes-or-no question (or at least I was creating the illusion of asking). Then, in the paradoxical way that children have, once they knew they had the chance to say no, they began to answer my question with tacit affirmations, tugging the door after them on the way out or kicking it shut behind them on the way in.

My problems with my kids are, of course, my own, but learning how to express and punctuate polite requests tends to be a problem for all of us. Consider, for a moment, the wording of those three signs, alike in all respects except for the final mark of punctuation. The version that ends with a period is really a quiet but nonetheless firm demand. There is no element of a question in it at all. The voice rises in an arc and then flattens out at the end on a note of resolution. In the version that ends with an exclamation point, the voice rises in a higher arc and resounds with greater intensity and force of feeling, but it, too, comes down at the end—this time with something of a bang. In the final version, the one with the question mark, the voice starts on an upward curve and then trails off, still on an upward note. Three different readings of the same words, each with a different impact on the reader—all evoked by three different punctuation marks at the end.

Once you become sensitive to the effects produced by these marks of punctuation, handling polite requests becomes quite simple. All you have to do is say the sentence aloud and listen to the sound of your own voice. If you end the sentence with your voice on an upward note, you know that a question mark is the right punctuation to use. If your voice comes down at the end, you know that you need a period. (And if you really feel forceful about it, you probably want an exclamation point.)

If there is any potential danger in so simple a rule, it is this: we sometimes express our requests orally as flat assertions ("Will you please do this for me.") when, as a matter of good taste and good manners, we ought to be asking a question ("Will you please do this for me?").

Now it is true that in the normal course of events we all make demands on one another, and though we tack on a "Will you please" for the sake of politeness, these are still demands, not questions. As long as your reader is not likely to consider them presumptuous, it is appropriate to punctuate these demands with periods:

Will you please sign both copies of the contract and return the original to me.

May I suggest that you confirm the departure time for your flight before you leave for the airport.

Will you please give my best regards to your family.

As opposed to these routine demands, there is the kind of polite request that asks the reader for a special favor. Here, if you really want to be polite, you will punctuate your request as a question so as to give your reader the chance to say no.

> May I please see you sometime next week?

> May I please get an advance copy of the confidential report you are doing?

> Will you please acknowledge all my correspondence for me while I'm away?

In these cases you are asking for things that the reader may be unable or unwilling to grant; therefore, you ought to pose these requests as questions. (If you try reading them as statements, you will observe how quickly they change into peremptory demands.) Suppose, however, that these requests were addressed to your subordinates. Under those conditions you would have the right to expect your reader to make the time to see you, to supply you with an advance copy of the confidential report, and to handle your mail for you; therefore, you would be justified in ending these sentences with periods. But even when you have this authority over your reader, you ought to consider the alternative of asking. The inspired public official who replaced the "Keep Off the Grass" signs with a simple "PLEASE?" understood people and how they like to be talked to. If a question mark will get faster results or establish a nicer tone, why not use it?

There are other myths that one could discuss, but these three are sufficient to permit me to make one central point. Mastery over the rules of punctuation depends to a considerable extent on cultivating a sensitivity to the way a sentence moves and the way it sounds.

Punctuating by ear has come to be frowned on—and with much justification—for it has come to mean punctuating solely by feeling, by instinct, by intuition, without much regard for (or knowledge of) the structure of the language and the function of punctuation. Yet the solution, it seems to me, is not to abandon the technique of punctuating by ear but to cultivate it, to develop in yourself a disciplined sense of the relationship between the sound and the structure and the mechanics of language. Many authorities on language, if pressed, have to concede that they often consider first whether a thing sounds right or looks right: only then do they utter a pronouncement as to why it is right. If they rely on their ears for this kind of assurance, then why don't you cultivate the same skill?

RE ABBREVS.

Sensitive environmentalists will tell you that emissions from smokestacks and automobile exhaust pipes are not the only forms of pollution that are potentially deadly to human beings. All about us are forces of depersonalization that continually menace the human touches that have previously graced our lives. Most of us have become reconciled to being numerical entities on computer printouts. Those of us who remember those elegant telephone exchanges (*PLaza 9, ASprinwall 7*) have had to reconcile ourselves to their numerical replacements (*759, 277*).

But new forms of pollutants continually appear on the atmospheric scene. We are beginning to choke—some of us—on the fog of initials and abbreviations and "memorable" acronyms that are intended to identify worthwhile examples of human endeavor. One gem is *HURRAH* (*H*elp *U*s *R*each & *R*ehabilitate *A*merica's *H*andicapped), an instance where a dignified cause is demeaned by a fatuous label, a hollow cheer, an irrelevant salute. Perhaps in self-defense I ought to found a group called *HELP* (*H*elp *E*liminate *L*inguistic *P*ollution).

To put matters in perspective, it may help to think of abbreviations as belonging to the same class of objects as instant coffee, powdered eggs, and TV dinners. They don't take up much space and they're great when you're in a hurry, but they never have the taste of the real thing. Abbreviations are always appropriate in highly expedient documents (such as invoices, purchase orders, low-level interoffice memos, and routine correspondence), where the emphasis is on precise communication of data in the briefest possible space without concern for style or elegance of expression. But in other kinds of writing, where some attention is given to the *effect* to be made on the reader, a more formal style prevails—and under these circumstances only certain kinds of abbreviations are acceptable.

Some that are always acceptable, even in the most formal contexts, are those that precede or follow personal names (*Mr., Mrs., Ms., Jr., Sr., Ph.D., Esq.*), those that are part of an organization's legal name (*Inc., Ltd., Co.*), those used in expressions of time (*a.m., p.m., PST, EDT*), and a few miscellaneous expressions (such as *B.C.* and *A.D.*).

Those venerable Latin abbreviations *etc., i.e., e.g.,* and the like are usually acceptable, but in writing that aspires to a certain elegance or formality they ought to be replaced, not by the full Latin expressions, but rather by the English expressions *and so forth* (or *and the like*), *that is, for example,* or appropriate equivalents.

Organizations with long names are now commonly identified by their initials in all but the most formal writing—*AFL-CIO, UNICEF, FBI, CBS.* Even the initials *U.S.* are now acceptable in all but the most formal writing when used in the names of federal agencies (such as the *U.S. Department of Labor*); however, using the initials by themselves (as in *throughout the U.S.*) is bad form.

Abbreviations of days of the week, of names of months, of geographic names, and of units of measure are appropriate only in business forms, in correspondence that is clearly expedient, and in tables where space is tight.

Although it may seem troublesome knowing *when* to abbreviate, it is often more troublesome knowing *how* to abbreviate. There are so many variations in style (involving the use of caps or small letters, the use or omission of periods, and the use or omission of internal space) that it is often difficult to find an authoritative source to follow. (The tenth edition of *Merriam-Webster's New Collegiate Dictionary*, for example, omits virtually all periods from its list of abbreviations, as if this were now the commonly accepted practice. Merriam-Webster, of course, uses periods with many of the abbreviations that appear in the main text. See ¶503, note.)

Here are a few safe guidelines:

1. An all-capital abbreviation made up of the initials of several words is normally written without periods and without internal space (for example, *IBM, UAW, BPOE, SEC, IQ*). The only major exceptions are geographic names (such as *U.S.A.*), academic degrees (such as *B.A., M.D.*), and a few odd expressions (such as *A.D., B.C.,* and *P.O.*).

2. A small-letter abbreviation that consists of the initials of several words is normally written *with* a period after each initial but *without* space after internal periods (for example, *a.m., e.g.*).

3. When an abbreviation can be styled in all caps (*COD, FOB*) or in small letters (*c.o.d., f.o.b.*), reserve the use of all caps for business forms and similar documents where the blatant look of the capitals will not matter.

4. When an abbreviation stands for several words and consists of more than initials, insert a period and a space after each element in the abbreviation (for example, *Lt. Col., op. cit.*). Academic degrees, however, are an exception: write them *with* the periods but *without* internal space (for example, *Ph.D., Ed.D., LL.B.*).

5. A person's initials are now usually written without periods and space (as in *JFK*) unless they are part of the full name (as in *J. F. Kennedy*).

So much, in brief, for abbreviations. Useful devices on many occasions, but—except for an *R.S.V.P.* delicately scripted in the lower left corner of a formal invitation—not very elegant.

THE
GREGG
REFERENCE
MANUAL

PART 1

GRAMMAR, USAGE, AND STYLE

SECTION 1
PUNCTUATION: MAJOR MARKS

———————

THE PERIOD (¶¶101–109)

THE QUESTION MARK (¶¶110–118)

THE EXCLAMATION POINT (¶¶119–121)

THE COMMA (¶¶122–175)

1

The Comma (*Continued*)

The Semicolon (¶¶176–186)

The Colon (¶¶187–199)

Punctuation marks are the mechanical means for making the meaning of a sentence easily understood. They indicate the proper relationships between words, phrases, and clauses when word order alone is not sufficient to make these relationships clear.

One important caution about punctuation: If you find it particularly hard to determine the appropriate punctuation for a sentence you have written, the chances are that the sentence is improperly constructed. To be on the safe side, recast your thought in a form you can handle with confidence. In any event, do not try to save a badly constructed sentence by means of punctuation.

Section 1 deals with the three marks of terminal punctuation (the period, the question mark, and the exclamation point) plus the three major marks of internal punctuation (the comma, the semicolon, and the colon). All other marks of punctuation are covered in Section 2.

THE PERIOD

At the End of a Statement or Command

101 Use a period to mark the end of a sentence that makes a statement or expresses a command. (Leave two spaces between the period and the start of the next sentence. For complete guidelines on spacing, see ¶299.)

> My friend Price tells me that his computer mouse has been eating his icons.
>
> John W. Hirsch, president of Seglin Controls Inc., has announced the company's plan to acquire Parker Associates before the end of this year.
>
> I question the need to cut advertising and promotion expenses at this time.
>
> All monthly expense reports must be submitted no later than the 10th of the following month.
>
> Make sure that Kate gets to the airport by 10 a.m. (The period that marks the end of the abbreviation also serves to mark the end of the sentence.)

102 **a.** Use a period to mark the end of an *elliptical* (condensed) expression that represents a complete statement or command. Elliptical expressions often occur as answers to questions or as transitional phrases.

> Yes.   No.   Of course.   Indeed.   By all means.
>
> Enough on that subject.   Now, to proceed to your next point.

b. Do not confuse elliptical expressions with sentence fragments. An elliptical expression represents a complete sentence. A sentence fragment is a word, phrase, or clause that is incorrectly treated as a separate sentence when it ought to be incorporated with adjacent words to make up a complete sentence.

> Great news! The laser printer arrived yesterday. After we had waited for six weeks. (*Great news* is an elliptical expression; it represents a complete sentence, *I have great news. After we had waited for six weeks* is a sentence fragment, incorrectly treated as a sentence in its own right; this dependent clause should be linked with the main clause that precedes it.)
>
> REVISED: Great news! The laser printer arrived yesterday, after we had waited for six weeks.

¶103

1

At the End of a Polite Request or Command

103   **a.** Requests, suggestions, and commands are often phrased as questions out of politeness. Use a period to end this kind of sentence if you expect your reader to respond *by acting* rather than by giving you a yes-or-no answer.

Will you please call us at once if we can be of further help.

Would you please send all bills to my bank for payment while I'm out of the country.

May I suggest that you put your request in writing and send it to Mr. Herzog for his approval.

If you can't attend the meeting, could you please send someone else in your place.

NOTE: Use a period only when you are sure that your reader is not likely to consider your request presumptuous.

b. If you are asking a favor or making a request that your reader may be unable or unwilling to grant, use a question mark at the end of the sentence. The question mark offers your reader a chance to say no to your request and helps to preserve the politeness of the situation.

May I ask a favor of you? Could you spare fifteen minutes to tell my son about career opportunities in your company?

Will you be able to have someone in your department help me on the Woonsocket project?

Will you please handle the production reports for me while I'm away?

c. If you are not sure whether to use a question mark or a period, reword the sentence so that it is clearly a question or a statement; then punctuate accordingly. For example, the sentence directly above could be revised as follows:

Would you be willing to handle the production reports for me while I'm away?

I would appreciate your handling the production reports for me while I'm away.

d. When you are addressing a request to someone who reports to you, you expect that person to comply. Therefore, a period can properly be used to punctuate such requests. However, since most people prefer to be *asked* to do something rather than be *told* to do it, a question mark establishes a nicer tone and often gets better results. Consider using a question mark when your request to a subordinate involves something beyond the routine aspects of the job.

Will you please let me know what your vacation plans are for the month of August. (Routine request to a subordinate.)

May I ask that you avoid scheduling any vacation time during August this year? I will need your help in preparing next year's forecasts and budgets. (Special request to a subordinate. The question mark suggests that the writer is sensitive to the problems this request could cause.)

NOTE: If you are unwilling to give your subordinate the impression that your request allows for a yes-or-no answer, simply drop the attempt at politeness and issue a straightforward command.

I must ask that you not schedule any vacation time during August this year. I will need your help in preparing next year's forecasts and budgets.

At the End of an Indirect Question

104 Use a period to mark the end of an indirect question. (See also ¶¶115–116.)

> Frank Wilcox has asked whether an exception can be made to our leave-of-absence policy.
>
> The only question she asked was when the report had to be on your desk.
>
> Why Janet Murray left the company so quickly has never been explained.
>
> We know what needs to be done; the question is how to pay for it.

With Decimals

105 Use a period (without space before or after it) to separate a whole number from a decimal fraction; for example, *$5.50, 33.33 percent.*

In Outlines and Displayed Lists

106 Use periods after numbers or letters that enumerate items in an outline or a displayed list—unless the numbers or letters are enclosed in parentheses. (See ¶¶107, 199c, 222, 223, 1357c–d, 1424f, 1724–1726 for illustrations.)

> **NOTE:** No periods are used after bullets that introduce items in a displayed list.

107 **a.** Use periods after independent clauses, dependent clauses, or long phrases that are displayed on separate lines in a list. Also use periods after short phrases that are essential to the grammatical completeness of the statement introducing the list. (In the following example the three listed items are all objects of the preposition *on* in the introductory statement.)

> Please get me year-end figures *on:* **OR** Please get me year-end figures *on:*
>
> a. Domestic sales revenues.   • Domestic sales revenues.
> b. Total operating costs.   • Total operating costs.
> c. Net operating income.   • Net operating income.

      b. No periods are needed after short phrases in a list if the introductory statement is grammatically complete (as in the first example below) or if the listed items are like those on an inventory sheet or a shopping list.

> The subnotebook computers in this price range offer the following features:
>
> 1. Light weight (between 4 and 5 pounds—including battery)
> 2. Backlit color screens
> 3. Big hard drives (120 MB to 200 MB)
> 4. At least 8 MB of RAM

> When you come to take the qualifying examination, please bring:
>
> 2 No. 2 pencils
> 1 ballpoint pen

With Headings

108 **a.** Use a period after a *run-in* heading (one that begins a paragraph and is immediately followed by text matter on the same line) unless some other mark of punctuation, such as a question mark, is required.

(Continued on page 8.)

Insuring Your Car. Automobile insurance is actually a package of six different types of coverage. . . .

How Much Will It Cost? How much automobile insurance will cost you depends on your driving record, your age, and how much shopping . . .

b. Omit the period if the heading is *freestanding* (displayed on a line by itself). However, retain a question mark or an exclamation point with a freestanding head if the wording requires it.

TAX-SAVING TECHNIQUES

Tax Elimination or Reduction

Nontaxable Income. Of the various types of nontaxable income, the most significant is the interest paid on municipal bonds. Investment in municipals has become one of the most popular ways to avoid . . .

Is It Legal? Investing your money so as to avoid taxes is perfectly legal. It is quite different from tax evasion, a deliberate attempt to . . .

NOTE: A period follows a run-in expression like *Table 6,* even though the heading as a whole is freestanding.

Table 6. SALARY RANGES   Figure 2-4. DEPARTMENTAL STAFF NEEDS

➤ *For the treatment of headings in reports and manuscripts, see ¶1425; for the treatment of headings in tables, see ¶¶1611–1614.*

A Few Don'ts

109 Don't use a period:

a. After letters used to designate persons or things (for example, *Manager A, Class B, Grade C, Brand X*). EXCEPTION: Use a period when the letter is the initial of a person's last name (for example, *Mr. A.* for *Mr. Adams*).

b. After contractions (for example, *cont'd;* see ¶505).

c. After ordinals expressed in figures (*1st, 2d, 3d, 4th*).

d. After roman numerals (for example, *Volume I, David Weild III*).

EXCEPTION: Periods follow roman numerals in an outline. (See ¶¶223, 1721–1726.)

➤ *Periods with abbreviations: see ¶¶506–513, 515.*
Periods with brackets: see ¶296.
Periods with dashes: see ¶¶213, 214a, 215a.
Periods with parentheses: see ¶¶224c, 225a, 225c, 226c.
Periods with quotation marks: see ¶¶247, 252, 253, 257, 258, 259.
Three spaced periods (ellipsis marks): see ¶¶274–280, 291, 299.
Spacing with periods: see ¶¶299, 1432e.

THE QUESTION MARK

To Indicate Direct Questions

110 **a.** Use a question mark at the end of a direct question. (Leave two spaces between the question mark and the start of the next sentence. For complete guidelines on spacing, see ¶299.)

Will you be able to meet with us after 5 p.m.?

Either way, how can we lose?

NOTE: Be sure to place the question mark at the *end* of the question.

How do you account for this entry: "Paid to E. M. Johnson, $300"?
(NOT: How do you account for this entry? "Paid to E. M. Johnson, $300.")

➤ *For the punctuation of indirect questions, see ¶¶104, 115, 116.*

b. Use a question mark (or, for special emphasis, an exclamation point) after a *rhetorical question,* a question to which no reply is expected.

Who wouldn't snap up an opportunity like that? (See also ¶119b.)

Wouldn't you rather be stuck in the sands of Florida this winter than in the snowdrifts of New England?

Isn't it incredible that people could fall for a scheme like that? (OR !)

NOTE: If the first clause of a compound sentence is a rhetorical question and the second clause is a statement, use a period to end the sentence.

Why don't you look at the attached list of tasks, and then let's discuss which ones you would like to take on.

111 Use a question mark at the end of an *elliptical* (condensed) *question,* that is, a word or phrase that represents a complete question.

Marion tells me that you are coming to the Bay Area. When? (The complete question is, "When are you coming?")

NOTE: Punctuate complete and elliptical questions separately, according to your meaning.

When will the job be finished? In a week or two?
(NOT: When will the job be finished in a week or two?)

Where shall we meet? At the airport? (With this punctuation, the writer allows for the possibility of meeting elsewhere.)

Where shall we meet at the airport? (With this punctuation, the writer simply wants to pinpoint a more precise location within the airport.)

112 Use a question mark at the end of a sentence that is phrased like a statement but spoken with the rising intonation of a question.

You expect me to believe this story?   He still intends to proceed?

113 A request, suggestion, or command phrased as a question out of politeness may not require a question mark. (See ¶103.)

To Indicate Questions Within Sentences

114 When a short direct question falls *within a sentence,* set the question off with commas and put a question mark at the end of the sentence. However, when a short direct question falls *at the end of a sentence,* use a comma before it and a question mark after.

I can alter the terms of my will, *can't I,* whenever I wish?

We aren't obligated to attend the meeting, *are we?*

NOTE: Short questions falling within a sentence may also be set off with dashes or parentheses in place of commas. (See ¶¶214b, 224d.)

115 When a longer direct question comes *at the end of a sentence,* it starts with a capital letter and is preceded by a comma or a colon. The question mark that ends the question also serves to mark the end of the sentence.

(Continued on page 10.)

NOTE: In the examples below and in ¶116, notice how a simple shift in word order converts a direct question to an indirect question. When the verb precedes the subject *(shall we, can we)*, the question is direct. When the verb follows the subject *(we shall, we can)*, the question is indirect.

> The key question is, Whom *shall we* nominate for next year's election?
>
> This is the key question: Whom *shall we* nominate for next year's election? (Use a colon if the introductory material is an independent clause.)
>
> **BUT:** We now come to the key question of whom *we shall* nominate for next year's election. (An indirect question requires no special punctuation or capitalization.)
>
> **OR:** We now come to the key question of whom to nominate for next year's election.

116 When a longer direct question comes *at the beginning of a sentence*, it is followed by a question mark (for emphasis) or simply a comma.

> How *can we* achieve these goals? is the next question. (Leave one space after a question mark within a sentence.)
>
> **OR:** How *can we* achieve these goals, is the next question.
>
> **BUT:** How *we can* achieve these goals is the next question. (Indirect question; no special punctuation is needed. See ¶115, note.)

117 **a.** A series of brief questions at the end of a sentence may be separated by commas or (for emphasis) by question marks. Do not capitalize the individual questions.

> Who will be responsible for drafting the proposal, obtaining comments from all the interested parties, preparing the final version, and coordinating the distribution of copies? (As punctuated, this sentence implies that one person may be asked to perform all these tasks.)
>
> **OR:** Who will be responsible for drafting the proposal? obtaining comments from all the interested parties? preparing the final version? coordinating the distribution of copies? (As punctuated, this sentence implies that a number of people may be asked to perform one or more of these tasks.)
>
> NOTE: Leave one space after a question mark within a sentence and two spaces after a question mark at the end of a sentence. For complete guidelines on spacing, see ¶299.

b. The brief questions in *a* above are all related to the same subject and predicate *(Who will be responsible for)*. Do not confuse this type of sentence pattern with a series of independent questions. Each independent question starts with a capital letter and ends with a question mark.

> Before you accept the job offer, think about the following: Will this job give you experience relevant to your real career goal? Will it permit you to keep abreast of the latest technology? Will it pay what you need?
>
> NOTE: Leave two spaces after a question mark that marks the end of an independent question. For complete guidelines on spacing, see ¶299.

c. Independent questions in a series are often elliptical (condensed) expressions. (See ¶111.)

> Has Walter's loan been approved? *When? By whom? For what amount?* (In other words: *When* was the loan approved? *By whom* was the loan approved? *For what amount* was the loan approved?)
>
> (**NOT:** Has Walter's loan been approved, when, by whom, and for what amount?)

To Express Doubt

118 A question mark enclosed in parentheses may be used to express doubt or uncertainty about a word or phrase within a sentence. Do not insert any space before the opening parenthesis; leave one space after the closing parenthesis unless another mark of punctuation is required at that point.

He joined the firm after his graduation from Columbia Law School in 1993(?).

NOTE: When dates are already enclosed within parentheses, question marks may be inserted as necessary to indicate doubt.

the explorer Verrazano (1485?–1528?)

➤ *Question marks with dashes: see ¶¶214b, 215a.*
  Question marks with parentheses: see ¶¶224d, 225a, 225d, 226c.
  Question marks with quotation marks: see ¶¶249, 252, 254, 257, 258, 259, 261.
  Spacing with question marks: see ¶¶299, 1432e.

THE EXCLAMATION POINT

The exclamation point is an "emotional" mark of punctuation that is most often found in sales and advertising copy. Like the word *very*, it loses its force when overused, so avoid using it wherever possible.

To Express Strong Feeling

119 **a.** Use an exclamation point at the end of a sentence (or an elliptical expression that stands for a sentence) to indicate enthusiasm, surprise, disbelief, urgency, or strong feeling. (Leave two spaces between the exclamation point and the start of the next sentence. For complete guidelines on spacing, see ¶299.)

Yes! We're selling our entire inventory below cost! Doors open at 9 a.m.!

No! I don't believe it!   Hang in there!   Incredible!

b. An exclamation point may be used in place of a question mark to express strong feeling. (See also ¶110b.)

How could you do it! What made you think I'd welcome a call at 2:30 a.m.!

c. The exclamation point may be enclosed in parentheses and placed directly after a word that the writer wants to emphasize. Do not insert any space before the opening parenthesis; leave one space after the closing parenthesis unless another mark of punctuation is required at that point.

We won exclusive(!) distribution rights in the Western Hemisphere.

120 **a.** A single word may be followed by an exclamation point to express intense feeling. The sentence that follows it is punctuated as usual.

Congratulations! Your summation at the trial was superb.

b. When such words are repeated for emphasis, an exclamation point follows each repetition.

Going! Going! Our bargains are almost gone!

c. When exclamations are mild, a comma or a period is sufficient.

Well, well, things could be worse.   No. I won't accept those conditions.

1

With *Oh* and *O*

121 The exclamation *oh* may be followed by either an exclamation point or a comma, depending on the emphasis desired. It is capitalized only when it starts a sentence. The capitalized *O*, the sign of direct address, is not usually followed by any punctuation.

Oh! I didn't expect that!	O Lord, help me!
Oh, what's the use?	O America, where are you headed?

➤ *Exclamation point with dashes: see ¶¶214b, 215a.*
 Exclamation point with parentheses: see ¶¶224d, 225a, 225d, 226c.
 Exclamation point with quotation marks: see ¶¶249, 252, 254, 257, 258,
   259, 261.
 Spacing with exclamation points: see ¶¶299, 1432e.

THE COMMA

The comma has two primary functions: it *sets off* nonessential expressions that interrupt the flow of thought from subject to verb to object or complement, and it *separates* elements within a sentence to clarify their relationship to one another. Two commas are typically needed to "set off," but only a single comma is needed to "separate."

The following paragraphs (¶¶122–125) present an overview of the rules governing the use of the comma. For a more detailed treatment of the specific rules, see ¶¶126–175.

Basic Rules for Commas That Set Off

122 Use commas to set off *nonessential expressions*—words, phrases, and clauses that are not necessary for the meaning or the structural completeness of the sentence.

IMPORTANT NOTE: In many sentences you can tell whether an expression is nonessential or essential by trying to omit the expression. If you can leave it out without affecting the meaning or the structural completeness of the sentence, the expression is nonessential and should be set off by commas.

NONESSENTIAL: Let's get the advice of Harry Stern, *who has in-depth experience with all types of personal computers.*

ESSENTIAL: Let's get the advice of someone *who has in-depth experience with all types of personal computers.* (Without the *who* clause, the meaning of the sentence would be incomplete.)

NONESSENTIAL: There is, *no doubt,* a reasonable explanation for his behavior at the board meeting.

ESSENTIAL: There is *no doubt* about her honesty. (Without *no doubt,* the structure of the sentence would be incomplete.)

However, in other sentences the only way you can tell whether an expression is nonessential or essential is by the way you would say it aloud. If your voice tends to *drop* as you utter the expression, it is nonessential; if your voice tends to *rise,* the expression is essential.

1

NONESSENTIAL: Finch and Helwig would prefer, *therefore,* to limit the term of the agreement to two years.

ESSENTIAL: Finch and Helwig would *therefore* prefer to limit the term of the agreement to two years.

➤ *For additional examples, see ¶141, note.*

a. **Interrupting Elements.** Use commas to set off words, phrases, and clauses when they break the flow of a sentence from subject to verb to object or complement. (See also ¶¶144–147.)

We can deliver the car on the day of your husband's birthday or, *if you wish,* on the Saturday before then. (When this sentence is read aloud, notice how the voice drops on the nonessential expression *if you wish.*)

They have sufficient assets, *don't they,* to cover these losses?

Let's take advantage of the special price and order, *say,* 200 reams this quarter instead of our usual quantity of 75.

Mary Cabrera, *rather than George Spengler,* has been appointed head of the New Albany office.

BUT: Mary Cabrera has been appointed head of the New Albany office *rather than George Spengler.* (The phrase is not set off when it does not interrupt.)

b. **Afterthoughts.** Use commas to set off words, phrases, or clauses loosely added onto the end of a sentence. (See also ¶144.)

Send us your check as soon as you can, *please.*

Grant promised to share expenses with us, *if I remember correctly.*

It is not too late to place an order, *is it?*

c. **Transitional Expressions and Independent Comments.** Use commas to set off transitional expressions (like *however, therefore, on the other hand*) and independent comments (like *obviously, in my opinion, of course*) when they interrupt the flow of the sentence. Do not set these elements off, however, when they are used to emphasize the meaning; the voice goes up in such cases. In the examples that follow, consider how the voice drops when the expression is nonessential and how it rises when the expression is essential. (See also ¶¶138–143.)

NONESSENTIAL: We are determined, *nevertheless,* to finish on schedule.

ESSENTIAL: We are *nevertheless* determined to finish on schedule.

NONESSENTIAL: It is, *of course,* your prerogative to change your mind. (Here the voice rises on *is* and drops on *of course.*)

ESSENTIAL: It is *of course* your prerogative to change your mind. (Here the voice rises on *of course.*)

d. **Descriptive Expressions.** When descriptive expressions *follow* the words they refer to and provide additional but nonessential information, use commas to set them off. (See also ¶¶148–153.)

NONESSENTIAL: His most recent article, "How to Make a Profit With High-Tech Investments," appeared in the June 1 issue of *Forbes.* (*His most recent* indicates which article is meant; the title gives additional but nonessential information.)

ESSENTIAL: The article "How to Make a Profit With High-Tech Investments" appeared in the June 1 issue of *Forbes.* (Here the title is needed to indicate which article is meant.)

(Continued on page 14.)

NONESSENTIAL: Thank you for your letter of April 12, in which you questioned our discount terms. (The date indicates which letter; the *in which* clause gives additional information. See also ¶152.)

ESSENTIAL: Thank you for your letter in which you questioned our discount terms. (Here the *in which* clause is needed to indicate which letter is meant.)

e. Dates. Use commas to set off the year in complete dates (for example, Sunday, May 1, *1996,* . . .). (See also ¶¶154–155.)

f. Names. Use commas to set off abbreviations that follow a person's name (Julie Merkin, *Ph.D.,* announces the opening . . .) and to set off names of states or countries following city names (Rye, *New York,* will host . . .). In personal names and company names, the trend is not to set off elements like *Jr., Sr., III, Inc.,* or *Ltd.* (for example, *Guy Tracy Jr.* and *Redd Inc.*); however, individual preferences should be respected when known. (See also ¶¶156–159.)

Basic Rules for Commas That Separate

123 Use a Single Comma:

a. To separate the two main clauses in a compound sentence when they are joined by *and, but, or,* or *nor.* (See also ¶¶126–129.)

We can't accept the marketing restrictions you proposed, *but* we think there is some basis for a mutually acceptable understanding.

b. To separate three or more items in a series—unless all the items are joined by *and* or *or.* (See also ¶¶162–167.)

It takes time, effort, *and* a good deal of money.

BUT: It takes time *and* effort *and* a good deal of money.

c. To separate two or more adjectives that both modify the same noun. (See also ¶¶168–171.)

We need to mount an *exciting, hard-hitting* ad campaign.

d. To separate the digits of numbers into groups of thousands. (See ¶461.)

Sales projections for the Southern Region next year range between $900,000 and $1,000,000.

e. To indicate the omission of key words or to clarify meaning when the word order is unusual. (See also ¶¶172–175.)

Half the purchase price is due on delivery of the goods; the balance, in three months. (The comma here signifies the omission of *is due.*)

What will happen, we don't know. (The comma here helps the reader cope with the unusual word order; it separates the object, *What will happen,* from the subject, *we,* which follows.)

124 Use a single comma after *introductory elements*—items that begin a sentence and come before the subject and verb of the main clause.

Yes, we can.   *Well,* that depends. (Introductory words.)

Taking all the arguments into consideration, we have decided to modernize these facilities rather than close them down. (Introductory participial phrase.)

To determine the proper mix of ingredients for a particular situation, see the table on page 141. (Introductory infinitive phrase.)

Before we can make a final decision, we will need to run another cost-profit analysis. (Introductory dependent clause.)

a. Use a comma after an *introductory request* or *command*.

Look, we've been through tougher situations before.

You see, the previous campaigns never did pan out.

Please remember, all expense reports must be on my desk by Friday.

BUT: *Please remember that* all . . . (When *that* is added, *please remember* becomes the main verb and is no longer an introductory element.)

b. Commas are not needed after *ordinary introductory adverbs* or *short introductory phrases* that answer such questions as:

WHEN:	tomorrow, yesterday, recently, early next week, in the morning, soon, in five years, in 1996
HOW OFTEN:	occasionally, often, frequently, once in a while
WHERE:	here, in this case, at the meeting
WHY:	for that reason, because of this situation

However, commas are used after introductory adverbs and phrases:

(1) When they function as *transitional expressions* (such as *well, therefore, however, for example, in the first place*), which provide a transition in meaning from the previous sentence.

(2) When they function as *independent comments* (such as *in my opinion, by all means, obviously, of course*), which express the writer's attitude toward the meaning of the sentence. (See also ¶¶138–143.)

In the morning things may look better. (Short prepositional phrase telling *when;* no comma needed.)

In the first place, they don't have sufficient capital. (Transitional expression; followed by comma.)

In my opinion, we ought to look for another candidate. (Independent comment; followed by comma.)

Recently we had a request for school enrollment trends. (Introductory adverb telling *when;* no comma needed.)

Consequently, we will have to cancel the agreement. (Transitional expression; followed by comma.)

Obviously, the request will have to be referred elsewhere. (Independent comment; followed by comma.)

NOTE: Many writers use commas after *all* introductory elements to avoid having to analyze each situation.

125 Separating commas are often improperly used in sentences. In the following examples the diagonal marks indicate points at which single commas *should not* be used.

a. Do not separate a subject and its verb.

The person she plans to hire for the job/ is Peter Crotty.

BUT: The person she plans to hire for the job, *I believe,* is Peter Crotty. (Use *two* commas to set off an interrupting expression.)

Whether profits can be improved this year/ depends on several key variables. (Noun clause as subject.)

BUT: *Anyone who contributes, contributes* to a most worthy cause. (In special cases like this, a comma may be required for clarity. See also ¶175b.)

(Continued on page 16.)

b. Do not separate a verb and its object or complement.

The test mailing *has not produced/ the results* we were hoping for. (Verb and object.)

Mrs. Paterra *will be/ the Hapworth Corporation's new director of marketing.* (Verb and complement.)

The equipment *is/ easy to operate, inexpensive to maintain, and built to give reliable service for many years.* (Verb and complement.)

Rebecca Hingham *said/ that the research data would be on your desk by Monday morning.* (Noun clause as object.)

BUT: Rebecca Hingham *said, "The research data will be on your desk by Monday morning."* (A comma ordinarily follows a verb when the object is a direct quotation. See also ¶256.)

OR: The question we really need to address *is, Do we have a better solution to propose?* (A comma also follows a verb when the object or complement is a direct question. See also ¶115.)

c. Do not separate an adjective from a noun that follows it.

The project requires a highly motivated, research-oriented, *cost-conscious/ manager.*

d. Do not separate a noun and a prepositional phrase that follows.

The board of directors/ of the Fastex Corporation will announce its decision this Friday.

BUT: The board of directors, *of necessity,* must turn down the merger at this time. (Use *two* commas to set off an interrupting expression.)

e. Do not separate a coordinating conjunction (*and, but, or,* or *nor*) and the following word.

You can read the draft of the division's medium-range plan now *or/ when* you get home tonight.

BUT: You can read the draft of the division's medium-range plan now or, *if you prefer,* when you get home tonight. (Use *two* commas to set off an interrupting expression.)

f. Do not separate *two* words or phrases that are joined by a coordinating conjunction.

The letters on the Gray case/ and *those concerning Mr. Pendleton* should be shown to Mrs. Almquist. (Two subjects.)

I *have read Ms. Berkowitz's capital spending proposal/* and *find it well done.* (Two predicates. See also ¶127.)

We hope *that you will visit our store soon/* and *that you will find the styles you like.* (Two noun clauses serving as objects of the verb *hope.*)

The CEO plans *to visit the Western Region/* and *call personally on the large accounts that have stopped doing business with us.* (Two infinitive phrases serving as objects of the verb *plans.*)

He may go on to graduate school at *Stanford/* or *Harvard.* (Two objects of the preposition *at.*)

BUT: *Frank Albano will handle the tickets,* and *Edna Hoehn will be responsible for publicity.* (A comma separates two independent clauses joined by a coordinating conjunction. See ¶126.)

The following rules (¶¶126–137) deal with the punctuation of clauses and phrases in sentences.

With Clauses in Compound Sentences

126 **a.** When a compound sentence consists of *two* independent clauses joined by a coordinating conjunction (*and, but, or,* or *nor*), place a separating comma before the conjunction. (See ¶129.)

Mrs. Fenster noticed a small discrepancy in the figures, *and* on that basis she began to reanalyze the data.

BUT: Mrs. Fenster noticed a small discrepancy in the figures *and* on that basis began to reanalyze the data. (See ¶127a–b.)

Show this proposal to Mr. Florio, *and* ask him for his reaction. (See ¶127c.)

Either we step up our promotion efforts, *or* we must be content with our existing share of the market.

Not only were we the developers of this process, *but* we were the first to apply it to the field of pollution control.

b. For special effect, the comma before the coordinating conjunction can be replaced by a period, a question mark, or an exclamation point. The coordinating conjunction is then capitalized, and the second independent clause is treated as a separate sentence. However, this treatment, if overused, can quickly lose its effectiveness. (See page 255 for a usage note on *and.*)

Is it self-confidence that makes you successful? Or is it success that makes you self-confident?

I told Callahan that we would not reorder from his company unless he cut his prices by 20 percent. And he did.

NOTE: Do not insert a comma directly after the coordinating conjunction unless a parenthetical element begins at that point.

I told Callahan that we would not reorder from his company unless he cut his prices by 20 percent. And, to my total amazement, he did.

c. When a compound sentence consists of *three* or more independent clauses, punctuate this series like any other series. (See also ¶162.)

Bob can deal with the caterer, Nora can handle publicity, and Bev and I can take care of the rest.

127 Do not confuse a *compound sentence* with a simple sentence containing a *compound predicate.*

a. A *compound sentence* contains at least two independent clauses, and each clause contains a subject and a predicate.

Barbara just got her master's, and she is now looking for a job in sales.

b. A sentence may contain one subject with a *compound predicate,* that is, two predicates connected by a coordinating conjunction. In such sentences no comma separates the two predicates.

Barbara *just got her master's* and *is now looking for a job in sales.* (When *she* is omitted from the example in *a* above, the sentence becomes a simple sentence with a compound predicate.)

Ogleby not only *wants a higher discount* but also *demands faster turnarounds on his orders.* (Compound predicate; no comma before *but.*)

BUT: *Ogleby not only wants a higher discount,* but *he also demands faster turnarounds on his orders.* (Compound sentence; comma before *but.*)

(Continued on page 18.)

c. When one or both verbs are in the imperative and the subject is not expressed, treat the sentence as a compound sentence and use a comma between the clauses.

Please look at the brochure I have enclosed, and then *get* back to me if you have additional questions.

You may not be able to get away right now, but *do plan* to stay with us whenever you find the time.

Call Ellen Chen sometime next week, and *ask* her whether she will speak at our conference next fall.

BUT: *Call* Ellen Chen and *ask* her whether she will speak at our conference next fall. (Omit the comma if either clause is short. See ¶129.)

d. When nonessential elements precede the second part of a *compound predicate*, they are treated as interrupting expressions and are set off by two commas. When these same expressions precede the second clause of a *compound sentence*, they are treated as introductory expressions and are followed by one comma.

We can bill you on our customary terms or, *if you prefer*, can offer you our new deferred payment plan. (Interrupting expression requires two commas.)

We can bill you on our customary terms, or *if you prefer*, we can offer you our new deferred payment plan. (Introductory expression requires one comma.)

Frank Bruchman went into the boardroom and, *without consulting his notes*, proceeded to give the directors precise details about our financial situation. (Interrupting expression.)

Frank Bruchman went into the boardroom, and *without consulting his notes*, he proceeded to give the directors precise details about our financial situation. (Introductory expression.)

➤ *See also ¶¶131c, 136a, 142.*

128 Do not use a comma between two independent clauses that are not joined by a coordinating conjunction *(and, but, or,* or *nor)*. This error of punctuation is known as a *comma splice* and produces a *run-on sentence.* Use a semicolon, a colon, or a dash (whichever is appropriate), or start a new sentence. (See ¶¶176, 187, 204–205.)

WRONG: Please review these spreadsheets quickly, I need them back tomorrow.

RIGHT: Please review these spreadsheets quickly; I need them back tomorrow.

OR: Please review these spreadsheets quickly. I need them back tomorrow.

129 If either clause of a compound sentence is short, the comma may be omitted before the conjunction.

Their prices are low and their service is efficient.

Please initial these forms and return them by Monday.

Consider leasing and see whether it costs less in the long run than buying.

Consider whether leasing costs more than buying and then decide.

With Clauses in Complex Sentences

A complex sentence contains one independent clause and one or more dependent clauses. *After, although, as, because, before, if, since, unless, when,* and *while* are among the words most frequently used to introduce dependent clauses. (See ¶132 for a longer list.)

130 Introductory Dependent Clauses

a. When a dependent clause *precedes* the independent clause, separate the clauses with a comma.

Before we can make a decision, we must have all the facts.

When you read the Weissberg study, look at Appendix 2 first.

If, however, they had watched their investments more closely, do you think they could have avoided bankruptcy?

After we have studied all aspects of the complaint, <u>we will make</u> a recommendation.

BUT: *Only after we have studied all aspects of the complaint* <u>will we make</u> a recommendation. (No comma follows the introductory clause when the word order in the main clause is abnormal. Compare the abnormal *will we make* here with the normal *we will make* in the preceding example.)

b. Be sure you can recognize an introductory dependent clause, even if some of the essential words are omitted from the clause. (Such constructions are known as *elliptical clauses.*)

Whenever possible, he leaves his office by six. (Whenever *it is* possible, . . .)

If so, I will call you tomorrow. (If *that is* so, . . .)

Should you be late, just call to let me know. (*If* you should be late, . . .)

c. Use a comma after an introductory clause when it serves as the *object* of a sentence (but not when it serves as the *subject*).

Whomever you nominate, I will support. (Introductory clause as object.)

Whomever you nominate will have my support. (Introductory clause as subject.)

That the department must be reorganized, I no longer question. (Introductory clause as object.)

That the department must be reorganized is no longer questioned. (Introductory clause as subject.)

d. Sentences like those shown in *a–c* above are often introduced by an expression such as *he said that, she believes that,* or *they know that.* In such cases use the same punctuation as prescribed in *a–c.*

Liz believes that *before we can make a decision,* we must have all the facts. (A separating comma follows the dependent clause, just as if the sentence began with the word *Before.* No comma precedes the dependent clause because it is considered introductory, not interrupting.)

I think that *when you read the Weissberg study,* you will gain a new perspective on the situation.

Harry says that *whenever possible,* he leaves his office by six.

Everyone knows that *whomever you nominate* will have my support in the next election.

BUT: He said that, *as you may already know,* he was planning to take early retirement. (Two commas are needed to set off an interrupting dependent clause. See also ¶131c.)

131 Dependent Clauses Elsewhere in the Sentence

When a dependent clause *follows* the main clause or *falls within* the main clause, commas are used or omitted depending on whether the dependent clause is essential (restrictive) or nonessential (nonrestrictive).

(Continued on page 20.)

1

a. An *essential* clause is necessary to the meaning of the sentence. Because it *cannot be omitted*, it should not be set off by commas.

The person *who used to be Englund's operations manager* is now doing the same job for Jenniman Brothers. (Tells which person.)

The Pennington bid arrived *after we had made our decision.* (Tells when.)

Damato's suggestion *that we submit the issue to arbitration* may be the only sensible alternative. (Tells which of Damato's suggestions is meant.)

Mrs. Foy said *that she would send us an advance program.* (Tells what was said.)

b. A *nonessential* clause provides additional descriptive or explanatory detail. Because it *can be omitted* without changing the meaning of the sentence, it should be set off by commas.

George Pedersen, *who used to be Englund's operations manager,* is now doing the same job for Jenniman Brothers. (The name indicates which person; the *who* clause simply gives additional information.)

The Pennington bid arrived on Tuesday, *after we had made our decision.* (*Tuesday* tells when; the *after* clause simply adds information.)

Damato's latest suggestion, *that we submit the issue to arbitration,* may be the only sensible alternative. (*Latest* tells which suggestion is meant; the *that* clause is not essential.)

c. A dependent clause occurring within a sentence must always be set off by commas when it *interrupts* the flow of the sentence.

We can review the wording of the announcement over lunch or, *if your time is short,* over the phone.

Please tell us when you plan to be in town and, *if possible,* where you will be staying. (The complete dependent clause is *if it is possible.*)

Senator Hemphill, *when offered the chance to refute his opponent's charges,* said he would respond at a time of his own choosing.

Ann Kourakis is the type of person who, *when you need help badly,* will be the first to volunteer.

If, *when you have weighed the alternatives,* you choose one of the models that cost over $500, we can arrange special credit terms for you.

BUT: He said that *if we choose one of the models that cost over $500,* his firm can arrange special credit terms for us. (See ¶130d for dependent clauses following *he said that, she knows that,* and similar expressions.)

132 The following list presents the words and phrases most commonly used to introduce dependent clauses. For most of these expressions two sentences are given: one containing an essential clause and one a nonessential clause. In a few cases only one type of clause is possible. If you cannot decide whether a clause is essential or nonessential (and therefore whether commas are required or not), compare it with the related sentences that follow.

After. ESSENTIAL: His faxed response came *after you left last evening.* (Tells when.)
NONESSENTIAL: His faxed response came this morning, *after the decision had been made.* (The phrase *this morning* clearly tells when; the *after* clause provides additional but nonessential information.)

All of which. ALWAYS NONESSENTIAL: The rumors, *all of which were unfounded,* brought about his defeat in the last election.

Although, even though, and **though.** ALWAYS NONESSENTIAL: She has typed her letter of resignation, *although I do not believe she will submit it.*

As. ESSENTIAL: The results of the mailing are *as you predicted they would be.*
NONESSENTIAL: The results of the mailing are disappointing, *as you predicted they would be.* (See page 256 for a usage note on *as.*)

As . . . as. ALWAYS ESSENTIAL: He talked *as* persuasively at the meeting *as* he did over the telephone. (See page 256 for a usage note on *as . . . as.*)

As if and **as though.** ESSENTIAL: She drove *as if* (or *as though*) *the road were a minefield.* (The *as if* clause tells how she drove.)
NONESSENTIAL: She drove cautiously, *as if* (or *as though*) *the road were a minefield.* (The adverb *cautiously* tells how she drove; the *as if* clause provides additional but nonessential information.)

As soon as. ESSENTIAL: We will fill your order *as soon as we receive new stock.*
NONESSENTIAL: We will fill your order next week, *as soon as we receive new stock.*

At, by, for, in, and **to which.** ESSENTIAL: I went to the floor *to which I had been directed.*
NONESSENTIAL: I went to the tenth floor, *to which I had been directed.*

Because. *Essential* or *nonessential,* depending on closeness of relation.
ESSENTIAL: She left *because she had another appointment.* (Here the reason expressed by the *because* clause is essential to complete the meaning.)
NONESSENTIAL: I need to have two copies of the final report by 5:30 tomorrow, *because I am leaving for Chicago on a 7:30 flight.* (Here the meaning of the main clause is complete; the reason expressed in the *because* clause offers additional but nonessential information.)

Compare these examples: I'm not taking that course of action, *because I distrust Harry's recommendations.* BUT: I'm not taking that course of action *because I distrust Harry's recommendations.* I based my decision on another reason altogether.

Before. ESSENTIAL: The shipment was sent *before your letter was received.*
NONESSENTIAL: The shipment was sent on Tuesday, *before your letter was received.* (*Tuesday* tells when the shipment was sent; the *before* clause provides additional but nonessential information.)

Even though. See *Although.*

For. ALWAYS NONESSENTIAL: He read the book, *for he was interested in psychology.* (A comma should always precede *for* as a conjunction to prevent misreading *for* as a preposition.)

If. ESSENTIAL: Let us hear from you *if you are interested.*
NONESSENTIAL: She promised to write from Toronto, *if I remember correctly.* (Clause added loosely.)

In order that. *Essential* or *nonessential,* depending on closeness of relation.
ESSENTIAL: Please notify your instructor *in order that a makeup examination may be scheduled.*
NONESSENTIAL: Please notify your instructor if you will be unable to attend the examination on Friday, *in order that a makeup examination may be scheduled.*

No matter what (why, how, etc.**).** ALWAYS NONESSENTIAL: The order cannot be ready by Monday, *no matter what the store manager says.*

None of which. ALWAYS NONESSENTIAL: We received five boxes of samples, *none of which are in good condition.*

None of whom. ALWAYS NONESSENTIAL: We have interviewed ten applicants, *none of whom were satisfactory.*

Not so . . . as. ALWAYS ESSENTIAL: The second copy was *not so* clear *as* the first one. (See page 256 for a usage note on *as . . . as—not so . . . as.*)

(Continued on page 22.)

Since. ESSENTIAL: We have taken no applications *since we received your memo.* NONESSENTIAL: We are taking no more applications, *since our lists are now closed.* (Clause of reason.)

So that. *Essential* or *nonessential,* depending on closeness of relation. ESSENTIAL: Examine all shipments *so that any damage may be detected promptly.* NONESSENTIAL: Examine all shipments as soon as they arrive, *so that any damage may be detected promptly.*

So . . . that. ALWAYS ESSENTIAL: The costs ran *so* high *that we could not make a profit.*

Some of whom. ALWAYS NONESSENTIAL: The agency has sent us five applicants, *some of whom seem promising.*

Than. ALWAYS ESSENTIAL: The employees seem to be more disturbed by the rumor *than they care to admit.*

That. When used as a relative pronoun, *that* refers to things; it also refers to persons when a class or type is meant. ALWAYS ESSENTIAL: Here is a picture of the plane *that I own.* She is the candidate *that I prefer.* (See also ¶1062.) When used as a subordinating conjunction, *that* links the dependent clause it introduces with the main clause. ALWAYS ESSENTIAL: We know *that we will have to make cuts in the budget.* (See page 274 for a usage note on *that.*)

Though. See *Although.*

Unless. ESSENTIAL: This product line will be discontinued *unless customers begin to show an interest in it.*
NONESSENTIAL: I plan to work on the Aspen proposal all through the weekend, *unless Cindy comes into town.* (Clause added loosely as an afterthought.)

Until. ALWAYS ESSENTIAL: I will continue to work *until my children are out of school.*

When. ESSENTIAL: The changeover will be made *when Mr. Ruiz returns from his vacation.*
NONESSENTIAL: The changeover will be made next Monday, *when Mr. Ruiz returns from his vacation.* (*Monday* tells when; the *when* clause provides additional but nonessential information.)

Where. ESSENTIAL: I plan to visit the town *where I used to live.*
NONESSENTIAL: I plan to stop off in Detroit, *where I used to live.*

Whereas. ALWAYS NONESSENTIAL: The figures for last year cover urban areas only, *whereas those for this year include rural areas as well.* (Clause of contrast.)

Which. Use *which* (rather than *who*) when referring to animals, things, and ideas. Always use *which* (instead of *that*) to introduce nonessential clauses: The revised report, *which was done by Mark,* is very impressive. *Which* may also be used to introduce essential clauses. (See ¶1062b, note.)

While. ESSENTIAL: The union has decided not to strike *while negotiations are still going on.* (Here *while* means "during the time that.")
NONESSENTIAL: The workers at the Apex Company have struck, *while those at the Powers Company are still at work.* (Here *while* means "whereas.")

Who. ESSENTIAL: All students *who are members of the Backpackers Club* will be leaving for Maine on Friday.
NONESSENTIAL: John Behnke, *who is a member of the Backpackers Club,* will be leading a group on a weekend trip to Maine.

Whom. ESSENTIAL: This package is for the friend *whom I am visiting.*
NONESSENTIAL: This package is for my cousin Amy, *whom I am visiting.*

Whose. ESSENTIAL: The prize was awarded to the employee *whose suggestion yielded the greatest cost savings.*
NONESSENTIAL: The prize was awarded to Joyce Bruno, *whose suggestion yielded the greatest cost savings.*

With Clauses in Compound-Complex Sentences

133 A compound-complex sentence typically consists of two independent clauses (joined by *and, but, or,* or *nor*) and one or more dependent clauses. To punctuate a sentence of this kind, first place a separating comma before the conjunction that joins the two main parts. Then consider each half of the sentence alone and provide additional punctuation as necessary.

> The computer terminals were not delivered until June 12, five weeks after the promised delivery date, and *when I wrote to complain to your sales manager,* it took another three weeks simply for him to acknowledge my letter. (No comma precedes *when* because the *when* clause is considered an introductory expression, not an interrupting expression. See also ¶127d.)

> Jeff Adler, the CEO of Marshfield & Duxbury, is eager to discuss a joint venture with my boss, *who is off on a six-week trip to the Far East,* but the earliest date I see open for such a meeting is Wednesday, October 20.

> **NOTE:** If a misreading is likely or a stronger break is desired, use a semicolon rather than a comma to separate the two main clauses. (See ¶177.)

134 When a sentence starts with a dependent clause that applies to both independent clauses that follow, do not use a comma to separate the independent clauses. (A comma would make the introductory dependent clause seem to apply only to the first independent clause.)

> Before you start to look for venture capital, you need to prepare an analysis of the market *and* you must make a detailed set of financial projections. (The *before* clause applies equally to the two independent clauses that follow; hence no comma before *and.*)

> **BUT:** Before you start to look for venture capital, you need to prepare an analysis of the market, *but* don't think that's all there is to it. (The *before* clause applies only to the first independent clause; hence a comma is used before *but.*)

With Participial, Infinitive, and Prepositional Phrases

135 Introductory Phrases

> **a.** Use a comma after an *introductory participial phrase.*

> *Seizing the opportunity,* I presented an overview of our medium-range plans.

> *Established in 1905,* our company takes great pride in its reputation for high-quality products and excellent service.

> *Having checked the statements myself,* I feel confident that they are accurate.

> **NOTE:** Watch out for phrases that look like introductory participial phrases but actually serve as the subject of the sentence or part of the predicate. Do not put a comma after these elements.

> *Looking for examples of good acknowledgment letters in our files* has taken me longer than I had hoped. (Gerund phrase as subject.)

> **BUT:** *Looking for examples of good acknowledgment letters in our files,* I found four that you can use. (Participial phrase used as an introductory element; the subject is *I.*)

(Continued on page 24.)

1

Following Mrs. Fahnstock's speech was a presentation by Ms. Paley. (With normal word order, the sentence would read, "A presentation by Ms. Paley was *following Mrs. Fahnstock's speech.*" The introductory phrase is actually part of the predicate; the subject is *a presentation by Ms. Paley.*)

BUT: *Following Mrs. Fahnstock's speech,* Ms. Paley made her presentation. (Participial phrase used as an introductory element; the subject is *Ms. Paley.*)

b. Use a comma after an *introductory infinitive phrase* unless the phrase is the subject of the sentence. (Infinitive phrases are introduced by *to.*)

To get the best results from your dishwasher, follow the printed directions. (The subject *you* is understood.)

To have displayed the goods more effectively, he should have consulted a lighting specialist. (The subject is *he.*)

BUT: *To have displayed the goods more effectively* would have required a lighting specialist. (Infinitive phrase used as subject.)

c. As a general rule, use a comma after all *introductory prepositional phrases.* A comma may be omitted after a *short* prepositional phrase if (1) the phrase does not contain a verb form, (2) the phrase is not a transitional expression or an independent comment, or (3) there is no sacrifice in clarity or desired emphasis. (Many writers use a comma after all introductory prepositional phrases to avoid analyzing each situation.)

In response to the many requests of our customers, we are opening a branch in Kenmore Square. (Comma required after a long phrase.)

In 1994 our entire inventory was destroyed by fire. (No comma required after a short phrase.)

BUT: *In 1994,* 384 cases of pneumonia were reported. (Comma required to separate two numbers. See ¶456.)

In preparing your report, be sure to include last year's figures. (Comma required after a short phrase containing a verb form.)

In addition, a 6 percent city sales tax must be imposed. (Comma required after a short phrase used as a transitional expression. See ¶¶138a, 139.)

In my opinion, your ads are misleading as they now appear. (Comma required after short phrase used as an independent comment. See ¶¶138b, 139.)

In legal documents, amounts of money are often expressed both in words and in figures. (Comma used to give desired emphasis to the introductory phrase.)

CONFUSING: After all you have gone through a great deal.
CLEAR: *After all,* you have gone through a great deal. (Comma required after a short phrase to prevent misreading.)

NOTE: Omit the comma after an introductory prepositional phrase if the word order in the rest of the sentence is inverted.

Out of an initial investment of $5000 came a stake that is currently worth over $2,500,000. (Normal word order: A stake that is currently worth over $2,500,000 came out of an initial investment of $5000.)

In an article I read in Time was an account of his trip. (Omit the comma after the introductory phrase when the verb in the main clause immediately follows.)

BUT: *In an article I read in Time,* there was an account . . .

d. When a compound sentence starts with a phrase that applies to both independent clauses, do not use a comma to separate the two clauses if doing so would make the introductory phrase seem to apply only to the first clause. (See also ¶134.)

In response to the many requests of our customers, we are opening a branch in Kenmore Square and we are extending our evening hours in all our stores.

136 Phrases at the Beginning of a Clause

a. When a participial, infinitive, or prepositional phrase occurs *at the beginning of a clause within the sentence,* insert or omit the comma following, just as if the phrase were an introductory element at the beginning of the sentence. (See ¶135.)

I was invited to attend the monthly planning meeting last week, and *seizing the opportunity,* I presented an overview of our medium-range plans. (A separating comma follows the participial phrase just as if the sentence began with the word *Seizing.* No comma precedes the phrase because the phrase is considered introductory, not interrupting. See also ¶127d.)

The salesclerk explained that *to get the best results from your dishwasher,* you should follow the printed directions.

We would like to announce that *in response to the many requests of our customers,* we are opening a branch in Kenmore Square.

Last year we had a number of thefts, and *in 1994* our entire inventory was destroyed by fire. (No comma is needed after a short introductory prepositional phrase.)

b. If the phrase interrupts the flow of the sentence, set it off with two commas.

Pamela is the type of person who, *in the midst of disaster,* will always find something to laugh about.

If, *in the attempt to push matters to a resolution,* you offer that gang new terms, they will simply dig in their heels and refuse to bargain.

137 Phrases Elsewhere in the Sentence

When a participial, infinitive, or prepositional phrase occurs *at some point other than the beginning of a sentence* (see ¶135) *or the beginning of a clause* (see ¶136), commas are omitted or used depending on whether the phrase is essential or nonessential.

a. An *essential* participial, infinitive, or prepositional phrase is necessary to the meaning of the sentence and cannot be omitted. Therefore, do not use commas to set it off.

The catalog *scheduled for release in November* will have to be delayed until January. (Participial.)

The decision *to expand our export activities* has led to a significant increase in profits. (Infinitive.)

The search *for a new general manager* is still going on. (Prepositional.)

b. A *nonessential* participial, infinitive, or prepositional phrase provides additional information but is not needed to complete the meaning of the sentence. Set off such phrases with commas.

This new collection of essays, *written in the last two years before his death,* represents his most distinguished work. (Participial.)

I'd rather not attend her reception, *to be frank about it.* (Infinitive.)

Morale appears to be much better, *on the whole.* (Prepositional.)

c. A phrase occurring within a sentence must always be set off by commas when it *interrupts* the flow of the sentence.

The commission, *after hearing arguments on the proposed new tax rate structure,* will consider amendments to the tax law.

The company, *in its attempt to place more women in high-level management positions,* is undertaking a special recruitment program.

¶138

1

The following rules (¶¶138–161) deal with the various uses of commas to set off nonessential expressions. See also ¶¶201–202 and ¶¶218–219 for the use of dashes and parentheses to set off these expressions.

With Transitional Expressions and Independent Comments

138   **a.** Use commas to set off *transitional expressions*. These nonessential words and phrases are called *transitional* because they help the reader mentally relate the preceding thought to the idea now being introduced. They express such notions as:

ADDITION:	additionally (see page 254), also, besides, furthermore, in addition, moreover, too (see ¶143), what is more
CONSEQUENCE:	accordingly, as a result, consequently, hence (see ¶139b), otherwise, so (see ¶179), then (see ¶139b), therefore, thus (see ¶139b)
SUMMARIZING:	after all, all in all, all things considered, briefly, by and large, in any case, in any event, in brief, in conclusion, in short, in summary, in the final analysis, in the long run, on balance, on the whole, to sum up
GENERALIZING:	as a rule, as usual, for the most part, generally, generally speaking, in general, ordinarily, usually
RESTATEMENT:	in essence, in other words, namely, that is, that is to say
CONTRAST AND COMPARISON:	by contrast, by the same token, conversely, instead, likewise, on one hand, on the contrary, on the other hand, rather, similarly, yet (see ¶¶139b, 179)
CONCESSION:	anyway, at any rate, be that as it may, even so, however, in any case, in any event, nevertheless, still, this fact notwithstanding
SEQUENCE:	afterward, at first, at the same time, finally, first, first of all, for now, for the time being, in conclusion, in the first place, in time, in turn, later on, meanwhile, next, second, then (see ¶139b), to begin with
DIVERSION:	by the by, by the way, incidentally
ILLUSTRATION:	for example, for instance, for one thing

NOTE: The coordinating conjunctions *and, but, or,* or *nor* are sometimes used as transitional expressions at the beginning of a sentence. (See ¶126b.)

➤ *See ¶¶139–142 for the punctuation of transitional expressions depending on where they occur in a sentence.*

b. Use commas to set off *independent comments,* that is, nonessential words or phrases that express the writer's attitude toward the meaning of the sentence. By means of these independent comments, the writer indicates that what he is about to say carries his wholehearted endorsement *(indeed, by all means)* or deserves only his lukewarm support *(apparently, presumably)* or hardly requires saying *(as you already know, clearly, obviously)* or represents only his personal views *(in my opinion, personally)* or arouses some emotion in him *(unfortunately, happily)* or presents his honest position *(frankly, actually, to tell the truth).* Such terms modify the meaning of the sentence as a whole rather than a particular word within the sentence.

AFFIRMATION:	by all means, indeed, of course, yes
DENIAL:	no
REGRET:	alas, unfortunately, regrettably
PLEASURE:	fortunately, happily
QUALIFICATION:	ideally, if necessary, if possible, literally, strictly speaking, theoretically, hopefully (see page 264)
PERSONAL VIEWPOINT:	according to her, as I see it, in my opinion, personally
ASSERTION OF CANDOR:	actually, frankly, in reality, to be honest, to say the least, to tell the truth
ASSERTION OF FACT:	as a matter of fact, as it happens, as you know, believe it or not, certainly, clearly, doubtless, in fact, naturally, needless to say, obviously, without doubt
WEAK ASSERTION:	apparently, perhaps, presumably, well

➤ *See ¶¶139–142 for the punctuation of independent comments depending on where they occur in a sentence.*

139 At the Beginning of a Sentence

a. When the words and phrases listed in ¶138a–b appear at the beginning of a sentence, they should be followed by a comma unless they are used as essential elements.

NONESSENTIAL: *After all,* you have done more for him than he had any right to expect.

ESSENTIAL: *After all* you have done for him, he has no right to expect more.

NONESSENTIAL: *However,* you look at the letter yourself to see whether you interpret it as I do.

ESSENTIAL: *However* you look at the letter, there is only one interpretation.

NONESSENTIAL: *Obviously,* the guest of honor was quite moved by the welcome she received.

ESSENTIAL: *Obviously* moved by the welcome she received, the guest of honor spoke with an emotion-choked voice. (Here *obviously* modifies *moved*. In the preceding sentence, *obviously* modifies the meaning of the sentence as a whole.)

b. When *hence, then, thus, so,* or *yet* occurs at the beginning of a sentence, the comma following is omitted unless the connective requires special emphasis or a nonessential element occurs at that point.

Thus they thought it wise to get an outside consultant's opinion.

Then they decided to go back to their original plan.

BUT: *Then,* after they rejected the consultant's recommendation, they decided to go back to their original plan.

➤ *See also ¶142a, note.*

c. When an introductory transitional expression or independent comment is incorporated into the flow of the sentence without any intervening pause, the comma may be omitted.

Of course I can handle it.   *Perhaps* she was joking.
No doubt he meant well.   *Indeed* she was not.

140 At the End of a Sentence

Use one comma to set off a transitional expression or an independent comment at the end of a sentence. However, be sure to distinguish between nonessential and essential elements.

> NONESSENTIAL: Philip goes to every employee reception, *of course.*
> ESSENTIAL: Philip goes to every employee reception as a matter *of course.*

> NONESSENTIAL: The deal is going to fall through, *in my opinion.*
> ESSENTIAL: She doesn't rank very high *in my opinion.*

141 Within the Sentence

Use two commas to set off a transitional expression or an independent comment when it occurs as a nonessential element *within the sentence.*

> I, *too,* was not expecting a six-month convalescence.
> The doctors tell me, *however,* that I will regain full use of my left leg.

If, however, the expression is used as an essential element, leave the commas out.

> NONESSENTIAL: Let me say, *to begin with,* that I think very highly of him.

> ESSENTIAL: If you want to improve your English, you ought *to begin with* a good review of grammar.

NOTE: In many sentences the only way you can tell whether an expression is nonessential or essential is by the way you say it. If your voice tends to *drop* as you utter the expression, it is nonessential and should be set off by commas.

> We concluded, *nevertheless,* that their offer was not serious.
> Millie understands, *certainly,* that the reassignment is only temporary.
> It is critical, *therefore,* that we rework all these cost estimates.

If your voice tends to *rise* as you utter the expression, it is essential and should not be set off by commas.

> We *nevertheless* concluded that their offer was not serious.
> Millie *certainly* understands that the reassignment is only temporary.
> It is *therefore* critical that we rework all these cost estimates.

If commas are inserted in the previous example, the entire reading of the sentence will be changed. The voice will rise on the word *is* and drop on *therefore.* (If this is actually the way you want the sentence to be read, then commas around *therefore* are appropriate.)

> It is, *therefore,* critical that we rework all these cost estimates.

142 At the Beginning of a Clause

a. When a transitional expression or independent comment occurs *at the beginning of the second independent clause* in a compound sentence and is *preceded by a semicolon,* use one comma following the expression.

> I would love to work in a side trip to Vail; *however,* I don't think I can pull it off.
> My boss just approved the purchase; *therefore,* let's confirm a delivery date.

In sentences like the two above, a period may be used in place of a semicolon. The words *however* and *therefore* would then be capitalized to mark the start of a new sentence, and they would be followed by a comma.

NOTE: When *hence, then, thus,* or *so* appears at the beginning of an independent clause, the comma following is omitted unless the connective requires special emphasis or a nonessential element occurs at that point. (See also ¶139b.)

Melt the butter over high heat; *then* add the egg.

BUT: Melt the butter over high heat; *then,* when the foam begins to subside, add the egg.

➤ *For the use of a semicolon before a transitional expression, see ¶¶178–180.*

b. When the expression occurs *at the beginning of the second independent clause* in a compound sentence and is *preceded by a comma and a coordinating conjunction,* use one comma following the expression. (See also ¶127d.)

The location of the plant was not easy to reach, and *to be honest about it,* I wasn't very taken with the people who interviewed me.

The job seemed to have no future, and *to tell the truth,* the salary was pretty low.

In the first place, I think the budget for the project is unrealistic, and *in the second place,* the deadlines are almost impossible to meet.

NOTE: If the expression is a simple adverb like *therefore,* the comma following the expression is usually omitted. (See also ¶180.)

The matter must be resolved by Friday, and *therefore* our preliminary conference must be held no later than Thursday.

All the general managers have been summoned to a three-day meeting at the home office, and *consequently* I have had to reschedule all my meetings.

c. If the expression occurs *at the beginning of a dependent clause,* either treat the expression as nonessential (and set it off with two commas) or treat it as essential (and omit the commas).

If, *moreover,* they do not meet the deadline, we have the right to cancel the contract.

If *indeed* they want to settle the dispute, why don't we suggest that they submit to arbitration?

He is a man who, *in my opinion,* will make a fine marketing director.

She is a woman who *no doubt* knows how to run a department smoothly and effectively.

The situation is so serious that, *strictly speaking,* bankruptcy is the only solution.

The situation is so serious that *perhaps* bankruptcy may be the only solution.

143 With the Adverb *Too*

a. When the adverb *too* (in the sense of "also") occurs at the end of a clause or a sentence, the comma preceding is omitted.

If you feel that way *too,* why don't we just drop all further negotiation?

They are after a bigger share of the market *too.*

b. When *too* (in the sense of "also") occurs elsewhere in the sentence, particularly between subject and verb, set it off with two commas.

You, *too,* could be in the Caribbean right now.

Then, *too,* there are the additional taxes to be considered.

c. When *too* is used as an adverb meaning "excessively," it is never set off with commas.

The news is almost *too* good to be believed.

1

With Interruptions and Afterthoughts

144   Use commas to set off words, phrases, or clauses that interrupt the flow of a sentence or that are loosely added at the end as an afterthought.

Pam is being pursued, *so I've been told,* by three headhunters.

Bob spoke on state-of-the-art financial software, *if I remember correctly.*

Our order processing service, *you must admit,* leaves much to be desired.

His research work has been outstanding, *particularly in the field of ergonomics.*

➤ *See also ¶¶131c, 136b, 137c.*

CAUTION: When enclosing an interrupting expression with two commas, be sure the commas are inserted accurately.

WRONG: That is the best, *though not the cheapest way,* to proceed.

RIGHT: That is the best, *though not the cheapest,* way to proceed.

WRONG: This book is better written, though less exciting than, her last book.

RIGHT: This book is better written, *though less exciting,* than her last book.

WRONG: Her work is as good, if not better than, that of the man she replaced.

RIGHT: Her work is as good as, *if not better than,* that of the man she replaced.

WRONG: Glen has a deep interest in, *as well as a great fondness,* for jazz.

RIGHT: Glen has a deep interest in, *as well as a great fondness for,* jazz.

With Direct Address

145   Names and titles used in direct address must be set off by commas.

We agree, *Mrs. Connolly,* that your order was badly handled.

No, *sir,* that is privileged information.

I count on your support, *Bob.*

With Additional Considerations

146   **a.** When a phrase introduced by *as well as, in addition to, besides, along with, including, accompanied by, together with, plus,* or a similar expression falls between the subject and the verb, it is ordinarily set off by commas. Commas may be omitted, however, if the phrase fits smoothly into the flow of the sentence or is essential to the meaning.

Everyone, *including the top corporate managers,* will be required to attend the in-house seminars on the ethical dimensions of business.

The business plan *including strategies for the new market segments we hope to enter* is better than the other plans I have reviewed. (The *including* phrase is needed to distinguish this plan from the others; hence no commas.)

One *plus* one doesn't always equal two, as we have seen in the Parker-Jackel merger. (The *plus* phrase is essential to the meaning; hence no commas.)

Claudia *as well as Nina* should be invited to participate in the sales meeting in Maui. (The *as well as* phrase flows smoothly in this sentence.)

➤ *For the effect these phrases have on the choice of a singular or a plural verb, see ¶¶1007; for a usage note on* as well as, *see page 257.*

b. When the phrase occurs elsewhere in the sentence, commas may be omitted if the phrase is closely related to the preceding words.

The refinancing terms have been approved by the trustees *as well as the creditors.*

BUT: I attended the international monetary conference in Bermuda, *together with five associates from our Washington office.*

With Contrasting Expressions

147 Contrasting expressions should be set off by commas. (Such expressions often begin with *but, not,* or *rather than.*)

> The Sanchezes are willing to sell, *but only on their terms.*
>
> He had changed his methods, *not his objectives,* we noticed.
>
> Paula, *rather than Al,* has been chosen for the job.
>
> The CEO and not the president will make that decision. (See ¶1006b.)

NOTE: When such phrases fit smoothly into the flow of the sentence, no commas are required.

> It was a busy *but enjoyable* trip.   They have chosen Paula *rather than Al.*

➤ *For the punctuation of balancing expressions, see ¶172c.*

The following rules (¶¶148–153) deal with descriptive expressions that immediately follow the words to which they refer. When nonessential, these expressions are set off by commas.

With Identifying, Appositive, or Explanatory Expressions

148 Use commas to set off expressions that provide additional but *nonessential* information about a noun or pronoun immediately preceding. Such expressions serve to further identify or explain the word they refer to.

> Harriet McManus, *an independent real estate broker for the past ten years,* will be joining our agency on Tuesday, *October 1.* (Phrases such as those following *Harriet McManus* and *Tuesday* are appositives.)
>
> Acrophobia, *that is, the fear of great heights,* can now be successfully treated. (See also ¶¶181–183 for other punctuation with *that is, namely,* and *for example.*)
>
> His first book, *written while he was still in graduate school,* launched a successful writing career.
>
> Our first thought, *to run to the nearest exit,* would have resulted in panic.
>
> Ms. Ballantine, *who has been a copywriter for six years,* will be our new copy chief.
>
> Everyone in our family likes outdoor sports, *such as tennis and swimming.* (See ¶149, note.)

NOTE: In some cases other punctuation may be preferable in place of commas.

> **CONFUSING:** Mr. Newcombe, *my boss,* and I will discuss this problem next week. (Does *my boss* refer to Mr. Newcombe, or are there three people involved?)
>
> **CLEAR:** Mr. Newcombe (my boss) and I will be discussing this problem next week. (Use parentheses or dashes instead of commas when an appositive expression could be misread as a separate item in a series.)
>
> There are two factors to be considered, *sales and collections.* (A colon or a dash could be used in place of the comma. See ¶¶189, 201.)
>
> **BUT:** There are three factors to be considered: sales, collections, and inventories. (When the explanatory expression consists of a series of *three* or more items and comes at the end of the sentence, use a colon or dash. See ¶¶189, 201.)
>
> **OR:** These three factors—sales, collections, and inventories—should be considered. (When the explanatory series comes within the sentence, set it off with dashes or parentheses. See ¶¶183, 202, 219.)

1

149 When the expression is *essential* to the completeness of the sentence, do not set it off. (In the following examples the expression is needed to identify which particular item is meant. If the expression were omitted, the sentence would be incomplete.)

The year *1997* marks the one hundredth anniversary of our company.

The word *liaison* is often misspelled.

The novelist *Anne Tyler* gave a reading last week from a work in progress.

The statement *"I don't remember"* was frequently heard in court yesterday.

The impulse *to get away from it all* is very common.

The notes *in green ink* were made by Mrs. Long.

The person *who takes over as general manager* will need everyone's support.

NOTE: Compare the following sets of examples:

Her article *"Color and Design"* was published in June. (The title is essential; it identifies *which* article.)

Her latest article, *"Color and Design,"* was published in June. (Nonessential; the word *latest* already indicates which article.)

Her latest article *on color and design* was published in June. (Without commas, this means she had earlier articles on the same subject.)

Her latest article, *on color and design,* was published in June. (With commas, this means her earlier articles were on other subjects.)

Everyone in our family likes such outdoor sports *as tennis and swimming.* (The phrase *as tennis and swimming* is essential; without it, the reader would not know which outdoor sports were meant.)

Everyone in our family likes outdoor sports, *such as tennis and swimming.* (The main clause, *Everyone in our family likes outdoor sports,* expresses a complete thought; the phrase *such as tennis and swimming* gives additional but nonessential information. Hence a comma is needed before *such as.*)

Words *such as peak, peek, and pique* can be readily confused. (The *such as* phrase indicates which words are meant.)

A number of Fortune 500 companies, *such as GE, TRW, and DuPont,* have introduced new programs to motivate their middle managers. (The *such as* phrase provides additional but nonessential information.)

150 A number of expressions are treated as essential simply because of a very close relationship with the preceding words. (If read aloud, the combined phrase sounds like one unit, without any intervening pause.)

After a while Gladys *herself* became disenchanted with the Washington scene.

We *legislators* must provide funds for retraining displaced workers.

My wife Eve has begun her own consulting business. (Strictly speaking, *Eve* should be set off by commas, since the name is not needed to indicate *which* wife. However, commas are omitted in expressions like these because they are read as a unit.)

My brother Paul may join us as well.
BUT: My brother, *Paul Engstrom,* may join us.

The composer *Stephen Sondheim* has many Broadway hits to his credit.
BUT: My favorite composer, *Stephen Sondheim,* has many Broadway hits . . .

The Story of English by Robert McCrum, William Cran, and Robert MacNeil has been made into a highly praised television series. (Unless there is another book with the same title, the *by* phrase identifying the authors is not essential and should be set off by commas. However, since a book title and a *by* phrase are typically read as a unit, commas are usually omitted.)

151 When *or* introduces a word or a phrase that identifies or explains the preceding word, set off the explanatory expression with commas.

> Determine whether the clauses are coordinate, *or of equal rank.* (The nonessential *or* phrase may also be set off by parentheses.)

However, if *or* introduces an alternative thought, the expression is essential and should not be set off by commas.

> Determine whether the clauses are coordinate *or noncoordinate.*

152 When a business letter is referred to by date, any related phrases or clauses that follow are usually nonessential.

> Thank you for your letter of February 27, *in which you questioned the balance on your account.* (The date is sufficient to identify which letter is meant; the *in which* clause simply provides additional but nonessential information. Of course, if one received more than one letter with the same date from the same person, the *in which* clause would be essential and the comma would be omitted.)

However, no comma is needed after the date if the following phrase is short and closely related.

> Thank you for your letter of February 27 *about the balance on your account.*

With Residence and Business Connections

153 Use commas to set off a *long phrase* denoting a person's residence or business connections.

> Gary Kendall, *of the Van Houten Corporation in Provo, Utah,* will be visiting us next week.
>
> Gary Kendall *of Provo, Utah,* will be visiting us next week. (Omit the comma before *of* to avoid too many breaks in a short phrase. The state name must always be set off by commas when it follows a city name. See also ¶160.)
>
> Gary Kendall *of the Van Houten Corporation* will be visiting us next week. (Short phrase; no commas.)
>
> Gary Kendall *of Provo* will be visiting us next week. (Short phrase; no commas.)

The following rules (¶¶154–161) deal with the "nonessential" treatment of certain elements in dates, personal names, company names, and addresses. These elements cannot truly be called nonessential, but the traditional style is to set them off with commas.

In Dates

154 a. Use two commas to set off the year when it follows the month and day.

> On October 31, *1998,* I plan to retire and open a bookshop in Maine.
>
> The November 28, *1994,* issue of *Business Week* forecast that home computer sales would explode as PCs turned into all-purpose information appliances.

b. When the month, day, and year are used as a nonessential expression, be sure to set the entire phrase off with commas.

> The conference scheduled to begin on Monday, *November 27, 1995,* has now been rescheduled to start on February 6, 1996.
>
> Payment of estimated income taxes for the fourth quarter of 1996 will be due no later than Wednesday, *January 15, 1997.*

155 Omit the commas when only the month and year are given.

> In *August 1997* Glen and I dissolved our partnership and went our independent ways.

> Isn't it about time for *Consumer Reports* to update the evaluation of cordless telephones that appeared in the *December 1994* issue?

➤ *For additional examples involving dates, see ¶410.*

With *Jr., Sr.,* Etc.

156 Do not use commas to set off *Jr., Sr.,* or roman or arabic numerals following a person's name unless you know that the person in question prefers to do so.

> Kelsey R. Patterson Jr.   Benjamin Hart 2d
>
> Christopher M. Gorman Sr.   Anthony Jung III
>
> John Bond Jr.'s resignation will be announced tomorrow.

NOTE: When a person prefers to use commas in his name, observe the following style:

> Peter Passaro, Jr. (Use one comma when the name is displayed on a line by itself.)
>
> Peter Passaro, Jr., director of . . . (Use two commas when other copy follows.)
>
> Peter Passaro, Jr.'s promotion . . . (Drop the second comma when a possessive ending is attached.)

157 Abbreviations like *Esq.* and those that stand for academic degrees or religious orders are set off by two commas when they follow a person's name.

> Address the letter to Helen E. Parsekian, *Esq.,* in New York.
>
> Roger Farrier, *LL.D.,* will address the Elizabethan Club on Wednesday.
>
> The Reverend James Hanley, *S.J.,* will serve as moderator of the panel.

158 When a personal name is given in inverted order, set off the inverted portion with commas.

> McCaughan, James W., Jr.

With *Inc.* and *Ltd.*

159 Do not use commas to set off *Inc., Ltd.,* and similar expressions in a company name unless you know that a particular company prefers to do so. (See also ¶¶1328–1329.)

> Time Inc.   Field Hats, Ltd.
>
> Time *Inc.* has expanded its operations beyond magazine publishing.
>
> Field Hats, *Ltd.,* should be notified about this mistake.

NOTE: When commas are to be used in a company name, follow this style:

> Alwyn & Hyde, Inc. (Use one comma when the name is displayed on a line by itself.)
>
> Alwyn & Hyde, Inc., announces the publication of . . . (Use two commas when other copy follows.)
>
> Alwyn & Hyde, Inc.'s annual statement . . . (Drop the second comma after a possessive ending.)

➤ *For the use of commas with other parts of a company name, see ¶163.*

In Geographic References and Addresses

160 Use two commas to set off the name of a state, a country, or the equivalent when it directly follows the name of a city or a county.

> Four years ago I was transferred from Bartlesville, *Oklahoma,* to Kinshasa, *Zaire.*
>
> Could Pickaway County, Ohio, become a haven for retired editors?
>
> Our Pierre, *South Dakota,* office is the one nearest to you.
>
> **OR:** Our Pierre (South Dakota) office is the one nearest to you. (Parentheses are clearer than commas when a city-state expression serves as an adjective.)
>
> Washington, *D.C.'s* transportation system has improved greatly since I was last there. (Omit the second comma after a possessive ending.)

161 When expressing complete addresses, follow this style:

> **IN SENTENCES:** During the month of August you can send material directly to me at 402 Woodbury Road, Pasadena, CA 91104, or you can ask my assistant to forward it. (Note that a comma follows the ZIP Code but does not precede it.)
>
> **IN DISPLAYED BLOCKS:** 402 Woodbury Road
> Pasadena, CA 91104

The following rules (¶¶162–175) deal with various uses of separating commas: to separate items in a series, to separate adjectives that precede a noun, and to clarify meaning in sentences with unusual word order or omitted words.

In a Series

162 When three or more items are listed in a series and the last item is preceded by *and, or,* or *nor,* place a comma before the conjunction as well as between the other items. (See also ¶126c.)

> Study the rules for the use of the comma, the semicolon, *and* the colon.
>
> The consensus is that your report is well written, that your facts are accurate, *and* that your conclusions are sound.
>
> The show will appeal equally to women and men, adults and children, *and* sophisticates and innocents. (See page 255 for a usage note on *and.*)

NOTE: If a nonessential element follows the conjunction *(and, or,* or *nor)* in a series, omit the comma before the conjunction to avoid excessive punctuation.

> We invited Ben's business associates, his friends and, of course, his parents.
>
> (**RATHER THAN:** . . . his friends, and, of course, his parents.)

163 For a series in an organization's name, always follow the style preferred by that organization.

> Merrill Lynch, Pierce, Fenner & Smith Inc.
> Legg Mason Wood Walker, Inc.

If you do not have the organization's letterhead or some other reliable resource at hand, follow the standard rule on commas in a series (see ¶162).

> Our primary supplier is *Ames, Koslow, Milke, and Company.*

NOTE: Do not use a comma before an ampersand (&) in an organization's name unless you know that a particular organization prefers to do so.

> Aspinwall, Bromley, Carruthers & Dalgleish

164 When an expression such as *and so on* or *etc.* closes a series, use a comma before and after the expression (except at the end of a sentence).

> Our sale of suits, coats, hats, *and so on,* starts tomorrow.

> Tomorrow morning we will start our sale of suits, coats, hats, *etc.*

➤ *For a usage note on* etc., *see page 261.*

165 Do not insert a comma after the last item in a series unless the sentence structure demands a comma at that point.

> May 8, June 11, and July 14 are the dates for the next three hearings.

> May 8, June 11, and July 14, 1997, are the dates for the next three hearings. (The comma after *1997* is one of the pair that sets off the year. See ¶154.)

166 When *and, or,* or *nor* is used to connect all the items in a series, do not separate the items by commas. (See also ¶123b.)

> Send copies to our employees *and* stockholders *and* major customers.

167 If a series consists of only two items, do not separate the items with a comma. (See also ¶125f.)

> We can send the samples to you *by regular mail* or *by one of the express services.*

NOTE: Use a comma, however, to separate two independent clauses joined by *and, but, or,* or *nor.* (See ¶126a.)

➤ *For the use of the semicolon in a series, see* ¶¶*184–185.*

With Adjectives

168 When two consecutive adjectives modify the same noun, separate the adjectives with a comma.

> Jean is a *generous, outgoing* person. (A person who is *generous and outgoing.*)

NOTE: Do *not* use a comma between the adjectives if they are connected by *and, or,* or *nor.*

> Jean is a *generous* and *outgoing* person.

169 When two adjectives precede a noun, the first adjective may modify the combined idea of the second adjective plus the noun. In such cases do not separate the adjectives by a comma.

> The estate is surrounded by an *old stone* wall. (A *stone* wall that is *old.*)

> Here is the *annual financial* statement. (A *financial* statement that is *annual.*)

TEST: To decide whether consecutive adjectives should be separated by a comma or not, try using them in a relative clause *after* the noun, with *and* inserted between them. If they read smoothly and sensibly in that position, they should be separated by a comma in their actual position.

> We need an *intelligent, enterprising* person for the job. (One can speak of "a person who is *intelligent* and *enterprising,*" so a comma is correct.)

> Throw out your *old down* coat. (One cannot speak of "a coat that is *old* and *down,*" so no comma should be used in the actual sentence.)

> You can purchase any of these printers with a *low down* payment. (In this case the adjective *low* modifies a compound noun, *down payment.*)

> To put it gently but plainly, I think Jason is a *low-down* scoundrel. (In this case *low-down* is a compound adjective and requires a hyphen to connect *low* and *down.* See ¶¶813–832 for a discussion of compound adjectives.)

170 When more than two adjectives precede a noun, insert a comma only between those adjectives where *and* could have been used.

> a relaxed, unruffled, confident manner (a relaxed *and* unruffled *and* confident manner)
>
> an experienced, efficient legal assistant (an experienced *and* efficient legal assistant)
>
> the established American political system (*and* cannot be inserted between these three adjectives)

171 Do not use a comma between the final adjective in a series and the following noun.

> I put in a long, hard, *demanding day* on Monday.
> (NOT: I put in a long, hard, *demanding, day* on Monday.)

To Indicate Omitted Words

172 **a. Omission of Repetitive Wording.** Use a comma to indicate the omission of repetitive wording in a compound sentence. (This use of the comma usually occurs when clauses are separated by semicolons.)

> Employees aged 55 and over are eligible for a complete physical examination every year; those between 50 and 54, every two years; and those under 50, every three years.

> NOTE: If the omitted words are clearly understood from the context, simpler punctuation may be used.

> Employees aged 55 and over are eligible for a complete physical examination every year, those between 50 and 54 every two years, and those under 50 every three years.

b. Omission of *That.* In some sentences the omission of the conjunction *that* creates a definite break in the flow of the sentence. In such cases insert a comma to mark the break.

> Remember, this offer is good only through May 31.
> The problem is, not all of these assumptions may be correct.
> The fact is, things are not working out as we had hoped.
> Chances are, the deal will never come off.

> NOTE: In sentences that are introduced by expressions such as *he said, she thinks, we feel,* or *they know,* the conjunction *that* is often omitted following the introductory expression. In such cases no comma is necessary because there is no break in the flow of the sentence.

> We know you can do it.   She said she would handle everything.
> They think our price is too high.   We believe we offer the best service.

c. Balancing Expressions. Use a comma to separate the two parts of a balancing expression from which many words have been omitted.

> First come, first served.   The more we give, the more they take.
> First in, last out.   GIGO: garbage in, garbage out.
> Here today, gone tomorrow.   The less I see of him, the better I like it.

> NOTE: The phrase *The sooner the better* usually appears without a separating comma.

To Indicate Unusual Word Order

173 In some colloquial sentences, clauses or phrases occur out of normal order and connective words may be omitted. Use a comma to mark the resulting break in the flow of the sentence.

> You must not miss the play, it was that good.
> (**NORMAL ORDER:** The play was so good that you must not miss it.)

> Why he took the money, I'll never understand.

> That the shipment would be late, we were prepared to accept; that you would ship the wrong goods, we did not expect.

NOTE: In formal writing, these sentences should be recast in normal word order.

➤ *See also ¶135c, note.*

For Special Emphasis

174 Individual words may be set off by commas for special emphasis.

> I have tried, *sincerely,* to understand your problems.

> They contend, *unrealistically,* that we can cut back on staff and still generate the same amount of output.

NOTE: The use of commas in the examples above forces the reader to dwell momentarily on the word that has been set off in each case. Without this treatment *sincerely* and *unrealistically* would not receive this emphasis.

For Clarity

175 **a.** Use a comma to prevent misreading.

> As you know, nothing came of the meeting.
> (**NOT:** As you know nothing came of the meeting.)

> To a liberal like Bill, Buckley seems hard to take.

> Soon after, the committee disbanded without accomplishing its goal.

b. Sometimes, for clarity, it is necessary to separate even a subject and a verb.

> All any insurance policy is, is a contract for services.

c. Use a comma to separate repeated words.

> It was a *long, long* time ago.

> That was a *very, very* old argument.

> *Well, well,* we'll find a way.

> *Now, now,* you don't expect me to believe that!

➤ *Commas with dashes: see ¶¶213, 215b.*
Commas in numbers: see ¶¶461–463.
Commas with questions within sentences: see ¶¶114–117.
Commas with parentheses: see ¶224a.
Commas inside closing quotation marks: see ¶247.
Commas at the end of quotations: see ¶¶253–255.
Commas preceding quotations: see ¶256.
Commas with quotations within a sentence: see ¶¶259–262.
Commas to set off interruptions in quoted material: see ¶262.
Spacing with commas: see ¶299.

THE SEMICOLON

Between Independent Clauses—
And, But, Or, or *Nor* Omitted

176 **a.** When a coordinating conjunction *(and, but, or,* or *nor)* is omitted between two independent clauses, use a semicolon—not a comma—to separate the clauses. (See ¶187.) If you prefer, you can treat the second clause as a separate sentence.

> Most of the stockholders favored the sale; the management did not.
> **OR:** Most of the stockholders favored the sale. The management did not.
> **(NOT:** Most of the stockholders favored the sale, the management did not.)

> Bob is going for his M.B.A.; Janet already has hers.

> Subnotebooks aren't just smaller; they're cheaper.
> **(NOT:** Subnotebooks aren't just smaller, they're cheaper.)

b. If the clauses are not closely related, treat them as separate sentences.

> **WEAK:** Thank you for your letter of September 8; your question has already been passed on to the manager of mail-order sales, and you should be hearing from Mrs. Livonia within three days.

> **BETTER:** Thank you for your letter of September 8. Your question has already been passed on to the manager of mail-order sales, and you should be ...

c. The omission of *but* between two independent clauses requires, strictly speaking, the use of a semicolon between the two clauses. However, when the clauses are short, a comma is commonly used to preserve the flow of the sentence.

> Not only was the food bad, the portions were minuscule.

Between Independent Clauses—
And, But, Or, or *Nor* Included

177 A comma is normally used to separate two independent clauses joined by a coordinating conjunction. However, under certain circumstances a semicolon is appropriate before the coordinating conjunction.

a. Use a semicolon in order to achieve a stronger break between clauses than a comma provides.

> **NORMAL BREAK:** Many people are convinced that they could personally solve the problem if given the authority to do so, but no one will come forward with a clear-cut plan that we can evaluate in advance.

> **STRONG BREAK:** Many people are convinced that they could personally solve the problem if given the authority to do so; but no one will come forward with a clear-cut plan that we can evaluate in advance.

b. Use a semicolon when one or both clauses have internal commas and a misreading might occur if a comma also separated the clauses.

> **CONFUSING:** I sent you an order for copier paper, computer paper, and No. 10 envelopes, and shipping tags, cardboard cartons, stapler wire, and binding tape were sent to me instead.

> **CLEAR:** I sent you an order for copier paper, computer paper, and No. 10 envelopes; and shipping tags, cardboard cartons, stapler wire, and binding tape were sent to me instead.

(Continued on page 40.)

c. If no misreading is likely, a comma is sufficient to separate the clauses, even though commas are also used within the clauses.

> On June 8, 1995, I discussed this problem with your customer service manager, Betty Dugan, but your company has taken no further action.

> All in all, we're satisfied with the job Bergquist Associates did, and in view of the tight deadlines they had to meet, we're pleased that they came through as well as they did.

➤ *For additional examples, see ¶133.*

With Transitional Expressions

178 When independent clauses are linked by transitional expressions (see a partial list below), use a semicolon between the clauses. (You can also treat the second independent clause as a separate sentence.)

accordingly	however	so (see ¶179)
besides	moreover	that is (see ¶181)
consequently	namely (see ¶181)	then
for example (see ¶181)	nevertheless	therefore
furthermore	on the contrary	thus
hence	otherwise	yet (see ¶179)

> They have given us an oral okay to proceed; *however,* we're still waiting for written confirmation. (**OR:** . . . okay to proceed. *However,* we're still . . .)

> Our costs have started to level off; our sales, *moreover,* have continued to grow.

> Let's give them another month; *then* we can pin them down on their progress.

NOTE: Use a comma after the transitional expression when it occurs at the start of the second clause. (See the first example above.) However, no comma is needed after *hence, then, thus, so,* and *yet* unless a pause is wanted at that point. (See the third example above.)

➤ *For the use of commas with transitional expressions, see ¶¶138–143.*

179 An independent clause introduced by *so* (in the sense of "therefore") or *yet* may be preceded by a comma or a semicolon. Use a comma if the two clauses are closely related and there is a smooth flow from the first clause to the second. Use a semicolon or a period if the clauses are long and complicated or if the transition between clauses calls for a long pause or a strong break.

> Sales have been good, *yet* profits are low.

> This report explains why production has slowed down; *yet* it does not indicate how to avoid future glitches.

> These sale-priced attaché cases are going fast, *so* don't delay if you want one.

> We have been getting an excessive number of complaints during the last few months about our service; *so* I would like each of you to review the operations in your department and indicate what corrective measures you think ought to be taken. (**OR:** . . . about our service. *So* I would like . . .)

180 If both a coordinating conjunction and a transitional expression occur at the start of the second clause, use a comma before the conjunction.

> The site has a number of disadvantages, *and furthermore* the asking price is quite high. (See ¶142b and note.)

REMEMBER: A semicolon is needed to separate independent clauses, not so much because a transitional expression is present but because a coordinating conjunction is absent.

With *For Example, Namely, That Is,* Etc.

181 Before an Independent Clause

a. In general, when two independent clauses are linked by a transitional expression such as *for example (e.g.), namely,* or *that is (i.e.),* use a semicolon before the expression and a comma afterward.

> She is highly qualified for the job; *for example,* she has had ten years' experience as a research chemist.

> **NOTE:** You can also replace the semicolon with a period and treat the second clause as a separate sentence.

> She is highly qualified for the job. *For example,* she has had . . .

b. If the first clause serves to anticipate the second clause and the full emphasis is to fall on the second clause, use a colon before the transitional expression.

> Your proposal covers all but one point: *namely,* who is going to foot the bill?

c. For a stronger but less formal break between clauses, the semicolon or the colon may be replaced by a dash.

> Hampton says he will help—*that is,* he will help if you ask him to.

NOTE: Use the abbreviated forms *e.g.* and *i.e.* only in informal, technical, or "expedient" material. (See ¶502.)

182 At the End of a Sentence

When *for example, namely,* or *that is* introduces words, phrases, or a series of clauses *at the end of a sentence,* the punctuation preceding the expression may vary as follows:

a. If the first part of the sentence expresses the complete thought and the explanation that follows seems to be added as an afterthought, use a semicolon before the transitional expression.

> Always use figures with abbreviations; *for example,* 6 m, 9 sq in, 4 p.m. (Here the earlier part of the sentence carries the main thought; the examples are a welcome but nonessential addition.)

b. If the first part of the sentence suggests that an important explanation or illustration will follow, use a colon before the transitional expression to throw emphasis on what *follows.*

> My assistant has three important duties: *namely,* attending all meetings, writing the minutes, and sending out notices. (The word *three* anticipates the enumeration following *namely.* The colon suggests that what follows is the main thought of the sentence.)

> **NOTE:** Use a comma before the transitional expression to throw emphasis on what *precedes.*

> I checked these figures with three people, *namely,* Alma, Andy, and Jim. (This punctuation emphasizes *three people* rather than the specific names.)

c. If the expression introduces an appositive that explains a word or phrase immediately preceding, a comma should precede the transitional expression.

> Do not use quotation marks to enclose an indirect quotation, *that is, a restatement of a person's exact words.* (Here again, a comma is used because what precedes the transitional expression is more important than what follows.)

(Continued on page 42.)

d. The semicolon, the colon, and the comma in the examples in ¶182a–c may be replaced by a dash or by parentheses. The dash provides a stronger but less formal break; the parentheses serve to subordinate the explanatory element. (See also ¶¶201–205, 219.)

183 Within a Sentence

When *for example, namely,* or *that is* introduces words, phrases, or clauses *within a sentence,* treat the entire construction as nonessential and set it off with commas, dashes, or parentheses. Dashes will give emphasis to the interrupting construction; parentheses will make the construction appear less important than the rest of the words in the sentence.

Many of the components, *for example, the motor,* are manufactured by outside suppliers.

Many of the components—*for example, the motor*—are manufactured by outside suppliers.

Many of the components (*for example, the motor*) are manufactured by outside suppliers.

NOTE: Commas can be used to set off the nonessential element so long as it contains no internal punctuation (other than the comma after the introductory expression). If the nonessential element is internally punctuated with several commas, set it off with either dashes or parentheses.

Many of the components—*for example, the motor, the batteries, and the cooling unit*—are manufactured . . . (Use dashes for emphasis. See ¶201.)

OR: Many of the components (*for example, the motor, the batteries, and the cooling unit*) are manufactured . . . (Use parentheses for subordination. See ¶219b.)

In a Series

184 Use a semicolon to separate items in a series if any of the items already contain commas.

The company will be represented on the Longwood Environmental Council by Martha Janowski, director of public affairs; Harris Mendel, vice president of manufacturing; and Daniel Santoya, director of environmental systems.

NOTE: As an alternative use parentheses to enclose the title following each name. Then use commas to separate the items in the series.

The company will be represented on the Longwood Environmental Council by Martha Janowski (director of public affairs), Harris Mendel (vice president of manufacturing), and Daniel Santoya (director of environmental systems).

185 Avoid starting a sentence with a series punctuated with semicolons. Try to recast the sentence so that the series comes at the end.

AWKWARD: New offices in Framingham, Massachusetts; Rochester, Minnesota; Metairie, Louisiana; and Bath, Maine, will be opened next year.

IMPROVED: Next year we will open new offices in Framingham, Massachusetts; Rochester, Minnesota; Metairie, Louisiana; and Bath, Maine.

With Dependent Clauses

186 Use semicolons to separate a series of parallel dependent clauses if they are long or contain internal commas. (However, a simple series of dependent clauses requires only commas, just like any other kind of series. For an illustration see the second example in ¶162.)

They promised that they would review the existing specifications, costs, and sales estimates for the project; that they would analyze Merkle's alternative figures; and that they would prepare a comparison of the two proposals and submit their recommendations.

If you have tried special clearance sales but have not been able to raise the necessary cash; if you have tried to borrow the money and have not been able to find a lender; if you have offered to sell part of the business but have not been able to find a partner, then it seems to me that your only course of action is to go out of business. (See ¶185.)

> *Semicolons with dashes: see ¶¶213, 215c.*
Semicolons with parentheses: see ¶224a.
Semicolons with quotation marks: see ¶248.
Spacing with semicolons: see ¶299.

THE COLON

Between Independent Clauses

187   **a.** Use a colon between two independent clauses when the second clause explains or illustrates the first clause and there is no coordinating conjunction or transitional expression linking the two clauses. (Leave two spaces after a colon. See also ¶299.)

I have a special fondness for the Maine coast: it reminds me of the many happy summers we spent there before our children went off to college.

I have two major hurdles to clear before I get my Ph.D.: pass the oral exam and write a dissertation.

NOTE: The second clause that explains or illustrates the first clause may itself consist of more than one independent clause.

It has been said that a successful project goes through three stages: it won't work, it costs too much, and I always knew it was a good idea.

b. Compare the use of the colon and the semicolon in the following sentences.

The job you have described sounds very attractive: the salary, the benefits, and the opportunities for advancement seem excellent. (Use a colon when the second clause explains the first.)

The job you have described sounds very attractive; it is the kind of job I have been looking for. (Use a semicolon when the second clause does not explain the first clause.)

The job you have described sounds very attractive; for example, the salary and the benefits are good, and the opportunities for advancement seem excellent. (Use a semicolon when a transitional expression links the clauses.)

c. If you aren't sure whether to use a semicolon or a colon between two independent clauses, you can always treat each clause as a separate sentence and use a period at the end of each.

The job you have described sounds very attractive. For example, the salary and the benefits are good, and the opportunities for advancement seem excellent.

Before Lists and Enumerations

188 Place a colon before such expressions as *for example, namely,* and *that is* when they introduce words, phrases, or a series of clauses anticipated earlier in the sentence. (See ¶¶181–182.)

> The company provides a number of benefits not commonly offered in this area: for example, free dental insurance, low-cost term insurance, and personal financial counseling services.

189 When a clause contains an anticipatory expression (such as *the following, as follows, thus,* and *these*) and directs attention to a series of explanatory words, phrases, or clauses, use a colon between the clause and the series.

> *These* are some of the new features in this year's models: a fuel economy indicator, a new rear suspension, and a three-year limited warranty.

> *The following* staff members have been selected to attend the national sales conference in Honolulu:
>
> > Frances Berkowitz
> > Thomas Gomez
> > Thomas Miscina

190 Use a colon even if the anticipatory expression is only implied and not stated.

> The house has attractive features: cross ventilation in every room, a two-story living room, and two terraces.

> Scientists have devised a most appropriate name for a physical property opposed to gravity: levity. (The colon may be used even when what follows is only a single word. See also ¶210.)

191 Do not use a colon in the following cases:

a. If the anticipatory expression occurs near the beginning of a long sentence.

> We have set *the following* restrictions on the return of merchandise, so please be aware of this new policy when dealing with customers. Goods cannot be returned after five days, and price tags must not be removed.

> **BUT:** We have set *the following* restrictions on the return of merchandise: goods cannot be returned . . .

b. If the sentence containing the anticipatory expression is followed by another sentence.

> Campers will find that *the following* small items will add much to their enjoyment. These articles may be purchased from a store near the camp.
>
> > Flashlight   Hot-cold food bag
> > Camera   Fishing gear

c. If an explanatory series follows an introductory clause that does not express a complete thought. (In such cases the introductory element often ends with a verb or a preposition.)

> **WRONG:** Some of the questions that this book answers are: How can you reduce your insurance expenses without sacrificing protection? How can you avoid being over- or underinsured? How can you file a claim correctly the first time around? (Here the introductory clause is incomplete. It has a subject, *Some,* and a verb, *are,* but it lacks a complement.)

> **RIGHT:** Some of the questions that this book answers are these: How can you . . . ? (Here the introductory clause is complete; hence a colon is acceptable.)

RIGHT: Here are some of the questions that this book answers: How can you . . . ? (Here again the introductory clause is complete; hence a colon is acceptable.)

WRONG: The panel consists of: Ms. Seidel, Mrs. Kitay, and Mr. Haddad.

RIGHT: The panel consists of Ms. Seidel, Mrs. Kitay, and Mr. Haddad.

RIGHT: The panel consists of the following people: Ms. Seidel, Mrs. Kitay, and Mr. Haddad.

WRONG: This set of china includes: 12 dinner plates, 12 salad plates, and 12 cups and saucers.

RIGHT: This set of china includes 12 dinner plates, 12 salad plates, and 12 cups and saucers.

RIGHT: This set of china includes the following items: 12 dinner plates, 12 salad plates, and 12 cups and saucers.

NOTE: A colon may be used after an incomplete introductory clause if the items in the series are listed on separate lines.

This set of china includes:	The panel consists of:
12 dinner plates	Ms. Seidel
12 salad plates .	Mrs. Kitay
12 cups and saucers	Mr. Haddad

In Expressions of Time and Proportions

192 When hours and minutes are expressed in figures, separate them with a colon, as in the expression *8:25*. (No space precedes or follows this colon. See also ¶299.)

193 A colon is used to represent the word *to* in proportions, as in the ratio *2:1*. (No space precedes or follows this colon. See also ¶299.)

After Salutations

194 In business letters, use a colon after the salutation (see also ¶1346). In social-business letters, use a comma (see also ¶1396b).

In References to Books or Publications

195 **a.** Use a colon to separate the title and the subtitle of a book.

William Least Heat Moon, in *Blue Highways: A Journey Into America*, has provided an extraordinary portrait of a country and its people.

b. A colon may be used to separate volume number and page number in footnotes and similar references. (Leave no space before or after the colon. See also ¶299.)

8:763–766 (meaning *Volume 8, pages 763–766*; see also ¶1512, note)

NOTE: A reference to chapter and verse in the Bible is handled the same way:

Is. 55:10 (meaning *Chapter 55, verse 10* in the Book of Isaiah)

Capitalizing After a Colon

196 Do not capitalize after a colon if the material that follows cannot stand alone as a sentence.

(Continued on page 46.)

1

All cash advances must be countersigned by me, with one exception: when the amount is less than $50. (Dependent clause following a colon.)

Two courses are required: algebra and English. (Words following a colon.)

EXCEPTION: Capitalize the first word after the colon if it is a proper noun, a proper adjective, or the pronoun *I*.

Two courses are required: English and algebra.

197 Do not capitalize the first word of an independent clause after a colon if the clause explains, illustrates, or amplifies the thought expressed in the first part of the sentence. (See ¶196, exception.)

Essential and nonessential elements require altogether different punctuation: the latter should be set off by commas; the former should not.

198 Capitalize the first word of an independent clause after a colon if it requires special emphasis or is presented as a formal rule. (In such cases the independent clause expresses the main thought; the first part of the sentence usually functions only as an introduction.)

Let me say this: If the company is to recover from its present difficulties, we must immediately devise an entirely new marketing strategy.

Here is the key principle: Nonessential elements must be set off by commas; essential elements should not.

199 Also capitalize the first word after a colon under these circumstances:

a. When the material following the colon consists of two or more sentences.

There are several drawbacks to this proposal: First, it will tie up a good deal of capital for the next five years. Second, the likelihood of a significant return on the investment has not been shown.

b. When the material following the colon is a quoted sentence.

Frederick Fontina responded in this way: "We expect to win our case once all the facts are brought out in the trial." (See ¶256 for the use of a colon before a quoted sentence.)

c. When the material following the colon starts on a new line (for example, the body of a letter following the salutation or the individual items displayed on separate lines in a list).

Dear John:	Capitalize the first word of:
I have read your latest draft, and I find it much improved. However, on page 4 I wish you would redo . . .	a. Every sentence. b. Direct quotations. c. Salutations in letters.

d. When the material *preceding* the colon is a short introductory word such as *Note, Caution, Remember,* or *Wanted.*

Note: All expense reports must be submitted no later than Friday.

Remember: All equipment must be turned off before you leave.

➤ *Colons with dashes: see ¶¶213, 215c.*
Colons with parentheses: see ¶224a.
Colons with quotation marks: see ¶¶248, 256.
Spacing with colons: see ¶¶299, 1432e.

SECTION 2
PUNCTUATION: OTHER MARKS

Quotation Marks (*Continued*)

UNDERLINING AND ITALICS (¶¶285–290)

OTHER MARKS OF PUNCTUATION (¶¶291–298)

SPACING WITH PUNCTUATION MARKS (¶299)

THE DASH

Although the dash has a few specific functions of its own, it most often serves in place of the comma, the semicolon, the colon, or parentheses. When used as an alternative to these other marks, it creates a much more emphatic separation of words within a sentence. Because of its versatility, some writers are tempted to use a dash to punctuate almost any break within a sentence. However, this indiscriminate use of dashes destroys the special forcefulness that a dash can convey. So please use the dash sparingly—and then only for deliberate effect.

In Place of Commas

201 Use dashes in place of commas to set off a nonessential element that requires special emphasis.

> At this year's annual banquet, the speakers—and the food—were superb.
>
> Of all the color samples you sent me, there was only one I liked—taupe.

202 If a nonessential element already contains internal commas, use dashes in place of commas to set the element off. (If dashes provide too emphatic a break, use parentheses instead. See ¶¶183, 219.)

> Our entire inventory of Oriental rugs—including a fine selection of Sarouks, Kashans, and Bokharas—will be offered for sale at a 40 percent discount.

203 To give special emphasis to the second independent clause in a compound sentence, use a dash rather than a comma before the coordinating conjunction.

> The information I sent you is true—and you know it!

In Place of a Semicolon

204 For a stronger but less formal break, use a dash in place of a semicolon between closely related independent clauses.

> I do the work—he gets the credit!
>
> The job needs to be done—moreover, it needs to be done well.
>
> Wilson is totally unqualified for a promotion—for example, he still does not grasp the basic principles of good management.

In Place of a Colon

205 For a stronger but less formal break, use a dash in place of a colon to introduce explanatory words, phrases, or clauses.

> I need only a few items for my meeting with Kaster—namely, a copy of his letter of May 18, a copy of the contract under dispute, and a bottle of aspirin.
>
> My arrangement with Gina is a simple one—she handles sales and promotion, and I take care of production.

In Place of Parentheses

206 Use dashes instead of parentheses when you want to give the nonessential element strong emphasis. (See ¶¶183, 219.)

> Call Mike Habib—he's with Jax Electronics—and get his opinion.

To Indicate an Abrupt Break or an Afterthought

207 Use a dash to show an abrupt break in thought or to separate an afterthought from the main part of a sentence. When a sentence breaks off after a dash, leave two spaces before the next sentence. (See ¶208.)

> I wish you would— Is there any point in telling you what I wish for you?
>
> We offer the best service in town—and the fastest!
>
> George Parrish's plane will be landing at O'Hare—or did he say Midway?

208 If a *question* or an *exclamation* breaks off abruptly before it has been completed, use a dash followed by a question mark or an exclamation point as appropriate and then two spaces. If the sentence is a *statement*, however, use a dash alone, followed by two spaces.

> Do you want to tell him or—? Suppose I wait to hear from you.
>
> If only— Yet there's no point in talking about what might have been.
> (NOT: If only—. Yet there's no point in talking about what might have been.)

➤ *For the use of ellipsis marks to indicate a break in thought, see ¶291b.*

To Show Hesitation

209 Use a dash to indicate hesitation, faltering speech, or stammering.

> The work on the Patterson project was begun—oh, I should say—well, about May 1—certainly no later than May 15.

To Emphasize Single Words

2

210 Use dashes to set off single words that require special emphasis.

> Jogging—that's what he lives for.
>
> There is, of course, a secret ingredient in my pasta sauce—fennel.

With Repetitions and Restatements

211 Use dashes to set off and emphasize words that repeat or restate a previous thought.

> Next week—on Thursday at 10 a.m.—we will be making an important announcement at a press conference.
>
> Don't miss this opportunity—the opportunity of a lifetime!

Before Summarizing Words

212 Use a dash before such words as *these, they,* and *all* when these words stand as subjects summarizing a preceding list of details.

> Network television, magazines, and newspapers—*these* will be the big gainers in advertising revenues next year.
>
> India, Korea, and Australia—*all* are important new markets for us.
>
> BUT: India, Korea, and Australia are all important new markets for us. (No dash is used when the summarizing word is not the subject.)

Punctuation Preceding an Opening Dash

213 Do not use a comma, a semicolon, or a colon before an opening dash. Moreover, do not use a period before an opening dash (except a period following an abbreviation).

> Quality circles boost productivity—and they pay off in higher profits too. (NOT: Quality circles boost productivity,—and they pay off in higher profits too.)
>
> The catalog proofs arrived before 11 a.m.—just as you promised.

Punctuation Preceding a Closing Dash

214 **a.** When a *statement* or a *command* is set off by dashes within a sentence, do not use a period before the closing dash (except a period following an abbreviation).

> Ernie Krauthoff—he used to have his own consulting firm—has gone back to his old job at Marker's.
>
> (NOT: Ernie Krauthoff—He used to have his own consulting firm.—has gone back to his old job at Marker's.)
>
> Your proposal was not delivered until 6:15 p.m.—more than two hours after the deadline.

b. When a *question* or an *exclamation* is set off by dashes within a sentence, use a question mark or an exclamation point before the closing dash.

The representative of the Hitchcock Company—do you know her?—has called again for an appointment.

The new sketches—I can't wait to show them to you!—should be ready by Monday.

NOTE: When a complete sentence is set off by dashes, do not capitalize the first word unless it is a proper noun, a proper adjective, the pronoun *I,* or the first word of a quoted sentence.

2

Punctuation Following a Closing Dash

215 When the sentence construction requires some mark of punctuation following a closing dash, either retain the dash or use the sentence punctuation—but do not use both marks together.

a. When a closing dash falls at the end of a sentence, it should be replaced by the punctuation needed to end the sentence—a period, a question mark, or an exclamation point. (See ¶208 for exceptions.)

Wheeler's Transport delivers the goods—on time!
(**NOT:** Wheeler's Transport delivers the goods—on time—!)

b. When a closing dash occurs at a point where the sentence requires a comma, retain the closing dash and omit the comma.

The situation has become critical—indeed dangerous—but no one seems to care. (Here the closing dash is retained, and the comma before the coordinating conjunction is omitted.)

If you feel you are qualified for the job—and you may very well be—you ought to take the employment test and go for an interview. (Here the closing dash is retained, and the comma that separates a dependent clause from an independent clause is omitted.)

Brophy said—and you can check with him yourself—"This office must be vacated by Friday." (Here the closing dash is retained, and the comma before the quotation is omitted.)

NOTE: Do not put a phrase in dashes if the closing dash occurs at a point where a comma is needed after an item in a series. Put the phrase in parentheses instead.

CONFUSING: I plan to ask Spalding, Crawford—Betty, not Harold—Higgins, and Martin to investigate why sales have fallen off so sharply.

CLEAR: I plan to ask Spalding, Crawford (Betty, not Harold), Higgins, and Martin to investigate why sales have fallen off so sharply.

c. If a closing dash occurs at a point where the sentence requires a semicolon, a colon, or a closing parenthesis, drop the closing dash and use the required sentence punctuation.

Please try to get your sales projections to us by Wednesday—certainly by Friday at the latest; otherwise, they will be of no use to us in planning next year's budget.

Here is what Marsha had to say—or at least the gist of it: look for new opportunities in niche marketing, and move quickly to capitalize on them.

You need a volunteer (for example, someone like Louis Morales—he's always cooperative) to play the part of the customer.

2

Constructing Dashes

216 If you are using word processing software, you will very likely have access to a special character called an *em dash*. (This is the dash that appears in all the examples in ¶¶201–215.) If you do not have access to this special character, you can construct a dash by striking the hyphen key *twice*, with no space before, between, or after the hyphens. For example:

```
Don't believe him--ever!   NOT: Don't believe him -- ever!
If only I had realized--  But now it's too late.
```
(Two spaces follow a dash when a statement breaks off abruptly. See ¶208.)

NOTE: Do not use a single hyphen with space before and after it.

217 Type a dash at the end of a line (rather than at the start of a new line).

```
He lives in Hawaii--       NOT: He lives in Hawaii
on Maui, I believe.             --on Maui, I believe.
```

NOTE: An *en dash* (half the length of an em dash but longer than a hyphen) is used in a phrase like *the years 1995–1999.* For other uses of an en dash, see ¶¶459–460 and 819b, note.

PARENTHESES

Parentheses and dashes serve many of the same functions, but they differ in one significant respect: parentheses can set off only nonessential elements, whereas dashes can set off essential and nonessential elements. **REMEMBER:** In setting off elements, dashes emphasize; parentheses de-emphasize.

With Explanatory Material

218 Use parentheses to enclose explanatory material that is independent of the main thought of the sentence. The material within parentheses may be a single word, a phrase, or even an entire sentence.

We called him Mr. B. for so long that when I ran into him last week, I couldn't remember his last name (Bertolucci). (A single word.)

By Friday (and sooner if possible) I will have an answer for you. (A phrase.)

Our competitors (we consistently underprice them) can't understand how we do it. (A sentence.)

NOTE: Be sure the parentheses enclose only what is truly parenthetical.

WRONG: I merely said I was averse (not violently opposed *to*) your suggestion.
RIGHT: I merely said I was averse (not violently opposed) *to* your suggestion.

219 Use parentheses to set off a nonessential element when dashes would be too emphatic and commas might create confusion.

a. Parentheses are clearer than commas when a city-state expression occurs as an adjective.

Sales are down in our Middletown (Connecticut) office.
BETTER THAN: Sales are down in our Middletown, Connecticut, office.

b. Parentheses are clearer than commas when the nonessential element already contains commas. (See ¶¶183, 202.)

In three of our factories (Gary, Detroit, and Milwaukee) output is up.

With References

220 Use parentheses to set off references and directions.

> When I last wrote to you (see my letter of July 8 attached), I enclosed photo-copies of checks that you had endorsed and deposited.

When a reference falls *at the end of a sentence*, it may be treated as part of the sentence or as a separate sentence.

> This point is discussed at greater length in Chapter 7 (see pages 90–101).
>
> **OR:** This point is discussed at greater length in Chapter 7. (See pages 90–101.)

➤ *See also the note following ¶225d.*

With Dates

221 Use parentheses to enclose dates that accompany a person's name, a publication, or an event.

> He claims that he can trace his family back to Charlemagne (742–814).
>
> The "Sin On" Bible (1716) got its name from an extraordinary typographical error: instead of counseling readers to "sin no more," it urged them to "sin on more."

With Enumerated Items

222 **a. Within a Sentence.** Use parentheses to enclose numbers or letters that accompany enumerated items within a sentence.

> We need the following information to complete our record of Ms. Pavlick's experience: (1) the number of years she worked for your company, (2) a de-scription of her duties, and (3) the number of promotions she received.
>
> **NOT:** . . . our record of Ms. Pavlick's experience: 1) the number of years she worked for your company, 2) a description of her duties, and 3) the number of promotions she received. (The only acceptable use of a single closing paren-thesis is in an outline. See ¶223.)
>
> **NOTE:** Letters are used to enumerate items within a sentence when the sentence itself is part of a *numbered* sequence.
>
> 3. Please include these items on your expense report: (a) the cost of your hotel room, (b) the cost of meals, and (c) the amount spent on travel.

b. In a Displayed List. If the enumerated items appear on separate lines, the letters or numbers are usually followed only by periods. (See ¶107.)

223 Subdivisions in outlines are often enclosed in parentheses. It is sometimes necessary to use a single closing parenthesis to provide another level of subdivision.

> 1. ....
>   a. ....
>   (1) ....
>   (a) ....
>   1) ....
>   a) ....

> I. ....
>   A. ....
>   1. ....
>   a. ....
>   (1) ....
>   (a) ....
>   1) ....
>   a) ....

NOTE: At every level of an outline there should be at least two items. If an item is labeled *A*, there must be at least one more item (labeled *B*) at the same level.

➤ *For guidelines on formatting outlines, see ¶¶1721–1726.*

Parenthetical Items Within Sentences

224 If the item in parentheses falls *within a sentence:*

a. Make sure that any punctuation that comes after the item (such as a comma, a semicolon, a colon, or a dash) falls *outside* the closing parenthesis.

Unless I hear from you within five working days (by May 3), I will turn this matter over to my attorney.

I tried to reach you last Monday (I called just before noon); however, no one in your office knew where you were.

For Jane there is only one goal right now (and you know it): getting that M.B.A.

I saw your picture in a magazine last week (in *People,* I think)—and how I laughed when I saw who was standing next to you!

NOTE: Do not insert a comma, a semicolon, a colon, or a dash *before* an opening parenthesis.

b. Do not capitalize the first word of the item in parentheses, even if the item is a complete sentence. **EXCEPTIONS:** Proper nouns, proper adjectives, the pronoun *I,* and the first word of a quoted sentence. (See examples in *c* and *d.*)

c. Do not use a period before the closing parenthesis except with an abbreviation.

Plan to stay with us (we're only fifteen minutes from the airport) whenever you come to New Orleans.

NOT: Plan to stay with us (We're only fifteen minutes from the airport.) whenever you come to New Orleans.

Paul Melnick (he's Boyd's new sales manager) wants to take you to lunch.

At last week's hearing (I had to leave at 4 p.m.), was the relocation proposal presented?

d. Do not use a question mark or an exclamation point before the closing parenthesis unless it applies solely to the parenthetical item *and* the sentence ends with a different mark of punctuation.

At the coming meeting (will you be able to make it on the 19th?), let's plan to discuss next year's budget. (Question mark used in parentheses because the sentence ends with a period.)

May I still get tickets to the show (and may I bring a friend), or is it too late? (Question mark omitted in parentheses because the sentence ends with a question mark.)

NOT: May I still get tickets to the show (and may I bring a friend?), or is it too late?

Parenthetical Items at the End of Sentences

225 If the item in parentheses is to be incorporated *at the end of a sentence:*

a. Place the punctuation needed to end the sentence *outside* the closing parenthesis.

Please return the payroll review sheets by Monday (October 8).

How can I reach Jan Weidner (she spoke at yesterday's seminar)?

What a prima donna I work with (you know the one I mean)!

b. Do not capitalize the first word of the item in parentheses, even if the item is a complete sentence. **EXCEPTIONS:** Proper nouns, proper adjectives, the pronoun *I*, and the first word of a quoted sentence. (See examples in *c* and *d* below.)

c. Do not use a period before the closing parenthesis except with an abbreviation.

Our office is open late on Thursdays (until 9 p.m.).

Our office is open late on Thursdays (we're here until nine).

NOT: Our office is open late on Thursdays (We're here until nine.).

d. Do not use a question mark or an exclamation point before the closing parenthesis unless it applies solely to the parenthetical element *and* the sentence ends with a different mark of punctuation.

My new assistant is Bill Romero (didn't you meet him once before?).

Be sure to send the letter to Portland, Oregon (not Portland, Maine!).

Then he walked out and slammed the door (can you believe it?)!

Do you know Ellen Smyth (or is it Smythe)?
NOT: Do you know Ellen Smyth (or is it Smythe?)?

I'm through with the job (and I mean it)!
NOT: I'm through with the job (and I mean it!)!

NOTE: When a complete sentence occurs within parentheses at the end of another sentence, it may be incorporated into the sentence (as in the examples above) so long as it is fairly short and closely related. If the sentence in parentheses is long or requires special emphasis, it should be treated as a separate sentence (see ¶226).

Parenthetical Items as Separate Sentences

226 If the item in parentheses is to be treated as a *separate sentence:*

a. The preceding sentence should close with a punctuation mark of its own.

b. The item in parentheses should begin with a capital letter.

c. A period, a question mark, or an exclamation point (whichever is appropriate) should be placed *before* the closing parenthesis.

d. No other punctuation mark should follow the closing parenthesis. Leave two spaces before the start of the next sentence.

Then Steven Pelletier made a motion to replace the board of directors. (He does this at every stockholders' meeting.) However, this year . . .

I was most impressed with the speech given by Helena Verdi. (Didn't you used to work with her?) She knew her subject and she knew her audience.

➤ *Parentheses around question marks: see ¶118.*
Parentheses around exclamation points: see ¶119c.
Parentheses around confirming figures: see ¶420.
Parentheses around area codes in telephone numbers: see ¶454.
Parenthetical elements within parenthetical elements: see ¶297.
Plural endings in parentheses: see ¶626.

QUOTATION MARKS

Quotation marks have three main functions: to indicate the use of someone else's exact words (see ¶¶227–234), to set off words and phrases for special emphasis (see ¶¶235–241), and to display the titles of literary and artistic works (see ¶¶242–244).

2

For guidance on how to position punctuation marks in relation to the closing quotation mark—*inside* or *outside*—see ¶¶247–251.

For more specific guidance on when to use punctuation with quoted material and which punctuation to use, refer to the following paragraphs:

> *Quotations standing alone: see ¶252.*
> *Quotations at the beginning of a sentence: see ¶¶253–255.*
> *Quotations at the end of a sentence: see ¶¶256–258.*
> *Quotations within a sentence: see ¶¶259–261.*
> *Quotations with interrupting expressions: see ¶¶262–263.*
> *Quotations within quotations: see ¶¶245–246.*
> *Long quotations: see ¶¶264–265.*
> *Quoted letters: see ¶266.*
> *Quoted poetry: see ¶¶267–268.*
> *Quoted dialogues and conversations: see ¶¶269–270.*
> *Quotation marks as a symbol for inches: see ¶432.*

With Direct Quotations

227 Use quotation marks to enclose a *direct quotation,* that is, the exact words of a speaker or a writer.

> Casey Stengel once said, "The secret of managing is to keep the guys who hate you from the guys who are undecided."
>
> When I asked Diana whether she liked the new format of the magazine, all she said was "No." (See ¶¶233, 256a.)

228 **a.** Do not use quotation marks for an *indirect quotation,* that is, a restatement or a rearrangement of a person's exact words. (An indirect quotation is often introduced by *that* or *whether* and usually differs from a direct quotation in person, verb tense, or word order.)

> **DIRECT QUOTATION:** Mrs. Knudsen asked her boss, "Am I still being considered for the transfer?"
>
> **INDIRECT QUOTATION:** Mrs. Knudsen asked her boss whether she was still being considered for the transfer.
>
> **DIRECT QUOTATION:** Her boss said, "You're still in the running, but don't expect a quick decision."
>
> **INDIRECT QUOTATION:** Her boss said that she was still in the running but should not expect a quick decision.
>
> **NOTE:** Sometimes *direct* quotations are introduced by *that.* See ¶¶256f and 272, note.

b. In some cases a person's exact words may be treated as either a direct or an indirect quotation, depending on the kind of emphasis desired.

The chairman himself said, "The staff should be told at once that the rumors about a new building have no foundation." (The use of quotation marks emphasizes that these are the chairman's exact words.)

The chairman himself said the staff should be told at once that the rumors about a new building have no foundation. (Without quotation marks, the emphasis falls on the message itself. The fact that the chairman used these exact words is not important.)

229 Do not use quotation marks to set off a *direct question* at the end of a sentence unless it is also a *direct quotation* (one that uses someone's exact words.)

DIRECT QUESTION: The question is, Who will pay for restoring the landmark?

DIRECT QUOTATION: Mrs. Burchall then asked, "Who will pay for restoring the landmark?"

DIRECT QUOTATION: Mrs. Burchall then replied, "The question is, Who will pay for restoring the landmark?" (See also ¶115.)

230 When only a word or phrase is quoted from another source, be sure to place the quotation marks only around the words extracted from the original source and not around any rearrangement of those words.

Tanya said she would need "more help" in order to finish your report by this Friday. (Tanya's exact words were, "How can he expect me to finish his report by this Friday without more help?")

NOTE: When a quoted word or phrase comes at the end of a sentence, the period goes *inside* the closing quotation mark.

Barbara described the plain white shift she wore to the masquerade party as a "Freudian slip." (See also ¶247a, particularly examples 2–4.)

231 Be particularly sure not to include such words as *a* and *the* at the beginning of the quotation or *etc.* at the end unless these words were actually part of the original material.

Ben thought you did a "super" job on the packaging design. (Ben's exact words were, "Tell Bonnie I thought the job she did on the packaging design was super.")

Explain the decision any way you want, but tell George I said, "I'm truly sorry about the way things turned out," etc., etc.

232 When quoting a series of words or phrases in the exact sequence in which they originally appeared, use quotation marks before and after the complete series. However, if the series of quoted words or phrases did not appear in this sequence in the original, use quotation marks around each word or phrase.

According to Selma, the latest issue of the magazine looked "fresh, crisp, and appealing." (Selma's actual words were, "I think the new issue looks especially fresh, crisp, and appealing.")

BUT: Selma thinks the magazine looks "fresh" and "crisp."
(NOT: Selma thinks the magazine looks "fresh and crisp.")

233 Do not quote the words *yes* and *no* unless you wish to emphasize that these were (or will be) the exact words spoken.

Please answer the question yes or no.

Don't say no until you have heard all the terms of the proposal.

You need to start saying no to cookies and yes to laps around the block.

(Continued on page 58.)

When asked if he would accept a reassignment, Nick thought for a moment; then, without any trace of emotion, he said "Yes." (The quotation marks imply that Nick said precisely this much and no more. See ¶256a, note, for the use or omission of a comma after *he said*.)

NOTE: When quoting the words *yes* and *no,* capitalize them if they represent a complete sentence.

All she said was "No."

I would have to answer that question by saying "Yes and no."
BUT: That question requires something more than a yes-or-no answer.

234 Do not use quotation marks with well-known proverbs and sayings. They are not direct quotations.

Sidney really believes that an apple a day keeps the doctor away.

For Special Emphasis

235 When using technical terms, business jargon, or coined words not likely to be familiar to your reader, enclose them in quotation marks when they are first used.

One computer support center reports that some software users become confused when they are directed to press any key. They call to complain that they cannot find the "any" key.

It takes Joe a long time to get himself "booted up" in the morning. (The quoted phrase refers to the technique whereby a computer gets itself up and running.)

236 a. Words used humorously or ironically may be enclosed in quotation marks. However, unless you are convinced your reader will otherwise miss the humor or the irony, omit the quotation marks.

I was totally underwhelmed by Joe's proposal to centralize all purchasing. (**RATHER THAN:** I was totally "underwhelmed" by Joe's proposal . . .)

HDL cholesterol is the good kind; it's LDL that's the bad kind. (**RATHER THAN:** . . . the "good" kind . . . the "bad" kind . . .)

Nothing would please me more than looking at the slides of Mike's tour of Egypt. (One might reasonably conclude that the writer takes unalloyed pleasure at the prospect.)

BUT: "Nothing" would please me more than looking at the slides of Mike's tour of Egypt. (When *Nothing* is enclosed in quotation marks, the writer makes it clear that doing nothing would be preferable to looking at Mike's slides.)

b. A slang expression, the use of poor grammar, or a deliberate misspelling is enclosed in quotation marks to indicate that such usage is not part of the writer's normal way of speaking or writing.

Now that his kids have run off to Europe with the college tuition money, Bob has stopped boasting about his close-knit "nucular" family. (The writer is mimicking Bob's habitual mispronunciation of *nuclear.*)

As far as I'm concerned, Polly Harrington's version of what happened "ain't necessarily so."

c. Quotation marks are not needed for colloquial expressions.

She cares less about the salary than she does about the perks—you know, chauffeured limousine, stock options, and all the rest of it. (*Perks* is short for *perquisites,* meaning "special privileges.")

Pam is planning to temp until she's sure about staying in Los Angeles. (*To temp* means "to do temporary work.")

237 a. Use quotation marks to enclose words and phrases that have been made to play an abnormal role in a sentence—for example, verb phrases made to function as adjectives.

We were all impressed by her "can do" attitude. (*Can do* is a verb phrase used here as an adjective modifying *attitude*.)

OR: We were all impressed by her can-do attitude. (A hyphen may also be used to hold together a phrase used as an adjective before a noun. See ¶828.)

BUT NOT: We were all impressed by her "can-do" attitude. (Do not use both quotation marks and a hyphen for the same purpose.)

I'm selling my car on an "as is" (**OR** as-is) basis.

NOTE: When a verb like *must* or a preposition-adverb like *in* becomes established as a noun or an adjective (as indicated in the dictionary), use quotation marks only in those constructions where confusion could otherwise result.

You have to read that book; it's a must.

BUT: You have to get that book; it's "must" reading.

Frank must have an in with their purchasing department.

BUT: I guess she thinks it's still the "in" thing to do.

b. Do not use quotation marks to enclose phrases taken from other parts of speech and now well established as nouns; for example, *haves and have-nots, pros and cons, ins and outs.* (See also ¶625.)

a helpful list of dos and don'ts

all the whys and wherefores

a lot of ifs, ands, or buts (see also ¶285)

238 When a word or an expression is formally defined, the word to be defined is usually italicized and the definition is usually quoted so that the two elements may be easily distinguished. (See ¶286.)

➤ *For guidelines on underlining, see ¶290.*

239 A word referred to as a word may be enclosed in quotation marks but is now more commonly italicized or underlined. (See ¶285.)

240 a. Words and phrases introduced by such expressions as *marked, labeled, signed,* and *entitled* are enclosed in quotation marks.

The carton was marked "Fragile."

He received a message signed "A Friend."

The article entitled "Write Your Senator" was in that issue. (See ¶260.)

NOTE: Titles of complete published works following the expression *entitled* require italics or underlining rather than quotation marks. (See ¶289 for titles to be italicized or underlined; ¶¶242–244 for titles to be quoted.)

b. Words and phrases introduced by *so-called* do not require quotation marks, italics, or underlining. The expression *so-called* is sufficient to give special emphasis to the term that follows.

The so-called orientation session struck me as an exercise in brainwashing.

241 The translation of a foreign expression is enclosed in quotation marks; the foreign word itself is italicized or underlined. (See ¶287.)

With Titles of Literary and Artistic Works

242 Use quotation marks around the titles that represent only *part* of a complete published work—for example, the titles of chapters, lessons, topics, sections, and parts within a book; the titles of articles and feature columns in newspapers and magazines; and the titles of essays, short poems, lectures, sermons, and conference themes. (Italicize or underline titles of *complete* published works. See ¶289.)

> The heart of her argument can be found in Chapter 3, "The Failure of Traditional Therapy." You'll especially want to read the section entitled "Does Father Know Best?"

> An exciting article—"Can Cancer Now Be Cured?"—appears in the magazine I'm enclosing. (See ¶¶260–261 for the use of commas, dashes, and parentheses with quoted titles.)

> The theme of next month's workshop is "Imperatives for the Nineties—From the Ragged Edge to the Cutting Edge."

> The title of my speech for next month's luncheon will be "Reforming Our Local Tax Policy."

> **BUT:** At next month's luncheon I will be talking about reforming our local tax policy. (Do not enclose the words with quotation marks when they describe the topic rather than signify the exact title.)

NOTE: The titles *Preface, Contents, Appendix,* and *Index* are not quoted, even though they represent parts within a book. They are often capitalized, however, for special emphasis.

> All the supporting data is given in the Appendix. (Often capitalized when referring to another section within the same work.)

> **BUT:** You'll find that the most interesting part of his book is contained in the appendix. (Capitalization is not required when reference is made to a section within another work.)

243 Use quotation marks around the titles of *complete but unpublished* works, such as manuscripts, dissertations, and reports.

> I would like to get a copy of Sandor's study, "Criteria for Evaluating Staff Efficiency."

> Thank you for giving us the chance to review "Working out of Your Home." I have given your manuscript to an editor with a good deal of personal experience in this field.

244 Use quotation marks around the titles of songs and other short musical compositions and around the titles of individual segments or programs that are part of a larger television or radio series. (Series titles are italicized or underlined.)

> Just once I would like to get through a company party without having to hear Reggie sing "Danny Boy."

> I understand that our company was briefly mentioned on the <u>Frontline</u> program entitled "Pentagon, Inc.," which was shown last Tuesday night.

Quotations Within Quotations

245 A quotation within another quotation is enclosed in single quotation marks. Use the apostrophe for a single quotation mark.

> Dorothy Parker once said, "The most beautiful words in the English language are 'check enclosed.' "

246   If a quotation appears within the single-quoted material, revert to double quotation marks for the inner portion.

> Mrs. DeVries then remarked, "I thought it a bit strange when Mr. Fowler said, 'Put these checks in an envelope marked "Personal Funds," and set them aside for me.' " (When single and double quotation marks occur together, do not insert any extra space between them.)

NOTE: For the positioning of punctuation in relation to a single quotation mark, see the following paragraphs:

> ➤ *For placement of periods and commas, see ¶247b.*
> *For placement of semicolons and colons, see ¶248b.*
> *For placement of question marks and exclamation points, see ¶249d.*
> *For placement of dashes, see ¶250b.*

The following rules (¶¶247–251) indicate how to position punctuation marks in relation to the closing quotation mark—inside *or* outside.

With Periods and Commas

247   **a.** Periods and commas always go *inside* the closing quotation mark. This is the preferred American style. (Some writers in the United States follow the British style: Place the period *outside* when it punctuates the whole sentence, *inside* when it punctuates only the quoted material. Place the comma *outside,* since it always punctuates the sentence, not the quoted material.)

> According to Edward Shepherd Mead, "Not even computers will replace committees, because committees buy computers."
> He wants to change "on or about May 1" to read "no later than May 1."
> The price tag on the leather sofa was clearly marked "Sold."
> Sign your name wherever you see an "X."
> "Let's go over the details again," she said.
> "The date stamp indicates that my copy arrived at 10:50 a.m.," he said.
> Their latest article, "Scanning the Future," will appear in next month's issue of *Inc.* magazine.
> "Witty," "clever," "amusing," and "hilarious" are only a few of the adjectives that are being applied to her new book.
> The package was labeled "Fragile," but that meant nothing to your delivery crew.

   b. Periods and commas also go *inside* the single closing quotation mark.

> Mr. Poston said, "Please let me see all the orders marked 'Rush.'"
> "All he would say was 'I don't remember,'" answered the witness.

NOTE: Do not confuse a single quotation mark with an apostrophe used to show possession. When a sentence requires the use of a comma or a period at the same point as an apostrophe showing possession, the comma or period *follows* the apostrophe.

> I recently took over the management of the Murrays', the Boyarskys', and the Cabots' investment portfolios.

With Semicolons and Colons

248 **a.** Semicolons and colons always go *outside* the closing quotation mark.

> Last Tuesday you said, "I will mail a check today"; it has not yet arrived.

> When the announcement of the changeover was made, my reaction was "Why?"; John's only reaction was "When?"

> Please send me the following items from the file labeled "In Process": the latest draft of the Berryman agreement and FASB Statement 33.

> The memo I sent you yesterday said that the new workstations would cost "a nominal egg"; it should have said "an arm and a leg."

b. Semicolons and colons also go *outside* the single quotation mark.

> Alice Arroyo called in from her country place to say, "Please send me the following items from the file labeled 'In Process': the latest draft of the Berryman agreement and FASB Statement 33."

With Question Marks and Exclamation Points

249 **a.** A question mark or an exclamation point goes *inside* the closing quotation mark when it applies only to the quoted material.

> His first question was, "How long have you worked here?" (Quoted question at the end of a statement.)

> Garland still ends every sales meeting by shouting, "Go get 'em!" (Quoted exclamation at the end of a statement.)

b. A question mark or an exclamation point goes *outside* the closing quotation mark when it applies to the entire sentence.

> When will she say, for a change, "You did a nice job on that"? (Quoted statement at the end of a question.)

> Stop saying "Don't worry"! (Quoted statement at the end of an exclamation.)

c. If the quoted material and the entire sentence each require the same mark of punctuation, use only one mark—the one that comes first. (See also ¶¶257–258.)

> Have you seen the advertisement that starts, "Why pay more?" (Quoted question at the end of a question.)

> Let's not panic and yell "Fire!" (Quoted exclamation at the end of an exclamation.)

d. These same principles govern the placement of a question mark or an exclamation point in relation to a single quotation mark.

> What prompted her to say, "Be careful in handling documents marked 'Confidential'"? (Quoted phrase within a quoted statement within a question.)

> Dr. Marks asked, "Was the check marked 'Insufficient Funds'?" (Quoted phrase within a quoted question within a statement.)

> Miss Parsons then said, "How did you answer him when he asked you, 'How do you know?'" (Quoted question within a quoted question within a statement.)

With Dashes

250 **a.** A dash goes *inside* the closing quotation mark to indicate that the speaker's or writer's words have broken off abruptly.

> It was tragic to hear Tom say, "If he had only listened—"

b. A dash goes *outside* the closing quotation mark when the sentence breaks off abruptly *after* the quotation.

> If I hear one more word about "boosting productivity"—

> **BUT:** Mrs. Halliday said, "If I hear one more word from the general manager about 'boosting productivity'—"

c. A closing dash goes *outside* the closing quotation mark when the quotation itself is part of a nonessential element being set off by a pair of dashes.

> Get the latest draft—it's the one with the notation "Let's go with this"—and take it to Gladys Pomeroy for her approval.

With Parentheses

251 **a.** The closing parenthesis goes *inside* the closing quotation mark when the parenthetical element is part of the quotation.

> Fox agreed to settle his account "by Friday (July 28)" when he last wrote us.

b. The closing parenthesis goes *outside* the closing quotation mark when the quotation is part of the parenthetical element.

> Joe Elliott (the one everyone calls "Harper's gofer") will probably get the job.

The following rules (¶¶252–270) indicate what punctuation to use with various kinds of quoted material.

Punctuating Quotations That Stand Alone

252 When a quoted sentence stands alone, put the appropriate mark of terminal punctuation—a period, a question mark, or an exclamation point—*inside* the closing quotation mark.

> "I think we should switch suppliers at once."
> "Can you send us your comments within two weeks?"
> "I won't accept that kind of response!"

Punctuating Quotations That Begin a Sentence

253 When a quoted *statement* occurs at the beginning of a sentence, omit the period before the closing quotation mark and use a comma instead.

> "I think we should switch suppliers at once," he said.
> (**NOT:** . . . at once.," he said.)

EXCEPTION: Retain the period if it accompanies an abbreviation.

> "I'm still planning to go on for an LL.B.," she said.

254 When a quoted *question* or *exclamation* occurs at the beginning of a sentence, retain the question mark or the exclamation point before the closing quotation mark and do *not* insert a comma.

> "Can you send us your comments within two weeks?" she asked.
> (**NOT:** . . . within two weeks?," she asked.)

> "I won't accept that kind of response!" I told him.
> (**NOT:** . . . that kind of response!," I told him.)

255 When a quoted *word* or *phrase* occurs at the beginning of a sentence, no punctuation should accompany the closing quotation mark unless required by the overall construction of the sentence.

> "An utter bore" was the general reaction to yesterday's speaker.

> "Managing Your Portfolio," the second chapter in the Klingenstein book, sets forth some guidelines I have never seen anywhere else. (The comma that follows the chapter title is the first of a pair needed to set off a nonessential expression.)

Punctuating Quotations That End a Sentence

256 **a.** When a quoted *statement, question,* or *exclamation* comes at the end of a sentence and is introduced by an expression such as *he said* or *she said,* a comma usually precedes the opening quotation mark.

> Mr. Kelley said, "We'll close early on Friday."

> In her letter Diana said, "I plan to arrive on Thursday at 6 p.m."

NOTE: If the quotation is quite short or is woven into the flow of the sentence, omit the comma.

> All she said was "No." **OR:** All she said was, "No." (The comma creates a slight pause and throws greater emphasis on the quotation.)

> Why does he keep saying "It won't work"?

b. Use a colon in place of a comma if the introductory expression is an independent clause.

> Jerry would say only this: "I'll send you my new address once I'm settled."

> When you can't make up your mind, remember Yogi Berra's sage advice: "If you come to a fork in the road, take it."

c. Use a colon in place of a comma if the quotation contains more than one sentence.

> Mr. Bowles then said: "If the legislation is passed by Congress, we have an excellent chance to compete effectively in international markets. However, if the legislation gets bottled up in committee, our competitive position will worsen."

d. Use a colon in place of a comma if the quotation is set off on separate lines as an extract. (See also ¶265.)

> Sheila's letter said in part:
>> I have greatly valued your assistance. You have always acted as if you were actually part of our staff, with our best interests in mind.

e. Do not use either a comma or a colon before an indirect quotation.

> Sheila said that she had always valued Bob's assistance on various projects.

f. Do not use either a comma or a colon when a direct quotation is introduced by *that* or is otherwise woven into the flow of the sentence.

> In a previous letter to you, I noted that "you have always acted as if you were actually part of our staff, with our best interests in mind."

NOTE: The first word of the quotation is not capitalized in this case, even though it was capitalized in the original. Compare *you* here with *You* in the example in *d* above. (See ¶272 for the rule on capitalizing the first word of a quoted sentence.)

257 When a quoted *sentence* (a statement, a question, or an exclamation) falls at the end of a larger sentence, do not use double punctuation—that is, one mark to end the quotation and another to end the sentence. Choose the stronger mark. (**REMEMBER:** *A question mark is stronger than a period; an exclamation point is stronger than a period or a question mark.*) If the same mark of punctuation is required for both the quotation and the sentence as a whole, use the first mark that occurs—the one within quotation marks.

Quoted Sentences at the End of a Statement

Bob said, "I can't wait to get back to work." (**NOT** .".)

Mrs. Fahey asked, "How long have you been away?" (**NOT** ?".)

Mr. Auden shouted, "We can't operate a business this way!" (**NOT** !".)

Quoted Sentences at the End of a Question

Did you say, "I'll help out"? (**NOT** ."?)

Why did Mary ask, "Will Joe be there?" (**NOT** ?"?)

Who yelled "Watch out!" (**NOT** !"?)

Quoted Sentences at the End of an Exclamation

How could you forget to follow up when you were specifically told, "Give this order special attention"! (**NOT** ."!)

Stop saying "How should I know"! (**NOT** ?"!)

How I'd like to walk into his office and say, "I quit!" (**NOT** !"!)

NOTE: When a quoted sentence ends with an abbreviation, retain the abbreviation period, even though a question mark or an exclamation point follows as the terminal mark of punctuation.

The reporter asked, "When did you first hear about the board's decision to sell Modem Inc.?"

Didn't Larry tell Meg, "I'll help you with the tuition for your M.D."?

However, if a period is required as the terminal mark of punctuation, use only one period to mark the end of the abbreviation and the end of the sentence.

Gloria said, "You can call as early as 6:30 a.m." (**NOT** .".)

➤ *For placement of periods, see ¶247.*
For placement of question marks and exclamation points, see ¶249.

258 When a quoted *word* or *phrase* occurs at the end of a sentence, punctuate according to the appropriate pattern in the following examples. (**NOTE:** If the quoted word or phrase represents a complete sentence, follow the patterns shown in ¶257.)

Quoted Words and Phrases at the End of a Statement

He says he is willing to meet "at your convenience." (**NOT** ".)

I thought her letter said she would arrive "at 10 p.m." (**NOT** .".)

I've been meaning to read "Who Pays the Bill?" (**NOT** ?".)

Critics have praised his latest article, "Freedom Now!" (**NOT** !".)

(Continued on page 66.)

Quoted Words and Phrases at the End of a Question

> Why is he so concerned about my "convenience"?
> Didn't she clearly state she would arrive "at 10 p.m."?
> Have you had a chance to read "Who Pays the Bill?" (NOT ?"?)
> What did you think of the article "Freedom Now!"?

Quoted Words and Phrases at the End of an Exclamation

> He couldn't care less about my "convenience"!
> You're quite mistaken—she clearly said "at 10 a.m."!
> Don't waste your time reading "Who Pays the Bill?"!
> What a reaction he got with his article "Freedom Now!" (NOT !"!)

Punctuating Quotations Within a Sentence

259 Do not use a comma before or after a quotation when it is woven into the flow of the sentence.

> Don't say "I can't do it" without trying.
> No considerate person would say "Why should I care?" under such desperate circumstances.
> The audience shouted "Bravo!" and "Encore!" at the end of Emanuel Ax's recital last night.

NOTE: In such cases do not use a period at the end of a quoted statement, but retain the question mark or the exclamation point at the end of a quoted question or exclamation (as illustrated in the examples above).

260 Do not use commas to set off a quotation that occurs within a sentence as an *essential* expression. (See ¶149.)

> The luxurious practice of booking passage between England and India on the basis of "Port Outward, Starboard Homeward" (so as to get a cabin on the cooler side of the ship) is said to be the origin of the word *posh*.
> The chapter entitled "Locating Sources of Venture Capital" will give you specific leads you can pursue.

261 **a.** When a quotation occurs within a sentence as a *nonessential* expression, use a comma before the opening quotation mark and before the closing quotation mark.

> His parting words, "I hardly know how to thank you," were sufficient.
> The next chapter, "The Role of Government," further clarifies the answer.

b. If the *nonessential* quoted matter requires a question mark or an exclamation point before the closing quotation mark, use a pair of dashes or parentheses (rather than commas) to set off the quoted matter.

> Your last question—"How can we improve communications between departments?"—can best be answered by you.

> RATHER THAN: Your last question, "How can we improve communications between departments?," can best be answered by you.

> NOTE: When some or all of the quoted items in a series end with a question mark or an exclamation point, display them in a list to avoid the awkwardness of inserting commas before the quotation marks.

Next month's issue will feature the following articles:

"Is the Age of the Mainframe Over?"

"Tax Law Changes—Again!"

"Whither Wall Street?"

RATHER THAN: Next month's issue will feature the following articles: "Is the Age of the Mainframe Over?," "Tax Law Changes—Again!," and "Whither Wall Street?"

c. If *essential* quoted material ends with a question mark or an exclamation point and occurs within a sentence where a comma would ordinarily follow (for example, at the end of an introductory clause or phrase), omit the comma.

Although we were all asked last week to read an article entitled "Can U.S. Manufacturers Prosper in Today's World Markets?" the topic was totally ignored in this week's seminar.

RATHER THAN: . . . an article entitled "Can U.S. Manufacturers Prosper in Today's World Markets?," the topic was . . .

NOTE: If the omission of a comma at this point could lead to confusion, reword the sentence to avoid the problem.

We were all asked last week to read an article entitled "Can U.S. Manufacturers Prosper in Today's World Markets?" Yet the topic was . . .

OR: We were all asked last week to read an article entitled "Can U.S. Manufacturers Prosper in Today's World Markets?"; yet the topic was . . .

Punctuating Quoted Sentences With Interrupting Expressions

262 When a quoted sentence is *interrupted* by an expression such as *he asked* or *she said,* use a comma and a closing quotation mark before the interrupting expression and another comma after it. Then resume the quotation with an opening quotation mark, and put the first word in small letters unless it is a proper noun, a proper adjective, or the pronoun *I.*

"During the past month," the memo said in part, "we have received some welcome news from our overseas branches."

263 If the interrupting expression ends the sentence and the quotation continues in a new sentence, put a period after the interrupting expression and start the new sentence with an opening quotation mark and a capital letter.

"Perhaps we should decline the invitation," he said. "It would be better not to go than to arrive late."

Punctuating Long Quotations

264 If a quotation consists of more than one sentence without any interrupting elements, use quotation marks only at the beginning and at the end of the quotation. Do not put quotation marks around each sentence within the quotation.

Here is the full text of the release he gave to the media: "I have decided to withdraw from the upcoming election. I wish to thank my supporters for their enormous help. I am sorry to disappoint them."

265 A long quotation that will make four or more lines may be handled in one of the following ways:

a. The preferred style for displaying the quoted material is to treat it as a single-spaced extract. Indent the extract a half inch from each side margin, and leave a blank line above and below the extract. Do not enclose the quoted material in quotation marks; the indention replaces the quotation marks. If any quoted material appears within the extract, retain the quotation marks around this material. If the extract consists of more than one paragraph, leave a blank line between paragraphs. (See page 313 for an illustration of an extract in the body of a letter.)

NOTE: Ordinarily, start the quoted material flush left on the shorter line length; however, if a paragraph indention was called for in the original, indent the first line a half inch. Indent the first line of any additional paragraphs a half inch also, but do not leave a blank line between indented paragraphs.

b. Use the same line length and spacing for the quoted material as for other text material on the page.

(1) If the quoted material consists of one paragraph only, place quotation marks at the beginning and end of the paragraph. Use the normal paragraph indention of a half inch.

(2) If the quoted material consists of two or more paragraphs, place a quotation mark *at the start* of each paragraph but at the end of only one paragraph—the last one.

(3) Change double quotation marks within the quoted material to single quotation marks, and vice versa. (See ¶¶245–246.)

> "When you are writing a letter that grants a request, you can follow this pattern:
>
> "First, express appreciation for the writer's interest in the company's product or service.
>
> "Next, give the exact information requested and, if possible, additional information that may be of interest.
>
> "Finally, express willingness to 'be of further help.'"

Quoting Letters

266 Letters and other business documents that are to be quoted word for word may be handled in one of the following ways:

a. Make a printout or a photocopy of the material. In this case no quotation marks are used.

b. If no equipment is available, type the material on a separate sheet of paper headed *COPY*. In this case no quotation marks are used.

c. The material, if short, may be treated like a long quotation (see ¶265). If you use a shorter line length, omit the quotation marks. If you use the same line length as you do for other material on the page, then place the opening quotation mark before the first word and the closing quotation mark after the last word.

Quoting Poetry

267 When quoting a complete poem (or an extended portion of one) in a letter or a report, type it line for line, single-spaced (except for stanza breaks). If the line length is shorter than that of the normal text above and below the poem, no quotation marks are needed; the poem will stand out sufficiently as an extract. If, however, quotation marks are needed to indicate the special nature of the material, place a quotation mark at the beginning of each stanza and at the end of only the last stanza. (See also ¶284b.)

268 A short extract from a poem is sometimes woven right into a sentence or a paragraph. In such cases use quotation marks at the beginning and end of the extract, and use a diagonal line (with one space before and after) to indicate where each line breaks in the actual poem.

> In a poem about the death of an American poet, Richard Wilbur refers scathingly to the more prominent notices given to a "cut-rate druggist, a lover of Giving, / A lender, and various brokers: gone from this rotten / Taxable world to a higher standard of living."

Quoting Dialogues and Conversations

269 When quoting dialogues and conversations, start the remarks of each speaker as a new paragraph, no matter how brief.

> "Waiter, what was in that glass?"
>
> "Arsenic, sir."
>
> *"Arsenic.* I asked you to bring me absinthe."
>
> "I thought you said arsenic. I beg your pardon, sir."
>
> "Do you realize what you've done, you clumsy fool? I'm dying."
>
> "I am extremely sorry, sir."
>
> "I DISTINCTLY SAID ABSINTHE."
>
> "I realize that I owe you an apology, sir. I am extremely sorry."
>
> —Myles na Gopaleen

270 In plays and court testimony, where the name of the speaker is indicated, quotation marks are not needed.

> CECILY: Uncle Jack is sending you to Australia.
>
> ALGER: Australia! I'd sooner die.
>
> CECILY: Well, he said at dinner on Wednesday night that you would have to choose between this world, the next world, and Australia.
>
> ALGER: Oh, well! The accounts I have received of Australia and the next world are not particularly encouraging. This world is good enough for me, cousin Cecily.
>
> —Oscar Wilde

The following rules (¶¶271–284) cover a number of stylistic matters, such as how to style quoted material (¶271), how to capitalize in quoted material (¶¶272–273), how to handle omissions in quoted material (¶¶274–280), how to handle insertions in quoted material (¶¶281–283), and how to align quotation marks (¶284).

Style in Quoted Material

271 In copying quoted material, follow the style of the extract exactly in punctuation, spelling, hyphenation, and number style. (See ¶283 for the use of [*sic*] to indicate errors in the original.)

Capitalization in Quoted Material

272 Ordinarily, capitalize the first word of every complete sentence in quotation marks.

> I overheard Ellis mutter, "Only a fool would make such a claim."

> Here is the key sentence in her memo: "Despite the understaffing in the department, everyone is expected to meet the goals established for the coming year."

NOTE: If the quoted sentence is preceded by *that* or is otherwise incorporated into the flow of a larger sentence, do not capitalize the first word (unless it is a proper noun, a proper adjective, or the pronoun *I*).

> I overheard Ellis mutter that "only a fool would make such a claim."

> In essence, she says that "despite the understaffing in the department, everyone is expected to meet the goals established for the coming year."

273 When quoting a word or phrase, do not capitalize the first word unless it meets *one* of these conditions:

a. The first word is a proper noun, a proper adjective, or the pronoun *I*.

> No one is terribly impressed by his "Irish temper."

b. The first word was capitalized in its original use.

> I watched her scrawl "Approved" and sign her name at the bottom of the proposal.

c. The quoted word or phrase occurs at the beginning of a sentence.

> "Outrageous" was the publisher's reaction to Maxon's attempt to duck the questions of the reporters. (Even if the expression was not capitalized in the original material, it is capitalized here to mark the start of the sentence.)

d. The first word represents a complete sentence.

> The Crawleys said "Perhaps"; the Calnans said "No way."

➤ *See ¶¶277–278 on capitalizing the first word of a quoted sentence fragment.*

Omissions in Quoted Material

274 If one or more words are omitted *within a quoted sentence,* use ellipsis marks (three spaced periods, with one space before and after each period) to indicate the omission.

> "During the past forty years . . . we have been witnessing a change in buying habits, particularly with respect to food."

NOTE: Omit any marks of internal punctuation (a comma, a semicolon, a colon, or a dash) on either side of the ellipsis marks unless they are required for the sake of clarity.

> **ORIGINAL VERSION:** "The objectives of the proposed bill are admirable, I will cheerfully concede; the tactics being used to gain support for the bill are not."

> **CONDENSED VERSION:** "The objectives of the proposed bill are admirable . . .; the tactics being used to gain support for the bill are not." (The comma preceding the omitted phrase is not needed; however, the semicolon following the omitted phrase must be retained for clarity.)

275 If one or more words are omitted *at the end of a quoted sentence,* use three spaced periods followed by the necessary terminal punctuation for the sentence as a whole.

"Can anyone explain why . . . ?" (The original question read, "Can anyone explain why this was so?")

"During the past forty years, starting in the late 1950s, we have been witnessing a change in buying habits . . . . Consumers have become more concerned with what's in the package rather than with the package itself." (The first three periods represent the omitted words "particularly with respect to food"; the fourth period marks the end of the sentence. Two spaces follow before the next sentence.)

NOTE: If the quotation is intended to trail off, use only three spaced periods at the end of the sentence. (See also ¶291b.)

His reaction was, "If I had only known . . ."

276   If one or more sentences are omitted *between other sentences* within a long quotation, use three spaced periods *after* the terminal punctuation of the preceding sentence.

"During the past forty years, starting in the late 1950s, we have been witnessing a change in buying habits, particularly with respect to food. . . . How far this pattern of change will extend cannot be estimated."

NOTE: There is no space between *food* and the first period because that period marks the end of a sentence. The remaining three periods signify the omission of one or more complete sentences. Two spaces follow before the next sentence.

277   If only a fragment of a sentence is quoted within another sentence, it is not necessary to use ellipsis marks to signify the omission of words before or after the fragment.

According to Robertson's report, there has been "a change in buying habits" during the past forty years.

Moreover, if the fragment as given can be read as a complete sentence, capitalize the first word in the quoted fragment, even though this word was not capitalized in the original. (Compare *We* in the following example with *we* in the example in ¶276.)

According to Robertson's report, "We have been witnessing a change in buying habits, particularly with respect to food."

278   If a displayed quotation starts in the middle of a sentence, use three spaced periods at the beginning of the quotation.

According to Robertson's report, there has been

. . . a change in buying habits, particularly with respect to food. . . . How far this pattern of change will extend cannot be estimated.

If the fragment, however, can be read as a complete sentence, capitalize the first word of the fragment and omit the ellipsis marks. (Compare *Starting* in the following example with *starting* in the example in ¶276.)

According to Robertson's report:

Starting in the late 1950s, we have been witnessing a change in buying habits, particularly with respect to food.

279   When a long quotation starts with a complete sentence and ends with a complete sentence, do not use three spaced periods at the beginning or the end of the quotation unless you need to emphasize that the quotation has been extracted from a larger body of material.

280   If one or more paragraphs are omitted within a long quotation, indicate the omission by adding three spaced periods *after* the terminal punctuation that concludes the preceding paragraph.

Insertions in Quoted Material

281 For clarity, it is sometimes necessary to insert explanatory words or phrases within quoted material. Enclose such insertions in brackets. (See also ¶¶296–298.)

> Miss Rawlings added, "At the time of the first lawsuit [1993], there was clear-cut evidence of an intent to defraud."

282 For special emphasis, you may wish to italicize words that were not so treated in the original. In such cases insert a phrase like *emphasis added* in brackets at the end of the quotation or immediately after the italicized words.

> In the course of testifying, she stated, "I never met Mr. Norman in my life, *to the best of my recollection.* [Emphasis added.]"

NOTE: If the equipment you are using does not provide *italic* type, underline the words to be emphasized. (See ¶290 for guidelines on underlining and italics.)

283 When the original wording contains a misspelling, a grammatical error, or a confusing expression of thought, insert the term *sic* (meaning "so" or "this is the way it was") in brackets to indicate that the error existed in the original material.

> As he wrote in his letter, "I would sooner go to jail then [*sic*] have to pay your bill."

NOTE: Italicize the word *sic* when it is used in this way. If you do not have access to an italic font, do not underline *sic.*

➤ *For simple interruptions such as* he said *or* she said, *see ¶¶262–263.*

Aligning Quotation Marks

284 **a.** In a list, any opening quotation mark should align with the first letter of the other items.

> I urge you to read the following materials (which I am sending to you under separate cover):
>
> *White-Collar Blues* by Charles Heckscher
> "Getting Comfortable With Couples in the Workplace" by Anne B. Fisher
> *Genderflex* by Judith C. Tingley

b. In poems, the opening quotation mark at the beginning of each stanza should clear the left margin so that the first letter of each line will be in alignment. (See also ¶267.)

> "So here I am, in the middle way, having had twenty years—
> Twenty years largely wasted, the years of *l'entre deux guerres*—
> Trying to learn to use words, and every attempt
> Is a wholly new start, and a different kind of failure
> Because one has only learnt to get the better of words
> For the thing one no longer has to say, or the way in which
> One is no longer disposed to say it. And so each venture
> Is a new beginning, a raid on the inarticulate
> With shabby equipment always deteriorating
> In the general mess of imprecision of feeling . . ."
> —T. S. Eliot

Underlining and Italics

IMPORTANT NOTE: *Italic type* (the counterpart of underlining or underscoring) is now widely available and is the preferred means of giving special emphasis to words and phrases and to the titles of literary and artistic works.

For Special Emphasis

285 A word referred to as a word is usually italicized or underlined. (Some writers prefer to enclose the word in quotation marks instead.) A word referred to as a word is often introduced by the expression *the term* or *the word*.

> The term *muffin-choker* refers to a bizarre item in the morning newspaper that you read as you eat your breakfast.
>
> Did you know that *ciao,* the Italian word used as an expression of greeting or farewell, literally means "I am your slave"?
>
> If you used fewer compound sentences, you wouldn't have so many *and*s (**OR** <u>and</u>s) in your writing. (Only the root word is italicized or underlined, not the *s.*)
>
> **BUT:** She refused to sign the contract because she said it had too many ifs, ands, or buts. (Neither italics nor underlining is required for the phrase *ifs, ands, or buts* because the writer is not referring literally to these words as words. The phrase means "too many conditions and qualifications.")

NOTE: Letters referred to as letters are usually italicized or underlined if they are not capitalized. In such cases underlining may be preferable since a single italic letter may not look sufficiently different to stand out.

> dotting your <u>i</u>'s (**OR** *i*'s)   the three Rs
> minding your <u>p</u>'s and <u>q</u>'s (**OR** *p*'s and *q*'s)   three Bs and one C
> solving for <u>x</u> when <u>y</u> = 3 (**OR** for *x* when *y*)   **BUT:** to the nth degree

➤ *For the plurals of letters such as* i'*s and* Rs, *see* ¶¶*622–623.*

286 In a formal definition, the word to be defined is usually italicized or underlined and the definition quoted. In this way the two elements may be easily distinguished.

> The verb *prevaricate* (a polite way of saying "to lie") comes from the Latin word *praevaricari,* which means "to go zigzag, to walk crookedly."

NOTE: An informal definition does not require any special punctuation.

> A wainwright is a person who makes or repairs wagons.
>
> Thomas Hobson was an English stablekeeper who insisted that every customer take the horse nearest the door. Hence the term *Hobson's choice* means that you really have no choice at all. (Because the definition is informal, it does not have to be set off in quotation marks. However, *Hobson's choice* is italicized or underlined, as indicated in ¶285, because the words are referred to as words.)

287 Italicize or underline foreign expressions that are not considered part of the English language. (Use quotation marks to set off translations of foreign expressions.)

> It's true, *n'est-ce pas?* (Meaning "isn't that so?")

NOTE: Once a foreign expression has become established as part of the English language, italics or underlining is no longer necessary. (Most dictionaries offer guidance on this point.) Here are some frequently used expressions that do not need italics or any other special display:

à la carte	de jure	magnum opus	pro tem
à la mode	double entendre	maven	quid pro quo
a priori	en masse	modus operandi	raison d'être
ad hoc	en route	modus vivendi	rendezvous
ad infinitum	esprit de corps	non sequitur	repertoire
ad nauseam	et al.	ombudsman	résumé
alfresco	etc.	op. cit.	savoir faire
alma mater	ex officio	per annum	sic (see ¶283)
alter ego	fait accompli	per capita	sine qua non
bona fide	habeas corpus	per diem	status quo
carte blanche	ibid. (see ¶1530)	per se	summa cum laude
caveat emptor	in absentia	prima facie	tête-à-tête
chutzpah	in toto	prix fixe	tour de force
cul-de-sac	joie de vivre	pro forma	vice versa
de facto	laissez-faire	pro rata	vis-à-vis

➤ *For the use of accents and other diacritical marks with foreign words, see ¶718.*

288 The *individual* names of ships, trains, airplanes, and spacecraft may be italicized or underlined for special display or written simply with initial caps.

The S.S. *Parlin* will sail on Thursday.   **or:** The S.S. Parlin . . .

but: I flew to Paris on a Concorde and came back on a DC-10. (No special display is needed for the names *Concorde* and *DC-10* because they identify classes of aircraft but are not the names of individual planes.)

With Titles of Literary and Artistic Works

289 **a.** Italicize or underline titles of *complete* works that are published as separate items—for example, books, pamphlets, long poems, magazines, and newspapers. Also italicize or underline titles of movies, plays, musicals, operas, television and radio series, long musical pieces, paintings, and works of sculpture.

Our ads in *The Wall Street Journal* have produced excellent results.

or: Our ads in The Wall Street Journal have produced excellent results.

You will particularly enjoy a cookbook entitled *The Supper of the Lamb.*

Next Friday we will hear Der Rosenkavalier (**or** . . . *Der Rosenkavalier*).

The painting that is popularly referred to as *Whistler's Mother* is actually entitled *Arrangement in Gray and Black No. 1.*

NOTE: Do not italicize, underline, or quote the titles of musical pieces that are identified by form (for example, *symphony, concerto, sonata*) or by key (for example, *A Major, B Flat Minor*). However, if a descriptive phrase accompanies this type of title, italicize or underline this phrase if the work is long; quote this phrase if the work is short.

Beethoven's Sonata No. 18 in E Flat Minor, Op. 31, No. 3

Tchaikovsky's Symphony No. 6 in B Flat Minor (the *Pathétique*)

Chopin's Etude No. 12 (the "Revolutionary" Etude)

b. Titles of complete works may be typed in all-capital letters as an alternative to italics or underlining.

Every executive will find RIGHT ON TIME! a valuable guide.

2

NOTE: The use of all-capital letters is acceptable when titles occur frequently (as in the correspondence of a publishing house) or when the use of all-capital letters is intended to have an eye-catching effect. In other circumstances use italics or underlining.

c. In material that is being prepared for publication, titles of complete works must be italicized or underlined. This special display indicates that the title must appear in italics in the final version.

Every executive will find *Right on Time!* a valuable guide.

d. In titles of magazines, do not italicize, underline, or capitalize the word *magazine* unless it is part of the actual title.

Time magazine   **BUT:** *The New York Times Magazine*

e. In some cases the name of the publishing company is the same as the name of the publication. Italicize or underline the name when it refers to *the publication* but not when it refers to *the company*.

I saw her column in *Business Week.*   I wrote to Business Week about a job.

Joe used to be *Fortune*'s management editor; now he works as a management consultant to half a dozen Fortune 500 companies.

f. Italicize or underline a subtitle (but not an edition number) that accompanies the main title of a book.

If you're looking for a good overview of the subject, get a copy of Bateman and Zeithaml's *Management: Function and Strategy,* Second Edition.

➤ *For the use of quotation marks with titles of literary and artistic works, see ¶¶242–244; for the treatment of titles of sacred works, see ¶350.*

Guidelines for Underlining and Italics

290 Underline or italicize as a unit whatever should be grasped as a unit—individual words, titles, phrases, or even whole sentences.

a. When you want to give special emphasis to a unit consisting of two or more words, be sure to underline or italicize the entire unit, including the space between words.

I would not use the phrase <u>in a nutshell</u> in the sentence where you sum up your feelings about the place where you work.

BUT: Do you understand the meaning of terms like <u>ipso facto</u>, <u>sine qua non</u>, and <u>pro forma</u>? (Only the individual units are emphasized in this case.)

b. Do not give special emphasis to a mark of *sentence punctuation* that comes directly after the emphasized material unless it is an integral part of the emphasized material.)

This week the Summertime Playhouse is presenting <u>Oklahoma!</u>, next week <u>Where's Charley?</u>, and the following week <u>My Fair Lady</u>.

c. Do not underline or italicize a possessive or plural ending that is added on to a word being emphasized.

the <u>Times-Picayune</u>'s editorial   too many <u>and</u>s

d. When giving special emphasis to an element that has to be divided at the end of a line, underline or italicize the dividing hyphen as well.

For a Wall Street exposé with "the suspense of a first-rate thriller," read <u>Barbarians at the Gate</u>.

OTHER MARKS OF PUNCTUATION

The Apostrophe (')

The use of the apostrophe is covered in the following paragraphs:

➤ *As a single quotation mark, see ¶¶245–246, 247b.*
To indicate the omission of figures in dates, see ¶¶412, 624.
As a symbol for feet, see ¶¶432, 543.
To form contractions, see ¶505.
To form plurals of figures, letters, etc., see ¶¶622–625.
To form possessives, see ¶¶247b, 627–651.
To form expressions derived from all-capital abbreviations, see ¶522c.

Ellipsis Marks (. . .)

291 **a.** Ellipsis marks (three spaced periods, with one space before and after each period) are often used, especially in advertising, to display individual items or to connect a series of loosely related phrases.

Where can you match these services—

. . . Free ticket delivery
. . . Flight insurance
. . . On-time departures

The Inn at the End of the Road . . . where you may enjoy the epicure's choicest offerings . . . by reservation only . . . closed Tuesdays.

b. Ellipsis marks are also used to indicate that a sentence trails off before the end. The three spaced periods create an effect of uncertainty or suggest an abrupt suspension of thought. (No terminal punctuation is used with ellipsis marks in this kind of construction.)

He could easily have saved the situation by . . .   But why talk about it?

➤ *For the use of ellipsis marks to indicate omissions in quoted material, see ¶¶274–280.*

The Asterisk (*)

292 The asterisk may be used to refer the reader to a footnote placed at the bottom of a page or a table. (See ¶¶1502f, 1636c.)

a. When the asterisk and some other mark of punctuation occur together within a sentence, the asterisk *follows* the punctuation mark, with no intervening space. (See also ¶1502b.)

b. In the footnote itself, leave no space after the asterisk.

293 Asterisks are used to replace words that are considered unprintable.

If the TV cameras had been present when Finney called Schultz a ***** (and about 50 other names as well), tonight's newscast would have contained the longest bleep in television history.

The Diagonal (/)

294 The diagonal occurs (without space before or after) in certain abbreviations and expressions of time.

B/S	bill of sale	w/	with
c/o	care of	n/30	net amount due in 30 days

The copy deadline for the fall '96/winter '97 catalog is April 15.

Please check the figures for fiscal year 1997/98.

I'm concerned about their P/E ratio. (Referring to the price-earnings ratio of a company's stock.)

295 a. The diagonal is used to express alternatives.

a go/no-go decision	an either/or proposition
input/output systems	meet on Monday and/or Tuesday
an AM/FM tuner	(see usage note for *and/or* on page 255)

b. The diagonal may be used to indicate that a person or thing has two functions or components.

the owner/manager	zoned for commercial/industrial activities
our secretary/treasurer	planning to hold a dinner/dance
a Time/CNN poll	a client/server network

NOTE: A hyphen may also be used in such expressions. (See ¶806.)

c. The diagonal is also used in writing fractions (for example, 4/5) and in some code and serial numbers (for example, 2S/394756).

➤ *For the use of the diagonal when quoting poetry, see ¶268.*
For the use of the diagonal in telephone numbers, see ¶454.

Brackets ([ ])

296 A correction or an insertion in a quoted extract should be enclosed in brackets. (See also ¶¶281–283.)

His final request was this: "Please keep me appraised [*sic*] of any new developments." (See ¶283, note.)

The transcript of his testimony contains this incredible statement: "I did not approach Commissioner Zajac *at any time* [emphasis added] while my petition was being considered."

"If we all pull together, we can bring a new level of political leadership to this state. [Extended applause.] Please give me your support in this campaign." (Note the capitalization of *Extended* and the use of a period before the closing bracket when the bracketed element is treated as a separate sentence. See also ¶226.)

297 When a parenthetical element falls within another parenthetical element, enclose the smaller element in brackets and enclose the larger element in parentheses.

Scalzo said on television yesterday that prices would begin to fall sharply. (However, in an article published in the *Times* [May 15, 1998], he was quoted as saying that prices would remain steady for the foreseeable future.)

298 If the equipment you are using does not provide brackets, either construct them (as shown in the illustration below) or leave a space at the point where each mark should appear and pen in the marks after you remove the paper from the machine.

"We returned to Salem /Massachusetts7 the following year."

NOTE: If the term to be enclosed in brackets has to be underlined, do the underlining on the machine and insert the brackets by hand.

Halliburton's press release stated, "If it hadn't been for a certain newspaper [The Tribune], we never would have lost the election."

SPACING WITH PUNCTUATION MARKS

299 Period (.)

No space *before.*

Two spaces *after* the end of a sentence. (See ¶1432e.)

Two spaces *after* a period when it follows a number or letter that indicates an enumeration.

One space *after* an abbreviation within a sentence. (See also ¶511.)

No space *after* a decimal point.

No space *after* when another mark of punctuation follows the period (for example, a closing quotation mark; a closing parenthesis; a closing dash, a comma, a semicolon, or a colon following an "abbreviation" period).

Question Mark (?) or Exclamation Point (!)

No space *before.*

Two spaces *after* the end of a sentence.

One space *after* a question mark within a sentence. (See ¶¶116–117.)

No space *after* when another mark of punctuation follows (for example, a closing quotation mark, a closing parenthesis, or a closing dash).

Comma (,)

No space *before.*

One space *after* unless a closing quotation mark follows the comma.

No space *after* commas within a number.

Semicolon (;)

No space *before;* one space *after.*

Colon (:)

No space *before.*

Two spaces *after* within a sentence.

No space *before* or *after* in expressions of time *(8:20 p.m.)* or in proportions *(2:1).*

Dash (—)

No space *before* or *after* a dash.

No space *before, between,* or *after* two hyphens used to represent a dash.

Two spaces *after* a dash at the end of a statement that breaks off abruptly. (See ¶¶207–208.)

Hyphen (-)

No space *before;* no space *after* except at the end of a line.

Opening Parenthesis (() or Bracket ([)

One space *before* when parenthetical material is within a sentence.

Two spaces *before* when parenthetical material follows a sentence. In this case the parenthetical material starts with a capital letter and closes with its own sentence punctuation. (See ¶¶226, 296.)

No space *after.*

Closing Parenthesis ( )) or Bracket ( ])

No space *before.*

One space *after* when parenthetical material is within a sentence.

Two spaces *after* when parenthetical material is itself a complete sentence and another sentence follows. (See ¶¶226, 296.)

No space *after* if another mark of punctuation immediately follows.

Opening Quotation Mark (")

Two spaces *before* when quoted material starts a new sentence or follows a colon.

No space *before* when a dash or an opening parenthesis precedes.

One space *before* in all other cases.

No space *after.*

Closing Quotation Mark (")

No space *before.*

Two spaces *after* when quoted material ends the sentence.

No space *after* when another mark of punctuation immediately follows (for example, a semicolon or colon).

One space *after* in all other cases.

Single Quotation Mark (' ')

No space between single and double quotation marks. (See ¶246.)

Apostrophe (')

No space *before,* either within a word or at the end of a word.

One space *after* only if it is at the end of a word within a sentence.

No space *after* when another mark of punctuation immediately follows (for example, a comma or a period).

Ellipsis Marks (. . .)

One space *before* and *after* each of the three periods within a sentence. (See ¶¶274–275.)

No space *before* when an *opening* quotation mark precedes ellipsis marks.

No space *after* when a *closing* quotation mark follows ellipsis marks. (See last example in ¶275.)

Two spaces *after* ellipsis marks that follow a period, a question mark, or an exclamation point at the end of a sentence. (See example in ¶276.)

Asterisk (*)

No space *before* an asterisk following a word or punctuation mark within a sentence or at the end of a sentence.

Two spaces *after* an asterisk at the end of a sentence.

One space *after* an asterisk following a word or punctuation mark within a sentence.

No space *after* an asterisk in a footnote. (See ¶292.)

Diagonal (/)

No space *before* or *after* a diagonal. (See ¶268 for an exception.)

SECTION 3

CAPITALIZATION

The function of capitalization is to give distinction, importance, and emphasis to words. Thus the first word of a sentence is capitalized to indicate distinctively and emphatically that a new sentence has begun. Moreover, proper nouns like *George, Chicago, Dun & Bradstreet, the Parthenon, January,* and *Friday* are capitalized to signify the special importance of these words as the official names of particular persons, places, and things. A number of words, however, may function either as proper nouns or as common nouns—for example, terms like *the board of directors* or *the company.* For words like these, capitalization practices vary widely, but the variation merely reflects the relative importance each writer assigns to the word in question.

Despite disagreements among authorities on specific rules, there is a growing consensus against overusing capitalization in business writing. When too many words are emphasized, none stand out. The current trend, then, is to use capitalization more sparingly—to give importance, distinction, or emphasis only when and where it is warranted.

3

The following rules of capitalization are written with ordinary situations in mind. If you work or study in a specialized field, you may find it necessary to follow a different style of capitalization.

BASIC RULES

First Words

301 Capitalize the first word of:

a. Every sentence. (See ¶302 for exceptions.)

Try to limit each of your e-mail messages to one screen (25 lines).

Will you be able to pull everything together by then?

The deadline we have been given is absolutely impossible!

b. An expression used as a sentence. (See also ¶¶102, 111, 119–120.)

So much for that.	Really?	No!
Enough said.	How come?	Congratulations!

c. A quoted sentence. (See also ¶¶272–273.)

Mrs. Eckstein herself said, "We surely have not heard the complete story."

d. An independent question within a sentence. (See also ¶¶115–117.)

The question is, Whose version of the argument shall we believe?

BUT: Have you approved the divisional sales forecasts? the expense projections? the requests for staff expansion? (See ¶117.)

e. Each item displayed in a list or an outline. (See also ¶¶107, 1357c, 1424e, 1725d.)

Here is a powerful problem-solving tool that will help you:

• Become an effective leader.
• Improve your relations with subordinates, peers, and superiors.
• Cope with stressful situations on the job.

(Continued on page 82.)

f. Each line in a poem. (Always follow the style of the poem, however.)

> From wrong to wrong the exasperated spirit
> Proceeds, unless restored by that refining fire
> Where you must move in measure, like a dancer.
>
> —T. S. Eliot

g. The salutation and the complimentary closing of a letter. (See also ¶¶1348, 1359.)

Dear Mrs. Pancetta: Sincerely yours,

302   **a.** When a sentence is set off by *dashes* or *parentheses* within another sentence, do not capitalize the first word following the opening dash or parenthesis unless it is a proper noun, a proper adjective, the pronoun *I*, or the first word of a quoted sentence. (See ¶¶214, 224–225 for examples.)

b. Do not capitalize the first word of a sentence following a colon except under certain circumstances. (See ¶¶196–199.)

Proper Nouns

303   Capitalize every *proper noun*, that is, the official name of a particular person, place, or thing. Also capitalize the pronoun *I*.

Martin Luther King, Jr.	Wednesday, February 8
Baton Rouge, Louisiana	the Great Depression
Xerox Corporation	the Civil Rights Act of 1964
the Red Cross	the Japanese
the Internet (OR the Net)	Jupiter and Uranus
Johns Hopkins University	French Literature 212
the World Trade Center	a Xerox copy
the Statue of Liberty	*Gone With the Wind*
the Center for Science in	the Smithsonian Institution
the Public Interest	United Farm Workers of America
a Pulitzer Prize	Flight 403
Microsoft Word	The House of Representatives

NOTE: Prepositions (like *of, for,* and *in*) are not capitalized unless they have four or more letters (like *with* and *from*). (See also ¶¶360–361.) The articles *a* and *an* are not capitalized; the article *the* is capitalized only under special circumstances. (See ¶324.) Conjunctions (like *and* and *or*) are also not capitalized. However, follow the capitalization style used by the owner of the name; for example, *3-In-One oil, One-A-Day vitamins, the poet e e cummings, Book-Of-The-Month Club, Diet Pepsi, diet Coke.*

304   Capitalize adjectives derived from proper nouns.

America (n.), American (adj.)	Machiavelli (n.), Machiavellian (adj.)
Norway (n.), Norwegian (adj.)	Hemingway (n.), Hemingwayesque (adj.)

EXCEPTIONS: Congress, congressional; the Senate, senatorial; the Constitution (U.S.), constitutional (see also ¶306)

305   Capitalize imaginative names and nicknames that designate particular persons, places, or things. (See ¶¶333–335 for imaginative place names; ¶344 for imaginative names of historical periods.)

the Founding Fathers	Bigfoot
the First Lady	Whoopi Goldberg
the White House	the Gray Panthers
the Oval Office	Big Mac
the Stars and Stripes	the Establishment
the Gopher State (Minnesota)	Down Under (Australia)
Mother Nature	Generation X
every state in the Union	the Little Dipper
Fannie Mae (from the initials *FNMA*,	the Information Superhighway
referring to the Federal National	the Middle Ages
Mortgage Association)	**BUT:** the space age

306 Some expressions that originally contained or consisted of proper nouns or adjectives are now considered common nouns and should not be capitalized. (See ¶309b.)

charley horse	napoleon	ampere	texas leaguer
plaster of paris	boycott	watt	arabic numbers
manila envelope	diesel	joule	roman numerals
bone china	macadam	kelvin	**BUT:** Roman laws

NOTE: Check an up-to-date dictionary to determine capitalization for words of this type.

Common Nouns

307 A *common noun* names a class of things (for example, *books*), or it may refer indefinitely to one or more things within that class (*a book, several books*). Nouns used in this way are considered general terms of classification and are often modified by indefinite words such as *a, any, every,* or *some*. Do not capitalize nouns used as general terms of classification.

a company	every board of directors
any corporation	some senators

308 A common noun may also be used to name a *particular* person, place, or thing. Nouns used in this way are often modified (a) by *the, this, these, that,* or *those* or (b) by possessive words such as *my, your, his, her, our,* or *their*. Do not capitalize a general term of classification, even though it refers to a particular person, place, or thing.

COMMON NOUN:	our doctor	the hotel	the river
PROPER NOUN:	Dr. Tsai	Hotel Algonquin	the Colorado River

309 **a.** Capitalize a common noun when it is part of a proper name but not when it is used alone in place of the full name. (For exceptions, see ¶310.)

Professor Perry	**BUT:** the professor
the Goodall Corporation	the corporation
the Easton Municipal Court	the court
Sunset Boulevard	the boulevard
the Clayton Antitrust Act	the act

NOTE: Also capitalize the plural form of a common noun in expressions such as *the Republican and the Democratic Parties, Main and Tenth Streets, the Missouri and Ohio Rivers,* and *the Atlantic and Pacific Oceans*.

(Continued on page 84.)

3

b. In a number of compound nouns, the first element is a proper noun or a proper adjective and the second element is a common noun. In such cases capitalize only the first element, since the compound as a whole is a common noun.

Brownie points	a Ferris wheel	a Rhodes scholar	a Labrador retriever
a Dutch oven	Danish pastry	French doors	Tex-Mex cooking

NOTE: Check an up-to-date dictionary for words of this type. After extensive usage the proper noun or adjective may become a common noun and no longer require capitalization. (See ¶306.)

310 Some *short forms* (common-noun elements replacing the complete proper name) are capitalized when they are intended to carry the full significance of the complete proper name. It is in this area, however, that the danger of overcapitalizing most often occurs. Therefore, do not capitalize a short form unless it clearly warrants the importance, distinction, or emphasis that capitalization conveys. The following kinds of short forms are commonly capitalized:

PERSONAL TITLES: Capitalize titles replacing names of high-ranking national, state, and international officials (but not ordinarily local officials or company officers). (See ¶313.)

ORGANIZATIONAL NAMES: Do not capitalize short forms of company names except in formal or legal writing. (See ¶321.)

GOVERNMENTAL NAMES: Capitalize short forms of names of national and international bodies (but not ordinarily state or local bodies). (See ¶¶326–327, 334–335.)

PLACE NAMES: Capitalize only well-established short forms. (See ¶¶332, 335.)

NOTE: Do not use a short form to replace a full name unless the full name has been mentioned earlier or will be understood from the context.

SPECIAL RULES

Personal Names

311 **a.** Treat a person's name—in terms of capitalization, spelling, punctuation, and spacing—exactly as the person does.

Alice Mayer	Charles Burden Wilson
Alyce Meagher	L. Westcott Quinn
Steven J. Dougherty, Jr.	R. W. Ferrari
Stephen J. Dockerty Jr.	Peter B. J. Hallman

➤ *For the treatment of initials such as FDR, see ¶516.*
For the use or omission of commas with terms such as Jr., see ¶156.

b. Respect individual preferences in the spelling of personal names.

Ann Marie, Anne Marie, Anna Marie, Annemarie, Annamarie, Anne-Marie, AnneMarie

Macmillan, MacMillan, Mac Millan, Macmillen, MacMillen, MacMillin, McMillan, Mc Millan, McMillen, McMillin, McMillon

c. In names containing the prefix *O'*, always capitalize the *O* and the letter following the apostrophe; for example, *O'Brian* or *O'Brien*.

d. Watch for differences in capitalization and spacing in names containing prefixes like *d', da, de, del, della, di, du, l', la, le, van,* and *von.*

D'Amelio, d'Amelio, Damelio   deLaCruz, DeLacruz, Dela Cruz, DelaCruz
LaCoste, Lacoste, La Coste   VanDeVelde, Van DeVelde, vandeVelde

e. When a surname with an uncapitalized prefix stands alone (that is, without a first name, a title, or initials preceding it), capitalize the prefix to prevent a misreading.

Paul de Luca   Mr. de Luca   P. de Luca   BUT: Is De Luca leaving?

f. When names that contain prefixes are to be typed in all-capital letters, follow these principles: If there is no space after the prefix, capitalize only the initial letter of the prefix. If space follows the prefix, capitalize the entire prefix.

NORMAL FORM: MacDonald   Mac Donald
ALL-CAPITAL FORM: MacDONALD   MAC DONALD

g. When a nickname or a descriptive expression precedes or replaces a person's first name, simply capitalize it. However, if the nickname or descriptive expression falls between a person's first and last names, enclose it either in quotation marks or in parentheses.

Ol' Blue Eyes   BUT: Frank "Ol' Blue Eyes" Sinatra
    OR: Frank (Ol' Blue Eyes) Sinatra

➤ *For the plurals of personal names, see ¶¶615–616.*
For the possessives of personal names, see ¶¶630–633.

Titles With Personal Names

312   **a.** Capitalize all official titles of honor and respect when they *precede* personal names.

PERSONAL TITLES:
Mrs. Norma Washburn (see ¶517)   Miss Popkin
Ms. Terry Fiske   Mr. Benedict

EXECUTIVE TITLES:
President Julia McLeod   Vice President Saulnier

PROFESSIONAL TITLES:
Professor Henry Pelligrino   Dr. Khalil (see ¶517)

CIVIC TITLES:
Governor Samuel O. Bolling   Ambassador Staedler
Mayor-elect Louis K. Uhl (see ¶317)   ex-Senator Hausner (see ¶317)

MILITARY TITLES:
Colonel Perry L. Forrester   Commander Comerford

RELIGIOUS TITLES:
the Reverend William F. Dowd   Rabbi Gelfand

b. Do not capitalize such titles when the personal name that follows is in apposition and is set off by commas. (Some titles, like that of the President of the United States, are always capitalized. See ¶313 for examples of such exceptions.)

Yesterday the *president,* Julia McLeod, revealed her plans to retire next June.
BUT: Yesterday *President* Julia McLeod revealed her plans to retire next June.

(Continued on page 86.)

3

c. Do not capitalize occupational titles (such as *author, surgeon, publisher,* and *lawyer*) preceding a name.

The reviews of *drama critic* Simon Ritchey have lost their bite.
(NOT: The reviews of *Drama Critic* Simon Ritchey have lost their bite.)

NOTE: Occupational titles can be distinguished from official titles in that only official titles can be used with a last name alone. Since one would not address a person as "Author Mailer" or "Publisher Johnson," these are not official titles and should not be capitalized.

d. Do not confuse a true title preceding a name (such as *Judge*) with a generic expression (such as *federal judge*).

Judge Ann Bly OR federal judge Ann Bly (BUT NOT: federal Judge Ann Bly)

President Julia McLeod OR company president Julia McLeod
(BUT NOT: company President Julia McLeod)

313 **a.** In general, do not capitalize titles of honor and respect when they *follow* a personal name or are used *in place of* a personal name.

Julia McLeod, *president* of McLeod Inc., has revealed her plans to retire next June. During her sixteen years as *president,* the company grew . . .

However, exceptions are made for important officials and dignitaries, as indicated in the following paragraphs.

b. Retain the capitalization in the titles of high-ranking national, state, and international officials when they *follow* or *replace* a specific personal name. Below are examples of titles that remain capitalized.

NATIONAL OFFICIALS: the *President,* the *Vice President,* Cabinet members (such as the *Secretary of State* and the *Attorney General*), the heads of government agencies and bureaus (such as the *Director* or the *Commissioner*), the *Chief Justice,* the *Ambassador,* the *Senator,* the *Representative.*

STATE OFFICIALS: the *Governor,* the *Lieutenant Governor.* (BUT: the *attorney general,* the *senator.*)

FOREIGN DIGNITARIES: the *Queen of England,* the *King,* the *Prime Minister.*

INTERNATIONAL FIGURES: the *Pope,* the *Secretary General of the United Nations.*

NOTE: Some authorities now recommend that even these titles not be capitalized.

c. Titles of local governmental officials and those of lesser federal and state officials are not usually capitalized when they follow or replace a personal name. However, these titles are sometimes capitalized in writing intended for a limited readership (for example, in a local newspaper, in internal communications within an organization, or in correspondence coming from or directed to the official's office), where the intended reader would consider the official to be of high rank.

The *Mayor* promised only last fall to hold the city sales tax at its present level. (Excerpt from an editorial in a local newspaper.)

BUT: Francis Fahey, *mayor* of Coventry, Rhode Island, appeared before a House committee today. The *mayor* spoke forcefully about the need to maintain federal aid to . . . (Excerpt from a national news service release.)

I would like to request an appointment with the *Attorney General.* (In a letter sent to the state attorney general's office.)

BUT: I have written for an appointment with the *attorney general* and expect to hear from his office soon.

d. Titles of *company officials* (for example, the *president,* the *general manager*) should not be capitalized when they follow or replace a personal name. Exceptions are made in formal minutes of meetings (see page 480) and in rules and bylaws.

The *president* will visit thirteen countries in a tour of company installations abroad. (Normal style.)

The *Secretary's* minutes were read and approved. (In formal minutes.)

NOTE: Some companies choose to capitalize these titles in all their communications because of the great respect the officials command within the company. However, this practice confers excessive importance on people who are neither public officials nor eminent dignitaries, and it should be avoided.

e. In general, do not capitalize job titles when they stand alone. However, in procedures manuals and in company memos and announcements, job titles are sometimes capitalized for special emphasis.

Marion Conroy has been promoted to the position of *senior accountant* (OR *Senior Accountant*).

f. Titles *following* a personal name or *standing alone* are sometimes capitalized in formal citations and acknowledgments.

314 Do not capitalize titles used as general terms of classification. (See ¶307.)

a United States senator   every king
a state governor   any ambassador

EXCEPTION: Because of the special regard for the office of the President of the United States, this title is capitalized even when used as a general term of classification (for example, every *President, Presidential* campaigns).

315 Capitalize any title (even if not of high rank) when it is used in *direct address* (that is, quoted or unquoted speech made directly to another person).

DIRECT ADDRESS: Please tell me, *Doctor,* what risks are involved in this treatment.

INDIRECT ADDRESS: I asked the *doctor* what risks were involved in this treatment.

NOTE: In direct address, do not capitalize a term like *madam, miss,* or *sir* if it stands alone without a proper name following.

Isn't it true, *sir,* that the defendant offered you money for trade secrets?

316 In the *inside address* of a letter, in the *writer's identification block,* and on an *envelope,* capitalize all titles whether they precede or follow the name. (See ¶¶1322–1325, 1362–1368, and the illustrations on page 353.)

317 Do not capitalize *former, late, ex-,* or *-elect* when used with titles. (See ¶363 for the style in headings.)

the late President Truman   ex-President Bush   Mayor-elect Bawley

Family Titles

318 Capitalize words such as *mother, father, aunt,* and *uncle* when they stand alone or are followed by a personal name.

Let me ask *Mother* and *Dad* if that date is open for them.

We'll be glad to put up *Aunt Peg* and *Uncle Fred* when they come to visit.

I hear that *Brother Bobby* has gone off the deep end again.

Do you think *Grandmother Harvey* will be pleased when she hears the news?

319 Do not capitalize family titles when they are preceded by possessives (such as *my, your, his, her, our,* and *their*) and simply describe a family relationship.

> Let me ask my *mother* and *dad* if that date is open for them.
>
> Do you think your *brother* Bobby would like to meet my *sister* Fern?

NOTE: If the words *uncle, aunt,* or *cousin* form a unit when used together with a first name, capitalize these titles, even when they are preceded by a possessive.

> Frank wants us to meet his *Uncle John.* (Here *Uncle John* is a unit.)
>
> **BUT:** Frank wants us to meet his *uncle,* John Cunningham. (Here *uncle* simply describes a family relationship.)
>
> I hope you can meet my *Cousin May.* (The writer thinks of her as *Cousin May.*)
>
> **BUT:** I hope you can meet my *cousin* May. (Here the writer thinks of her as *May;* the word *cousin* merely indicates relationship.)

Names of Organizations

320 **a.** Capitalize the names of companies, unions, associations, societies, independent committees and boards, schools, political parties, conventions, foundations, fraternities, sororities, clubs, and religious bodies.

NationsBank Corporation	the Hopewell Chamber of Commerce
the Transport Workers Union of America	the University of North Dakota
the American Society for Training and Development	the Democratic and Liberal Parties
the Committee for Economic Development	the Republican National Convention
the Financial Accounting Standards Board	the Andrew W. Mellon Foundation
	the Overseas Press Club of America
	Sigma Chi Fraternity
	St. Mark's United Methodist Church
	Parents Anonymous

NOTE: Try to follow the style established by the organization itself, as shown in the letterhead or some other written communication from the organization.

Disney World   Kmart Corporation   **BUT:** Toys "R" Us, Inc. (don't try
BUT: Disneyland   U-Haul International   to replicate the backward *R*)

FULL NAME: E. I. du Pont de Nemours and Company   **SHORT FORM:** DuPont

b. Also capitalize imaginative names used to refer to specific organizations. (See also ¶333b.)

Big Blue (IBM)   the Big Board (the New York Stock Exchange)
Ma Bell (AT&T)   the Baby Bells (the U.S. regional phone companies)

➤ *For the treatment of articles (like* the*), prepositions (like* of *or* for*), and conjunctions (like* and*), see ¶303, note. For the capitalization of abbreviations and acronyms used as organizational names, see ¶¶520, 522.*

321 When the common-noun element is used in place of the full name (for example, *the company* in place of *the Andersen Hardware Company*), do not capitalize the short form unless special emphasis or distinction is required (as in legal documents, minutes of meetings, bylaws, and other formal communications, where the short form is intended to invoke the full authority of the organization). In most cases, however, capitalization is unnecessary because the short form is used only as a general term of classification. (See ¶¶307–308.)

The *company* has always made a conscientious effort to involve itself in community affairs. However, our *company* policy specifically prohibits our underwriting any activity in support of a candidate for public office. (As used here, *company* is a term of general classification.)

BUT: On behalf of the *Company,* I am authorized to accept your bid. (Here the full authority of the company is implied; hence *Company* is spelled with a capital *C.*)

Mr. Weinstock has just returned from a visit to Haverford College. He reports that the *college* is planning a new fund-raising campaign to finance the construction of the new media center.

BUT: The *College* hopes to raise an additional $10,000,000 this year to finance the construction of the new media resource center. (Announcement in the alumni bulletin.)

NOTE: Do not capitalize the short form if it is modified by a word other than *the.* In constructions such as *our company, this company,* and *every company,* the noun is clearly a general term of classification. (See also ¶308.)

322 Common organizational terms such as *advertising department, manufacturing division, finance committee,* and *board of directors* are ordinarily capitalized when they are the actual names of units within the writer's own organization. These terms are not capitalized when they refer to some other organization unless the writer has reason to give these terms special importance or distinction.

The *Board of Directors* will meet next Thursday at 2:30. (From a company memo.)

BUT: Julia Perez, senior vice president of the Mulholland Bancorp, has been elected to the *board of directors* of the Kensington Trade Corporation. (From a news release intended for a general audience.)

The *Finance Committee* will meet all week to review next year's budget. (Style used by insiders.)

BUT: Gilligan says his company can give us no encouragement about the sponsorship of a new art center until its *finance committee* has reviewed our proposal. (Style normally used by outsiders.)

The *Advertising Department* will unveil the fall campaign this Friday. (Style used by insiders.)

BUT: The *advertising department* of Black & London will unveil its fall campaign this Friday. (Style used by outsiders.)

NOTE: Do not capitalize these organizational terms when they are modified by a word other than *the.* Constructions such as *this credit department, their credit department, every credit department, your credit department,* and *our credit department* are terms of general classification and should not be capitalized. (See also ¶321, note.)

Black & London always seems to have a great deal of turnover in *its advertising department.*

We don't have as much turnover in *our advertising department* as you may think. (Some insiders prefer to write "our Advertising Department" because of the special importance they attach to their own organizational structure.)

I would like to apply for the position of copywriter that is currently open in *your advertising department.* (Some outsiders might write "your Advertising Department" if they wanted to flatter the reader by giving special importance to the reader's organizational structure.)

323 Capitalize such nouns as *marketing, advertising,* or *promotion* when they are used alone to designate a department within an organization.

> Paul Havlicek in *Corporate Communications* is the person to talk with.
>
> I want to get a reaction from our people in *Marketing* first.
>
> **BUT:** I want to talk to our *marketing* people first. (Here *marketing* is simply a descriptive adjective.)

324 Capitalize the word *the* preceding the name of an organization only when it is part of the legal name of the organization.

> The Associated Press   The New York Times (see ¶289d)
> The Gap   The Wall Street Journal

a. Even when part of the organizational name, *the* is often uncapitalized except in legal or formal contexts where it is important to give the full legal name.

b. Do not capitalize *the* when the name is used as a modifier or is given in the form of an abbreviation.

> the Associated Press report   the AP   works for the Times

Names of Government Bodies

325 Capitalize the names of countries and international organizations as well as national, state, county, and city bodies and their subdivisions.

> the United Nations   the Utah Bureau of Air Quality
> the Clinton Administration   the Ohio Legislature
> the Cabinet   the Court of Appeals of the State of
> the Ninety-ninth Congress   Wisconsin (see ¶303, note)
>   (see ¶363)   the New York State Board of Education
> the House of Representatives the Coe County Shade Tree Commission
> **BUT:** the federal government   the Boston City Council
>   (see ¶¶328–329)   the Small Business Development Agency

➤ *For city and state names, see ¶¶334–335.*

326 Capitalize short forms of names of national and international bodies and their major divisions.

> the House (referring to the House of Representatives)
>
> the Department (referring to the Department of Justice, the State Department, the Department of the Treasury, etc.)
>
> the Bureau (referring to the Bureau of the Budget, the Federal Bureau of Investigation, the Bureau of the Census, etc.)
>
> the Court (referring to the United States Supreme Court, the International Court of Justice, etc.)
>
> the Fed (referring to the Federal Reserve Board)
>
> **BUT:** the feds (referring to federal regulators)

As a rule, do not capitalize short forms of names of state or local governmental groups except when special circumstances warrant emphasis or distinction. (See ¶327.)

327 Common terms such as *police department, board of education,* and *county court* need not be capitalized (even when referring to a specific body), since they are terms of general classification. However, such terms should be capitalized when the writer intends to refer to the organization in all of its official dignity.

The *Police Department* has announced the promotion of Robert Boyarsky to the rank of sergeant. (The short form is capitalized here because it is intended to have the full force of the complete name, the *Cranfield Police Department*.)

BUT: The Cranfield *police department* sponsors a youth athletic program that we could well copy. (No capitalization is used here because the writer is referring to the department in general terms and not by its official name.)

NOTE: Do not capitalize the short form if it is not actually derived from the complete name. For example, do not capitalize the short form *police department* if the full name is *Department of Public Safety*.

328 Capitalize *federal* only when it is part of the official name of a federal agency, a federal act, or some other proper noun.

the *Federal* Reserve Board the *Federal* Insurance Contributions Act

BUT: ... subject to *federal,* state, and local laws.

329 The terms *federal government* and *government* (referring specifically to the United States government) are now commonly written in small letters because they are considered terms of general classification. In government documents, however, and in other types of communications where these terms are intended to have the force of an official name, they are capitalized.

330 Capitalize the words *union* and *commonwealth* only when they refer to a specific government.

Wilkins has lectured on the topic in almost every state in the *Union.*

Names of Places

331 Capitalize the names of places, such as streets, buildings, parks, monuments, rivers, oceans, and mountains. Do not capitalize short forms used in place of the full name. (See ¶332 for a few exceptions.)

Montgomery Street	**BUT:** the street
Empire State Building	the building
Stone Mountain Park	the park
Sacramento River	the river
Lake Pontchartrain	the lake
Colony Surf Hotel	the hotel
Rittenhouse Square	the square
Riverside Drive	the drive
Bighorn Mountain	the mountain
Shoshone Falls	the falls
the Washington Monument	the monument
Stapleton Airport	the airport
the Fogg Art Museum	the museum
Golden Gate Bridge	the bridge
Nicollet Mall	the mall

➤ *For plural expressions like* the Atlantic and Pacific Oceans, *see* ¶*309a, note. For the treatment of prepositions and conjunctions in proper names, see* ¶*303, note.*

332 A few short forms are capitalized because of clear association with one place.

the Coast (the West Coast)	the Hill (Capitol Hill)
the Continent (Europe)	the Street (Wall Street)
the Channel (English Channel)	the Village (Greenwich Village)

333 **a.** Capitalize imaginative names that designate specific places or areas.

the Bay Area (around San Francisco)	the Right Bank (in Paris)
the Second City (Chicago)	the South Lawn of the White House
the Big Apple (New York)	inside the Beltway (Washington, D.C.)
the Big D (Dallas)	Tinseltown (Hollywood)
Back Bay (in Boston)	the Big Muddy (the Missouri River)
the Pacific Rim	the Beehive State (Utah)
	the French Quarter (in New Orleans)

NOTE: The terms *Sunbelt* and *Frostbelt* are now commonly spelled as one word; the terms *Farm Belt*, *Bible Belt*, and *Rust Belt* are still commonly spelled as two words. Within the same context treat these terms the same way—as two words; for example, *in the Farm Belt and the Frost Belt*.

b. Some place names are used imaginatively to refer to types of businesses or institutions.

Silicon Valley (the cluster of high-tech industries south of San Francisco)
Madison Avenue (the advertising industry)
Wall Street (the financial industry)
Off-Off-Broadway (experimental theater in New York City)
Foggy Bottom (the U.S. State Department)

334 Capitalize the word *city* only when it is part of the corporate name of the city or part of an imaginative name.

Kansas City   **BUT:** the city of Dallas   the Windy City (Chicago)

335 Capitalize *state* only when it follows the name of a state or is part of an imaginative name.

New York *State* is also called the Empire *State*.

The *state* of Alaska is the largest in the Union.

Washington *State* entered the Union in 1889, the forty-second *state* to do so.

Next year we plan to return to the *States*. (Meaning the *United States*.)

NOTE: Do not capitalize *state* when used in place of the actual state name.

He is an employee of the *state*. (People working for the state government, however, might write *State*.)

336 Capitalize *the* only when it is a part of the official name of a place.

The Dalles	**BUT:** the Bronx
The Hague	the Netherlands

337 Capitalize the words *upper* and *lower* only when they are part of an actual place name or a well-established imaginative name.

Upper Peninsula	Lower East Side
Upper West Side	Newton Lower Falls

Points of the Compass

338 **a.** Capitalize *north, south, east, west,* and derivative words when they designate definite regions or are an integral part of a proper name.

in the North	the Far North	the North Pole
down South	the Deep South	the South Side
out West	the Far West	the West Coast
back East	the Middle East	the Eastern Seaboard

b. Do not capitalize these words when they merely indicate direction or general location.

Many factories have relocated from the *Northeast* to the *South*. (Region.)
BUT: They maintain a villa in the *south* of France. (General location.)
OR: Go *west* on Route 517 and then *south* on I-95. (Direction.)

John is coming back *East* after three years on the *West Coast*. (Region.)
BUT: The *west coast* of the United States borders on the Pacific. (Referring only to the shoreline, not the region.)

Most of our customers live on the *East Side*. (Definite locality.)
BUT: Most of our customers live on the *east side* of town. (General location.)

339 Capitalize such words as *Northerner, Southerner,* and *Midwesterner.*

340 Capitalize such words as *northern, southern, eastern,* and *western* when they refer to the people in a region or to their political, social, or cultural activities. Do not capitalize these words when they merely indicate general location or refer to the geography or climate of the region.

Eastern bankers	**BUT:** the eastern half of Pennsylvania
Southern hospitality	southern temperatures
Western civilization	westerly winds
the Northern vote	a northern winter

The *Northern* states did not vote as they were expected to. (Political activities.)
BUT: The drought is expected to continue in the *northern* states. (Climate.)

My sales territory takes in most of the *southeastern* states. (General location.)

NOTE: When terms like *western region* and *southern district* are used to name organizational units within a company, capitalize them.

The *Western Region* (referring to a part of the national sales staff) reports that sales are 12 percent over budget for the first six months this year.

341 When words like *northern, southern, eastern,* and *western* precede a place name, they are not ordinarily capitalized because they merely indicate general location within a region. However, when these words are actually part of the place name, they must be capitalized. (Check an atlas or the geographic listings in a dictionary when in doubt.)

Preceding a Place Name	**Part of a Place Name**
northern New Jersey	**BUT:** Northern Ireland
western Massachusetts	Western Australia

NOTE: Within certain regions it is not uncommon for many who live there to capitalize the adjective because of the special importance they attach to the regional designation. Thus people who live in southern California may prefer to write *Southern California*.

Days of the Week, Months, Holidays, Seasons, Events, Periods

342 Capitalize names of days, months, holidays, and religious days.

Tuesday	Mother's Day	Good Friday
February	the Fourth of July	All Saints' Day
New Year's Eve	Kwanza	Christmas
April Fools' Day	Kamehameha Day	Rosh Hashanah
Veterans Day	Ramadan	Yom Kippur

343 Do not capitalize the names of the seasons unless they are personified.

> We hold our regional sales conferences during the *fall* and *winter*, but our national conference always takes place early in the *spring*.

> We do not plan to announce our new line of software applications until our fall '97/winter '98 catalog.

> > BUT: And this you can see is the bolt. The purpose of this
> > Is to open the breech, as you see. We can slide it
> > Rapidly backwards and forwards: we call this
> > Easing the spring. And rapidly backwards and forwards
> > The early bees are assaulting and fumbling the flowers:
> > They call it easing the Spring.
>
> > —Henry Reed

344 **a.** Capitalize the names of historical events and imaginative names given to historical periods.

the American Revolution	the Renaissance
World War II	the Counter-Reformation
the Holocaust	Prohibition
Fire Prevention Week	the Great Depression

b. References to cultural *ages* are usually capitalized. However, contemporary references are not usually capitalized unless they appear together with a capitalized reference.

the Bronze Age	BUT: the space age
the Dark Ages	the atomic age
the Middle Ages	the nuclear age

The course spans the development of civilization from the *Stone Age* to the *Space Age*.

c. References to cultural *eras* are usually capitalized, but references to cultural periods are usually not.

the Christian Era	BUT: the romantic period
the Victorian Era	the colonial period

345 Do not capitalize the names of decades and centuries.

during the fifties	in the twenty-first century
in the nineteen-nineties	during the nineteen hundreds

NOTE: Decades are capitalized, however, in special expressions.

the Gay Nineties	the Roaring Twenties

Acts, Laws, Bills, Treaties

346 **a.** Capitalize formal titles of acts, laws, bills, and treaties, but do not capitalize common-noun elements that stand alone in place of the full name.

the Americans With Disabilities Act	the act
Public Law 480	the law
the Treaty of Versailles	the treaty
the First Amendment	the amendment
the Constitution of the United States	BUT: the Constitution (see ¶304)

b. Do not capitalize generic or informal references to existing or pending legislation except for proper nouns and adjectives.

environmental protection laws	the Brady gun control law

c. "Laws" that make humorous or satirical observations about human and organizational behavior are capitalized to suggest that they carry the same authority as an actual piece of legislation.

Parkinson's Law states that work expands to fill the time that has been allotted for its completion.

Murphy's Law holds that if something can go wrong, it will.

The *Peter Principle* maintains that people in an organization tend to be promoted until they reach their level of incompetence.

According to *Fudd's First Law of Opposition,* if you push something hard enough, it will fall over.

d. In the names of authentic scientific laws, capitalize only proper nouns and adjectives.

Gresham's law   Newton's first law of motion
Mendel's law   the first law of thermodynamics

Programs, Movements, Concepts

347 a. Do not capitalize the names of programs, movements, or concepts when used as general terms.

social security benefits   the civil rights movement
BUT: the Social Security Administration BUT: the Civil Rights Act
medicare payments   the big bang theory
BUT: the Medicare Act   existentialism and rationalism

b. Capitalize proper nouns and adjectives that are part of such terms.

the Socratic method   Newtonian physics
Keynesian economics   Marxist-Leninist theories

c. Capitalize imaginative names given to programs and movements.

the New Deal   the New Frontier
the Great Society   the War on Poverty

d. Capitalize terms like *democrat, socialist,* and *communist* when they signify formal membership in a political party but not when they merely signify belief in a certain philosophy.

a lifelong *Democrat* (refers to a person   a lifelong *democrat* (refers to
  who consistently votes for candidates   a person who believes in the
  of the Democratic Party)   principles of democracy)
independent voters   leftists
the right wing   fascist tendencies

Races, Peoples, Languages

348 Capitalize the names of races, peoples, tribes, and languages.

Caucasians   Americans   Native Americans   BUT: the blacks
the Japanese   Hispanics   Mandarin Chinese   the whites

NOTE: Do not hyphenate terms like *African Americans* or *French Canadians* when they are used as nouns, because the first word in each case modifies the second. However, hyphenate such terms when they are used as adjectives; for example, *African-American enterprises, French-Canadian voters.* Moreover, hyphenate such terms when the first element is a prefix; for example, *an Afro-American style, the Anglo-Saxons, the Indo-Chinese.*

➤ *For a usage note on ethnic references, see pages 261–262.*

Religious References

349 **a.** Capitalize all references to a supreme being.

God	the Supreme Being	Allah
the Lord	the Messiah	Yahweh
the Holy Spirit	the Almighty	Providence

NOTE: The word *God* is capitalized in such compound expressions as *God-fearing* and *Godspeed* but not in such terms as *godforsaken* and *god-awful*.

b. Capitalize personal pronouns referring to a supreme being when they stand alone, without an antecedent nearby.

Offer thanks unto *Him*.   BUT: Ask the Lord for *his* blessing.

NOTE: Some writers capitalize these personal pronouns under all circumstances.

c. Capitalize references to persons revered as holy.

the Prince of Peace	Buddha	John the Baptist
the Good Shepherd	the Prophet	Saint Peter (see ¶518e)
the Blessed Virgin	the Apostles	Luke the Evangelist

d. Capitalize the names of religions, their members, and their buildings.

Reform Judaism	Mormons	Saint Mark's Episcopal Church
Zen Buddhism	Methodists	Temple Beth Sholom

the Roman Catholic *Church* (meaning the institution as a whole)

BUT: the Roman Catholic *church* on Wyoming Avenue (referring to a specific building)

e. Capitalize references to religious events. (See also ¶342.)

the Creation	the Exodus	the Crucifixion
the Flood	the Second Coming	the Resurrection

f. In general, do not capitalize references to specific religious observances and services. However, if you are writing from the perspective of a particular religion, follow the capitalization style of that religion.

bar mitzvah	baptism	BUT: the Eucharist
seder	christening	the Mass

350 Capitalize (but do not quote, underline, or italicize) references to works regarded as sacred.

the King James Bible	the Koran	the Ten Commandments
BUT: biblical sources	the Talmud	the Sermon on the Mount
the Revised Standard Version	the Torah	Psalms 23 and 24
the Old Testament	the Our Father	Kaddish
the Book of Genesis	the Lord's Prayer	Hail Mary
	Hebrews 13:8	the Apostles' Creed

Celestial Bodies

351 Capitalize the names of planets (*Jupiter, Mars*), stars (*Polaris, the North Star*), and constellations (*the Big Dipper, the Milky Way*). However, do not capitalize the words *sun, moon,* and *earth* unless they are used in connection with the capitalized names of other planets or stars.

With the weather we've been having, we haven't seen much of the *sun*.

We have gone to the ends of the *earth* to assemble this collection of jewelry.

Compare the orbits of *Mars, Venus,* and *Earth*.

Course Titles, Subjects, Academic Degrees

352 Capitalize the names of specific course titles. However, do not capitalize names of subjects or areas of study (except for any proper nouns or adjectives in such names).

> *American History 201* meets on Tuesdays and Thursdays. (Course title.)
>
> Harriet got a bachelor's degree in *American history*. (Area of study.)

353 Do not capitalize academic degrees used as general terms of classification. However, capitalize a degree used after a person's name.

> a bachelor of arts degree   received his bachelor's (see ¶644)
> a master of science degree   working for a master's
> a doctor of laws degree   will soon receive her doctorate
>
> **BUT:** Claire Hurwitz, Doctor of Philosophy

354 In references to academic years, do not capitalize the words *freshman*, *sophomore, junior,* and *senior*. In references to grade levels, capitalize the word *grade* when a number follows but not when a number precedes.

> All incoming *freshmen* must register by September 4.
>
> Harriet spent her *junior* year in Germany.
>
> Our oldest child is in *Grade 6;* our second child is in the *third grade*.

Commercial Products

355 Capitalize trademarks, brand names, proprietary names, names of commercial products, and market grades. The common noun following the name of a product should not ordinarily be capitalized; however, manufacturers and advertisers often capitalize such words in the names of their own products to give them special emphasis.

> Elmer's glue   **BUT:** Krazy Glue

NOTE: Be alert to the correct spelling of proper nouns.

> Macintosh computers   **BUT:** McIntosh apples

356 Capitalize all trademarks except those that have become clearly established as common nouns. To be safe, check an up-to-date dictionary or consult The International Trademark Association (1133 Avenue of the Americas, New York, NY 10036).

> Xerox, Photostat; **BUT:** photocopy, fax
> DeskWriter, LaserJet; **BUT:** laser printer
> Express Mail, Yellow Pages, Filofax
>   **BUT:** e-mail, voice mail, videotex
> Scotch tape, Post-it notes, Rolodex
> Acrilan, Dacron, Lycra, Orlon,
>   Ultrasuede; **BUT:** nylon, spandex,
> Levi's, Windbreaker, Snugli, L'eggs
> Loafers, Air Jordan, 'Boks
> Jeep, Dumpster, Hide-A-Bed
> Airbus, Learjet, AAdvantage
> Teflon, Velcro, Ziploc, Baggies, GLAD
> AstroTurf, Styrofoam, Lucite, Mylar
> Fiberglas; **BUT:** fiberglass
> Jacuzzi, Disposall, Frigidaire, Freon
> Laundromat, Dustbuster, Drygas
> Crock-Pot, Pyrex dish, Dixie cup
>
> Off!, Oh Henry!, $H_2OH!$, Guess?
> Band-Aid, Ace bandage, Q-Tips
> Kleenex, Vaseline, Chap Stick
> Tylenol, Novocain, Demerol,
>   Valium; **BUT:** aspirin
> Nicoderm, NyQuil, Adrenalin
>   **BUT:** penicillin, ampicillin
> diet Coke, Diet Pepsi, Kool-Aid,
>   7UP, Gatorade, Sanka
> Kitty Litter, Seeing Eye dog
> Day-Glo colors, Technicolor
> Discman, Walkman, Polaroid
>   **BUT:** camcorder
> Jazzercise, Ski-Doo, Hula Hoop
> Frisbee, Ping-Pong, Rollerblades
> Scrabble, Trivial Pursuit
> Realtor; **BUT:** real estate agent

Advertising Material

357 Words ordinarily written in small letters may be capitalized in advertising copy for special emphasis. (This style is inappropriate in all other kinds of written communication.)

> Save money now during our *Year-End Clearance Sale.*
>
> It's the event *Luxury Lovers* have been waiting for . . . from Whitehall's!

Legal Documents

358 In legal documents, many words that ordinarily would be written in small letters are written with initial capitals or all capitals—for example, references to parties, the name of the document, special provisions, and sometimes spelled-out amounts of money (see ¶420b).

> THIS AGREEMENT, made this 31st day of January 1995 . . .
>
> . . . hereinafter called the SELLER . . .
>
> WHEREAS the Seller has this day agreed . . .
>
> WITNESS the signatures . . .

Nouns With Numbers or Letters

359 Capitalize a noun followed by a number or a letter that indicates sequence. **EXCEPTIONS:** Do not capitalize the nouns *line, note, page, paragraph, size, step,* and *verse.*

Account 66160	Check 181	Invoice 270487	Policy 394857
Act 1	Class 4	Item 9859D	Room 501
Appendix A	Column 1	Lesson 20	Route 46
Article 2	Diagram 4	line 4	Rule 3
Book III	Exercise 8	Model B671-4	Section 1
Building 4	Exhibit A	note 1	size 10
Bulletin T-119	Extension 2174	page 158	step 3
Car 8171	Figure 9	paragraph 2a	Table 7
Channel 55	Flight 626	Part Three	Unit 2
Chapter V	Illustration 19	Plate XV	verse 3
Chart 3	Interstate 71	Platform 3	Volume II

NOTE: It is often unnecessary to use *No.* before the number. (See ¶455a.)

> Purchase Order 4713 (**RATHER THAN:** Purchase Order *No.* 4713)

Titles of Literary and Artistic Works; Headings

360 In titles of literary and artistic works and in displayed headings, capitalize all words with *four or more* letters. Also capitalize words with fewer than four letters except:

> **ARTICLES:** *the, a, an*
>
> **SHORT CONJUNCTIONS:** *and, as, but, if, or, nor*
>
> **SHORT PREPOSITIONS:** *at, by, for, in, of, off, on, out, to, up*

NOTE: Be sure to capitalize short verb forms like *Is* and *Be.* However, do not capitalize *to* when it is part of an infinitive.

> *How to Succeed in Business Without Really Trying*
>
> "Redevelopment Proposal Is Not Expected to Be Approved"

361 Even articles, short conjunctions, and short prepositions should be capitalized under the following circumstances:

a. Capitalize the first and last word of a title.

"*A* Home to Be Proud *Of*"

CAUTION: Do not capitalize *the* at the beginning of a title unless it is actually part of the title.

For further details check *the Encyclopaedia Britannica.*

This clipping is from *The New York Times.*

b. Capitalize the first word following a dash or colon in a title.

Abraham Lincoln—The Early Years

The Treaty of Versailles: A Reexamination

c. Capitalize short words like *in, out, off,* and *up* in titles when they serve as adverbs rather than as prepositions. (These words may occur as adverbs in verb phrases or in hyphenated compounds derived from verb phrases. See ¶¶803, 1070.)

"AT&T Chalks *Up* Record Earnings for the Year"

"LeClaire Is Runner-*Up* in Election" (see also ¶363)

BUT: "Sailing *up* the Mississippi"

The Spy Who Came In From the Cold

"Foxworth Is Considered a Shoo-*In* for Governor"

BUT: "Pollsters Project an Easy Win for Foxworth *in* Heavy Voter Turnout"

d. Capitalize short prepositions like *in* and *up* when used together with prepositions having four or more letters.

"Sailing *Up* and *Down* the Mississippi"

"Happenings *In* and *Around* Town"

"Mall Opening *On* or *About* May 1"

e. When a title or heading is displayed on more than one line, do not capitalize the first word of any turnover line unless it needs to be capitalized on the basis of the preceding guidelines.

Should You Invest for the Long Pull	Millions	Income
or Should You Trade Continually?	*of* Dollars	*per* Capita

➤ *For the capitalization of* Preface, Contents, Appendix, *and* Index, *see* ¶242, *note; for the use of all-capital letters with titles, see* ¶289b.

362 Do not capitalize a book title when it is incorporated into a sentence as a descriptive phrase.

In his book on *economics* Samuelson points out that . . .

BUT: In his book *Economics* Samuelson points out that . . .

Hyphenated Words

363 *Within a sentence,* capitalize only those elements of a hyphenated word that are proper nouns or proper adjectives. *At the beginning of a sentence,* capitalize the first element in the hyphenated word but not other elements unless they are proper nouns or proper adjectives. *In a heading or title,* capitalize all the elements except articles, short prepositions, and short conjunctions. (See ¶360.)

(Continued on page 100.)

Within Sentences	Beginning Sentences	In Headings and Titles
e-mail	E-mail	E-Mail
up-to-date	Up-to-date	Up-to-Date
Spanish-American	Spanish-American	Spanish-American
English-speaking	English-speaking	English-Speaking
mid-September	Mid-September	Mid-September
ex-President Bush	Ex-President Bush	Ex-President Bush
Senator-elect Murray	Senator-elect Murray	Senator-Elect Murray
self-confidence	Self-confidence	Self-Confidence
de-emphasize	De-emphasize	De-Emphasize
follow-up	Follow-up	Follow-Up (see ¶361c)
Ninety-ninth Congress	Ninety-ninth Congress	Ninety-Ninth Congress
one-sixth	One-sixth	One-Sixth
post-World War II	Post-World War II	Post-World War II

Awards and Medals

364 Capitalize the names of awards and medals.

Pulitzer Prize winners	the Congressional Medal of Honor
the Nobel Prize	the Distinguished Service Medal
Oscars and Emmys	the Purple Heart

Computer Terminology

365 **a.** The names of many programming languages are written in all capitals.

BASIC	FORTRAN	BUT: Pascal
COBOL	APL	Ada
SNOBOL	LISP	Logo

  b. The names of many operating systems are also written in all-capital letters.

MS-DOS	UNIX	BUT: Macintosh OS
PC-DOS	OS/2	Microsoft Windows

  c. The names of many software applications are compound nouns that are written solid but with a capital letter at the beginning of each element. (Follow the manufacturer's style in each case.)

WordPerfect	PageMaker	BUT: Microsoft Word
OmniPage	ZipZapp	dBASE for Windows
VirusScan	QuarkXPress	CorelDRAW

> *Capitalization of questions within sentences: see ¶¶115, 117.*
> *Capitalization after a colon: see ¶¶196–199.*
> *Capitalization after an opening bracket: see ¶296.*
> *Capitalization after an opening dash: see ¶214, note.*
> *Capitalization after an opening parenthesis: see ¶¶224–226.*
> *Capitalization after an opening quotation mark: see ¶¶272–273.*
> *Capitalization of abbreviations: see ¶514.*

SECTION 4

NUMBERS

¶401

There is a significant difference between using figures and using words to express numbers. Figures are big (like capital letters) and compact and informal (like abbreviations); when used in a sentence, they stand out clearly from the surrounding words. By contrast, numbers expressed in words are unemphatic and formal; they do not stand out in a sentence. It is this functional difference between figures and words that underlies all aspects of number style.

BASIC RULES

The rules for expressing numbers would be quite simple if writers would all agree to express numbers entirely in figures or entirely in words. But in actual practice the exclusive use of figures is considered appropriate only in tables and statistical matter, whereas the exclusive use of words to express numbers is found only in ultraformal documents (such as proclamations and social invitations). In writing that is neither ultraformal nor ultratechnical, most style manuals call for the use of both figures and words in varying proportions. Although authorities do not agree on details, there are two sets of basic rules in wide use: the *figure style* (which uses figures for most numbers above 10) and the *word style* (which uses figures for most numbers above 100). Unless you deal with a very limited type of business correspondence, you should be familiar with both styles and be prepared to use each appropriately as the situation demands.

Figure Style

The figure style is most commonly used in ordinary business correspondence (dealing with sales, production, finance, advertising, and other routine commercial matters). It is also used in journalistic and technical material and in academic work of a technical or statistical nature. In writing of this kind, most numbers represent significant quantities or measurements that should stand out for emphasis or quick comprehension.

401 Spell out numbers from 1 through 10; use figures for numbers above 10. This rule applies to both exact and approximate numbers.

> I would like *ten* copies of this article, but I need only *two* or *three* right away.
>
> At the convention we got over *75* requests for a copy of your report.
>
> We expect about *30* to *35* employees to sign up for the graphic arts course.
>
> The advertising is deliberately pitched at the *40-plus* age group.
>
> My letter in last Sunday's paper apparently provoked over *25* letters and some *60-odd* phone calls.
>
> One bookstore chain has already ordered *2500* copies. (See ¶461, note, on the omission of commas in four-digit figures.)
>
> The exhibition drew more than *12,000* people in the first month.
>
> We send out about 200,000 catalogs almost every month, but our year-end holiday catalog is mailed to over 1,000,000 households. (See ¶403b.)

a. Use all figures—even for the numbers 1 through 10 (as in this sentence)—when they have technical significance or need to stand out for quick comprehension. This all-figure style is used in tables, in statistical material, and in expressions of dates *(May 3)*, money *($6)*, clock time *(4 p.m.)*, proportions and ratios *(a 5-to-1 shot)*, sports scores *(3 to 1)*, academic grades *(95)*, and percentages *(8 percent)*. This style is also used with abbreviations and symbols *(12 cm, 8°F)*, with numbers referred to as numbers *(think of a number from 1 to 10)*, with highway designations *(U.S. Route 1, I-80)*, and with technical or emphatic references to age *(a tristate clinical study of 5-year-olds)*, periods of time *(a 6-month loan)*, measurements *(parcels over 3 pounds)*, and page numbers *(page 1)*.

b. In isolated cases spell out a number above 10 in order to de-emphasize the number or make it seem indefinite.

Jonathan could give you *a thousand and one* reasons for his inability to find a job that's right for him.

I have *a hundred* things to do today. (In this context *100 things* would seem too precise, too exact.)

NOTE: Also use words for numbers at the beginning of a sentence, for most ordinals *(our twenty-fifth anniversary)*, for fractions *(one-third of our sales)*, and for nontechnical or nonemphatic references to age *(my son just turned twelve)*, periods of time *(twenty years ago)*, and measurements *(I need to lose another thirty pounds)*.

➤ *For rules on how to express numbers in figures, see ¶¶461–464. For rules on how to express numbers in words, see ¶¶465–467.*

402 Use the same style to express *related* numbers above and below 10. If any of the numbers are above 10, put them all in figures.

We used to have *two* dogs, *one* cat, and *one* rabbit.

BUT: We now have *5* dogs, *11* cats, and *1* rabbit. (The rabbit is male.)

Our *four* sons consumed a total of *18* hamburgers, *5* large bottles of diet Coke, *12* DoveBars, and about *2000* cookies—all at *one* sitting. (Figures are used for all the related items of food; the other numbers—*four* and *one*—are spelled out, since they are not related and are not over 10.)

NOTE: In the names of companies and products, follow the organization's style.

a 7-Eleven store	a can of 7UP	A.1. steak sauce
3-In-One oil	V8 juice	9-Lives cat food
Lotus 1-2-3 software	3M office products	One-A-Day vitamins

403 For fast comprehension, numbers in the *millions* or higher may be expressed as follows:

21 million (in place of 21,000,000)
3 billion (in place of 3,000,000,000)
14½ million (in place of 14,500,000)
2.4 billion (in place of 2,400,000,000)

Bindel & Boggs is placing an order for *2.4 million* barrels of oil.

BUT: Bindel & Boggs is placing a *2.4-million-barrel* order. (See ¶817.)

a. This style may be used only when the amount consists of a whole number with nothing more than a simple fraction or decimal following. A number such as *4,832,067* must be written all in figures.

b. Treat related numbers alike.

Last year we sold *21,557,000* items; this year, nearly *23,000,000*. (**NOT:** 21,557,000 . . . 23 million.)

➤ *For examples involving money, see ¶416.*

¶404

Word Style

The word style of numbers is used in high-level executive correspondence (see ¶¶1395–1396) and in nontechnical material, where the writing is of a more formal or literary nature and the use of figures would give numbers an undesired emphasis and obtrusiveness. Here are the basic rules for the word style.

404 Spell out all numbers, whether exact or approximate, that can be expressed in one or two words. (A hyphenated compound number like *twenty-one* or *twenty-nine* counts as one word.) In effect, spell out all numbers from 1 through 100 and all round numbers above 100 that require no more than two words (such as *sixty-two thousand* or *forty-five million*).

> Mr. Ryan received *twenty-three* letters praising his talk last Wednesday at the Rotary Club.

> Last year more than *twelve million* people attended the art exhibition our company sponsored.

> Some *sixty-odd* people have called to volunteer their services.

> Over *two hundred* people attended the reception for Helen and Frank Russo.

> **BUT:** Over *250* people attended the reception. (Use figures when more than two words are required.)

> **NOTE:** In writing of an ultraformal nature—proclamations, social invitations, and many legal documents—even a number that requires more than two words is spelled out. However, as a matter of practicality the word style ordinarily uses figures when more than two words are required.

➤ *For rules on how to express numbers in words, see ¶¶465–467.*

405 Express related numbers the same way, even though some are above 100 and some below. If any must be in figures, put all in figures.

> We sent out *three hundred* invitations and have already received over *one hundred* acceptances.

> **BUT:** We sent out *300* invitations and have already received *125* acceptances. (**NOT:** three hundred . . . 125.)

406 Numbers in the millions or higher *that require more than two words when spelled out* may be expressed as follows:

> 231 million (in place of 231,000,000)
> 9¾ billion (in place of 9,750,000,000)
> 671.4 million (in place of 671,400,000)

Even a two-word number such as *sixty-two million* should be expressed as *62 million* when it is related to a number such as *231 million* (which cannot be spelled in two words). Moreover, it should be expressed as *62,000,000* when it is related to a number such as *231,163,520*.

SPECIAL RULES

The preceding rules on figure style (¶¶401–403) and word style (¶¶404–406) are basic guidelines that govern in the absence of more specific principles. The following rules cover those situations that require special handling (for example, expressions of dates and money). In a number of cases where either figures or words are acceptable, your choice will depend on whether you are striving for emphasis or formality.

Dates

The following rules apply to dates in sentences. See ¶1314 for date lines in business correspondence.

407 When the day *precedes* the month or *stands alone,* express it either in ordinal figures (*1st, 2d, 3d, 4th,* etc.) or in ordinal words (the *first,* the *twelfth,* the *twenty-eighth*).

> **FOR EMPHASIS:** This year's international sales conference runs from Monday, the *2d* of August, through Thursday, the *5th.*

> **FOR FORMALITY:** We leave for Europe on the *third* of June and don't return until the *twenty-fifth.*

408 When the day *follows* the month, use a cardinal figure (*1, 2, 3,* etc.) to express it.

> on March *6* (**NOT:** March *6th* **OR** March *sixth*)

409 **a.** Express complete dates in month-day-year sequence.

> March 6, 1998

> **NOTE:** In United States military correspondence and in letters from foreign countries, the complete date is expressed in day-month-year sequence.

> 6 March 1998

b. The form *3/6/98* (representing a *month*-day-year sequence) is acceptable on business forms and in informal letters and memos. Avoid this form, however, if there is any chance your reader could misinterpret it as a *day*-month-year sequence.

c. Avoid the following forms: *March 6th, 1998; Mar. 6, 1998; the 6th of March, 1998; the sixth of March, 1998.*

410 Note the use of commas and other punctuation with expressions of dates.

> On *August 13, 1996,* my husband and I received the bank loan that permitted us to start our own restaurant. (Two commas set off the year following the month and day.)

> We set a formal opening date of *November 15, 1996;* we actually opened on *March 18, 1997* (because of the flash fire that virtually destroyed the restaurant and forced us to start from scratch). (Note that the second comma is omitted after *1996* and *1997* because in each case some other punctuation mark—a semicolon or an opening parenthesis—is required at that point.)

> Sales for *February 1997* hit an all-time low. (Omit commas around the year when it follows the month alone.)

> **BUT:** Once we introduced our new product line in *September 1996,* it was clear that we were finally on the road to a strong recovery. (The comma following *1996* is needed to separate an introductory dependent clause from the rest of the sentence, not because of the date.)

> The *May 1996* issue of *The Atlantic* carries an excerpt from Brenda's forthcoming book. (No commas are used when the month-year expression serves as an adjective.)

> **BUT:** The *May 6, 1996,* issue of *Newsweek* broke the story. (Use two commas to set off the year when a complete date serves as an adjective. See ¶154.)

(Continued on page 106.)

4

In *1995* we opened six branch offices in . . . (No comma follows the year in a short introductory phrase unless a nonessential element follows immediately.)

On *February 28* we will decide . . . (No comma follows the month and day in a short introductory phrase unless a nonessential element follows immediately.)

BUT: On *February 28,* the date of the next board meeting, we will decide . . . (Insert a comma when a nonessential element follows immediately.)

On *February 28,* 27 managers from the Iowa plant will . . . (Insert a comma when another figure follows immediately. See ¶456.)

Yesterday, *April 3,* I spoke to a group of exporters in Seattle. On Tuesday, *April 11,* I will be speaking at an international trade fair in Singapore. (Set off a month-day expression when it serves as an appositive. See ¶148.)

➤ *For the use or omission of a comma when a date is followed by a related phrase or clause, see ¶152.*

411 In formal legal documents, formal invitations, and proclamations, spell out the day and the year. A number of styles may be used:

May twenty-first	nineteen hundred and ninety-eight
the twenty-first of May	one thousand nine hundred and ninety-eight
this twenty-first day of May	in the year of our Lord one thousand nine hundred and ninety-eight

4

412 **a.** Class graduation years and well-known years in history may appear in abbreviated form.

the class of '99   the winter of '98   **BUT:** the San Francisco 49ers

b. Years also appear in abbreviated form in certain business expressions. (See also ¶294.)

FY 1996/97 **OR** fiscal year 1996/97
the fall '97/'98 catalog

➤ *For the expression of centuries and decades, see ¶¶438–439; for dates in a sequence, see ¶¶458–460.*

Money

413 **a.** Use figures to express exact or approximate amounts of money.

$7	about $1500	over $5,000,000 a year	a $50 bill
$13.50	nearly $50,000	a $5,000,000-a-year account	$350 worth

b. When amounts of money from different countries are referred to in the same context, the unit of currency in each case usually appears as an abbreviation or symbol (or both) before the numerical amount.

US$10,000	(refers to 10,000 U.S. dollars)
Can$10,000	(refers to 10,000 Canadian dollars)
Mex$10,000	(refers to 10,000 Mexican pesos)
DM10,000	(refers to 10,000 German deutsche marks)
£10,000	(refers to 10,000 British pounds)
¥ 10,000	(refers to 10,000 Japanese yen)

NOTE: If you are using software with special character sets, you can access the symbols for the British pound and the Japanese yen. If your equipment does not have the capability to print the symbols £ and ¥, you may be able to construct them as follows: To form the symbol for the British pound, type a capital *L* over a small *f*: £. To form the symbol for the Japanese yen, type a capital Y over an equal sign (=): ¥.

c. An isolated, nonemphatic reference to money may be spelled out.

two hundred dollars	a half-dollar
nearly a thousand dollars	half a million dollars
a twenty-dollar bill	five thousand dollars' worth (note
a million-dollar beach house	the apostrophe with *dollars*)

414 Spell out indefinite amounts of money.

a few million dollars   many thousands of dollars

415 It is not necessary to add a decimal point or zeros to a *whole* dollar amount that occurs in a sentence.

I am enclosing a check for *$125* as payment in full.

This model costs $12.50; that one costs *$10*.

In a column, however, if any amount contains cents, add a decimal point and two zeros to all *whole* dollar amounts to maintain a uniform appearance. (See also ¶1628.)

$150.50
25.00
8.05
——
$183.55

416 Money in round amounts of a million or more may be expressed partially in words. (The style given in the first column is preferred.)

$12 million	**OR**	12 million dollars			
$10½ million	**OR**	10½ million dollars			
$10.5 million	**OR**	10.5 million dollars			
$6¼ billion	**OR**	6¼ billion dollars	**OR**	$6250 million	
$6.25 billion	**OR**	6.25 billion dollars	**OR**	6250 million dollars	

a. This style may be used only when the amount consists of a whole number with nothing more than a simple fraction or decimal following.

10.5 million dollars   **BUT:** $10,235,000

b. Express related amounts the same way.

from $500,000 to $1,000,000 (**NOT:** from $500,000 to $1 million)

c. Repeat the word *million* (*billion*, etc.) with each figure to avoid misunderstanding.

$5 million to $10 million (**NOT:** $5 to $10 million)

417 Fractional expressions of large amounts of money should be either completely spelled out (see ¶427) or converted to an all-figure style.

one-quarter of a million dollars   **OR** $250,000
(**BUT NOT:** ¼ of a million dollars   **OR** $¼ million)

a half-billion dollars   **OR** $500,000,000
(**BUT NOT:** ½ billion dollars   **OR** $½ billion)

418 a. For amounts under a dollar, ordinarily use figures and the word *cents*.

I am sure that customers will not pay more than *50 cents* for this item.

This machine can be fixed with *80 cents'* worth of parts. (Note the apostrophe with *cents*.)

These *25-cent* tokens can be used at all tollbooths.

NOTE: An isolated, nonemphatic reference to cents may be spelled out.

I wouldn't give *two cents* for that car.

(Continued on page 108.)

b. Do not use the style *$.75* in sentences except when related amounts require a dollar sign.

> It will cost you *$4.84* a copy to do the company manual: *$.86* for the paper, *$1.54* for the printing, and *$2.44* for the special binder.

c. The cent sign (*¢*) may be used in technical and statistical material.

> The price of lead, approximately *15.5¢* a pound in 1970, now runs around *37¢* a pound; zinc, averaging *15¢* a pound in 1970, now sells for *60¢* a pound.

419 When using the dollar sign or the cent sign with a price range or a series of amounts, use the sign with each amount.

> $5,000 to $10,000 $10 million to $20 million
> 10¢ to 20¢   (**BUT NOT:** $10 to $20 million)

> These three properties are valued at $832,900, $954,500, and $1,087,000, respectively.

> If the term *dollars* or *cents* is to be spelled out, use the term only with the final amount.

420 In legal documents, amounts of money are often expressed first in words and then, within parentheses, in figures. (See also ¶¶465–467.)

> One Hundred Dollars ($100)   **OR**   One Hundred (100) Dollars
> **BUT NOT:** One Hundred ($100) Dollars

> Three Thousand One Hundred and 50/100 Dollars ($3100.50)

a. When spelling out amounts of money, omit the *and* between hundreds and tens of dollars if *and* is used before the fraction representing cents.

> Six Hundred Thirty-two and 75/100 Dollars
> (**NOT:** Six Hundred *and* Thirty-two and 75/100 Dollars)

> **NOTE:** In whole dollar amounts, the use of *and* between hundreds and tens of dollars is optional.

> Six Hundred Thirty-two Dollars   **OR**   Six Hundred and Thirty-two Dollars

b. The capitalization of spelled-out amounts may vary. Sometimes the first letter of each main word is capitalized (as in the examples in ¶420a); sometimes only the first letter of the first word is capitalized (as on checks); sometimes the entire amount is in all-capital letters.

The following rules (¶¶421–428) cover situations in which numbers are usually spelled out: at the beginning of sentences and in expressions using indefinite numbers, ordinal numbers, and fractions.

At the Beginning of a Sentence

421 Spell out a number that begins a sentence, as well as any related numbers.

> *Thirty-four* former students of Dr. Helen VanVleck came from all parts of the country to honor their professor on the occasion of her retirement.

> *Eight hundred* people have already signed the recall petition.

> *Forty* to *fifty* percent of the people polled on different occasions expressed disapproval of the mayor's performance in office.

> (**NOT:** *Forty* to *50* percent . . .)

422   If the number requires more than two words when spelled out or if figures are preferable for emphasis or quick reference, reword the sentence.

> You ought to consider *486* processors if you want to boost productivity.
> (**NOT:** *486* processors are worth considering . . .)
>
> The company sent out *298* copies of its consumer guidelines last month.
> (**NOT:** *Two hundred and ninety-eight* copies of its consumer guidelines were sent
> out by the company last month.)
>
> We had a good year in *1997*.
> (**NOT:** *Nineteen hundred ninety-seven* [**OR** *1997*] was a good year for us.)
>
> Our mining operations in Nevada provide *60* to *70* percent of our revenues.
> (**NOT:** *Sixty* to *seventy* percent of our revenues come from our mining opera-
> tions in Nevada.)

Indefinite Numbers and Amounts

423   Spell out indefinite numbers and amounts.

> several hundred investors   hundreds of inquiries
> a few thousand acres   thousands of readers
> a multimillion-dollar sale   many millions of dollars
> a man in his late forties   a roll of fifties and twenties

> ➤ *For approximate numbers, see ¶401 (figure style) and ¶404 (word style).*

Ordinal Numbers

424   In general, spell out all ordinal numbers (*first, second, third,* etc.) that can
be expressed in one or two words. (A hyphenated number like *twenty-first*
counts as one word.)

> in the twenty-first century   the firm's one hundredth anniversary
> twentieth-century art (see ¶817)   (**BUT:** the firm's 125th anniversary)
> on the forty-eighth floor   the Ninety-ninth Congress (in text)
> on my fifty-fifth birthday   the Ninety-Ninth Congress (in head-
> the Fourteenth Ward   ings and titles; see ¶363)
> the two millionth visitor   the 104th Congress
>   to EPCOT   the Eighteenth Amendment

> ➤ *For the rule on how to express ordinal numbers in words, see ¶465; for the
> distinction between ordinals and fractions, see ¶427d.*

425   Use figures for ordinals in certain expressions of dates (see ¶¶407–409),
in numbered street names above 10 (see ¶1333b), and in situations calling for special emphasis.

In Advertising Copy

> Come to our *25th* Anniversary Sale! (Figures for emphasis.)
>
> Come to our *Twenty-fifth* Anniversary Sale! (Words for formality.)

In Ordinary Correspondence

> Watkins & Glenn is having a *twenty-fifth* anniversary sale.

NOTE: Ordinal figures are expressed as follows: *1st, 2d* or *2nd, 3d* or *3rd,
4th,* etc. Do not use an "abbreviation" period following an ordinal figure.

> ➤ *For the use of* 2d *in preference to* 2nd, *see ¶503.*

426 Ordinals that follow a person's name may be expressed in arabic or roman numerals. As a rule, use arabic numerals unless you know that the person in question prefers roman numerals.

> James A. Wilson 3d   **OR**   James A. Wilson III
> C. Roy Post 4th   **OR**   C. Roy Post IV

➤ *For the use of commas with numerals after a person's name, see ¶156.*

Fractions

427 Fractions Standing Alone

a. Ordinarily, spell out a fraction that stands alone (without a whole number preceding); for example, *one-third.* Use figures, however, if the spelled-out form is long and awkward or if the fraction is used in a technical measurement or some type of computation.

> one-half the audience (see ¶427c)   three-fourths of the profits
> two-thirds of our employees   nine-tenths of a mile away
> multiply by 2/5   a quarter pound of butter
> 3/4-yard lengths (**BETTER THAN:** three-quarter-yard lengths)
> 5/32 inch (**BETTER THAN:** five thirty-seconds of an inch)
> He came back *a half hour* later (**OR** *half an hour* later).

NOTE: Hyphenate *half dozen* or *half a dozen* when this phrase is used as a compound modifier before a noun. (See also ¶817a.)

> I'll take a *half-dozen* eggs (**OR** *half-a-dozen* eggs).
> **BUT:** I'll take *a half dozen* (**OR** *half a dozen*).

b. When a fraction is spelled out, hyphenate the numerator and the denominator unless either element already contains a hyphen.

> five-eighths   thirteen thirty-seconds   twenty-seven sixty-fourths

NOTE: Some authorities hyphenate *simple fractions* (those that require only a single word for the numerator and the denominator) when they are used as adjectives but not as nouns.

> a *two-thirds* majority
> **BUT:** *two thirds* of the voters

c. In constructions involving the balanced phrases *one half . . . the other half,* do not hyphenate *one half.*

> *One half* of the shipment was damaged beyond use; *the other half* was salvageable.

d. Distinguish between large spelled-out fractions (which are hyphenated) and large spelled-out ordinals (which are not).

> The difference is less than *one-hundredth* of 1 percent. (Hyphenated fraction meaning *1/100.*)
>
> **BUT:** This year the company will be celebrating the *one hundredth* anniversary of its founding. (Unhyphenated ordinal meaning *100th.*)

e. Fractions expressed in figures should not be followed by endings like *sts, ds, nds,* or *ths* or by an *of* phrase.

> 3/200 (**NOT:** 3/200ths)   9/64 inch (**NOT:** 9/64ths of an inch)

If a sentence requires the use of an *of* phrase following the fraction, spell the fraction out.

> three-quarters of an hour (**NOT:** 3/4 of an hour)

4

428 Fractions in Mixed Numbers

a. Ordinarily use figures to express a mixed number (a whole number plus a fraction); for example, *3¼*. Spell out a mixed number at the beginning of a sentence.

> Our sales are now *4½* times what they were in 1987.
>
> *Two and a quarter* (**OR** *Two and one-quarter*) inches of rain fell over the weekend. (Note the use of *and* between the whole number and the fraction.)

b. When constructing fractions that do not appear on the keyboard or in a special character set with word processing software, use the diagonal (/). Separate a whole number from a fraction by means of a space (not with a hyphen).

> I can remember when an *8 5/8* percent mortgage seemed high.
> (**NOT:** . . . an 8-5/8 percent mortgage.)

c. In the same sentence, do not mix ready-made fractions (½, ¼) with those that you construct yourself (7/8, 5/16).

> The rate on prime commercial paper has dropped from *11 1/2* percent a year ago to *8 3/4* percent today.
> (**NOT:** 11½ . . . 8 3/4.)

> **NOTE:** To simplify typing, convert constructed fractions (and simpler ones used in the same context) to a decimal form whenever feasible.

> The rate on prime commercial paper has dropped from *11.5* percent a year ago to *8.75* percent today.

The following rules (¶¶429–442) deal with measurements and with expressions of age and time (elements that often function as measurements). When these elements have technical or statistical significance, they are expressed in figures; otherwise, they are expressed in words.

Measurements

429

Most measurements have a technical significance and should be expressed in figures (even from 1 through 10) for emphasis or quick comprehension. However, spell out an isolated measurement that lacks technical significance.

> A higher rate is charged on parcels over *2 pounds*.
> **BUT:** I'm afraid I've gained another *two pounds* this week.
>
> Add *1 quart* of sugar for each *4 quarts* of strawberries.
> **BUT:** Last weekend we picked *four quarts* of strawberries from our own patch.
>
> There is no charge for delivery within a *30-mile* radius of Chicago.
> **BUT:** It's only a *thirty-mile* drive up to our summer place.

> **NOTE:** Dimensions, sizes, and exact temperature readings are always expressed in figures.

> I'm looking for a *4- by 6-foot* rug for my reception room. (See also ¶432.)
>
> Please send me a half-dozen blue oxford shirts, size *17½/33*.
>
> The thermometer now stands at 32°F, a drop of five degrees in the past hour.
>
> **BUT:** The temperature has been in the low *thirties* (**OR** *30s*) all week. (An indefinite reference to the temperature may be spelled out or expressed in figures.)

430 When a measurement consists of several elements, do not use commas to separate the elements. The measurement is considered a single unit.

> The package weighed *8 pounds 11 ounces.*
> The punch bowl holds *4 quarts 1 pint.*
> Hal is *6 feet 8 inches* tall in his stocking feet.

NOTE: If this type of measurement is used as a compound modifier before a noun, use hyphens to connect all the elements as a single unit. (See also ¶817.)

> a *6-foot-8-inch* man

431 The unit of measurement may be abbreviated (for example, *12 ft*) or expressed as a symbol (for example, *12′*) in technical material or in tables. If either an abbreviation or a symbol is used, the number must be expressed as a figure.

> ➤ *For the style of abbreviations for units of measure, see* ¶¶*535–538.*
> *For the use of figures with abbreviations and symbols, see* ¶*453.*

4

432 Dimensions may be expressed as follows:

GENERAL USAGE:	a room 15 by 30 feet	a 15- by 30-foot room
TECHNICAL USAGE:	{ a room 15 × 30 ft a room 15′ × 30′	a 15- × 30-ft room a 15′ × 30′ room
GENERAL USAGE:	a room 5 by 10 meters	a 5- by 10-meter room
TECHNICAL USAGE:	a room 5 × 10 m	a 5- × 10-m room
GENERAL USAGE:	15 feet 6 inches by 30 feet 9 inches	
TECHNICAL USAGE:	15 ft 6 in × 30 ft 9 in OR 15′ 6″ × 30′ 9″	

Ages and Anniversaries

433 Express ages in figures (including 1 through 10) when they are used as significant statistics or as technical measurements.

> Ethel Kassarian, *38,* has been promoted to executive director of marketing services.
> The attached printout projects the amount of the monthly retirement benefit payable *at the age of 65.* (See the entry for *Age–aged–at the age of* on page 254.)
> A computer literacy program is being offered in the schools to all *8- and 9-year-olds.* (See ¶832.)
> This insurance policy is specially tailored for people in the *50-plus* age group.
> You cannot disregard the job application of a person *aged 58.* (NOT: age 58.)

NOTE: When age is expressed in years, months, and days, do not use commas to separate the elements; they make up a single unit.

> On January 1 she will be *19 years 4 months and 17 days old.* (The *and* linking months and days may be omitted.)

434 Spell out ages in nontechnical references and in formal writing.

> My son is *three years old* and my daughter is *two.*
> Shirley is in her early *forties;* her husband is in his *mid-sixties.*
> Have you ever tried keeping a group of *five-year-olds* happy and under control at the same time?

435 Spell out ordinals in references to birthdays and anniversaries except where special emphasis or more than two words are required. (See also ¶¶424–425.)

on my thirtieth birthday   her forty-first class reunion
our twenty-fifth anniversary   the company's 135th anniversary

Periods of Time

436 Use figures (even from 1 through 10) to express periods of time when they are used as technical measurements or significant statistics (as in discounts, interest rates, and credit terms).

a 35-hour workweek   a 30-year mortgage   a note due in 6 months

437 Spell out nontechnical references to periods of time unless the number requires more than two words.

a twenty-minute wait   in twenty-four months   three hundred years ago
eight hours later   in the last thirty years   **BUT:** 350 years ago
twelve days from now   forty-odd years ago   two thousand years ago

438 Centuries may be expressed as follows:

the 1900s **OR** the nineteen hundreds
the twenty-first century   twentieth-century art

439 Decades may be expressed as follows:

the 1990s **OR** the nineteen-nineties **OR** the nineties **OR** the '90s

the mid-1960s **OR** the mid-sixties **OR** the mid-'60s

during the years 1988–1998 **OR** from 1988 to 1998 (see ¶459)

OR between 1988 and 1998

NOTE: Decades are not capitalized except in special expressions such as *the Gay Nineties, the Roaring Twenties.*

Clock Time

440 With *a.m., p.m., Noon,* and *Midnight*

a. Always use figures with *a.m.* or *p.m.*

We take off at *8:45 a.m.*   The bus is due at *2 p.m.*

By *8 p.m.,* CST, the first election returns should be in.

OR: By *8 p.m.* (CST) the first election returns should be in.

b. In printed material, *a.m.* and *p.m.* usually appear in small capitals without internal space (A.M., P.M.). In other material, *a.m.* and *p.m.* typically appear in small letters without internal space; however, you can use small capitals if you have that option. Avoid the use of all-capital letters.

c. For time "on the hour," zeros are not needed to denote minutes.

Our store is open from 9:30 *a.m.* to *6 p.m.* (**NOT:** 6:00 p.m.)
BUT: Our store is always open until 6:00. (See ¶442 for the use of zeros when *a.m.* or *p.m.* is omitted.)

We always close from *12 noon* to 1:30 *p.m.*

You can buy your tickets between *9* and *10 a.m.*

(Continued on page 114.)

In tables, however, when some entries are given in hours and minutes, add a colon and two zeros to exact hours to maintain a uniform appearance. (For more complex illustrations showing the alignment of clock times in columns, see ¶1626b.)

Arr.	Dep.
8:45	9:10
9:00	9:25
9:50	10:00

d. Do not use *a.m.* or *p.m.* unless figures are used.

this morning   tomorrow afternoon
(**NOT:** this a.m.)   (**NOT:** tomorrow p.m.)

e. Do not use *a.m.* or *p.m.* with *o'clock*.

6 o'clock **OR** 6 p.m.   ten o'clock **OR** 10 a.m.
(**NOT:** 6 p.m. o'clock)   (**NOT:** 10 a.m. o'clock)

NOTE: The expression *o'clock* is more formal than *a.m.* or *p.m.*

f. Do not use *a.m.* or *p.m.* with the expressions *in the morning, in the afternoon, in the evening,* and *at night.* The abbreviations themselves already convey one of these meanings.

at 9 p.m. **OR** at nine in the evening   (**NOT:** at 9 p.m. in the evening)

g. Use a colon (without space before or after) to separate hours from minutes (as in *3:22*).

h. The times *noon* and *midnight* may be expressed in words alone. However, use the forms *12 noon* and *12 midnight* when these times are given with other times expressed in figures.

Dinner is served in the main dining room until *midnight.*
BUT: Dinner is served from *6 p.m.* until *12 midnight.*

441   With *O'Clock*

a. With *o'clock,* use figures for emphasis or words for formality.

3 o'clock (for emphasis)   three o'clock (for formality)

b. To express hours and minutes with *o'clock,* use this style:

half past four o'clock **OR** half after four o'clock
(**BUT NOT:** four-thirty o'clock)

c. Expressions of time containing *o'clock* may be reinforced by such phrases as *in the morning, in the afternoon,* and the like.

10 o'clock at night   seven o'clock in the morning

For quick comprehension, use the forms *10 p.m.* and *7 a.m.*

442   Without *a.m., p.m.,* or *O'Clock*

When expressing time without *a.m., p.m.,* or *o'clock,* either spell the time out or—for quick comprehension—convert the expression to an all-figure style.

arrive at eight **OR** arrive at 8:00 (**NOT:** at 8)
five after six **OR** 6:05
a quarter past ten **OR** 10:15
twenty of four **OR** 3:40
a quarter to five **OR** a quarter of five **OR** 4:45
half past nine **OR** nine-thirty **OR** 9:30
nine forty-two **OR** 9:42

NOTE: A hyphen is used between hours and minutes (*seven-thirty*) but not if the minutes must be hyphenated (*seven thirty-five*).

The following rules (¶¶443–455) deal with situations in which numbers are always expressed in figures.

Decimals

443 Always write decimals in figures. Never insert commas in the decimal part of a number.

> 665.3184368 (no comma in decimal part of the number)
> 58,919.23785 (comma used in whole part of the number)

➤ *For the metric style of writing decimals, see ¶461b.*

444 When a decimal stands alone (without a whole number preceding the decimal point), insert a zero before the decimal point. (Reason: The zero keeps the reader from overlooking the decimal point.)

> 0.55 inch   0.08 gram   EXCEPTIONS: a Colt .45; a .36 caliber revolver

445 Ordinarily, drop the zero at the end of a decimal (for example, write *2.787* rather than *2.7870*). However, retain the zero (*a*) if you wish to emphasize that the decimal is an exact number or (*b*) if the decimal has been rounded off from a longer figure. In a column of figures add zeros to the end of a decimal in order to make the number as long as other numbers in the column. (For illustrations, see ¶¶1626, 1628, 1629, 1631.)

446 Do not begin a sentence with a decimal figure.

> The temperature was *63.7*.
> (NOT: *63.7* was the temperature.)

Percentages

447 Express percentages in figures, and spell out the word *percent*. (See ¶¶421–422 for percentages at the beginning of a sentence.)

> When your mortgage rate goes from *6 percent* to *6.6 percent*, it may have increased by less than 1 percentage point, but you'll pay *10 percent* more in interest.
>
> Yogi Berra once said, "Baseball is *90 percent* mental. The other half is physical."
>
> My client expected a *25 percent* discount. (NOT: a 25-percent discount.)
>
> Our terms are *2 percent* 10 days, net 30 days. (These credit terms may be abbreviated as *2/10, n/30* on invoices and other business forms.)

NOTE: The % symbol may be used in tables, on business forms, and in statistical or technical material.

448 **a.** Fractional percentages *under 1 percent* may be expressed as follows:

> one half of 1 percent   OR   0.5 percent (see ¶444)

   b. Fractional percentages *over 1 percent* should be expressed in figures.

> 7½ percent   OR   7.5 percent   9¼ percent   OR   9.25 percent

449 In a range or series of percentages, the word *percent* follows the last figure only. If the symbol % is used (see ¶447, note), it must follow each figure.

> Price reductions range from *20 to 50 percent*. (BUT: from 20% to 50%.)
> We give discounts of *10, 20, and 30 percent*. (BUT: 10%, 20%, and 30%.)

➤ *For the use of % in a column of figures, see ¶1629; for the use of* percent *and* percentage, *see page 270.*

Ratios and Proportions

450 As a rule, write ratios and proportions in figures.

a proportion of 5 to 1 **OR** a 5-to-1 ratio **OR** a 5:1 ratio
the odds are 100 to 1 **OR** a 100-to-1 shot

NOTE: A nontechnical reference may be spelled out.

a *fifty-fifty* chance of success **OR** a *50-50* chance of success

Scores and Voting Results

451 Use figures (even for 1 through 10) to express scores and voting results.

a score of 85 on the test   a vote of 17 to 6
New York 8, Chicago 6   **BUT:** a 17-6 vote

Numbers Referred to as Numbers

452 Always use figures to express numbers referred to as numbers.

pick a number from 1 to 10   divide by 16
the number 7 is considered lucky   multiply by ⅞

Figures With Abbreviations and Symbols

453 **a.** Always use figures with abbreviations and symbols.

$50   10:15 a.m.   43%   2 in **OR** 2″   FY1995 (see ¶1615c)
65¢   6 p.m.   No. 631   I-95   200 km (see ¶537)

b. If a symbol is used in a range of numbers, it should be repeated with each number. A full word or an abbreviation used in place of the symbol is given only with the last number.

20°–30°C   **BUT:** 20 to 30 degrees Celsius (see ¶537, note)
5½″ × 8″   5½ by 8 inches **OR** 5½ × 8 in
9′ × 12′   9 by 12 feet **OR** 9 × 12 ft
30%–40%   30 to 40 percent
50¢–60¢   50 to 60 cents
$70–$80   seventy to eighty dollars

NOTE: A symbol should be used with each number in a series.

discounts of 5%, 10%, and 15%   **BUT:** discounts of 5, 10, and 15 percent

Telephone Numbers

454 **a.** Insert a hyphen after the first three digits of a telephone number; for example, *284-1789.* If a company chooses to express its phone number partially or entirely in words, follow the company's style; for example, *345-GIFT, 4-ANGIES, JOB-HUNT, CASH-NOW, GOFEDEX, PICK-UPS.*

b. When the area code precedes a phone number, use a hyphen or a diagonal (with no space on either side) between the two elements, or enclose the area code in parentheses (followed by one space).

707-555-3998 **OR** 707/555-3998 **OR** (707) 555-3998

NOTE: When the area code and the telephone number as a unit have to be enclosed in parentheses, use either a hyphen or a diagonal after the area code.

➤ *For the various uses of phone numbers, see* ¶¶*1311–1312.*

You can always reach me by phone (517-555-6939) between 8:30 and 11:30 a.m.

OR: . . . by phone (517/555-6939) between 8:30 and 11:30 a.m.

BUT NOT: . . . by phone ((517) 555-6939) between 8:30 and 11:30 a.m.

c. When an access code precedes the area code and the phone number, it is customary to use a hyphen to connect all the elements.

Please use our toll-free, 24-hour phone number: 1-800-555-6400.

NOTE: International phone numbers typically contain a series of special access codes. Hyphens are used to connect all the elements.

011-64-9-555-1523

└── international access code from the United States
    └── country access code
      └── city access code

d. When providing a telephone extension along with the main number, use the following form: *555-4890, Ext. 6041.* (In formal correspondence, spell out *Extension.*)

No. or # With Figures

455 If the term *number* precedes a figure, express it as an abbreviation (singular: *No.;* plural: *Nos.*). At the beginning of a sentence, however, spell out *Number* to prevent misreading.

Our check covers the following invoices: *Nos.* 8592, 8653, and 8654.

Number 82175 has been assigned to your new policy. (NOT: No. 82175 . . .)

Our manager says the Southern Region has to be No. 1 in sales—or else!

a. If an identifying noun precedes the figure (such as *Invoice, Check, Room, Box,* or the like), the abbreviation *No.* is usually unnecessary.

Our check covers *Invoices* 8592, 8653, and 8654.

EXCEPTION: License No. HLM 744 (see ¶463 for other exceptions)

b. The symbol # may be used on business forms (such as invoices) and in technical material.

➤ *For the capitalization of nouns preceding figures, see ¶359.*

The following rules (¶¶456–470) deal with two technical aspects of style: (1) treating numbers that are adjacent or in a sequence and (2) expressing numbers in figures, words, or roman numerals.

Adjacent Numbers

456 When two numbers come together in a sentence and both are in figures or both are in words, separate them with a comma.

In *1995, 78* percent of our field representatives exceeded their sales goal.

Although the meeting was scheduled for *two, ten* people did not show up.

On page *192, 25* problems are provided for review purposes.

On Account *53512, $125.40* is the balance outstanding.

On May *8, 18* customers called to complain.

(Continued on page 118.)

NOTE: No comma is necessary when one number is in figures and the other is in words.

On May *9 seven* customers called to complain.

457 When two numbers come together and one is part of a compound modifier (see ¶817), express one of the numbers in figures and the other in words. As a rule, spell the first number unless the second number would make a significantly shorter word.

two 8-room houses   **BUT:** 500 four-page leaflets
sixty $5 bills   150 five-dollar bills

Numbers in a Sequence

458 Use commas to separate numbers that do not represent a continuous sequence.

on pages 18, 20, and 28   the years 1989, 1993, and 1997

459 **a.** An en dash in computer-generated material (or a hyphen in typewritten material) may be used in place of the word *to* to link two figures that represent a continuous sequence. Do not leave any space before or after the en dash or hyphen. (See ¶¶216–217.)

on pages 18–28   in Articles I–III
during the week of May 15–21   during the years 1987–1997

     b. Do not use the en dash (or hyphen) if the sequence is introduced by the word *from* or *between*.

from 1995 to 1998   between 1994 and 1997
(**NOT:** from 1995–1998)   (**NOT:** between 1994–1997)

460 **a.** In a continuous sequence of figures connected by an en dash or a hyphen, the second figure may be expressed in abbreviated form. This style is used for sequences of page numbers or years when they occur quite frequently. In isolated cases, do not abbreviate. (See ¶¶216–217.)

1990–98 (**OR** 1990–1998)   pages 110–12 (**OR** pages 110–112)
1901–2 (**OR** 1901–1902)   pages 101–2 (**OR** pages 101–102)

     b. Do not abbreviate the second number when the first number ends in two zeros.

1900–1997 (**NOT:** 1900–97)   pages 100–101 (**NOT:** pages 100–1)

     c. Do not abbreviate the second number when it starts with different digits.

1890–1902 (**NOT:** 1890–02)   pages 998–1004 (**NOT:** pages 998–04)

     d. Do not abbreviate the second number when it is under 100.

46–48 A.D. (see pages 253–254)   pages 46–48

Expressing Numbers in Figures

461 **a.** When numbers run to five or more figures, use commas to separate thousands, hundreds of thousands, millions, etc., in *whole* numbers. Do not use commas in the decimal part of a number. (See also ¶443.)

12,375   147,300 $11,275,478   4,300,000,000   **BUT:** 70,650.37248

NOTE: The comma is now commonly omitted in four-digit whole numbers except in columns with larger numbers that require commas.

3500 OR 3,500 $2000.50 OR $2,000.50

b. In metric quantities, use a space (not a comma) to separate digits into groups of three. Separate whole numbers and decimal fractions, counting from the decimal point.

12 945 181 (RATHER THAN: 12,945,181)   0.594 31 (RATHER THAN: 0.59431)

NOTE: When a four-digit number is used as a metric quantity, do not leave a space unless the number is used in a column that has larger numbers.

5181 OR 5 181   0.3725 OR 0.372 5

462 Do not use commas in year numbers, page numbers, house or building numbers, room numbers, ZIP Code numbers, telephone numbers, heat units, and decimal parts of numbers.

1986	8760 Sunset Drive	New York, New York 10021	1500°C
page 1246	Room 1804	602-555-2174 (see ¶454)	13,664.9999

463 Serial numbers (for example, invoice, style, model, or lot numbers) are usually written without commas. However, some serial numbers are written with hyphens, spaces, or other devices. In all cases follow the style of the source.

Invoice 38162   **BUT:** Social Security No. 152-22-8285
Model G-43348   License No. SO14 785 053
Lot 75/23512   Patent No. 222,341

➤ For the capitalization of nouns before numbers, see ¶359.
For the use of No., see ¶455.

464 To form the plurals of figures, add *s*. (See ¶624.)

in the '90s (decades)   in the 90s (temperature)

Expressing Numbers in Words

465 When expressing numbers in words, hyphenate all compound numbers between *21* and *99* (or *21st* and *99th*), whether they stand alone or are part of a number over 100.

twenty-one   twenty-one hundred
twenty-first   twenty-one hundredth

seven hundred and twenty-five (*and* may be omitted)

five thousand seven hundred and twenty-five (no commas)

Do not hyphenate other words in a spelled-out number over 100.

one hundred   nineteen hundred
two thousand   three hundred thousand
four million   six hundred million
twenty-three billion   fifty-eight trillion

➤ For the capitalization of hyphenated numbers, see ¶363.

466 When there are two ways to express a number in words, choose the simpler form. For example, use the form *fifteen hundred* rather than *one thousand five hundred*. (The longer form is rarely used except in formal expressions of dates. See ¶411 for examples.)

467 To form the plurals of spelled-out numbers, add *s* or *es*. (For numbers ending in *y*, change the *y* to *i* before *es*.)

ones	twos	threes	sixes	twenty-fives
thirds	sixths	eighths	twenties	thirty-seconds

➤ *For spelled-out dates, see ¶411; for spelled-out amounts of money, see ¶¶413c, 414, 417, 418, 420; for spelled-out fractions, see ¶¶427–428.*

Expressing Numbers in Roman Numerals

468 Roman numerals are used chiefly for the important divisions of literary and legislative material, for main topics in outlines, in dates on public buildings, and in proper names.

Chapter VI	World Wars I and II	Roy Ward II
Volume III	MCMXCVIII (1998)	Pope John XXIII

NOTE: Pages in the front section of a book or a formal report (such as the preface and table of contents) are usually numbered in small roman numerals: *iii, iv, v,* etc. Other pages are numbered in arabic numerals: *1, 2, 3,* etc. (See ¶¶1420, 1426.)

4

469 To form roman numerals, consult the following table.

1	I	13	XIII	60	LX	1100	MC
2	II	14	XIV	70	LXX	1400	MCD
3	III	15	XV	80	LXXX	1500	MD
4	IV	19	XIX	90	XC	1600	MDC
5	V	20	XX	100	C	1900	MCM
6	VI	21	XXI	200	CC	2000	MM
7	VII	24	XXIV	400	CD	5000	$\overline{\text{V}}$
8	VIII	25	XXV	500	D	10,000	$\overline{\text{X}}$
9	IX	29	XXIX	600	DC	50,000	$\overline{\text{L}}$
10	X	30	XXX	800	DCCC	100,000	$\overline{\text{C}}$
11	XI	40	XL	900	CM	500,000	$\overline{\text{D}}$
12	XII	50	L	1000	M	1,000,000	$\overline{\text{M}}$

NOTE: A dash appearing over any roman numeral indicates that the original value of the numeral is to be multiplied by 1000.

Expressing Large Numbers in Abbreviated Form

470 In technical and informal contexts and in material where space is tight (such as tables and classified ads), large numbers may be abbreviated.

ROMAN STYLE: 48M (48,000); 6.3$\overline{\text{M}}$ (6,300,000)

METRIC STYLE: 31K (31,000); K stands for *kilo,* signifying thousands

5.2M (5,200,000); M stands for *mega,* signifying millions

8.76G (8,760,000,000); G stands for *giga,* signifying billions

9.4T (9,400,000,000,000); T stands for *tera,* signifying trillions

➤ *Division of larger numbers at the end of a line: see ¶915.*
House, street, and ZIP Code numbers: see ¶¶1332–1333, 1339, 1341c.

SECTION 5

ABBREVIATIONS

BASIC RULES

When to Use Abbreviations

501 An abbreviation is a shortened form of a word or phrase used primarily to save space. Abbreviations occur most frequently in technical writing, statistical material, tables, and notes.

502 In business writing, abbreviations are appropriate in "expedient" documents (such as business forms, catalogs, and routine memos and letters between business offices), where the emphasis is on communicating data in the briefest form. In other kinds of writing, where a more formal style is appropriate, use abbreviations sparingly. When in doubt, spell it out.

a. Some abbreviations are always acceptable, even in the most formal contexts: those that precede or follow personal names (such as *Mr., Ms., Mrs., Jr., Sr., Esq., Ph.D., S.J.*); those that are part of an organization's legal name (such as *Co., Inc., Ltd.*); those used in expressions of time (such as *a.m., p.m., CST, EDT*); and a few miscellaneous expressions (such as *A.D.* and *B.C.*).

b. Organizations with long names are now commonly identified by their initials in all but the most formal writing (for example, *NAACP, SEC*).

c. Days of the week, names of the months, geographic names, and units of measure should be abbreviated only on business forms, in "expedient" correspondence, and in tables, lists, and narrow columns of text (for example, in a newsletter or brochure) where space is tight.

d. When an abbreviation is only one or two keystrokes shorter than the full word (for example, *Pt.* for *Part*), do not bother to abbreviate except to achieve consistency in a context where similar terms are being abbreviated. (See also ¶532 for abbreviations of months.)

503 Consult a dictionary or an authoritative reference work for the acceptable forms of abbreviations. When a term may be abbreviated in several ways, choose the form that is shortest without sacrifice of clarity.

continued:	Use *cont.* rather than *contd.*
2 pounds:	Use *2 lb* rather than *2 lbs* (see ¶620).
Enclosures 2:	Use *Enc. 2* rather than *Encs. 2* or *Encl. 2.*
second, third:	Use *2d, 3d* rather than *2nd, 3rd* (see also ¶425, note).
megabyte, kilobyte	Use *MB, KB* for clarity rather than *M, K.*

NOTE: *Merriam-Webster's Collegiate Dictionary,* Tenth Edition, the basic authority for all spelling in this manual, shows virtually every abbreviation without any periods, even though in actual practice many abbreviations are still written with periods.* Thus, for example, unless your Latin is very good, you may not realize that in the expression *et al.,* the word *et* is a full word (meaning "and") and requires no period, whereas *al.* is short for *alii* (meaning "others") and does require a period. Under these circumstances, for specific abbreviations not shown in this manual, you will need to consult another up-to-date dictionary.

---

*It is interesting to note that Merriam-Webster itself uses periods with certain abbreviations (for example, *masc., fem., trans., fr., prob., lit.,* and *ca.*) when they occur functionally within the main text of the dictionary, even though these same abbreviations are given *without* periods in the section on abbreviations at the back of the dictionary.

The forms shown here reflect the spellings found in Merriam-Webster, but the punctuation is based on observations of actual practice and is consistent with the style recommended by other authorities.

504 Be consistent within the same material: do not abbreviate a term in some sentences and spell it out in other sentences. Moreover, having selected one form of an abbreviation (say, *c.o.d.*), do not use a different style *(COD)* elsewhere in the same material. (See ¶542.)

NOTE: When using an abbreviation that may not be familiar to the reader, spell out the full term along with the abbreviation when it is first used.

> At the end of *fiscal year (FY)* 1997, we showed a profit of $1.2 million; at the end of FY1998, however, we showed a loss of $1.8 million.
>
> OR: At the end of *FY1997 (fiscal year 1997)* . . .

505 a. Given a choice between an abbreviation and a contraction, choose the abbreviation. It not only looks better but is easier to read.

> cont. (RATHER THAN: cont'd)   govt. (RATHER THAN: gov't)
> dept. (RATHER THAN: dep't)   mfg. (RATHER THAN: m'f'g)

b. When a word or phrase is shortened by contraction, an apostrophe is inserted at the exact point where letters are omitted and no period follows the contraction except at the end of a sentence.

> you're   doesn't   don't
> let's   could've   rock 'n' roll
> ma'am   o'clock   ne'er-do-well

NOTE: Respect a company's preference when it uses a contraction in its corporate name or in the name of a product.

> Wash'n Dri   Puss'N Boots   Dunkin' Donuts
> Sweet'n Low   Linens N' Things   Cap'n Crunch
> Shake 'n Bake   Ship 'n' Shore   Chock Full o' Nuts
> Light n' Lively   Bran'nola   Land O Lakes

c. As a rule, contractions are used only in informal writing or in tables where space is limited. However, contractions of verb phrases (such as *can't* for *cannot*) are commonly used in business letters where the writer is striving for an easy, colloquial tone. In formal writing, contractions are not used (except for *o'clock,* which is considered a more formal way to express time than *a.m.* or *p.m.*).

d. Be sure to distinguish certain contractions from possessive pronouns that sound the same but do not use an apostrophe.

> Ron has been pushing the Kirschner proposal for all *it's* worth. (In other words, for all *it is* worth.)
>
> Let's get an outside consultant to analyze the Kirschner proposal and assess *its* worth. (Here *its* is a possessive pronoun; no apostrophe should be used.)

➤ *See ¶1056e for further examples and a test on how to determine the correct form.*

e. Note that certain contractions can have more than one meaning.

> What's her name? (What *is* her name?)
> What's he do for a living? (What *does* he do for a living?)
> What's been happening? (What *has* been happening?)
> When's the last time you saw her? (When *was* the last time you saw her?)
> Let's find out. (Let *us* find out.)

Punctuation and Spacing
With Abbreviations

506 The abbreviation of a single word requires a period at the end.

Mrs.	Jr.	Corp.	pp.	Wed.
misc.	Esq.	Inc.	Nos.	Oct.

NOTE: Units of measurement are now commonly written without periods. (See ¶¶535a, 538a.)

507 Almost all small-letter abbreviations made up of single initials require a period after each initial but no space after each internal period.

a.m.	i.e.	f.o.b.	**BUT:** rpm	mpg
p.m.	e.g.	e.o.m.	cpi	mph

➤ *For the omission of periods with abbreviations of units of measure, see* ¶*535a. For the definition of business abbreviations like* f.o.b. *and* e.o.m., *see* ¶*541.*

508 All-capital abbreviations made up of single initials normally require no periods and no internal space.

CBS	AMA	AICPA	IRS	VIP
MIT	UAW	NFL	UN	PSAT

EXCEPTIONS: Retain the periods in abbreviations of geographic names (such as *U.S.A.*), academic degrees (such as *B.A., M.S.*), and a few miscellaneous expressions (such as A.D., B.C., P.O., and V.P.).

509 If an abbreviation of two or more words consists of more than single initials, insert a period and a space after each element in the abbreviation.

N. Mex.	Lt. Col.	Rt. Rev.	loc. cit.	nol. pros.

EXCEPTIONS: Academic abbreviations, such as *Ph.D.*, (doctor of philosophy), *LL.B.* (bachelor of law), and *Litt.D.* (doctor of letters), are written with periods but no spaces. Units of measurement such as *sq ft* and *cu cm* are written with spaces but no periods.

510 A number of shortened forms of words are not abbreviations and should not be followed by a period. (See ¶236c and ¶524, note.)

caps	exam	limo	prefab	specs
combo	expo	logo	prep	stereo
comp	fax	memo	promo	sync
condo	high-tech	micros	repro	temp
co-op	hype	perks	req	typo
deli	info	phone	sales rep	before the 2d
demo	lab	photo	sci-fi	after the 5th

A number of the *sales reps* have sent a *fax,* asking for some *info* on this year's incentive *comp* plans.

When you check the *repros* for *typos,* please watch out for the problems we had with *caps* in our last *promo* piece, and make sure our *logo* is not left off this time.

Also check everything against the original *specs,* and tell me what the total *prep* costs amount to.

511 *One space* should follow an abbreviation within a sentence unless another mark of punctuation follows immediately.

You ought to talk to your CPA about that problem.

Dr. Wilkins works in Washington, D.C., but his home is in Bethesda.

Please call tomorrow afternoon (before 5:30 p.m.).

When Jonas asked, "When do you expect to finish your Ph.D.?" Fred looked embarrassed. (See ¶261c regarding the omission of a comma after an introductory dependent clause.)

I'm waiting for some word on Harrison, Inc.'s stock repurchase plan. (See ¶¶638–639 for possessive forms of abbreviations.)

512 *Two spaces* should follow an abbreviation at the end of a sentence that makes a statement. If the abbreviation ends with a period, that period also serves to mark the end of the sentence. If the abbreviation ends without a period, insert one to mark the end of the sentence and then leave two spaces.

Helen has just returned from a trip to Washington, D.C.   Next year . . .

We're flying over on Air France and coming back on KLM.   If you . . .

513 *No space* should follow an abbreviation at the end of a question or an exclamation. The question mark or the exclamation point should come directly after the abbreviation.

Did you see Jack Hainey being interviewed last night on CBS?

Because of bad weather our flight didn't get in until 4 *a.m.*!

Capitalization

514 Most abbreviations use the same capitalization as the full words for which they stand.

Mon.	Monday	e-mail	electronic mail
Btu	British thermal unit	D.C.	District of Columbia

EXCEPTIONS: CST   Central standard time
A.D.   anno Domini (see pages 253–254)

➤ *For abbreviations with two forms (for example,* COD *or* c.o.d.*), see* ¶542.

The following rules (¶¶515–549) offer guidance on how to treat specific types of abbreviations.

SPECIAL RULES

Personal Names and Initials

515 Use periods with abbreviations of first or middle names but not with nicknames.

Thos.	Jos.	Robt.	Benj.	Jas.	Wm.	Saml.	Edw.
Tom	Joe	Bob	Ben	Jim	Bill	Sam	Ed

NOTE: Do not abbreviate first and middle names unless (1) you are preparing a list or table where space is tight or (2) a person uses such abbreviations in his or her legal name. (See also ¶1321a, note.)

516 **a.** Each initial in a person's name should be followed by a period and one space.

W. E. B. Du Bois
J. T. Noonan & Co.

Mr. L. Bradford Anders
L. B. Anders Inc. (see also ¶159)

(Continued on page 126.)

NOTE: Respect the preference of (1) the individual or (2) the company that uses a person's initials in its corporate name.

Harry S Truman	BFGoodrich	FAO Schwarz
L.L. Bean, Inc.	JCPenney	S.C. Johnson

b. When personal initials stand alone, type them preferably without periods or space. If periods are used, omit the internal space.

JTN   OR   J.T.N.

c. For names with prefixes, initials are formed as follows:

JDM (for John D. MacDonald)   FGO (for Frances G. O'Brien)

NOTE: If you know that an individual prefers some other form (for example, *FGO'B* rather than *FGO*), respect that preference.

d. Do not use a period when the initial is only a letter used in place of a real name. (See also ¶109a.)

I have selected three case studies involving a Ms. A, a Mr. B, and a Miss C. (Here the letters are used in place of real names, but they are not abbreviations of those names.)

BUT: Call Mrs. *G.* when you get a chance. (Here *G.* is an initial representing an actual name like *Galanos.*)

e. The abbreviation *NMI* is sometimes used on forms and applications to indicate that an individual has <u>no</u> <u>m</u>iddle <u>i</u>nitial.

5

Abbreviations With Personal Names

517   **a.** Always abbreviate the following titles when they are used with personal names:

SINGULAR: { Mrs. (for Mistress)   Ms.   Mr.   Dr.
          { Mme. (for Madame)

PLURAL: Mmes. OR Mesdames   Mses. OR Mss.   Messrs.   Drs.

Mr. and *Mrs.* Pollo both speak highly of *Dr.* Fry.

Ms. Harriet Porter will serve as a consultant to the Finance Committee.

NOTE: The abbreviation *Ms.* is used (1) when a woman has indicated that she prefers this title, (2) when a woman's marital status is unknown, or (3) when a woman's marital status is considered not relevant to the situation. Always respect the individual woman's preference. If her preference is unknown, use the title *Ms.* or omit the title altogether. (See also ¶¶618, 1322b, 1366a.)

➤ *For the proper use of the singular and plural forms of these titles, see ¶618; for the use of* Dr. *with degrees, see ¶519c.*

b. The titles *Miss* and *Misses* are not abbreviations and should not be followed by periods.

c. In general, spell out all other titles used with personal names.

Vice President Howard Morse	Professor Harriman
Mayor Wilma Washington	Father Hennelly
Governor Warren R. Fishback	Dean Castaneda

d. Long military, religious, and honorable titles are spelled out in formal situations but may be abbreviated in informal situations as long as the surname is accompanied by a first name or initials.

Formal	**Informal**
Brigadier General Percy J. Cobb	Brig. Gen. P. J. Cobb
Lieutenant Governor Nancy Pulaski	Lt. Gov. Nancy Pulaski

(BUT NOT: Brig. Gen. Cobb, Lt. Gov. Pulaski)

NOTE: Do not abbreviate *Reverend* or *Honorable* when these words are preceded by *the*.

Formal	**Informal**
the Reverend William R. Bullock	Rev. W. R. Bullock
the Honorable Sarah T. McCormack	Hon. Sarah T. McCormack

➤ *For the treatment of titles in addresses, see ¶¶1322–1323; for the treatment of titles in salutations, see ¶¶1347–1350.*

518

a. Always abbreviate *Jr., Sr.,* and *Esq.* when these terms follow personal names.

b. The forms *Jr.* and *Sr.* should be used only with a full name or initials but not with a surname alone. A title like *Mr.* or *Dr.* may precede the name.

Mr. Henry J. Boardman *Jr.*

OR: Mr. H. J. Boardman *Jr.*

(BUT NOT: Mr. Boardman Jr.)

➤ *For the use or omission of commas with* Jr. *and* Sr., *see ¶156.*

c. The form *Esq.* should also be used only with a full name or initials, but no title should precede the name. (See ¶157.)

George W. LaBarr, *Esq.*

NOT: Mr. George W. LaBarr, Esq.

NOTE: In the United States the form *Esq.* is used primarily by lawyers. Although by derivation the title applies strictly to males, it is now common practice for women who are lawyers to use the title as a professional designation.

d. The terms *2d* or *II* and *3d* or *III* following personal names are not abbreviations and should not be used with periods.

e. When the word *Saint* is part of a person's name, follow that person's preference for abbreviating or spelling out the word.

Yves Saint-Laurent	Ruth St. Denis
Camille Saint-Saëns	St. John Perse

NOTE: When used with the name of a person revered as holy, the word *Saint* is usually spelled out, but it may be abbreviated in informal contexts and in lists and tables where space is tight.

Saint Martin	Saint Thérèse
Saint Francis	Saint Catherine

➤ *For the treatment of* Saint *in place names, see ¶529b.*

5

Academic Degrees, Religious Orders, and Professional Designations

519 **a.** Abbreviations of academic degrees and religious orders require a period after each element in the abbreviation but no internal space.

B.S.	LL.B.	B.Ch.E.	M.D.	S.J.
M.B.A.	Litt.D.	B.Arch.	D.D.S.	O.S.B.
Ph.D.	Ed.D.	M.Div.	R.N.	S.N.D.

NOTE: The term *ABD* (without periods) is often used to identify a graduate student who has completed all the requirements for a doctorate except the dissertation. (The initials stand for *all but dissertation.*)

So far we have received résumés from two *Ph.D.s* and seven *ABDs.* (See ¶622a for guidelines on forming the plurals of these abbreviations.)

b. The term *M.B.A.* is now commonly written without periods when it is used to signify an executive with a certain type of training rather than the degree itself.

We have just hired two Stanford *MBAs* and one from Harvard.

BUT: After I get my *M.B.A.,* I plan to go on to law school.

c. When academic degrees follow a person's name, do not use such titles as *Dr., Mr., Ms., Miss,* or *Mrs.* before the name.

Dr. Helen Garcia   OR   Helen Garcia, M.D.

(BUT NOT: Dr. Helen Garcia, M.D.)

However, other titles may precede the name as long as they do not convey the same meaning as the degree that follows.

Professor Rex Ford, Ph.D.	the Reverend John Day, D.D.
President Jean Dill, L.H.D.	OR: the Reverend Dr. John Day
Dean May Ito, J.S.D.	(BUT NOT: the Reverend Dr. John Day, D.D.)

➤ *See also ¶¶1324c, 1324d, 1364a.*

d. Academic degrees standing alone may be abbreviated except in very formal writing.

I am now completing my *Ph.D.* thesis.

She received her *M.A.* degree last year.
OR . . . her *master of arts* degree last year. (See also ¶353.)

e. Professional designations such as *CPA* (certified public accountant), *CPS* (certified professional secretary), *CFP* (certified financial planner), *CLU* (chartered life underwriter), and *FACS* (fellow of the American College of Surgeons) are commonly written *without* periods when they are used alone but *with* periods when they are used with academic degrees.

Anthony Filippo, CPA	BUT: Anthony Filippo, B.S., M.B.A., *C.P.A.*
Ruth L. Morris, CLU	Ruth L. Morris, B.A., *C.L.U.*

Names of Organizations

520 Names of well-known business organizations, labor unions, societies, associations (trade, professional, charitable, and fraternal), and government agencies are often abbreviated except in the most formal writing. When these abbreviations consist of all-capital initials, they are typed without periods or spaces.

AFL-CIO	American Federation of Labor and Congress of Industrial Organizations
ILGWU	International Ladies' Garment Workers' Union
NAACP	National Association for the Advancement of Colored People
NYSE	New York Stock Exchange
NAM	National Association of Manufacturers
NIMH	National Institute of Mental Health
YMCA	Young Men's Christian Association
IRS	Internal Revenue Service
SEC	Securities and Exchange Commission

521 The following terms are often abbreviated in the names of business organizations. However, follow the individual company's preference for abbreviating or spelling out.

Mfg.	Manufacturing	Co.	Company	Inc.	Incorporated
Mfrs.	Manufacturers	Corp.	Corporation	Ltd.	Limited

Acronyms

522 **a.** An acronym—for example, *NOW*—is a shortened form derived from the initial letters of the words that make up the complete form. Thus *NOW* is derived from *National Organization for Women*. Like all-capital abbreviations such as *IRS* and *NAM*, acronyms are usually written in all capitals and without periods; however, unlike those abbreviations, which are pronounced letter by letter, acronyms are pronounced like words. Because they have been deliberately coined to replace the longer expressions they represent, acronyms are appropriate for use on all occasions.

5

CARE	Cooperative for American Relief to Everywhere
ASCAP	American Society of Composers, Authors, and Publishers
AMEX	American Stock Exchange (see ¶522b for *AmEx*)
ZIP (Code)	Zone Improvement Plan
PIN	personal identification number
EMILY's List	a political fund-raising group based on the concept that early money is like yeast (and makes the dough rise)
SADD	Students Against Drunk Driving
NASDAQ	National Association of Security Dealers Automated Quotations
OSHA	Occupational Safety and Health Administration
ESOP	employee stock ownership plan
EPCOT	Experimental Prototype Community of Tomorrow
FONZ	Friends of the National Zoo
AIDS	acquired immune deficiency syndrome
NIMBY	not in my backyard (as in *a NIMBY protest*)
SOHO	small office, home office (as in *the SOHO market*)
WATS	Wide-Area Telecommunications Service
MEGO	my eyes glaze over
BOGSAT	bunch of guys sitting around table (an ad hoc decision-making process)

NOTE: In a few cases acronyms derived from initial letters are written entirely in small letters without periods.

scuba	self-contained underwater breathing apparatus
laser	light amplification by stimulated emission of radiation

(Continued on page 130.)

b. Some coined names use more than the first letters of the words they represent. Such names are usually written with only the first letter capitalized.

Ameslan	American Sign Language
Delmarva	an East Coast peninsula made up of Delaware and parts of Maryland and Virginia
radar	radio detecting and ranging
sonar	sound navigation ranging
modem	modulator and demodulator
canola (oil)	Canada, oil low acid
op ed page	the page that is opposite the editorial page
BUT: AmEx	American Express
FedEx	Federal Express
INTELPOST	International Electronic Postal Service

c. In a few cases all-capital abbreviations such as *MC* (for *master of ceremonies*) or DJ (for *disc jockey*) may also be spelled out in an uncapitalized form (*emcee* and *deejay*). The spelled-out forms are preferable when such abbreviations are used as verbs.

Fran Zangwill *emceed* (**RATHER THAN:** MC'd) the fund-raiser kickoff dinner.

Who has been *okaying* (**RATHER THAN:** OK'ing) these bills? (See ¶548.)

BUT: You'd find it easier to get up in the morning if you didn't *OD* on TV every night. (Here the choice is between *OD* and *overdose,* not *oh-dee.*)

5 Names of Broadcasting Stations and Systems

523 The names of radio and television broadcasting stations and the abbreviated names of broadcasting systems are written in all-capital letters without periods and without spaces.

Portsmouth:	WRAP-AM	San Antonio:	KISS-FM
Houston:	KILT-FM	New Orleans:	WYES-TV

According to *ABC* and *CBS,* the earthquake registered 6.8 on the Richter scale.

Names of Government and International Agencies

524 The names of well-known government and international agencies are often abbreviated. They are written without periods or spaces.

FNMA	the Federal National Mortgage Association (often referred to as "Fannie Mae," the result of trying to sound out the initials *FNMA*)
FEMA	the Federal Emergency Management Agency
EEOC	the Equal Employment Opportunity Commission
WHO	the World Health Organization

NOTE: Expressions such as *the Fed* (for the Federal Reserve Board) and *the Ex-Im Bank* (for the U.S. Export-Import Bank) involve shortened forms rather than true abbreviations and thus are written without periods.

525 The name *United States* is usually abbreviated when it is part of the name of a government agency. When used as an adjective, the name is often abbreviated, though not in formal usage. When used as a noun, the name is spelled out.

U.S. Department of Agriculture	USDA
U.S. Air Force	USAF
the United States government	the U.S. government
United States foreign policy	U.S. foreign policy

throughout the United States (NOT: throughout the U.S.)

Geographic Names

526 Do not abbreviate geographic names except in tables, business forms, and "expedient" correspondence (see ¶502) and in place names with *Saint.* (See ¶529b.)

NOTE: In informal writing, the city of Washington may be referred to as *D.C.* and Los Angeles as *L.A.* In general, however, spell these names out.

INFORMAL CONTEXT: Did you know that Liz has been transferred from the *D.C.* office to the branch in *L.A.?*

OTHER CONTEXTS: Did you know that Liz has been transferred from the *Washington, D.C.,* office to the branch in *Los Angeles?*

527 **a.** When abbreviating state names *in addresses,* use the two-letter abbreviations (without periods) shown in ¶1341 and on the inside back cover.

b. *In all situations other than addresses,* use the following abbreviations (with periods and spacing as shown).

Alabama	Ala.	North Carolina	N.C.
Arizona	Ariz.	North Dakota	N. Dak.
Arkansas	Ark.	Oklahoma	Okla.
California	Calif.	Oregon	Oreg.
Canal Zone	C.Z.	Pennsylvania	Pa.
Colorado	Colo.	Puerto Rico	P.R.
Connecticut	Conn.	Rhode Island	R.I.
Delaware	Del.	South Carolina	S.C.
District of		South Dakota	S. Dak.
Columbia	D.C.	Tennessee	Tenn.
Florida	Fla.	Texas	Tex.
Georgia	Ga.	Vermont	Vt.
Illinois	Ill.	Virgin Islands	V.I.
Indiana	Ind.	Virginia	Va.
Kansas	Kans.	Washington	Wash.
Kentucky	Ky.	West Virginia	W. Va.
Louisiana	La.	Wisconsin	Wis.
Maryland	Md.	Wyoming	Wyo.
Massachusetts	Mass.	Alberta	Alta.
Michigan	Mich.	British Columbia	B.C.
Minnesota	Minn.	Manitoba	Man.
Mississippi	Miss.	New Brunswick	N.B.
Missouri	Mo.	Newfoundland	Nfld.
Montana	Mont.	Northwest Territories	N.W.T.
Nebraska	Nebr.	Nova Scotia	N.S.
Nevada	Nev.	Ontario	Ont.
New Hampshire	N.H.	Prince Edward Island	P.E.I.
New Jersey	N.J.	Quebec	P.Q. or Que.
New Mexico	N. Mex.	Saskatchewan	Sask.
New York	N.Y.	Yukon Territory	Y.T. or Yuk.

NOTE: Alaska, Guam, Hawaii, Idaho, Iowa, Maine, Ohio, and Utah are not abbreviated.

5

528 a. Geographic abbreviations made up of single initials require a period after each initial but *no* space after each internal period.

U.K.   United Kingdom   N.A.   North America

NOTE: When a company uses a geographical abbreviation in its corporate name or in the name of a product, respect the company's style.

U.S.A.   **BUT:** *USA Today*   U.S.   **BUT:** U S WEST Communications

b. If the geographic abbreviation contains more than single initials, space once after each internal period.

N. Mex.   N. Dak.   W. Va.   W. Aust.

529 a. In place names, do not abbreviate *Fort, Mount, Point,* or *Port* except in tables and lists where space is tight.

Fort Wayne   Mount Pleasant   Point Pleasant   Port Arthur
Fort Myers   Mount Rainier   Point Pelee   Port Ludlow

b. In U.S. place names, abbreviate *Saint.* For other place names involving *Saint,* follow the style shown in an authoritative dictionary or atlas.

St. Louis, Missouri   St. Lawrence River
St. Petersburg, Florida   St. Charles Avenue

➤ *For the abbreviation or the spelling out of names of streets, cities, states, and countries, see also ¶¶1334–1337, 1340–1341, 1343.*

5 Compass Points

530 a. Spell out compass points used as ordinary nouns and adjectives.

The company has large landholdings in the *Southwest.*

We purchased a lot at the *southwest* corner of Green and Union Streets.

➤ *For the capitalization of compass points, see ¶¶338–341.*

b. Spell out compass points included in street names except in lists and tables where space is tight. (See also ¶1334.)

143 South Mountain Avenue   1232 East Franklin Street

531 a. Abbreviate compass points without periods when they are used *following* a street name to indicate the section of the city. (See also ¶1335.)

1330 South Bay Boulevard, SW

NOTE: In some communities the predominant style is to use periods in such abbreviations; for example, *S.W., N.E.* (See ¶1335.)

b. In technical material (especially pertaining to real estate and legal or nautical matters), abbreviate compass points without periods.

N   north   NE   northeast   NNE   north-northeast

Days and Months

532 Do not abbreviate names of days of the week and months of the year except in tables or lists where space is limited. In such cases the following abbreviations may be used:

Sun.	Thurs., Thu.	Jan.	May	Sept., Sep.
Mon.	Fri.	Feb.	June, Jun.	Oct.
Tues., Tue.	Sat.	Mar.	July, Jul.	Nov.
Wed.		Apr.	Aug.	Dec.

NOTE: When space is extremely tight, as in the column heads of some computer reports, the following one- and two-letter abbreviations may be used.

Su M Tu W Th F Sa
Ja F Mr Ap My Je Jl Au S O N D

Time and Time Zones

533 Use the abbreviations *a.m.* and *p.m.* in expressions of time. These abbreviations most commonly appear in small letters, but you may use small capitals (A.M., P.M.) if you have that option. (See ¶440.) For more formal expressions of time, use *o'clock* (see ¶441).

534 **a.** The standard time zones in the continental United States are abbreviated as follows:

EST (Eastern standard time)   MST (Mountain standard time)
CST (Central standard time)   PST (Pacific standard time)

➤ *See ¶440a for examples.*

NOTE: When daylight saving time is in effect, use DST (daylight saving time) or one of the following forms:

EDT (Eastern daylight time)   MDT (Mountain daylight time)
CDT (Central daylight time)   PDT (Pacific daylight time)

b. Puerto Rico and the U.S. Virgin Islands are in the Atlantic standard time zone (AST). Hawaii is in the Hawaii-Aleutian time zone (abbreviated simply as HST with reference to Hawaii). Alaska falls in the Alaska time zone (which is commonly abbreviated as YST, referring to an earlier designation, the Yukon time zone). Within these areas only Alaska observes daylight saving time (YDT).

Customary Measurements

535 Abbreviate units of measure when they occur frequently, as in technical and scientific work, on invoices and other business forms, and in tables.

a. Units of measure are now commonly abbreviated without periods. The abbreviations are the same for the singular and the plural.

yd (yard, yards)   oz (ounce, ounces)   rpm (revolutions per minute)
ft (foot, feet)   gal (gallon, gallons)   cpi (characters per inch)
mi (mile, miles)   lb (pound, pounds)   mph (miles per hour)

NOTE: The abbreviation *in* (for *inch* or *inches*) may be written without a period if it is not likely to be confused with the preposition *in*.

8 in OR 8 in.   BUT: 8 sq in   8 ft 2 in

b. In a set of simple dimensions or a range of numbers, use an abbreviation only with the last number. Repeat a symbol with each number.

a room 10 × 15 ft BUT: a room 10′ × 15′ (see ¶543b)
35° to 45°F OR 35°–45°F (see ¶¶538c, 543b)

NOTE: In a set of complex dimensions, where more than one unit of measure is involved, repeat the abbreviations with each number.

a room 10 ft 6 in × 19 ft 10 in OR a room 10′ 6″ × 19′ 10″ (see ¶432)

536 In nontechnical writing, spell out units of measure.

a 20-gallon container   8½ by 11 inches
a 150-acre estate   an 8½- by 11-inch book (see ¶817)

Metric Measurements

The following rules of style are based on the *Metric Editorial Guide*, published by the American National Metric Council (Washington, D.C.). For a full listing of metric terms, consult a dictionary.

537 The most common metric measurements are derived from three basic units and several prefixes indicating multiples or fractions of a unit, as shown below. The abbreviations for these terms appear in parentheses in the first column below.

Basic Units

meter (m)   One meter is 10 percent longer than a yard (39.37 inches).
gram (g)   A thousand grams (a *kilogram*) is 10 percent heavier than 2 pounds (2.2 pounds).
liter (L)   A liter is about 5 percent bigger than a quart (1.057 quarts).

Prefixes Indicating Fractions

deci (d)   1/10   A *decimeter* (dm) equals 1/10 meter.
centi (c)   1/100   A *centigram* (cg) equals 1/100 gram.
milli (m)   1/1000   A *milliliter* (mL) equals 1/1000 liter.

Prefixes Indicating Multiples

deka (da)   10   A *dekameter* (dam) equals 10 meters (about 11 yards).
hecto (h)   100   A *hectogram* (hg) equals 100 grams (about 3½ ounces).
kilo (k)   1000   A *kilometer* (km) equals 1000 meters (about 5/8 mile).

NOTE: Temperatures are expressed in terms of the Celsius scale (abbreviated *C*).

Water freezes at 0°C (32°F) and boils at 100°C (212°F).

With a temperature of 37°C (98.6°F), you can't be very sick.

The temperature here on the island stays between 20° and 30°C (68° and 86°F).

➤ *For the use of spaces in figures expressing metric quantities, see ¶461b.*

538 Metric units of measurement, like the customary units of measurement described in ¶535, are abbreviated in technical and scientific work, on business forms, and in tables. In nontechnical writing, metric units are ordinarily spelled out, but some expressions typically appear in abbreviated form (for example, *35-mm film*).

a. Abbreviations of metric units of measurement are written without periods except at the end of a sentence.

100-mm cigarettes (10 centimeters or about 4 inches)
a 30-cm width (about 12 inches or 1 foot)
an office 5 × 3 m (about 5.5 by 3.3 yards)
a 1000-km trip (620 miles)
weighs 100 kg (about 220 pounds)
50 to 75 kg (about 110 to 165 pounds)
feels like 10°C weather (50°F weather)

NOTE: In abbreviations of expressions like *kilometers per hour*, a diagonal is used to express *per*.

an 80 km/h speed limit (50 miles per hour)

b. Metric abbreviations are the same for the singular and the plural.

1 kg (1 kilogram)   5 kg (5 kilograms)

c. When expressing temperatures, leave no space between the number and the degree symbol or between the degree symbol and the abbreviation for Celsius.

14°C (NOT: 14° C)

d. In printed material, metric measurements for area and volume are usually expressed with raised numbers.

m² square meter   cm³ cubic centimeter

If the equipment you are using makes it difficult or awkward to create raised numbers, use the following forms:

sq m square meter   cu cm cubic centimeter

NOTE: In material that uses raised numbers for footnote references, use the forms *sq m* and *cu cm* to avoid the possibility of confusion.

Chemical and Mathematical Expressions

539 Do not use a period after the symbols that represent chemical elements and formulas.

K (potassium)   NaCl (sodium chloride—table salt)

The chemical notations H_2O and CO_2 stand for "dihydrogen oxide" (namely, water) and "carbon dioxide." They do not refer, as one student observed, to hot water and cold water.

540 Do not use a period after such mathematical abbreviations as *log* (for *logarithm*) and *tan* (for *tangent*).

Business Expressions

541 A number of terms are commonly abbreviated on business forms, in tables, and in routine business correspondence. (See also ¶¶544–546.)

acct.	account	BS OR	bill of sale
ack.	acknowledge	B/S	
addl.	additional	B-school	graduate school of
agt.	agent		business
AI	artificial intelligence	bu	bushel(s)
a.k.a.	also known as	C	100; Celsius
amt.	amount		(temperature)
anon.	anonymous	CDC	community development
AP	accounts payable		corporation
approx.	approximately	CEO	chief executive officer
AR	accounts receivable	CFO	chief financial officer
ASAP	as soon as possible	cg	centigram(s)
Assn.	Association	chg.	charge
assoc.	associate(s)	c.i.f. OR	cost, insurance, and
asst.	assistant	CIF	freight (see ¶542)
att.	attachment	CIO	chief information officer
Attn.	Attention	cm	centimeter(s)
avg.	average	Co.	Company
bal.	balance	c/o	care of
bbl	barrel(s)	c.o.d. OR	cash (or collect) on
bl	bale(s)	COD	delivery (see ¶542)
BL OR	bill of lading	COLA	cost-of-living adjustment
B/L		cont.	continued
bldg.	building	COO	chief operating officer

(Continued on page 136.)

5

Corp.	Corporation	HQ	headquarters
CPA	certified public accountant (see ¶519e)	hr	hour(s)
		in OR in.	inch(es) (see ¶535a, note)
CPI	consumer price index	Inc.	Incorporated
cr.	credit	incl.	including, inclusive
ctn.	carton	ins.	insurance
cwt.	hundredweight	intl.	international
d.b.a. OR DBA	doing business as (see ¶542)	inv.	invoice
		ips	inches per second
dept.	department	kg	kilogram(s)
dis.	discount	km	kilometer(s)
dist.	district	km/h	kilometers per hour
distr.	distributor, distribution, distributed	L	liter(s) (see ¶537)
		l., ll.	line, lines
div.	division	lb	pound(s)
DJIA	Dow Jones industrial average	LBO	leveraged buyout
		l.c.l. OR LCL	less-than-carload lot (see ¶542)
doz.	dozen		
dr.	debit	LIFO	last in, first out
dstn.	destination	Ltd.	Limited
dtd.	dated	m	meter(s) (see ¶537)
ea.	each	M	1000
EEO	equal employment opportunity	M&A	mergers and acquisitions
		max.	maximum
enc.	enclosed, enclosure	mdse.	merchandise
e.o.m. OR EOM	end of month (see ¶542)	mfg.	manufacturing
		mfr.	manufacturer
Esq.	Esquire	mg	milligram(s)
ETA	estimated time of arrival	mgr.	manager
ETD	estimated time of departure	mgt. OR mgmt.	management
exec.	executive	MHz	megahertz
F	Fahrenheit (temperature)	min	minute(s)
		min.	minimum
f.a.s. OR FAS	free alongside ship (see ¶542)	misc.	miscellaneous
		mL	milliliter(s)
f.b.o. OR FBO	for the benefit of (see ¶542)	mm	millimeter(s)
		mo	month(s)
FIFO	first in, first out	MO	mail order, money order
f.o.b. OR FOB	free on board (see ¶542)	mpg	miles per gallon
		mph	miles per hour
ft	foot, feet	mtg.	mortgage
ft-tn	foot-ton(s)	n/30	net in 30 days
fwd.	forward	NA	not applicable, not available
FY	fiscal year (see ¶504)		
FYI	for your information	n.d.	no date
g	gram(s) (see ¶537)	No., Nos.	number(s) (see ¶455)
GAAP	generally accepted accounting principles	nt. wt.	net weight
		NV	no value
		OAG	*Official Airline Guide*
gal	gallon(s)	opt.	optional
GM	general manager	OS	out of stock
gr.	gross	OTC	over the counter
gr. wt.	gross weight	oz	ounce(s)
hdlg.	handling	p., pp.	page, pages
HMO	health maintenance organization	P&H	postage and handling
		P&L OR P/L	profit and loss (statement)
HP OR hp	horsepower		

PC	personal computer, politically correct	ROE	return on equity
P.C.	professional corporation	ROI	return on investment
pd.	paid	rpm	revolutions per minute
P.E.	professional engineer	S&H	shipping and handling
PERT	program evaluation and review technique	SASE	self-addressed, stamped envelope
pkg.	package(s)	sec	second(s)
PO	purchase order	sec.	secretary
P.O.	post office	shtg.	shortage
p.o.e. OR POE	port of entry (see ¶542)	SO	shipping order
		std.	standard
PP	parcel post	stge.	storage
ppd.	postpaid, prepaid (postage paid in advance)	stmt.	statement
		treas.	treasury, treasurer
pr.	pair(s)	UPC	Universal Product Code
PS, PS.	postscript	VAT	value-added tax
pt	pint(s)	V.P.	vice president
pt.	part, point(s), port	vs.	versus (v. in legal citations)
qt	quart(s)		
qtr.	quarter(ly)	w/	with
qty.	quantity	whsle.	wholesale
recd.	received	w/o	without, week of
reg.	registered, regular	wt.	weight
ret.	retired	yd	yard(s)
rev.	revised	yr	year(s)
ROA	return on assets	YTD	year to date

542 A few common business abbreviations listed in ¶541 are frequently typed in small letters (with periods) when they occur within sentences but are typed in all-capital letters (without periods) when they appear on business forms. For example,

c.i.f.	OR	CIF		f.o.b.	OR	FOB
c.o.d.	OR	COD		l.c.l.	OR	LCL
e.o.m.	OR	EOM		p.o.e.	OR	POE

Symbols

543 A number of symbols are often used on business forms, in tables and statistical material, and in informal business communications. If you are using software with special character sets, you can access these symbols.

@	at	°	degree(s)	#	number (before a figure)
&	and	=	equals	#	pounds (after a figure)
%	percent	′	feet	¶	paragraph
$	dollar(s)	″	inches; ditto	×	by, multiplied by
¢	cent(s)	§	section		

a. Leave one space before and after the following symbols:

@	order 200 @ $49.95	=	if $a = 7$ and $b = 9$
&	Kaye & Elman Inc.	×	a room 12 × 18 ft

NOTE: As a rule, do not leave space before and after an ampersand (&) in all-capital abbreviations.

AT&T pursues a wide range of R&D [research and development] activities.

(Continued on page 138.)

At the next shareholders' meeting we need to anticipate some tough queries during the Q&A [question and answer] session about our M&A [merger and acquisition] activities.

I have an uncontrollable passion for M&M's [candy].

b. Do not leave space between a figure and one of the following symbols:

%	a 65% sales increase	#	use 50# paper for the job
¢	about 30¢ a pound	'	a 9′ × 12′ Oriental carpet
°	reduce heat to 350°	″	an 8½″ × 11″ sheet of paper

c. Do not leave any space after these symbols when they are followed by a figure:

$	in the $250–$500 range	¶¶	as explained in ¶¶1218–1220
#	reorder #4659 and #4691	§	will be covered in §14.26

Computer Abbreviations and Acronyms

544 The following list presents some of the abbreviations and acronyms commonly used in references to computers and the Internet.

ASCII	American Standard Code for Information Interchange (pronounced *as-kee*)
BASIC	Beginner's All-Purpose Symbolic Instruction Code
BBSs	bulletin board services (see ¶622a)
BCD	binary coded decimal
BIOS	basic input/output system
bit	binary digit
BLOB	binary large object
bps	bits per second
CAD	computer-aided design
CAI	computer-aided instruction
CAM	computer-aided manufacturing
CAR	computer-assisted retrieval
CD-ROM	compact disc–read-only memory
CGA	color graphics adapter
CPU	central processing unit
CRT	cathode-ray tube
DBMS	database management system
DOS	disk operating system
dpi	dots per inch
DTP	desktop publishing
e-mail	electronic mail
EOF	end of file
FAQ	frequently asked questions (pronounced *fak*)
FAT	file allocation table
FTP	file transfer protocol
GIGO	garbage in, garbage out
GUI	graphical user interface (pronounced *goo-ee*)
IC	integrated circuit
I/O	input/output
KB OR K	kilobyte
LAN	local area network
LQ	letter quality
MB OR M	megabyte
MICR	magnetic ink character reader
NLQ	near letter quality
OCR	optical character recognition OR reader
OS	operating system
PC	personal computer

PIC	personal intelligent communicator
PPP	point-to-point protocol
RAM	random-access memory
RISC	reduced instruction set computer
ROM	read-only memory
SCSI	small computer system interface port (pronounced *scuzzy*)
SLIP	serial line Internet protocol
TCP/IP	transmission control protocol/Internet protocol
VDT	video display terminal
VM	voice mail
WAIS	wide area information server (pronounced *ways*)
WAN	wide area network
WORM	write once—read many times
WWW	World Wide Web
WYSIWYG	what you see is what you get (pronounced *wiz-ee-wig*)
XGA	extended graphics array

➤ *For a glossary of computer terms, see Appendix B.*
For the capitalization of computer terms, see ¶365.

Foreign Expressions

545 Many foreign expressions contain or consist of short words, some of which are abbreviations and some of which are not. Use periods only with abbreviations.

ad hoc	meaning "for a particular purpose"
ad val.	*ad valorem,* meaning "according to the value"
c. **OR** ca.	*circa,* meaning "approximately"
cf.	*confer,* meaning "compare"
Cie.	*Compagnie,* meaning "Company"
e.g.	*exempli gratia,* meaning "for example"
et al.	*et alii,* meaning "and other people"
etc.	*et cetera,* meaning "and other things," "and so forth"
ibid.	*ibidem,* meaning "in the same place"
idem	meaning "the same"
i.e.	*id est,* meaning "that is"
infra	meaning "below"
inst.	*instans,* meaning "the current month"
loc. cit.	*loco citato,* meaning "in the place cited"
M.O.	*modus operandi,* meaning "the way in which something is done"
N.B.	*nota bene,* meaning "note well"
nol. pros.	*nolle prosequi,* meaning "to be unwilling to prosecute"
non seq.	*non sequitur,* meaning "it does not follow"
op. cit.	*opere citato,* meaning "in the work cited"
p.a. **OR** PA	*per annum,* meaning "for each year"
p.d. **OR** PD	*per diem,* meaning "for each day"
pro tem	*pro tempore,* meaning "for the time being"
prox.	*proximo,* meaning "in the next month"
Q.E.D.	*quod erat demonstrandum,* meaning "which was to be demonstrated"
q.v.	*quod vide,* meaning "which see"
re **OR** in re	meaning "in the matter of," "concerning"
R.S.V.P. **OR** R.s.v.p.	*Répondez s'il vous plaît,* meaning "please reply"
supra	meaning "above"
ult.	*ultimo,* meaning "in the last month"

5

Miscellaneous Expressions

546 The following list of expressions presents common abbreviations acceptable in general usage.

A-OK	very definitely OK	our morale is A-OK
A1	first-rate	his heart is now in A1 condition
ATM	automated teller machine	get $50 from the nearest ATM
AV	audiovisual	a list of AV materials
CAT	clear-air turbulence	a plane crash caused by CAT
CATV	community antenna television	an improvement in CATV programming
CB	citizens band	called in on her CB radio
CD	certificate of deposit, compact disc	investing in 6% CDs / the quality of a CD recording
DAT	digital audio tape	the superior quality of DATs
ESP	extrasensory perception	their manager must have ESP
GDP	gross domestic product	the GDP for the fourth quarter
HDTV	high-definition television	the screen needed for HDTV
ID	identification data	show your user ID card
IOU	I owe you	holds my IOU for $500
IQ	intelligence quotient	take an IQ test
IRA	individual retirement account	make a tax-deductible deposit to your IRA
PA	public address	a problem with our PA system
PR	public relations	work on your PR campaign
R&D	research and development	need a bigger R&D budget
S&L	savings and loan association	a small S&L mortgage
SOP	standard operating procedure	find out the SOP for submitting expense reports
SRO	standing room only	an SRO audience at our show
TLC	tender, loving care	give this customer some TLC
TV	television	watch for it on TV
UFO	unidentified flying object	took off like a UFO
VCR	videocassette recorder	play this tape on your VCR
VIP	very important person	treat these dealers like VIPs

547 Do not use periods with letters that are not abbreviations. (See also ¶109a.)

Brand X	T-bill	f-stop	I-beam pointer	V-chip
X ray	T square	y-axis	U-turn	B picture

548 The abbreviation *OK* is written without periods. In sentences, the forms *okay, okayed,* and *okaying* look better than *OK, OK'd,* and *OK'ing,* but the latter forms may be used.

549 The dictionary recognizes *x* as a verb; however, *cross out, crossed out,* and *crossing out* look better than *x out, x-ed out,* and *x-ing out.*

➢ *Plurals of abbreviations: see ¶¶619–623.*
Possessives of abbreviations: see ¶¶638–639.

SECTION 6

PLURALS AND POSSESSIVES

Forming Plurals

When you are uncertain about the plural form of a word, consult a dictionary. If no plural is shown, form the plural according to the rules in ¶¶601–626.

Basic Rule

601 Plurals are regularly formed by adding *s* to the singular form.

suburb	suburbs	quota	quotas
fabric	fabrics	idea	ideas
yield	yields	committee	committees
egg	eggs	freebie	freebies
length	lengths	league	leagues
check	checks	alibi	alibis
rhythm	rhythms	menu	menus
flight	flights	bayou	bayous

NOTE: A few words have the same form in the plural as in the singular. (See ¶¶603, 1013, 1016, 1017.)

Nouns Ending in S, X, CH, SH, or Z

602 When the singular form ends in *s*, *x*, *ch*, *sh*, or *z*, the plural is formed by adding *es* to the singular.

virus	viruses	sketch	sketches
summons	summonses	wish	wishes
business	businesses	quartz	quartzes
fax	faxes	**BUT:** quiz	quizzes

603 Singular nouns ending in silent *s* do not change their forms in the plural. (However, the *s* ending is pronounced when the plural form is used.)

one corps   two corps   a rendezvous   many rendezvous

Nouns Ending in Y

604 When a singular noun ends in *y* preceded by a *consonant*, the plural is formed by changing the *y* to *i* and adding *es* to the singular.

copy	copies	liability	liabilities
policy	policies	proxy	proxies

605 When a singular noun ends in *y* preceded by a *vowel*, the plural is formed by adding *s* to the singular.

delay	delays	guy	guys
attorney	attorneys	**BUT:** soliloquy	soliloquies
boy	boys	colloquy	colloquies

Nouns Ending in O

606 Singular nouns ending in *o* preceded by a *vowel* form their plurals by adding *s* to the singular.

stereo	stereos	shampoo	shampoos
ratio	ratios	boo	boos
portfolio	portfolios	tattoo	tattoos
scenario	scenarios	duo	duos

607 Singular nouns ending in *o* preceded by a *consonant* form their plurals in different ways.

a. Some nouns in this category simply add *s*.

ego	egos	memo	memos
photo	photos	placebo	placebos
macro	macros	two	twos
typo	typos	weirdo	weirdos
logo	logos	hairdo	hairdos

b. Some add *es*.

potato	potatoes	hero	heroes
tomato	tomatoes	embargo	embargoes
echo	echoes	fiasco	fiascoes

c. Some have two plural forms. (The preferred form is given first.)

cargo	cargoes, cargos	zero	zeros, zeroes
no	nos, noes	tuxedo	tuxedos, tuxedoes
motto	mottoes, mottos	innuendo	innuendos, innuendoes
proviso	provisos, provisoes	ghetto	ghettos, ghettoes

d. Singular musical terms ending in *o* form their plurals by adding *s*.

soprano	sopranos	piano	pianos
alto	altos	cello	cellos
basso	bassos	banjo	banjos

➤ *For foreign nouns ending in* o, *see* ¶*614*.

Nouns Ending in *F, FE,* or *FF*

608 **a.** Most singular nouns that end in *f, fe,* or *ff* form their plurals by adding *s* to the singular form.

belief	beliefs	safe	safes
proof	proofs	tariff	tariffs

b. Some commonly used nouns in this category form their plurals by changing the *f* or *fe* to *ve* and adding *s*.

half	halves	self	selves
wife	wives	shelf	shelves
leaf	leaves	knife	knives
thief	thieves	life	lives

c. A few of these nouns have two plural forms. (The preferred form is given first.)

scarf	scarves, scarfs	dwarf	dwarfs, dwarves

Nouns With Irregular Plurals

609 The plurals of some nouns are formed by a change of letters within.

wom*a*n	wom*e*n	f*oo*t	f*ee*t
m*ouse*	m*ice**	g*oo*se	g*ee*se

610 A few plurals end in *en* or *ren*.

ox	oxen	brother	brethren (*an alternative*
child	children		*plural to* brothers)

*Mice refers to computer devices as well as to rodents.

Compound Nouns

611 When a compound noun is a *solid* word, pluralize the final element in the compound as if it stood alone.

print*out*	print*outs*	birth*day*	birth*days*
flash*back*	flash*backs*	photo*copy*	photo*copies*
wine*glass*	wine*glasses*	grand*child*	grand*children*
hat*box*	hat*boxes*	foot*hold*	foot*holds*
eye*lash*	eye*lashes*	fore*foot*	fore*feet*
straw*berry*	straw*berries*	tooth*brush*	tooth*brushes*
book*shelf*	book*shelves*	mouse*trap*	mouse*traps*
BUT: *passer*by	*passers*by	work*man*	work*men*
stand*by*	stand*bys*	BUT: talisman	talisman*s*
	(NOT: standbies)		(NOT: talismen)

612 **a.** The plurals of *hyphenated* or *spaced* compounds are formed by pluralizing the chief element of the compound.

father-in-law	*fathers*-in-law	couch *potato*	couch *potatoes*
senator-elect	*senators*-elect	*rule* of thumb	*rules* of thumb
looker-on	*lookers*-on	*letter* of credit	*letters* of credit
runner-up	*runners*-up	*account* payable	*accounts* payable
grant-in-aid	*grants*-in-aid	*attorney* at law	*attorneys* at law
bill of lading	*bills* of lading	deputy *chief* of staff	deputy *chiefs* of staff
editor in chief	*editors* in chief	lieutenant *general*	lieutenant *generals*
BUT: time-*out*	time-*outs*	BUT: chaise *longue**	chaise *longues*

> ➤ *See ¶614 for the plurals of foreign compound words.*

b. When a hyphenated compound does not contain a noun as one of its elements, simply pluralize the final element.

go-*between*	go-*betweens*	two-by-*four*	two-by-*fours*
get-*together*	get-*togethers*	no-*no*	no-*nos*
hang-*up*	hang-*ups*	has-*been*	has-*beens*
hand-me-*down*	hand-me-*downs*	have-*not*	have-*nots* (see ¶625a)
drive-*in*	drive-*ins*	know-it-*all*	know-it-*alls*
fade-*out*	fade-*outs*	so-and-*so*	so-and-*sos*
come-*on*	come-*ons*	do-it-*yourselfer*	do-it-*yourselfers*
show-*off*	show-*offs*	shoot-'em-*up*	shoot-'em-*ups*
run-*through*	run-*throughs*	no-see-*um*	no-see-*ums*

c. Some of these compounds have two recognized plural forms. (The first plural form shown below is preferred because it adds the plural sign to the chief element of the compound.)

court-martial	*courts*-martial, court-*martials*
notary public	*notaries* public, notary *publics*
attorney general	*attorneys* general, attorney *generals*

d. When the first element of a compound is a *possessive,* simply pluralize the final element.

collector's item	collector's items
traveler's check	traveler's checks
rabbit's foot	rabbit's feet
proofreaders' mark	proofreaders' marks
farmers' market	farmers' markets
witches' brew	witches' brews
finder's fee	finder's fees
visitor's permit	visitor's permits

---

*Note that the correct spelling of this word is *longue* (not *lounge*).

NOTE: Do not convert a singular possessive form into a plural unless the context clearly requires it. (See also ¶651.)

> The number of *driver's licenses* issued last year was 15 percent ahead of the number issued the year before.

> **BUT:** As a result of the highway checkpoints set up by the state police, more than 200 *drivers' licenses* have been revoked in the past four weeks.

613 The plurals of compounds ending in *ful* are formed by adding *s*.

armful	armfuls	handful	handfuls
cupful	cupfuls	teaspoonful	teaspoonfuls

Compare the difference in meaning in these phrases:

> six *cupfuls* of sugar (a quantity of sugar that would fill one cup six times)

> six *cups full* of sugar (six separate cups, each filled with sugar)

Foreign Nouns

614 Many nouns of foreign origin retain their foreign plurals, others have been given English plurals, and still others have two plurals—an English and a foreign one. When two plural forms exist, one may be preferred to the other or there may be differences in meaning that govern the use of each. Consult your dictionary to be sure of the plural forms and the meanings attached to them.

➤ *For agreement of foreign-plural subjects with verbs, see ¶1018.*

WORDS ENDING IN *US*

Singular	English Plural	Foreign Plural
alumnus (m.)		alumni
apparatus	apparatuses*	apparatus
cactus	cactuses	cacti*
census	censuses	
corpus		corpora
focus	focuses*	foci†
genus		genera
nucleus	nucleuses	nuclei*
opus	opuses	opera*
prospectus	prospectuses	
radius	radiuses	radii*
status	statuses	
stimulus		stimuli
syllabus	syllabuses	syllabi*
terminus	terminuses	termini*

WORDS ENDING IN *A*

Singular	English Plural	Foreign Plural
agenda	agendas	
alumna (f.)		alumnae
antenna	antennas (of radios)	antennae (of insects)
formula	formulas*	formulae
minutia		minutiae
schema	schemas*	schemata†
stigma	stigmas	stigmata*
vertebra	vertebras	vertebrae*

---

*Preferred form.   †Merriam-Webster shows this form first.   (Continued on page 146.)

WORDS ENDING IN *UM*

Singular	English Plural	Foreign Plural
addendum		addenda
auditorium	auditoriums*	auditoria
bacterium		bacteria
colloquium	colloquiums*	colloquia
cranium	craniums*	crania
curriculum	curriculums*	curricula†
datum	datums	data* (see ¶1018)
erratum		errata
gymnasium	gymnasiums*	gymnasia
maximum	maximums*	maxima†
medium	mediums (spiritualists)	media (for advertising and communication)
memorandum	memorandums*	memoranda
millennium	millenniums*	millennia†
minimum	minimums*	minima†
momentum	momentums*	momenta†
optimum	optimums*	optima†
referendum	referendums*	referenda†
stadium	stadiums*	stadia†
stratum		strata
symposium	symposiums*	symposia†
ultimatum	ultimatums*	ultimata

WORDS ENDING IN *O*

Singular	English Plural	Foreign Plural
concerto	concertos	concerti*
graffito		graffiti
libretto	librettos*	libretti
paparazzo		paparazzi
tempo	tempos	tempi (in music)
virtuoso	virtuosos*	virtuosi

WORDS ENDING IN *ON*

Singular	English Plural	Foreign Plural
automaton	automatons*	automata
criterion	criterions	criteria*
phenomenon	phenomenons	phenomena*

WORDS ENDING IN *X*

Singular	English Plural	Foreign Plural
apex	apexes*	apices
appendix	appendixes*	appendices
codex		codices
crux	cruxes*	cruces
index	indexes (of books)	indices (math symbols)
larynx	larynxes	larynges*
matrix	matrixes	matrices*
vertex	vertexes	vertices*
vortex	vortexes	vortices*

---

*Preferred form.   †Merriam-Webster shows this form first.

WORDS ENDING IN *IS*

Singular	English Plural	Foreign Plural
analysis		analyses
axis		axes
basis		bases
crisis		crises
diagnosis		diagnoses
ellipsis		ellipses
emphasis		emphases
hypothesis		hypotheses
parenthesis		parentheses
synopsis		synopses
synthesis		syntheses
thesis		theses

WORDS ENDING IN *EAU*

Singular	English Plural	Foreign Plural
beau	beaus	beaux*
bureau	bureaus*	bureaux
plateau	plateaus*	plateaux
tableau	tableaus	tableaux*
trousseau	trousseaus	trousseaux*

NOTE: The *x* ending for these foreign plurals is pronounced like *z*.

COMPOUND WORDS

Singular	English Plural	Foreign Plural
chaise longue	chaise longues*	chaises longues
coup d'état		coups d'état
éminence grise		éminences grises
fait accompli		faits accomplis
hors d'oeuvre	hors d'oeuvres*	hors d'oeuvre
idiot savant	idiot savants	idiots savants*
maître d'hôtel		maîtres d'hôtel
maître d'	maître d's	
nouveau riche		nouveaux riches
pas de deux		pas de deux

Proper Names

615 **a.** Most *surnames* are pluralized by the addition of *s*.

Mr. and Mrs. Brinton	the Brintons
Mr. and Mrs. Romano	the Romanos

b. When a surname ends in *s, x, ch, sh,* or *z*, add *es* to form the plural.

Mr. and Mrs. Banks	the Bankses
Mr. and Mrs. Van Ness	the Van Nesses
Mr. and Mrs. Maddox	the Maddoxes
Mr. and Mrs. March	the Marches
Mr. and Mrs. Welsh	the Welshes
Mr. and Mrs. Katz	the Katzes
Mr. and Mrs. Jones	the Joneses
Mr. and Mrs. James	the Jameses
Mr. and Mrs. Barnes	the Barneses

*Preferred form.

(Continued on page 148.)

NOTE: Omit the *es* ending if it makes the plural surname awkward to pronounce.

the Hodges (NOT: Hodgeses) the Hastings (NOT: Hastingses)

c. Never change the original spelling of a surname when forming the plural. Simply add *s* or *es*, according to ¶615*a* and *b*.

Mr. and Mrs. McCarthy	the McCarthys (NOT: McCarthies)
Mr. and Mrs. Wolf	the Wolfs (NOT: Wolves)
Mr. and Mrs. Martino	the Martinos (NOT: Martinoes)
Mr. and Mrs. Goodman	the Goodmans (NOT: Goodmen)
Mr. and Mrs. Lightfoot	the Lightfoots (NOT: Lightfeet)
Mr. and Mrs. Fairchild	the Fairchilds (NOT: Fairchildren)

d. When a surname is followed by *Jr.*, *Sr.*, or a number like *2d* or *II*, the plural can be formed two ways:

ORDINARY USAGE: the Roy Van Allen *Jrs.* the Ellsworth Hadley *3ds*
FORMAL USAGE: the Roy Van *Allens* Jr. the Ellsworth *Hadleys* 3d

616 To form the plurals of *first names*, add *s* or *es* but do not change the original spellings.

Marie	Maries	Douglas	Douglases	Timothy	Timothys
Ralph	Ralphs	Dolores	Doloreses	Beatrix	Beatrixes
Waldo	Waldos	Gladys	Gladyses	Fritz	Fritzes

617 To form the plural of other proper names, add *s* or *es* but do not change the original spelling.

three Texans	two Christmases ago
the Norwegians	checked our Rolodexes
the Dakotas	bought six Macintoshes
Februarys	Marches (*es* after *ch* sound)
the two Kansas Citys (NOT: Cities)	Czechs (*s* after *k* sound)

EXCEPTIONS:

the Alleghenies (for Allegheny Mountains)
the Rockies (for Rocky Mountains)

Personal Titles

618 a. The plural of *Mr.* is *Messrs.;* the plural of *Ms.* is *Mses.* or *Mss.;* the plural of *Mrs.* or *Mme.* is *Mmes.* (for *Mesdames*); the plural of *Miss* is *Misses* (no period follows). However, the use of plural titles normally occurs only in formal situations. In ordinary usage, simply retain the singular form and repeat it with each name.

Formal Usage	**Ordinary Usage**
Messrs. Rae and Tate	Mr. Rae and Mr. Tate
Mmes. (OR Mesdames) Byrd and Clyde	Mrs. Byrd and Mrs. Clyde
Misses Russo and Dupree	Miss Russo and Miss Dupree
Mses. (OR Mss.) Lai and Cohen	Ms. Lai and Ms. Cohen

b. When personal titles apply to two or more people with the same surname, the plural may be formed in two ways: (a) pluralize only the title (formal usage); (b) pluralize only the surname (ordinary usage).

Formal Usage	**Ordinary Usage**
the Messrs. Steele	the Mr. Steeles
the Mmes. (OR Mesdames) Bergeret	the Mrs. Bergerets
the Misses Conroy	the Miss Conroys
the Mses. (OR Mss.) Purdy	the Ms. Purdys

6

Abbreviations, Letters, Numbers, Words, and Symbols

619 Form the plurals of most abbreviations by adding *s* to the singular.

apt.	apts.	vol.	vols.	No.	Nos.	Dr.	Drs.
bldg.	bldgs.	par.	pars.	Co.	Cos.	401(k)	401(k)s

620 **a.** The abbreviations of many customary units of weight and measure, however, are the same in both the singular and plural.

oz (ounce **OR** ounces) ft (foot **OR** feet)
deg (degree **OR** degrees) in (inch **OR** inches)
bbl (barrel **OR** barrels) mi (mile **OR** miles)

NOTE: For a number of these abbreviations, two plural forms have been widely used: for example, *lb* or *lbs* (meaning "pounds"), *yd* or *yds* (meaning "yards"), *qt* or *qts* (meaning "quarts"). However, the trend is toward using *lb, yd,* and *qt* to signify the plural.

b. The abbreviations of metric units of weight and measure are the same in both the singular and plural. (See also ¶¶537–538.)

km (kilometer **OR** kilometers) cg (centigram **OR** centigrams)
mL (milliliter **OR** milliliters) dam (dekameter **OR** dekameters)

➤ *For the omission of periods with abbreviations of measurements, see ¶¶535a, 538a.*

621 **a.** The plurals of a few single-letter abbreviations (such as *p.* for *page* and *f.* for *the following page*) consist of the same letter doubled.

p. 64 (page 64) c. copy
pp. 64–72 (pages 64 through 72) cc. copies

pp. 9 f. (page 9 and the following page) n. 3 (note 3)
pp. 9 ff. (page 9 and the following pages) nn. 3–4 (notes 3 and 4)

l. 23 (line 23)
ll. 23–24 (lines 23 through 24)

b. Plurals of certain symbols consist of the same symbol doubled.

¶ paragraph ¶¶ paragraphs § section §§ sections

622 **a.** Capital letters and abbreviations ending with capital letters are pluralized by adding *s* alone.

three Rs	HMOs	BBSs	V.P.s
four Cs	POs	IQs	M.D.s
five VIPs	S&Ls	PTAs	Ph.D.s

b. Some authorities still sanction the use of an apostrophe before the *s* (for example, *four C's, PTA's*). However, the apostrophe is functionally unnecessary except where confusion might otherwise result.

three A's too many I's two U's

BUT: His report card showed three As, two Bs, and one C. (When the context is clear, no apostrophes are necessary.)

623 For the sake of clarity, uncapitalized letters and uncapitalized abbreviations are pluralized by adding an apostrophe plus *s*. (See ¶285, note.)

dotting the *i*'s *p*'s and *q*'s four c.o.d.'s wearing pj's

NOTE: When initials are spelled out, the plurals are formed normally.

emcees deejays okays Jaycees

624 Numbers expressed in figures are pluralized by the addition of *s* alone. (See, however, ¶622b.)

> in the 1990s   in the '90s (decade)   in the 90s (temperature)   sort the W2s

Numbers expressed in words are pluralized by the addition of *s* or *es*.

> ones   twos   threes   sixes   twenties   twenty-fives

625 **a.** When words taken from other parts of speech are used as nouns, they are usually pluralized by the addition of *s* or *es*.

ifs, ands, or buts	ins and outs	pros and cons	whereabouts
dos and don'ts	ups and downs	the haves and	whys and
yeses and nos	yeas and nays	the have-nots	wherefores

b. If the pluralized form is unfamiliar or is likely to be misread, use an apostrophe plus *s* to form the plural.

> which's and that's   or's and nor's

c. If the singular form already contains an apostrophe, simply add *s* to form the plural.

> ain'ts   mustn'ts   don'ts   ma'ams

➤ *For the use of italics or underlining with words referred to as words, see ¶¶ 285, 290c.*

Plural Endings in Parentheses

626 When referring to an item that could be either singular or plural, enclose the plural ending in parentheses.

> Please send the appropriate *form(s)* to the appropriate state *agency(ies)*.

6

FORMING POSSESSIVES

Possession Versus Description

627 A noun ending in the sound of *s* is usually in the possessive form if it is followed immediately by another noun. (An apostrophe alone or an apostrophe plus *s* is the sign of the possessive. See ¶¶630–640.)

> *Hodgkins'* product line (meaning the product line *of the Hodgkins Company*)
> *Faulkner's* novels (meaning the novels *written by Faulkner*)
> *McTavish's* property (meaning the property *belonging to McTavish*)
> a two *weeks'* vacation (meaning a vacation *for* or *lasting two weeks*)
> **BUT:** a *two-week* vacation (see ¶817a, note)

NOTE: To be sure that the possessive form should be used, try substituting an *of* phrase or making a similar substitution as in the examples above. If the substitution works, the possessive form is correct.

628 Do not mistake a descriptive form ending in *s* for a possessive form.

> sales effort (*sales* describes the kind of effort)
> savings account (*savings* describes the kind of account)
> news release (*news* describes the type of press release)
> earnings record (*earnings* describes the type of record)

NOTE: Some cases can be difficult to distinguish. Is it *the girls basketball team* or *the girls' basketball team*? Try substituting an irregular plural like *women.* You wouldn't say *the women basketball team;* you would say *the women's basketball team.* By analogy, *the girls' basketball team* is correct.

➤ *For descriptive and possessive forms in organizational names, see ¶640.*

629 In a number of cases only a slight difference in wording distinguishes a descriptive phrase from a possessive phrase.

Descriptive	Possessive
a six-month leave of absence	a six months' leave of absence
the California climate	California's climate
the Burgess account	Burgess's account
the Crosby children	the Crosbys' children
	OR: Mr. and Mrs. Crosby's children

Singular Nouns

630 To form the possessive of a singular noun *not* ending in an *s* sound, add an apostrophe plus *s* to the noun.

my lawyer's advice	Illinois's highways
a child's game	Arkansas's mountains
Gloria's career	Des Moines's mayor
Mr. and Mrs. Goodwin's party	the corps's leadership

631 To form the possessive of a singular noun that ends in an *s* sound, be guided by the way you pronounce the word.

a. If a new syllable is formed in the pronunciation of the possessive, add an apostrophe plus *s*.

your boss's approval	Mr. and Mrs. Morris's plane tickets
the witness's reply	Phoenix's suburbs
Congress's intention	Ms. Lopez's application
Dallas's business district	Mr. Marsh's office
St. Louis's airport	my coach's training regimen

b. If the addition of an extra syllable would make a word ending in an *s* hard to pronounce, add the apostrophe only.

Mrs. Phillips' request	Jesus' parables
Mr. Hastings' proposal	Moses' flight from Egypt
the Burroughs' condominium	for goodness' sake (see ¶646)
Los Angeles' freeways	Achilles' heel
New Orleans' restaurants	BUT: Achilles tendon

NOTE: Individual differences in pronunciation will affect the way some of these possessives are written. For example, if you pronounce the possessive form of *Perkins* as two syllables, you will write *Mr. Perkins' kindness;* if you pronounce the possessive of *Perkins* as three syllables, you will write *Mr. Perkins's kindness.* The important thing is to listen to your own pronunciation. When you hear yourself pronounce the possessive of *boss* as two syllables *(boss's)* and the possessive of *witness* as three *(witness's),* you will not be tempted to write *your boss' approval* or *the witness' reply.* Naturally, tradition should take precedence over your ear. For example, the U.S. ambassador to Great Britain is appointed to the *Court of St. James's* (not, as you might expect, *Court of St. James).*

c. When forming the possessive of any noun ending in *s* (for example, *Mr. Hodges*), always place the apostrophe at the end of the original word, never within it.

Mr. Hodges' message (**NOT:** Mr. Hodge's message)

Plural Nouns

632 **a.** For a *regular* plural noun (one that ends in *s* or *es*), add only an apostrophe to form the plural possessive. (See ¶¶639–640 for the use of the apostrophe in organizational names.)

investors' objectives
the witnesses' contradictions
the United States' policy

attorneys' fees
the agencies' conflicting rules
the Gaineses' legal residence

b. Since the singular and plural possessives for the same word usually sound exactly alike, pay particularly close attention to the meaning in order to determine whether the noun in question is singular or plural.

An *investor's* objectives should largely define investment strategy.
BUT: *Investors'* objectives are often not clearly defined.

We will need a ride to Mr. and Mrs. *Gaines's* party.
BUT: We will need a ride to the *Gaineses'* party.

I especially want to hear the last witness's testimony.
BUT: I especially want to hear the last two witnesses' testimony.

NOTE: In some cases only a dictionary can help you determine whether the possessive form should be singular or plural. For example, a plural possessive is used in *Legionnaires' disease,* but a singular possessive is used in *Hodgkin's disease* since the discoverer's name was Dr. Hodgkin (and not, as you might have expected, the more common name Hodgkins). Unlike the term *deacon's bench* (which uses a singular possessive), the term *Parsons table* involves no possessive form at all.

633 For an *irregular* plural noun (one that does not end in *s*), add an apostrophe plus *s* to form the plural possessive.

women's blouses   men's shirts
children's toys   **BUT:** menswear
(originally, men's wear)

the alumni's reunion
the alumnae's contribution

IMPORTANT NOTE: To avoid mistakes in forming the possessive of plural nouns, form the plural first; then apply the rule in ¶632 or ¶633, whichever fits.

Singular	Plural	Plural Possessive
boy	boys (regular)	boys'
boss	bosses (regular)	bosses'
hero	heroes (regular)	heroes'
Mr. and Mrs. Fox	the Foxes (regular)	the Foxes'
child	children (irregular)	children's
alumnus	alumni (irregular)	alumni's
alumna	alumnae (irregular)	alumnae's

Compound Nouns

634 To form the *singular* possessive of a compound noun (whether solid, spaced, or hyphenated), add an apostrophe plus *s* to the last element of the compound.

my son-in-law's job prospects
the secretary-treasurer's report
the owner-manager's policies
a do-it-yourselfer's obsession

my stockbroker's advice
the notary public's seal
an eyewitness's account
the attorney general's decision

635 To form the *plural* possessive of a compound noun, first form the plural.

a. If the plural form ends in *s,* add only an apostrophe.

Singular	Plural	Plural Possessive
stockholder	stockholders	stockholders'
vice president	vice presidents	vice presidents'
clerk-typist	clerk-typists	clerk-typists'
salesclerk	salesclerks	salesclerks'

b. If the plural form does not end in *s,* add an apostrophe plus *s.*

Singular	Plural	Plural Possessive
editor in chief	editors in chief	editors in chief's
brother-in-law	brothers-in-law	brothers-in-law's

NOTE: To avoid the awkwardness of a plural possessive such as *editors in chief's* or *brothers-in-law's,* rephrase the sentence.

AWKWARD: We may have to invite my three *sisters-in-law's* parents too.
BETTER: We may have to invite the parents of my three *sisters-in-law* too.

AWKWARD: Mr. Ahmed's statement agrees with both *attorneys general's* views.
BETTER: Mr. Ahmed's statement agrees with the views of both *attorneys general.*

Pronouns

636 The possessive forms of *personal pronouns* and of the relative pronoun *who* do not require the apostrophe. These pronouns have their own possessive forms.

I: my, mine	she: her, hers	they: their, theirs
you: your, yours	it: its	who: whose
he: his	we: our, ours	

My copy of the letter arrived last week, so she should háve received *hers* by now. (NOT: her's.)

Each unit comes carefully packed in *its* own carton. (NOT: it's.)

The two products look so much alike that it's [it is] hard to tell *ours* from *theirs.* (NOT: our's from their's.)

CAUTION: Do not confuse personal possessive pronouns with similarly spelled contractions. (See ¶1056e for examples.)

637 Some *indefinite pronouns* have regular possessive forms.

one's choice	the other's claim	anybody's guess
anyone else's job	the others' claim	no one's responsibility
one another's time	each other's claim	someone's chance

For those indefinite pronouns that do not have possessive forms, use an *of* phrase.

Although the children in this group seem very much alike, the needs *of each* are different. (NOT: each's needs.)

Abbreviations

638 To form the singular possessive of an abbreviation, add an apostrophe plus *s.* To form the plural possessive, add an *s* plus an apostrophe to the singular form. (See also ¶639.)

Singular	Plural
Mr. C.'s opinion	the M.D.s' diagnoses
PBS's programming	the Ph.D.s' theses
this HMO's doctors	the CPAs' meeting

Personal, Organizational, and Product Names

639 To form the possessive of a personal or an organizational name that ends with an abbreviation, a number, or a prepositional phrase, add an apostrophe plus *s* at the end of the complete name.

the Winger Co.'s new plant Hyde & Sikh Inc.'s dividends
the Knights of Columbus's drive David Weild II's retirement
United Bank of Arizona's loan rates Walter Frick Jr.'s campaign

NOTE: If *no* extra *s* sound is created when you pronounce the possessive form, add only an apostrophe.

the Gerald Curry Jrs.' yacht

➤ *For the treatment of possessive forms when terms like* Jr. *and* Inc. *are set off by commas, see* ¶¶ *156 and 159.*

640 The names of many organizations and products contain words that could be considered either possessive or descriptive terms.

a. As a rule, use an apostrophe if the term is a singular possessive noun or an irregular plural noun.

McCall's *Harper's Bazaar* *Women's Wear Daily* Children's Hospital
McDonald's Levi's jeans Macy's Reese's Pieces

b. Do not use an apostrophe if the term is a regular plural.

American Bankers Association Chemical Workers Union
Government Employees Insurance Company Investors Trust Company
U.S. Department of Veterans Affairs Underwriters Laboratories Inc.

c. In all cases follow the organization's preference when known.

Investor's Management Services, Inc. Mrs. Paul's frozen foods
International Ladies' Garment Workers' Union Mrs. Fields cookies
Ladies' Home Journal Little Charlies pizza
Reader's Digest Thomas' English muffins
Lay's potato chips Taster's Choice
Folgers coffee Bakers Choice
Diners Club membership M&M's candy
Lands' End catalogs Planters peanuts

d. When adding the sign of the possessive to a phrase that must be italicized or underlined, do not italicize or underline the possessive ending. (See also ¶290c.)

Gone With the Wind's main characters *The Wind in the Willows'* author

Nouns in Apposition

641 Sometimes a noun that ordinarily would be in the possessive is followed by an *appositive*, a closely linked explanatory word or phrase. In such cases add the sign of the possessive to the appositive.

Rockport, *Massachusetts'* beauty attracts many painters. (Note that the comma that normally follows an appositive is omitted after a possessive ending.)

You will faint when you see Paul *the plumber's* bill. (If the noun and the appositive are closely linked as a unit, even the first comma is omitted. See also ¶150.)

NOTE: To avoid an awkward construction, use an *of* phrase instead.

You will need to get the signature *of Mr. Bartel,* the executor.
(**BETTER THAN:** You will need to get Mr. Bartel, *the executor's* signature.)

6

Separate and Joint Possession

642   **a.** To indicate separate possession, add the sign of the possessive to the name of each individual.

> the buyer's and the seller's signatures   the Joneses' and the Browns' houses
>
> **NOTE:** Repeating *the* with each name emphasizes that ownership is separate.

b. If one or both of the individuals' names are replaced by a possessive pronoun, watch out for awkwardness and reword if necessary.

> **AWKWARD:** my and the seller's signatures
> **BETTER:**   the seller's and my signatures
> **OR:**   the seller's signature and mine
>
> **AWKWARD:** their and our houses
> **BETTER:**   their house and ours
>
> **AWKWARD:** your and your husband's passports
> **BETTER:**   the passports for you and your husband

643   **a.** To indicate joint (or common) ownership, add the sign of the possessive to the *final* name alone.

> the Barneses and the Terrys' property line
>
> **NOTE:** In organizational names, follow the company's preference.
>
> Ben & Jerry's ice cream   Kroch's & Brentano's bookstores

b. If one of the owners is identified by a pronoun, make each name and pronoun possessive.

> Karen's and my ski lodge   **BUT:** Karen and Brian's ski lodge

Possessives Standing Alone

644   Sometimes the noun that the possessive modifies is not expressed but merely understood.

> Fred is getting a *master's* [degree] in international economics.
>
> Ask for it at your *grocer's* [store].
>
> Wear your oldest shirt and *Levi's* [jeans]. (The trademark *Levi's* is a singular possessive form.)
>
> We have been invited to dinner at the *Furnesses'* [house].
>
> **BUT:** We always enjoy an evening with the *Furnesses*. (The people themselves are referred to; hence no possessive.)

NOTE: The possessive form must be used in the following construction in order to keep the comparison parallel.

> This year's product line is pulling better than *last year's* [product line].
>
> **NOT:** This year's product line is pulling better than *last year*. (Incorrectly compares *product line* with *last year*.)

Inanimate Possessives

645   As a rule, nouns referring to inanimate things should not be in the possessive. Use an *of* phrase instead.

> the bottom of the barrel (**NOT:** the barrel's bottom)
> the wording of the agreement (**NOT:** the agreement's wording)
> the lower level of the terminal (**NOT:** the terminal's lower level)

646 In many common expressions that refer to time and measurements, however, and in phrases implying personification, the possessive form has come to be accepted usage. (See also ¶817a.)

one day's notice	a dollar's worth	a stone's throw
a nine days' wonder	several dollars' worth	for heaven's sake
an hour's work	two cents' worth	for conscience' sake
two years' progress	at arm's length	(see ¶631b)
the company's assets	New Year's resolutions	the earth's atmosphere
the computer's memory	this morning's news	in today's world

NOTE: Be sure to distinguish possessive expressions like those above from similar wording where no possessive relation is involved.

two weeks' salary   BUT: two weeks ago, two weeks later, two weeks overdue

I bought *five dollars' worth* of chocolate truffles.

BUT: I found *five dollars lying* on the sidewalk.

Possessives Preceding Verbal Nouns

647 **a.** When a noun or a pronoun modifies a *gerund* (the *ing* form of a verb used as a noun), the noun or pronoun should be in the possessive.

What was the point of *our* asking any further questions? (NOT: of us asking.)

NOTE: The use of a possessive form before a gerund can produce a sentence that is grammatically correct but awkward nonetheless. In such cases reword the sentence.

AWKWARD: He wanted to be reassured about his *children's* being given a ride home.

BETTER: He wanted to be reassured that his children would be given a ride home.

b. Not every noun or pronoun preceding the *ing* form of a verb should be in the possessive form. Compare the following pairs of examples:

I heard *you* singing at the party. (Here the emphasis is on *you*, the object of *heard; singing* is a participle that modifies *you*.)

I liked *your* singing at the party. (Here the emphasis is on *singing*, a gerund that is the object of *liked;* the pronoun *your* is in the possessive form because it modifies *singing*.)

Our success in this venture depends on *Allen* acting as the coordinator. (This suggests that the success depends on Allen himself rather than on the role he is playing. Even if Allen's role should change, success seems likely as long as he is associated with the project in some way.)

Our success in this venture depends on *Allen's* acting as the coordinator. (This puts the emphasis squarely on Allen's acting in a certain role. If he ceases to function as the coordinator, the venture may not succeed.)

Possessives in *Of* Phrases

648 **a.** The object of the preposition *of* should not ordinarily be in the possessive form, since the *of* phrase as a whole expresses possession. However, possessives are used in a few idiomatic expressions.

Tony and Fiona are good friends of *ours* as well as our *children's*.

Did you know that Polly and Fred are neighbors of the *Joneses'*?

Bobby Busoni is a business associate of *Gordon's*.

b. Note the difference in meaning in the following phrases:

a statue of Rodin (a statue showing the likeness of the sculptor Rodin)
a statue of Rodin's (a statue created by Rodin)

a controversial view of the President (a view held by someone else)
a controversial view of the President's (a view held by the President)

c. Avoid adding the sign of the possessive to an *of* phrase.

AWKWARD: A *friend of mine's house* burned down last night.

BETTER: The *house of a friend of mine* burned down last night.

AWKWARD: *One of my friends' son* has been named a Rhodes scholar. (NOT: One of my friend's son.)

BETTER: The *son of one of my friends* has been named a Rhodes scholar.

NOTE: Attaching the sign of the possessive to an *of* phrase can sometimes create humorous confusion in addition to awkwardness.

CONFUSING: You must negotiate the purchase price with the owner of the horse's wife.

CLEAR: You must negotiate the purchase price of the horse with the owner's wife.

Possessives Modifying Possessives

649 Avoid attaching a possessive form to another possessive. Change the wording if possible.

AWKWARD: I have not yet seen the *utility company's lawyer's* petition.

BETTER: I have not yet seen the petition of the *utility company's lawyer*.

Possessives in Holidays

650 Possessives in names of holidays are usually singular.

New Year's Eve	Valentine's Day	BUT: Presidents' Day
Lincoln's Birthday	Saint Patrick's Day	April Fools' Day
Mother's Day	Saint Agnes' Eve	All Saints' Day

NOTE: Some holiday names contain a plural form rather than a plural possessive; for example: *Armed Forces Day, Veterans Day, United Nations Day.*

Miscellaneous Expressions

651 A number of common expressions contain possessive forms. Most of these involve singular possessives.

driver's license	proofreaders' mark
traveler's check	lovers' lane
collector's item	workers' compensation (see ¶809a)
visitor's permit	witches' brew
seller's market	women's room
BUT: farmers' market	BUT: woman's rights
finder's fee	states' rights
dog's life	BUT: state's evidence
cat's-paw	citizen's arrest
rabbit's foot	BUT: citizens band
bull's-eye	teacher's pet
monkey's uncle	BUT: teachers college

➤ *For the plural forms of expressions like these, see ¶612d.*

SECTION 7

SPELLING

Section 7 offers three kinds of assistance: ¶¶701–718 present the basic guidelines for correct spelling; ¶719 provides a list of look-alike and sound-alike words for review and fast reference; ¶720 presents a list of troublesome words.

The authority for spelling in this manual is the 1993 printing of *Merriam-Webster's Collegiate Dictionary*, Tenth Edition, and *Webster's Third New International Dictionary*. Whenever two spellings are allowable, only the first form is usually given here.

NOTE: The dictionaries and spell checkers that are built into word processing software may not always agree with the dictionaries that serve as the authority for spelling in this manual. A spell checker will flag any word not listed in its own dictionary or in a supplemental dictionary you create, even if the word is spelled correctly. Reduce the number of "false alarms" by expanding your dictionary to include frequently used terms and names. In addition, always proofread carefully since no spell checker will flag words spelled correctly but used incorrectly. (See ¶1202b.) For example, if you write "Summer is our peek season for swimwear," the spell checker will not question *peek* because it is spelled correctly. You will have to find the error yourself or suffer the embarrassing consequences.

SPELLING GUIDES

When a Final Consonant Is Doubled

701 When a word of one syllable ends in a single consonant (ba*g*) preceded by a single vowel (b*a*g), double the final consonant before a suffix beginning with a vowel (bagg*age*) or before the suffix y (bagg*y*). (See ¶703.)

rub	rub*b*ed	swim	swim*m*er	slip	slip*p*age
glad	glad*d*en	skin	skin*n*y	star	star*r*ing
if	if*f*y	clan	clan*n*ish	bet	bet*t*or

EXCEPTIONS:

yes	yeses	dew	dewy	fix	fixed
bus	buses	bow	bowed	box	boxy

NOTE: When a one-syllable word ends in *y* preceded by a single vowel, do not double the *y* before a suffix beginning with a vowel. (See ¶711.)

pay	payee	joy	joyous	toy	toying
key	keyed	boy	boyish	buy	buyer

702 When a word of more than one syllable ends in a single consonant (refe*r*) preceded by a single vowel (ref*e*r) and the accent falls on the last syllable of the root word (re*fer*), double the final consonant before a suffix beginning with a vowel (referr*ed*). (See ¶704.)

forbid	forbid*d*en	begin	begin*n*ing	infer	inferr*ed*
unclog	unclog*g*ed	unzip	unzip*p*ed	occur	occur*r*ing
control	control*l*er	concur	concur*r*ent	regret	regret*t*able

EXCEPTIONS (SEE ¶711):

display	displaying	obey	obeyed	enjoy	enjoyable

NOTE: When a suffix beginning with a vowel is added, do not double the final consonant if the accent *shifts* from the second syllable.

refer	referred	prefer	preferred	transfer	transferred
BUT: reference		**BUT:** preferable		**BUT:** transferee	

When a Final Consonant Is Not Doubled

7

703 When a word of one syllable ends in a single consonant (ba*d*) preceded by a single vowel (b*a*d), *do not* double the final consonant before a suffix beginning with a *consonant* (bad*ly*).

glad	glad*ness*	star	star*dom*	play	play*ful*
ten	ten*fold*	wit	wit*less*	joy	joy*fully*
ship	ship*ment*	flag	flag*ship*	boy	boy*hood*

704 When a word of more than one syllable ends in a single consonant (bene-fi*t*) preceded by a single vowel (benef*i*t) and the accent *does not* fall on the last syllable of the root word (*bene*fit), *do not* double the final consonant before a suffix beginning with a vowel (benefit*ed*).

catalog	cataloged, cataloging	differ	differed, different
total	totaled, totaling	credit	credited, creditor
cancel	canceled, canceling	profit	profited, profiting
	(**BUT:** cancellation)	benefit	benefited, benefiting
diagram	diagramed, diagraming	borrow	borrowed, borrowing
worship	worshiped, worshiper	index	indexed, indexing

(Continued on page 160.)

EXCEPTIONS:

program	programmed, programming	kidnap	kidnapped, kidnapping
format	formatted, formatting		
overstep	overstepped, overstepping	handicap	handicapped, handicapping
outfit	outfitted, outfitting		

705 When a word of one or more syllables ends in a single consonant (clou*d*, repea*t*) preceded by more than one vowel (cl*ou*d, rep*ea*t), *do not* double the final consonant before any suffix, whether it begins with a consonant (cloud*less*) or a vowel (repeat*ing*).

gain	gain*ful*	bias	bias*ed*	wool	wool*en*
haul	haul*ing*	chief	chief*ly*		(**BUT:** wool*ly*)
dream	dream*y*	riot	riot*ous*	loud	loud*ness*
cheer	cheer*y*	broad	broad*ly*	equal	equal*ed*
deceit	deceit*ful*	poet	poet*ic*	duel	duel*ing*
feud	feud*al*	toil	toil*some*	buoy	buoy*ant*

EXCEPTIONS:

equip	equipped, equipping (**BUT:** equipment)	quit	quitting
quiz	quizzed, quizzing, quizzical	squat	squatter

706 When a word of one or more syllables ends with more than one consonant (wo*rk*, deta*ch*), *do not* double the final consonant before any suffix (work*day*, detach*ed*).

comb	comb*ing*	back	back*ward*	shirr	shirr*ing*
hand	hand*y*	curl	curl*y*	mass	mass*ive*
self	self*ish*	warm	warm*ly*	slant	slant*wise*
swing	swing*ing*	return	return*ed*	jinx	jinx*ed*
wish	wish*ful*	harp	harp*ing*	blitz	blitz*ing*

NOTE: Words ending in *ll* usually retain both consonants before a suffix. However, when adding the suffix *ly*, drop one *l* from the root word. When adding the suffix *less* or *like*, insert a hyphen between the root and the suffix to avoid three *l*'s in a row.

skill	skillful	full	fully	hull	hull-less
install	installment	dull	dully	shell	shell-like

Final Silent *E*

7

707 **a.** Words ending in silent *e* usually *drop* the *e* before a suffix beginning with a vowel.

sale	sal*able*	sense	sens*ible*	propose	propos*ition*
move	mov*able*	argue	argu*ing*	execute	execut*ive*
store	stor*age*	issue	issu*ing*	sincere	sincer*ity*
arrive	arriv*al*	blue	blu*ish*	desire	desir*ous*
accuse	accus*ation*	true	tru*ism*	use	us*ual*

EXCEPTIONS:

agree	agreeing	mile	mileage	dye	dyeing
see	seeing	acre	acreage	hoe	hoeing

b. Words ending in silent *e* usually *drop* the *e* before the suffix *y*.

ease	easy	ice	icy	edge	edgy
chance	chancy	bounce	bouncy	range	rangy

EXCEPTIONS:

cage	cagey	dice	dicey	price	pricey

c. Words ending in *ce* or *ge* usually *retain* the *e* before a suffix beginning with *a* or *o* (so as to preserve the soft sound of the *c* or *g*).

enforce	enforce*able*	courage	courag*eous*
notice	notice*able*	outrage	outrag*eous*
peace	peace*able*	change	change*able*
replace	replace*able*	knowledge	knowledge*able*
service	service*able*	manage	manage*able*
advantage	advantag*eous*	marriage	marriage*able*

EXCEPTIONS:

| pledge | pledgor | | mortgage | mortgagor |

NOTE: Before suffixes beginning with *i*, the *e* is usually dropped.

| force | for*cible* | college | colleg*ial* | age | ag*ing* |
| reduce | redu*cible* | finance | finan*cial* | enforce | enfor*cing* |

EXCEPTIONS:

| singe | singeing | tinge | tingeing | age | ageism |

708 Words ending in silent *e* usually *retain* the *e* before a suffix beginning with a consonant.

hope	hope*ful*	flame	flame*proof*
care	care*less*	trouble	trouble*some*
sincere	sincere*ly*	nine	nine*ty*
manage	manage*ment*	subtle	subtle*ty*
like	like*ness*	edge	edge*wise*

EXCEPTIONS:

wise	wisdom	judge	judgment
awe	awful	acknowledge	acknowledgment
true	truly	subtle	subtly
due	duly	nine	ninth
gentle	gently	whole	wholly

709 Words ending in *ie* change the *ie* to *y* before adding *ing*.

| die dying | tie tying | lie lying |

When Final *Y* Is Changed to *I*

710 Words ending in *y* preceded by a consonant change the *y* to *i* before any suffix except one beginning with *i*.

vary	vari*able*		accompany	accompani*ment*
custody	custodi*al*		happy	happi*ness*
Italy	Itali*an*		fallacy	fallac*ious*
defy	defi*ant*		try	try*ing*
carry	carri*ed*		thirty	thirty*ish*
fly	fli*er*		lobby	lobby*ist*
easy	easi*er*		Kennedy	Kennedy*ite*
heavy	heavi*est*	**BUT:** dry	dry*ly*
fifty	fifti*eth*		shy	shy*ly*
fancy	fanci*ful*		country	country*wide*
likely	likeli*hood*		academy	academ*ic*
ordinary	ordinari*ly*		economy	econom*ist*

711 Words ending in *y* preceded by a vowel usually retain the *y* before any suffix.

okay	okay*ed*	convey	convey*ance*	employ	employ*able*
clay	clay*ey*	obey	obey*ing*	joy	joy*ful*
display	display*ing*	survey	survey*or*	buy	buy*er*

EXCEPTIONS:

| pay | paid | day | daily | gay | gaily |
| lay | laid | say | said | slay | slain |

EI and *IE* Words

712 According to the old rhyme:
Put *i* before *e*
Except after *c*
Or when sounded like *a*
As in *neighbor* and *weigh*.

I Before E

believe	brief	field	niece	**BUT:** either	height
relieve	chief	wield	piece	neither	leisure
belief	thief	yield	anxiety	seize	foreign
relief	friend	view	variety	weird	forfeit

After C

deceive	receive	conceive	perceive	**BUT:** ancient	species
deceit	receipt	conceit	ceiling	science	financier

Sounded Like A

freight	their	eight	vein
weight	heir	sleigh	skein

Words Ending in *ABLE* and *IBLE*

713 **a.** The ending *able* is more commonly used.

admirable	dependable	likable	probable	salable
advisable	doable	movable	reasonable	transferable
changeable	knowledgeable	payable	receivable	valuable

➤ *See ¶707 on dropping or retaining silent* e *before the ending.*

b. However, a number of frequently used words end in *ible*.

compatible	eligible	irrepressible	possible	susceptible
convertible	feasible	irresistible	responsible	terrible
credible	flexible	legible	sensible	visible

Words Ending in *ANT, ANCE, ENT,* and *ENCE*

714 Words ending in *ant, ance, ent,* and *ence* follow no clear-cut pattern. There-fore, consult a dictionary when in doubt.

exist*ent*	persist*ent*	defend*ant*	descend*ant*	occurr*ence*
insist*ent*	resist*ant*	depend*ent*	transcend*ent*	recurr*ence*
assist*ance*	mainten*ance*	relev*ance*	surveill*ance*	intellig*ence*

Words Ending in *IZE, ISE,* and *YZE*

715 **a.** Most words end in *ize*.

apologize	criticize	minimize	realize	summarize
authorize	economize	organize	recognize	vandalize
characterize	emphasize	prize	specialize	visualize

b. A number of common words end in *ise*.

advertise	compromise	enterprise	improvise	supervise
advise	devise	exercise	merchandise	surprise
arise	disguise	franchise	revise	televise

c. Only a few words end with *yze*.

analyze	paralyze	catalyze

7

Words Ending in *CEDE, CEED,* and *SEDE*

716 **a.** Only *one* word ends in *sede: supersede.*

b. Only *three* words end in *ceed: exceed, proceed, succeed.* (Note, however, that derivatives of these three words are spelled with only one *e: excess, procedure, success.*)

c. All other words ending with the sound of "seed" are spelled *cede: precede, secede, recede, concede, accede, intercede.*

Words Ending in *C*

717 Words ending in *c* usually take the letter *k* before a suffix so as to preserve the hard sound of the *c.*

mimic   mimicked, mimicking (**BUT:** mimicry)
panic   panicked, panicking, panicky
picnic   picnicked, picnicking, picnicker
shellac   shellacked, shellacking
traffic   trafficked, trafficking

BUT: arc   arced, arcing

Words With Diacritical Marks

718 Many French words are now considered part of the English language and no longer require italics or underlining (see ¶287). Some of these words still retain diacritical marks from the French form. If you are using software with special character sets, you can access these diacritical marks. Otherwise, you will have to insert them by hand.

a. Acute Accent. An acute accent (´) over the letter *e* (*é*) signifies that the letter is to be pronounced "ay" (as in *may*). Moreover, it signifies that at the end of a word the letter *é* is to be pronounced as a separate syllable.

attaché	crudités	fiancé (m.)	risqué
blasé	détente	fiancée (f.)	sauté
café	éclat	habitué	touché
cliché	élan	née	**BUT:** matinee
communiqué	entrée	outré	melee
consommé	exposé	passé	puree

A few words call for two acute accents:

résumé   protégé   décolleté   déclassé

NOTE: The word *forte* (meaning "one's strong point") does not have an acute accent over the *e.* It should be pronounced as if it were spelled *fort* (not *fortay*).

b. Grave Accent. A few expressions taken from the French retain a grave accent (`` ` ``).

à la carte	vis-à-vis	déjà vu	pièce de résistance
à la mode	pied-à-terre	voilà	cause célèbre

c. The Circumflex. A few phrases derived from the French still retain a circumflex (^).

maître d'hôtel	raison d'être	pâté	papier-mâché
table d'hôte	tête-à-tête	bête noire	**BUT:** fete

WORDS THAT SOUND ALIKE OR LOOK ALIKE

719 The following list contains two types of words: (a) words that are pronounced *exactly alike* though spelled differently, and (b) words that look and sound *somewhat alike*.

NOTE: For additional words that are frequently confused, see Section 11.

accede to comply with; to give consent
exceed to surpass

accent stress in speech or writing
ascent act of rising
assent consent

accept to take; to receive
except (v.) to exclude; (prep.) excluding (see page 263)

access admittance
excess surplus

ad short for *advertisement*
add to join

adapt to adjust
adept proficient
adopt to choose

addenda (see *agenda*)

addition something added
edition one version of a printed work

adherence attachment
adherents followers

adverse harmful; hostile; unfavorable (see page 254)
averse opposed (to)

advice (n.) information; recommendation
advise (v.) to recommend to give counsel

affect to influence; to change; to assume (see page 254)
effect (n.) result; impression; (v.) to bring about

agenda list of things to be done
addenda additional items

aid (n.) a form of help; (v.) to help
aide an assistant

ail to be in ill health
ale a drink much like beer

air atmosphere
heir one who inherits

aisle (see *isle*)

allot to assign or distribute a share of something (see page 253)
a lot a great deal; NOT: alot

allowed permitted
aloud audibly

allusion an indirect reference
illusion an unreal vision; misapprehension
delusion a false belief
elusion adroit escape

almost nearly (see page 255)
all most all very much

already previously (see page 255)
all ready all prepared

altar part of a church
alter to change

alternate (n.) substitute; (v.) to take turns
alternative (n.) one of several things from which to choose

altogether entirely (see page 255)
all together everyone in a group

always at all times (see page 255)
all ways all means or methods

annual yearly
annul to cancel

ante- a prefix meaning "before"
anti- a prefix meaning "against"

antecedence priority
antecedents preceding things; ancestors

anyone anybody (see ¶1010)
any one any one person in a group

anyway in any case (see page 256)
any way any method

apportion (see *portion*)

appraise to set a value on (see page 256)
apprise to inform

arc something arched or curved
ark a ship; a place of protection and safety

are (see *hour*)

area surface; extent
aria a melody
arrears that which is due but unpaid

arrange to put in order
arraign to call into court

ascent (see *accent*)

assay to test, as an ore or a chemical
essay (n.) a treatise; (v.) to attempt

assent (see *accent*)

assistance help
assistants those who help

assure (see *ensure*)

ate past tense of *eat*
eight a number

attain to gain; to achieve
attend to be present at

attendance presence
attendants escorts; followers; companions; associates

aught (see *ought*)

averse (see *adverse*)

awhile (adv.) for a short time (see page 257)
a while (phrase) a short period of time

bail (n.) security; the handle of a pail; (v.) to dip water
bale a bundle

baloney nonsense
bologna smoked sausage

bare (adj.) naked; empty; (v.) to expose
bear (n.) an animal; (v.) to carry; to endure; to produce

base (n.) foundation; (adj.) mean
bass a fish (pronounced like *mass*); lower notes in music (pronounced like *base*)

bases plural of *base* and of *basis*
basis foundation

bazaar (see *bizarre*)

beat (n.) throb; tempo; (v.) to strike
beet a vegetable

berry a fruit
bury to submerge; to cover over

berth a bed
birth being born

beside by the side of; separate from (see page 257)
besides in addition to; also

bibliography list of writings pertaining to a given subject or author
biography written history of a person's life

billed charged
build to construct

birth (see *berth*)

bizarre fantastic; extravagantly odd
bazaar a place for selling goods

blew past tense of *blow*
blue a color

block (n.) a solid piece of material; (v.) to obstruct
bloc an interest group pursuing certain political or economic goals

board a piece of wood; an organized group; meals
bored penetrated; wearied

boarder one who pays for meals and often for lodging as well
border edge

bolder more daring
boulder a large rock

born brought into life
borne carried; endured

boy a male child
buoy a float

brake (n.) a retarding device; (v.) to retard
break (n.) an opening; a fracture; (v.) to shatter; to divide

bread food
bred brought up

breath respiration
breathe (v.) to inhale and exhale
breadth width

bridal concerning the bride or the wedding
bridle (n.) means of controlling a horse; (v.) to take offense

broach to open; to introduce

brooch ornamental clasp

build (see *billed*)

bullion uncoined gold or silver
bouillon broth

buoy (see *boy*)

bury (see *berry*)

cache (see *cash*)

calendar a record of time
calender a machine used in finishing paper and cloth
colander a strainer

callous (adj.) hardened
callus (n.) a hardened surface

7

cannot usual form (meaning "to be unable")
can not two words in the phrase *can not only* (where *can* means "to be able")

canvas (n.) a coarse cloth
canvass (v.) to solicit

capital (n.) city serving as the seat of government; a principal sum of money; a large-sized letter; (adj.) chief; foremost; punishable by death
capitol the building in which a state legislative body meets
Capitol the building in which the U.S. Congress meets

carton a pasteboard box
cartoon a caricature

cash ready money
cache a hiding place

casual incidental
causal causing

cease to stop
seize to grasp

cede to grant; to give up
seed that from which anything is grown

ceiling top of a room; any overhanging area
sealing closing

cell (see *sell*)

cellar (see *seller*)

census statistics of population
senses mental faculties

cent (see *scent*)

cereal any grain food
serial arranged in a series

cession a yielding up
session the sitting of a court or other body

choose to select
chose did choose (past tense of *choose*)
chews masticates

chord combination of musical tones
cord string or rope

chute (see *shoot*)

cite (v.) to quote; to summon
sight a view; vision
site a place

click a slight, sharp noise
clique an exclusive group
cliché a trite phrase

climatic referring to climate
climactic referring to a climax

clothes garments
cloths fabrics
close (n.) the end; (v.) to shut

coarse rough; common
course direction; action; a way; part of a meal

colander (see *calendar*)

collision a clashing
collusion a scheme to defraud

coma an unconscious state
comma a mark of punctuation

command (n.) an order; (v.) to order
commend to praise; to entrust

commence (v.) to begin
comments (n.) remarks

complement something that completes
compliment (n.) a flattering remark; (v.) to praise (see page 259)

comprehensible understandable
comprehensive extensive

confidant a friend; an adviser (feminine form: *confidante*)
confident sure; positive

confidently certainly; positively
confidentially privately

conscience (n.) the sense of right and wrong
conscious (adj.) cognizant; sensible; aware

conservation preservation
conversation a talk

consul (see *council*)

consular (see *councillor*)

continual occurring steadily but with occasional breaks
continuous uninterrupted; unbroken

cooperation working together
corporation a form of business organization

cord (see *chord*)

core the central part; the heart
corps a group of persons with a common activity

correspondence letters
correspondents those who write letters; journalists
corespondents certain parties in divorce suits

costume dress
custom habit

7

council an assembly

counsel (n.) an attorney; advice; (v.) to give advice

consul a foreign representative

councillor a member of a council

counselor one who advises

consular (adj.) of a consul

course (see *coarse*)

courtesy a favor; politeness

curtesy a husband's life interest in the lands of his deceased wife

curtsy a gesture of respect

credible believable

creditable meritorious; deserving of praise

credulous ready to believe

critic one who makes judgments

critique (n.) a critical assessment; (v.) to judge; to criticize

cue a hint

queue a line of people

currant a berry

current (adj.) belonging to the present; (n.) a flow of water or electricity

curser one who curses

cursor a symbol used as a pointer on a computer screen

custom (see *costume*)

dairy source of milk products

diary daily record

deceased dead

diseased sick

decent proper; right

descent going down

dissent disagreement

decree a law

degree a grade; a step

deduce to infer

deduct to subtract

defer to put off

differ to disagree

deference respect; regard for another's wishes

difference dissimilarity; controversy

delusion (see *allusion*)

deposition a formal written statement

disposition temper; disposal

depraved morally debased

deprived taken away from

deprecate to disapprove

depreciate to lessen in estimated value

desert (n.) barren land; (plural) a deserved reward; (v.) to abandon

dessert the last course of a meal

desolate lonely; sad

dissolute loose in morals

detract to take away from

distract to divert the attention of

device (n.) a contrivance

devise (v.) to plan; to convey real estate by will

dew (see *do*)

diary (see *dairy*)

die (n.) mold; (v.) to cease living

dye (n.) that which changes the color of; (v.) to change the color of

differ (see *defer*)

difference (see *deference*)

disapprove to withhold approval

disprove to prove the falsity of

disassemble to take apart

dissemble to disguise; to feign

disburse to pay out

disperse to scatter

discreet prudent

discrete distinct; separate

diseased (see *deceased*)

disinterested unbiased; impartial

uninterested bored; unconcerned

disposition (see *deposition*)

disprove (see *disapprove*)

dissemble (see *disassemble*)

dissent (see *decent*)

dissolute (see *desolate*)

distract (see *detract*)

divers (adj.) various or sundry; (n.) plural of *diver*

diverse different

do to perform

due owing

dew moisture

done finished

dun to demand payment

dose a measured quantity

doze to sleep lightly

dual double

duel a combat

due (see *do*)

dye (see *die*)

7

dying near death
dyeing changing the color of

edition (see *addition*)

effect (see *affect*)

eight (see *ate*)

elapse (see *lapse*)

elicit to draw forth
illicit unlawful

eligible qualified
illegible unreadable

elusion (see *allusion*)

elusive baffling; hard to catch
illusive misleading; unreal

emerge to rise out of
immerge to plunge into

emigrate to go away from a country
immigrate to come into a country

eminent well-known; prominent
imminent threatening; impending
emanate to originate from; to come out of

en route (see *root*)

ensure to make certain (see page 261)
insure to protect against loss
assure to give confidence to someone

envelop (v.) to cover; to wrap
envelope (n.) a wrapper for a letter

equable even; tranquil
equitable just; right

erasable capable of being erased
irascible quick-tempered

especially to an exceptional degree
specially particularly, as opposed to generally

essay (see *assay*)

everyday ordinary (see page 262)
every day each day

everyone each one (see ¶1010)
every one each one in a group

ewe (see *you*)

exalt to glorify
exult to be joyful

exceed (see *accede*)

except (see *accept*)

excess (see *access*)

expand to increase in size
expend to spend

expansive capable of being extended
expensive costly

expatiate to enlarge on
expiate to atone for

explicit clearly expressed
implicit implied

extant still existing
extent measure

exult (see *exalt*)

facet aspect
faucet a tap

facetious witty
factitious artificial
fictitious imaginary

facilitate to make easy
felicitate to congratulate

facility ease
felicity joy

faint (adj.) dim; weak; (v.) to pass out
feint a trick; a deceptive move

fair (adj.) favorable; just; (n.) an exhibit
fare (n.) cost of travel; food; (v.) to go forth

farther at a greater distance, referring to *actual* distance (see page 263)
further to a greater extent or degree, referring to *figurative* distance; moreover; in addition

faucet (see *facet*)

faze to disturb
phase a stage in development

feet plural of *foot*
feat an act of skill or strength

fictitious (see *facetious*)

finale the end
finally at the end
finely in a fine manner

fineness delicacy
finesse tact

fir a tree
fur skin of an animal

fiscal (see *physical*)

flair aptitude
flare a light; a signal

flaunt to display showily
flout to treat with contempt

flew did fly
flue a chimney
flu short for *influenza*

flounder to move clumsily
founder to collapse; to sink; one who establishes something

flour ground meal
flower blossom

for a preposition
fore first; preceding; the front
four numeral

forbear to bear with
forebear an ancestor

forgo to relinquish; to let pass
forego to go before

formally in a formal manner
formerly before

fort a fortified place
forte (n.) area where one excels; (adv.) loud (musical direction)

forth away; forward
fourth next after third

forward ahead
foreword preface

foul unfavorable; unclean
fowl a bird

founder (see *flounder*)

four (see *for*)

fur (see *fir*)

further (see *farther*)

genius talent
genus a classification in botany or zoology

gibe (n.) a sarcastic remark; (v.) to scoff at
jibe to agree

grate (n.) a frame of bars (as in a fireplace); (v.) to scrape; to irritate
great large; magnificent

guessed past tense of *guess*
guest visitor

hail (n.) a shower of icy pellets; (v.) to call out to
hale (adj.) healthy; (v.) to compel to go

hall a corridor
haul to drag

heal to cure
heel part of a foot or a shoe

healthful promoting health (e.g., a *healthful* food)
healthy being in good health (e.g., a *healthy* person)

hear to perceive by ear
here in this place

heard past tense of *hear*
herd a group of animals

heir (see *air*)

higher at a greater height
hire to employ; to use someone's services

holy sacred
holey full of holes
wholly entirely
holly a tree

hour sixty minutes
our belonging to us
are a form of *to be* (as in *we are, you are, they are*)

human pertaining to humanity
humane kindly

hypercritical overcritical
hypocritical pretending virtue

ideal a standard of perfection
idle unoccupied; without worth
idol object of worship
idyll a description of rural life

illegible (see *eligible*)

illicit (see *elicit*)

illusion (see *allusion*)

illusive (see *elusive*)

imitate to resemble; to mimic
intimate (adj.) innermost; familiar; (v.) to hint; to make known

immerge (see *emerge*)

immigrate (see *emigrate*)

imminent (see *eminent*)

implicit (see *explicit*)

imply to suggest (see page 265)
infer to deduce; to guess; to conclude

inane senseless
insane of unsound mind

incidence range of occurrence
incidents occurrences; happenings

incinerate to burn
insinuate to imply

incite (v.) to arouse
insight (n.) understanding

indict to charge with a crime
indite to compose; to write

indifferent without interest (see page 265)
in different in other

indigenous native
indigent needy
indignant angry

indirect not direct (see page 265)
in direct *in* (preposition) + *direct* (adjective)

7

infer (see *imply*)

ingenious clever
ingenuous naive

insane (see *inane*)

insight (see *incite*)

insinuate (see *incinerate*)

insoluble incapable of being dissolved
insolvable not explainable
insolvent unable to pay debts

instants short periods of time
instance an example

insure (see *ensure*)

intelligent possessed of understanding
intelligible understandable

intense acute; strong
intents aims

interstate between states
intrastate within one state
intestate dying without a will

intimate (see *imitate*)

into, in to (see page 265)

irascible (see *erasable*)

isle island
aisle passage between rows

its possessive form of *it*
it's contraction of *it is* or *it has* (see ¶1056e)

jibe (see *gibe*)

key a means of gaining entrance or under-standing
quay a wharf (also pro-nounced *key*)

knew understood
new fresh; novel

know to understand
no not any

lapse to become void
elapse to pass
relapse to slip back into a former condition

last final (see page 266)
latest most recent

later more recent; after a time
latter second in a series of two (see page 266)

lath a strip of wood
lathe a wood-turning machine

lay to place (see page 267)
lie (n.) a falsehood; (v.) to recline; to tell an untruth
lye a strong alkaline solution

lead (n.) heavy metal (pronounced like *led*); (v.) to guide (pro-nounced *leed*)
led guided (past tense of *to lead*)

lean (adj.) thin; (v.) to incline
lien a legal claim

leased rented
least smallest

legislator a lawmaker
legislature a body of law-makers

lend to allow the use of temporarily
loan (n.) something lent; (v.) to lend
lone solitary

lessee a tenant
lesser of smaller size
lessor one who gives a lease

lessen (v.) to make smaller
lesson (n.) an exercise assigned for study

levee embankment of a river
levy (v.) to raise a collec-tion of money; (n.) the amount that is thus collected

liable responsible
libel defamatory statement

lie (see *lay*)

lien (see *lean*)

lightening making lighter
lightning accompaniment of thunder
lighting illumination

loan, lone (see *lend*)

loath (adj.) reluctant
loathe (v.) to detest

local (adj.) pertaining to a particular place
locale (n.) a particular place

loose (adj.) not bound; (v.) to release
lose (v.) to suffer the loss of; to part with unin-tentionally
loss something lost

lye (see *lay*)

made constructed
maid a servant

magnificent having splendor
munificent unusually generous

mail correspondence
male masculine

main (adj.) chief; (n.) a conduit
mane long hair on the neck of certain animals

manner a way of acting (as in "to the manner born")
manor an estate

marital pertaining to marriage
martial military
marshal (n.) an official; (v.) to arrange

maybe perhaps (see page 268)
may be a verb consisting of two words

mean (adj.) unpleasant; (n.) the midpoint; (v.) to intend
mien appearance

meat flesh of animals
meet (v.) to join; (adj.) proper
mete to measure

medal a badge of honor
meddle to interfere
metal a mineral
mettle courage; spirit

mien (see *mean*)

miner a worker in a mine
minor (adj.) lesser, as in size, extent, or importance; (n.) a person who is under legal age

mist haze
missed failed to do

mite a tiny particle
might (n.) force; (v.) past tense of *may*

mood disposition
mode fashion; method

moral virtuous
morale spirit

morality virtue
mortality death rate

morning before noon
mourning grief

munificent (see *magnificent*)

naught (see *ought*)

new (see *knew*)

no (see *know*)

nobody no one (see page 268)
no body no group

none not one (see ¶1013)
no one nobody (see ¶1010)

oculist an ophthalmologist or an optometrist
ophthalmologist a doctor who treats eyes
optician one who makes or sells eyeglasses
optometrist one who measures vision

official authorized
officious overbold in offering services

one a single thing
won did win

ordinance a local law
ordnance arms; munitions

ought should
aught anything; all
naught nothing; zero

our (see *hour*)

overdo to do too much
overdue past due

packed crowded
pact an agreement

pail a bucket
pale (adj.) light-colored; (n.) an enclosure

pain suffering
pane window glass

pair two of a kind
pare to peel
pear a fruit

parameter a quantity with an assigned value; a constant
perimeter the outer boundary

partition division
petition prayer; a formal written request

partly in part
partially to some degree

past (n.) time gone by; (adj., adv., or prep.) gone by
passed moved along; transferred (past tense of *pass*)

patience composure; endurance
patients sick persons

peace calmness
piece a portion

peak the top
peek to look slyly at
pique (n.) resentment; (v.) to offend; to arouse
piqué cotton fabric

peal to ring out
peel (n.) the rind; (v.) to strip off

pear (see *pair*)

pedal (adj.) pertaining to the foot; (n.) a treadle
peddle to hawk; to sell

peek (see *peak*)

peer (n.) one of equal rank or age; (v.) to look steadily
pier a wharf

perfect without fault
prefect an official

perimeter (see *parameter*)

perpetrate to be guilty of
perpetuate to make perpetual

perquisite privilege
prerequisite a preliminary requirement

7

persecute to oppress
prosecute to sue

personal private
personnel the staff

perspective a view in correct proportion
prospective anticipated

peruse to read
pursue to chase

petition (see *partition*)

phase (see *faze*)

physic a medicine
physique bodily structure
psychic (adj.) pertaining to the mind or spirit; (n.) a medium

physical relating to the body
fiscal pertaining to finance (see page 263)
psychical mental

piece (see *peace*)

pier (see *peer*)

pique, piqué (see *peak*)

plain (adj.) undecorated; (n.) prairie land
plane (n.) a level surface, an airplane; (v.) to make level

plaintiff party in a lawsuit
plaintive mournful

pleas plural of *plea*
please to be agreeable

pole a long, slender piece of wood or metal
poll (n.) the casting of votes by a body of persons; (v.) to register the votes of

poor (adj.) inadequate; (n.) the needy
pore to study; to gaze intently
pour to flow

populace the common people; the masses
populous thickly settled

portend (see *pretend*)

portion a part
proportion a ratio of parts
apportion to allot

practicable workable; feasible
practical useful

pray to beseech
prey a captured victim

precede to go before
proceed to advance

precedence priority
precedents established rules

prefect (see *perfect*)

preposition a part of speech
proposition an offer

prerequisite (see *perquisite*)

prescribe to designate
proscribe to outlaw

presence bearing; being present
presents gifts

presentiment a foreboding
presentment a proposal

pretend to make believe
portend to foreshadow

principal (adj.) chief; leading; (n.) a capital sum of money that draws interest; chief official of a school
principle a general truth; a rule; integrity

proceed (see *precede*)

profit gain
prophet one who forecasts

prophecy a prediction
prophesy to foretell

propose to suggest
purpose intention

proposition (see *preposition*)

proscribe (see *prescribe*)

prosecute (see *persecute*)

prospective (see *perspective*)

psychic (see *physic*)

purpose (see *propose*)

pursue (see *peruse*)

quay (see *key*)

queue (see *cue*)

quiet calm; not noisy
quite entirely; wholly
quit to stop

rain falling water
rein part of a bridle; a curb
reign (n.) the term of a ruler's power; (v.) to rule

raise to lift something (see page 270)
raze to destroy
rays beams

rap to knock
wrap (n.) a garment; (v.) to enclose

read to perform the act of reading
reed a plant; a musical instrument
red a color

real actual
reel (n.) a spool; a dance; (v.) to whirl

reality actuality
realty real estate

receipt an acknowledgment of a thing received

recipe a formula for mixing ingredients

recent (adj.) relating to a time not long past
resent (v.) to feel hurt by

reference that which refers to something
reverence profound respect

reign, rein (see *rain*)

relapse (see *lapse*)

residence a house
residents persons who reside in a place

respectably in a manner worthy of respect
respectfully in a courteous manner
respectively in the order indicated

right (adj.) correct; (n.) a privilege
rite a ceremony
wright a worker; a maker (used as a combining form, as in *playwright*)
write to inscribe

role a part in a play
roll (n.) a list; a type of bread; (v.) to revolve

root (n.) underground part of a plant; (v.) to implant firmly
route (n.) an established course of travel; (v.) to send by a certain route
en route on or along the way
rout (n.) confused flight; (v.) to defeat

rote repetition
wrote did write

sail (n.) part of a ship's rigging; (v.) to travel by water
sale the act of selling

scene a setting; an exhibition of strong feeling
seen past participle of *to see*

scent odor
sent did send
cent penny
sense meaning

sealing (see *ceiling*)

seam a line of junction
seem to appear

seed (see *cede*)

seize (see *cease*)

sell to transfer for a price
cell a small compartment

seller one who sells
cellar an underground room

sense, sent (see *scent*)

senses (see *census*)

serge a kind of cloth
surge (n.) a billow; (v.) to rise suddenly

serial (see *cereal*)

serve to help (see page 271)
service to keep in good repair

session (see *cession*)

sew (see *so*)

shear to cut; to trim
sheer transparent; unqualified, utter

shoot to fire
chute a slide

shown displayed; revealed; past participle of *show*
shone gave off light; did shine

sight, site (see *cite*)

simple plain; uncomplicated
simplistic oversimplified; falsely simple

sleight dexterity, as in "sleight of hand"
slight (adj.) slender; scanty; (v.) to make light of

so therefore
sew to stitch
sow to scatter seed

soar (see *sore*)

soared did fly
sword weapon

sole one and only
soul the immortal spirit

soluble having the ability to dissolve in a liquid
solvable capable of being solved or explained

some a part of
sum a total

someone somebody (see ¶1010)
some one some person in a group

sometime at some unspecified time (see page 273)
some time a period of time
sometimes now and then

son male child
sun the earth's source of light and heat

sore painful
soar to fly

7

soul (see *sole*)

sow (see *so*)

spacious having ample room

specious outwardly correct but inwardly false

specially (see *especially*)

staid grave; sedate

stayed past tense and past participle of *to stay*

stair a step

stare to look at

stake (n.) a pointed stick; the prize in a contest; (v.) to wager

steak a slice of meat or fish

stationary fixed

stationery writing materials

statue a carved or molded figure

stature height

statute a law

steal to take unlawfully

steel a form of iron

straight not crooked; directly

strait a water passageway; (plural) a distressing situation

suit (n.) a legal action; clothing; (v.) to please

suite a group of things forming a unit

sweet having an agreeable taste; pleasing

sum (see *some*)

sun (see *son*)

superintendence management

superintendents supervisors

surge (see *serge*)

sweet (see *suit*)

sword (see *soared*)

tack (n.) direction; (v.) to change direction (see page 274)

tact considerate way of behaving so as to avoid offending others

tail the end

tale a story

tare allowance for weight

tear (n.) a rent or rip (pronounced like *tare*); a secretion from the eye (pronounced like *tier*); (v.) to rip

tier a row or layer

taught did teach

taut tight; tense

team a group

teem to abound

tenant one who rents property

tenet a principle

than conjunction of comparison (see page 274)

then (adv.) at that time

their belonging to them (see ¶1056e)

there in that place

they're contraction of *they are*

theirs possessive form of *they*, used without a following noun (see ¶1056e)

there's contraction of *there is* or *there has*

therefor for that thing

therefore consequently

throes a painful struggle

throws hurls; flings

through by means of; from beginning to end; because of

threw did throw

thorough carried through to completion

tier (see *tare*)

to (prep.) toward

too (adv.) more than enough; also

two one plus one

tortuous winding; twisty; devious

torturous cruelly painful

track a trail

tract a treatise; a piece of land

trial examination; an experiment; hardship

trail a path

undo to open; to render ineffective

undue improper; excessive

uninterested (see *disinterested*)

urban pertaining to the city

urbane polished; suave

vain proud; conceited; futile

vane a weathercock

vein a blood vessel; a bed of mineral materials

vale a valley

veil a concealing cover or cloth

vendee purchaser

vendor seller

veracious truthful

voracious greedy

veracity truthfulness

voracity ravenousness; greediness

7

vice wickedness; a prefix used with nouns to designate titles of office (see ¶808b)
vise a clamp

waist part of the body
waste (n.) needless destruction; useless consumption; (v.) to expend uselessly

wait to stay
weight heaviness

waive (v.) to give up
wave (n.) a billow; a gesture; (v.) to swing back and forth

waiver the giving up of a claim
waver to hesitate

want (n.) a need; (v.) to lack; to desire
wont a custom (pronounced like *want*)
won't contraction of *will not*

ware goods
wear to have on
were form of *to be*
where at the place in which

wave (see *waive*)

way direction; distance; manner
weigh to find the weight

weak not strong
week seven days

weather (n.) state of the atmosphere; (v.) to come through safely
whether if (see page 265)

weight (see *wait*)

whoever anyone who
who ever *two words* (see page 276)

wholly (see *holy*)

whose possessive of *who*
who's contraction of *who is* or *has* (see ¶1063)

won (see *one*)

wont, won't (see *want*)

wood lumber
would an auxiliary verb form (as in *they would like some*)

wrap (see *rap*)

wright, write (see *right*)

wrote (see *rote*)

yoke a crosspiece that holds two things together; an oppressive constraint
yolk the yellow part of an egg

you second-person pronoun
yew an evergreen tree or bush
ewe a female sheep

your belonging to *you* (see ¶1056e)
you're contraction of *you are*

TROUBLESOME WORDS

720   The following list presents a selection of words that business writers often misspell or stop and puzzle over. In some cases the difficulty results from the inability to apply an established rule; for such words, references to the rules are given. In many other instances, however, errors result from the peculiar spelling of the words themselves; in such cases the only remedy is to master the correct spelling of such words on an individual basis.

NOTE: For troublesome words that sound alike or look alike, see ¶719 and Section 11. For troublesome compound words, see Section 8.

abscess
absence
accessory
accidentally (see page 253)
accommodate
accompanying
achievement
acknowledgment (see ¶708)
acquaintance
acquiesce

acquire
acquisition
across
adjacent
advantageous (see ¶707)
adviser
aegis
affidavit
aggressive
aging (see ¶707)

Albuquerque
algorithm
alignment
all right (see page 255)
alleged
already (see page 255)
amateur
amortize (see ¶715a)
analogous
analysis

analyze (see ¶715c)
anomalous
answer
antecedent
appall
apparatus
architect
argument (see ¶708)
assistance (see ¶714)
asthma
attendance
attorney
autumn
auxiliary
bachelor
bankruptcy
bargain
basically
believe (see ¶712)
beneficiary
benefited (see ¶704)
benign
Berkeley (California)
biased (see ¶705)
biscuit
bizarre
boundary
breakfast
brochure
buoyant
bureau
business
busy
calendar
caliber
calorie
campaign
canceled (see ¶704)
cancellation (see ¶704)
candor
Caribbean
carriage
catalog
category
ceiling
cemetery
census
chaise longue (see ¶612a)
changeable (see ¶707)
chronological
Cincinnati
circuit
coincidence
collateral
colonel
colossal
column
comparison
concede (see ¶716c)
conceive

condemn
Connecticut
connoisseur
conscience
conscientious
conscious
consensus
corduroy
correspondent
courtesy
debt
debtor
deductible
de-emphasize
defendant (see ¶714)
defense
deficit
definite
dependent (see ¶714)
Des Moines
descendant (see ¶714)
describe
desperately
detrimental
develop
dictionary
dilemma
disappear
disappoint
disastrous
dissatisfied
dissimilar
doctrinaire
dossier
double
ecstasy
eighth
either
eliminate
embarrass
emphasize
empty
entrepreneur
enumerate
environment
erroneous
escrow
exaggerate
exceed (see ¶716b)
excellent
exercise
exhaustible
exhibition
exhilarate
exonerate
exorbitant
extension
extraordinary
eyeing
facsimile

familiar
fantasy
fascinating
fatigue
February
fiery
financier
fluorescent
forbade
foreign (see ¶712)
foresee
forfeit
forty
fourteen
fourth
freight
fulfill
gauge
glamorous
glamour
goodwill
government
grammar
grateful
gray
grievous
gruesome (see ¶708)
guarantee
guardian
handkerchief
harass
height (see ¶712)
hemorrhage
heterogeneous
hindrance
hors d'oeuvre
hygiene
hypocrisy
impasse
inasmuch as
incidentally
indict
indispensable
innocuous
innuendo
inoculate
interim
intern
irrelevant (see ¶714)
itinerary
jeopardy
judgment (see ¶708)
khaki
labeled (see ¶704)
laboratory
league
ledger
leisure
liable
liaison

7

library
license
lien
lieutenant
lightning
liquefy
literature
maintenance
maneuver
marriage
marshaled
martyr
medieval
mediocre
memento
mileage (see ¶707)
milieu
millennium
millionaire
miniature
minuscule
miscellaneous
mischievous
misspell
mnemonic
mortgage
motor
necessary
negotiate
neighbor
neither (see ¶712)
nickel
niece (see ¶712)
ninety
ninth
noticeable (see ¶707)
nuclear
obsolescent
offense
omelet
omission
ophthalmology
pamphlet
panicky (see ¶717)
paradigm
parallel
parliament
pastime
patience
permissible (see ¶713b)
perseverance
persistent
persuade
phase
phenomenal
Philippines
phony
physician
picnicking (see ¶717)
Pittsburgh

plagiarism
potato, potatoes
practically
practice
prairie
preceding (see ¶716c)
preferable (see ¶702)
prerogative
presumptuous
pretense
privilege
procedure (see ¶716b)
proceed (see ¶716b)
programmed (see ¶704)
prohibition
pronunciation
protégé
psalm
pseudonym
psychiatric
psychological
publicly
pursue
quantity
questionnaire
queue
rarefy
receipt
receive (see ¶712)
recommend
reconnaissance
recruit
reinforce
relevant (see ¶714)
renaissance
rendezvous
renowned
rescind
resistance (see ¶714)
restaurant
résumé (see ¶718)
rhapsody
rhetorical
rhyme
rhythm
rhythmic
sacrilegious
salable (see ¶707)
San Francisco
sandwich
satellite
schedule
scissors
secretary
seize (see ¶712)
separate
sergeant
siege (see ¶712)
sieve
similar

simultaneous
sincerely (see ¶708)
skeptic
skillful
souvenir
specimen
sponsor
stratagem
strength
subpoena
subtlety
subtly
succeed
summary
superintendent
supersede (see ¶716a)
surgeon
surprise
surreptitious
surveillance (see ¶714)
synagogue
tariff
taxiing
technique
temperament
temperature
tempt
theater
their (see ¶712)
theory
thoroughly
threshold
through
totaled (see ¶704)
tragedy
traveler (see ¶704)
Tuesday
unctuous
unique
unmanageable (see ¶707)
unwieldy (see ¶712)
usage (see ¶707)
vaccinate
vacillate
vacuum
vegetable
victim
vinyl
volume
warrant
Wednesday
weird (see ¶712)
whether
whiskey
wholly
wield (see ¶712)
withhold
woeful
woolly (see ¶705)
yield (see ¶712)

7

SECTION 8

COMPOUND WORDS

Some compound words are written as solid words, some are written as separate words, and some are hyphenated. As in other areas of style, authorities do not agree on the rules. Moreover, style is continually changing: many words that used to be hyphenated are now written solid or as separate words. The only complete guide is an up-to-date dictionary. However, a careful reading of the following rules will save you many a trip to the dictionary.

NOTE: The spellings in this section agree with those in the 1993 printing of *Merriam-Webster's Collegiate Dictionary,* Tenth Edition, and *Webster's Third New International Dictionary* unless otherwise indicated.

COMPOUND NOUNS

801 Compound nouns follow no regular pattern. Some are written solid, some are spaced, and some are hyphenated.

airfreight	air bag	air-conditioning
checklist	check mark	check-in
closeout	close shave	close-up
crossroad	cross section	cross-reference
daytime	day care	day-tripper
doubleheader	double take	double-dipper
eyewitness	eye shadow	eye-opener
freelance	free fall	free-marketer
goodwill	good sense	good-bye
halftime	half hour	half-truth
jobholder	job action	job-hopper
lightbulb	light meter	light-year
moneylender	money market	money-grubber
placeholder	place mat	place-name
pocketbook	pocket money	pocket-handkerchief
showbiz	show business	show-off
sickroom	sick pay	sick-out
timetable	time deposit	time-saver
trademark	trade name	trade-off
bondholder	bond paper	
bookstore	book review	
bylaw	by-product	
cashbook	cash flow	
handbook	hand truck	
homeowner	home port	
lifestyle	life span	
masterpiece	master plan	
paperwork	paper clip	
payroll	pay dirt	
salespeople	sales tax	
schoolteacher	school board	
standby	stand-in	
voiceprint	voice-over	
wageworker	wage earner	
workstation	work stoppage	

8

NOTE: To be sure of the spelling of a compound noun, check a dictionary. If the noun is not listed, treat the components as separate words. For the spelling of compounds in company names, check letterheads for possible variations. (Compare, for example, *United Airlines* with *Delta Air Lines.*)

802 Some solid and hyphenated compound nouns closely resemble verb phrases. Be sure, however, to treat the elements in a verb phrase as separate words.

Nouns	Verb Phrases
a *breakdown* in communications	when communications *break down*
a thorough *follow-up* of the report	to *follow up* on your recommendation
operate a *drive-in*	*drive in* to your dealer's
a high school *dropout*	don't *drop out* of high school
at the time of *takeoff*	planes cannot *take off* or land
when they give us a *go-ahead*	we can *go ahead* with the plan
come to a *standstill*	we can't *stand still*
let's have a *run-through*	let's *run through* the plan
plan a *get-together*	plan to *get together*
they have the *know-how*	they *know how* to handle it
expect a *turnaround* in sales	once our sales *turn around*
we have to make a *getaway*	we have to *get away*
to attempt a *takeover* of their firm	to attempt to *take over* their firm
I was a *standby* on Flight 968A	we can't *stand by* and do nothing
Paul's speech was merely a *put-on*	your requisition was *put on* hold
protect data with regular *backups*	always *back up* the data in the file
after you complete the *log-on*	after you *log on* to the program
devise another plan as a *fallback*	we can always *fall back* on Plan B
need to reduce staff *turnover*	need to *turn over* a new leaf

803 **a.** *Up* **Words.** Compound nouns ending in *up* are either solid or hyphenated. For example:

backup	linkup	call-up	mock-up
blowup	makeup	catch-up	runner-up
breakup	markup	close-up	send-up
brushup	pasteup	cover-up	shake-up
buildup	pileup	flare-up	sign-up
checkup	roundup	follow-up	start-up
cleanup	setup	grown-ups	tie-up
holdup	slipup	hang-up	toss-up
hookup	speedup	higher-ups	touch-up
letup	warmup*	jam-up	wrap-up
lineup	windup	mix-up	write-up

b. *Down* **Words.** Most compound nouns ending in *down* are solid. For example:

breakdown	lowdown	shakedown	**BUT:** dressing-down
closedown	markdown	showdown	put-down
comedown	meltdown	shutdown	sit-down
countdown	phasedown	slowdown	step-down
crackdown	rubdown	sundown	wind-down
letdown	rundown	turndown	write-down

c. *In* **Words.** Compound nouns ending in *in* are typically hyphenated. For example:

break-in	fill-in	shoo-in	trade-in
cave-in	lead-in	shut-in	turn-in
check-in	log-in	sit-in	walk-in
drive-in	phone-in	stand-in	weigh-in
fade-in	run-in	tie-in	write-in

---

*Merriam-Webster shows this as a hyphenated word, but it frequently appears as a solid word in business.

8

d. *Out* Words. Compound nouns ending in *out* are typically solid. For example:

bailout	foldout	readout	**BUT:**	cop-out
blackout	handout	rollout		diner-out
blowout	hangout	sellout		fade-out
breakout	hideout	shakeout		falling-out
burnout	holdout	shutout		lights-out
buyout	layout	standout		log-out
carryout	lockout	tryout		shoot-out
checkout	lookout	turnout		sick-out
closeout	payout	walkout		time-out
dropout	phaseout	washout		
fallout	printout	workout		

e. *On* Words. Compound nouns ending in *on* are typically hyphenated. For example:

add-on	come-on	hangers-on	run-on
carry-on	follow-on	log-on	slip-on
carryings-on	goings-on	put-on	turn-on

f. *Off* Words. Compound nouns ending in *off* are either solid or hyphenated. For example:

checkoff	liftoff	brush-off	send-off
cutoff	payoff	drop-off	show-off
falloff	runoff	log-off	sign-off
kickoff	shutoff	play-off	spin-off
knockoff	standoff	rake-off	tip-off
layoff	takeoff	rip-off	trade-off
leadoff	turnoff	sell-off	write-off

g. *Over* Words. Compound nouns ending in *over* are typically solid. For example:

carryover	layover	slipover		turnover
changeover	leftover	spillover		walkover
crossover	pushover	stopover	**BUT:**	going-over
hangover	rollover	switchover		once-over
holdover	runover	takeover		voice-over

h. *Back* Words. Compound nouns ending in *back* are typically solid. For example:

buyback	fallback	payback	rollback
callback	feedback	piggyback	setback
comeback	flashback	playback	snapback
drawback	kickback	pullback	throwback

i. *Away* Words. These compounds are typically solid. For example:

breakaway	giveaway	runaway	straightaway
getaway	hideaway	stowaway	throwaway

j. Compounds Ending in *About*, *Around*, and *By*. These compounds are typically solid. For example:

knockabout	turnabout	runaround	passersby
layabout	whereabouts	turnaround	standbys

k. Compounds Ending in *Between*, *Through*, and *Together*. These compounds are typically hyphenated. For example:

go-between	follow-through	walk-through	get-together
in-between	run-through	**BUT:** breakthrough	

804   **a.** Hyphenate a compound noun that lacks a noun as one of its elements.

the also-rans	know-it-alls	a set-to
a big to-do	hand-me-downs	a lean-to
a cure-all	the well-to-do	a talking-to
a go-getter	a shoot-'em-up	give-and-take
a has-been	do-it-yourselfers	a five-and-ten
the have-nots	a good-for-nothing	half-and-half
know-how	a ne'er-do-well	my one-and-only
a look-alike	a merry-go-round	on the up-and-up
make-believe	a free-for-all	show-and-tell
say-so	the be-all and end-all	the old so-and-so
two-by-fours	hide-and-seek	**BUT:** ups and downs
the old one-two	no get-up-and-go	wear and tear
a nine-to-fiver	a sing-along	wannabes

b. Words coined from repeated syllables or rhyming syllables are typically hyphenated. Other coined words may be hyphenated or solid.

boo-boo	culture-vulture	one-upmanship
goody-goody	hurly-burly	stick-to-itiveness
no-no	nitty-gritty	comeuppance
yo-yo	walkie-talkie	whodunit
hanky-panky	**BUT:** wingding	twofers
hocus-pocus	mumbo jumbo	a gofer

c. Many compound nouns that end with a prepositional phrase are hyphenated.

ambassador-at-large	stick-in-the-mud	**BUT:** bill of lading
attorney-at-law	man-about-town	editor in chief
brother-in-law	right-of-way	line of credit
grants-in-aid	stay-at-home	power of attorney
jack-of-all-trades	stock-in-trade	rule of thumb
Johnny-on-the-spot	theater-in-the-round	standard of living

805   Treat a compound noun like *problem solving* as two words unless your dictionary specifically shows it as solid or hyphenated. (Most words of this pattern are not shown in a dictionary. However, the solid and hyphenated examples below have been taken from the 1993 printing of *Merriam-Webster's Collegiate Dictionary,* Tenth Edition, published by Merriam-Webster.)

bean counting	brainstorming	belt-tightening
data processing	downloading	consciousness-raising
decision making	downsizing	house-sitting
number crunching	housewarming	name-dropping
problem solving	letterspacing	sight-seeing
profit sharing	logrolling	soul-searching
skill building	safekeeping	speed-reading
skin diving	trailblazing	whistle-blowing
(**BUT:** skydiving)	troubleshooting	witch-hunting

➤ *For words like* air conditioning, *which are derived from hyphenated infinitives like* air-condition, *see* ¶812.

806   Hyphenate two nouns when they signify that one person or one thing has two functions. (See also ¶¶295b, 818b.)

actor-director	director-producer	secretary-treasurer
dinner-dance	owner-manager	wheeler-dealer

807 Compound nouns that have a single letter as their first element are either hyphenated or written as two words.

A-frame	f-stop	I beam	T square	X ray
B-school	G suit	J-bar lift	U-turn	x-axis
D-mark	H-bomb	T-shirt	V neck	y-coordinate

NOTE: The term *X ray* (which is two words when used as a noun) is hyphenated when used as a verb or an adjective. (See also ¶815a.)

808 **a.** Do not hyphenate civil and military titles of two or more words.

Chief of Police Potenza   Attorney General Leibowitz
General Manager Werner   Rear Admiral Byrd

b. Hyphenate compound titles containing *ex* and *elect.*

ex-President Bush   Vice President-elect Jordan

NOTE: Also use a hyphen when *ex* is attached to a noun (*ex-wife, ex-convict*), but omit the hyphen in Latin phrases (*ex officio, ex cathedra*).

➤ *For the capitalization of titles with* ex *and* elect, *see ¶¶317 and 363; for the correct usage of* ex, *see the entry for* Ex–former *on page 263.*

c. The hyphen is still customary in *vice-chancellor* and *vice-consul*, but it is gone from *vice president* and *vice admiral* (for example, *Vice President* Gore).

809 Compound nouns containing *man* or *men* as an element were traditionally used generically to refer to males and females alike. For example:

not for the average *layman*	the history of *mankind*
of concern to all *businessmen*	reduce the number of *man-hours*
write your *congressman*	a new source of *manpower*

a. The *generic* use of such terms is now widely considered unacceptable, because the masculine bias of these terms makes then unsuitable for reference to women. Therefore, avoid using such terms. The following list suggests appropriate alternatives.

In Place of the Generic Term	**Use**
layman	layperson
businessmen	business owners, business executives, business managers, business people
congressmen	members of Congress, representatives
mankind	people, humanity, the human race, human beings
man-hours	worker-hours
manpower	work force, human resources, staff
salesmen	salespeople, sales representatives, salespersons, salesclerks, sales staff, sales force, sales associates
foremen	supervisors
policemen	police officers, the police
mailmen	mail carriers
workmen	workers

NOTE: *Workmen's compensation insurance* (or *workmen's comp*) is now commonly referred to as *workers' compensation insurance* (or *workers' comp*).

➤ *See ¶840 for alternatives to words ending with feminine suffixes.*

(Continued on page 184.)

¶810

b. Whenever possible, replace a word like *salesmanship* with an alternative expression (for example, *selling skills*). However, words such as *craftsmanship, workmanship, sportsmanship, grantsmanship, brinkmanship,* and *one-upmanship* are still widely used because of the difficulty in devising alternative expressions.

c. When naming a job or role, avoid the use of compound terms ending in *man* or *woman* unless the term refers to a specific person whose gender is known.

> There are ten candidates seeking election to the City *Council.* (**NOT:** ... seeking election as city *councilmen.*)
>
> **BUT:** *Councilwoman* Walters and *Councilman* Holtz will study the proposal.
>
> Write to your *representative in Congress.* (**NOT:** Write to your *congressman.*)
>
> **BUT:** I was very much impressed by *Congresswoman* Schroeder of Colorado.
>
> Who will be appointed as *head* of the committee? **OR** Who will be appointed to *chair* the committee? (**NOT:** ... appointed *chairman* of the committee?)
>
> **BUT:** Robert Haas has been appointed *chairman* of the committee.

NOTE: Words like *chairperson* and *spokesperson* have been coined as a means of avoiding the generic use of masculine compound nouns. Personal taste or institutional policy will dictate whether to use these terms or not.

810 Terms like *doctor, lawyer,* and *nurse* are generic—that is, they apply equally to women and men. Therefore, do not use compound nouns like *woman lawyer* and *male nurse* unless there is a legitimate reason for making a distinction according to gender.

> Next Wednesday there will be a seminar on the special problems facing *women lawyers* in the courtroom.

➤ *Capitalization of hyphenated compound nouns: see ¶363.*
Plurals of compound nouns: see ¶¶611–613.
Possessives of compound nouns: see ¶¶634–635.

COMPOUND VERBS

811 a. Compound verbs are usually hyphenated or solid.

to air-condition	to fine-tune	to backstop	to mastermind
to baby-sit	to off-load	to bulldoze	to moonlight
to blue-pencil	to pinch-hit	to buttonhole	to pinpoint
to color-code	to rubber-stamp	to downgrade	to proofread
to custom-tailor	to second-guess	to download	to sandbag
to deep-six	to shrink-wrap	to downsize	to shortchange
to double-click	to soft-pedal	to ghostwrite	to sidetrack
to double-space	to spot-check	to hamstring	to troubleshoot
to dry-clean	to test-drive	to handpick	to waterproof
to field-test	to window-shop	to highlight	to whitewash

NOTE: If you try to check the spelling of a compound verb in a dictionary and do not find the verb listed, hyphenate the components.

b. Do not hyphenate verb phrases such as *make up, slow down, tie in.* (See ¶802 for examples.)

812 **a.** If the infinitive form of a compound verb has a hyphen, retain the hyphen in other forms of the verb. (See *b* below for an exception.)

Would you like to *air-condition* your entire house?
The theater was not *air-conditioned.*
We need an *air-conditioning* expert to advise us.

You need to *double-space* all these reports.
Please *double-space* this letter.
This material should not be *double-spaced.*
BUT: Leave a *double space* between paragraphs. (No hyphen in *double space* as a compound noun.)

b. The gerund derived from a hyphenated compound verb requires no hyphen unless it is followed by an object.

Dry cleaning is the best way to treat this garment.
BUT: *Dry-cleaning* this *sweater* will not remove the spot.

Double spacing would make this table easier to read.
BUT: *Double-spacing* this *table* would make it easier to read.

Spot checking is all we have time for.
BUT: In *spot-checking* the *data,* I found some disturbing errors.

COMPOUND ADJECTIVES

No aspect of style causes greater difficulty than compound adjectives. When a compound adjective is shown hyphenated in the dictionary, you can assume only that the expression is hyphenated when it occurs directly *before* a noun. When the same combination of words falls elsewhere in the sentence, the use or omission of hyphens depends on how the words are used.

For the basic rules, see ¶¶813–815. For detailed comments, see the following paragraphs:

➤ *Adjective + noun (as in* short-term *note): see* ¶816.
Compound with number or letter (as in 40-hour *week): see* ¶817.
Compound noun (as in high school *graduate): see* ¶818.
Proper name (as in Madison Avenue *agencies): see* ¶819.
Noun + adjective (as in tax-free *imports): see* ¶820.
Noun + participle (as in time-consuming *details): see* ¶821.
Adjective + participle (as in nice-looking *layout): see* ¶822.
Adjective + noun + ed (as in quick-witted *assistant): see* ¶823.
Adverb + participle (as in privately owned *stock): see* ¶824a.
Adverb + participle (as in well-known *facts): see* ¶824b.
Adverb + adjective (as in very exciting *test results): see* ¶825.
Participle + adverb (as in warmed-over *ideas): see* ¶826.
Adjective + adjective (as in black leather *notebook): see* ¶827.
Verb + verb (as in stop-and-go *traffic): see* ¶828.
Verb + adverb (as in read-only *memory): see* ¶829.
Verb + noun (as in take-home *pay): see* ¶830.
Phrasal compound (as in up-to-date *accounts): see* ¶831.

NOTE: If you try to check the spelling of a compound adjective in a dictionary and do not find it listed, match up the components with one of the patterns shown above and follow the standard style for that pattern.

Basic Rules

813 A compound adjective consists of two or more words that function as a unit and express a single thought. These one-thought modifiers are derived from (and take the place of) adjective phrases and clauses. In the following examples the left column shows the original phrase or clause; the right column shows the compound adjective.

Adjective Phrase or Clause	Compound Adjective
terminals *installed at the point of sale*	*point-of-sale* terminals
a career *moving along a fast track*	a *fast-track* career
a guarantee *to give you your money back*	a *money-back* guarantee
a woman *who speaks quietly*	a *quiet-spoken* woman
an actor *who is well known*	a *well-known* actor
a conference *held at a high level*	a *high-level* conference
a building *ten stories high*	a *ten-story* building
a report *that is up to date*	an *up-to-date* report
an article *that is as long as a book*	a *book-length* article
an environment *where people work under high pressure*	a *high-pressure* environment

NOTE: In the process of becoming compound adjectives, the adjective phrases and clauses are usually reduced to a few essential words. In addition, these words frequently undergo a change in form (for example, *ten stories high* becomes *ten-story*); sometimes they are put in inverted order (for example, *who speaks quietly* becomes *quiet-spoken*); sometimes they are simply extracted from the phrase or clause without any change in form (for example, *well-known, high-level*).

814 Hyphenate the elements of a compound adjective that occurs *before* a noun. (**REASON:** The words that make up the compound adjective are not in their normal order or a normal form and require hyphens to hold them together.)

high-tech equipment (equipment *that reflects a high level of technology*)

a *worst-case* scenario (a scenario *based on the worst case that could occur*)

an *old-fashioned* dress (a dress *of an old fashion*)

a *$20,000-a-year* salary (a salary *of $20,000 a year*)

long-range plans (plans *projected over a long range of time*)

machine-readable copy (copy *readable by a machine*)

an *eye-catching* display (a display *that catches the eye*)

a *high-ranking* official (an official *who ranks high in the organization*)

same-day service (service *completed the same day you bring the item in*)

a *black-tie* affair (an affair *at which men must wear formal clothes with a black tie*)

the *rubber-chicken* circuit (a circuit or series *of banquets at which speeches are given and rubbery chicken or some equally bad food is served*)

revolving-door management (a management *with such rapid turnover that managers seem to be arriving and departing through a continuously revolving door*)

bottom-line results (the results that are *shown on the bottom line of a financial statement*)

EXCEPTIONS: A number of compounds like *real estate* and *high school* do not need hyphens when used as adjectives before a noun. (See ¶818.)

815 **a.** When these expressions occur *elsewhere in the sentence,* drop the hyphen if the individual words occur in a normal order and in a normal form. (In such cases the expression no longer functions as a compound adjective.)

Before the Noun	Elsewhere in Sentence
an *X-ray* treatment	This condition can be treated by *X ray.* (Object of preposition.)
an *up-to-date* report	Please bring the report *up to date.* (Prepositional phrase.)
a *follow-up* letter	Let's *follow up* at once with a letter. (Verb + adverb.)
a *high-level* decision	The decision must be made at a *high level.* (Object of preposition.)
a *never-to-be-forgotten book*	Your latest book is *never to be forgotten.* (Adverb + infinitive phrase.)
an *off-the-record* comment	The next comment is *off the record.* (Prepositional phrase.)
a *no-nonsense* attitude	Marion will tolerate *no nonsense* from you. (Object of verb.)
a *low-key* sales approach	Christopher pitches his sales approach in a *low key.* (Object of preposition.)
a *cause-and-effect* relationship	Is there a relationship of *cause and effect* in this case? (Object of preposition.)
a *four-color* cover	Is this cover printed in *four colors?* (Object of preposition.)

b. When these expressions occur elsewhere in the sentence *but are in an inverted word order or an altered form,* retain the hyphen.

Before the Noun	Elsewhere in Sentence
a *tax-exempt* purchase	The purchase was *tax-exempt.* **BUT:** The purchase was *exempt from taxes.*
government-owned lands	These lands are *government-owned.* **BUT:** These lands are *owned by the government.*
a *friendly-looking* watchdog	That watchdog is *friendly-looking.* **BUT:** That watchdog *looks friendly.*
high-priced goods	These goods are *high-priced.* **BUT:** These goods carry a *high price.*

NOTE: The following kinds of compound adjectives almost always need to be hyphenated:

➤ *Noun + adjective (for example,* tax-exempt*): see* ¶820.
Noun + participle (for example, government-owned*): see* ¶821.
Adjective + participle (for example, friendly-looking*): see* ¶822.
Adjective + noun + ed (for example, high-priced*): see* ¶823.

8

Adjective + Noun (see also ¶¶817–819)

816 **a.** Hyphenate an adjective and a noun when these elements serve as a compound modifier *before* a noun. Do not hyphenate these elements when they play a normal role *elsewhere in the sentence* (for example, as the object of a preposition or of a verb). However, if the expression continues to function as a compound adjective, retain the hyphen.

(Continued on page 188.)

Before the Noun	Elsewhere in Sentence
high-speed printers	These printers run at *high speed*. (Object of preposition.)
a *plain-paper* fax	Please be sure to order a fax that uses *plain paper*. (Object of verb.)
red-carpet treatment	They plan to roll out the *red carpet*. (Object of infinitive.)
a *closed-door* discussion	The discussion was held behind *closed doors*. (Object of preposition.)
an *all-day* seminar	The seminar will last *all day*. (Normal adverbial phrase.)
a *long-term* investment in bonds	This investment in bonds runs for a *long term*. (Object of preposition.)
	BUT: This investment in bonds is *long-term*. (Compound adjective.)
a *part-time* job	This job is *part-time*. (Compound adjective.)
	I work *part-time*. (Compound adverb.)
	I travel *part of the time*. (Normal adverbial phrase.)

NOTE: Combinations involving comparative or superlative adjectives plus nouns follow the same pattern.

Before the Noun	Elsewhere in Sentence
a *larger-size* shirt	He wears a *larger size*. (Object of verb.)
the *finest-quality* goods	These goods are of the *finest quality*. (Object of preposition.)

b. A few compound adjectives in this category are now written solid—for example, *a commonsense solution, a freshwater pond, a surefire success.*

Compound With Number or Letter

817 **a.** When a number and a noun form a one-thought modifier *before* a noun (as in *six-story building*), make the noun singular and hyphenate the expression. When the expression has a normal form and a normal function *elsewhere in the sentence,* do not hyphenate it.

Before the Noun	Elsewhere in Sentence
a *one-way* street	a street that runs only *one way*
a *first-person* account	a story written in the *first person*
a *first-rate* job	a job that deserves the *first* (or highest) *rating*
	BUT: a job that is *first-rate*
a *two-piece* suit	a suit consisting of *two pieces*
a *three-ring* circus	a circus with *three rings*
a *four-point* program	a program containing *four points*
a *5-liter* container	a container that holds *5 liters*
an *8-foot* ceiling	a ceiling *8 feet* above the floor
a *20-year* mortgage	a mortgage running for *20 years*
twentieth-century art	art of the *twentieth century*
a *50-cent* fee	a fee of *50 cents*
an *$85-a-month* charge	a charge of *$85 a month*
a *100-meter* sprint	a sprint of *100 meters*
an *8½- by 11-inch* book (see ¶832)	a book *8½ by 11 inches*
a *55-mile-an-hour* speed limit	a speed limit of *55 miles an hour*

Before the Noun	Elsewhere in Sentence
a *2-million-ton* shipment	a shipment of *2 million tons*
a *10-inch-thick* panel	a panel *10 inches thick*
a *7-foot-2-inch* basketball player	a basketball player *7 feet 2 inches* tall (see ¶430)
24-hour-a-day service	service *24 hours a day*
600-dpi graphics	graphics composed of *600 dpi* (dots per inch)

EXCEPTIONS: a *15 percent* decline, a *$4 million* profit, a *twofold* increase (BUT: a *12-fold* increase), a *secondhand* car (BUT: a *second-degree* burn)

➤ *For the hyphenation of fractional expressions serving as compound adjectives* (*like* half-dozen *or* 1/4-inch), *see* ¶427a.

NOTE: A hyphenated compound adjective and an unhyphenated possessive expression often provide *alternative* ways of expressing the same thought. Do not use both styles together.

a *one-year* extension	a *two-week* vacation
OR: a *one year's* extension	OR: a *two weeks'* vacation
(BUT NOT: a one-year's extension)	(BUT NOT: a two-weeks' vacation)

b. Hyphenate compound adjectives involving a number and *odd* or *plus*.

The embezzlement occurred some *twenty-odd* years ago.

I now give my age simply as *forty-plus*.

c. Compound adjectives involving two numbers (as in ratios and scores) are expressed as follows:

a *50-50* (OR *fifty-fifty*) chance	a *1000-to-1* possibility
20/20 (OR *twenty-twenty*) vision	a *3-to-1* ratio OR a *3:1* ratio
an *18-7* victory over the Giants	BUT: a ratio of *3 to 1*

➤ *See also* ¶450–451.

d. Other compound expressions involving a number or letter are expressed as follows:

our *number-one** (OR *No. 1*) priority	*Class A* materials
BUT: our goal is to be *number one*	a grade of *A plus* (OR *A+*)
in *A1* condition	BUT: does *A-plus* (OR *A+*) work
BUT: *A.1.* steak sauce	a passing mark of *D minus* (OR *D−*)
Title IX provisions	BUT: a *D-minus* (OR *D−*) student

Compound Noun

818 **a.** A number of adjective-noun combinations (such as *real estate* or *social security*) and noun-noun combinations (such as *life insurance* or *money market*) are actually well-established compound nouns serving as adjectives. Unlike *short-term, low-risk,* and the examples in ¶816, these expressions refer to well-known concepts or institutions. Because they are easily grasped as a unit, they *do not* require a hyphen.

accounts payable records	*life insurance* policy	*public relations* adviser
branch office reports	*mass production* techniques	*real estate* agent
high school diploma	*money market* funds	*social security* tax
income tax return	*nuclear energy* plant	*word processing* center

EXCEPTION: a *mail-order* business

---

*Merriam-Webster does not hyphenate *number-one* before a noun.

(Continued on page 190.)

NOTE: When dictionaries do not provide guidance on a specific adjective-noun combination, consider whether the expression is more like a well-known compound such as *social security* or more like *short-term*. Then space the combination or hyphenate it accordingly.

b. When a noun-noun combination involves two words of relatively equal rank, hyphenate the combination. (See also ¶295.)

the *price-earnings* ratio   the *space-time* continuum   an *air-sea* search
cost-benefit analyses   *labor-management* relations   a *sand-gravel* mixture

c. As a general rule, when a compound noun is used as a compound adjective, the decision to hyphenate or not will depend on how familiar you think your reader is with the term in question. Thus a term like *small business owner* would not be hyphenated if you feel your reader is familiar with the concept of *small business*. However, if your reader could misinterpret *small business owner* as a reference to the size of the person rather than to the size of the business, write *small-business owner*.

d. A compound noun like *African American* is hyphenated when used as an adjective. (See ¶348, note.)

Proper Name

819 **a.** Do not hyphenate the elements in a proper name used as an adjective.

a *Supreme Court* decision   a *Rodeo Drive* location
a *Saks Fifth Avenue* store   *Mickey Mouse* procedures

b. When two or more distinct proper names are combined to form a one-thought modifier, use a hyphen to connect the elements.

a *German-American* restaurant   the cuisine is *German-American*

the *New York-Chicago-Los Angeles* flight (no hyphens within *New York* and *Los Angeles*)   BUT: the flight to *New York, Chicago, and Los Angeles*

NOTE: If one of the elements already contains a hyphen, use an en dash in computer-generated material (two hyphens in typewritten material) to connect the two proper names.

the *Winston-Salem–Atlanta* bus trip   the Scranton–Wilkes-Barre area

Noun + Adjective

820 **a.** When a compound adjective consists of a noun plus an adjective, hyphenate this combination whether it appears before or after the noun. (See ¶815b.)

accident-prone	ice-cold	price-conscious	tone-deaf
bone-dry	knee-deep	scot-free	top-heavy
brain-dead	machine-readable	sky-high	trigger-happy
capital-intensive	paper-thin	street-smart	user-friendly
class-conscious	pitch-dark	tax-exempt	water-repellent
color-blind	power-hungry	toll-free	year-round

Your suggestion is ingenious but not *cost-effective.*

You are trying to solve an *age-old* problem.

She wants everything to be *letter-perfect.*

We import these *water-repellent* fabrics *duty-free.*

I want a computer that is *IBM-compatible.*

NOTE: Retain the hyphen in a noun plus an adjective combination when the expression functions as an adverb rather than as an adjective.

ADJECTIVE: Please call me on my *toll-free* number.
ADVERB: You can always call me *toll-free.*

ADJECTIVE: The information is encoded on *paper-thin* wafers.
ADVERB: The wafers have to be sliced *paper-thin.*

b. A few words in this category are now written solid. For example:

-wide:	worldwide, nationwide, countrywide, statewide, countywide, citywide, communitywide, industrywide, companywide, storewide
-proof:	waterproof, fireproof, shatterproof, weatherproof, childproof
-worthy:	praiseworthy, newsworthy, trustworthy, creditworthy
-sick:	homesick, airsick, carsick, heartsick
-long:	daylong, nightlong, yearlong, lifelong, agelong

Noun + Participle

821 **a.** When a compound adjective consists of a noun plus a participle, hyphenate this combination whether it appears before or after the noun. (See ¶815b.)

awe-inspiring	law-abiding	panic-stricken
bell-shaped	market-tested	smoke-filled
decision-making	mind-boggling	tailor-made
hair-raising	muscle-bound	tax-sheltered
interest-bearing	nerve-racking	Windows-based

This *number-crunching* software uses *eye-popping* graphics.

Computer-aided design was one of the great breakthroughs of the 1980s.

Buying *custom-tailored* suits can easily become *habit-forming.*

b. When an open compound noun is combined with a participle to form a one-thought modifier, insert a hyphen only before the participle.

U.S. *government-owned* lands	a *Pulitzer Prize-winning* play
a *Labor Department-sponsored* conference	*health care-related* expenditures
a *Dayton, Ohio-based* consortium	*solar energy-oriented* research
a *Frank Lloyd Wright-designed* building	*Pentium processor-based* PCs

NOTE: Combining an open compound noun with a participle to form a compound adjective can often lead to awkward constructions. Reword to eliminate this problem.

AWKWARD: This software is *Novell network-compatible.*

BETTER: This software can also be used on a Novell network.

c. A few words in this category are now written solid. For example:

hand-:	handmade, handpicked, handwoven, handwritten
heart-:	heartbreaking, heartbroken, heartfelt, heartrending, heartwarming
home-:	homebound, homegrown, homemade, homespun
time-:	timesaving, timeserving, timeworn BUT: time-consuming, time-honored, time-sharing, time-tested
pain-:	painkilling, painstaking

8

Adjective + Participle (see also ¶824b)

822 a. When a compound adjective consists of an adjective plus a participle, hyphenate this combination whether it appears before or after the noun. (See ¶815b.)

clean-cut	high-ranking	rough-hewn
friendly-looking (see ¶824a)	long-standing	smooth-talking
half-baked	odd-sounding	soft-spoken
hard-hitting	ready-made	sweet-smelling

EXCEPTIONS: easygoing, halfhearted

I'm *half-tempted* to apply for the Singapore opening myself.

He is a *smooth-talking* operator who never delivers what he promises.

Betty was anything but *soft-spoken* in arguing against the new procedures.

b. Retain the hyphen even when a comparative or superlative adjective is combined with a participle—for example, *nicer-looking, best-looking, oddest-sounding, better-tasting.*

As the *highest-ranking* official present, Mrs. Egan took charge of the meeting.

This year's brochure is *better-looking* than last year's.

Why can't we attract *better-qualified* people to our company?

Adjective + Noun + *ED*

823 a. When a compound adjective consists of an adjective plus a noun plus *ed*, hyphenate this combination whether it appears before or after the noun. (See ¶815b.)

broad-minded	empty-handed	open-ended
empty-headed	light-fingered	closed-captioned
quick-witted	two-fisted	low-pitched
hot-tempered	loose-jointed	high-priced
good-humored	double-breasted	middle-aged
high-spirited	long-winded	old-fashioned
fair-haired	good-hearted	short-lived (pronounced ''līvd'')
dog-eared	wasp-waisted	pint-sized (see ¶823d)
two-faced	deep-seated	fast-paced
clear-eyed	swivel-hipped	broad-based
hard-nosed	clean-limbed	coarse-grained
tight-mouthed	weak-kneed	double-edged
thin-lipped	long-legged	single-spaced (see ¶812)
sharp-tongued	flat-footed	deep-rooted
gap-toothed	hot-blooded	high-powered
red-cheeked	thin-skinned	one-sided
round-shouldered	full-bodied	BUT: lopsided

Our success was *short-lived:* the business folded after six months. (*Short-lived* is derived from the phrase *of short life.* For that reason the *i* in *lived* is pronounced like the long *i* in *life*, not like the short *i* in *given.*)

These symptoms commonly occur in *middle-aged* executives.

I'm too *old-fashioned* to be that *broad-minded.*

b. Retain the hyphen in comparative or superlative forms—for example, *smaller-sized, highest-priced, best-natured.*

Our *higher-priced* articles sold well this year.
These goods are *higher-priced* than the samples you showed me.

Fred is the *longest-winded* speaker I ever heard.
Fred's speech was the *longest-winded* I ever heard.

8

c. Some words in this category are now written solid. For example:

-headed: bareheaded, bullheaded, chowderheaded, clearheaded, fatheaded, hardheaded, hotheaded, levelheaded, muddleheaded, pigheaded, redheaded, softheaded, thickheaded, woodenheaded, wrongheaded
BUT: bald-headed, empty-headed, light-headed

-hearted: bighearted, brokenhearted, coldhearted, halfhearted, heavyhearted, lighthearted, openhearted, softhearted, stouthearted, tenderhearted, warmhearted, wholehearted
BUT: good-hearted, hard-hearted, single-hearted

-mouthed: closemouthed, openmouthed, widemouthed, bigmouthed, loudmouthed
BUT: tight-mouthed

-fisted: hardfisted, tightfisted, closefisted
BUT: two-fisted

-sighted: nearsighted, shortsighted, farsighted
BUT: clear-sighted, sharp-sighted

-brained: birdbrained, featherbrained, lamebrained, scatterbrained

-minded: feebleminded
BUT: broad-minded, civic-minded, high-minded, like-minded, low-minded, open-minded, serious-minded, single-minded, small-minded, strong-minded

d. Compound adjectives such as *pint-sized, pocket-sized, life-sized, full-sized, giant-sized, king-sized, queen-sized,* and *twin-sized* may also be written without the final *d.*

Adverb + Participle (see also ¶825)

824 a. Do not hyphenate an adverb-participle combination if the adverb ends in *ly.*

a *poorly constructed* house	a *wholly owned* corporation
a *highly valued* employee	a *newly formed* division
a *clearly defined* set of terms	an *extremely tiring* trip

NOTE: Hyphenate adjectives ending in *ly* when they are used with participles. (See ¶822.)

a *friendly-sounding* voice   a *motherly-looking* woman

➤ *To distinguish between adjectives and adverbs ending in* ly, *see ¶1069.*

b. Other adverb-participle compounds are hyphenated *before* the noun. When these same combinations occur in the predicate, drop the hyphen if the participle is part of the verb.

Before the Noun	Elsewhere in Sentence
a *well-known* consultant	This consultant *is* well *known*.
much-needed reforms	These reforms *were* much *needed*.
the *above-mentioned* facts	These facts *were mentioned* above.
the *ever-changing* tides	The tides *are* ever *changing*.
a *long-remembered* tribute	Today's tribute *will be* long *remembered*.
a *soon-forgotten* achievement	Her achievement *was* soon *forgotten*.

(Continued on page 194.)

However, if the participle does not become part of the verb and continues to function with the adverb as a one-thought modifier in the predicate, retain the hyphen.

Before the Noun	Elsewhere in Sentence
a *well-behaved* child	The child is *well-behaved*.
a *clear-cut* position	Their position was *clear-cut*.
a *well-intentioned* proposal	The proposal was *well-intentioned*.

NOTE: You couldn't say, "The child is behaved" or "Their position was cut" or "The proposal was intentioned." Since the participle is not part of the verb, it must be treated as part of a compound adjective. Compare the use of *fast-moving* in the following examples.

Before the Noun	Elsewhere in Sentence
a *fast-moving* narrative	The narrative is *fast-moving*.
	BUT: The narrative *is* fast *moving* toward a climax.

c. A hyphenated adverb-participle combination like those in *b* retains the hyphen even when the adverb is in the comparative or superlative.

a *better-known* brand	the *hardest-working* manager
the *best-behaved* child	a *faster-moving* stock clerk

d. A few words in this category are now written solid. For example:

-going ongoing, outgoing, thoroughgoing

far- farseeing, farsighted **BUT:** far-fetched, far-flung, far-reaching

free- freehanded, freehearted, freestanding, freethinking, freewheeling **BUT:** free-floating, free-spoken, free-swinging

wide- widespread **BUT:** wide-eyed, wide-ranging, wide-spreading

Adverb + Adjective

825 a. A number of adverb-adjective combinations closely resemble the adverb-participle combinations described in ¶824. However, since an adverb normally modifies an adjective, do not use a hyphen to connect these words.

a *not too interesting* report	a *very moving* experience
a *rather irritating* delay	a *quite trying* day

NOTE: In these examples you can omit the adverb and speak of an *interesting* report, an *irritating* delay, a *moving* experience, and a *trying* day; hence no hyphen is needed. However, in the first set of examples at the top of this page, you cannot speak of a *behaved* child, a *cut* position, or an *intentioned* proposal; for that reason, the adverb preceding *behaved, cut,* and *intentioned* must be linked by a hyphen.

b. Do not hyphenate a comparative or superlative form when the adverb *more, most, less,* or *least* is combined with an adjective.

a *more determined* person	a *less complicated* transaction
the *most exciting* event	the *least interesting* lecture

Participle + Adverb

826 Hyphenate a participle-adverb combination *before* the noun but not when it occurs elsewhere in the sentence.

Before the Noun	Elsewhere in Sentence
filled-in forms	These forms should be *filled in.*
worn-out equipment	The equipment was *worn out.*
a *tuned-up* engine	The engine has been *tuned up.*
a *scaled-down* proposal	The proposal must be *scaled down.*
baked-on enamel	This enamel has been *baked on.*
a *cooling-off* period	Don't negotiate without *cooling off* first.
unheard-of bargains	These bargains were *unheard of.*
an *agreed-upon* date	We *agreed upon* a date.
warmed-over ideas	His ideas were *warmed over* for the occasion.

➤ *See also the examples in ¶831.*

Adjective + Adjective

827 **a.** Do not hyphenate independent adjectives preceding a noun.

a *long* and *tiring* trip (*long* and *tiring* each modify *trip*)

a *warm, enthusiastic* reception (*warm* and *enthusiastic* each modify *reception;* a comma marks the omission of *and*)

a *distinguished public* orator (*public* modifies *orator; distinguished* modifies *public orator*)

➤ *For the use of commas with adjectives, see ¶¶168–171, especially the final examples in ¶169.*

b. In a few special cases two adjectives joined by *and* are hyphenated because they function as one-thought modifiers. These, however, are rare exceptions to the rule stated in *a.*

a *cut-and-dried* presentation	an *out-and-out* lie
a *hard-and-fast* rule	an *up-and-coming* lawyer
a *high-and-mighty* attitude	a *lean-and-mean* approach
a *tried-and-true* method	a *rough-and-tumble* environment
an *open-and-shut* case	a *spick-and-span* kitchen

Henry views the matter in *black-and-white* terms. (A one-thought modifier.)

BUT: Sue wore a *black and white* dress to the Mallory party. (Two independent adjectives.)

c. Hyphenate two adjectives that express the dual nature of the thing that they refer to. (See also ¶¶295b, 806.)

a *true-false* test   a *compound-complex* sentence
BUT: a *bittersweet* ending

d. Hyphenate expressions such as *blue-black, green-gray, snow-white,* and *red-hot* before and after a noun. However, do not hyphenate expressions such as *bluish green, dark gray,* or *bright red* (where the first word clearly modifies the second).

Sales have been *red-hot* this quarter.   Her dress was *bluish green.*

Verb + Verb

828 **a.** Hyphenate a compound adjective consisting of two verbs (sometimes joined by *and* or *or*) when the adjective appears *before* the noun.

(Continued on page 196.)

point-and-click navigating

the *cut-and-paste* procedure

a *hit-or-miss* marketing strategy

a *make-or-break* financial decision

stop-and-go production lines

a *wait-and-see* attitude

graded on a *pass-fail* basis

a *can-do* spirit

a *do-or-die* commitment

a *live-and-let-live* philosophy

b. Do not hyphenate these elements when they play a normal function *elsewhere in the sentence.* However, retain the hyphen if these expressions continue to function as a compound adjective.

They're never sure whether they'll *hit or miss* their marketing targets.

BUT: Their marketing strategy can best be described as *hit-or-miss.*

Verb + Adverb

829 a. Hyphenate a compound adjective consisting of a verb plus an adverb when the adjective appears *before* the noun.

our *break-even* point

a *read-only* memory

the *trickle-down* theory of financing

a *get-well* card

a *mail-in* rebate

a *pop-up* menu

a *twist-off* cap

a *drop-dead* party dress

a *come-hither* look

a *zip-out* lining

a *tow-away* zone

run-on sentences

carry-on luggage

a *drive-through* window

b. Do not hyphenate these elements when they play a normal function *elsewhere in the sentence.*

At what point will we *break even?*

Does this lining *zip out?*

Verb + Noun

830 a. Hyphenate a compound adjective consisting of a verb plus a noun (or pronoun) when the adjective appears *before* the noun.

take-home pay

a *take-charge* kind of person

a *thank-you* note

a *show-me* kind of attitude

BUT: a *turnkey* computer system

a *lackluster* approach

b. Do not hyphenate these elements when they play a normal function *elsewhere in the sentence.*

In terms of salary it's not so much what you gross as it is what you *take home.*

Betsy is inclined to *take charge* of any situation in which she finds herself.

Phrasal Compound

831 a. Hyphenate phrases used as compound adjectives *before* a noun. Do not hyphenate such phrases when they occur normally elsewhere in the sentence.

Before the Noun	Elsewhere in Sentence
up-to-date expense figures	The expense figures are *up to date.*
down-to-earth projections	These projections appear to be *down to earth.*
on-the-job training	I got my training *on the job.*
off-the-shelf software	You can buy that software *off the shelf.*
an *in-service* workshop	Modify only the equipment currently *in service.*
a *going-out-of-business* sale	Is Chelsea's Drugs *going out of business?*

Before the Noun	Elsewhere in Sentence
an *out-of-the-way* location	Why is the shopping mall so far *out of the way?*
over-the-counter stocks	These stocks are sold only *over the counter.*
under-the-table payments	Don't make any payments *under the table.*
an *above-average* rating	Our unit's performance was rated *above average.*
below-the-line charges	These charges will show up *below the line.*
a *middle-of-the-road* position	His political position never strays far from the *middle of the road.*
before-tax earnings	What were our earnings *before taxes?*
after-dinner speeches	Speeches *after dinner* ought to be prohibited.
around-the-clock service	We provide order service *around the clock.*
across-the-board cuts	The CEO wants budget cuts *across the board.*
a *between-the-lines* reading	When you read *between the lines,* Jan's memo takes on a completely different interpretation.
behind-the-scenes contract negotiations	Contract negotiations are still going on *behind the scenes.*
a *state-of-the-art* installation	This model reflects the current *state of the art.*
a *spur-of-the-moment* decision	Barra's decision to resign was made on the *spur of the moment.*
a *change-of-address* form	Please show your *change of address.*
a *matter-of-fact* approach	Jan accepted the situation as a *matter of fact.*
a *dog-in-the-manger* attitude	Joe's attitude reminds me of the fable about the *dog in the manger.*
straight-from-the-shoulder talk	I gave it to him *straight from the shoulder.*
made-to-order wall units	These wall units were *made to order.*
a *pay-as-you-go* tax plan	The new tax plan requires you to *pay as you go.*
a *would-be* expert	Roy hoped he *would be* accepted as an expert.
coast-to-coast flights	I fly *coast to coast* about three times a month.
bumper-to-bumper traffic	The traffic stood *bumper to bumper.*
a *case-by-case* analysis	We must resolve these problems *case by case.*
a *by-invitation-only* seminar	Attendance at the seminar is *by invitation only.*
a *$150,000-a-year* fee	Our legal fees run about *$150,000 a year.*
a *well-thought-of* designer	Our former designer was *well thought of.*
a *well-thought-out* plan	The plan was *well thought out.*
a *much-talked-about* party	Your party was *much talked about.*
BUT: in the *not too distant* future (see ¶825a)	
a *nine-year-old* girl	Michelle is only *nine years old.*
BUT: a *9½-year-old* girl	Michelle is only *9½ years old.* (See ¶428a.)
(**NOT:** a nine-and-a-half-year-old girl)	

b. When two nouns joined by *and* are used as a compound adjective before a noun, hyphenate the phrase.

a *cock-and-bull* story	a *trial-and-error* approach
a *dog-and-pony* show	a *mom-and-pop* operation
a *chicken-and-egg* situation	a *carrot-and-stick* proposal
a *life-and-death* matter	a *meat-and-potatoes* kind of guy
a *cat-and-mouse* relationship	a *cause-and-effect* hypothesis

(Continued on page 198.)

c. As a rule, do not hyphenate foreign phrases used as adjectives before a noun. (See also ¶287.)

an *ad hoc* committee	an *ex officio* member
an *à la carte* menu	a *pro rata* assessment
a *bona fide* transaction	a *per diem* fee

EXCEPTIONS: an *ad-lib* speech, a *laissez-faire* economic policy

d. When a compound modifier consists of two or more hyphenated phrases, separate the phrases with a comma.

a *penny-wise, pound-foolish* approach to handling money
a *knock-down, drag-out** fight over ownership of the company
the *first-in, first-out** method of accounting
a *first-come, first-served* policy of seating
a *chin-up, back-straight, stomach-in* posture
an *on-again, off-again* wedding

BUT: a *go/no-go** decision (see also ¶295a)

e. Hyphenate repeated or rhyming words used before a noun.

a *go-go* attitude	an *artsy-craftsy* boutique
a *rah-rah* spirit	a *fancy-schmancy* wedding
a *buddy-buddy* relationship	a *rinky-dink* setup
a *teeny-weeny* salary increase	a *ticky-tacky* operation

Suspending Hyphen

832 a. When a series of hyphenated adjectives has a common basic element and this element is shown only with the last term, insert a "suspending" hyphen after each of the incomplete adjectives to indicate a relationship with the last term.

long- and *short-term* securities	*8½-* by *11-inch* paper
private- and *public-sector* partnerships	*10-* and *20-year* bonds
single-, double-, or *triple-spaced* copy	a *three-* or *four-color* cover

b. Use one space after each suspending hyphen unless a comma is required at that point.

a *six-* to *eight-week* delay	*3-, 5-,* and *8-gallon* buckets
a *10-* to *12-hour* trip	*6-, 12-,* and *24-month* CDs

c. When two or more solid compound adjectives with a common element are used together (for example, *lightweight* and *heavyweight*) and the common element is shown only with the last term, use a suspending hyphen with the incomplete forms to indicate a relationship with the common element.

This product is available in *light-* and *heavyweight* versions.
Please provide *day-* and *nighttime* phone numbers.

NOTE: Repeat the common element with each word if the use of the suspending hyphen looks odd or confusing; for example, *boyfriend or girlfriend* (rather than *boy-* or *girlfriend*).

➤ *See ¶833d–e for the use of a suspending hyphen with prefixes or suffixes.*

---

*Merriam-Webster treats this word differently.

8

Prefixes and Suffixes

833 **a.** In general, do not use a hyphen to set off a prefix at the beginning of a word or a suffix at the end of a word. (See ¶808b for two exceptions: *ex-* and *-elect.*)

*after*taste	*mini*bike	change*able*
*ambi*dextrous	*mis*spell	patron*age*
*ante*date	*mono*syllable	free*dom*
*anti*trust (see ¶834)	*multi*purpose	six*fold*
*audio*visual	*non*essential	meaning*ful*
*bi*weekly	*off*beat	cable*gram*
*by*line (**BUT:** by-product)	*out*run	photo*graph*
*circum*locution	*over*confident	convert*ible*
*co*author (see ¶835)	*para*medical	misspell*ing*
*counter*balance	*poly*syllabic	fifty*ish*
*de*centralize (see ¶835)	*post*test	thank*less*
*extra*legal	*pre*requisite (see ¶835)	book*let*
*fore*front	*pro*active	child*like*
*hyper*sensitive	*pseudo*scientific	induce*ment*
*hypo*critical	*re*organize (see ¶837)	upper*most*
*il*legal	*retro*active	happi*ness*
*im*material	*semi*annual (see ¶834)	computer*nik*
*in*defensible	*sub*division	fire*proof*
*infra*structure	*super*natural	censor*ship*
*inter*office	*supra*natural	hand*some*
*intra*mural (see ¶834)	*trans*continental	home*stead*
*intro*version	*ultra*conservative (see ¶834)	back*ward*
*macro*economics	*un*accustomed	nation*wide* (see ¶820b)
*micro*processor	*under*current	edge*wise*
*mid*stream	*up*shot	trust*worthy*

NOTE: Although a hyphen is not usually used to set off the prefix *mid-*, a hyphen normally follows *mid* in expressions involving numbers (as in *mid-sixties*). (See ¶¶434, 439.) Also, in the addition of the suffix *less* or *like*, if three *l*'s occur in succession, a hyphen should be used; for example, *shell-less, bell-like.* (See ¶706, note.)

b. Whenever necessary, use a hyphen to prevent one word from being mistaken for another. (See ¶837.)

lock the *coop*	*multiply* by 12	a *unionized* factory
buy a *co-op*	a *multi-ply* fabric	an *un-ionized* substance

c. As a rule, when adding a prefix to a hyphenated or spaced compound word, use a hyphen after the prefix. (See ¶818.)

pre-high school texts	*non*-interest-bearing notes
post-bread-winning years	*non*-computer-literate adults
ex-attorney general	*non*-civil service position

EXCEPTIONS: coeditor in chief, unair-conditioned, unself-conscious

d. When two or more prefixes have a common element and this element is shown only with the final prefix, insert a "suspending" hyphen after each of the unattached prefixes to indicate a relationship with the common element.

pre- and *post*natal care	*maxi-, midi-,* and *mini*skirts
macro- and *micro*economics	*inter-* and *intra*office networks
pro- and *anti*union forces	*over-* and *under*qualified job applicants

(Continued on page 200.)

8

e. When two or more suffixes have a common element, it is possible to leave one of the suffixes unattached and insert a "suspending" hyphen to indicate the relationship with the common element; for example, *servicemen and -women.* However, to avoid confusion or awkwardness, it is usually better to repeat the common element with each suffix.

AWKWARD: I thought Nancy's reaction was more *thoughtless* than *-ful.*
BETTER: I thought Nancy's reaction was more *thoughtless* than *thoughtful.*

AWKWARD: I would characterize his behavior as *childlike* rather than *-ish.*
BETTER: I would characterize his behavior as *childlike* rather than *childish.*

834 When the prefix ends with *a* or *i* and the base word begins with the same letter, use a hyphen after the prefix to prevent misreading.

ultra-active	anti-intellectual	semi-independent
intra-abdominal	anti-inflationary	semi-indirect

835 **a.** When the prefix ends with *e* or *o* and the base word begins with the same letter, the hyphen is almost always omitted.

coordinate	reeducate	preeminent	de-emphasize
cooperate	reelect	preemployment	de-escalate
BUT: co-op	reemphasize	preempt	
co-opt	reemploy	preexisting	
co-owner	reenforce	BUT: pre-engineered	

b. In a few cases a hyphen follows *co,* even though the base word begins with a letter other than *o.*

co-edition	BUT: coauthor	coeditor	copromoter
co-occurrence	cocaptain	cofounder	copublisher
co-officiate	cochair	coholder	cosigner
co-organizer	cocontributor	copartner	cosponsor
co-payment	codefendant	copilot	costar
	codeveloper	coproducer	coworker

836 **a.** Use a hyphen after *self* when it serves as a prefix.

self-addressed	self-evident	self-important	self-study
self-confidence	self-fulfilling	self-paced	self-supporting
self-destruct	self-help	self-serving	self-worth

b. Omit the hyphen when *self* serves as the base word and is followed by a suffix.

selfdom	selfhood	selfness
selfish	selfless	selfsame

c. Avoid the expression *him- or herself.* Use *himself or herself.*

837 As a rule, the prefix *re* (meaning "again") should not be followed by a hyphen. A few words require the hyphen so that they can be distinguished from other words with the same spelling but a different meaning.

to *re-collect* the slips	to *recollect* the mistake
to *re-cover* a chair	to *recover* from an illness
to *re-form* the class	to *reform* a sinner
to *re-lease* the apartment	to *release* the hostage
she *re-marked* the ticket	as he *remarked* to me
to *re-press* the jacket	to *repress* one's emotions
to *re-sort* the cards	to *resort* to violence
to *re-sign* the contracts	to *resign* the position
to *re-treat* the cloth	to *retreat* to safer ground
a *re-creation* of the original sketches	a *recreation* program for employees

838 When a prefix is added to a word that begins with a capital letter, use a hyphen after the prefix.

| anti-American | mid-January | pre-Revolutionary War days |
| non-Asiatic | trans-Canadian | post-World War II period |

BUT: transatlantic, transpacific, the Midwest

839 Always hyphenate family terms involving the prefix *great* or the suffix *in-law*, but treat terms involving *step* and *grand* solid.

| my great-grandfather | my grandmother | your brother-in-law |
| their great-aunt | his grandchild | my stepdaughter |

840 Avoid feminine suffixes like *ess, ette,* and *trix.*

She has an established reputation as an *author* and a *poet.* (**NOT:** *authoress* and *poetess.*)

If you have any questions, ask your *flight attendant.* (**NOT:** *steward* or *stewardess.*)

NOTE: A few terms with feminine suffixes are still widely used; for example, *hostess, heroine, fiancée,* and *waitress.*

841 Use a hyphen after *quasi* when an adjective follows.

| quasi-judicial | quasi-public |
| quasi-legislative | **BUT:** quasi corporation |

SOMETIMES ONE WORD, SOMETIMES TWO WORDS

842 A number of common words may be written either as one solid word or as two separate words, depending on the meaning. See individual entries listed alphabetically in ¶1101 (unless otherwise indicated) for the following words:

Almost–all most
Already–all ready
Altogether–all together
Always–all ways
Anyone–any one (see ¶1010, note)
Any more–anymore
Anytime–any time
Anyway–any way
Awhile–a while
Everyday–every day
Everyone–every one (see ¶1010, note)
Indifferent–in different
Indirect–in direct

Into–in to (see *In*)
Maybe–may be
Nobody–no body
None–no one (see ¶1013)
Onto–on to (see *On*)
Someday–some day
Someone–some one (see ¶1010, note)
Sometime–sometimes–some time
Upon–up on (see *On*)
Whoever–who ever

> *Hyphens in spelled-out numbers: see ¶¶427, 465.*
> *Hyphens in spelled-out dates: see ¶411.*
> *Hyphens in spelled-out amounts of money: see ¶420.*
> *Hyphens in spelled-out fractions: see ¶427.*
> *Hyphens in numbers representing a continuous sequence: see ¶¶459–460.*

SECTION 9

WORD DIVISION

Automatic hyphenation is a feature of many word processing programs. When the automatic hyphenation feature is turned on, the program consults its electronic dictionaries to determine where to insert a hyphen when dividing a word at the end of a line. The electronic dictionaries may not always agree with the authority for word divisions shown in this manual (the 1993 printing of *Merriam-Webster's Collegiate Dictionary,* Tenth Edition). Moreover, some of the electronic word divisions may break the "unbreakable" rules in ¶¶901–906. Therefore, always review all electronic word-division decisions and adjust them as necessary. You may want to wait until you have edited your document before you turn on the automatic hyphenation feature. In that way you can review all word divisions at the same time. (See ¶1203a.)

When the automatic hyphenation feature is turned on, the hyphen that divides a word at the end of a line is a *soft hyphen* (that is, a nonpermanent hyphen). If you subsequently change your text so that the divided word no longer falls at the end of a line, the soft hyphen will disappear. If you are typing an expression in which a hyphen must always appear, use a *regular hyphen.* If such an expression crosses the end of a line, it will be divided after the hyphen. If you are typing a hyphenated expression (such as a phone number) that should not be divided at the end of a line, use a *hard hyphen.* In that way the complete expression will remain on the same line.

Whenever possible, avoid dividing a word at the end of a line. Word divisions are unattractive and they may sometimes confuse a reader. However, an extremely ragged right margin is also very unattractive. When word division is unavoidable, try to divide at the point that is least likely to disrupt the reader's grasp of the word. The following word division rules include (1) those that must never be broken (¶¶901–906) and (2) those that should be followed whenever space permits a choice (¶¶907–920).

Basic Rules

901 Divide words only between syllables. Whenever you are unsure of the syllabication of a word, consult a dictionary. (See also ¶¶921–922 for some guides to correct syllabication.)

> **NOTE:** Some syllable breaks shown in the dictionary are not acceptable in typed material as points of word division. (See ¶¶903–904.)

902 Do not divide one-syllable words. Even when *ed* is added to some words, they still remain one-syllable words and cannot be divided.

stressed	through	spring	hour
planned	thoughts	straight	rhythm

903 Do not set off a one-letter syllable at the beginning or the end of a word.

amaze (**NOT:** a- maze)	media (**NOT:** medi- a)
ideal (**NOT:** i- deal)	lucky (**NOT:** luck- y)

> **NOTE:** So as to discourage word division at the beginning or end of a word, some dictionaries no longer mark one-letter syllables at these points.

904 Do not divide a word unless you can leave a syllable of at least three characters (the last of which is the hyphen) on the upper line and you can carry a syllable of at least three characters (the last may be a punctuation mark) to the next line.

ad- mit	*de-* ter	*un-* der	*in-* ert
do- *ing*	re- *new*	set- *up,*	happi- *ly.*

> **NOTE:** Whenever possible, avoid dividing any word with fewer than six letters.

905 Do not divide abbreviations.

ACTION	UNICEF	AMVETS	NASDAQ
irreg.	approx.	assoc.	introd.

> **NOTE:** An abbreviation like *AFL-CIO* may be divided after the hyphen.

906 Do not divide contractions.

haven't	shouldn't	mustn't	o'clock

Preferred Practices

While it is acceptable to divide a word at any syllable break shown in the dictionary, it is often better to divide at some points than at others in order to obtain a more intelligible grouping of syllables. The following rules indicate preferred practices whenever you have sufficient space left in the line to permit a choice.

907 Divide a solid compound word between the elements of the compound.

eye- witness	time- saving	photo- copy	socio- economic

908 Divide a hyphenated compound word at the point of the hyphen.

self- confidence	father- in-law	cross- reference	senator- elect

909 Divide a word *after* a prefix (rather than within the prefix).

Preferred		Acceptable	
....	intro-	....	in-
duce	inter-	troduce	in-
national ...	super-	ternational ...	su-
sonic	circum-	personic	cir-
stances	ambi-	cumstances ...	am-
dextrous		bidextrous	

However, avoid divisions like the following, which can easily confuse a reader.

Confusing		Better	
....	inter-	....	in-
rogate	super-	terrogate	su-
lative	circum-	perlative	cir-
ference ...	ambi-	cumference	am-
tious	hyper-	bitious	hy-
bole	extra-	perbole	ex-
neous	coin-	traneous	co-
cide		incide	

NOTE: The word *extraordinary* can be divided after *ex-*, after *extraor-*, or after *extraordi-*, but not after *extra-*.

910 Divide a word *before* a suffix (rather than within the suffix).

appli- cable (RATHER THAN: applica- ble)

comprehen- sible (RATHER THAN: comprehensi- ble)

911 When a word has both a prefix and a suffix, choose the division point that groups the syllables more intelligibly.

replace- ment (RATHER THAN: re- placement)

The same principle applies when a word contains a suffix added on to a suffix. Choose the division point that produces the better grouping.

helpless- ness (RATHER THAN: help- lessness)

912 Whenever you have a choice, divide after a prefix or before a suffix (rather than within the root word).

over- active (RATHER THAN: overac- tive)

success- ful (RATHER THAN: suc- cessful)

NOTE: Avoid divisions that could confuse a reader.

re- address (RATHER THAN: read- dress)
re- allocate (RATHER THAN: real- locate)
re- apportion (RATHER THAN: reap- portion)
re- arrange (RATHER THAN: rear- range)
re- invest (RATHER THAN: rein- vest)
co- insure (RATHER THAN: coin- sure)
co- operate (RATHER THAN: coop- erate)

9

913 When a one-letter syllable occurs within the root of a word, divide *after* it (rather than before it).

impera- tive	pene- trate	simi- lar	congratu- late
nega- tive	reme- dies	apolo- gize	salu- tary

914 When two separately sounded vowels come together in a word, divide between them.

recre- *ation*	medi- *ation*	pro- *active*	situ- *ated*
pre- *eminent*	experi- *ence*	po- *etic*	influ- *ential*
spontane- *ity*	ant*i*- *intellectual*	auto- *immune*	ingenu- *ity*
courte- *ous*	patr*i*- *otic*	co- *opting*	continu- *ous*

NOTE: Do not divide between two vowels when they are used together to represent one sound.

m*ai*n- t*ai*ned	tr*ea*- surer	en- cr*oa*ching	ac- q*uai*nt
extr*ao*r- dinary	es- t*ee*med	ap- p*oi*nt	g*ue*ss- ing
pa- t*ie*nce	sur- g*eo*n	ty- c*oo*n	acq*ui*t- tal
por- t*io*n	n*eu*- tral	pro- n*ou*nce	mis- q*uo*ted

915 When necessary, an extremely long number can be divided after a comma; for example, *24,358,- 692,000.* Try to leave at least four digits on the line above and at least six digits on the line below, but always divide after a comma.

916 Try not to end more than two consecutive lines in hyphens.

917 Try not to divide at the end of the first line or at the end of the last full line in a paragraph.

918 Do not divide the last word on a page.

Breaks Within Word Groups

919 Try to keep together certain kinds of word groups that need to be read together—for example, page and number, month and day, month and year, title and surname, surname and abbreviation (or number), number and abbreviation, or number and unit of measure.

page 203	September 1997	Paula Schein, J.D.	10:30 a.m.
April 29	Mrs. Connolly	Adam Hagerty Jr.	465 miles

NOTE: If you are using word processing software, insert a *hard space* between the elements of a word group that should not be broken at the end of a line. The complete word group will remain on the same line.

920 When necessary, longer word groups may be broken as follows:

a. *Dates* may be broken between the day and year.

.... November 14, 1997, ... **NOT:** .... November 14, 1997, ...

b. *Street addresses* may be broken between the name of the street and *Street, Avenue,* or the like. If the street name consists of two or more words, the break may come between words in the street name.

.... 1024 Westervelt Boulevard .... **NOT:** .... 1024 Westervelt Boulevard ....

.... 617 North Fullerton Street .... **NOT:** .... 617 North Fullerton Street ....

c. *Names of places* may be broken between the city and the state or between the state and the ZIP Code. If the city or state name consists of two or more words, the break may come between these words.

.... Portland, Oregon 97229, ... **OR:** .... Portland, Oregon 97229, ...

.... Grand Rapids, MI 49505, ... **OR:** .... Grand Forks, North Dakota, ...

9

d. *Names of persons* may be broken between the given name (including middle initial if given) and surname.

.... Mildred R.   **NOT:** .... Mildred
Palumbo ....   R. Palumbo ....

NOTE: If it is absolutely necessary, a person's name may be divided. Follow the same principles given for dividing ordinary words.

Eisen- hower   Spil- lane (see ¶922c)   **BUT:** Spell- man (see ¶922a)

e. *Names preceded by long titles* may be broken between the title and the name (preferably) or between words in the title.

.... Assistant Commissioner   **OR:** .... Assistant
Roy N. Frawley.............................   Commissioner Roy N. Frawley...

f. *A numbered or lettered enumeration* may be broken before (but not directly after) any number or letter.

.... these points: **NOT:** .... these points: (1)
(1) All cards should ....   All cards should ....

g. *A sentence with a dash in it* may be broken after the dash.

.... Early next year—   **NOT:** .... Early next year
say, in March—let's ....   —say, in March—let's ....

h. *A sentence with ellipsis marks in it* may be broken after the ellipsis marks.

Tennis . . . health spa . . . golf . . .   **NOT:** Tennis . . . health spa . . . golf
and more.   . . . and more.

Guides to Correct Syllabication

921   Syllabication is generally based on pronunciation rather than on roots and derivations.

knowl- edge (**NOT:** know- ledge)   prod- uct (**NOT:** pro- duct)
chil- dren (**NOT:** child- ren)   ser- vice (**NOT:** serv- ice)

Note how syllabication changes as pronunciation changes.

Verbs	**Nouns**
pre- sent (to make a gift)	pres- ent (a gift)
re- cord (to make an official copy)	rec- ord (an official copy)
pro- ject (to throw forward)	proj- ect (an undertaking)

922   The following paragraphs offer some guides to syllabication.

a. If a word ends in double consonants *before* a suffix is added, you can safely divide *after* the double consonants (so long as the suffix creates an extra syllable).

sell- ers   bless- ing   staff- ing   buzz- ers   **BUT:** filled, distressed

b. If a final consonant of the base word is doubled *because* a suffix is added, you can safely divide *between* the double consonants (so long as the suffix creates an extra syllable).

ship- ping   omit- ted   begin- ner   refer- ral   **BUT:** shipped, referred

c. When double consonants appear elsewhere *within* the base word (but not as the final consonants), you can safely divide between them.

bub- bling	dif- fer	recom- mend	cur- rent
suc- cess	strug- gle	con- nect	neces- sary
mid- dle	mil- lion	sup- pose	bet- ter

9

SECTION 10

GRAMMAR

¶1001

Pronouns (¶¶1049–1064)

Adjectives and Adverbs (¶¶1065–1073)

Negatives (¶¶1074–1076)

Prepositions (¶¶1077–1080)

Sentence Structure (¶¶1081–1086)

➤ *For definitions of grammatical terms, see the appropriate entries in the Glossary of Grammatical Terms (Appendix A).*

SUBJECTS AND VERBS

Basic Rule of Agreement

1001 a. A verb must agree with its subject in number and person.

> *I am* eager to get back to work. (First person singular subject *I* with first person singular verb *am*.)

> *It seems* odd that *Farmer has* not *followed up* on our last conversation. (Third person singular subjects *it* and *Farmer* with third person singular verbs *seems* and *has* not *followed up.*)

10

He is coming to stay with us for a week. (Third person singular subject *he* with third person singular verb *is coming*.)

She does intend to call you this week. (Third person singular subject *she* with third person singular verb *does intend*.)

We were delighted to read about your promotion. (First person plural subject *we* with first person plural verb *were*.)

They are convinced that the *Foys are* worth millions. (Third person plural subjects *they* and *Foys* with third person plural verbs *are convinced* and *are*.)

Your *order* for six laptop computers *was shipped* last Friday. (Third person singular subject *order* with third person singular verb *was shipped*.)

Our *efforts* to save the business *have been* unsuccessful. (Third person plural subject *efforts* with third person plural verb *have been*.)

NOTE: A plural verb is always required after *you*, even when *you* is singular, referring to only one person.

You alone *have understood* the full dimensions of the problem. (Second person singular subject *you* with second person plural verb *have understood*.)

You both *have been* a great help to us. (Second person plural subject *you* with second person plural verb *have been*.)

You do enjoy your work, don't you? (Second person singular subject *you* with second person plural verb *do enjoy*.)

b. Although *s* or *es* added to a *noun* indicates the plural form, *s* or *es* added to a verb indicates the third person singular. (See ¶1035.)

Singular	Plural
The price *seems* reasonable.	The prices *seem* reasonable
The tax *applies* to everyone.	The taxes *apply* to everyone.

Subjects Joined by *And*

1002 a. If the subject consists of two or more words that are connected by *and* or by *both . . . and,* the subject is plural and requires a plural verb.

Ms. Rizzo and *Mr. Bruce have received* promotions.

Both the *collection* and the *delivery* of mail *are* to be curtailed as of July 1. (The repetition of *the* with the second subject emphasizes that two different items are meant.)

The *general managers* and the *controllers are attending* a three-day meeting in Chicago this week.

The *director of marketing* and the *product managers are reviewing* the advertising budgets for next year.

The *sales projections* and the *cost estimate do* not *have* to be revised.

b. Use a singular verb when two or more subjects connected by *and* refer to the same person or thing. (See also ¶1028a, fourth example.)

Our *secretary and treasurer is* Frances Eisenberg. (One person.)

Corned beef and cabbage was his favorite dish. (One dish.)

Wear and tear has to be expected when you're in the rental business. (One type of damage.)

c. Use a singular verb when two or more subjects connected by *and* are preceded by *each, every, many a,* or *many an.* (See also ¶1009b.)

Every computer, printer, and fax machine *is marked* for reduction.

Many a woman and man *has responded* to our plea for contributions.

10

¶1003

Subjects Joined by *Or* or Similar Connectives

1003 If the subject consists of two or more *singular* words that are connected by *or, either . . . or, neither . . . nor,* or *not only . . . but also,* the subject is singular and requires a singular verb.

Either *July* or *August is* a good time for the sales conference.

Neither the *Credit Department* nor the *Accounting Department has* the file.

Not only a cost-profit *analysis* but also a marketing *plan needs* to be developed.

1004 If the subject consists of two or more *plural* words that are connected by *or, either . . . or, neither . . . nor,* or *not only . . . but also,* the subject is plural and requires a plural verb.

Neither the regional *managers* nor the *salesclerks have* the data you want.

Not only the *dealers* but also the *retailers are* unhappy about our new policy.

1005 If the subject is made up of both singular and plural words connected by *or, either . . . or, neither . . . nor,* or *not only . . . but also,* the verb agrees with the nearer part of the subject. Since sentences with singular and plural subjects usually sound better with plural verbs, try to locate the plural subject closer to the verb whenever this can be done without sacrificing the emphasis desired.

Either *Miss Hertig* or her *assistants have* copies of the new catalog. (The verb *have* agrees with the nearer subject, *assistants.*)

Neither the *buyers* nor the *sales manager is* in favor of the system. (The verb *is* agrees with the nearer subject, *sales manager.*)

BETTER: Neither the *sales manager* nor the *buyers are* in favor of the system. (The sentence reads better with the plural verb *are.* The subjects *sales manager* and *buyers* have been rearranged without changing the emphasis.)

Not only the *teachers* but also the *superintendent is* in favor of the plan. (The verb *is* agrees with the nearer subject, *superintendent.* With the use of *not only . . . but also,* the emphasis falls on the subject following *but also.*)

Not only the *superintendent* but also the *teachers are* in favor of the plan. (When the sentence is rearranged, the nearer subject, *teachers,* requires the plural verb *are.* However, the emphasis has now changed.)

Not only my *colleagues* but *I am* in favor of the plan. (The first person verb *am* agrees with the nearer subject, *I.* Rearranging this sentence will change the emphasis.)

NOTE: When the subjects reflect different grammatical persons (first, second, or third), the verb should agree in person as well as number with the nearer subject. If the result seems awkward, reword as necessary.

ACCEPTABLE: Neither you nor *I am* in a position to pay Ben's legal fees.
BETTER: Neither *one* of us *is* in a position to pay Ben's legal fees. (See ¶1009a.)

ACCEPTABLE: Neither you nor *she has* the time to take on the Fuller case.
ACCEPTABLE: Neither she nor *you have* the time to take on the Fuller case.
BETTER: *She* and *you are* each too busy to take on the Fuller case. (See ¶1009c.)

AWKWARD: If you or Gary *is coming* to the convention, please visit our booth.
BETTER: If Gary or you *are coming* to the convention, please visit our booth.

➤ *For* neither . . . nor *constructions following* there is, there are, there was, *or* there were, *see the last four examples in* ¶1028a; *for examples of subject-verb-pronoun agreement in these constructions, see* ¶1049c.

Intervening Phrases and Clauses

1006 a. When establishing agreement between subject and verb, disregard intervening phrases and clauses.

The *purchase order* for new diskettes *has* not *been found*. (Disregard *for new diskettes. Purchase order* is the subject and takes the singular verb *has* not *been found*.)

The *prices* shown in our catalog *do* not *include* sales tax.

Only *one* of the items that I ordered *has been delivered*. (See also ¶1008.)

Her *experience* with banks and brokerage houses *gives* her excellent qualifications for the position.

Several *phases* of our order processing system *are* out of sync.

A key *factor*, the company's assets, *is* not *being given* sufficient weight in the analysis. (The subject *factor*, not the intervening appositive, determines that the verb should be singular in this case.)

BUT: The company's *assets*, a key factor, *are* not *being given* sufficient weight in the analysis.

NOTE: When certain indefinite pronouns (*all, none, any, some, more, most*) and certain fractional expressions (for example, *one-half of, a part of, a percentage of*) are used as subjects, you may have to look at an intervening phrase or clause to determine whether the verb should be singular or plural. See ¶¶1013 and 1025 for examples.

b. When a sentence has both a positive and a negative subject, make the verb agree with the positive subject. Set off the negative subject with commas unless it is preceded by *and* or *but*.

Profit and not sales *is* the thing to keep your eye on. (The verb *is* agrees with the positive subject *profit*.)

The *design* of the container, not the contents, *determines* what the consumer's initial reaction to the product will be.

The *members* of the Executive Committee and not the president *wield* the real power in the corporation.

It is not the president but the *members* of the Executive Committee who *wield* the real power in the corporation. (In the main clause the verb *is* agrees with the subject *it;* the verb *wield* in the *who* clause is plural to agree with the antecedent of *who*, the positive subject *members*. See ¶1062c.)

BUT: It is the *president* and not the members of the Executive Committee who *wields* the real power in the corporation. (In this sentence the positive subject is *president*, a singular noun; therefore, the verb *wields* in the *who* clause must also be singular.)

1007 The number of the verb is not affected by the insertion between subject and verb of phrases beginning with such expressions as:

along with	as well as	plus	except
together with	in addition to	besides	rather than
and not (see ¶1006b)	accompanied by	including	not even

If the subject is singular, use a singular verb; if the subject is plural, use a plural verb.

This *study*, along with many earlier reports, *shows* that the disease can be arrested if detected in time.

Mr. and Mrs. Swenson, together with their son and daughters, *are going* to New Mexico.

(Continued on page 212.)

10

No one, not even the executive vice presidents, *knows* whether the CEO plans to resign. (See ¶1010.)

The *director* of finance, not the divisional controllers, *is authorized* to approve unbudgeted expenditures over $5000. (See ¶1006b.)

NOTE: When the construction of a sentence like those above requires a singular verb but a plural verb would sound more natural, reword the sentence to create a plural subject.

CORRECT: The national sales *report,* along with the regional breakdowns you specifically requested plus the individual performance printouts, *was sent* to you last week.

BETTER: The national sales *report,* the regional *breakdowns* you specifically requested, and the individual performance *printouts were sent* to you last week. (The three subjects joined by *and—report, breakdowns,* and *printouts*—call for a plural verb.)

One of . . .

1008 a. Use a singular verb after a phrase beginning with *one of* or *one of the;* the singular verb agrees with the subject *one.* (Disregard any plural that follows *of* or *of the.*)

One of my backup disks *has been lost.*

One of the reasons for so many absences *is* poor motivation.

One of us *has* to take over the responsibility for in-service training.

One of you *is* to be nominated for the office.

One of the interviewers *is going* to call you early next week.

b. The phrases *one of those who* and *one of the things that* are followed by plural verbs because the verbs refer to *those* or *things* (rather than to *one*).

She is one of *those* who *favor* increasing the staff. (In other words, of *those* who *favor* increasing the staff, she is one. *Favor* is plural to agree with *those.*)

He is one of our *employees* who *are* never late. (Of our *employees* who *are* never late, he is one.)

I ordered one of the new *copiers* that *were advertised* in Monday's paper. (Of the new *copiers* that *were advertised* in Monday's paper, I ordered one.)

You are one of *those* rare individuals who *are* always honest with *themselves.* (Of those rare *individuals* who *are* always honest with *themselves,* you are one.)

EXCEPTION: When the words *the only* precede such phrases, the meaning is singular and a singular verb is required. Note that both words, *the* and *only,* are required to produce a singular meaning.

John is *the only one* of the staff members who *is going* to be transferred. (Of the staff members, John is *the only one* who *is going* to be transferred. Here the singular verb *is* is required to agree with *one.*)

BUT: John is only one of the *staff members* who *are going* to be transferred. (Of the *staff members* who *are going* to be transferred, John is only one.)

Indefinite Pronouns Always Singular

1009 a. The words *each, every, either, neither, one, another,* and *much* are always singular. When they are used as subjects or as adjectives modifying subjects, a singular verb is required.

10

Each has a clear-cut set of responsibilities.

Each employee was informed of the new policy well in advance.

One shipment was sent yesterday; *another is* to leave the warehouse tomorrow morning.

Neither one of the applicants *is* eligible.
OR: *Neither applicant is* eligible.

Much remains to be done on the Belgravia project.
OR: *Much work remains* to be done on the Belgravia project.

➤ *For the use of* either . . . or *and* neither . . . nor, *see* ¶¶*1003–1005.*

b. When *each, every, many a,* or *many an* precedes two or more subjects joined by *and,* the verb should be singular.

Every customer and supplier *has been notified.*

➤ *See* ¶ *1002c for other examples.*

c. When *each* follows a plural subject, keep the verb plural. In that position, *each* has no effect on the number of the verb. To test the correctness of such sentences, mentally omit *each.*

The *members* each *feel* their responsibility.

They each *have* high expectations.

Twelve each of these items *are required.*

1010 The following compound pronouns are always singular and require a singular verb:

anybody	everybody	somebody	nobody
anything	everything	something	nothing
anyone	everyone	someone	no one
OR any one	**OR** every one	**OR** some one	

Everyone is required to register in order to vote.

Something tells me I'm wrong.

NOTE: Spell *anyone, everyone,* and *someone* as two words when these pronouns are followed by an *of* phrase or are used to mean "one of a number of things."

Every one of us (each person in the group) *likes* to be appreciated.

BUT: *Everyone* (everybody) *likes* to be appreciated.

1011 Use a singular verb when two compound pronouns joined by *and* are used as subjects.

Anyone and *everyone is entitled* to a fair hearing.

Nobody and *nothing is going* to stop me.

Indefinite Pronouns Always Plural

1012 The words *both, few, many, others,* and *several* are always plural. When they are used as subjects or as adjectives modifying subjects, a plural verb is required.

Several members were invited; the *others were overlooked.*

Both books are out of print.

Many were asked, but *few were* able to answer.

10

¶1013

Indefinite Pronouns Singular or Plural

1013 a. *All, none, any, some, more,* and *most* may be singular or plural, depending on the noun that they refer to. (The noun often occurs in an *of* phrase that follows immediately.)

All of the manuscript *has been finished.*
All of the reports *have been handed* in.

Some was acceptable. (Meaning some of the manuscript.)
Some were acceptable. (Meaning some of the reports.)

Is there *any* (money) left?
Are there *any* (bills) to be paid?

Do any of you *know* John Ferguson well? (*Any* is plural because it refers to the plural *you;* hence the plural verb *do know.*)

Does any one of you *know* John Ferguson well? (*Any* is singular because it refers to the singular *one;* hence the singular verb *does know.*)

More than one customer *has complained* about that item. (*More* refers to the singular noun *customer;* hence the singular verb *has complained.*)

More than five customers *have complained* . . . (*More* refers to the plural noun *customers;* hence the plural verb *have complained.*)

Most of the stock *has been sold.*
More of these computer stands *are* due.

Some of the software *seems* too high-priced.
Some of the videotapes *seem* too high-priced.

b. In formal usage, *none* is still considered a singular pronoun. In general usage, however, *none* is considered singular or plural, depending on the number of the noun to which it refers. *No one* or *not one* is often used in place of *none* to stress the singular idea.

None of the merchandise *was stolen.*
None of the packages *were* properly *wrapped.*
None were injured. (Meaning none of the passengers.)
Not one of the associates *has* a good word to say about the managing partner.

NOTE: The relative pronouns *who, which,* and *that* (like the indefinite pronouns discussed in *a* above) may be singular or plural, depending on the noun they refer to. (See ¶1062c.)

Nouns Ending in S

1014 Some nouns appear to be plural but are actually singular. When used as subjects, these nouns require singular verbs.

news *(no plural)*	measles *(no plural)*
lens *(plural:* lenses)	summons *(plural:* summonses)

The *news* from overseas *is* very discouraging.

The *lens has* to be reground.

1015 A number of nouns are always considered plural, even though they each refer to a single thing. As subjects, they require plural verbs.

assets	dues	grounds	proceeds	savings
belongings	earnings	odds	quarters	thanks
credentials	goods	premises	riches	winnings

The *premises are* now available for inspection.

My *earnings* this year *are* not what I had counted on.

10

NOTE: The following nouns are considered plural: *glasses, scissors, pliers, pants,* and *trousers.* However, when they are preceded by the phrase *pair of,* the entire expression is considered singular.

> These *scissors need* sharpening. **BUT:** This *pair of scissors needs* sharpening.

1016 A few nouns (not all of which end in *s*) have the same form in the plural as in the singular. When used as subjects, these nouns take singular or plural verbs according to the meaning.

series	means	chassis	headquarters	deer
species	gross	corps	sheep	moose

> The *series* of concerts planned for the spring *looks* very exciting. (One series.)
> Three *series* of tickets *are going* to be issued. (Three series.)

> One *means* of breaking the impasse *is* to offer more money.
> Other *means* of solving the problem *have* not *come* to mind.

> *Headquarters is* not pleased with the performance of the Northeastern Region. (Referring to top management or central authority.)

> The Pesco Corporation *headquarters are located* at the intersection of Routes 80 and 287. (Referring to the offices of top management.)

Nouns Ending in *ICS*

1017 Many nouns ending in *ics* (such as *acoustics, economics, ethics, politics,* and *statistics*) take singular or plural verbs, depending on how they are used. When they refer to a body of knowledge or a course of study, they are *singular.* When they refer to qualities or activities, they are *plural.*

> *Economics* (a course of study) *is* a prerequisite for advanced business courses.
> The *economics* (the economic aspects) of his plan *are* not very sound.

> *Statistics is* the one course I almost failed.
> The *statistics indicate* that the market for this product line is shrinking.

> *Acoustics will* not *be listed* in next year's course offerings.
> The *acoustics* in the new concert hall *are* remarkably good.

Nouns With Foreign Plurals

1018 Watch for nouns with foreign-plural endings (see ¶614). Such plural nouns, when used as subjects, require plural verbs.

> No *criteria have been established.*
> **BUT:** No *criterion has been established.*

> *Parentheses are required* around such references.
> **BUT:** The closing *parenthesis was omitted.*

> The *media* through which we reach our clients *are* quality magazines and radio broadcasts.
> **BUT:** The *medium* we find most effective *is* television.

NOTE: The noun *data,* which is plural in form, is commonly followed by a plural verb in technical and scientific usage. In general usage, *data* in the sense of "information" is followed by a singular verb; in the sense of "distinct bits of information," it is followed by a plural verb.

> The *data* obtained after two months of experimentation *is* now *being analyzed.* (Here *data* means "information.")

> **BUT:** The *data* assembled by six researchers *are* now *being compared.* (Here *data* refers to several distinct bits of information.)

10

¶1019

Collective Nouns

1019 The following rules govern the form of verb to be used when the subject is a collective noun. (A *collective noun* is a word that is singular in form but represents a group of persons, animals, or things; for example, *army, audience, board, cabinet, class, committee, company, corporation, council, department, faculty, firm, group, jury, majority, minority, public, school, society.*)

a. If the group is acting as a unit, use the singular form of the verb.

The *Board of Directors meets* Friday.   The *firm is* one of the oldest in the field.

The *committee has agreed* to submit *its* report on Monday. (The pronoun *its* is also singular to agree with *committee.*)

b. If the members of the group are acting separately, use a plural verb.

A *group* of researchers *are coming* from all over the world for the symposium next month. (The members of the group are acting separately in the process of coming together from all over the world.)

BUT: A *group* of researchers *is meeting* in Geneva next month. (The members of the group are acting as a unit in the process of meeting.)

NOTE: The use of a collective noun with a plural verb often produces an awkward sentence. Whenever possible, recast the sentence by inserting a phrase like *the members of* before the collective noun.

AWKWARD: The *committee are* not in agreement on the action *they* should take. (The verb *are* and the pronoun *they* are plural to agree with the plural *committee.*)

BETTER: The *members* of the committee *are* not in agreement . . .

c. In a number of constructions, the choice of a singular or plural verb often depends on whether you wish to emphasize the group as a unit or as a collection of individuals. However, once the choice has been made, treat the collective noun consistently within the same context. If the resulting sentence sounds awkward, recast it as necessary.

I hope your *family is* well. (Emphasizes the family as a whole.)
OR: I hope your *family are* all well. (Emphasizes the individuals in the family.)
SMOOTHER: I hope all the *members* of your family *are* well.
OR: I hope *everyone* in your family *is* well.

The *couple was married* (**OR** *were married*) last Saturday.
OR: *Bob and Pauline were married* last Saturday.

The *couple have moved* into *their* new house. (More idiomatic than: "The *couple has moved* into *its* new house.")
OR: The *Goodwins have moved* into *their* new house.

NOTE: The expression *a couple of* is usually plural in meaning.

A *couple* of customers *have* already *reported* the error in our ad.

A *couple* of orders *have been shipped* to the wrong address.

BUT: A *couple* of days *is* all I need to complete the report. (When the phrase refers to a period of time, an amount of money, or a quantity that represents a total amount, treat the phrase as singular. See also ¶1024.)

Organizational Names

1020 Organizational names may be treated as either singular or plural. Ordinarily, treat the name as singular unless you wish to emphasize the individuals who make up the organization; in that case, use the plural. Once a choice has been made, use the singular or plural form consistently within the same context.

10

Brooks & Rice *has lost its* lease. *It is* now *looking* for a new location.

OR: Brooks & Rice *have lost their* lease. *They are* now *looking* for . . .

(**BUT NOT:** Brooks & Rice *has lost its* lease. *They are* now *looking* for . . .)

NOTE: If the organization is referred to as *they* or *who,* use a plural verb with the company name. If the organization is referred to as *it* or *which,* use a singular verb. (See ¶1049a.)

Geographic Names

1021 Geographic names that are plural in form are treated as *singular* if they refer to only one thing.

The *Netherlands is* the first stop on my itinerary.

The *Virgin Islands consists* of three large islands (St. John, St. Croix, and St. Thomas) and about fifty smaller islands.

The *United States has undertaken* a new foreign aid program.

BUT: These *United States are bound* together by a common heritage of political and religious liberty.

Names of Publications and Products

1022 The name of a publication or product is considered singular, even though it may be plural in form.

Physicians & Computers is one magazine you should consider if you want to market your software to doctors.

Consumer Reports is publishing an update on automobile insurance costs.

Changing Times is offering new subscribers a special rate for a limited time.

The Number; A Number

1023 The expression *the number* has a singular meaning and requires a singular verb; *a number* has a plural meaning and requires a plural verb.

The number of branch offices we have in the Southeast *has increased* in each of the last five years.

A number of our branch offices *are* now *located* in suburban malls rather than in the central business district.

Expressions of Time, Money, and Quantity

1024 When subjects expressing periods of time, amounts of money, or quantities represent *a total amount,* use singular verbs. When these subjects represent *a number of individual units,* use plural verbs.

Three months is too long a time to wait.
BUT: *Three months have passed* since our last exchange of letters.

That *$10,000 was* an inheritance from my uncle.
BUT: *Thousands* of dollars *have* already *been spent* on the project.

Ten acres is considered a small piece of property in this area.
BUT: *Ten acres were plowed* last spring.

A psychotic is convinced that *2 and 2 equals* 5, whereas a neurotic recognizes that *2 plus 2 is* 4 but can't stand it.

10

Fractional Expressions

1025 When the subject is an expression such as *one-half of, two-thirds of, a part of, a majority of, a percentage of, a portion of,* or *the rest of:*

a. Use a *singular verb* if a *singular noun* follows *of* or is implied.

Three-fourths of the *mailing list has been checked.*

Part of our Norfolk *operation is being closed down.*

A *majority* of *2000 signifies* a landslide in this town. (The noun *2000* is considered singular because it is a total amount. See ¶1024.)

A large *percentage has* to be retyped. (Referring to a manuscript.)

b. Use a *plural verb* when a *plural noun* follows *of* or is implied.

Two-thirds of our *customers live* in the suburbs.

Part of the *walls are* to be papered.

A *majority* of our *employees have contributed* to the United Way fund drive.

A large *percentage work* part-time. (Referring to the students at a college.)

NOTE: Consider the word *half* as a condensed version of *one-half of.*

Over *half* the *staff have signed up* for the additional benefits. (In this case *half* is considered plural because the collective noun *staff*, though singular in form, takes a plural verb when it is plural in meaning. See ¶1019b.)

Phrases and Clauses as Subjects

1026 When a phrase or clause serves as the subject, the verb should be singular.

Analyzing financial reports takes all my time these days.

Whether the decision was right or not is no longer important.

That they will accept the offer is far from certain.

Whomever you support is likely to be elected.

Whatever sales brochure they mail me goes directly into the circular file.

EXCEPTION: Clauses beginning with *what* may be singular or plural, according to the meaning.

What we need *is* a new *statement* of policy. (The *what* clause refers to *statement;* hence the verb is singular.)

What we need *are* some *guidelines* on personal time off. (Here the *what* clause refers to *guidelines;* hence the verb is plural.)

Subjects in Inverted Sentences

1027 Whenever the verb precedes the subject, make sure they agree.

Attached are two *copies* of the January mailing piece.

What *were* your *reasons* for resigning?

Where *is* (**OR** Where's) this *strategy going* to take us?

Where *are* the *reviews* of the Kelly book?
NOT: Where *is* (**OR** Where's) the *reviews* of the Kelly book?

What *is missing* from the report *is* the *rationale* for the decision.

What *appear* to be problems *are* often *opportunities.*

Should a *position become* available, we will let you know. (In this case the helping verb *should* precedes the subject. If written in normal word order, this sentence would read: If a *position should become* available. . . .)

10

1028 a. In a sentence beginning with *there is, there are, here is, here are,* or a similar construction, the real subject follows the verb. Use *is* when the real subject is singular, *are* when it is plural.

There *is* a vast *difference* between the two plans.
There *are* a great many *angles* to this problem.

Here *are* two *catalogs* and an *order blank*. (See ¶¶1002a, 1028b.)
Here *is* an old *friend* and former *partner* of mine. (The subject, *friend and partner,* is singular because only one person is referred to. See ¶1002b.)

There *is many an investor* who regrets not having bought our stock when it was only $5 a share. (See ¶1002c.)

There *is* a *branch office* or an *agency* representing us in every major city in the country. (See ¶1003.)

There *is* not only a 5 percent *state tax* but also a 2.5 percent *city tax.* (See ¶1003.)

There *is* the *cost* of your own time in addition to the substantial outlay for materials that must be figured in. (See ¶1007.)

There's (There *is*) *more* than one *way* to solve the problem. (See ¶1013a.)
There're (There *are*) *more* than six *candidates* running for mayor. (See ¶1056e.)
(**NOT:** There's more than six candidates running for mayor.)

There *are a number* of problems to be resolved. (See also ¶1023.)
Here *is the number* of orders received since Monday.

Here *is ten dollars* as a contribution. (See also ¶1024.)
Here *are ten* silver *dollars* for your collection.

There *is* neither a *hospital* nor a *clinic* on the island. (See ¶1003 for two singular subjects joined by *neither . . . nor.*)

There *are* neither *motel rooms* nor *condominiums* available for rent this late in the season. (See ¶1004 for two plural subjects joined by *neither . . . nor.*)

There *were* neither *tennis courts* nor a *swimming pool* in the hotel where we finally found a room. (*Were* agrees with the nearer subject, *tennis courts.* See also ¶1005 for singular and plural subjects joined by *neither . . . nor.*)

There *was* neither central *air conditioning* nor *fans* for any of the rooms in the hotel. (*Was* agrees with the nearer subject, *air conditioning.* See also ¶1005.)

b. When the subject consists of two or more singular nouns—or several nouns, the first of which is singular—*there is* or *here is* usually sounds more idiomatic (despite the fact that the subject is plural) than *there are* or *here are.* If you do not feel comfortable with this idiomatic construction, change the wording as necessary.

In the higher-priced model there *is* a more powerful *processor,* a 9.5-inch *color display,* and a 250 MB *hard drive.* (In this construction, *there is* is understood to be repeated before the second and third subjects.)

OR: In the higher-priced model there *are* the following *features:* a more powerful *processor,* a 9.5-inch *color display,* and a 250 MB *hard drive.* (In this version *are* agrees with the plural subject *features;* the three subjects in the sentence above are now simply appositives modifying *features.*)

Within a mile of the airport there *is* a full-service *hotel* and three *motels.*

OR: Within a mile of the airport there *is* a full-service hotel *plus* (**OR** *in addition to* **OR** *as well as*) three motels. (By changing the connective from *and* to *plus* or something similar, you are left with a singular subject, *hotel,* that calls for the singular verb *is.*)

OR: Within a mile of the airport there *are* three *motels* and a full-service *hotel.* (When the first subject in the series is plural, the verb *are* not only is grammatically correct but also sounds natural.)

10

Subjects and Predicate Complements

1029 Sentences containing a linking verb (such as *become* or some form of *to be*) sometimes have a plural subject and a singular complement or a singular subject and a plural complement. In such cases make sure that the verb agrees with the *subject* (and not with the complement).

> *Bicycles are* the only product we make.   The key *issue is* higher wages.
>
> *One* of the things we have to keep track of *is* entertainment expenses. (Use *is* to agree with *one*, the subject.)
>
> *It is* they who are at fault. (Use *is* to agree with *it*, the subject.)

NOTE: Do not confuse the last two examples with the *inverted* sentences shown in ¶1028. In a sentence beginning with *here is* or *there is*, the subject *follows* the linking verb. In a sentence beginning with *it is* or *one . . . is*, the subject *precedes* the linking verb.

VERBS

This section deals with the correct use of verb tenses and other verb forms. For the rules on agreement of verbs with subjects, see ¶¶1001–1029.

Principal Parts

1030 The principal parts of a verb are the four simple forms upon which all tenses and other modifications of the verb are based.

a. For most verbs, form the past and the past participle simply by adding *d* or *ed* to the present; form the present participle by adding *ing* to the present. (Some verbs require a minor change in the ending of the present form before *ed* or *ing* is added.)

Present	Past	Past Participle	Present Participle	
taxi	taxied	taxied	taxiing	
drop	dropped	dropped	dropping	(see ¶701)
occur	occurred	occurred	occurring	(see ¶702)
offer	offered	offered	offering	(see ¶704)
need	needed	needed	needing	(see ¶705)
fill	filled	filled	filling	(see ¶706)
warm	warmed	warmed	warming	(see ¶706)
issue	issued	issued	issuing	(see ¶707)
die	died	died	dying	(see ¶709)
try	tried	tried	trying	(see ¶710)
obey	obeyed	obeyed	obeying	(see ¶711)
panic	panicked	panicked	panicking	(see ¶717)

b. Many frequently used verbs, however, have principal parts that are irregularly formed. For example:

Present	Past	Past Participle	Present Participle	
choose	chose	chosen	choosing	
do	did	done	doing	
forget	forgot	forgotten	forgetting	
		OR forgot		
go	went	gone	going	
lay	laid	laid	laying	(see page 267)
lie	lay	lain	lying	(see page 267)
see	saw	seen	seeing	
write	wrote	written	writing	

10

NOTE: Dictionaries typically show the principal parts for all *irregular* verbs. If you are in doubt about any form, consult your dictionary. If the principal parts are not shown, the verb is regular. (See ¶1030a.)

c. The past participle and the present participle, if used as a part of a verb phrase, must *always* be used with one or more helping verbs, also known as auxiliary verbs. The most common helping verbs are:

is	was	can	do	has	have	might	shall	will
are	were	could	did	had	may	must	should	would

Verb Tenses

1031 The first principal part of the verb (the *present tense*) is used:

a. To express *present time*.

We *fill* all orders promptly.   She *does* what is expected of her.

b. To make a statement that is *true at all times*.

There *is* an exception to every rule (including this one).

c. With *shall* or *will* to express *future time*.

We *will order* (**OR** *shall order*) new stock next week. (For the use of the helping verbs *shall* and *will* in the future tense, see page 272.)

➤ *For the third person singular form of the present tense, see ¶1035.*

1032 a. The second principal part of the verb (the *past tense*) is used to express *past time*. (No helping verb is used with this form.)

We *filled* the order yesterday.   She *did* what was expected of her.

b. Do not use a past participle form to express the past tense.

He *drank* his coffee. (**NOT:** He *drunk* his coffee.)

I *saw* it. (**NOT:** I *seen* it.)

They *began* it together. (**NOT:** They *begun* it together.)

He was the one who *did* it. (**NOT:** He was the one who *done* it.)

I can't believe this sweater *shrank*. (**NOT:** . . . this sweater *shrunk.*)

Jill *brought* me up to date on the Cox project. (**NOT:** Jill *brung* me . . .)

Someone *sneaked* into my office last night. (**NOT:** Someone *snuck* . . .)

1033 The third principal part of the verb (the *past participle*) is used:

a. To form the *present perfect tense*. This tense indicates action that was started in the past and has recently been completed or is continuing up to the present time. It consists of the verb *have* or *has* plus the past participle.

We *have filled* the orders. (**NOT:** We *have filled* the orders yesterday.)

She *has* always *done* what we expect of her.

Consumers *have become* an articulate force in today's business world.

b. To form the *past perfect tense*. This tense indicates action that was completed *before another past action*. It consists of the verb *had* plus the past participle.

We *had filled* the orders before we saw your letter.

She *had finished* the job before we arrived.

10

(Continued on page 222.)

c. To form the *future perfect tense.* This tense indicates action that will be completed *before a certain time in the future.* It consists of the verb *shall have* or *will have* plus the past participle.

We *will have filled* the orders by that time. (See page 272 for a usage note on *shall* and *will.*)

She *will have finished* the job by next Friday.

NOTE: Be careful not to use a past tense form (the second principal part) in place of a past participle.

I have *broken* the racket. (**NOT:** I have *broke* the racket.)

The dress has *shrunk.* (**NOT:** The dress has *shrank.*)

Prices have *risen* again. (**NOT:** Prices have *rose* again.)

He has *worn* his shoes out. (**NOT:** He has *wore* his shoes out.)

1034 The fourth principal part of the verb (the *present participle*) is used:

a. To form the *present progressive tense.* This tense indicates action still in progress. It consists of the verb *am, is,* or *are* plus the present participle.

We *are filling* all orders as fast as we can.

She *is doing* all that can be expected of her.

b. To form the *past progressive tense.* This tense indicates action in progress sometime in the past. It consists of the verb *was* or *were* plus the present participle.

We *were waiting* for new stock at the time your order came in.

She *was doing* a good job when I last checked her work.

c. To form the *future progressive tense.* This tense indicates action that will be in progress in the future. It consists of the verb *shall be* or *will be* plus the present participle.

We *will be working* overtime for the next two weeks. (See page 272 for a usage note on *shall* and *will.*)

They *will be receiving* additional stock throughout the next two weeks.

d. To form the *present perfect progressive,* the *past perfect progressive,* and the *future perfect progressive tenses.* These tenses convey the same meaning as the simple perfect tenses (see ¶1033) except that the progressive element adds the sense of continuous action. These tenses consist of the verbs *has been, have been, had been, shall have been,* and *will have been* plus the present participle. Compare the following examples with those in ¶1033.

We *have been filling* these orders with Model 212A instead of 212. (Present perfect progressive.)

We *had been filling* these orders with Model 212A until we saw your directive. (Past perfect progressive.)

By next Friday we *will have been working* overtime for two straight weeks. (Future perfect progressive.)

1035 The first principal part of the verb undergoes a change in form to express the third person singular in the present tense.

a. Most verbs simply add *s* in the third person singular.

he feels	**BUT:** I feel, you feel, we feel, they feel
she thinks	I think, you think, we think, they think
it looks	I look, you look, we look, they look

10

b. Verbs ending in *s, x, z, sh, ch,* or *o* add *es.*

he misses	it buzzes	she watches
she fixes	he wishes	it does

c. Verbs ending in a vowel plus *y* add *s;* those ending in a consonant plus *y* change *y* to *i* and add *es.*

say: he says	employ: she employs	try: it tries
convey: she conveys	buy: he buys	apply: she applies

d. Verbs ending in *i* simply add *s.*

taxi: he taxis	ski: she skis

e. The verb *to be* is irregular since *be,* the first principal part, is not used in the present tense.

I am	we are
you are	you are
he, she, it is	they are

f. A few verbs remain unchanged in the third person singular.

PRESENT TENSE:	he may	she can	it will
PAST TENSE:	he might	she could	it would

➤ *See page 260 for a usage note on* Don't.

Passive Forms

1036 The passive forms of a verb consist of some form of the helping verb *to be* plus the past participle of the main verb.

it is intended (present passive of *intend*)
we were expected (past passive of *expect*)
they will be audited (future passive of *audit*)
she has been notified (present perfect passive of *notify*)
you had been told (past perfect passive of *tell*)
he will have been given (future perfect passive of *give*)

1037 A *passive* verb directs the action toward the subject. An *active* verb directs the action toward an object.

ACTIVE: Melanie (*subject*) will lead (*verb*) the discussion (*object*).
PASSIVE: The discussion (*subject*) will be led (*verb*) by Melanie.

➤ *For additional examples, see the entry for* Voice *on page 525.*

a. The passive form of a verb is appropriate (1) when you want to emphasize the *receiver* of the action (by making it the subject) or (2) when the *doer* of the action is not important or is deliberately not mentioned.

I was seriously injured as a result of your negligence. (Emphasizes *I,* the receiver of the action. **RATHER THAN:** Your negligence seriously injured me.)

This proposal is based on a careful analysis of all available research studies. (Emphasizes the basis for the proposal; the name of the person who drafted the proposal is not important.)

Unfortunately, the decision was made without consulting any of the board members. (Emphasizes how the decision was made and deliberately omits the name of the person responsible.)

Fred Allen once defined a conference as a gathering of important people who "singly can do nothing but together can decide that nothing can be done."

10

(Continued on page 224.)

b. In all other cases use active verb forms to achieve a simpler and more vigorous style. Except in those circumstances cited in ¶1037a, passive verb forms typically produce awkward or stilted sentences.

WEAK PASSIVES: It *has been decided* by the Human Resources Committee that full pay *should be given* to you for the period of your hospitalization.

STRONG ACTIVES: The Human Resources Committee *has decided* that you *should receive* full pay for the period of your hospitalization.

c. Watch out for passive constructions that unintentionally point to the wrong *doer* of the action.

CONFUSING: Two computers were reported stolen over the weekend by the head of corporate security.

CLEAR: The head of corporate security reported that two computers were stolen over the weekend.

CONFUSING: One of our second-shift workers was found injured by a Good Samaritan outside the parking lot entrance last night.

CLEAR: Last night one of our second-shift workers was injured outside the parking lot entrance and was found there by a Good Samaritan.

Verbs Following Clauses of Necessity, Demand, Etc.

1038 Sentences that express *necessity, demand, strong request, urging,* or *resolution* in the main clause require a *subjunctive* verb in the dependent clause that follows.

a. If the verb in the dependent clause requires the use of the verb *to be,* use the form *be* with all three persons (not *am, is,* or *are*).

NECESSITY: It is necessary (OR important OR essential) that these questions *be answered* at once. (NOT: are answered.)

DEMAND: I insist that I *be allowed* to present a minority report at the next board meeting. (NOT: am allowed.)

REQUEST: They have asked that you *be notified* at once if matters do not proceed according to plan. (NOT: are notified.)

URGING: We urged (OR suggested) that he *be given* a second chance to prove himself in the job. (NOT: is given.)

RESOLUTION: The committee has resolved (OR decided OR ruled) that the decision *be deferred* until the next meeting. (NOT: is deferred.)

b. If the verb in the dependent clause is a verb other than *be,* use the ordinary *present tense* form for all three persons. However, do not add *s* (or otherwise change the form) for the third person singular.

NECESSITY: It is essential that he *arrive* on time. (NOT: arrives.)

DEMAND: They insist that he *do* the work over. (NOT: does.)

REQUEST: They have asked that she *remain* on the committee until the end of the year. (NOT: remains.)

URGING: I suggested that she *type* the material triple-spaced to allow room for some very heavy editing. (NOT: types.)

RESOLUTION: They have resolved that Fred *represent* them. (NOT: represents.)

➢ *See the entry for* Mood, subjunctive *in Appendix A.*

10

Verbs Following *Wish* Clauses

1039 Sentences that start with *I wish, she wishes,* and so on, require a subjunctive verb in the dependent clause that follows.

    a. To express *present* time in the dependent clause, put the verb in the *past tense.*

        I wish I *knew* how to proceed.

        I wish I *could attend.*

        NOTE: If the verb is *to be,* use *were* for all three persons.

        I wish I *were going* to the reception. (**NOT:** was going.)

        I wish he *were going* with me.

    b. To express *past* time in the dependent clause, put the verb in the *past perfect tense.*

        I wish that she *had invited* me.

        I wish that I *had been* there.

        I wish that I *could have attended.*

    c. To express *future* time in the dependent clause, use the helping verb *would* instead of *will.*

        I wish he *would arrive* on time.

        I wish she *would make* more of an effort.

Verbs in *If* Clauses

1040 When an *if* clause states a condition that is *highly improbable, doubtful,* or *contrary to fact,* the verb in the *if* clause requires special treatment, like that described in ¶1039: *to express present time, use the past tense; to express past time, use the past perfect tense.* (In the following examples note the relationship of tenses between the dependent clause and the main clause.)

    If I *knew* the answer (but I don't), I *would* not *ask* you.

    If I *had known* the answer (but I didn't), I *would* not *have asked* you.

    If I *were* you (but I am not), I *would take* the job.

    If I *had been* in your shoes (but I wasn't), I *would have taken* the job.

    If he *were invited* (but he isn't), he *would be* glad to go.

    If he *had been invited* (but he wasn't), he *would have been* glad to go.

    NOTE: Do not use *would have* for *had* in an *if* clause. See page 276 for a usage note on *would have.*

1041 When an *if* clause states a condition that is *possible* or *likely,* the verb in the *if* clause requires no special treatment. *To express present time, use the present tense; to express past time, use the past tense.* Compare the following pairs of examples. Those labeled "Probable" reflect the verb forms described here in ¶1041. Those labeled "Improbable" reflect the verb forms described in ¶1040.

    PROBABLE: If I *leave* this job (and I may do so), I *will take* a full-time teaching position.

    IMPROBABLE: If I *left* this job (but I probably won't), I *would take* a full-time teaching position.

(Continued on page 226.)

10

PROBABLE: If I *go* to San Francisco (and I may), I *will want* you to go with me.

IMPROBABLE: If I *were going* to San Francisco (but I probably won't), I *would want* you to go with me.

PROBABLE: If she *was* in yesterday (and she may have been), I *did* not *see* her.

IMPROBABLE: If she *had been* in yesterday (but she wasn't), I *would have seen* her.

Verbs in *As If* or *As Though* Clauses

1042 When an *as if* or *as though* clause expresses a condition *contrary to fact*, the verb in the clause requires special treatment, like that described in ¶1040.

She acts as if she *were* the only person who mattered. (But she isn't.)

He talks as if he *knew* the facts of the situation. (But he doesn't.)

You act as though you *hadn't* a care in the world. (But you have.)

1043 *As if* or *as though* clauses are now often used to express a condition that is *highly probable*. In such cases do not give the verb special treatment. *Use the present tense to express present time, the future tense to express future time, and the past tense to express past time.*

It looks as if it *will* rain. (OR: It looks as if it *is going* to rain.)

She acted as if she *planned* to look for another job.

Infinitives

1044 An infinitive is the form of the verb preceded by *to* (for example, *to write, to do, to be*). When two or more infinitives are used in a parallel construction, the word *to* may be omitted after the first infinitive unless special emphasis is desired.

Ask Ruth Gonzales *to sign* both copies of the contract, *return* the original to us, and *keep* the other copy. (*Return* and *keep* are infinitives without *to*.)

I would like you *to explain* the job to Harry, *to give* him help if he needs it, and *to see* that the job is done properly. (For emphasis, *to* is used with all three infinitives—*explain, give,* and *see*.)

NOTE: The word *to* is usually dropped when the infinitive follows such verbs as *see, hear, feel, let, help,* and *need.*

Will you please help me *prepare* the report? (RATHER THAN: help me *to prepare*)

You need not *return* the clipping. (OR: You do not need *to return* the clipping.)

1045 a. Infinitives have two main tense forms: the present infinitive and the perfect infinitive.

(1) The perfect infinitive is used to express action that has been completed before the time of the main verb.

I *am sorry to have caused* you so much trouble last week. (The act of causing trouble was completed before the act of expressing regret; therefore, the perfect infinitive is used.)

(2) The present infinitive is used in all other cases.

I planned *to leave* early. (NOT: *to have left*. The act of leaving could not have been completed before the act of planning, so the present infinitive is used.)

b. The passive form of the present infinitive consists of *to be* plus the past participle. Do not omit *to be* in such constructions.

This office needs *to be repainted*. (NOT: This office needs *repainted*.)

10

1046 *Splitting an infinitive* (that is, inserting an adverb between *to* and the verb) should be avoided because (a) it typically produces an awkward construction and (b) the adverb usually functions more effectively in another location.

> **WEAK:** It was impossible to *even* see a foot ahead.
>
> **BETTER:** It was impossible to see *even* a foot ahead.
>
> **WEAK:** He always tries to *carefully* do the work.
>
> **BETTER:** He always tries to do the work *carefully*.

However, split the infinitive when alternative locations of the adverb produce an awkward or weakly constructed sentence.

a. Before splitting an infinitive, first try to place the adverb *after the object* of the infinitive. In many instances the adverb functions most effectively in that location.

> You ought *to review* these plans *thoroughly*.
> (**BETTER THAN:** You ought to thoroughly review these plans.)
>
> I need *to make* the decision *quickly*.
> (**BETTER THAN:** I need to quickly make the decision.)

b. If step *a* does not produce an effective sentence, try to locate the adverb directly *before* or directly *after* the infinitive. In some cases the adverb functions effectively in this position; in other cases the resulting sentence is awkward.

> **CONFUSING:** I want you *to supervise* the work that is to be done *personally*. (When the object of the infinitive is long or involved, it is difficult to place the adverb after the object without creating confusion. Here *personally* seems to modify *to be done* when in fact it should modify *to supervise*.)
>
> **AWKWARD:** I want you to supervise *personally* the work that is to be done.
>
> **GOOD:** I want you *personally* to supervise the work that is to be done.

c. If steps *a* and *b* fail to produce an effective sentence, try splitting the infinitive. If a good sentence results, keep it; if not, try rewording the sentence.

> **CONFUSING:** I want you *to consider* Jenkins' proposal to handle all our deliveries *carefully*. (When *carefully* is located after the complete object, it no longer clearly refers to *to consider*.)
>
> **AWKWARD:** I want you *carefully* to consider Jenkins' proposal to handle all our deliveries.
>
> **AWKWARD:** I want you to consider *carefully* Jenkins' proposal to handle all our deliveries.
>
> **GOOD:** I want you to *carefully* consider Jenkins' proposal . . .

d. When an infinitive consists of *to be* plus a past or present participle of another verb, inserting an adverb before the participle is not considered splitting an infinitive. Nevertheless, in many such sentences it may be possible to locate the adverb to better advantage elsewhere in the sentence.

> These plans need to be *thoroughly* reviewed.
>
> Claude appears to be *continually* turning up with last-minute objections to any decision I make.

(Continued on page 228.)

10

NOTE: By the same token, it is perfectly acceptable to position an adverb between a helping verb and a past or present participle. It is even acceptable to position an adverb *within* the elements of a helping verb.

This new technology has *already* been *effectively* applied in many industries.
I hear that Martha has been *seriously* considering early retirement.

➤ *For dangling infinitive phrases, see also* ¶*1082b.*

Sequence of Tenses

1047 When the verb in the main clause is in the past tense, the verb in a dependent *that* clause should also express past time. Compare the tenses in the following pairs of examples:

She *says* (present) that she *is* now *working* (present) for CBS.
She *said* (past) that she *was* now *working* (past) for CBS.

He *says* (present) that he *has seen* (present perfect) your résumé.
He *said* (past) that he *had seen* (past perfect) your résumé.

I *think* (present) that he *will see* (future) you tomorrow.
I *thought* (past) that he *would see* (past form of *will see*) you tomorrow.

EXCEPTION: The verb in the dependent clause should remain in the present tense if it expresses a general truth.

Our legal adviser *pointed out* (past) that all persons under 18 *are* (present) legally considered minors. (General truth.)

Omitting Parts of Verbs

1048 When compound verbs in the same sentence share a common element, that element does not need to be repeated.

We *have* received your letter and forwarded it to our St. Louis office. (The helping verb *have* is shared by the two main verbs, *received* and *forwarded.*)

We can and will *achieve* these goals. (The main verb *achieve* is shared by the two helping verbs, *can* and *will.*)

However, do not omit any element when different parts of the main verb are required.

WRONG: I never have and I never will forget what you have done for me.
RIGHT: I never have *forgotten* and I never will *forget* . . .

WRONG: We have and still are asking for an accounting of the assets.
RIGHT: We have *asked* and still are *asking* for . . .

Troublesome Verbs

➤ *See individual entries listed alphabetically in Section 11 for the following verbs:*

Affect–effect	Don't	Of–have
Ain't	Ensure–insure–assure	Raise–rise
Appraise–apprise	Enthused over	Serve–service
Appreciate	Graduated–was graduated	Set–sit
Bring–take	Help	Shall–will
Come–go	Imply–infer	Should–would
Come and	Lay–lie	Supposed to
Complement–compliment	Learn–teach	Try and
Comprise–compose	Leave–let	Type–key
Could not care less	May–can (might–could)	Used to
Done	Maybe–may be	Would have

10

PRONOUNS

Agreement With Antecedents: Basic Rules

1049 a. A pronoun must agree with its *antecedent* (the word for which the pronoun stands) in number, gender, and person.

I must stand by *my* client, just as *you* must stand by *yours.*

Frank said that *he* could do the job alone.

Alice wants to know whether *her* proposal has been approved.

The *company* has not decided whether to change *its* policy on vacations. (See ¶¶1019–1020.)

We plan to explain *our* shift in corporate strategy at the next shareholders' meeting.

The company's *auditors* will issue *their* report tomorrow.

The *Vanderveers* are giving a party at *their* house.

The *grand jury* has completed *its* investigation. (See ¶1019 for collective nouns.)

Why not have *each witness* write *his* or *her* version of the accident? (See ¶1053 for indefinite pronouns as antecedents.)

It is *I* who *am* at fault. (*Who* agrees in person and number with the antecedent *I;* the verb *am* also agrees with *I.*)

It is *she* who *is* willing to compromise.

It is *we,* the individual taxpayers, who *have* to make up for the loss of commercial ratables.

It is *they* who *are* behind schedule.

It is *you* who *are* to blame. (*Who* refers to *you;* hence the verb is *are* to agree with *you.* See ¶1001a, note.)

BUT: You are the *person* who *is* to blame. (Here *who* refers to *person;* hence the verb is *is* to agree with *person.*)

b. Use a plural pronoun when the antecedent consists of two nouns or pronouns joined by *and.*

Can *Mary* and *you* give us *your* decision by Monday?

Sonia and *Dave* say *they* will attend.

The *Montaignes* and the *Reillys* have sent *their* regrets.

Are *you* and *I* prepared to say that *we* can handle the assignment?

c. Use a singular pronoun when the antecedent consists of two *singular* nouns joined by *or* or *nor.* Use a plural pronoun when the antecedent consists of two *plural* nouns joined by *or* or *nor.* (See also ¶¶1003–1005.)

Either *Will* or *Ed* will have to give up *his* office. (**NOT:** their.)

Neither *Joan* nor *Helen* wants to do *her* share. (**NOT:** their.)

Either the *Kopecks* or the *Henleys* will bring *their* videocassette recorder.

NOTE: When *or* or *nor* joins a singular noun and a plural noun, a pronoun that refers to this construction should agree in number with the nearer noun. However, a strict application of this rule can lead to problems in sentence structure and meaning. Therefore, always try to make this kind of construction plural by locating the plural subject nearer the verb.

10

(Continued on page 230.)

Neither Mr. Wing nor his *employees have* reached *their* goal. (The plural pronoun *their* is used to agree with the nearer noun, *employees;* the verb *have* is also in the plural.)

NOT: Neither the employees nor *Mr. Wing has* reached *his* goal. (The sentence follows the rule—*his* agrees with *Mr. Wing,* the nearer noun, and the verb *has* is singular; however, the meaning of the sentence has been distorted.)

d. Make sure that the pronouns you use refer to the antecedents you intend. To avoid confusion, reword as necessary.

CONFUSING: Unrealistic deadlines, excessive pressures, and unsafe working conditions can be very damaging to your employees. You must do everything you can to eliminate them. (The employees or the destructive conditions?)

CLEAR: Unrealistic deadlines, excessive pressures, and unsafe working conditions can be very damaging to your employees. You must do everything you can to eliminate these destructive conditions.

Agreement With Common-Gender Antecedents

1050 Nouns that apply to both males and females have a *common* gender.

parent	doctor	boss	writer
child	lawyer	supervisor	speaker
customer	professor	employee	listener
manager	instructor	student	consultant

When a singular noun of common gender serves as a *definite* antecedent (one that names a specific person whose gender is known), use the pronoun *he* or *she* as appropriate.

My *boss* [previously identified as Robert Hecht] prefers to open *his* own mail.

Ask your *doctor* [known to be a woman] to sign *her* name on this form.

1051 When a singular noun of common gender serves as an *indefinite* antecedent *(a doctor, any doctor, every doctor)* or as a *generic* antecedent *(the doctor,* meaning "doctors in general"), the traditional practice has been to use *he* as a generic pronoun applying equally to males and females.

The *writer* should include a table of contents with *his* manuscript.

When an indefinite or generic antecedent names an occupation or a role in which women predominate (for example, *the teacher, the secretary, the nurse*), the traditional practice has been to use *she* as a generic pronoun.

A *secretary* needs to organize *her* work and set priorities each day.

This traditional use of *he* and *she* as generic pronouns (as described above) is offensive to many people, who feel that the masculine bias in the word *he* makes it unsuitable as a pronoun that applies equally to women and men. Moreover, they feel that the generic use of *she* serves to reinforce stereotyped notions about women's occupations or roles. The ideal solution would be a new generic pronoun without masculine or feminine connotations. However, until such a pronoun has been devised and accepted into common usage, consider various alternatives to the generic use of *he* or *she.* (See ¶1052.)

1052 a. Use *he or she, his or her,* or *him or her.* This solution works well in isolated cases but can be clumsy if repeated frequently in the same context. (In any case, avoid the use of *he/she, s/he,* and similar constructions.)

10

An *instructor* should offer *his or her* students challenging projects.

(**RATHER THAN:** An instructor should offer *his* students . . .)

b. Change the wording from singular to plural.

Parents of teenage children often *wonder* where *they* went wrong.

(**RATHER THAN:** The *parent* of a teenage child often *wonders* where *he or she* went wrong.)

c. Reword to avoid the generic pronoun.

When a customer calls, be sure to ask for a phone number.

(**RATHER THAN:** When a customer calls, ask *him or her* to leave *his or her* phone number.)

An assistant tries to anticipate the needs of the boss.

(**RATHER THAN:** An assistant tries to anticipate the needs of *his or her* boss.)

d. If the application of these various alternatives produces wordiness or an unacceptable shift in meaning or emphasis, then as a last resort use the generic *he* or the generic *she* as described in ¶1051. However, try to avoid doing so whenever possible.

Agreement With Indefinite-Pronoun Antecedents

1053 a. Use a singular pronoun when the antecedent is a singular indefinite pronoun. The following indefinite pronouns are always singular. They are typically used as nouns, but a few (such as *each* and *every*) are used as adjectives.

anyone	everyone	someone	no one
anybody	everybody	somebody	nobody
anything	everything	something	nothing
each	every	either	one
each one	many a	neither	another

Every company has *its* own vacation policy. (**NOT:** their.)

Neither one of the campaigns did as well as *it* was supposed to. (**NOT:** they were.)

NOTE: These singular indefinite forms often call for the generic use of *he* or *she* (see ¶¶1051–1052). The following sentences use alternative wording to show how the generic *he* or *she* can be avoided. The last sentence presents a situation for which no reasonable alternative exists.

Everyone should submit *his* expense report by Friday.
BETTER: All staff *members* should submit *their* expense reports by Friday.
OR: *Everyone* should submit *his or her* expense report by Friday.

If *anyone* should ask for me, tell *him* that I won't return until Monday.
BETTER: If anyone should ask for me, say that I won't return . . .

While the conference is in session, does *every assistant* know how *she* is to handle *her boss's* calls?
BETTER: . . . do *all the assistants* know how *they* are to handle *their bosses'* calls?

Nobody could have helped *himself* in a situation like that.

➤ *For agreement of these indefinite pronouns with verbs, see ¶¶1009–1011; for possessive forms of these pronouns, see ¶637.*

(Continued on page 232.)

10

b. Use a plural pronoun when the antecedent is a plural indefinite form. The following indefinite pronouns are always plural:

many   few   several   others   both

Many customers prefer to help *themselves; others* usually like to have a salesperson wait on *them.*

A *few* of the directors have not yet taken *their* vacations.

Several sales representatives in the Southern Region made *their* annual goals in nine months.

Both managers have said that *they* want to be considered for Mr. Hall's job when he retires next year.

➤ *For agreement of these indefinite pronouns with verbs, see ¶1012.*

c. The following indefinite forms may be singular or plural, depending on the noun to which they refer.

all   none   any   some   more   most

When these words are used as antecedents, determine whether they are singular or plural. Then make the pronouns that refer to them agree in number.

Some of the *employees* have not yet had *their* annual physical checkup. (*Some* refers to *employees* and is plural; *some* is the antecedent of *their.*)

Some of the *manuscript* has been typed, but *it* has not been proofread. (*Some* refers to *manuscript* and is singular; *some* is the antecedent of *it* in the second clause.)

➤ *For agreement of these indefinite pronouns with verbs, see ¶1013.*

d. Since indefinite forms express the third person, pronouns referring to these antecedents should also be in the third person *(he, she, it, they).*

If *anyone* wants a vacation pay advance, *he* or *she* should apply for it in writing. (**NOT**: If *anyone* wants a vacation pay advance, *you* should apply for it . . .)

If the indefinite form is modified so that it strongly expresses the first or second person, the personal pronoun must also agree in number. Compare the following examples:

Most parents want *their* children to go to college. (Third person.)
Most of us want *our* children to go to college. (First person.)

A *few* have missed *their* deadlines. (Third person.)
A *few of you* have missed *your* deadlines. (Second person.)

Each employee knows how much *he* or *she* ought to contribute to the United Way fund drive. (Third person.)
BUT: *Each of us* knows how much *he* or *she* ought to contribute to the United Way fund drive. (Third person. In this sentence, *of us* does not shift the meaning to the first person; the emphasis is on what the individual contributes, not on what *we* contribute.)

IMPORTANT NOTE: **Pronouns take different forms, not only to indicate a difference in person** *(I, you, he)*, **number** *(he, they)*, **and gender** *(he, she)* **but also to indicate a difference in case** *(nominative, possessive, objective)*. **Although a pronoun must agree with its antecedent in person, number, and gender, it does *not* necessarily agree with its antecedent in case. The case of a pronoun depends on its own relation to the other words in the sentence. The rules in ¶¶1054–1064 indicate how to choose the right case for pronouns.**

10

Personal Pronouns

1054 Nominative Forms of Personal Pronouns

Use *I, we, you, he, she, it, they:*

a. When the pronoun is the subject of a verb.

I wrote to Eileen McIntyre, but *she* hasn't answered.

Debbie and *I* can handle the job ourselves.
(**NOT:** Debbie and me **OR:** me and Debbie.)

Either *he* or *I* can work late tonight. (**NOT:** him or me.)

NOTE: In sentences like the last two above, try each subject alone with the verb. You would not say "Me can handle the job" or "Him can work late tonight." Therefore, *I* and *he* must be used.

b. When the pronoun appears in the predicate after some form of the verb *to be (am, is, are, was, were)* or after a verb phrase containing some form of *to be* (see the list below). Pronouns that follow these verb forms should be in the nominative.

shall (**OR** will) be	have (**OR** has) been
should (**OR** would) be	had been
shall (**OR** will) have been	may (**OR** might) be
should (**OR** would) have been	may (**OR** might) have been
can (**OR** could) be	must (**OR** ought to) be
could have been	must have (**OR** ought to have) been

It could have been *they.*

It is *I.*

Was it *he* or *she* who phoned?

This is *she.*

NOTE: A sentence like *It could have been they,* while grammatically correct, would sound better if reworded in idiomatic English: *They could have been the ones.* Moreover, a sentence like *It's me* is acceptable in colloquial speech but not in writing. When you hear a telephone caller ask for you by name, do not respond by saying *This is him* or *This is her.* If you wish to respond correctly (and somewhat pompously), say *This is he* or *This is she.* If you wish to respond correctly (and sound more natural), say *This is . . .* and then give your name.

➤ *For special rules governing pronouns with the infinitive* to be, *see ¶1064.*

1055 Objective Forms of Personal Pronouns

Use *me, us, you, him, her, it, them:*

a. When the pronoun is the direct or indirect object of a verb.

Larry gave Maris and *us* tickets for the opening.

They invited my husband and *me* for the weekend.

NOTE: When *my husband and* is mentally omitted, the objective form *me* is clearly the correct pronoun ("They invited *me* for the weekend").

b. When the pronoun is the object of a preposition.

This is for *you* and *her.*

No one knows except *you* and *me.* (**NOT:** except you and I.)

Between *you* and *me,* that decision is unfair. (**NOT:** between you and I.)

EXCEPTION: He is a friend of *mine (yours, his, hers, ours, theirs).* (See ¶648.)

(Continued on page 234.)

10

c. When the pronoun is the subject or object of an infinitive. (See ¶1064.)

> The department head asked *him* to resign. (*Him* is the subject of *to resign.*)
>
> Did you ask Janet to call *me*? (*Me* is the object of *to call.*)

1056 Possessive Forms of Personal Pronouns

a. Most personal pronouns have two possessive forms:

my	your	his	her	its	our	their
mine	yours	....	hers	...	ours	theirs

b. Use *my, your, his, her, its, our,* or *their* when the possessive pronoun immediately precedes the noun it modifies.

> That is *my* book.   It was *their* choice.   George is *her* neighbor.

c. Use *mine, yours, his, hers, its, ours,* or *theirs* when the possessive pronoun stands apart from the noun it refers to.

> That book is *mine.*   The choice was *theirs.*   George is a neighbor of *hers.*

NOTE: Do not insert an apostrophe before the final *s* in possessive pronouns.

> yours (**NOT:** your's)   ours (**NOT:** our's)
> hers (**NOT:** her's)   theirs (**NOT:** their's)

d. A pronoun that modifies a *gerund* (a verbal noun ending in *ing*) should be in the possessive. (See ¶647.)

> I appreciated *your shipping* the order so promptly.
> (**NOT:** I appreciated *you shipping* the order so promptly.)
>
> I was not happy about *his telling* the media why he had resigned.
> (**NOT:** I was not happy about *him telling* the media why he had resigned.)

e. Do not confuse certain possessive pronouns with contractions and other phrases that sound like the possessive pronouns.

its (possessive)	it's (it is **OR** it has)
their (possessive)	they're (they are) **OR** there're (there are)
theirs (possessive)	there's (there is **OR** there has)
your (possessive)	you're (you are)

As a test for the correct form, try to substitute *it is, it has, they are, there are, there is, there has,* or *you are,* whichever is appropriate. If the substitution does not make sense, use the corresponding possessive form.

> The firm must protect *its* assets. ("Protect it is assets" makes no sense.)
> **BUT:** *It's* time to take stock of our achievements.
>
> How would you go about estimating *its* worth?
> **BUT:** How much would you say *it's* worth?
>
> *Their* investing in high-tech stocks was a shrewd idea.
> **BUT:** *They're* investing in high-tech stocks.
>
> *Their* complaints have proved to be unfounded.
> **BUT:** *There are* complaints that have proved to be unfounded.
>
> *Theirs* no longer works; that's why they borrow ours.
> **BUT:** *There's* no use expecting him to change.
>
> *Your* thinking is sound, but we lack the funds to underwrite your proposal.
> **BUT:** *You're* thinking of applying for a transfer, I understand.

➤ *For other possessive pronouns, see also ¶¶636–637.*

10

1057 When a pronoun follows *than* or *as* in a comparison, determine the correct form of the pronoun by mentally supplying any missing words. To avoid correct but awkward sentences, actually supply the missing words.

> She writes better than *I*. (She writes better than *I do*.)
>
> I like you better than *him*. (I like you better than *I like him*.)
> **BUT:** I like you better than *he*. (I like you better than *he does*.)
>
> Joe is not as talented as *she*. (Joe is not as talented as *she is*.)

1058 When a pronoun is used to identify a noun or another pronoun, it is either nominative or objective, depending on how the antecedent is used.

> The committee has asked *us*, Ruth and *me*, to present the report. (Since *us* is objective, the identifying pronoun *me* is also objective.)
>
> The explanation was for the *newcomers*, Marie and *me*. (Was for *me*.)
>
> The exceptions were the *newcomers*, Marie and *I*. (Exception was *I*.)
>
> Let's *you* and *me* schedule a brown-bag lunch. (*Let's* is a contraction for *let us*. Since *us* is the objective form, the pronouns *you* and *me* are also objective.)

> **NOTE:** In sentences like the following, mentally omit the noun *(employees)* to determine the correct form.

> The company wants *us* employees to work on Saturdays. (The company wants *us* to work on Saturdays.)
>
> *We* employees need to confer. (*We* need to confer.)

1059 Some writers consistently use *we* instead of *I* to avoid a seeming overemphasis on themselves. However, it is preferable to use *we* only when you are speaking on behalf of an organization you represent and to use *I* when speaking for yourself alone.

> *We* shall prepare the necessary forms as soon as you send *us* a signed release. (This writer is speaking on behalf of the firm.)
>
> It is *my* opinion that this patient may be discharged at once. (This writer is speaking only for himself. Under these circumstances it would sound pompous to say, "It is *our* opinion.")

Compound Personal Pronouns

1060 The *self-* or *selves*-ending pronouns *(myself, yourself, himself, herself, itself, ourselves, yourselves, themselves)* should be used:

a. To direct the action expressed by the verb back to the subject.

> *She* found *herself* the only one in favor of the move.
>
> *We* have satisfied *ourselves* as to the wisdom of the action.
>
> We think that *they* have insured *themselves* against a possible loss.

b. To emphasize a noun or pronoun already expressed.

> The *trainees themselves* arranged the program.
>
> *I* will write her *myself*.
>
> *I myself* am bewildered. (**BUT NOT:** *I myself* am *personally* bewildered. Using *myself* and *personally* in the same sentence creates redundancy rather than emphasis.)

> **NOTE:** Do not use a compound personal pronoun unless the noun or pronoun to which it refers is expressed in the same sentence.

> The tickets are for the Wrights and *me*. (**NOT:** myself.)
>
> Henry and *I* can handle all the mail. (**NOT:** Henry and myself.)

10

¶1061

Interrogative and Relative Pronouns

1061 *Who* and *Whom; Whoever* and *Whomever*

a. These pronouns are both *interrogative* pronouns (used in asking questions) and *relative* pronouns (used to refer to a noun in the main clause).

Who is going? (Interrogative.)

Mr. Sears is the one *who* is going. (Relative, referring to *one.*)

To *whom* shall I deliver the message? (Interrogative.)

Ms. DeAngelis, *whom* I have never met, is in charge of the program. (Relative, referring to *Ms. DeAngelis.*)

b. These pronouns may be either singular or plural in meaning.

Who is talking? (Singular.)   *Whom* do you prefer for this job? (Singular.)

Who are going? (Plural.)   *Whom* do you prefer for these jobs? (Plural.)

c. *Who* (or *whoever*) is the nominative form. Use *who* whenever *he, she, they, I,* or *we* could be substituted in the *who* clause. (If in doubt, mentally rearrange the clause as is done in parentheses after each of the following examples.)

Who is arranging the teleconference? (*She* is arranging the teleconference.)

Who booked our sales conference in a honeymooners' hideaway? (*He* booked the sales conference.)

Who shall I say is calling? (I shall say *he* is calling.)

Who did they say was chosen? (They did say *she* was chosen.)

Who could it have been? (It could have been *he.*)

The matter of *who* should pay was not decided. (*He* should pay.)

Everybody wants to know *who* you think should be appointed. (You think *she* should be appointed.)

Whoever wins the primary will win the election. (*She* wins the primary.)

We will select *whoever* meets our minimum qualifications. (*He* meets our minimum qualifications.)

I will speak to *whoever* answers the phone. (*He* answers the phone.)

Please write at once to *whoever* you think can supply the information desired. (You think *she* can supply the information desired.)

Gloria is the one *who* can best do the job. (*She* can best do the job.)

James is the one *who* we expect will win. (We expect *he* will win.)

Please vote for the member *who* you believe has done the most for the firm. (You believe *he* has done the most for the firm.)

You are free to vote for *whoever* appeals to you. (*She* appeals to you.)

You are free to vote for *whomever* you wish. (You wish to vote for *him.*)

We have referred your claim to our attorney, *who* we are sure will reply soon. (We are sure *she* will reply soon.)

We have sent this order blank to all *who* we have reason to believe are interested in our book. (We have reason to believe *they* are interested . . .)

d. *Whom* (or *whomever*) is the objective form. Use *whom* whenever *him, her, them, me,* or *us* could be substituted as the object of the verb or as the object of a preposition in the *whom* clause.

Whom did you see today? (You did see *her* today.)

To *whom* were you talking? (You were talking to *him.*)

10

Whom were you talking about? (You were talking about *him*.)

Whom did you say you wanted to see? (You did say you wanted to see *her*.)

It depends on *whom* they mean. (They mean *him*.)

The question of *whom* we should charge is at issue. (We should charge *her*.)

Whomever you designate will get the promotion. (You designate *him*.)

I will hire *whomever* I can find. (I can find *her*.)

I will speak to *whomever* you suggest. (You suggest *her*.)

I will give the job to *whomever* you think you can safely recommend. (You think you can safely recommend *him*.)

BUT: I will give the job to *whoever* you think can be safely recommended. (You think *he* can be safely recommended.)

I need a cashier *whom* I can trust. (I can trust *her*.)

The man to *whom* I was referring is Ed Meissen. (I was referring to *him*.)

The person *whom* I was thinking of doesn't have all those qualifications. (I was thinking of *her*.)

The person *whom* we invited to address the committee cannot attend. (We invited *him* to address the committee.)

Jo Fry is the nominee *whom* they plan to support. (They plan to support *her*.)

Steve Koval is the person *whom* we all thought the committee would nominate. (We all thought the committee would nominate *him*.)

Elaine Gerrity, *whom* I considered to be their most promising representative, resigned. (I considered *her* to be their most promising representative.)

1062 *Who, Which,* and *That*

a. *Who* and *that* are used when referring to persons. Select *who* when the individual person or the individuality of a group is meant and *that* when a class, species, or type is meant.

She is the only one of my managers *who* can speak Japanese fluently.

He is the kind of student *that* should take advanced math.

b. *Which* and *that* are used when referring to places, objects, and animals. *Which* is always used to introduce nonessential clauses, and *that* is ordinarily used to introduce essential clauses.

Laura's report on employee benefits, *which* I sent you last week, should be of some help. (*Which* introduces a nonessential clause.)

The report *that* I sent you last week should be of some help. (*That* introduces an essential clause.)

NOTE: Many writers now use either *which* or *that* to introduce an essential clause. Indeed, *which* is to be preferred to *that* (1) when there are two or more parallel essential clauses in the same sentence, (2) when *that* has already been used in the sentence, or (3) when the essential clause is introduced by an expression such as *this . . . which, that . . . which, these . . . which,* or *those . . . which.*

Vivian is taking courses *which* will earn her a higher salary rating in her current job and *which* will qualify her for a number of higher-level jobs.

That is a movie *which* you must not miss.

We need to reinforce *those* ideas *which* were presented in earlier chapters.

(Continued on page 238.)

10

c. The verb in a relative clause introduced by *who, which,* or *that* should agree in number with the subject of the relative clause. In many cases the subject is clearly expressed.

The laser printer that *you have ordered* will be delivered in two weeks. (The subject of the relative clause is *you,* which requires a plural verb, *have ordered.*)

However, when the relative pronoun *who, which,* or *that* is itself the subject of the relative clause, the verb in the relative clause must agree with the antecedent of the relative pronoun.

The laser *printer* that *was ordered* on May 4 will be delivered in two weeks. (The relative pronoun *that* is the subject of the relative clause and refers to a singular antecedent, *printer.* Therefore, the verb in the relative clause—*was ordered*— must be singular.)

BUT: The laser *printers* that *were ordered* . . .

Sometimes it is difficult to determine the antecedent of the relative pronoun. In such cases mentally rearrange the wording, as is done in the following example.

Hyphenate the *elements* of a *compound adjective* that occur?/occurs? before a noun. (To determine whether the antecedent of *that* is the plural term *elements* or the singular term *compound adjective,* recast the sentence: "When a *compound adjective occurs* before a noun, hyphenate the elements." This makes it clear that in the original sentence *compound adjective* is the antecedent of *that;* thus the verb in the relative clause must be singular: *occurs.*)

Hyphenate the elements of a *compound adjective* that *occurs* before a noun.

d. *Which, that,* and *who* may be used to refer to organizations. When you are referring to the organization as a single entity (in other words, as *it*), then use *which* or *that* as indicated in ¶1062b. However, when you are thinking of the organization in terms of the individuals who make up the organization (in other words, when you think of the organization as *they*), you may use *who* or *that* as indicated in ¶1062a. (See also ¶1020.)

Although you are free to choose your own doctor, medical care is also available through an HMO [a health maintenance organization] with *which* the company has a special contract. (Since the HMO is referred to as a single entity, use *with which,* not *with whom.*)

Whenever we run short of computer supplies, the Brown & Weiner Company is the one *that* gives us the best service and the best prices.

We really like doing business with the people at the Brown & Weiner Company. They are a customer-oriented group *who* give us the best service and the best prices. (*That* may also be used in this sentence in place of *who.*)

1063 *Whose* and *Who's*

Do not confuse *whose* (the possessive form of *who*) with *who's* (a contraction meaning "who is" or "who has").

Whose house is it? (It is *his.*)

Who's the owner of that house? (*She* is.)

Who's had the most experience in that position? (*She* has had the most experience in that position.)

Who's the most experienced person in that position? (*She* is the most experienced person in that position.)

Whose experience is best suited to that position? (*Her* experience is.)

10

Pronouns With *To Be*

1064 a. If a pronoun is the subject of *to be,* use the *objective* form.

I want *her* to be successful.   I expected *them* to be late.

Whom do you consider to be the more expert driver? (You do consider *whom* to be the more expert driver?)

b. If *to be* has a subject and is followed by a pronoun, put that pronoun in the *objective* case.

They mistook the *visitors* to be *us.* (*Visitors,* the subject of *to be,* is in the objective; therefore, the predicate pronoun following *to be* is objective—*us.*)

They took *her* to be *me.*

Whom did you take *him* to be? (You did take *him* to be *whom?*)

c. If *to be* has *no* subject and is followed by a pronoun, put that pronoun in the *nominative* case.

The *caller* was thought to be *I.* (*I* agrees with the subject, *caller.*)

The *Macauleys* were thought to be *we.*

Who was *he* thought to be? (*He* was thought to be *who?*)

NOTE: The examples above are all grammatically correct, but they also sound quite awkward. Whenever possible, use more idiomatic wording. For example, the three sentences above could be recast as follows:

They thought I was the one who called.

The Macauleys were mistaken for us.

Who did they think he was?

Troublesome Pronouns

➤ *See the paragraphs indicated for each of the following pronouns. Entries listed in Section 11 are in alphabetic order.*

All of (see ¶1101)	Each other–one another (see ¶1101)	Someone–some one (see ¶1010, note)
Anyone–any one (see ¶1010, note)	Everyone–every one (see ¶1010, note)	That–which–who (see ¶1062)
Between you and me (see ¶1055b)	Most (see ¶1101)	These sort–these kind (see ¶1101)
Both–each (see ¶1101)	Nobody–no body (see ¶1101)	Who–whom (see ¶1061)
Both alike (see ¶1101)	None–no one (see ¶¶1013b and 1101)	Whoever–who ever (see ¶1061)

ADJECTIVES AND ADVERBS

For definitions of the terms *adjective* and *adverb,* see the appropriate entries in the Glossary of Grammatical Terms (Appendix A).

1065 Only an adverb can modify an adjective.

Packard's will give you a *really* good buy on calculators.

(**NOT:** Packard's will give you a *real* good buy on calculators.)

10

1066 When a word in the predicate refers to the *action of the verb*, use an *adverb* (not an adjective).

> We guarantee *to ship* the portfolios *promptly.*
>
> They *were injured badly* in the accident.

TEST: If *in a . . . manner* can be substituted for the *ly*-ending word, choose the adverb.

> *Read* the directions *carefully* (in a careful manner).

1067 When a word in the predicate describes the *subject* of the sentence, use an *adjective* (not an adverb). Verbs of the *senses* (*feel, look, sound, taste, smell*) and *linking* verbs (the various forms of *be, seem, appear, become*) are followed in most cases by adjectives. A few other verbs (such as *grow, prove, get, keep, remain,* and *turn*) are sometimes followed by adjectives.

> I feel *bad* (**NOT** badly). He has grown *tall.*
>
> She looked *happy.* The work proved *hard.*
>
> Your voice sounded *strong.* I got *lucky.*
>
> He seemed (**OR** appeared) *shy.* Let's all keep (**OR** remain) *calm.*
>
> They became *famous.* The weather has turned *cold.*

TEST: If *is, are, was, were,* or some other form of *be* can be substituted for the verb, choose the adjective.

> He *looks happy.* He *is happy.*

NOTE: In the following group of examples, verbs of the senses and linking verbs are used as verbs of action (¶1066). Since the modifier refers to the action of the verb (and does not describe the subject), the modifier must be an adverb.

> She *looked suspiciously* at the visitor in the reception room.
>
> He *felt carefully* along the ledge for the key.
>
> Our market share *has grown quickly.*
>
> He *appeared quietly* in the doorway.

1068 Several of the most frequently used adverbs have two forms.

close, closely	fair, fairly	loud, loudly	short, shortly
deep, deeply	hard, hardly	quick, quickly	slow, slowly
direct, directly	late, lately	right, rightly	wide, widely

a. In a number of cases the two forms have different meanings.

> Ship the goods *direct.* (Meaning "straight," "without detour.")
> They were *directly* responsible. (Meaning "without any intervention.")

> They arrived *late.* The truck stopped *short.*
> I haven't seen her *lately.* You will hear from us *shortly.*

> You've been working too *hard.* Turn *right* at the first traffic light.
> I could *hardly* hear him. I don't *rightly* remember.

b. In some cases the choice is largely a matter of idiom. Some verbs take the *ly* form; others take the short form.

dig deep	go slow	open wide	come close	play fair
wound deeply	proceed slowly	travel widely	watch closely	treat fairly

c. In still other cases the choice is simply one of formality. The *ly* forms are more formal.

> sell cheap **OR** sell cheaply talk loud **OR** talk loudly

10

1069 a. Although the *ly* ending usually signifies an adverb, a few adjectives also end in *ly*—for example, *costly, orderly, timely, motherly, fatherly, friendly, neighborly, worldly, earthly, lively, lovely, lonely.*

> Let's look for a less *costly* solution.
>
> Her offer to help you was intended as a *friendly* gesture.

b. A few common *ly*-ending words are used both as adjectives and adverbs—for example, *early, only, daily, weekly, monthly, yearly.*

> I always try to leave for work at an *early* hour. (Adjective.)
>
> The surge in sales began *early* last month. (Adverb.)

1070 Words such as *up, in, out, on,* and *off*—commonly recognized as prepositions—also function as adverbs, especially in verb phrases where these words are needed to complete the meaning of the verb. (See also ¶802.)

	Used as Adverbs	**Used as Prepositions**
up:	to look *up* the definition	to jog *up* the hill
down:	to *take down* your name	to walk *down* the street
in:	to *trade in* your old car	to see *in* the dark
out:	to phase *out* operations	to look *out* the window
on:	to put *on* a performance	to act *on* the stage
off:	to write *off* our losses	to drive *off* the road

NOTE: When used in headings and titles as *adverbs*, these short words are capitalized; when used as *prepositions*, they are not. (See ¶361c–d.)

1071 Problems of Comparison

a. Form the comparative degree of *one-syllable* adjectives and adverbs by adding *er* to the positive form. Form the superlative degree by adding *est*. (See ¶1071e for a few exceptions.)

> thin: thinner, thinnest   soon: sooner, soonest

b. Form the comparative degree of *two-syllable* adjectives and adverbs either by adding *er* to the positive form or by inserting either *more* or *less* before the positive form. Form the superlative degree by adding *est* in some cases or by inserting *most* or *least* before the positive form.

> happy: happier, more (**OR** less) happy
> likely: likeliest, most (**OR** least) likely
> often: oftener, more (**OR** less) often
> highly: highest, most (**OR** least) highly

NOTE: If the positive form ends in a consonant plus *y* (for example, *happy, likely*), change the *y* to *i* before adding *er* or *est*. Some *ly*-ending words drop the *ly* in the comparative and superlative (for example, *highly, higher, highest; deeply, deeper, deepest*). (See also ¶710.)

c. Form the comparative degree of adjectives and adverbs containing *three or more syllables* by inserting *more* or *less* before the positive form. Form the superlative degree by inserting *most* or *least* before the positive form.

> competent: more competent   adventurous: less adventurous
> acceptable: most acceptable   carefully: least carefully

d. Avoid double comparisons.

> cheaper (**NOT:** more cheaper)   unkindest (**NOT:** most unkindest)

(Continued on page 242.)

10

e. A few adjectives and adverbs have irregular comparisons. For example:

Positive	Comparative	Superlative
good **OR** well (see page 264)	better	best
bad **OR** ill	worse	worst
far	farther, further (see ¶719)	farthest, furthest
late	later, latter (see ¶719)	latest, last
little	littler, less, lesser	littlest, least
many, much	more	most

f. Some adjectives and adverbs—for example, *square, round, unique, completely, universally, correct, perfect, always, never, dead*—do not logically permit comparison. A square cannot be any *squarer;* a circle cannot be the *roundest* of all circles. Nevertheless, a number of these words may be modified by *more, less, nearly, hardly, virtually,* and similar adverbs to suggest something less than absolute perfection in each case.

Next year we hope to do a *more complete* study.

He is looking for a *more universally* acceptable solution.

Handicraft of this caliber is *virtually unique* these days.

We *almost never* increase our prices more than once a year.

g. When referring to *two* persons, places, or things, use the comparative form; when referring to *more than two,* use the superlative form.

That is the *finer* piece of linen. (Only two pieces are involved.)
This is the *finest* piece of linen I could find. (Many pieces are involved.)

Of the two positions open, you have chosen the *more* promising.
Of the three positions open, you have chosen the *most* promising.

That is the *more* efficient of the two methods.
This is the *most* efficient method that could be devised.

I like Evelyn's plan *better* than Joe's or Betty's. (Although three things are involved, they are being compared two at a time; hence the comparative.)

NOTE: In a few idiomatic expressions (such as *Put your best foot forward* and *May the best man win*), the superlative form is used, even though only two things are referred to.

h. When comparing a person or a thing *within* the group to which it belongs, use the superlative. When comparing a person or a thing with individual members of the group, use the comparative and the words *other* or *else.*

Susan is the *most* conscientious employee on the staff.

Susan is *more* conscientious than any *other* employee on the staff. (Without the word *other,* the sentence would imply that Susan is not on the staff.)

Los Angeles is the *largest* city in California.

Los Angeles is *larger* than any *other* city in California. (Without *other,* the sentence would imply that Los Angeles is not in California.)

Bert's proposal was the *best* of all that were presented to the committee.

Bert's proposal was *better* than anyone *else's.* (**NOT:** anyone's.)

i. Be sure to compare like things. (See also ¶644, note.)

This year's output is lower than last year's. (In other words, "This year's *output* is lower than last year's *output.*")
NOT: This year's output is lower than last year. (Incorrectly compares *this year's output* with *last year.*)

10

1072 Adverbs such as *only, nearly, almost, ever, scarcely, merely, too,* and *also* should be placed as close as possible to the word modified—usually directly before it. Putting the adverb in the wrong position may change the entire meaning of the sentence.

> Our list of depositors numbers *almost* 50,000. (**NOT:** almost numbers.)

> *Only* the board can nominate the three new officers. (Cannot be nominated by anyone else.)

> The board can *only* nominate the three officers. (They cannot elect.)

> The board can nominate *only* the three officers. (They cannot nominate anyone else.)

> Elvira and Frank Mancuso have been married for *not quite* two years.
> (**NOT:** Elvira and Frank Mancuso have *not quite* been married for two years.)

1073 Do not use an adverb to express a meaning already contained in the verb.

assemble (**NOT:** assemble together)
begin (**NOT:** first begin)
cancel (**NOT:** cancel out)
continue (**NOT:** continue on)
convert (**NOT:** convert over)
cooperate (**NOT:** cooperate together)

finish (**NOT:** finish up or off)
follow (**NOT:** follow after)
refer (**NOT:** refer back)
repeat (**NOT:** repeat again)
return (**NOT:** return back)
revert (**NOT:** revert back)

Troublesome Adjectives and Adverbs

➤ *For the following adjectives and adverbs, see the entries listed alphabetically in* ¶*1101.*

A–an
Accidentally
Adverse–averse
All right
Almost–all most
Already–all ready
Altogether–all together
Always–all ways
Anxious–eager
Anymore–any more
Anytime–any time
Anyway–any way
Awhile–a while
Bad–badly
Complementary–complimentary
Different–differently

Equally as good
Everyday–every day
Ex–former
Farther–further
Fewer–less
Fiscal–financial
First–firstly, etc.
Flammable–inflammable
Former–first
Good–well
Hardly
Healthy–healthful
Hopefully
Incidentally
Indifferent–in different
Indirect–in direct
Last–latest
Latter–last

Maybe–may be
More important–more importantly
Only
Real–really
Said
Same
Scarcely
Someday–some day
Sometime–sometimes–some time
Sure–surely
This here
Unique
Up
Very
Wise

NEGATIVES

1074 To express a negative idea in a simple sentence, use only one negative expression in the sentence. (A *double negative*—two negative expressions in the same sentence—gives a *positive* meaning.)

> We can sit by and do *nothing*.

> We can*not* sit by and do *nothing*. (The *not* and *nothing* create a double negative; the sentence now has a positive meaning: "We ought to do something.")

(Continued on page 244.)

10

Jim is *un*aware of the facts. (Here the negative element is the prefix *un*.)

Jim is *not un*aware of the facts. (With the double negative, the sentence means "Jim *is* aware of the facts.")

NOTE: A double negative is not wrong in itself. As the examples above indicate, a double negative may offer a more effective way of expressing a *positive thought* than a straightforward positive construction would. However, a double negative *is* wrong if the sentence is intended to have a negative meaning. Remember, two negatives make a positive.

1075 A negative expression gives a negative meaning to the *clause* in which it appears. In a simple sentence, where there is only one clause, the negative expression affects the entire sentence (see ¶1074). In a sentence where there are two or more clauses, a negative expression affects only the clause in which it appears. Therefore, each clause may safely contain one negative expression. A double negative results when there are two negative expressions within the *same* clause.

If Mr. Bogosian can*not* lower his price, there is *no* point in continuing the negotiations. (The *if* clause contains the negative *not;* the main clause contains the negative *no*. Each clause has its own negative meaning.)

I have *not* met Halliday, and I have *no* desire to meet him.
OR: I have *not* met Halliday, *nor* do I have *any* desire to meet him. (When the negative conjunction *nor* replaces *and*, the adjective *no* changes to *any* so as to avoid a double negative in the second clause.)

We have *never* permitted, *nor* will we permit, any lowering of our standards. (Here the second clause interrupts the first clause. If written out in full, the sentence would read, "We have *never* permitted any lowering of our standards, *nor* will we permit any lowering of our standards.")

NOTE: A second negative expression may be used in a clause to repeat or intensify the first negative expression. This construction is not a double negative.

No, I did *not* make that statement.

He would *never, never* do a thing like that. That's a *no-no*.

1076 To preserve the *negative* meaning of a clause, follow these basic principles:

a. If the clause has a *negative verb* (a verb modified by *not* or *never*), do not use an additional negative expression, such as *nor, neither . . . nor, no, none, no one,* or *nothing*. Instead, use the corresponding positive expression, such as *or, either . . . or, any, anyone,* or *anything*.

I have *not* invited *anyone*. (**WRONG:** I have *not* invited *no one*.)

She does *not* want *any*. (**WRONG:** She does *not* want *none*.)

Mary did *not* have *anything* to do. (**WRONG:** Mary did *not* have *nothing* to do.)

I can*not* find *either* the letter *or* the envelope. (**WRONG:** I can*not* find *neither* the letter *nor* the envelope.)

He did *not* say whether he would mail the money to us *or* whether he would bring it himself. (**WRONG:** He did *not* say whether he would mail the money to us *nor* whether he would bring it himself.)

b. If a clause contains any one of the following expressions—*no, no one, none, nothing,* or *neither . . . nor* (this counts as one expression)—make sure that the verb and all other words are *positive*.

I see *nothing* wrong with *either* proposal. (**NOT:** neither proposal.)

Neither Martha Gutowski *nor* Yvonne Christopher *can* handle the meeting for me next Thursday. (**NOT:** cannot.)

c. The word *nor* may be used alone as a conjunction (see the second and third examples in ¶1075) or together with *neither.* Do not use *nor* in the same clause with any other negative; use *or* instead.

There are *neither* diskettes *nor* printer cartridges in the stockroom.
BUT: There are *no* diskettes *or* printer cartridges in the stockroom.
(**NOT:** There are *no* diskettes *nor* printer cartridges.)

There are *no* clear-cut rights *or* wrongs in the situation.
(**NOT:** There are *no* clear-cut rights *nor* wrongs in the situation.)

Francine has *not* called *or* written us for some time.
(**NOT:** Francine has *not* called *nor* written us for some time.)

Never try to argue *or* debate with Larry.
(**NOT:** *Never* try to argue *nor* debate with Larry.)

➤ *For* hardly, only, *and* scarcely, *which have a negative meaning, see the appropriate entries in ¶1101.*

PREPOSITIONS

Words Requiring Certain Prepositions

1077 Usage requires that certain words be followed by certain prepositions. Some of the most frequently used combinations are given in the following list.

account for something or someone: I find it hard to *account for* his behavior.

account to someone: You will have to *account to* Anne for the loss of the key.

agree on or **upon** (reach an understanding): We cannot *agree on* the price.

agree to (accept another person's plan): Will you *agree to* their terms?

agree with (concur with a person or an idea): I *agree with* your objectives.

angry at or **about** something: He was *angry about* the total disorder of the office.

angry with someone: You have every right to be *angry with* me.

apply for a position: You ought to *apply for* Harry's job, now that he has left.

apply to someone or something: You must *apply* yourself *to* the job in order to master it. I am thinking of *applying to* the Field Engineering Company.

argue about something: We *argued about* the terms of the contract.

argue with a person: It doesn't pay to *argue with* Bremer.

compare to (assert a likeness): She *compared* my writing *to* E. B. White's. (She said I wrote like E. B. White.)

compare with (analyze for similarities and differences): When she *compared* my writing *with* E. B. White's, she said that I had a similar kind of humor but that my sentences lacked the clean and easy flow of White's material.

conform to (preferred to *with*): These copies do not *conform to* the originals.

consists in (exists in): Happiness largely *consists in* wanting what you have, not having what you want.

consists of (is made up of): Their new formula for a wage settlement *consists of* the same old terms expressed in different language.

convenient for (suitable): What time will be most *convenient for* you?

convenient to (near at hand): Our plant is *convenient to* all transportation facilities in the area.

(Continued on page 246.)

10

correspond to (agree with): The shipment does not *correspond to* the sample.

correspond with (exchange letters with): It may be better to see him in person than to *correspond with* him.

differ about (something): We *differed about* means but not about objectives.

differ from (something else): This job *differs* very little *from* the one that I had.

differ with (someone): I *differ with* you over the consequences of our plan.

different from: This product is *different from* the one I normally use.

different than: I view the matter in a *different* way *than* you do. (Although *from* is normally preferred, *than* is acceptable in order to avoid sentences like "I view the matter in a different way from the way in which you do.")

identical with (not *to*): This $180 suit is *identical with* one advertised for $235 at other stores.

independent of (not *from*): He wants to be *independent of* his family's money.

interested in: We are *interested in* discussing the matter further with you at the conference in July.

retroactive to (not *from*): This salary adjustment is *retroactive to* May 1.

speak to (tell something to): You must *speak to* them about their absences.

speak with (discuss with): It was good to *speak with* you yesterday.

Superfluous Prepositions

1078 Omit prepositions that add nothing to the meaning—as in the following examples. (See also page 254 for a usage note on *all of*.)

Where is she [at]?

Where did that paper go [to]?

The new applicant seems to be [of] about sixteen years of age.

She could not help [from] laughing.

His office is opposite [to] hers.

Your chair is too near [to] your terminal.

Why don't we meet at about one o'clock? (Omit either *at* or *about*.)

The carton apparently fell off [of] the truck.

The strike is now over [with].

We need to focus [in] on ways to boost sales.

I'm not [for] sure that I can go with you to Rome.

Necessary Prepositions

1079 Conversely, do not omit essential prepositions.

I need to buy a couple *of* books.
(**NOT:** I need to buy a couple books.)

Of what use is this gadget?
(**NOT:** What use is this gadget?)

We don't stock that type *of* filter.
(**NOT:** We don't stock that type filter.)

You have a great interest *in*, as well as a deep respect *for*, fine antiques.
(**NOT:** You have a great interest, as well as a deep respect *for*, fine antiques.)

She frequently appears in movies, *in* plays, and on television.
(**NOT:** She frequently appears in movies, plays, and on television.)

NOTE: The preposition *of* is understood in expressions such as *what color cloth* and *what size shoes*.

10

Prepositions at the End of Sentences

1080 Whether or not a sentence should end with a preposition depends on the emphasis and effect desired.

> **INFORMAL:** I wish I knew which magazine her article appeared *in*.
>
> **FORMAL:** I wish I knew *in which* magazine her article appeared.
>
> **STILTED:** It is difficult to know *about* what you are thinking.
>
> **NATURAL:** It is difficult to know what you are thinking *about*.

Short questions and statements frequently end with prepositions.

How many can I count *on?*	What is this good *for?*
What is this made *of?*	We need tools to work *with*.
Where did he come *from?*	That's something we must look *into*.
He has nothing to worry *about*.	That's the car I want to look *at*.

Troublesome Prepositions

> *For the following prepositions, see individual entries listed alphabetically in Section 11.*

At about	From–off	Off
Beside–besides	In–into–in to	On–onto–on to
Between–among	In regards to	On–upon–up on
Due to–because of–	Indifferent–in different	Opposite
on account of	Indirect–in direct	Per–a
Except	Like–as, as if	Toward–towards
	Of–have	

> *For the treatment of words that can function as both prepositions and adverbs, see ¶¶802, 1070. For the capitalization of such words, see ¶361c–d.*

SENTENCE STRUCTURE

Parallel Structure

1081 Express parallel ideas in parallel form.

a. Adjectives should be paralleled by adjectives, nouns by nouns, dependent clauses by dependent clauses, and so on.

> **WRONG:** Your new sales training program was *stimulating* and a *challenge*. (Adjective and noun.)
>
> **RIGHT:** Your new sales training program was *stimulating* and *challenging*. (Two adjectives.)

> **WRONG:** The sales representatives have already started *using the new techniques* and *to produce higher sales*. (Participial phrase and infinitive phrase.)
>
> **RIGHT:** The sales representatives have already started *using the new techniques* and *producing higher sales*. (Two participial phrases.)
>
> **RIGHT:** The sales representatives have already started *to use the new techniques* and *produce higher sales*. (Two infinitive phrases.)

> **WRONG:** This desk copier is *easy* to operate, *efficient*, and *it is relatively inexpensive*. (Two adjectives and a clause.)
>
> **RIGHT:** This desk copier is *easy* to operate, *efficient*, and relatively *inexpensive*. (Three adjectives.)

10

(Continued on page 248.)

NOTE: Parallelism is especially important in displayed enumerations.

POOR: This article will discuss:

1. How to deal with corporate politics.
2. Coping with stressful situations.
3. What the role of the manager should be in the community.

BETTER: This article will discuss:

1. *Ways* to deal with corporate politics.
2. *Techniques* of coping with stressful situations.
3. The *role* of the manager in the community.

OR: This article will tell managers how to:

1. *Deal* with corporate politics.
2. *Cope* with stressful situations.
3. *Function* in the community.

b. Correlative conjunctions (*both . . . and, either . . . or, neither . . . nor, not only . . . but also, whether . . . or*, etc.) should be followed by elements in parallel form.

WRONG: Kevin is not only gifted as a painter but also as a sculptor.
RIGHT: Kevin is gifted not only *as a painter* but also *as a sculptor.*

WRONG: We are flying both to Chicago and San Francisco.
RIGHT: We are flying to both *Chicago* and *San Francisco.*
RIGHT: We are flying both *to Chicago* and *to San Francisco.*

WRONG: He would neither apologize nor would he promise to reform.
RIGHT: He would neither *apologize* nor *promise to reform.*
RIGHT: *He would not apologize,* nor *would he promise to reform.*

Dangling Constructions

1082 When a sentence begins with a participial phrase, an infinitive phrase, a gerund phrase, or an elliptical clause (one in which essential words are missing), make sure that the phrase or clause logically agrees with the subject of the sentence; otherwise, the construction will "dangle." To correct a dangling construction, make the subject of the sentence the doer of the action expressed by the opening phrase or clause. If that is not feasible, use an entirely different construction.

a. Participial Phrases

WRONG: Stashed away in the attic for the past hundred years, the *owner* of the painting has decided to auction it off. (Who was stashed in the attic: the owner of the painting?)

RIGHT: The owner of the painting that has been stashed away in the attic for the past hundred years has decided to auction it off.

WRONG: Having studied your cost estimates, a few *questions* occur to me about your original assumptions. (As worded, this version implies that the *questions* have studied the cost estimates.)

RIGHT: Having studied your cost estimates, I would like to ask you a few questions about your original assumptions. (In the correct version, the person who studied the cost estimates is now the subject of the sentence and is the one asking the questions.)

10

WRONG: Putting the matter of costs aside, the *matter* of production delays remains to be discussed.

RIGHT: Putting the matter of costs aside, *we* must still discuss the matter of production delays.

NOTE: A few words ending in *ing* (such as *concerning, considering, pending,* and *regarding*) have now become established as prepositions. Therefore, when they introduce phrases at the start of a sentence, it is not essential that they refer to the subject of the sentence.

Considering how long the lawsuit has dragged on, it might have been wiser not to sue.

b. Infinitive Phrases

WRONG: To appreciate the full significance of Fox's latest letter, all the previous correspondence should be read.

RIGHT: To appreciate the full significance of Fox's latest letter, you should read all the previous correspondence.

WRONG: To obtain this free booklet, the enclosed coupon should be mailed at once.

RIGHT: To obtain this free booklet, mail the enclosed coupon at once.

c. Prepositional-Gerund Phrases

WRONG: By installing a computerized temperature control system, a substantial saving in fuel costs was achieved.

RIGHT: By installing a computerized temperature control system, we achieved a substantial saving in fuel costs.

WRONG: In analyzing these specifications, several errors have been found.

RIGHT: In analyzing these specifications, I have found several errors.

d. Elliptical Clauses

WRONG: If ordered before May 1, a 5 percent discount will be allowed on these goods.

RIGHT: If these goods are ordered before May 1, a 5 percent discount . . .

WRONG: When four years old, my family moved to Omaha.

RIGHT: When I was four years old, my family moved to Omaha.

e. Absolute Phrases

Absolute phrases (typically involving passive participles) are not considered to "dangle," even though they come at the beginning of a sentence and do not refer to the subject. Such constructions, though grammatically correct, are usually awkward and should be avoided.

WEAK: The speeches having been concluded, we proceeded to take a vote.

BETTER: After the speeches were concluded, we proceeded to take a vote.

1083 When verbal phrases and elliptical clauses fall elsewhere in the sentence, look out for illogical or confusing relationships. Adjust the wording as necessary.

WRONG: I saw two truck drivers get into a fistfight while jogging down the street.

RIGHT: While jogging down the street, I saw two truck drivers get into a fistfight.

10

1084 A prepositional phrase will dangle at the beginning of a sentence if it leads the reader to expect a certain word as the subject and then another word is used instead.

> **WRONG:** As head of the program committee, we think you should make immediate arrangements for another speaker. (The head of the committee is *you*, not *we*.)
> **RIGHT:** We think that as head of the program committee you should make immediate arrangements for another speaker.

> **WRONG:** As a young boy, the woman I was destined to marry did not appeal to me in any way. (That woman never was a "young boy.")
> **RIGHT:** When I was a young boy, the woman I was destined to marry did not appeal to me in any way.

> **WRONG:** You voted for change. As your next governor, you will get change. (The voters are not going to be the next governor.)
> **RIGHT:** You voted for change. As your next governor, I will see to it that you get change!

1085 A verbal phrase will dangle at the end of a sentence if it refers to the meaning of the main clause as a whole rather than to the doer of the action.

> **WRONG:** Our sales have been steadily declining for the past six months, thus creating a sharp drop in profits. (As worded, the sentence makes it appear that *our sales,* by themselves, have created the drop in profits. Actually, it is *the fact* that our sales have been declining which has created the drop in profits.)

> **RIGHT:** The steady decline in our sales for the past six months has created a sharp drop in profits.

> **RIGHT:** Our sales have been steadily declining for the past six months. As a result, we have experienced a sharp drop in profits.

Misplaced Modifiers

1086 Watch out for misplaced modifiers (either words or phrases) that provide the basis for unintended (and sometimes humorous) interpretations.

> **WRONG:** I suspect that my assistant accidentally dropped the report I had been drafting in the wastebasket. (What an uncomfortable location in which to draft a report!)
> **RIGHT:** The report I had been drafting has disappeared. I suspect that my assistant accidentally dropped it in the wastebasket.

> **WRONG:** Here are some helpful suggestions for protecting your valuables from our hotel security staff. (Can no one be trusted?)
> **RIGHT:** Here are some helpful suggestions from our hotel security staff for protecting your valuables.

> **WRONG:** One of our assistant vice presidents has been referred to a personal finance counselor with serious credit problems. (Would you consult such a counselor?)
> **RIGHT:** One of our assistant vice presidents has serious credit problems and has been referred to a personal finance counselor.

10

SECTION 11

USAGE

A–An
A Lot–Alot–Allot
A–Of
Accidentally
A.D.–B.C.
Additionally
Adverse–Averse
Affect–Effect
Age–Aged–At the Age of
Ain't
All of
All Right
Almost–All Most
Already–All Ready
Altogether–All Together
Always–All Ways
Amount–Number
And
And Etc.
And/Or
Anxious–Eager
Anymore–Any More
Anyone–Any One
Anytime–Any Time
Anyway–Any Way
Appraise–Apprise
Appreciate
As
As . . . as–Not so . . . as
As Far as
As Well as
At About

Awhile–A While
Bad–Badly
Balance
Being That
Beside–Besides
Between–Among
Between You and Me
Biannual–Biennial–Semiannual
Biweekly–Bimonthly
Both–Each
Both Alike–Equal–Together
Bring–Take
But . . . However
But What
Cannot Help but
Come–Go
Come and
Complement–Compliment
Complementary–Complimentary
Comprise–Compose
Could Not Care Less
Data
Different–Differently
Different From–Different Than
Done
Don't (Do Not)
Doubt That–Doubt Whether
Due to–Because of–On Account of
Each Other–One Another
Ensure–Insure–Assure
Enthused Over
Equally as Good

251

Etc.
Ethnic References
Everyday–Every Day
Everyone–Every One
Ex–Former
Except
Farther–Further
Fewer–Less
First–Firstly, etc.
Fiscal–Financial
Flammable–Inflammable
Former–First
From–Off
Good–Well
Graduated–Was Graduated
Hardly
Healthy–Healthful
Help
Hopefully
However
If–Whether
Imply–Infer
In–Into–In to
In Regards to
Incidentally
Indifferent–In Different
Indirect–In Direct
Individual–Party–Person–People
Irregardless
Is Where–Is When
Its–It's
Kind
Kind of–Sort of
Kind of a
Last–Latest
Latter–Last
Lay–Lie
Learn–Teach
Leave–Let
Like–As, As if
Literally
May–Can (Might–Could)
Maybe–May Be
Media
More Important–More Importantly
Most
Nobody–No Body
None–No One
Of–Have

Off
On–Onto–On to
On–Upon–Up on
Only
Opposite
Per–A
Percent–Percentage
Plus
Raise–Rise
Real–Really
Reason Is Because
Retroactive to
Said
Same
Scarcely
Serve–Service
Set–Sit
Shall–Will
Should–Would
So–So That
Someday–Some Day
Someone–Some One
Sometime–Sometimes–Some Time
Supposed to
Sure–Surely
Sure and
Tack–Tact
Than–Then
That
That–Which–Who
These Sort–These Kind
This Here
Toward–Towards
Try and
Type–Key
Unique
United Kingdom–Great Britain–England
Up
Used to
Very
Vicious Circle
Ways
Where–That
Who–Which–That
Who–Whom
Whoever–Who Ever
Wise
Would Have

➤ *See ¶719 for a list of words that are frequently misused because they sound alike or look alike.*

1101 The following entries will help you avoid a number of common mistakes in usage.

A–an. In choosing *a* or *an*, consider the sound (not the spelling) of the following word. Use the article *a* before all *consonant* sounds, including sounded *h*, long *u*, and *o* with the sound of *w* (as in *one*).

a day	a home	a unit	a youthful spirit	a one-week delay
a week	a house	a union	a euphoric feeling	a 60-day note
a year	a hotel	a uniform	a European trip	a CPA

Use *an* before all *vowel* sounds except long *u* and before words beginning with silent *h*.

an asset	an AT&T product
an essay	an EPA ruling
an input	an f.o.b. order
an outcome	an HMO physician
an upsurge	an IRS audit
an eyesore	an L.A.-based firm
an heir	an M.B.A. degree
an hour	an NBC news report
an honor	an OPEC price cut
an 8-hour day	an ROI objective
an 80-year-old man	an SRO performance
an 11 a.m. meeting	an X-ray reading

NOTE: In speech, both *a historic occasion* and *an historic occasion* are correct, depending on whether the *h* is sounded or left silent. In writing, *a historic occasion* is the form more commonly used.

A lot–alot–allot. The phrase *a lot* (meaning "to a considerable quantity or extent") always consists of two words. Do not spell this phrase as one word (*alot*).

Thanks *a lot* (NOT *alot*) for all your help on this year's budget.

Do not confuse this phrase with the verb *allot* (meaning "to distribute or assign a share of something").

You will have to *allot* a portion of next year's budget to cover unforeseen expenses, even though you are not likely to have *a lot* of money left over after you cover your basic operations.

A–of. Do not use *a* in place of *of.*

What sort *of* turnout did you have at your seminar?
(NOT: What sort *a* turnout did you have at your seminar?)

The weather has been kind *of* cool for this time of year.
(NOT: The weather has been *kinda* cool for this time of year.)

➤ *See* **Kind of–sort of** *and* **Kind of a.**

A–per. See *Per–a.*

Accidentally. Note that this word ends in *ally.* (The form *accidently* is incorrect.)

A.D.–B.C. *A.D.* (abbreviation of *anno Domini,* Latin for "in the year of our Lord") and *B.C.* ("before Christ") are usually written in all-capital letters, with a period following each letter and with no internal space. Do not use a comma to separate *B.C.* or *A.D.* from the year.

150 B.C.	465 A.D. (ordinary usage)
in the first century B.C.	A.D. 465 (formal usage)

(Continued on page 254.)

NOTE: You may also put *A.D.* and *B.C.* in small caps (A.D., B.C.) if the equipment you are using provides that option.

Additionally. Avoid the use of *additionally* as a transitional expression. Use *in addition, moreover, furthermore,* or *besides* instead. (See ¶138a.)

> AWKWARD: *Additionally,* the new packaging will reduce costs by 20 percent.
> BETTER: *Moreover,* the new packaging will reduce costs by 20 percent.

Adverse–averse. *Adverse* means "unfavorable, harmful, hostile." *Averse* means "opposed (to), having a feeling of distaste (for)."

> This research report will have an *adverse* (unfavorable) effect on our sales.
> The medication you are taking could have *adverse* (harmful) side effects.
> I am not *averse* (opposed) to working on weekends for the next month.
> I am *averse* (opposed) to exercise in any form.
> BUT: I have *adverse* (hostile) feelings about exercise in any form.

Affect–effect. *Affect* is normally used as a verb meaning "to influence, change, assume." *Effect* can be either a verb meaning "to bring about" or a noun meaning "result, impression."

> The court's decision in this case will not *affect* (change) the established legal precedent.
> She *affects* (assumes) an unsophisticated manner.
> It is essential that we *effect* (bring about) an immediate improvement in sales.
> It will be months before we can assess the full *effect* (result) of the new law.

NOTE: In psychology, *affect* is used as a noun meaning "feeling, emotion," and the related adjective *affective* means "emotional." Because of the limited context in which these terms are likely to be used with these meanings, it should be easy to distinguish them from *effect* as a noun and the related adjective *effective.*

> We need to analyze the *effects* (results) of this new marketing strategy.
> We need to analyze the *affects* (emotions) produced by this conflict.
>
> Which technique is *effective* (capable of producing the desired results)?
> Let's deal with the *affective* (emotional) factors first.

Age–aged–at the age of

> I interviewed a man *aged 52* for the job. (NOT: a man age 52.)
> I don't plan to retire *at the age of 65.* (NOT: at age 65.)

NOTE: Elliptical references to age—for example, *at age 65*—should not be used except in technical writing such as human resources manuals.

> See the chart on page 64 for the schedule of retirement benefits for employees who retire *at age 65.*

Ain't. *Ain't* has long been considered nonstandard usage, but it is acceptable in certain idiomatic expressions.

> Making that many mistakes in one document *ain't* easy.
> Two thousand dollars for a thirty-minute speech? That *ain't* hay!
> If it *ain't broke,* don't fix it. (*If it isn't broken* is grammatically correct, but it lacks the punch of the original.)

All of. *Of* is not needed after *all* unless the following word is a pronoun.

> *All* the staff members belong to the softball team.
> (ALSO: *All of* the staff members belong to the softball team.)
> *All of* us belong to the softball team.

All right. Like *all wrong,* the expression *all right* should be spelled as two words. (While some dictionaries list *alright* without comment, this spelling is not generally accepted as correct.)

Almost–all most. See also *Most.*

The plane was *almost* (nearly) three hours late.

We are *all most* pleased (all very much pleased) with the new schedule.

Already–all ready

The order had *already* (previously) been shipped.

The order is *all ready* (all prepared) to be shipped.

Altogether–all together

He is *altogether* (entirely) too lazy to be a success.

The papers are *all together* (all in a group) in the binder I sent you.

Always–all ways

She has *always* (at all times) done good work.

We have tried in *all ways* (by all methods) to keep our employees satisfied.

Among–between. See *Between–among.*

Amount–number. Use *amount* for things in bulk, as in "a large amount of lumber." Use *number* for individual items, as in "a large number of inquiries."

And. Retain *and* before the last item in a series, even though that last item consists of two words joined by *and.*

We need to increase our expense budgets for advertising, staff training, *and* research and development.

(**NOT:** We need to increase our expense budgets for advertising, staff training, research and development.)

Beginning a sentence with *and* or some other coordinating conjunction (*but, or,* or *nor*) can be an effective means—*if not overused*—of giving special attention to the thought that follows the conjunction. No comma should follow the conjunction at the start of a new sentence unless a parenthetical element occurs at that point.

Last Friday George promised to submit the market analysis this Monday. *And* then he took off on a two-week vacation.

Tell him to return to the office at once. *Or* else.

BUT: George just called from Lake Tahoe to say that the report was undergoing some last-minute changes and would be on my desk by 11 a.m. *And,* to my delight, it was!

NOTE: Each of the sentences above illustrates how this device can be effectively used. However, these sentences also illustrate, when taken as a whole, how quickly the overuse of this device dissipates its effectiveness.

And etc. Never use *and* before *etc.* (See *Etc.*)

And/or. Try to avoid this legalistic term in ordinary writing.

Anxious–eager. Both *anxious* and *eager* mean "desirous," but *anxious* also implies fear or concern.

I'm *anxious* to hear whether we won the bid or not.

I'm *eager* (**NOT** *anxious*) to hear about your new house.

Anymore–any more

We used to vacation in Bermuda, but we don't go there *anymore* (any longer).

Please call me if you have *any more* (any additional) suggestions.

Anyone–any one. See ¶1010, note.

Anytime–any time

Come see us *anytime* you are in town. (One word meaning "whenever.")

Did you have dealings with Crosby at *any time* in the past? (Two words after a preposition such as *at*.)

Can you spend *any time* (any amount of time) with Jill and me when you next come to Tulsa?

Anyway–any way

Anyway (in any case), we can't spare him now.

If we can help in *any way* (by any method), please phone.

Appraise–apprise

We would like to *appraise* (set a value on) Mrs. Ellsworth's estate.

I will *apprise* (inform) you of any new developments.

Appreciate. When used with the meaning "to be thankful for," the verb *appreciate* requires an object.

NOT: We would appreciate if you could give us your decision by May 1.

BUT: We would appreciate *it* if you could give us your decision by May 1. (Pronoun as object.)

OR: We would appreciate *your* (**NOT** *you*) *giving us your decision by May 1.* (Noun clause as object. See ¶647b on the use of *your* before *giving*.)

We will always appreciate the *help* you gave us. (Noun as object.)

I will appreciate *whatever you can do for us.* (Noun clause as object.)

As. Do not use *as* for *that* or *whether*.

I do not know *whether* (**NOT** *as*) I can go.

Use *because, since,* or *for* rather than *as* in clauses of reason.

I cannot attend the meeting in Omaha, *because* (**NOT** *as*) I will be out on the West Coast that day.

As–as if. See *Like–as, as if*.

As . . . as–not so . . . as. The term *as . . . as* is now commonly used in both positive and negative comparisons. Some writers, however, prefer to use *not so . . . as* for negative comparisons.

Bob is every bit *as* bright *as* his older sister. (Positive comparison.)

It is *not as* important *as* you think. **OR:** . . . *not so* important *as* you think. (Negative comparison.)

As far as. *As far as* may be used as a preposition or as a subordinating conjunction.

I can drive you *as far as* Spokane. (Used as a preposition.)

I would recommend this template *as far as* format is concerned. (Used as a subordinating conjunction.)

BUT NOT: I would recommend this template *as far as* format. (Either create a clause following *as far as*, as in the example above, or change *as far as* to *on the basis of* or a similar expression: *I would recommend this template on the basis of format.*)

As well as. When using *as well as,* be on guard against the possibility of misleading your reader.

CONFUSING: Ms. Paglia plans to meet with Mr. Pierce and Mrs. Hamer as well as Ms. Fieno. (Is Ms. Paglia planning to meet with three people, or are Ms. Paglia and Ms. Fieno both planning to meet with two people?)

CLEAR: Ms. Paglia plans to meet *with* Mr. Pierce and Mrs. Hamer as well as *with* Ms. Fieno. (Repeating the preposition *with* makes it clear that Ms. Paglia will meet with three people.)

CLEAR: Ms. Paglia *as well as Ms. Fieno* plans to meet with Mr. Pierce and Mrs. Hamer. (Rearranging the word order makes it clear that both Ms. Paglia and Ms. Fieno will meet with two people. Note that an *as well as* phrase following the subject, *Ms. Paglia,* does not affect the number of the verb. See ¶1007.)

Assure. See *Ensure–insure–assure.*

At about. Use either *at* or *about* but not both words together. For example, ''Plan to arrive *at* ten'' OR ''Plan to arrive *about* ten.'' (BUT NOT: Plan to arrive *at about* ten.)

Awhile–a while. One word as an adverb; two words as a noun.

You may have to wait *awhile.* (Adverb.)

You may have to wait for *a while.* (Noun; object of the preposition *for.*)

I ran into him *a while* back.

Bad–badly. Use the adjective *bad* (not the adverb *badly*) after the verb *feel* or *look.* (See ¶1067.)

I feel *bad* (NOT *badly*) about the mistake.

BUT: He was hurt *badly.*

NOTE: The only way you can ''feel badly'' is to have your fingertips removed first.

Balance. Do not use *balance* to mean ''rest'' or ''remainder'' except in a financial or accounting sense.

I plan to use the *rest* of my vacation time next February.

(NOT: I plan to use the *balance* of my vacation time next February.)

BUT: The *balance* of the loan falls due at the end of this quarter.

B.C.–A.D. See *A.D.–B.C.*

Because. See *Reason is because.*

Because of. See *Due to–because of–on account of.*

Being that. Do not use *being that* for *since* or *because.*

Because I arrived late, I could not get a seat.

(NOT: *Being that* I arrived late, I could not get a seat.)

Beside–besides

I sat *beside* (next to) Mr. Parrish's father at the meeting.

Besides (in addition), we need your support of the measure.

Between–among. Ordinarily, use *between* when referring to *two* persons or things and *among* when referring to *more than* two persons or things.

The territory is divided evenly *between* the two sales representatives.

The profits are to be evenly divided *among* the three partners.

(Continued on page 258.)

Use *between* with more than two persons or things when they are being considered in pairs as well as in a group.

> There are distinct differences *between* New York, Chicago, and Dallas.
>
> In packing china, be sure to place paper *between* the plates.
>
> The memo says something different when you read *between* the lines.
>
> *Between* you, me, and the gatepost, we don't stand a chance of making budget.

Between you and me (not *I*). See ¶1055b.

Biannual–biennial–semiannual. *Biannual* and *semiannual* both mean "occurring twice a year." *Biennial* means "occurring every two years." Because of the possible confusion between *biannual* and *biennial,* use *semiannual* when you want to describe something that occurs twice a year.

> **PREFERRED:** our *semiannual* sales conference
> **CLEARER THAN:** our *biannual* sales conference

If you think that your reader could misconstrue *biennial,* avoid the term and use *every two years* instead.

> Within our global organization each national company holds its own sales conferences *on a semiannual basis* (**OR** *semiannually*); an international sales conference is scheduled *on a biennial basis* (**OR** *biennially* **OR** *every two years*).

Biweekly–bimonthly. These two words do not mean the same thing. Moreover, *bimonthly* has two quite different meanings, which could confuse your readers.

> If you are paid *biweekly* (every two weeks), you get 26 checks a year.
>
> If you are paid *bimonthly* (twice a month), you get only 24 checks a year.
>
> **OR:** If you are paid *bimonthly* (every two months), you get only 6 checks a year.

NOTE: To keep your meaning clear, avoid *bimonthly* and say "twice a month" or "every two months." You may also use *semimonthly* to mean "twice a month."

Both–each. *Both* means "the two considered together." *Each* refers to the individual members of a group considered separately.

> *Both* designs are acceptable.
> The designs are *each* acceptable.
>
> *Each* sister complained about the other.
> (**NOT:** *Both* sisters complained about the other.)

Both alike–equal–together. *Both* is unnecessary when used with *alike, equal,* or *together.*

> These laser printers are *alike.* (**NOT:** *both alike.*)
>
> These tape systems are *equal* in cost. (**NOT:** *both equal.*)
>
> We will travel *together* to Japan. (**NOT:** *both* travel *together.*)

Bring–take. *Bring* indicates motion toward the speaker. *Take* indicates motion away from the speaker.

> Please *bring* the research data with you when you next come to the office.
>
> Please *take* the enclosed letter to Farley when you go to see him.
>
> You may *take* my copy with you if you will *bring* it back by Friday.

➤ *See note under* Come–go.

Britain. See *United Kingdom–Great Britain–England.*

But . . . however. Use one or the other.

> We had hoped to see the show, *but* we couldn't get tickets.
> OR: We had hoped to see the show; *however,* we couldn't get tickets.
> (BUT NOT: . . . *but* we couldn't get tickets, *however.*)

But what. Use *that.*

> I do not doubt *that* (NOT *but what*) he will be elected.

Can–could. See *May–can (might–could).*

Cannot help but. This expression is a confusion of two others, namely, *can but* and *cannot help.*

> I *can but* try. (BETTER: I *can only* try.)

> I *cannot help* feeling sorry for her. (NOT: *cannot help but* feel.)

Class. See *Kind.*

Come–go. The choice between verbs depends on the location of the speaker. *Come* indicates motion *toward; go,* motion *away from.* (See also *Bring–take.*)

> When Bellotti *comes* back, I will *go* to the airport to meet him.

> *A manager speaking over the phone to an outsider:* Will it be convenient for you to *come* to our office tomorrow?

NOTE: When discussing your travel plans with a person at your destination, adopt that person's point of view and use *come.*

> *An outsider speaking over the phone to a manager:* Will it be convenient for me to *come* to your office tomorrow?

> *Midwesterner to Californian:* I am *coming* to California during the week of the 11th. I will *bring* the plans with me if they are ready.

However, if you are discussing your travel plans with someone who is *not* at your destination, observe the regular distinction between *come* and *go.*

> *An outsider speaking to an outsider:* I hope it will be convenient for me to *go* to their office tomorrow.

> *Midwesterner to Midwesterner:* I am *going* to California during the week of the 11th. I will *take* the plans with me if they are ready.

Come and. In formal writing, use *come to* instead of the colloquial *come and.*

> Come *to* see me. (NOT: Come *and* see me.)

Complement–compliment. *Complement* as a noun means "something that completes" or "one of two mutually completing parts"; as a verb it means "to complete, to be complementary to." *Compliment* as a noun means "an admiring or flattering remark"; as a verb it means "to praise, to pay a compliment to."

> A simple dessert of berries and sherbet makes a fine *complement* to an elaborate meal with several rich courses.

> The CEO was full of *compliments* for your sales presentation yesterday.

Complementary–complimentary. *Complementary* means "serving to complete" or "mutually supplying what each other lacks." *Complimentary* means "flattering" or "given free."

(Continued on page 260.)

Our top two executives work so well as a team because they bring *complementary* skills and expertise to their jobs.

The CEO had many *complimentary* things to say about your sales presentation.

May I get a *complimentary* copy of your new book?

Comprise–compose. *Comprise* means "to include, contain, consist of"; *compose* means "to make up." The parts *compose* (make up) the whole; the whole *comprises* (includes) the parts; the whole *is composed of* (**NOT** *is comprised of*) the parts.

The parent corporation *comprises* (consists of) three major divisions.

Three major divisions *compose* (make up) the parent corporation.

The parent corporation *is composed of* (is made up of) three major divisions.

Could not care less. To say that you "could not care less" means that you do not care at all. To say that you "could care less" implies that your ability to care has not yet reached rock bottom. If the first meaning is the one you wish to communicate, do not omit *not*.

Couldn't–hardly. See *Hardly*.

Data. See ¶1018, note.

Different–differently. When the meaning is "in a different manner," use the adverb *differently*.

I wish we had done it *differently*.

It came out *differently* than we expected. (See ¶1077.)

After linking verbs and verbs of the senses, the adjective *different* is correct. (See ¶1067.)

That music sounds completely *different*.

He seems (appears) *different* since his promotion.

Don't believe anything *different*. (Meaning "anything that is different.")

Different from–different than. See ¶1077.

Done. Do not say "I *done* it." Say "I *did* it." (See also ¶1032b.)

Don't (do not). Do not use *don't* with *he, she,* or *it;* use *doesn't*.

He *doesn't* talk easily.	**BUT:** I *don't* think so.
She needs help, *doesn't* she?	They *don't* want any help.
It *doesn't* seem right to penalize them.	We *don't* understand.

Doubt that–doubt whether. Use *doubt that* in negative statements and in questions. Use *doubt whether* in all other cases. (See also *If–whether.*)

We do not *doubt that* she is capable. (Negative statement.)

Does anyone *doubt that* the check was mailed? (Question.)

I *doubt whether* I can go.

Due to–because of–on account of. *Due to* introduces an adjective phrase and should modify nouns. It is normally used only after some form of the verb *to be* (*is, are, was, were,* etc.).

Her success is *due to* talent and hard work. (*Due to* modifies *success*.)

Because of and *on account of* introduce adverbial phrases and should modify verbs.

He resigned *because of* ill health. (*Because of* modifies *resigned*.)

(**NOT:** He resigned *due to* ill health.)

Each–both. See *Both–each.*

Each other–one another. Use *each other* to refer to two persons or things; *one another* for more than two.

> The two partners had great respect for *each other's* abilities.

> The four winners congratulated *one another.*

Eager–anxious. See *Anxious–eager.*

Effect–affect. See *Affect–effect.*

England. See *United Kingdom–Great Britain–England.*

Ensure–insure–assure. *Ensure* means "to make certain." *Insure* means "to protect against loss." *Assure* means "to give someone confidence"; the object of this verb should always refer to a person.

> I want to *ensure* (make certain) that nothing can go wrong tomorrow.

> I want to *insure* this necklace (protect it against loss) for $5000.

> I want to *assure* you (give you confidence) that nothing will go wrong.

Enthused over. Use *was* or *were enthusiastic about* instead.

> The sales staff *was enthusiastic about* (**NOT** enthused over) next year's styles.

Equal. See *Both alike–equal–together.*

Equally as good. Use either *equally good* or *just as good.*

> This model is newer, but that one is *equally good.* (**NOT:** equally as good.)

> Those are *just as good* as these. (**NOT:** equally as good.)

Etc. This abbreviation of *et cetera* means "and other things." Therefore, do not use *and* before *etc.* Use a comma before and after *etc.* (unless the expression falls at the end of a sentence or requires a stronger mark of punctuation, such as a semicolon). In formal writing, avoid the use of *etc.;* use a phrase such as *and the like* or *and so on* instead.

NOTE: Do not use *etc.* or an equivalent expression at the end of a series introduced by *such as.* The term *such as* implies that only a few selected examples will be given; therefore, it is unnecessary to add *etc.* or *and so on,* which suggests that further examples could be given.

> As part of its employee educational program, the company offers courses in report writing, business communication, grammar and style, *and so on.*

> **OR:** . . . the company offers courses *such as* report writing, business communication, and grammar and style.

> (**BUT NOT:** . . . the company offers courses *such as* report writing, business communication, grammar and style, *and so on.*)

➤ *For the use or omission of a comma before* such as, *see* ¶¶*148–149.*

Ethnic references. When identifying U.S. citizens or residents as members of a certain ethnic group, use great care in choosing an appropriate term. There is often disagreement within the group about which terms are acceptable and which are offensive, so always respect individual preferences if you know what they are. (See ¶348.)

a. Use *African Americans* or *Afro-Americans* to refer to black people of African ancestry. The terms *Negroes* and *colored people* are rarely used today except in the names of long-established organizations (for example, the United Negro College Fund and the National Association for the Advancement of Colored People). Use the term *blacks* only in context where you might also refer to *whites.* Use a term like *African*

Americans (which reflects ethnic ancestry rather than skin color) in a context where you are also referring to other ethnic groups such as Latinos.

the votes of Latinos and *African Americans*
(**RATHER THAN:** the votes of Latinos and *blacks*)

b. Use *Hispanics* to refer broadly to people who trace their roots to Latin America or Spain. Use *Latinos* to refer to people of Latin-American ancestry (that is, from Central or South America). The term *Chicanos* may be used to refer to people of Mexican ancestry; however, since some members of this group consider the term offensive, a safer alternative is *Mexican Americans.*

NOTE: Within the groups designated *Hispanic, Latino,* or *Chicano,* some people are white and some black. Therefore, do not use these terms in the same context with *white* or *black.*

the buying patterns of Hispanics and *African Americans*
(**RATHER THAN:** the buying patterns of Hispanics and *blacks*)

c. The terms *Anglo-Americans* and *Anglos* are used in some parts of the United States to refer to white people who have an English-speaking background.

Are there significant differences in the consumer preferences of Latinos, African Americans, and *Anglos?* (Note that all three groups are identified here by ethnic ancestry and not by color.)

Ideally, the term *whites* should be used only in a context where you might also refer to *blacks.* However, in the absence of a more widely accepted term than *Anglos* or *Anglo-Americans,* use *whites* even though other groups are identified by ethnic ancestry in the same context.

Are there significant differences in the consumer preferences of Latinos, African Americans, and *whites?*

d. Use *Asian Americans* to refer to people of South and East Asian ancestry. When referring to people who live in Asia, use *Asians* (rather than *Asiatics* or *Orientals,* which many now consider offensive).

e. The term *Native American* is now the preferred way to refer to people who trace their ancestry back to the earliest inhabitants of the Americas. Although some members of this group still refer to themselves as Indians (or American Indians), use the term *Indians* to refer only to people who live in India.

f. The term *people of color* refers broadly to people who trace their roots to non-European countries—for example, African Americans, Native Americans, and Asian Americans.

g. Many ethnic references consist of two words, the second of which is *American.* Do not hyphenate terms like *an African American, a German American,* or *a Chinese American* when they are used as nouns, because the first element in each case modifies the second. Hyphenate such terms, however, when they are used as adjectives: *African-American entrepreneurs, a German-American social club, Chinese-American restaurants.* Also hyphenate such terms when the first element is a prefix; for example, *Afro-Americans, Anglo-Americans.*

Everyday – every day

You'll soon master the *everyday* (ordinary) routine of the job.

He has called *every day* (each day) this week.

Everyone–every one. See ¶1010, note.

Ex–former. Use *ex-* with a title to designate the person who *immediately* preceded the current titleholder in that position; use *former* with a title to designate an earlier titleholder.

> Charles Feldman is the *ex-president* of the Harrisburg Chamber of Commerce. (Held office immediately before the current president.)
>
> **BUT:** . . . is a *former* president of the Harrisburg Chamber of Commerce. (Held office sometime before the current president and that person's immediate predecessor.)

Except. When *except* is a preposition, be sure to use the objective form of a pronoun that follows. (See also ¶1055b.)

> Everyone has been notified *except* Jean and *me.* (**NOT:** except Jean and *I.*)

Farther–further. *Farther* refers to actual distance; *further* refers to figurative distance and means "to a greater degree" or "to a greater extent."

> The drive from the airport was *farther* (in actual distance) than we expected.
>
> Let's plan to discuss the proposal *further* (to a greater extent).

Fewer–less. *Fewer* refers to number and is used with *plural* nouns. *Less* refers to degree or amount and is used with *singular* nouns.

> *Fewer* accidents (a smaller number) were reported than we expected.
>
> *Less* effort (a smaller degree) was put forth by the organizers, and thus *fewer* people (a smaller number) attended.

The expression *less than* (rather than *fewer than*) precedes plural nouns referring to periods of time, amounts of money, and quantities.

> less than ten years ago   **FORMAL:** fewer than 60 people
>
> less than $1 million   **COLLOQUIAL:** less than 60 people

The expression *or less* (rather than *or fewer*) is used after a reference to a number of items.

> in 100 words or less   in groups of six people or less

First–firstly, etc. In enumerations, use the forms *first, second, third* (**NOT** *firstly, secondly, thirdly*).

Fiscal–financial. The adjective *fiscal* (as in *fiscal year* or *FY*) can be used to refer to all types of financial matters—those of governments and private businesses. However, with the exception of *fiscal year,* it is better to use *fiscal* only in connection with government matters and to use *financial* in all other situations.

Flammable–inflammable. Both terms mean "easily ignitable, highly combustible." However, since some readers may misinterpret *inflammable* to mean "*non*flammable," *flammable* is the clearer form.

Former–ex. See *Ex–former.*

Former–first. *Former* refers to the first of two persons or things. When more than two are mentioned, use *first.* (See also *Latter–last.*)

> This item is available in wool and in Dacron, but I prefer the *former.*
>
> This item is available in wool, in Dacron, and in Orlon, but I prefer the *first.*

From–off. Use *from* (**NOT** *off*) with persons.

> I got the answer I needed *from* Margaret. (**NOT:** *off* Margaret.)

Go–come. See *Come–go.*

Good–well. *Good* is an adjective. *Well* is typically used as an adverb but may be used as an adjective to refer to the state of someone's health.

> Marie got *good* grades in school. (Adjective.)
>
> I will do the job as *well* as I can. (Adverb.)
>
> He admits he does not feel *well* today. (Adjective.)
>
> The security guards look *good* in their new uniforms. (Adjective.)

NOTE: *To feel well* means "to be in good health." *To feel good* means "to be in good spirits."

Graduated–was graduated. Both forms are acceptable. However, use *from* after either expression.

> My daughter *graduated from* MIT last year.
>
> (NOT: My daughter *graduated* MIT last year.)

Great Britain. See *United Kingdom–Great Britain–England.*

Hardly. *Hardly* is negative in meaning. To preserve the negative meaning, do not use another negative with it.

> You *could hardly* (NOT *couldn't hardly*) expect him to agree.

Have–of. See *Of–have.*

Healthy–healthful. People are *healthy;* a climate or food is *healthful.*

> You ought to move to a more *healthful* (NOT *healthier*) climate.

Help. Do not use *from* after the verb *help.* For example, "I couldn't *help* (NOT *help from*) telling her she was wrong."

Hopefully. Although the subject of much controversy, the use of *hopefully* at the beginning of a sentence is no different from the use of *obviously, certainly, fortunately, actually, apparently,* and similar words functioning as independent comments (see ¶138b). These adverbs express the writer's attitude toward what he is about to say; as such they modify the meaning of the sentence as a whole rather than a particular word.

> *Hopefully,* the worst is over and we will soon see a strong upturn in sales and profits.

However. Whether *however* should begin a sentence or not has been the subject of much controversy, with distinguished authorities on both sides of the issue. *Webster's Dictionary of English Usage* surveys the range of opinion on this matter and concludes:

> The only point that needs to be made is that there is no absolute rule for the placement of *however;* each writer must decide each instance on its own merits, and place the word where it best accomplishes its purpose. (Merriam, Springfield, Mass., 1989, pp. 514–515.)

However (like other transitional expressions, such as *therefore* and *moreover*) helps readers relate the thought being introduced to the thoughts that went before. Many readers find it more helpful if they encounter the transitional expression at the beginning of the sentence. In that way they can tell from the start the direction in which the new sentence is proceeding. Compare these examples:

> When you are addressing a request to someone who reports to you, you expect that person to comply. A period can be properly used, *therefore,* to punctuate such requests. Since most people prefer to be asked to do something rather than be told to do it, *however,* a question mark establishes a nicer tone and often gets better results.

When you are addressing a request to someone who reports to you, you expect that person to comply. *Therefore,* a period can properly be used to punctuate such requests. *However,* since most people prefer to be asked to do something rather than be told to do it, a question mark establishes a nicer tone and often gets better results.

In any case, the location of a transitional expression in a sentence must be determined by the individual writer. (For a list of transitional expressions, see ¶138a.)

➤ *For the entry* But . . . however, *see page 259.*

If–whether. *If* is often used colloquially for *whether* in such sentences as "He doesn't know *whether* he will be able to leave tomorrow." In written material, use *whether,* particularly in such expressions as *see whether, learn whether, know whether,* and *doubt whether.* Also use *whether* when the expression *or not* follows or is implied.

Find out *whether* (**NOT** *if*) this format is acceptable *or not.*

Imply–infer. *Imply* means "to suggest"; you imply something by *your own* words or actions.

Verna *implied* (suggested) that we would not be invited.

Infer means "to assume, to deduce, to arrive at a conclusion"; you infer something from *another person's* words or actions.

I *inferred* (assumed) from Verna's remarks that we would not be invited.

In–into–in to

The correspondence is *in* the file. (*In* implies position within.)

He walked *into* the outer office. (*Into* implies entry or change of form.)

All sales reports are to be sent *in to* the sales manager. (*In* is an adverb in the verb phrase *are to be sent in; to* is a simple preposition.)

Mr. Boehme came *in to* see me. (*In* is part of the verb phrase *came in; to* is part of the infinitive *to see.*)

In regards to. Substitute *in regard to, with regard to, regarding,* or *as regards.*

I am writing *in regard to* (**NOT** *in regards to*) your letter of May 1.

Incidentally. Note that this word ends in *ally.* Never spell it *incidently.*

Indifferent–in different

She was *indifferent* (not caring one way or the other) to the offer.

He liked our idea, but he wanted it expressed in *different* (in other) words.

Indirect–in direct

Indirect (not direct) lighting will enhance the appearance of this room.

This order is *in direct* (the preposition *in* plus the adjective *direct*) conflict with the policy of this company.

Individual–party–person–people. Use *individual* to refer to someone whom you wish to distinguish from a larger group of people.

We wish to honor those *individuals* who had the courage to speak out at a time when popular opinion was defending the status quo.

Use *party* only to refer to someone involved in a legal proceeding.

All the *parties* to the original agreement must sign the attached amendment.

(Continued on page 266.)

Use *person* to refer to a human being in all other contexts.

> Please tell me the name of the *person* in charge of your credit department.

If reference is made to more than one person, the term *people* usually sounds more natural than the plural form *persons*. In any event, always use *people* when referring to a large group.

> If you like, I can send you a list of all the *people* in our corporation who will be attending this year's national convention.

Infer. See *Imply–infer.*

Inflammable–flammable. See *Flammable–inflammable.*

Insure. See *Ensure–insure–assure.*

Irregardless. Use *regardless.*

Is where–is when. Do not use these phrases to introduce definitions.

> A dilemma is a situation in which you have to choose between equally unsatisfactory alternatives.

> (NOT: A dilemma *is where* you have to choose between equally unsatisfactory alternatives.)

However, these phrases may be correctly used in other situations.

> The Ritz-Carlton *is where* the dinner-dance will be held this year.

> Two o'clock *is when* the meeting is scheduled to begin.

Its–it's. See ¶1056e.

Kind. *Kind* is singular; therefore, write *this kind, that kind, these kinds, those kinds* (**BUT NOT** *these kind, those kind*). The same distinctions hold for *class, type,* and *sort.*

Kind of–sort of. These phrases are sometimes followed by an adjective (for example, *kind of sorry, sort of baffled*). Use this kind of expression only in informal writing. In more formal situations, use *rather* or *somewhat* (*rather sorry, somewhat baffled*).

> I was *somewhat* (**NOT** *kind of, sort of*) surprised.

> She seemed *rather* (**NOT** *kind of, sort of*) tired.

NOTE: When *kind of* or *sort of* is followed by a noun, the expression is appropriate in all kinds of situations.

> What *sort of business* is Vern Forbes in?

➢ *See* A–of *and* Kind of a.

Kind of a. The *a* is unnecessary. For example, "That *kind of* (**NOT** *kind of a*) material is very expensive."

Last–latest. *Last* means "after all others"; *latest,* "most recent."

> Mr. Lin's *last* act before leaving was to recommend Ms. Roth's promotion.

> Attached is the *latest* report we have received from the Southern Region.

Latter–last. *Latter* refers to the second of two persons or things mentioned. When more than two are mentioned, use *last.* (See also *Former–first.*)

> July and August are good vacation months, but the *latter* is more popular.

> June, July, and August are good vacation months, but the *last* is the most popular.

Lay–lie. *Lay* (principal parts: *lay, laid, laid, laying*) means "to put" or "to place." This verb requires an object to complete its meaning.

> Please *lay* the *boxes* on the pallets with extreme care.

> I *laid* the *message* right on your desk.

> I *had laid* two other *notes* there yesterday.

> He *is* always *laying* the *blame* on his assistants. (Putting the blame.)

> The dress *was laid* in the box. (A passive construction implying that someone *laid* the dress in the box.)

Lie (principal parts: *lie, lay, lain, lying*) means "to recline, rest, or stay" or "to take a position of rest." It refers to a person or thing as either assuming or being in a reclining position. This verb cannot take an object.

> Now he *lies* in bed most of the day.

> The mountains *lay* before us as we proceeded west.

> This letter *has lain* unanswered for two weeks.

> Today's mail *is lying* on the receptionist's desk.

TEST: In deciding whether to use *lie* or *lay* in a sentence, substitute the word *place, placed,* or *placing* (as appropriate) for the word in question. If the substitute fits, the corresponding form of *lay* is correct. If it doesn't, use the appropriate form of *lie.*

> I will *(lie* or *lay?)* down now. (You could not say, "I will *place* down now." Therefore, write "I will *lie* down now.")

> I *(laid* or *lay?)* the pad on his desk. ("I *placed* the pad on his desk" works. Therefore, write "I *laid* the pad.")

> I *(laid* or *lay?)* awake many nights. ("I *placed* awake" doesn't work. Write "I *lay* awake.")

> These files have *(laid* or *lain?)* untouched for some time. ("These files have *placed* untouched" doesn't work. Write "These files have *lain* untouched.")

> He has been *(laying* or *lying?)* down on the job. ("He has been *placing* down on the job" doesn't work. Write "He has been *lying* down.")

NOTE: When the verb *lie* means "to tell a falsehood," it has regularly formed principal parts *(lie, lied, lied, lying)* and is seldom confused with the verbs just described.

Learn–teach. *Learn* (principal parts: *learn, learned, learned, learning*) means "to acquire knowledge." *Teach* (principal parts: *teach, taught, taught, teaching*) means "to impart knowledge to others."

I *learned* from a master teacher.	A first-rate instructor *taught* me how.
(**NOT:** I *was learned* by a master teacher.)	I was *taught* by a first-rate instructor.

Leave–let. *Leave* (principal parts: *leave, left, left, leaving*) means "to move away, abandon, or depart." *Let* (principal parts: *let, let, let, letting*) means "to permit or allow." **TEST:** In deciding whether to use *let* or *leave,* substitute the appropriate form of *permit.* If *permit* fits, use *let;* if not, use *leave.*

> I now *leave* you to your own devices. (Abandon you.)

> Mr. Morales *left* on the morning train. (Departed.)

> *Let* me see the last page. (Permit me to see.)

> *Leave* me alone. **OR:** *Let* me alone. (Either is acceptable.)

Less–fewer. See *Fewer–less.*

Lie. See *Lay.*

Like–as, as if. *Like* is correctly used as a preposition. Although *like* is also widely used as a conjunction in colloquial speech, use *as, as if,* or a similar expression in written material.

> We need to hire another person *like* you.
> Kate, *like* her predecessor, will have to cope with the problem.
> *As* (**NOT** *Like*) I told you earlier, we will not reorder for six months.
>
> It looks *like* snow.
> It looks *as if* (**NOT** *like*) it will snow.
>
> Mary looks *like* her mother.
> Mary looks *as* (**NOT** *like*) her mother did at the same age.
> **BETTER:** Mary looks the way her mother did at the same age.

Literally. This adverb means "actually, truly." Do not use it in the sense of "almost" to modify a reference to an exaggerated or unreal situation.

> **NOT:** When Jensen got the bill for all the "minor changes" made at the last minute, he *literally* hit the ceiling. (Omit the word *literally* or change it to *almost* unless Jensen actually exploded out of his chair and hit the ceiling headfirst.)

May–can (might–could). *May* and *might* imply permission or possibility; *can* and *could,* ability or power.

> You *may* send them a dozen cans of paint on trial. (Permission.)
>
> The report *may* be true. (Possibility.)
>
> *Can* he present a workable plan? (Has he the ability?)
>
> Miss Kovacs said I *might* (permission) have the time off if I *could* (had the ability to) finish my work in time.
>
> Please call me if you think I *can* be of any help. (Emphasizes the ability to help.)
>
> Please call me if you think I *may* be of any help. (Emphasizes the possibility of helping.)

Maybe–may be. *Maybe* is an adverb; *may be* is a verb.

> If we don't receive a letter from them today, *maybe* (an adverb meaning "perhaps") we should call.
>
> Mr. Boston *may be* (a verb) out of town next week.

Media. *Media,* referring to various channels of communication and advertising, is a plural noun. *Medium* is the singular. (See ¶1018.)

More important–more importantly. *More important* is often used as a short form for "what is more important," especially at the beginning of a sentence. *More importantly* means "in a more important manner."

> *More important,* we need to establish a line of credit very quickly. (What is more important.)
>
> The incident was treated *more importantly* than it deserved. (In a more important manner.)

Most. Do not use *most* for *almost.*

> *Almost all* the money is gone.
> **OR:** *Most* of the money is gone.
> (**BUT NOT:** *Most all* of the money is gone.)

Nobody–no body

> There was *nobody* (no person) at the information desk when I arrived.
>
> *No body* (no group) of employees is more cooperative than yours.

NOTE: Spell *no body* as two words when it is followed by *of*. (See also ¶1010.)

None–no one. See ¶1013.

Not so . . . as. See *As . . . as–not so . . . as.*

Number. See *Amount–number.*

Of–a. See *A–of.*

Of–have. Do not use *of* instead of *have* in verb forms. The correct forms are *could have, would have, should have, might have, may have, must have, ought to have,* and so forth.

> What *could have* happened? (**NOT:** What *could of* happened?)

Off. Do not use *off of* or *off from* in place of *off*. (See also ¶1078.)

> The papers fell *off* the desk. (**NOT:** *off of* the desk.)

Off–from. See *From–off.*

On–onto–on to

> It's dangerous to drive *on* the highway shoulder. (*On* implies position or movement over.)
>
> He lost control of the car and drove *onto* the sidewalk. (*Onto* implies movement toward and then over.)
>
> Let's go *on to* the next problem. (*On* is an adverb in the verb phrase *go on; to* is a preposition.)
>
> She then went *on to* tell about her experiences in Asia. (*On* is part of the verb phrase *went on; to* is part of the infinitive *to tell.*)

On–upon–up on

> His statements were based *on* (**OR** *upon*) experimental data. (*On* and *upon* are interchangeable.)
>
> Please follow *up on* the Updegraff case. (*Up* is part of the verb phrase *follow up; on* is a preposition.)

On account of. See *Due to–because of–on account of.*

One another–each other. See *Each other–one another.*

Only. The adverb *only* is negative in meaning. Therefore, do not use another negative with it unless you want a positive meaning. (See ¶1072 for the placement of *only* in a sentence.)

> I use this letterhead *only* for foreign correspondence. (I do not use this letterhead for anything else.)
>
> **BUT:** I do not use this letterhead *only* for foreign correspondence. (I use it for a number of other things as well.)

Opposite. When used as a noun, *opposite* is followed by *of*.

> Her opinion is the *opposite of* mine.

In other uses, *opposite* is followed by *to* or *from* or by no preposition at all.

> Her opinion is *opposite to* (**OR** *from*) mine.
>
> She lives *opposite* the school.

Party. See *Individual–party–person–people.*

Per–a. *Per,* a Latin word, is often used to mean "by the," as in *28 miles per gallon (mpg)* or *55 miles per hour (mph).* Whenever possible, substitute *a* or *an;* for example, *at the rate of $8 an hour, 75 cents a liter. Per* must be retained, of course, in Latin phrases—for example, *per diem* (by the day) or *per capita* (for each person; literally, by the head).

NOTE: Do not use *per* in the sense of "according to" or "in accordance with."

> We are sending you samples *as you requested.* (**NOT:** *per your request.*)

Percent–percentage. In ordinary usage, *percent* should always be accompanied by a number; for example, *20 percent, 0.5 percent, 150 percent.* In a table, a column of figures representing percentages may be headed *Percent of Total* or something comparable. In all other cases, use the term *percentage.*

> A large *percentage* of the calls we got yesterday came from customers who misread our ad. (**NOT:** A large *percent* of the calls . . .)

> What *percentage* of our subscribers are in the 30–49 age group? (See ¶1025.)

NOTE: In the percentage formula used in mathematics (base × rate = amount), the rate is called a *percent* and the amount is called a *percentage.* Thus you might be asked to calculate the *percentage* if a sales tax of 6 percent (the rate) was applied to a purchase of $50 (the base). By the same token, you might be asked to calculate the *percent* (the rate) if you knew that a tax of $5 (the amount, or percentage) had been paid on an order of $200. Apart from this special context, *percent* and *percentage* should be used as noted above.

Person–people. See *Individual–party–person–people.*

Plus. *Plus* can be correctly used as a noun, an adjective, or a preposition. However, do not use it as a conjunction (with the sense of "and").

> Your presence at the hearing was a real *plus* for our cause. (*Plus* used correctly as a noun.)

> The decision to offer a 10 percent discount on all orders received by June 1 was a *plus* factor in the campaign. (*Plus* used correctly as an adjective.)

> Your willingness to innovate *plus* your patient perspective on profits has permitted this company to grow at an astonishing rate. (*Plus* used correctly as a preposition. Note that a *plus* phrase following the subject of a sentence does not affect the number of the verb. See ¶1007.)

> **BUT NOT:** You have always been willing to innovate, *plus* you have been patient about the profits to be derived from the innovations. (Do not use *plus* as a conjunction; use *and* instead.)

Raise–rise. *Raise* (principal parts: *raise, raised, raised, raising*) means "to cause to lift" or "to lift something." This verb requires an object to complete its meaning.

> Mr. Pinelli *raises* a good *question.*

> Most growers *have raised* the *price* of coffee.

> We *are raising money* for the United Fund.

> Our rent *has been raised.* (A passive construction implying that someone *has raised* the rent.)

Rise (principal parts: *rise, rose, risen, rising*) means "to ascend," "to move upward by itself," or "to get up." This verb cannot be used with an object.

> We will have to *rise* to the demands of the occasion.

> The sun *rose* at 6:25 this morning.

The river *has risen* to flood level.

The temperature *has been rising* all day.

TEST: Remember, you cannot "rise" anything.

Real–really. *Real* is an adjective; *really,* an adverb. Do not use *real* to modify another adjective; use *very* or *really.*

One taste will tell you these cookies were made with *real* butter. (Adjective.)

We were *really* expecting a lower price from you this year. (Adverb.)

BUT: It was *very* nice (**NOT:** real nice) to see you and your family again.

Reason is because. Replace *because* with *that.*

The *reason* for such low sales *is that* (**NOT** *because*) prices are too high.

Retroactive to. After *retroactive* use *to* (**NOT** *from*).

These improvements in benefits under the company dental plan will be *retroactive to* July 1. (See also ¶1077.)

Said. The use of *said* in a phrase like "the *said* document" is appropriate only in legal writing. In normal usage write "the document referred to above." (In many cases the document being referred to will be clear to the reader without the additional explanation.)

Same. Do not use *same* to refer to a previously mentioned thing.

We are now processing your order and will have *it* ready for you Monday. (**NOT:** We are now processing your order and will have *same* ready . . .)

Scarcely. The adverb *scarcely* is negative in meaning. To preserve the negative meaning, do not use another negative with it. (See ¶1072 for the placement of *scarcely.*)

I *scarcely* recognized (**NOT** *didn't scarcely* recognize) you.

Semiannual. See *Biannual–biennial–semiannual.*

Serve–service. Things can be *serviced,* but people are *served.*

We take great pride in the way we *serve* (**NOT** *service*) our clients.

For a small additional charge we will *service* the equipment for a full year.

Set–sit. *Set* (principal parts: *set, set, set, setting*) means "to place something somewhere." In this sense, *set* requires an object to complete its meaning. **REMEMBER:** You cannot "sit" anything.

It's important to *set* down your *recollections* while they are still fresh.

I must have dropped my wallet when I *set* my *suitcase* down.

I *have set* my *alarm* for six in the morning.

The crew *was setting* the *stage* for the evening performance.

The date *was set* some time ago. (A passive construction implying that someone *set* the date.)

NOTE: *Set* has a few other meanings in which the verb does *not* require an object, but these meanings are seldom confused with *sit.*

They *set* out on the trip in high spirits.

The sun *set* at 5:34 p.m. Wednesday.

Allow a full hour for the mixture to *set.*

(Continued on page 272.)

Sit (principal parts: *sit, sat, sat, sitting*) means "to be in a position of rest" or "to be seated." This verb cannot be used with an object.

> So here we *sit*, waiting for a decision from top management.
>
> I *sat* next to Ebbetsen at the board meeting.
>
> They *had sat* on the plane a full hour before the flight was canceled.
>
> They *will be sitting* in the orchestra.

Shall–will. The helping verb *shall* has largely given way to the verb *will* in all but the most formal writing and speech. The following rules reflect both ordinary and formal usage:

a. To express simple future time:

    (1) In *ordinary* circumstances use *will* with all three persons.

> *I* (**or** *we*) *will* be glad to help you plan the program.
>
> *You will* want to study these recommendations before the meeting.
>
> *He* (**or** *she, it, they*) *will* arrive tomorrow morning.

    (2) In *formal* circumstances use *shall* with the first person *(I, we)* and *will* with the second and third persons *(you, he, she, it, they)*.

> *I* (**or** *we*) *shall* be glad to answer all inquiries promptly.
>
> *You will* meet the McGinnesses at the reception this evening.
>
> *They* (**or** *he, she*) *will* not find the trip too tiring.

b. To indicate *determination, promise, desire, choice,* or *threat:*

    (1) In *ordinary* circumstances use *will* with all three persons.

    (2) In *formal* circumstances use *will* for the first person *(I, we)* and *shall* for the second and third persons *(you, he, she, it, they)*.

> In spite of the risk, *I will* go where I please. (Determination.)
>
> *They shall* not interfere with my department. (Determination.)
>
> *I will* send my check by the end of the week. (Promise.)
>
> *We will* report you to the authorities if this is true. (Threat.)
>
> *You shall* regret your answer. (Threat.)
>
> *He shall* study or *he shall* leave college. (Threat.)

c. To indicate *willingness* (to be willing, to be agreeable to) in both *ordinary* and *formal* circumstances, use *will* with all persons.

> Yes, I *will* meet you at six o'clock.

Should–would. *Should* and *would* follow the same rules as *shall* and *will* (see preceding entry) in expressions of future time, determination, and willingness. The distinctions concerning ordinary and formal usage also apply here.

> ORDINARY: I *would* like to hear from you.
>
> FORMAL: I *should* like to hear from you.

> ORDINARY: We *would* be glad to see her.
>
> FORMAL: We *should* be glad to see her.

> ORDINARY: I *would* be pleased to serve on that committee.
>
> FORMAL: I *should* be pleased to serve on that committee.

a. Always use *should* in all persons to indicate "ought to."

I *should* study tonight.

You *should* report his dishonesty to the manager.

He *should* pay his debts.

b. Always use *would* in all persons to indicate customary action.

Every day I *would* swim half a mile.

They *would* only say, "No comment."

She *would* practice day after day.

c. Use *should* in all three persons to express a condition in an *if* clause.

If I *should* win the prize, I will share it with you.

If you *should* miss the train, please call me collect.

d. Use *would* in all three persons to express willingness in an *if* clause.

If he *would* apply himself, he could win top honors easily.

If you *would* delay your decision, I could offer you more attractive terms.

So–so that. *So* as a conjunction means "therefore"; *so that* means "in order that."

The work is now finished, *so* you can all go home. (See also ¶179.)

Please finish what you are doing *so that* we can all go home.

Someday–some day

Please set up a meeting with Al and Jerry *someday* (on an unspecified day) next week.

BUT: Please set up a meeting with Al and Jerry *for some day* next week. (Two words when used as the object of a preposition such as *for*.)

Someone–some one. See ¶1010, note.

Sometime–sometimes–some time

The order will be shipped *sometime* (at some unspecified time) next week.

Sometimes (now and then) reports are misleading.

It took me *some time* (a period of time) to complete the job.

I saw him *some time* ago (a long time ago).

NOTE: Spell *some time* as two words when the term follows a preposition.

We will be happy to reconsider your proposal *at some time* in the future.

I've been thinking about retiring *for some time*.

Sort. See *Kind*.

Sort of–kind of. See *Kind of–sort of*.

Such as . . . etc. See *Etc*.

Supposed to. Be sure to spell *supposed* with a *d*.

Under the circumstances what was I *supposed to* think? (**NOT:** *suppose to*.)

Sure–surely. *Sure* is an adjective, *surely* an adverb.

I am *sure* that I did not make that mistake. (Adjective.)

You can *surely* count on our help. (Adverb.)

(Continued on page 274.)

Do not use *sure* as an adverb; use *surely* or *very*.

> I was *very* glad to be of help. (NOT: *sure* glad.)

Sure and. In written material use *sure to* in place of the colloquial *sure and*.

> Be *sure to* give my best regards to the Meltzers.
>
> (NOT: Be *sure and* give my best regards to the Meltzers.)

Tack–tact. Use *tack* (not *tact*) in the expression *to take a different tack* (meaning "to move in a different direction"). *Tact* means "a considerate way of behaving so as to avoid offending others."

> We may have to take a different *tack* in our negotiations with Firebridge.
>
> Please use a great deal of *tact* when you reply to Korbman's letter.

Take–bring. See *Bring–take*.

Teach–learn. See *Learn–teach*.

Than–then. *Than* is a conjunction introducing a dependent clause of comparison. *Then* is an adverb meaning "at that time" or "next."

> The compulsory retirement age is higher now *than* it was *then*.
>
> They *then* asserted that they could handle the account better *than* we. (See ¶1057 for the case of pronouns following *than*.)

NOTE: Remember that *then* (like *when*) refers to time.

That. As a subordinating conjunction, *that* links the dependent clause it introduces with the main clause. *That* is often omitted (but understood).

> We realize *that* our bargaining position is not a strong one.
>
> OR: We realize our bargaining position is not a strong one.

However, under certain circumstances *that* should not be omitted:

a. When the word or phrase following *that* could be misread as the object of the verb in the main clause.

> NOT: I heard your speech next Wednesday had to be rescheduled.
>
> BUT: I heard *that* your speech next Wednesday had to be rescheduled.

b. When *that* introduces two or more parallel clauses.

> NOT: Hilary said she had narrowed the applicants for the job down to three people and *that* she would announce her choice by this Friday.
>
> BUT: Hilary said *that* she had narrowed the applicants for the job down to three people and *that* she would announce her choice by this Friday.

c. When an introductory or interrupting element comes between *that* and the subject of the dependent clause.

> NOT: I think whenever possible, you should consult everyone involved before making your decision.
>
> BUT: I think *that* whenever possible, you should consult everyone involved before making your decision. (See ¶130d.)

NOTE: If you are in doubt, do not omit *that*.

That–where. See *Where–that*.

That–which–who. See ¶1062.

11

These sort—these kind. Incorrect; the correct forms are *this* sort, *this* kind, these *sorts*, these *kinds*. (See also *Kind*.)

This here. Do not use *this here* for *this*.

> *this* computer (**NOT** this here computer)

Together. See *Both alike—equal—together.*

Toward—towards. *Toward* is more common, but both forms are correct.

Try and. In written material use *try to* rather than the colloquial *try and.*

> Please *try to* be here on time.
> (**NOT:** Please *try and* be here on time.)

Type. See *Kind.*

Type—key. The verb *type* has traditionally been used to refer to actions performed on a typewriter keyboard. The verb *key* was introduced to refer to actions performed on a computer keyboard. However, *type* has supplanted *key* in many software manuals and even appears in screen displays.

Unique. Do not use *unique* in the sense of "unusual." A unique thing is one of a kind. (See ¶1071f.)

United Kingdom—Great Britain—England. *The United Kingdom* (or *the U.K.*) refers to England, Wales, Scotland, and Northern Ireland. *Great Britain* (or *Britain*) refers to England, Wales, and Scotland. *England* refers to England and Wales.

Up. Many verbs (for example, *end, rest, lift, connect, join, hurry, settle, burn, drink, eat*) contain the idea of "up"; therefore, the adverb *up* is unnecessary. In the following sentences, *up* should be omitted.

> You need to rest (up) for a bit.　　Save $50 if you join (up) now.
> Let's divide (up) the work load.　　I will call him (up) tomorrow.

Upon—up on. See *On—upon—up on.*

Used to. Be sure to spell *used* with a *d*.

> We *used* to use Forsgate as our main supplier. (**NOT:** We *use* to use . . .)

Very. This adverb can be used to modify an adjective, another adverb, a present participle, or a "descriptive" past participle.

> We are *very happy* with the outcome. (Modifying an adjective.)
> This finish dries *very quickly*. (Modifying an adverb.)
> It was a *very disappointing* showing. (Modifying a present participle.)
> I was *very pleased* with the pictures. (Modifying a descriptive past participle.)

When the past participle expresses action rather than description, insert an adverb like *much* after *very.*

> They are *very much opposed* to your plan. (*Opposed* is part of the complete verb *are opposed* and expresses action rather than description.)
> (**NOT:** They are *very opposed* to your plan.)

Vicious circle. The correct form of this expression is *vicious circle* (**NOT** *vicious cycle*).

Ways. Do not use *ways* for *way* in referring to distance. For example, "I live a short *way* (**NOT** *ways*) from here."

Well—good. See *Good—well.*

Where–that.   Do not use *where* in place of *that*.

I saw in yesterday's paper *that* Schuster's had changed its mind about closing its midtown store.

(NOT: I saw in yesterday's paper *where* Schuster's had changed its mind about closing its midtown store.)

Whether–if.   See *If–whether*.

Who–which–that.   See ¶1062.

Who–whom.   See ¶1061.

Whoever–who ever

Whoever (anyone who) made such a statement should be fired.

Who ever made such a statement? (*Ever* is an adverb.)

Will–shall.   See *Shall–will*.

Wise.   Avoid the temptation to coin new words by attaching the suffix *wise* to various nouns. (Stylewise, it's considered bad form.)

NOT: *Costwise*, we're already 20 percent over budget.

BUT: We're already 20 percent over budget on costs.

NOT: *Sizewise*, what comes after extralarge? Gross? (Even when used in a conscious attempt at humor, the approach leaves much to be desired. Once again, avoid the temptation.)

BUT: *In terms of size*, what comes after extralarge? Gross?

Would–should.   See *Should–would*.

Would have.   Note that the second word in this verb phrase is *have*. (The spelling *would of* is wrong.)

I myself *would have* (NOT *would of*) taken a different tack.

In a clause beginning with *if*, do not use *would have* in place of *had*.

If you *had* come early, you could have talked with Dr. Fernandez yourself.

NOT: If you *would have* come early, you could have talked with Dr. Fernandez yourself.

PART 2

TECHNIQUES AND FORMATS

———————

SECTION 12

Editing, Proofreading, and Filing

278

EDITING AND PROOFREADING

In the traditional business world, *editing* and *proofreading* have been considered activities quite distinct from the act of *composing* (whether letters, memos, reports, or some other documents). In this environment one person composes the document—either in the form of a written draft or in the form of dictated material on tape—and someone else assumes the responsibility for editing and proofreading the material and producing the final document. Although this separation of responsibilities still exists in many offices, only higher-level executives typically continue to enjoy this arrangement.

In the modern business world, the widespread use of computers has greatly affected the way in which documents are prepared and produced. Many people are now responsible both for composing and for producing the final document themselves. In this new environment editing and proofreading become fully integrated into the overall writing process.

Individuals approach the writing process in different ways. Some begin by planning what they want to say in the form of an outline (see ¶¶1718–1723). Then, on the basis of this outline, they compose a first draft of the document. Many other people find it difficult to plan and outline before they begin to write. For such people the first stage of writing is the means by which they discover what they are trying to say. They typically begin by jotting their thoughts down in random order, knowing that the result of this first effort may literally be a mess that needs to be cleaned up. People who are paralyzed by the sight of a blank screen or a blank sheet of paper find it comforting to begin the *serious* job of writing by looking at something already on the screen or on paper. (They may even find it helpful to pretend that someone else has created the mess that they are about to clean up.)

However writers arrive at a first draft—whether through careful planning and outlining or by means of a random outpouring of thoughts—they must now apply editing techniques to the writing process in order to determine what material to add or leave out, how to organize the material that remains, and how to adjust the wording so as to achieve their objective. As they edit, they must also correct any problems they encounter in grammar, usage, and style. And as they go through one or more additional drafts, they must also apply proofreading techniques to confirm that each draft accurately presents the material in the intended form. When writers proceed in this way, editing and proofreading become totally integrated in the writing process almost from the very beginning.

Whether you are working on material composed by someone else or you are responsible for all phases of the writing process, the following guidelines on editing and proofreading should help you achieve a higher level of quality in the documents you produce.

1201 The Editing and Proofreading Process

    a. *Proofreading* is the process by which you look at copy that you or someone else has written and confirm that this version faithfully reproduces the original material in the intended form. If the copy deviates in any way from the original, you have to mark it for correction. Once the corrections are made, you have to read the copy again to ensure that everything is now as it should be.

(Continued on page 280.)

12

NOTE: Ordinarily, one person can handle the task of comparing the copy against the original and noting any necessary corrections. However, if the material is complex or involves many statistics or formulas, it is wise for two people to share the proofreading function: one (known as the *copyholder*) reads the original material aloud and also indicates the intended punctuation, capitalization, and paragraphing, as well as other significant details of style and format, while the other person (the *proofreader*) examines the copy closely to ensure that everything appears as it ought to.

b. *Editing* is the process by which you look at material that you or someone else has written and evaluate it on its own terms (either in its original form or at a later stage). You question the material on the grounds of accuracy, clarity, coherence, consistency, and effectiveness. If you have drafted the material yourself, you may have to revise it several times in order to resolve all the problems you find. If you encounter problems while editing material that someone else has written, you resolve the ones you are equipped and authorized to handle. You refer the other problems (with suggestions for changes when possible) to the author of the original material, who will then decide how to resolve these problems.

c. If you encounter a set of figures as a proofreader, your responsibility—strictly speaking—is only to ensure that the figures on the copy agree with the corresponding figures in the original. However, as an editor, you may question whether the figures in the original are correct as given or even the best figures that might be supplied. By the same token, if you examine text material as a proofreader, your only responsibility is to confirm that the copy agrees with the original in wording, style, and format. However, as an editor, you might question—and change—the wording, the format, and the style in the interests of accuracy, clarity, coherence, consistency, and effectiveness.

d. Many people often function simultaneously as editors and proofreaders without realizing that they are operating at two different levels—one essentially *mechanical* (checking for similarities and differences) and the other essentially *analytical* and *judgmental* (looking for problems and solving them). Ideally, editing should be done on the original material so that all problems of substance, grammar, style, and format are resolved before a copy is executed in final form. However, it would be a mistake to read the final copy merely as a mechanical proofreader, assuming that the original is perfect and that you only need to look for places where the copy deviates from the original. On the chance that problems may have gone undetected in the earlier editing, you need to read the final copy in that challenging, questioning way that distinguishes editing from simple proofreading. You may be able to edit and proofread at the same time, or you may need to make several readings, focusing each time on different things. The following paragraphs will suggest the kinds of things you should be looking for when you proofread and edit.

1202 What to Look For When Proofreading

When *proofreading* a document, be especially watchful for the following types of mistakes.

a. Repeated words (or parts of words), especially at the end of one line and the beginning of the next.

What are the chances of your your coming to see us sometime this summer?	I have been awaiting some indi- indication of a willingness to compromise.
I can help you in the event in the event you have more work than you can handle.	We are looking forward to the to the reception you are planning for the Lockwoods.

NOTE: A spell checker may highlight some of these mistakes, but don't assume that it will find all of them. You must do your own careful checking as well.

b. Substitutions and omissions, especially those that change the meaning.

Original Material	Erroneous Copy
The courts have clearly ruled that this kind of transaction is now legal.	The courts have clearly ruled that this kind of transaction is not legal.
In my opinion, there is no reason to suspect Fred.	In my opinion, there is reason to suspect Fred.
I hereby agree to pay you $87.50 in full settlement of your claim.	I hereby agree to pay you $8750 in full settlement of your claim.
Tom has probably reached the acme of his career.	Tom has probably reached the acne of his career.
When provoked, Gail has been known to turn violent.	When provoked, Gail has been known to turn violet.
We want our managers to live in the communities where our plants are located.	We want our managers to lie in the communities where our plants are located.
He is quite proud of his flat stomach.	He is quite proud of his fat stomach.
The company needs a good turnaround strategy, but what that will be is still undetermined.	The company needs a good turnaround strategy, but what that will be is still undermined.
My son was ticketed yesterday for reckless driving.	My son was ticketed yesterday for wreckless driving.
I'll gladly give you the job if you'll do it in a week and if you'll reduce your price by $200.	I'll gladly give you the job if you'll reduce your price by $200.

NOTE: No spell checker is likely to pick up these mistakes, because nothing is misspelled. Only an alert reader can identify them. Hopefully, that reader will be you and not the person to whom the material is sent.

(Continued on page 282.)

c. Errors in copying key data.

	Original Material	Erroneous Copy
NAMES:	Katharine Ann Jorgensen	Katherine Anne Jorgenson
TITLES:	Ms. Margaret A. Kelley	Mrs. Margaret A. Kelly
ADDRESSES:	1640 Vauxhall Road Union, NJ 07083	140 Vauxhall Road Union, NH 07803
DATES:	October 13, 1996	October 31, 1997
PHONE NOS.:	419-555-1551	418-555-1515
AMOUNTS OF MONEY:	$83,454,000,000	$38,454,000
DECIMALS:	sales fell 5.2 percent	sales fell 52 percent
CLOCK TIME:	arrive at 4:15 p.m.	arrive at 4:51 p.m.
PERIODS OF TIME:	boil for 2 minutes	boil for 20 minutes

d. Transpositions in letters, numbers, and words as well as other typographical errors.

Original Material	Erroneous Copy
I'll buy two boats this May.	I'll buy tow boats this May.
a process of trial and error	a process of trail and error
Let's form a committee to re- view our pricing policy.	Let's from a committee to re- biew our pricing policy.
We'll need 82 binders for the seminar beginning July 12.	We'll need 28 binders for the seminar beginning July 21.
How can we thank you all for your thoughtfulness?	How can we thank you for all your thoughtfulness?
Capitalize the first letter of each word.	Capitalize the first word of each letter.

e. Errors in spacing and inconsistencies in format (for example, indenting some paragraphs but not others, leaving too little or too much space between words or after punctuation, improperly aligning lines).

Original Material	Erroneous Copy
Dear Mrs. Neilson:	Dear Mrs. Neilson:
Thank you for your letter of April 24. Let me try to answer each of the questions you raised.	Thankyou for your letter of April 24. Let me try to answer each of the questions you raised.
First, we do not sell the components separately; they only come packaged as a set.	First,we do not sell the com- ponents separately; they only come pack aged as a set.

NOTE: As a final step in proofreading, check the appearance of the document. Is the document printed clearly? Are there any smudges or marks that need to be cleaned up? Does each page as a whole look attractive? Apply standards that are appropriate for the occasion. Documents prepared for higher management and for clients or customers of your organization should meet the highest standards of appearance. On the other hand, manuscripts, drafts, and even rush memos to coworkers can be sent forward with minor corrections neatly inserted by hand. Naturally, if you are using a computer, you can make the corrections and quickly obtain a clean (and correct) page. (See ¶¶1203–1204.)

12

1203 What to Look For When Editing

When *editing* a document at any stage in the writing process, consider the material in light of the following factors.

➤ *For an explanation of the proofreaders' marks used to indicate the necessary corrections in the following examples, see ¶1205.*

a. Check for errors in *spelling* (see Section 7). Give special attention to compound words (see Section 8) and those with plural and possessive endings (see Section 6). When the material is in its final form, confirm the correctness of all word divisions. (See Section 9.)

```
We had a similar break down in communications last May

when a high-level executive failed to inform us that the

                         ⁀eys
corporation/s attornies had advised against it's proceed-
                  ati
ing with merger negotions.  However, that was only the
              e
tip of the icebrg.
```

NOTE: Use a spell checker if you have one. However, since spell checkers are not infallible, keep an up-to-date dictionary at hand.

b. Make sure that every necessary mark of *punctuation* is correctly inserted. (See Sections 1 and 2.)

```
How do you account for the fact that whenever we are

about to launch a new product, the company cuts the mar-

keting dollars we need to promote the product?
```

c. Inspect the material for possible errors in *capitalization, number,* and *abbreviation style.* (See Sections 3, 4, and 5.)

```
Please be sure to attend the Managers' meeting scheduled
                        3
for june 4th at three p.m.  There will be 5 announce-

ments of special interest.
```

d. Correct any errors in *grammar* and *usage.* (See Sections 10 and 11.)

```
         #                          has        fewer
Everyone of the sales representatives have made less
                                   a
calls in the past six months then they did in the

previous six-month period.
```

12

e. Be on the lookout for *inconsistencies in the wording* of the document. If you are editing someone else's material, resolve any problems that you can and refer the rest to the author of the original material.

When I met with you, Harry Mills, and Paula Fierro on

May 8, we agreed that . . . Ed: Wasn't Paula at the 5/8 meeting?

I think that you ought to fill Paula Fierro in on what

happened at our May 8 meeting and get her thoughts about

how we ought to proceed.

NOTE: Be especially alert to wording that conveys a meaning you did not intend.

BAD: We take pride in offering excellent food and service every day except Sunday. (Does this mean that on Sundays the food and service are perfectly dreadful?)

BETTER: We take pride in offering excellent food and service. We are open every day except Sunday.

BAD: To enjoy our specially priced pretheater menu, you must be seated by 6 p.m. Remember, the early bird gets the worm. (Does the menu offer anything more appetizing?)

BETTER: To enjoy our specially priced pretheater menu, you must be seated by 6 p.m. Please try to come earlier if you can.

NOTE: Also look out for *inconsistencies in format*. Make sure that comparable elements in the document (for example, text, titles, headings, displayed extracts, and numbered or bulleted lists) have been treated the same way in terms of typeface, type size, placement, and so on.

f. Look for problems in *organization* and *writing style*. The material could be entirely correct in terms of grammar, style, and usage and still contain unclear or repetitive wording, clumsy sentences, a weak organization, or a tone that is not appropriate for the occasion. By using reference materials (for example, a thesaurus, a dictionary, or a style manual), you can improve the wording and structure of the document.

g. Look at the document as a whole, and consider whether it is likely to accomplish its *objective*. If the document is intended to persuade readers to accept a recommendation that they currently tend to oppose, has the writer (you or someone else) anticipated their objections and dealt with them? Or has the writer ignored the existence of such objections and thereby created the need for a follow-up document—or, what is worse, made it likely that the readers' negative leanings will harden into a flat rejection of the writer's recommendations?

NOTE: If you are editing material you yourself have written, consider all the points noted in ¶1203a–g. However, if you are editing material written by someone else, the extent of your editing will depend on your experience and your relationship with the writer. If you are working for a literate boss, determine whether your boss has any special preferences with regard to matters of style. (What may look like an error to you could be an acceptable practice that you are not familiar with.) On the other hand, a boss who does not pretend to grasp the technical points of style will no doubt welcome your editing for such things as spelling, punctuation, capitalization, grammar, usage, and inconsistencies (see ¶1203a–e).

How much your boss—or anyone else for that matter—will appreciate your comments about the organization, writing style, and effectiveness of the material (see ¶1203f–g) will depend not only on your relationship with the writer but also on the tact with which you make your comments. Do not assume that because you have a close relationship with the writer, you can speak bluntly. Indeed, the closer the relationship, the more tact you may need to exercise.

12

1204 Editing and Proofreading at the Computer

The computer provides some wonderful enhancements to the editing process. You can insert new copy, kill old copy, rearrange copy as many times as you like, and then print a clean version without any evidence of all the foregoing changes. Yet in the process of all this electronic "cutting and pasting," you may have failed to remove every bit of the old version you rejected; you may have changed the subject of a sentence from singular to plural without realizing the effect this change would have on the verb; you may even have inserted new copy in the wrong place and thus unintentionally produced pure gibberish. It is imperative, therefore, that copy that has been rewritten and edited on a computer be carefully proofread. Try to catch and correct as many errors as you can when reviewing copy on the screen. However, experienced users report that it is difficult to find every error when proofing on the screen. They stress the importance of giving the printout a very careful reading as well.

NOTE: Whether you are dealing with material that you or someone else has written, edit it carefully in light of all the factors noted in ¶1203.

To maximize the benefits from a computer and minimize the drawbacks, follow these guidelines.

a. If you are composing at the computer, be especially careful when reviewing your work. Experienced writers recognize that when they read what they have written, they have a tendency to see what they intended to write rather than what is actually there. That's why even good writers always need good editors.

NOTE: If someone else will be editing your material and preparing the final document, you may be tempted to deliver the material (whether on disk or in some other electronic format) in rough, first-draft form and expect the other person to resolve any problems that remain in your material. However, experience demonstrates that the most effective communication takes place when the writer takes full responsibility for the document, even though editorial and administrative assistance is provided.

b. If you are typing material from hard copy, first edit it carefully. If someone else wrote the copy, then before you type it, get the writer's help in resolving any questions about content and style that you do not feel equipped or authorized to resolve yourself. By carefully editing this material prior to typing it, you greatly reduce the likelihood of undetected errors in the final document.

c. If you are transcribing from recorded input, you may have to consider the first version you print as a draft that must be shown to the dictator for alteration or approval.

(Continued on page 286.)

12

PROOFREADERS' MARK		DRAFT	FINAL COPY
ss☐	Single-space	ss⌈I have heard⌊he is leaving.	I have heard he is leaving.
ds☐	Double-space	ds⌈When will you⌊have a decision?	When will you have a decision?
+|ℓ#→	Insert 1 line space	<u>Percent of Change</u> +|ℓ#——⌐16.25	<u>Percent of Change</u> 16.25
−|ℓ#→	Delete (remove) 1 line space	Northeastern −|ℓ#→ regional sales	Northeastern regional sales
◡	Delete space	to͡gether	together
#	Insert space	It∧may ͔be	It may not be
◠	Move as shown	it is ⟨not⟩ true	it is true
∿	Transpose	belei͡vable	believable
		⟨is／it⟩ so	it is so
◯	Spell out	②years ago	two years ago
		16 Elm ⟨St.⟩	16 Elm Street
∧ OR ⋏	Insert a word	How much∧*is* it?	How much is it?
⅄ OR —	Delete a word or a punctuation mark	it may n̲o̲t̲ be true ⅄	it may be true
∧ OR ⋏	Insert a letter	temper*a*∧ture	temperature
ℬ OR ⱬ	Delete a letter and close up	commit𝓉ment to buẙy	commitment to buy
◡	Add on to a word	a real∧*ly* good day	a really good day
⅄ OR /	Change a letter	this superꜱedes	this supersedes
⅄ OR —	Change a word	*but* ͢and if you *can't* w̶o̶n̶'̶t̶	but if you can't

d. By the same token, if you receive input in the form of a disk or via a modem, you may want to give the person who originated the document a chance to review and alter the document before you undertake the final editing and proofreading.

e. Before you print the material, run it through the spell checker and the grammar checker and make the necessary corrections. Also scan the material on the screen for any obvious mistakes (such as those noted in ¶¶1202 and 1203), and make the necessary changes. However, do not assume that no further editing or proofreading will be required. Spell checkers and grammar checkers are not infallible, and your earlier review of copy on the screen may not have detected every error. (See ¶1201d.)

NOTE: If you have transcribed from recorded dictation, you will have no original copy to proofread against. Moreover, in the act of transcribing, it is easy to misinterpret and mispunctuate words and phrases or to omit them altogether. Therefore, while you should try to identify and correct as many errors on the screen as you can, you need to recognize that the editing you have done at this stage is not likely to be sufficient.

¶1205

PROOFREADERS' MARK	DRAFT	FINAL COPY
⋯ Stet (don't delete)	I was ~~very~~ glad	I was very glad
/ Lowercase a letter (make it a small letter)	Federal Government	federal government
≡ Capitalize	Janet L. greyston	Janet L. Greyston
∨ Raise above the line	in her new book*	in her new book*
∧ Drop below the line	H2SO4	H₂SO₄
⊙ Insert a period	Mr Henry Grenada	Mr. Henry Grenada
∧ Insert a comma	a large old house	a large, old house
∨ Insert an apostrophe	my childrens car	my children's car
∜ Insert quotation marks	he wants a loan	he wants a "loan"
= Insert a hyphen	a first=rate job	a first-rate job
	ask the coowner	ask the co-owner
OR ⊥ / M̄ Insert a dash or change a hyphen to a dash	Success at last! Here it is cash	Success--at last! Here it is—cash
___ Insert italics	Do it _now_, Bill!	Do it _now_, Bill!
no ital Delete italics	Do it now!	Do it now!
___ Insert underline	an issue of Time	an issue of Time
Delete underline	a very long day	a very long day
( ) Insert parentheses	left today (May 3)	left today (May 3)
¶ Start a new paragraph	¶If that is so	If that is so
2⌐ Indent 2 spaces	Net investment in tangible assets	Net investment in tangible assets
⊐ Move to the right	$38,367,000	$38,367,000
⊏ Move to the left	Anyone can win!	Anyone can win!
= Align horizontally	TO: Bob Muller	TO: Bob Muller
‖ Align vertically	Jon Peters Ellen March	Jon Peters Ellen March

f. After you print the material, examine it carefully for all types of errors as well as possible instances of inconsistency and incoherence. Make the necessary corrections, and then review the new material—first on the screen and then again on the final printout—to make sure that the corrections have been properly executed in the proper location. Also make sure that you have not introduced any new errors inadvertently.

1205 Proofreaders' Marks

Whether you are editing or proofreading, use the proofreaders' marks shown on page 286 and above to indicate the corrections that need to be made. Minor variations in the way these marks are formed are unimportant as long as the marks clearly indicate what corrections have to be made.

RULES FOR ALPHABETIC FILING

There are three types of alphabetic filing: (1) letter by letter (in which spaces between words are disregarded); (2) word by word; and (3) unit by unit (in which every word, abbreviation, and initial is considered a separate unit. The Association of Records Managers and Administrators (ARMA) recommends the use of the unit-by-unit method.

The basic principles of the unit-by-unit method (see ¶¶1206–1208) and the more specific rules that follow (see ¶¶1209–1221) are consistent with ARMA standards.* There are, however, many acceptable alternative rules and variations that are currently in use. The important thing to remember is that the goal of any set of filing standards and rules is to establish a consistent method of sorting and storing materials so that you and others you work with can retrieve these materials quickly and easily. Therefore, it makes sense to modify or change the following rules as necessary to accommodate the specific needs of your office or organization. Make sure, however, that everyone with access to your files knows what the modifications are so that a consistent set of standards can be maintained.

➤ *For guidelines on how to create a computerized file name, see ¶1372.*

IMPORTANT NOTE: Before names can be placed in alphabetic order, they must be *indexed;* that is, each name must be broken down into units, and the units must be arranged in a certain sequence. Once indexing is completed, the names can be compared unit by unit and alphabetic order thus established.

Each of the following rules is accompanied by a chart that shows names in two ways: the first column (headed *Name*) shows the full name in a *standard* format, that is, as it would appear in an inside address of a letter; the remaining group of columns (headed *Unit 1, Unit 2,* and so on) shows the name in an *indexed* format, arranged unit by unit in a sequence appropriate for alphabetizing. Note that the ''inside address'' format presents the names in capital and small letters, with punctuation as necessary. The indexed format presents the names in all-capital letters because for purposes of alphabetizing, the differences between capital and small letters should be ignored. Moreover, the indexed format ignores punctuation; in some cases it even ignores a space or a hyphen between parts of a name.

If you want to use a computer (1) to print names in alphabetic order and (2) to insert names in inside addresses as well as ordinary text, you may have to create two name fields—one using the standard format, the other using the indexed format—as shown in the following charts.

Basic Principles

1206 Alphabetizing Unit by Unit

    a. Alphabetize names by comparing the first units letter by letter.

---

*Alphabetic Filing Rules, Association of Records Managers and Administrators, Inc., Prairie Village, Kansas, 1996.

Name	Unit 1	Unit 2	Unit 3
AlphaNumerics	ALPHANUMERICS		
Butterfield	BUTTERFIELD		
Eagleton	EAGLETON		
Eaton	EATON		
Eberhardt	EBERHARDT		
Eberhart	EBERHART		
ERGOnomics	ERGONOMICS		
Office Space Designers	OFFICE	SPACE	DESIGNERS
Offices Incorporated	OFFICES	INCORPORATED	
Official Stationers	OFFICIAL	STATIONERS	
OFFshore Vacations	OFFSHORE	VACATIONS	

b. Consider second units only when the first units are identical.

Name	Unit 1	Unit 2
Foley Associates	FOLEY	ASSOCIATES
Foley Enterprises	FOLEY	ENTERPRISES
Foley Industries	FOLEY	INDUSTRIES
Foley Mills	FOLEY	MILLS

c. Consider additional units only when the first two units are identical.

Name	Unit 1	Unit 2	Unit 3	Unit 4
Fox Hill Company	FOX	HILL	COMPANY	
Fox Hill Farm	FOX	HILL	FARM	
Fox Hill Farm Supplies	FOX	HILL	FARM	SUPPLIES
Fox Hill Incorporated	FOX	HILL	INCORPORATED	

NOTE: If two names are identical, they may be distinguished on the basis of geographical location. (See ¶1219.)

1207 Nothing Comes Before Something

a. A single letter comes before a name that begins with the same letter.

Name	Unit 1
O	O
Oasis	OASIS
Oberon	OBERON

(Continued on page 290.)

b. A name consisting of one word comes before a name that consists of the same word plus one or more other words.

Name	Unit 1	Unit 2	Unit 3
Operations	OPERATIONS		
Operations Management Consultants	OPERATIONS	MANAGEMENT	CONSULTANTS
Operations Technologies	OPERATIONS	TECHNOLOGIES	

c. A name consisting of two or more words comes before a name that consists of the same two or more words plus another word, and so on.

Name	Unit 1	Unit 2	Unit 3	Unit 4
Oak Creek	OAK	CREEK		
Oak Creek Home Furnishings	OAK	CREEK	HOME	FURNISHINGS
Oak Creek Homes	OAK	CREEK	HOMES	

1208 Deciding Which Name to Use

ARMA advocates filing "under the most commonly used name or title." This helpful principle provides the basis for choosing which name you should use for a person or an organization when alternatives exist. Select the form most likely to be used and then provide cross-references for the alternatives. In that way anyone who is searching for material under an alternative name will be referred to the primary name being used for filing purposes. (See ¶¶1212c, 1214e, 1215a, note, and 1216a, note for specific instances in which this principle can be applied.)

Personal Names

1209 Rule 1: Names of Persons

a. Treat each part of the name of a person as a separate unit, and consider the units in this order: last name, first name or initial, and any subsequent names or initials. Ignore any punctuation following or within an abbreviation.

Name	Unit 1	Unit 2	Unit 3	Unit 4
Jacobs	JACOBS			
L. Jacobs	JACOBS	L		
L. Mitchell Jacobs	JACOBS	L	MITCHELL	
Stephen Jacobson	JACOBSON	STEPHEN		
Stephen Brent Jacobson	JACOBSON	STEPHEN	BRENT	
Steven O'K. Jacobson	JACOBSON	STEVEN	OK	
B. Jacoby	JACOBY	B		
B. T. Jacoby	JACOBY	B	T	
Bruce Jacoby	JACOBY	BRUCE		
C. Bruce Hay Jacoby	JACOBY	C	BRUCE	HAY

b. When you are dealing with a foreign personal name and cannot distinguish the last name from the first name, consider each part of the name in the order in which it is written. Naturally, whenever you can make the distinction, consider the last name first.

Name	Unit 1	Unit 2	Unit 3
Kwong Kow Ng	KWONG	KOW	NG
Ng Kwong Cheung	NG	KWONG	CHEUNG
Philip K. Ng	NG	PHILIP	K

c. In a name like *María López y Quintana,* the last name consists of three separate words. For purposes of alphabetizing, treat these separate words as a single unit (for example, *LOPEZYQUINTANA*).

NOTE: If you are using a computer, insert a hard space between the parts of a name such as *Lopez y Quintana.* Then the last name will be sorted as though it were typed without spaces, but it will appear *with spaces* in the alphabetized list of names.

➤ *For the treatment of hyphenated personal names, see ¶1211.*

1210 Rule 2: Personal Names With Prefixes

a. Consider a prefix as part of the name, not as a separate unit. Ignore variations in spacing, punctuation, and capitalization in names that contain prefixes (for example, *d', D', Da, de, De, Del, De la, Des, Di, Du, El, Fitz, L', La, Las, Le, Les, Lo, Los, M', Mac, Mc, Saint, San, Santa, Santo, St., Ste., Ten, Ter, Van, Van de, Van der, Von,* and *Von Der*).

NOTE: If you are using a computer, insert a hard space between the parts of a name such as *De La Cruz* or *De Voto.* Then the last name will be sorted as though it were typed without spaces, but it will appear *with spaces* in the alphabetized list of names.

Name	Unit 1	Unit 2	Unit 3
A. Serafino Delacruz	DELACRUZ	A	SERAFINO
Anna C. deLaCruz	DELACRUZ	ANNA	C
Michael B. DeLacruz	DELACRUZ	MICHAEL	B
Victor P. De La Cruz	DELACRUZ	VICTOR	P
LaVerne F. Delano	DELANO	LAVERNE	F
Angela G. D'Elia	DELIA	ANGELA	G
Pierre Des Trempes	DESTREMPES	PIERRE	
Brian K. De Voto	DEVOTO	BRIAN	K

b. Consider the prefixes *M', Mac,* and *Mc* exactly as they are spelled, but ignore the apostrophe in *M'.* Consider a name such as *O'Keefe* as one word, and ignore the apostrophe.

NOTE: If you are using a computer, insert a hard space between the parts of a name such as *Mac Kay.* Then the last name will be sorted as though it were typed without a space, but it will appear *with a space* in the alphabetized list of names.

(Continued on page 292.)

Name	Unit 1	Unit 2	Unit 3
Marilyn R. Mack	MACK	MARILYN	R
Irene J. MacKay	MACKAY	IRENE	J
Roy F. Mackay	MACKAY	ROY	F
Walter G. Mac Kay	MACKAY	WALTER	G
F. Timothy Madison	MADISON	F	TIMOTHY
Agnes U. M'Cauley	MCAULEY	AGNES	U
Patrick J. McKay	MCKAY	PATRICK	J
Andrew W. McLain	MCLAIN	ANDREW	W

c. Treat the prefixes *Saint, San, Santa, Santo, St.,* and *Ste.* exactly as they are spelled.

> **NOTE:** If you are using a computer, insert a hard space between the parts of a name such as *Saint Clair* or *San Marco.* Then the last name will be sorted as though it were typed without a space, but it will appear *with a space* in the alphabetized list of names.

Name	Unit 1	Unit 2	Unit 3
George V. Sahady	SAHADY	GEORGE	V
Kyle N. Saint Clair	SAINTCLAIR	KYLE	N
Jeffrey T. Sakowitz	SAKOWITZ	JEFFREY	T
Annette San Marco	SANMARCO	ANNETTE	
Felix Santacroce	SANTACROCE	FELIX	
Peter St. Clair	STCLAIR	PETER	
O. M. Ste. Marie	STEMARIE	O	M

1211 Rule 3: Hyphenated Personal Names

Consider the hyphenated elements of a name as a single unit. Ignore the hyphen.

Name	Unit 1	Unit 2	Unit 3
S. T. Laverty-Powell	LAVERTYPOWELL	S	T
Victor Puentes-Ruiz	PUENTESRUIZ	VICTOR	
Jean V. Vigneau	VIGNEAU	JEAN	V
Jean-Marie Vigneau	VIGNEAU	JEANMARIE	
Jean-Pierre Vigneau	VIGNEAU	JEANPIERRE	

1212 Rule 4: Abbreviated Personal Names, Nicknames, and Pseudonyms

a. Treat an abbreviated part of a name (such as *Wm.* for *William*) or a nickname (such as *Al* or *Kate*) as written if that is how the person is known. Ignore any punctuation used with the abbreviation.

Name	Unit 1	Unit 2	Unit 3
Chas. E. Kassily	KASSILY	CHAS	E
Bubbles Leaden	LEADEN	BUBBLES	
Peggy Sue Marker	MARKER	PEGGY	SUE
B. J. Purcell	PURCELL	B	J

b. If a person is known by a nickname alone (without a surname) or by a pseudonym, consider each word in the nickname or pseudonym as a separate unit. If the name begins with *The*, treat *The* as the last unit.

Name	Unit 1	Unit 2	Unit 3
Big Al	BIG	AL	
Coolio	COOLIO		
The Fat Lady	FAT	LADY	THE
Handy Joe Bob	HANDY	JOE	BOB
Harry the Horse	HARRY	THE	HORSE
Heavy D	HEAVY	D	
Mad Man Marko	MAD	MAN	MARKO
Madonna	MADONNA		
Mr. Bill (see ¶1213b)	MR	BILL	
Tiny Tim	TINY	TIM	

c. When you have to decide whether to file material under a person's formal name or under a nickname, pseudonym, or some abbreviated form, choose the form that best reflects how you and others you work with are most likely to look the person up. You should also enter the person's alternative names in the appropriate alphabetic sequence and make cross-references to the primary name you have selected. (See also ¶1208.)

1213 Rule 5: Personal Names With Titles and Suffixes

a. A title (such as *Dr., Major, Mayor, Miss, Mr., Mrs.,* or *Ms.*) may be used as the *last* filing unit in order to distinguish two or more names that are otherwise identical. Treat any abbreviated titles as written, but ignore any punctuation.

Name	Unit 1	Unit 2	Unit 3	Unit 4
Dr. Leslie G. Mabry	MABRY	LESLIE	G	DR
Miss Leslie G. Mabry	MABRY	LESLIE	G	MISS
Mr. Leslie G. Mabry	MABRY	LESLIE	G	MR
Mrs. Leslie G. Mabry	MABRY	LESLIE	G	MRS
Ms. Leslie G. Mabry	MABRY	LESLIE	G	MS
Major Felix Novotny	NOVOTNY	FELIX	MAJOR	
Mayor Felix Novotny	NOVOTNY	FELIX	MAYOR	

(Continued on page 294.)

b. When a title is used with only one part of a person's name, treat it as the *first* unit. (See ¶1208.)

Name	Unit 1	Unit 2
Dr. Ruth	DR	RUTH
Grandma Moses	GRANDMA	MOSES
King Hussein	KING	HUSSEIN
Miss Manners	MISS	MANNERS
Mother Teresa	MOTHER	TERESA
Prince Andrew	PRINCE	ANDREW
Saint Elizabeth	SAINT*	ELIZABETH

*Note that *Saint* as a title is considered a separate unit, whereas *Saint* as a prefix in a personal name is considered only part of a unit. (See ¶1210c for examples of *Saint* as a prefix.)

c. Ordinarily, alphabetize a married woman's name on the basis of her own first name. However, consider the title *Mrs.* (as abbreviated) if a woman uses her husband's name and you do not know her first name.

Name	Unit 1	Unit 2	Unit 3	Unit 4
Mrs. June Y. Nearing	NEARING	JUNE	Y	
Mr. Peter J. Nearing	NEARING	PETER	J	
Mr. Harry L. Norton	NORTON	HARRY	L	MR
Mrs. Harry L. Norton *(whose own first name is unknown)*	NORTON	HARRY	L	MRS

d. Consider a seniority term (such as *Jr., Sr., 2d, 3d, II,* or *III*), a professional or academic degree (such as *CPA, M.D.,* or *Ph.D.*), or any other designation following a person's name in order to distinguish names that are otherwise identical. Numeric designations precede alphabetic designations. Moreover, arabic numerals precede roman numerals, and each set of numbers is sequenced in numeric order. When dealing with ordinal numbers such as *3d* or *4th*, ignore the endings.

Name	Unit 1	Unit 2	Unit 3	Unit 4
James R. Foster 2d	FOSTER	JAMES	R	2
James R. Foster 3d	FOSTER	JAMES	R	3
James R. Foster III	FOSTER	JAMES	R	III
James R. Foster IV	FOSTER	JAMES	R	IV
James R. Foster, D.D.	FOSTER	JAMES	R	DD
James R. Foster Jr.	FOSTER	JAMES	R	JR
James R. Foster, M.B.A.	FOSTER	JAMES	R	MBA
James R. Foster, M.D.	FOSTER	JAMES	R	MD
James R. Foster, Mr.	FOSTER	JAMES	R	MR
James R. Foster, Ph.D.	FOSTER	JAMES	R	PHD
James R. Foster, S.J.	FOSTER	JAMES	R	SJ
James R. Foster, Sr.	FOSTER	JAMES	R	SR

NOTE: If you are using a computer, all names in which the first significant unit consists of arabic numerals will be sequenced in numeric order and will precede all names with a comparable unit composed of letters of the alphabet (as shown in the preceding chart).

There is a problem, however, with roman numerals. Since roman numerals are written with letters of the alphabet, a computer will consider them as letters (and not as numerals) and position them accordingly in an alphabetic sequence of names. Thus, if a computer were sequencing the names shown in the preceding chart, the name ending with *D.D.* (for *Doctor of Divinity*) would be inserted before the name ending with *III*. To avoid this outcome, you will have to override the computer and move the name ending with *D.D.* to the correct position (after *IV*, as shown in the preceding chart).

Organizational Names

1214 Rule 6: Names of Organizations

a. Treat each word in the name of an organization as a separate unit, and consider the units in the same order as they are written on the company letterhead or some other authoritative document.

Name	Unit 1	Unit 2	Unit 3	Unit 4
American Data Control	AMERICAN	DATA	CONTROL	
American Data Processing Corporation	AMERICAN	DATA	PROCESSING	CORPORATION
Computer Enterprises	COMPUTER	ENTERPRISES		
Computer Systems Unlimited	COMPUTER	SYSTEMS	UNLIMITED	
I Deal Card Shops	I	DEAL	CARD	SHOPS
Ideal Printers	IDEAL	PRINTERS		

b. When alphabetizing, ignore all punctuation—for example, periods, commas, hyphens, apostrophes, and diagonals. When words are joined by a hyphen or a diagonal, treat the phrase as a single unit.

Name	Unit 1	Unit 2	Unit 3
Baskins Advertising Agency	BASKINS	ADVERTISING	AGENCY
Baskins' Artworks	BASKINS	ARTWORKS	
Baskin's Basket Shop	BASKINS	BASKET	SHOP
Baskin-Shaw Films	BASKINSHAW	FILMS	
Baskin/Shaw Foods	BASKINSHAW	FOODS	
Curtis Imports	CURTIS	IMPORTS	
Curtis's China Gallery	CURTISS	CHINA	GALLERY
Curtiss Couriers	CURTISS	COURIERS	
Curtis's Marina	CURTISS	MARINA	
Oleander's Displays!	OLEANDERS	DISPLAYS	
O'Leary's Camera Shop	OLEARYS	CAMERA	SHOP
What's New?	WHATS	NEW	

(Continued on page 296.)

c. Treat prepositions (such as *of* and *in*), conjunctions (such as *and* and *or*), and articles (*the*, *a*, and *an*) as separate units. When *the*, *a*, or *an* is the first word in a name, treat it as the last unit.

Name	Unit 1	Unit 2	Unit 3	Unit 4
In-Plant Catering	INPLANT	CATERING		
Over the Rainbow Gifts	OVER	THE	RAINBOW	GIFTS
The Pen and Pencil	PEN	AND	PENCIL	THE
Photos in a Flash	PHOTOS	IN	A	FLASH
A Touch of Glass	TOUCH	OF	GLASS	A

d. When a compound expression is written as one word or hyphenated, treat it as a single unit. If the compound expression is written with spaces, treat each element as a separate unit.

Name	Unit 1	Unit 2	Unit 3
Aero Space Systems	AERO	SPACE	SYSTEMS
Aerospace Research	AEROSPACE	RESEARCH	
Aero-Space Unlimited	AEROSPACE	UNLIMITED	
Foy Brothers Associates	FOY	BROTHERS	ASSOCIATES
Foy North-South Properties	FOY	NORTHSOUTH	PROPERTIES
Foy-Brothers Financial Planners	FOYBROTHERS	FINANCIAL	PLANNERS
Pay Fone Systems	PAY	FONE	SYSTEMS
Paychex Incorporated	PAYCHEX	INCORPORATED	
Pay-O-Matic Company	PAYOMATIC	COMPANY	
South East Condos	SOUTH	EAST	CONDOS
Southeast Chemicals	SOUTHEAST	CHEMICALS	
South-East Medical Labs	SOUTHEAST	MEDICAL	LABS
Southeastern Medical Supplies	SOUTHEASTERN	MEDICAL-	SUPPLIES

e. Although the words in an organizational name should normally be considered in the same order in which they are written, there are occasions when it makes good sense to allow exceptions to this rule. (See also ¶1208.) Suppose the name in question is *Hotel Plaza*. Strictly speaking, *Hotel* should be the first unit. However, if you and others are more likely to look for stored material in the P section of the files, choose *Plaza* as the first unit and *Hotel* as the second. On the other hand, suppose the name in question is *Motel 6*. Most people would look for material in the M section. Thus it would be best to treat this name exactly as written.

The formal name of a South Bend academic institution is the *University of Notre Dame*. Yet most people would not look for the name in the U section (as the formal rule suggests) but would turn instead to the Ns. However, for the *University of the South*, most people would turn to the U section rather than the S section.

CAUTION: When introducing exceptions to the basic rule for organizational names, be sure that these exceptions are supported by cross-references for the sake of those who may search the files for an alternative name.

1215 Rule 7: Personal Names Within Organizational Names

a. When an organizational name includes a person's name, consider the parts of the personal name in the order in which they are written. Ignore any punctuation.

Name	Unit 1	Unit 2	Unit 3	Unit 4
Frank Balcom Construction Company	FRANK	BALCOM	CONSTRUCTION	COMPANY
Frank Balcom, Jr., Paving	FRANK	BALCOM	JR	PAVING
M. Clausen Optical Supplies	M	CLAUSEN	OPTICAL	SUPPLIES
M. G. Clausen Autos	M	G	CLAUSEN	AUTOS
Mark Clausen Interiors	MARK	CLAUSEN	INTERIORS	
Mark G. Clausen Homes	MARK	G	CLAUSEN	HOMES
Mark G. Clausen Hotel	MARK	G	CLAUSEN	HOTEL
Mark G. Clausen Roofing	MARK	G	CLAUSEN	ROOFING

NOTE: A more traditional rule that is still widely followed requires that a person's name within an organizational name be considered in the same way as if the person's name stood alone—namely, last name first. (See ¶1209.) Regardless of which approach you are following, there are specific situations in which it would be wise to make exceptions, depending on the way you (and others with access to your files) are likely to look the name up.

For example, even if you follow the ARMA standard for personal names in organizational names (first name first), you might want to make an exception for the *John F. Kennedy Presidential Library,* since most people would look for the file under the Ks rather than the Js. Similarly, the file for the *Bernard J. Baruch College* might be more easily found if sequenced according to the surname, *Baruch,* rather than the first name, *Bernard.*

On the other hand, those who follow the last-name-first approach might be wiser to locate the *Sarah Lawrence College* file in the S section rather than the L, to file materials on the *John Hancock Mutual Life Insurance Company* in the J section rather than the H, to store the *Fred Astaire Dance Studios* file under F rather than A, and to put the *Mary Kay Cosmetics* file under M rather than K.

The key here is to consider the way in which the name is most likely to be looked up and then provide cross-references between the alternative form and the primary form that has been selected. (See also ¶1208.)

(Continued on page 298.)

b. If a prefix is used in a personal name that is part of an organizational name, do not treat the prefix as a separate unit. (See ¶1210.)

Name	Unit 1	Unit 2	Unit 3	Unit 4
A. de La Cruz Securities Company	A	DELACRUZ	SECURITIES	COMPANY
A. D'Elia Boat Sales	A	DELIA	BOAT	SALES
Peter Saint Clair Boatels	PETER	SAINTCLAIR	BOATELS	
Peter St. Clair Insurance Agency	PETER	STCLAIR	INSURANCE	AGENCY
R. San Marco Environmental Controls	R	SANMARCO	ENVIRONMENTAL	CONTROLS

c. If a hyphenated personal name is part of an organizational name, treat the hyphenated elements as a single unit. (See ¶1211.)

Name	Unit 1	Unit 2	Unit 3	Unit 4
Mary Tom Packaging Consultants	MARY	TOM	PACKAGING	CONSULTANTS
Mary Tom-Katz Production Company	MARY	TOMKATZ	PRODUCTION	COMPANY

d. Consider a title in an organization's name as a separate unit in the order in which it occurs. Treat abbreviated titles as they are written and ignore punctuation.

Name	Unit 1	Unit 2	Unit 3	Unit 4
Capt. Jack Seafood	CAPT	JACK	SEAFOOD	
Captain Ahab Tours	CAPTAIN	AHAB	TOURS	
Dr. Popper Vision Services	DR	POPPER	VISION	SERVICES
Ma Blake Food Shops	MA	BLAKE	FOOD	SHOPS
Miss Celeste Sportswear	MISS	CELESTE	SPORTSWEAR	
Mother Goose Nurseries	MOTHER	GOOSE	NURSERIES	
Mr. George Limousine Service	MR	GEORGE	LIMOUSINE	SERVICE
Mrs. Ellis Bakeries	MRS	ELLIS	BAKERIES	
Princess Diana Gowns	PRINCESS	DIANA	GOWNS	
Saint Ann Thrift Shop	SAINT*	ANN	THRIFT	SHOP

*When *Saint* is used as a title rather than as a prefix in a personal name, treat it as a separate unit. (See ¶1213b.)

1216 Rule 8: Abbreviations, Acronyms, Symbols, and Letters in Organizational Names

a. Treat an abbreviation as a single unit. Consider it exactly as it is written, and ignore any punctuation.

Name	Unit 1	Unit 2	Unit 3	Unit 4
AFL-CIO	AFLCIO			
ILGWU	ILGWU			
NAACP	NAACP			
Smyly Grain Corp.	SMYLY	GRAIN	CORP	
Smyly Industries Inc.	SMYLY	INDUSTRIES	INC	
Smyth Data Systems Co.	SMYTH	DATA	SYSTEMS	CO
Smyth Datafax Ltd.	SMYTH	DATAFAX	LTD	
U. S. Data Sources*	U	S	DATA	SOURCES
U S Datalink	U	S	DATALINK	
U. S. Grant Foundation	U	S	GRANT	FOUNDATION
U.S. Data Files	US	DATA	FILES	
US Data Tracers	US	DATA	TRACERS	

*For the treatment of an abbreviation consisting of spaced letters (for example, U. S.), see ¶1216d.

NOTE: When organizations are better known by their abbreviated names (*AFL-CIO* and *NAACP*) or acronyms (*NOW, NYNEX, UNESCO*) than by their formal names, use these short forms for filing purposes and provide cross-references as necessary. (See also ¶¶520, 522.)

b. Treat acronyms and the call letters of radio and TV stations as single units.

Name	Unit 1	Unit 2	Unit 3
NASDAQ	NASDAQ		
NOW	NOW		
NYNEX	NYNEX		
OSHA	OSHA		
UNESCO	UNESCO		
VISTA	VISTA		
WBBM Radio Station	WBBM	RADIO	STATION

c. When the symbol & occurs in a name, consider it as if it were spelled out (that is, as *and*). If the symbol is freestanding (that is, with space on either side), treat it as a separate filing unit.

Name	Unit 1	Unit 2	Unit 3	Unit 4
A & L Fabrics	A	AND	L	FABRICS
A&B Publications	AANDB	PUBLICATIONS		
Allen & Korn	ALLEN	AND	KORN	
AT&T	ATANDT			

d. Treat single letters as separate units. If two or more letters in a sequence are written solid or are connected by a hyphen or a diagonal, treat the sequence as a single unit.

(Continued on page 300.)

Name	Unit 1	Unit 2	Unit 3	Unit 4
A & D Terminals	A	AND	D	TERMINALS
A D S Graphics	A	D	S	GRAPHICS
AAA	AAA			
A&D Printers Inc.	AANDD	PRINTERS	INC	
ADS Reports	ADS	REPORTS		
A/V Resources	AV	RESOURCES		
A-Z Rental Corp.	AZ	RENTAL	CORP	
Triple A Realty Trust	TRIPLE	A	REALTY	TRUST
W Z Leasing Co.	W	Z	LEASING	CO
W. Y. Yee (*person's name*)	YEE	W	Y	

1217 Rule 9: Geographic Names Within Organizational Names

a. Treat each part of a geographic name as a separate unit. However, treat hyphenated parts of a geographic name as a single unit.

Name	Unit 1	Unit 2	Unit 3	Unit 4
Big Sur Tours	BIG	SUR	TOURS	
Lake of the Woods Camping Store*	LAKE	OF	THE	WOODS
New Jersey Shore Rentals	NEW	JERSEY	SHORE	RENTALS
Puerto Rico Sugar Traders	PUERTO	RICO	SUGAR	TRADERS
United States Telecom	UNITED	STATES	TELECOM	
West New York Bedding	WEST	NEW	YORK	BEDDING
Wilkes-Barre Mills	WILKESBARRE	MILLS		

*The words *Camping* and *Store* represent the fifth and sixth filing units in this name.

b. When a geographic name begins with a prefix followed by a space or hyphen, treat the prefix and the following word as a single unit. (See ¶1210a for a list of prefixes.)

Name	Unit 1	Unit 2	Unit 3
El Cajon Editorial Services	ELCAJON	EDITORIAL	SERVICES
La Crosse Graphics	LACROSSE	GRAPHICS	
Las Vegas Lenders	LASVEGAS	LENDERS	
Le Mans Auto Repairs	LEMANS	AUTO	REPAIRS
Los Angeles Film Distributors	LOSANGELES	FILM	DISTRIBUTORS
San Francisco Cable Systems	SANFRANCISCO	CABLE	SYSTEMS
Santa Fe Hotel Supplies	SANTAFE	HOTEL	SUPPLIES
Ste.-Julie Inn	STEJULIE	INN	
St. Louis Water Filters	STLOUIS	WATER	FILTERS

NOTE: A name like *De Kalb* or *Des Moines* is considered a single unit, whereas a name like *Fond du Lac* should be treated as three units (since the prefix *du* does not come at the beginning of the geographic name).

1218 Rule 10: Numbers in Organizational Names

a. Arabic numerals (*1, 3, 5*) and roman numerals (*IV, XIX*) are considered separate units. Treat ordinal numbers such as *1st, 3d,* and *5th* as if they were written *1, 3,* and *5.*

b. Units that contain arabic numerals precede units expressed as roman numerals and those consisting of letters of the alphabet (as shown below). Arrange the units containing arabic numerals in numeric order.

NOTE: For sequencing purposes most computer programs will consider arabic numerals from the left. Given the arabic units below, a computer will place *1218* before *21* and *210.* To avoid this outcome, add zeros to the left of *21* and *210* to make them the same length as *1218: 0021, 0210, 1218.* Then the computer will sequence these units in the correct order.

Name	Unit 1	Unit 2	Unit 3	Unit 4
21st Century Travel	21	CENTURY	TRAVEL	
210th St. Assn.	210	ST	ASSN	
1218 Corp.	1218	CORP		
III Brothers Outlets	III	BROTHERS	OUTLETS	
The VII Hills Lodge	VII	HILLS	LODGE	THE
The IX Muses Bookshop	IX	MUSES	BOOKSHOP	THE
AAA Leasing Company	AAA	LEASING	COMPANY	
ILGWU Local 134	ILGWU	LOCAL	134	
ILGWU Local 145	ILGWU	LOCAL	145	
Seventh Heaven Vacations	SEVENTH	HEAVEN	VACATIONS	
Sixth Street Fashions	SIXTH	STREET	FASHIONS	
Third Avenue Elegance	THIRD	AVENUE	ELEGANCE	

c. Units that contain roman numerals follow those with arabic numerals but precede those consisting of letters of the alphabet (as shown above). Arrange units containing roman numerals in numeric order.

NOTE: For sequencing purposes most computer programs will consider roman numerals as letters of the alphabet and position them accordingly. If a computer were sequencing the names shown above, the name beginning with *III* would fall between *AAA* and *ILGWU.* The name beginning with *VII* would come after *Third.* The name beginning with *IX* would fall between *ILGWU* and *Seventh.* To avoid having the roman numerals scattered in this way, you would have to override the program and move these names to the positions shown in the chart above.

d. Units containing numbers expressed in words are sequenced (along with other units containing words or letters) in alphabetic order.

(Continued on page 302.)

e. When a number is written with a hyphen (*Seventy-Six*), ignore the hyphen and treat the number as a single unit (*SEVENTYSIX*).

Name	Unit 1	Unit 2	Unit 3	Unit 4
The Turtle Back Inn	TURTLE	BACK	INN	THE
Twelve Eighteen Realty Co.	TWELVE	EIGHTEEN	REALTY	CO
Twentieth Century Press	TWENTIETH	CENTURY	PRESS	
Twenty-Eight Benbow Street Studios	TWENTYEIGHT	BENBOW	STREET	STUDIOS
Twenty-Five Hundred Club	TWENTYFIVE	HUNDRED	CLUB	
The Warren 200 Colony	WARREN	200	COLONY	THE
The Warren House	WARREN	HOUSE	THE	
Warren Sixty-Fourth Street Salon	WARREN	SIXTYFOURTH	STREET	SALON

f. When a phrase consists of a number (in figures or words) linked by a hyphen or a diagonal to a letter or word (for example, *1-A, A-1, 1-Hour, 4/Way, One-Stop*), ignore the punctuation and treat the phrase as a single unit.

g. When the phrase consists of a figure linked to another figure by means of a hyphen or a diagonal (for example, *80-20* or *50/50*), consider only the number that precedes the punctuation.

NOTE: Most computer programs will consider the complete number and any punctuation.

h. When a phrase consists of a figure plus a letter or word (for example, *3M*) without any intervening space or punctuation, treat the phrase as a single unit.

1-A Physical Trainers	1A	PHYSICAL	TRAINERS	
3 Pro Corp.	3	PRO	CORP	
3M	3M			
4X Investment Group	4X	INVESTMENT	GROUP	
5-10 Household Wares	5	HOUSEHOLD	WARES	
5 Star Video Arcade	5	STAR	VIDEO	ARCADE
5-Corners Pasta Dishes	5CORNERS	PASTA	DISHES	
7-Eleven Food Store	7ELEVEN	FOOD	STORE	
20/20 Eye Care	20	EYE	CARE	
The 30-45 Singles Club	30	SINGLES	CLUB	THE
A-1 Autos Inc.	A1	AUTOS	INC	
Adam's 10-Minute Pizza Service	ADAMS	10MINUTE	PIZZA	SERVICE
Adams' One-Hour Photos	ADAMS	ONEHOUR	PHOTOS	
Adam's One-Stop Shop	ADAMS	ONESTOP	SHOP	
The Fifty-Fifty Co-op	FIFTYFIFTY	COOP	THE	
The Tarragon Tree	TARRAGON	TREE	THE	
Three-Hour Cleaners	THREEHOUR	CLEANERS		

i. When a symbol appears with a number, treat the two elements as a single unit only if there is no space between the symbol and the number. Consider the symbol as if it were spelled out; for example, & (*and*), ¢ (*cent* or *cents*), $ (*dollar* or *dollars*), # (*number* or *pounds*), % (*percent*), and + (*plus*).

NOTE: Most computer programs will consider these symbols on the basis of where they occur in the sequence of character sets. If you convert the symbol to a spelled-out form (as shown above), it will be sequenced in the correct alphabetic order.

Name	Unit 1	Unit 2	Unit 3	Unit 4
The $50 Outerwear Shop	50DOLLAR*	OUTERWEAR	SHOP	THE
50% Off Clothing Outlet	50PERCENT	OFF	CLOTHING	OUTLET
The 50+ Retirement Community	50PLUS	RETIREMENT	COMMUNITY	THE
The #1 Pizza Parlor	NUMBER1	PIZZA	PARLOR	THE
The Original 5&10	ORIGINAL	5AND10	THE	
Plaza 5 & 10	PLAZA	5	AND	10

*When a $ sign precedes a number, consider the number and then the word *DOLLAR* (or *DOLLARS*) in that order.

1219 Rule 11: Alphabetizing by Addresses

When two organizational names are otherwise identical, alphabetize them according to address.

a. First alphabetize by city.

b. If the city names are the same, consider the state. (For example, *Charleston, South Carolina*, comes before *Charleston, West Virginia*.)

Name	Unit 1	Unit 2	Unit 3	Unit 4
McDonald's Durango, Colorado	MCDONALDS	DURANGO		
McDonald's Springfield, Missouri	MCDONALDS	SPRINGFIELD	MISSOURI	
McDonald's Springfield, South Dakota	MCDONALDS	SPRINGFIELD	SOUTH	DAKOTA
McDonald's Torrington, Connecticut	MCDONALDS	TORRINGTON	CONNECTICUT	

c. If both the city and the state are identical, alphabetize by street name.

d. If the street name is a number, treat it exactly as written. Numbered street names expressed *in figures* precede street names (numbered or otherwise) expressed *in words*. Numbered street names *in figures* are

¶12

sequenced in numeric order. Numbered street names *in words* are sequenced (along with other street names in words) in alphabetic order.

Name	Unit 1	Unit 2	Unit 3	Unit 4
McDonald's 17th Street Tallahassee, Florida	MCDONALDS	TALLAHASSEE	17	STREET
McDonald's 41st Street Tallahassee, Florida	MCDONALDS	TALLAHASSEE	41	STREET
McDonald's Appleyard Drive Tallahassee, Florida	MCDONALDS	TALLAHASSEE	APPLEYARD	DRIVE
McDonald's Third Avenue Tallahassee, Florida	MCDONALDS	TALLAHASSEE	THIRD	AVENUE

e. If the street names are also the same, alphabetize by direction if it is part of the address (for example, *north, south, northeast, southwest*).

Name	Unit 1	Unit 2	Unit 3	Unit 4	Unit 5
McDonald's N. 16th Street Tallahassee, Florida	MCDONALDS	TALLAHASSEE	N	16	STREET
McDonald's S. 16th Street Tallahassee, Florida	MCDONALDS	TALLAHASSEE	S	16	STREET
McDonald's Swan Avenue East Tallahassee, Florida	MCDONALDS	TALLAHASSEE	SWAN	AVENUE	EAST
McDonald's Swan Avenue West Tallahassee, Florida	MCDONALDS	TALLAHASSEE	SWAN	AVENUE	WEST

f. If all the foregoing units are identical, consider the house or building numbers and sequence them in numeric order.

McDonald's 23 Tier Street Tallahassee, Florida	MCDONALDS	TALLAHASSEE	TIER	STREET	23
McDonald's 870 Tier Street Tallahassee, Florida	MCDONALDS	TALLAHASSEE	TIER	STREET	870

Governmental Names

1220 Rule 12: Federal Government Names

a. For any organization that is part of the federal government, consider *United States Government* as the first three units.

b. If necessary, consider the name of the department, transposing *Department of* to the end. (For example, treat *Department of Labor* as three separate units: *LABOR DEPARTMENT OF*.)

c. Next consider the name of the office or bureau within the department. Transpose opening phrases such as *Office of* and *Bureau of* to the end. (For example, treat *Bureau of Labor Statistics* as four separate units: *LABOR STATISTICS BUREAU OF.*)

NOTE: It is permissible to omit the names of departments (as is done in the following examples) and move directly from *United States Government* to the name of the office or bureau.

Name	Unit 4*	Unit 5	Unit 6	Unit 7
Office of Consumer Affairs	CONSUMER	AFFAIRS	OFFICE	OF
Federal Bureau of Investigation	FEDERAL	BUREAU	OF	INVESTIGATION
Food and Drug Administration	FOOD	AND	DRUG	ADMINISTRATION
General Accounting Office	GENERAL	ACCOUNTING	OFFICE	
National Labor Relations Board	NATIONAL	LABOR	RELATIONS	BOARD
National Park Service	NATIONAL	PARK	SERVICE	

*The first three units are *United States Government.*

1221 Rule 13: State and Local Government Names

a. For any organization (except an educational institution) that is part of a state, county, city, or town government, first consider the distinctive place name (for example, *Idaho* or *Sandpoint*).

b. Then consider the name of the department, bureau, or other subdivision, transposing elements (if necessary) as was done with federal departments and bureaus in ¶1220.

NOTE: Do not add *state, city,* or a similar term after the distinctive place name unless it is necessary to distinguish such names as *New York State, New York County,* and *New York City.* Moreover, do not add *of, of the,* or a similar expression unless it is part of the official name.

Name	Unit 1	Unit 2	Unit 3	Unit 4	Unit 5
Illinois State Board of Education	ILLINOIS	STATE	EDUCATION	BOARD	OF
Iowa Division of Labor	IOWA	LABOR	DIVISION	OF	
Water Commission, City of Yuma	YUMA	CITY	OF	WATER	COMMISSION
Registry of Deeds, Yuma County	YUMA	COUNTY	DEEDS	REGISTRY	OF

SECTION 13

LETTERS AND MEMOS

ENVELOPES (¶¶1388–1391)

13

MEMOS (¶¶1392–1394)

SOCIAL-BUSINESS CORRESPONDENCE (¶¶1395–1396)

LABELS (¶1397)

Word processing programs typically provide templates that greatly simplify the task of formatting letters, memos, and other documents. As the letter template illustrations on page 308 show, you simply insert the necessary copy as directed by the bracketed notes on the template and type your message. The computer then completes the formatting and prints a final document.

If you want to modify the templates or create your own format for letters and memos, Section 13 will provide you with helpful guidelines. These guidelines are not intended as inflexible rules. They can—and should—be modified to fit specific occasions as good sense and good taste require.

NOTE: You can also store *macro* commands in the template. Macro commands allow you to record keystrokes that you use repeatedly—for example, the name of a person or an organization, a frequently used phrase or sentence, a whole paragraph, or even the closing section of a letter (see ¶1301). Whenever you need to type the repetitive material, you simply run the macro by means of a few keystrokes. Using macros not only saves time but prevents errors.

(Continued on page 308.)

Letter template provided by **WordPerfect 6 for Windows**, using default specifications of 12 point Times New Roman and 1-inch top, side, and bottom margins.

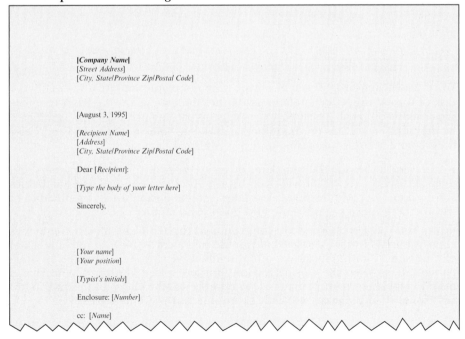

\<Organization\>

\<Address\> ☐ \<City, State Zip\> ☐ \<Telephone\> ☐ Fax: \<Fax\>

[Date]

[Name of Recipient]
[Title]
[Company]
[Address]
[City, State Zip]

Dear [Salutation]

Sincerely,

\<Name\>
\<Title\>

Letter template provided by **Microsoft Word 6 for Windows**, using default specifications of 10 point Times New Roman, 1.25-inch side margins, and a 1-inch top and bottom margin.

[Company Name]
[Street Address]
[City, State/Province Zip/Postal Code]

[August 3, 1995]

[Recipient Name]
[Address]
[City, State/Province Zip/Postal Code]

Dear *[Recipient]*:

[Type the body of your letter here]

Sincerely,

[Your name]
[Your position]

[Typist's initials]

Enclosure: *[Number]*

cc: *[Name]*

LETTERS

Parts of Letters

1301 A business letter has four parts with a variety of features:

Parts	Standard Features	Optional Features
HEADING:	Letterhead or return address (¶¶1311–1313)	Personal or confidential notation (¶1315)
	Date line (¶1314)	Reference notations (¶1316)
OPENING:	Inside address (¶¶1317–1343)	Attention line (¶¶1344–1345)
	Salutation (¶¶1346–1351)	
BODY:	Message (¶¶1354–1357)	Subject line (¶¶1352–1353)
CLOSING:	Complimentary closing (¶¶1358–1360)	Company signature (¶1361)
	Writer's identification (¶¶1362–1369)	File name notation (¶1372)
		Enclosure notation (¶¶1373–1374)
	Reference initials (¶¶1370–1371)	Delivery notation (¶1375)
		Copy notation (¶¶1376–1380)
		Postscript (¶1381)

➤ *Each of these features is illustrated in the model letters on pages 310–314.*

1302 A business letter is usually arranged in one of the following styles:

a. Modified-Block Style—Standard Format. The date line, the complimentary closing, the company signature, and the writer's identification all begin at center. All other lines begin at the left margin. (See page 310 for an illustration.)

NOTE: Current surveys indicate that this is still the style most commonly used.

b. Modified-Block Style—With Indented Paragraphs. This style is exactly the same as the standard format described in *a* above except for one additional feature: the first line of each paragraph is indented 0.5 inch (5 spaces on a typewriter). (See page 312 for an illustration.)

c. Block Style. All lines typically begin at the left margin. Nothing is indented except for displayed quotations, tables, and similar material. (See page 313 for an illustration.)

NOTE: This is the style most commonly used in the letter templates provided by word processing software.

d. Simplified Style. As in the block style, all lines begin at the left margin. However, the simplified style has these additional features: the salutation is replaced by an all-capital subject line, the complimentary closing is omitted, the writer's identification is typed in all-capital letters on one line, and open punctuation (see ¶1309b) is always used. (See page 314 for an illustration.)

Stationery Sizes

1303 The three sizes of stationery most commonly used are standard (8½″ × 11″), monarch or executive (7¼″ × 10½″), and baronial (5½″ × 8½″).

13

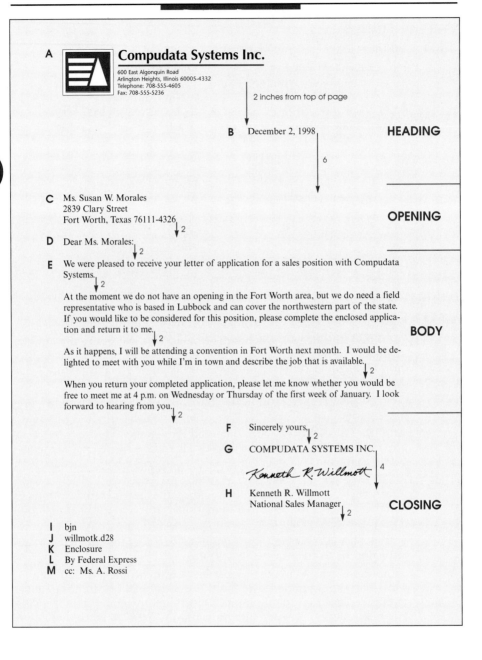

A **Compudata Systems Inc.**

600 East Algonquin Road
Arlington Heights, Illinois 60005-4332
Telephone: 708-555-4605
Fax: 708-555-5236

2 inches from top of page

B December 2, 1998

HEADING

6

C Ms. Susan W. Morales
2839 Clary Street
Fort Worth, Texas 76111-4326

2

OPENING

D Dear Ms. Morales:

2

E We were pleased to receive your letter of application for a sales position with Compudata Systems.

2

At the moment we do not have an opening in the Fort Worth area, but we do need a field representative who is based in Lubbock and can cover the northwestern part of the state. If you would like to be considered for this position, please complete the enclosed application and return it to me.

2

BODY

As it happens, I will be attending a convention in Fort Worth next month. I would be delighted to meet with you while I'm in town and describe the job that is available.

2

When you return your completed application, please let me know whether you would be free to meet me at 4 p.m. on Wednesday or Thursday of the first week of January. I look forward to hearing from you.

2

F Sincerely yours,

2

G COMPUDATA SYSTEMS INC.

4

Kenneth R. Willmott

H Kenneth R. Willmott
National Sales Manager

2

CLOSING

I bjn
J willmotk.d28
K Enclosure
L By Federal Express
M cc: Ms. A. Rossi

A **Letterhead.** The company's name and address, along with other information (such as a telephone number and a fax number). (See ¶¶1311–1312.)

B **Date Line.** The date (month, day, and year) on which the letter is typed; starts at center on the third line below the letterhead or on the first line below the top margin of 2 inches (12 lines on a typewriter). (See ¶1314.)

C **Inside Address.** The name and address of the person you are writing to. (See ¶¶1317–1343.)

D **Salutation.** An opening greeting like *Dear Ms. Morales.* (See ¶¶1346–1351.)

E **Message.** The text of the letter; all paragraphs are typed single-spaced with no indentions; leave 1 blank line between paragraphs. (See ¶¶1354–1357.)

F **Complimentary Closing.** A parting phrase like *Sincerely* or *Sincerely yours;* starts at center. (See ¶¶1358–1360.)

G **Company Signature.** An indication that the writer is acting on behalf of the company. (See ¶1361.)

H **Writer's Identification.** The writer's name and title. (See ¶¶1362–1369.)

I **Reference Initials.** The initials of the typist and sometimes those of the writer as well. (See ¶¶1370–1371.)

J **File Name Notation.** A coded notation that indicates where the document is stored in computer memory. (See ¶1372.)

K **Enclosure Notation.** A reminder that the letter is accompanied by an enclosure. (See ¶¶1373–1374.)

L **Delivery Notation.** An indication that the letter has been sent a special way. (See ¶1375.)

M **Copy Notation.** The names of those who will receive copies of this letter. (See ¶¶1376–1380.)

Modified-Block Style—With Indented Paragraphs

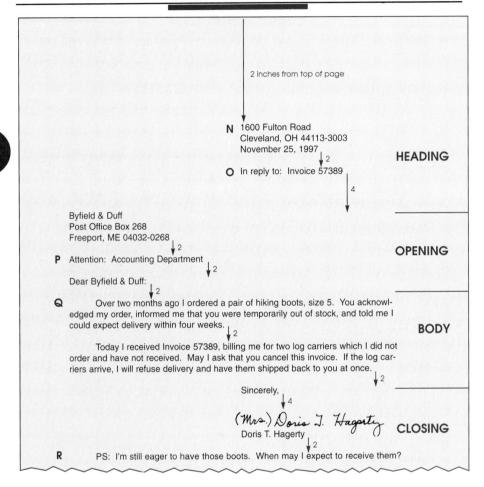

N   1600 Fulton Road
Cleveland, OH 44113-3003
November 25, 1997 ↓2

HEADING

O   In reply to: Invoice 57389

↓4

Byfield & Duff
Post Office Box 268
Freeport, ME 04032-0268 ↓2

OPENING

P   Attention: Accounting Department ↓2

Dear Byfield & Duff: ↓2

Q   Over two months ago I ordered a pair of hiking boots, size 5. You acknowledged my order, informed me that you were temporarily out of stock, and told me I could expect delivery within four weeks. ↓2

BODY

Today I received Invoice 57389, billing me for two log carriers which I did not order and have not received. May I ask that you cancel this invoice. If the log carriers arrive, I will refuse delivery and have them shipped back to you at once. ↓2

Sincerely, ↓4

(Mrs.) *Doris T. Hagerty*
Doris T. Hagerty ↓2

CLOSING

R   PS: I'm still eager to have those boots. When may I expect to receive them?

2 inches from top of page

N   Return Address. The arrangement that is used in a personal-business letter, when an individual writes on blank stationery from home. (For an alternative placement of the return address and other details, see ¶1313.) A person using word processing software can transform the return address into a professional-looking letterhead. (See ¶1312.)

O   Reference Notation. A filing code used by the writer or the addressee. (See ¶1316.)

P   Attention Line. A means of directing the letter to a particular person or a specific department, even though the letter is addressed to an organization as a whole. (For an alternative placement of the attention line and other details, see ¶¶1344–1345.)

Q   Paragraph indentions. Customarily 0.5 inch (5 spaces on a typewriter). (See ¶1356a.)

R   Postscript. A device for presenting a final idea or an afterthought. (See ¶1381.)

BLOCK STYLE

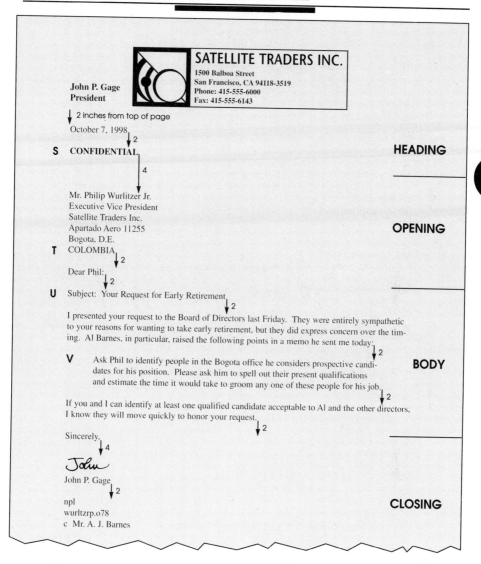

SATELLITE TRADERS INC.
1500 Balboa Street
San Francisco, CA 94118-3519
Phone: 415-555-6000
Fax: 415-555-6143

John P. Gage
President

↓ 2 inches from top of page
October 7, 1998
↓2

S CONFIDENTIAL
↓4

Mr. Philip Wurlitzer Jr.
Executive Vice President
Satellite Traders Inc.
Apartado Aero 11255
Bogota, D.E.
T COLOMBIA
↓2

Dear Phil:
↓2

U Subject: Your Request for Early Retirement
↓2

I presented your request to the Board of Directors last Friday. They were entirely sympathetic to your reasons for wanting to take early retirement, but they did express concern over the timing. Al Barnes, in particular, raised the following points in a memo he sent me today:
↓2

V   Ask Phil to identify people in the Bogota office he considers prospective candidates for his position. Please ask him to spell out their present qualifications and estimate the time it would take to groom any one of these people for his job.
↓2

If you and I can identify at least one qualified candidate acceptable to Al and the other directors, I know they will move quickly to honor your request.
↓2

Sincerely,
↓4

John

John P. Gage
↓2

npl
wurltzrp.o78
c Mr. A. J. Barnes

HEADING

OPENING

BODY

CLOSING

13

S **Confidential Notation.** A note indicating that the letter should be read only by the person addressed. (See ¶1315.)

T **International Address.** The name of the country typed in all-capital letters on a line by itself. (See ¶1343.)

U **Subject Line.** A means of stating what the letter is about. (See ¶¶1352–1353.)

V **Displayed Extract.** Copy set off from the rest of the letter for emphasis; indented 0.5 inch (5 spaces on a typewriter) from the left and right margins. (See ¶1357a.)

SIMPLIFIED STYLE

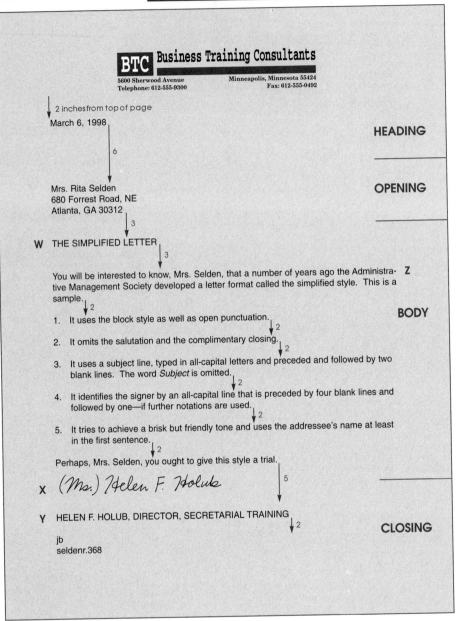

BTC **Business Training Consultants**

5600 Sherwood Avenue   Minneapolis, Minnesota 55424
Telephone: 612-555-9300   Fax: 612-555-0492

2 inches from top of page

March 6, 1998   **HEADING**

6

Mrs. Rita Selden   **OPENING**
680 Forrest Road, NE
Atlanta, GA 30312

3

W   THE SIMPLIFIED LETTER

3

You will be interested to know, Mrs. Selden, that a number of years ago the Administra- **Z**
tive Management Society developed a letter format called the simplified style. This is a
sample.

2

1. It uses the block style as well as open punctuation.   **BODY**

2

2. It omits the salutation and the complimentary closing.

2

3. It uses a subject line, typed in all-capital letters and preceded and followed by two
   blank lines. The word *Subject* is omitted.

2

4. It identifies the signer by an all-capital line that is preceded by four blank lines and
   followed by one—if further notations are used.

2

5. It tries to achieve a brisk but friendly tone and uses the addressee's name at least
   in the first sentence.

2

Perhaps, Mrs. Selden, you ought to give this style a trial.

X   *(Ms.) Helen F. Holub*   5

Y   HELEN F. HOLUB, DIRECTOR, SECRETARIAL TRAINING

2

CLOSING

jb
seldenr.368

W   **Subject Line.** Replaces the salutation; typed in all-capital letters on the
third line below the inside address.
(See also ¶1352.)

X   **Complimentary Closing.** Omitted.
(See also ¶¶1358–1360.)

Y   **Writer's Identification.** Typed on
one line in all-capital letters. (See also
¶1363.)

Z   **Justified Right Margin.** Makes each
line in the body of the letter end at
the same point. (See ¶1356b.)

Letter Placement

1304 Top Margin

a. First Page. If you are using stationery with a printed letterhead, place the date (the first element to be typed) on the third line below the letterhead or position it on the first line below the top margin of 2 inches (12 lines on a typewriter). If you are using a word processing letter template, your software will automatically position the current date.

NOTE: If you are using a return address rather than a printed letterhead, begin typing on the first line below the top margin of 2 inches (12 lines on a typewriter). (See ¶1313.)

b. Continuation Pages. Use a top margin of 1 inch (6 lines on a typewriter) on each continuation page of a letter. These pages are always typed on unprinted stationery (even if the first page is prepared on a printed letterhead). (See also ¶¶1382–1387.)

1305 Side Margins

a. If you are using word processing software, determine the default (preset) side margins. For standard and monarch (executive) stationery, WordPerfect 6 for Windows has 1-inch default side margins; Microsoft Word 6 for Windows has 1.25-inch default side margins.

b. The use of 1-inch side margins with standard ($8\frac{1}{2}'' \times 11''$) stationery yields a 6.5-inch line for the text and permits you to fit a great deal of copy on a page. However, a letter typed with wider side margins is more attractive and easier to read. The following table shows the extent to which you can widen standard side margins to produce a more open look.

Stationery	Standard (Default) Side Margins	Text Line	Adjusted Side Margins for Shorter Text Line	Shortest Text Line
Standard ($8\frac{1}{2}'' \times 11''$)	WordPerfect: 1" Word: 1.25"	6.5" 6"	Up to 1.75"	5"
Monarch (Executive) ($7\frac{1}{4}'' \times 10\frac{1}{2}''$)	WordPerfect: 1" Word: 1.25"	5.25" 4.75"	Up to 1.5"	4.25"
Baronial ($5\frac{1}{2}'' \times 8\frac{1}{2}''$)	WordPerfect:* Word:*	— —	—	3.5"

*Neither WordPerfect nor Microsoft Word provides default side margins for baronial stationery. The use of 0.75" side margins will yield a text line of 4"; the use of 1" side margins will yield a text line of 3.5". No other adjustments in the side margins are recommended for baronial stationery.

c. If you are using letterhead stationery with a column of printed copy running down the left side of the page, set the left margin 0.5 inch to the right of this copy and set the right margin at 1 inch.

d. Once you have established the side margins, the number of characters you can fit on a line of text will depend on the type size and typeface you select. The following chart displays some common typefaces in two sizes so that you can see the variation in the number of characters in an inch.

Common Type Sizes and Typefaces	Characters in 1 Inch
12 Point Times New Roman	abcdefghijklm
10 Point Times New Roman	abcdefghijklmnop
12 Point Univers	abcdefghijkl
10 Point Univers	abcdefghijklmn
12 Point Courier	abcdefghij
10 Point Courier	abcdefghijkl

NOTE: The default specification for WordPerfect 6 for Windows is 12 point Times New Roman. For Microsoft Word 6 for Windows it is 10 point Times New Roman, a very small typeface that some people will find hard to read. Review the typeface and type size options that are available to you, and select the one that best meets your needs.

1306 Bottom Margin

a. Leave a bottom margin of at least 1 inch (6 lines on a typewriter).

b. If the letter requires more than one page, you can increase the bottom margin on the first page up to 2 inches (12 lines on a typewriter).

c. If you are using letterhead stationery with a band of printed copy running across the bottom of the page, leave a minimum margin of 0.5 inch (3 lines on a typewriter) between the last line of text and the band of printed copy.

➤ *For guidelines on carrying a letter over from one page to the next, see ¶¶ 1382–1387.*

1307 Lengthening a Short Letter

To *spread* a short letter (under 75 words or about 8 lines of text) over one page, use any combination of the following techniques:

a. Increase the side margins. (See the table on page 315.)

b. Change the paper size from standard to monarch or baronial.

c. If you are using word processing software, increase the type size or select a typeface that yields fewer characters to an inch.

d. Lower the date line by as many as 6 lines.

e. Leave up to 9 blank lines between the date and the inside address.

f. Leave up to 6 blank lines for the signature.

g. Lower the reference initials 1 or 2 lines.

1308 Shortening a Long Letter

To *condense* a long letter (over 225 words or 23 lines of text), use any combination of the following techniques:

a. If you have been using wide side margins, reduce them to 1 inch on standard and monarch stationery and to 0.75 inch on baronial.

b. If you have been using monarch or baronial stationery, change to standard stationery.

c. If you are using word processing software, consider using a slightly smaller typeface or one that yields more characters to an inch. You can also reduce the space between words and letters. (Be sure, however, that after all such adjustments the type is still quite readable.)

d. If you are using printed stationery, type the date on the third line below the letterhead. On a blank page on which you are printing a letterhead or typing a return address, leave a top margin of only 1 inch (6 lines on a typewriter).

e. Reduce the space between the date and the inside address to 2 or 3 blank lines (instead of the customary 5).

f. Reduce the space for the signature from 3 blank lines to 2.

g. Position the reference initials on the same line as the writer's identification.

13

Punctuation Patterns

1309 The message in a business letter is always punctuated with normal punctuation (see Sections 1 and 2). The other parts may be punctuated according to one of the following patterns:

a. Standard (Mixed) Pattern. Use a colon after the salutation and a comma after the complimentary closing. (This is the style most commonly used.)

May 4, 1998

Mr. Bernard Krause Jr.
The Bergen Press Inc.
313 North Street
San Jose, CA 95113

Dear Mr. Krause:

Sincerely,

HUDSON COMPANY

Lee Brower

Lee Brower
Sales Manager

mr
krauseb.548
Enclosure
cc: Ms. Loo

(Continued on page 318.)

b. **Open Pattern.** Use no punctuation at the end of any line outside the body of the letter unless that line ends with an abbreviation.

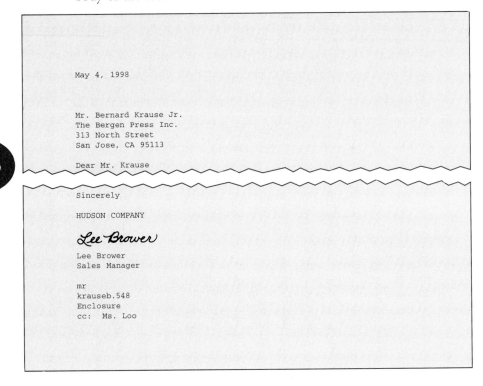

```
May 4, 1998


Mr. Bernard Krause Jr.
The Bergen Press Inc.
313 North Street
San Jose, CA 95113

Dear Mr. Krause
```

```
Sincerely

HUDSON COMPANY


Lee Brower
Sales Manager


mr
krauseb.548
Enclosure
cc:  Ms. Loo
```

Spacing

1310 Type all letters single-spaced. Leave 1 blank line between paragraphs. (See the illustrations on pages 310–314.)

The following rules (¶¶1311–1316) deal with the *heading* of a letter. The heading must always include two elements: a letterhead or a return address (¶¶1311–1313) and a date line (¶1314). It may also include a personal or confidential notation (¶1315) and reference notations (¶1316). The model letters shown on pages 310–314 illustrate the position of these elements in the heading.

Letterhead or Return Address

1311 Using a Printed Letterhead

a. The first page of a standard business letter is customarily written on stationery with a *printed letterhead* containing at least these elements: the organization's name, the street address or post office box number (or both), and the city, state, and ZIP Code. Most letterheads for organizations also provide the following elements as appropriate: a telephone number, a fax number, an e-mail address, a cable address, and a logo or some other graphic element. (See the illustration at the top of page 319.) Top executives may have special letterheads showing their name and title. (See page 313 for an illustration of a top executive's stationery.)

Cole, Steele & Backus

1800 Avenue of the Stars **Los Angeles, CA 90067-4201**

Telephone: (213) 555-4345   E-Mail: CSB150A@prodigy.com
Fax: (213) 555-4265   Cable: COSTEBA

13

b. Do not use abbreviations in a letterhead except those that are part of the organization's name or that represent a state name.

c. Even if your organization uses a post office box number as its primary mailing address, show a street address as well. In that way others will know where to direct ordinary mail (the post office) and where to direct express mail (the organization's office). If the two addresses have different ZIP Codes, be sure to provide this information.

1312 Creating a Letterhead

a. In place of printed stationery, you can use word processing templates and various typefaces and type sizes to create a professional-looking letterhead on plain paper.

The following illustrations show two computer-generated letterheads—one designed for a company and one designed for an individual working from home.

ALBERS AND PARKER INC.

11 West 19th Street   Box 3291, Old Chelsea Station
New York, NY 10011-4285   New York, NY 10011-9998
Telephone: 212-555-9897   Fax: 212-555-9803

Merle C. Forrest

SECOND WIND ★ 28 BISCAY ROAD ★ DAMARISCOTTA, MAINE 04531 ★ 207-555-9097

NOTE: Individuals who want to make themselves available to clients and customers at all hours may insert additional elements in their letterheads beyond those listed in ¶1311—for example, a home phone number (in addition to a business phone number), a mobile phone number, a pager number, or a voice mail number.

b. If you are using a typewriter to create a business letterhead, type the elements you wish to include in a series of centered double-spaced lines or in some other attractive arrangement. Begin typing the letterhead on the seventh line from the top of the page.

1313 Using a Return Address

If you are using plain paper for a *personal-business letter* (one you write as an individual from your home), you can supply the necessary address information in the form of a *return address*. There are two formats you can choose from.

a. Traditionally, the return address appears at the top of the page starting on the first line below the top margin of 2 inches (12 lines on a typewriter). Provide the following information on three or more single-spaced lines: (1) the street address; (2) the city, state, and ZIP Code; (3) the phone number (if you want the addressee to have it); and (4) the date (see ¶1314).

```
Apartment 2B             OR  212 West 22d Street, Apt. 2B
212 West 22d Street          New York, NY 10011-2706
New York, NY 10011-2706      212-555-9097
212-555-9097                 January 24, 1997
January 24, 1997
```

NOTE: For the *modified-block* letter style, start each line of the return address at the center of the page. (See page 312.) For the *block* and *simplified* styles, start each line at the left margin. (See pages 313–314.)

b. An alternative style locates the return address in the *closing* section of the letter, starting on the line directly below the writer's typed name.

```
Sincerely,  ↓4
```

```
Josephine C. Carbonara
Apartment 2B
212 West 22d Street
New York, NY 10011-2706
212-555-9097
```

NOTE: Each line of the return address begins at the same point as the complimentary closing and the writer's typed name—at the center of the page for the *modified-block* style and at the left margin for the *block* and *simplified* styles.

Date Line

1314 a. The date line consists of the *name of the month* (written in full—never abbreviated or represented by figures), the *day* (written in figures and followed by a comma), and the *complete year*.

December 28, 1998 (**NOT** Dec. 28, 1998 **OR** December 28th, 1998)

NOTE: Do not use the style *12/28/98* or *'98* in the date line of a business letter.

b. Some writers write the date line in this order: day, month, year. This is the style typically used in military correspondence and letters from abroad.

28 December 1998

c. If you are using the date feature of a word processing program, you can automatically insert the current day's date.

NOTE: A similar feature, called a *date code,* will enter the current day's date not only when you first input the letter but whenever you subsequently display the document or print it. Using the date code is helpful when you are sending out a form letter frequently; you will always want such letters to carry the current date. However, if you plan to store a letter and want to ensure that the original date line will not change, do not use a date code.

d. If you are formatting a letter yourself and using letterhead stationery, position the date line on the third line below the letterhead or on the first line below the top margin of 2 inches (12 lines on a typewriter).

NOTE: For the *modified-block* letter style, you may start the date line at the center or you may type it in some other position that is attractive in relation to the letterhead (so long as it still stands out). For the *block* and *simplified* letter styles, always start the date at the left margin.

e. When using a return address at the top of the letter, position the date as shown in ¶1313a. If the return address is placed at the bottom of the letter (as in ¶1313b), position the date on the first line below the top margin of 2 inches (12 lines on a typewriter).

➢ *See the illustrations on pages 310–314.*

Personal or Confidential Notation

1315 If a letter is of a personal or confidential nature, provide the appropriate notation on the second line below the date, at the *left* margin. Type the notation in all-capital letters, using boldface if you have that option. (See the illustration on page 313.)

PERSONAL   **CONFIDENTIAL**

Reference Notations

1316 a. Printed letterheads for large organizations sometimes contain a line in the upper right corner that reads *When replying, refer to:* or something similar. When using this kind of letterhead, type the appropriate reference number or other code 2 spaces after the colon, aligned at the bottom with the printed words. (You may insert a file name notation here instead of at the bottom of the letter. See ¶1372.)

NOTE: If the guide words *When replying, refer to:* are not printed on the stationery but are desired, type them on the second line below the date (or on the second line below any notation that follows the date). Start typing at the same point as the date.

When replying, refer to: watsonnd.369

(Continued on page 322.)

b. When you are replying to a letter that contains a reference number or when you want to emphasize the fact that your letter concerns an insurance policy, an order, or a similar document, type a reference notation on the second line below the date (or on the second line below any notation that follows the date). Start typing at the same point as the date. (See the illustration on page 312.)

```
In reply to:  G241 782 935    Refer to:  Policy 234844
```

c. When there are two reference notations to be given, type your own reference notation first (as indicated in ¶1316a). Then type the addressee's reference notation on the second line below.

```
When replying, refer to:  dingesc.524

Your reference:  blockagc.747
```

NOTE: Some writers prefer to give the addressee's reference notation in a subject line. (See ¶1353e.)

The following rules (¶¶1317–1351) deal with the opening of a letter. The opening typically includes two elements: the inside address (¶¶1317–1343) and the salutation (¶¶1346–1351). It may also include an attention line (¶¶1344–1345).

Inside Address

1317 Letters to an Individual

a. The inside address for a letter to an individual's home should include the following information: (1) the name of the person to whom you are writing; (2) the street address, the post office box number or mail-stop code (see ¶1338), or the rural route number (see ¶1317c); and (3) the city, state, and ZIP Code (see ¶1339).

```
Dr. Margaret P. Vanden Heuvel  Mr. James R. Drum Jr.
615 University Boulevard       General Delivery
Albuquerque, NM 87106-4553     Nobleboro, Maine 04555
```

➤ *For the placement of the inside address, see ¶1319a; for the use of the nine-digit ZIP Code, see ¶1339, note.*

b. If the person lives in an apartment building, give the apartment number after the street address or on the line above.

```
Miss Susan H. Ellington     Mrs. Lorraine Martineau
Apartment 2104              6834 Creston Road, Apt. 4D
11740 Wiltshire Boulevard  Edina, MN 55435
Los Angeles, CA 90025
```

c. If you are writing to someone with a rural route address or a highway contract route address, do not use *rural route, highway contract route, number, No.,* or *#* in the address. Use the abbreviation *RR* or *HC* plus a box number. For example:

```
RR 2, Box 454     HC 67, Box 21A
```

The U.S. Postal Service prefers that a street name not be used in conjunction with an *RR* or *HC* address. If one is used, place it on the line above the *RR* or *HC* address.

NOTE: If you are using word processing software, you can create a macro containing the inside address and salutation for any individual or organization that you frequently write to.

1318 Letters to an Organization

a. The inside address for a letter to an organization should include the following information: (1) the name of the business or organization, (2) a street address or a post office box number, and (3) the city, state, and ZIP Code. Whenever possible, address the letter to a specific person in the organization and include that person's job title and department (if known). If you do not have the name of a specific person, use a title instead (for example, *Director of Marketing*).

```
Mr. Arthur L. Quintero        Director of Research
National Sales Manager        Stanton Chemical Company
Paragon Industries            Post Office Box 21431
211 North Ervay Street        Chattanooga, TN 37421-0431
Dallas, Texas 75201
```

➤ *For the placement of the inside address, see ¶1319a; for the use of the nine-digit ZIP Code, see ¶1339, note.*

b. When a room number or a suite number is included in the inside address, the following arrangements are acceptable:

```
Ms. Alice G. Alvarez          James W. Chiverton, M.D.
Werler Construction Company   Suite 1200
416 12th Street, Room 12      1111 West Mockingbird Lane
Columbus, Georgia 31901-2528  Dallas, TX 75247-3158


Mr. Raymond Kermian           Miss Pauline Leggett
Contemporary Tours Inc.       Steele & Leggett
Room 304, Tower Building      503 Hanna Building
2506 Willowbrook Parkway      1422 Euclid Avenue
Indianapolis, IN 46205        Cleveland, Ohio 44115
```

1319 a. Whether a letter is going to an individual's home or to an organization, start the inside address at the left margin, on the *sixth* line below the date. If a notation falls between the date and the inside address (see ¶¶1315–1316), start the inside address on the *fourth* line below the notation.

➤ *See the illustrations on pages 310–314.*

NOTE: You may need to modify these guidelines if you are planning to use a window envelope (see ¶¶1389i, 1391d).

b. In social-business correspondence (see ¶¶1395–1396), type the inside address at the bottom of the letter, aligned at the left margin and starting on the *sixth* line below the writer's signature or title (whichever comes last). In a purely personal letter, no inside address is given at all.

c. Single-space the inside address and align each line at the left.

1320 a. If a letter is addressed to two or more people at different addresses, type the individual address blocks one under the other (with 1 blank line between) or position the address blocks side by side. If the address blocks take up too much space at the opening of the letter, type them at the end of the letter, starting on the second line below the final notation at the left or, if there are no notations, on the *sixth* line below the signature block.

(Continued on page 324.)

b. If a letter is addressed to two or more people at the same address, list each name on a separate line. Do not show a position title for each person unless it is short and can go on the same line as the name. Moreover, omit the names of departments unless the persons are in the same department. In effect, type only those parts of the address that are common to the people named at the start. (On the respective envelopes for each individual, give the full address for that individual and omit all reference to others named in the inside address.)

```
Dr. Paul J. Rogers
Mr. James A. Dawes
Research Department
Sloan and Hewitt Advertising
700 North Harding Avenue
Chicago, Illinois 60624-1002
```

13

The following rules (¶¶1321–1343) provide additional details concerning the parts of inside addresses. See also the models in Section 18 for special forms of address used for individuals, couples, organizations, professional people, education officials, government officials, diplomats, military personnel, and religious dignitaries.

Name of Person and Title

1321 When writing the name of a person in an inside address or elsewhere in a letter, be sure to follow that person's preferences in the spelling, capitalization, punctuation, and spacing of the name. (See ¶311.)

a. Do not abbreviate or use initials unless the person to whom you are writing prefers that style. For example, do not write *Wm. B. Sachs* or *W. B. Sachs* if the person to whom you are writing used *William B. Sachs* in his correspondence.

b. When writing to a married woman, follow her preference for first and last names if you know it. She may have decided not to adopt her husband's last name for business purposes (or for any purposes) and prefer to be addressed by her original name (for example, *Ms. Joan L. Conroy*). If you do know that she is using her husband's last name, continue to use her own first name and middle initial (for example, *Mrs. Joan L. Noonan*). The form that uses her husband's first name as well (for example, *Mrs. James W. Noonan*) is acceptable only for social purposes. It should never be used when addressing a business letter to a married woman, and it should not be used when a married woman becomes a widow unless she indicates that is her preference.

1322 In general, use a title before the name of a person in an inside address. (See ¶517 for appropriate abbreviations of such titles.)

a. If the person has no special title (such as *Dr., Professor,* or *The Honorable*), use the courtesy title *Mr., Ms., Mrs.,* or *Miss.* (See also ¶1801.)

b. In selecting *Ms., Mrs.,* or *Miss,* always respect the individual woman's preference. If her preference is unknown, use the title *Ms.* or omit the courtesy title altogether. (See also ¶1801b–c.)

NOTE: Follow the same practice in the salutation. (See ¶1349.)

c. If you do not know whether the person addressed is a man or a woman, do not use any courtesy title. (See also ¶1801d.) Follow the same practice in the salutation. (See ¶1349.)

NOTE: People who use initials in place of their first and middle names or who have ambiguous names (like *Marion, Leslie, Hilary,* and *Lee*) should always use a courtesy title when they sign their letters so that others may be spared the confusion over which title to use. (See also ¶¶1365–1366.)

d. Address teenage girls as *Ms.* or *Miss,* and respect the individual's preference if you know it. For girls younger than 13, *Ms.* or *Miss* may be used or omitted.

e. Address teenage boys as *Mr.* For boys younger than 13, omit the title. (*Master* is now rarely used except with the names of very young boys.)

13

1323 a. A letter to a husband and wife is traditionally addressed in this form:

```
Mr. and Mrs. Harold D. Bennisch Jr. (NOT: Mr. & Mrs.)
```

b. If the husband has a special title such as *Dr.* or *Professor,* the couple is addressed as follows:

```
Dr. and Mrs. Thomas P. Geiger
```

c. List the names of a married couple on separate lines when (1) the wife alone has a special title, (2) both spouses have special titles, or (3) they have different surnames.

```
Dr. Eleanor V. Eberhardt-Ball        Ms. Eloise Baum
Mr. Joseph L. Eberhardt-Ball         Mr. Philip O'Connell

Dean Walter O. Goetz          OR: Mrs. Eloise Baum
Professor Helen F. Goetz              Mr. Philip O'Connell
```

d. Some married couples prefer a style of address which uses the first names of the spouses and omits *Mr. and Mrs.* Those who use this style typically do so because it treats both spouses as equals and does not imply that the wife can only be identified by her husband's name. Respect such preferences when you are aware of them.

```
Janet and Arnold Rogon
(RATHER THAN: Mr. and Mrs. Arnold Rogon)
```

➤ *For other forms of address to use for couples in special circumstances, see* ¶*1802.*

1324 a. When *Jr., Sr.,* or a roman numeral such as *III* is typed after a name, omit the comma before this element unless you know that the person being addressed prefers the use of a comma. (See also ¶156.)

b. Do not use a title before a name if the term *Esq.* follows the name. (See also ¶¶518c, 1804a.)

```
Rita A. Henry, Esq. (NOT: Ms. Rita A. Henry, Esq.)
```

NOTE: A comma separates the last name from the term *Esq.*

c. As a rule, do not use an academic degree with a person's name in an inside address. However, some doctors of medicine and divinity prefer the use of the degree after their names (rather than the title *Dr.* before). (See also ¶1804b.)

(Continued on page 326.)

NOTE: If an academic degree follows the person's name, separate it from the last name with a comma. Also omit the titles *Dr., Miss, Mr., Mrs.,* and *Ms.* before the name. Another title (for example, *Professor, The Reverend, Captain, Dean*) may be used before the name as long as it does not convey the same meaning as the degree that follows. (See ¶519c.)

```
Reva C. Calhoun, M.D.
The Reverend Ernest G. Wyzanski, D.D.
```

d. Abbreviations of religious orders, such as *S.J.* and *S.N.D.,* are typed after names and preceded by a comma. An appropriate title should precede the name, even though the abbreviation follows the name; for example, *The Reverend John DeMaio, O.P.* (See also ¶1809.)

1325 a. A title of position, such as *Vice President* or *Sales Manager,* may be included in an inside address. If a title is to be used, place it on the line following the name; if the title requires a second line, indent the turnover 2 or 3 spaces. Capitalize the first letter of every word in the title except (1) prepositions under four letters (like *of, for,* and *in*), (2) conjunctions under four letters (like *and*), and (3) the articles *the, a,* and *an* when they appear *within* the title.

```
Mrs. Martha Hansen          Mr. Ralph Nielsen
Executive Vice President    Vice President and (NOT &)
                              General Manager

Mr. Harry F. Benjamin       Ms. Evangeline S. Palmer
Chairman of the Board       Director of In-Service
                              Training
```

NOTE: In the last example above, *In* is capitalized because it is the first element in a compound adjective (rather than a pure preposition as in *Editor in Chief*). By the same token, in the title *Coordinator of On-the-Job Training, On* is capitalized as the first element in a compound adjective but *of* and *the* are not.

b. If the title is very short, it may be typed on the same line as the person's name or the person's department in order to balance the length of the lines in the address. However, do not type a title on the same line as the name of an organization. (See ¶1327.)

```
Mr. J. C. Lee, President      Mrs. Lucinda Hollingsworth
Merchants National Bank       Manager, Support Services
                              E. J. Haines & Company

Mr. Armand F. Aristides    NOT: Mr. Armand F. Aristides
Controller                      Controller, Dahl, Inc.
Dahl, Inc.
```

In Care of . . .

1326 Sometimes a letter cannot be sent to the addressee's home or place of business; it must be directed instead to a third person who will see that the letter reaches the addressee. In such cases use an "in care of" notation as shown below.

```
Professor Eleanor Marschak    OR Professor Eleanor Marschak
In care of Henry Ward, Esq.      c/o Henry Ward, Esq.
```

Name of Organization

1327 Type the organization's name on a line by itself. If the name of a division or a department is needed in the address, it should precede the name of the organization on a line by itself.

```
Ms. Laura J. Kidd
Assistant Vice President
Department of Corporate Planning
Holstein, Brooks & Co.
```

1328 When writing the name of an organization in an inside address, always follow the organization's style for spelling, punctuation, capitalization, spacing, and abbreviations. The letterhead on incoming correspondence is the best source for this information. Note the variations in style in these names.

America Online, Inc.	BankAmerica Corp.
Sierra On-Line, Inc.	Rogers Cablesystems of America, Inc.
Time Inc.	USLife Corp.
Newsweek, Inc.	U S WEST Communications
Prudential Securities	Luce, Forward, Hamilton & Scripps
Incorporated	Dean Witter Reynolds Inc.
Hewlett-Packard Company	Browning-Ferris Industries
Charles Schwab & Co., Inc.	Ply*Gem Industries
PepsiCo, Inc.	Ex-Cell-O Corporation
Xerox Corporation	La-Z-Boy Chair Co.
Engelhard Corp.	1 Potato 2 Inc.
Parker Pen USA Limited	Toys "R" Us, Inc. (see ¶320a)
Frye & Smith Ltd.	!%@: Directory of Electronic Mail
Fujitsu, Ltd.	Addressing & Networks

NOTE: If the name is long and requires more than one line, indent any turnover line 2 or 3 spaces. (See ¶1329e for examples.)

1329 If you do not have some way of determining the official form of a company name, follow these rules:

a. Spell out the word *and*. Do not use an ampersand (&).

Haber, Curtis, and Hall Inc.

b. Write *Inc.* for *Incorporated* and *Ltd.* for *Limited*. Do not use a comma before the abbreviation.

c. As a rule, spell out *Company* or *Corporation;* if the name is extremely long, however, use the abbreviation *Co.* or *Corp.*

d. Do not use the word *the* at the beginning of a name unless you are sure it is part of the official name; for example, *The Wall Street Journal* (as illustrated at the top of page 328.)

e. Capitalize the first letter of every word except (1) prepositions under four letters (like *of* and *for*), (2) conjunctions under four letters (like *and*), and (3) the articles *the, a,* and *an* when they appear *within* the organization's name.

```
Department of Health and        American Society for the
   Human Services                  Prevention of Cruelty
200 Independence Avenue, SW         to Animals
Washington, DC 20201-0001        424 East 92d Street
                                 New York, New York 10128
```

(Continued on page 328.)

NOTE: In the following example note that the article *the* is capitalized because it comes at the start of the organization's official name. Note also that the name of the newspaper is not italicized or underlined because it refers to the organization rather than to the actual newspaper. (See also ¶289e.)

```
The Wall Street Journal
200 Liberty Street
New York, NY 10281-1099
```

➤ *For the use or omission of apostrophes in company names, see ¶640.*

Building Name

1330 If the name of a building is included in the inside address, type it on a line by itself immediately above the street address. A room number or a suite number should accompany the building name.

```
Room 118, Acuff Building         858 Park Square Building
904 Bob Wallace Avenue, SW       31 St. James Avenue
Huntsville, AL 35801             Boston, MA 02116-4255
```

➤ *For additional examples, see ¶1318b.*

Street Address

1331 Always type the street address on a line by itself, immediately preceding the city, state, and ZIP Code. (See ¶¶1317–1318 for examples.)

1332 Use figures for house and building numbers. Do not include the abbreviation *No.* or the symbol # before such numbers. **EXCEPTION:** For clarity, use the word *One* instead of the figure *1* in a house or building number; for example, *One Park Avenue.*

NOTE: Some house numbers contain a hyphen or a fraction; for example, *220-03 46th Street, 234½ Elm Street.*

1333 Numbers used as street names are written as follows:

a. Spell out the numbers 1 through 10; for example, *177 Second Avenue.*

b. Use figures for numbers over 10; for example, *627 East 202d Street* or *144 65th Street.* (See also ¶425, note.)

c. Some grid-style addresses require a period in a numbered street name; for example, *26.2 Road.*

1334 When a compass point (for example, *East, West, Southeast, Northwest*) appears *before* a street name, do not abbreviate it except in a very long street address when space is tight.

```
330 West 42d Street              3210 Northwest Grand Avenue
```

1335 When a compass point appears *after* a street name, follow the local style that predominates. In the absence of a local style, follow these guidelines:

a. Abbreviate compound directions (*NE, NW, SE, SW*) that represent a section of the city. Do not use a period with these abbreviations (see ¶531a). Insert a comma before them.

```
817 Peachtree Street, NE         120 112th Street, NW
```

b. Spell out *North, South, East,* and *West* following a street name, and omit the comma. (In such cases these compass points are typically an integral part of the street name rather than a designation of a section of the city.)

```
10 Park Avenue South              2049 Century Park East
```

1336 Use the word *and,* not an ampersand (&), in a street address; for example, *Tenth and Market Streets.* However, avoid the use of such "intersection" addresses if a house or building number plus a single street name is available (such as *304 Tenth Street*).

1337 Avoid abbreviating such words as *Street* and *Avenue* in inside addresses. (It may be necessary to abbreviate in envelope addresses. See ¶1390.)

> *For apartment and room numbers with street addresses, see ¶¶1317b, 1318b, 1330.*

13

Box Number

1338 a. A post office box number may be used in place of the street address.

```
Post Office Box 1518  OR  P.O. Box 1518  OR  Box 1518
```

NOTE: The U.S. Postal Service prefers that a designation such as *Drawer L* be changed to *Post Office Box L.*

b. A station name, if needed, should follow the post office box number (and a comma) on the same line. If very long, the station name may go on the line above.

```
Box 76984, Sanford Station    Linda Vista Station
Los Angeles, CA 90076-0984    P.O. Box 11215
                              San Diego, CA 92111
```

c. Some organizations show both a street address and a post office box number in their mailing address. When you are writing to an organization with two addresses, use the post office box number for ordinary mail and the street address for express mail.

d. If you are writing to someone who rents a mailbox from a private company, insert a *mailstop code* (representing the private box number) on the line *above* the name of the person you are writing to. Use the abbreviation *MSC* plus the box number. For example:

```
MSC 216
Ms. Robin B. Kantor
621 Bloomfield Avenue
Verona, NJ 07044
```

The delivery address that appears *below* the name of the recipient is the address of the private company where the mailbox is located. Do not put the mailstop code in that location.

City, State, and ZIP Code

1339 Always type the city, state, and ZIP Code on one line, immediately following the street address. Type the name of the city (followed by a comma and 1 space), the state (followed by 1 space but no comma), and the ZIP Code.

```
Denver, Colorado 80217  OR  Denver, CO 80217-9999
```

(Continued on page 330.)

(Continued on page 330.)

NOTE: The U.S. Postal Service encourages the use of a nine-digit ZIP Code (consisting of the basic five digits followed immediately by a hyphen and another four digits); hence the designation ZIP+4 Code. The use of the additional four digits is voluntary, but as an inducement the Postal Service offers discounts on postage fees. To qualify for a discount, mailers must submit a minimum of 500 *first-class* letters or postcards at one time; moreover, the envelope addresses must be readable by electronic (OCR) equipment (see ¶¶1389–1390) and satisfy a number of other criteria.

13

1340 When writing the name of a city in an inside address:

a. Do not use an abbreviation (for example, *L.A.* for *Los Angeles*).

b. Do not abbreviate the words *Fort, Mount, Point,* or *Port.* Write the name of the city in full; for example, *Fort Worth, Mount Vernon, Point Pleasant, Port Huron.* (See also ¶529a.)

c. Abbreviate the word *Saint* in the names of American cities; for example, *St. Louis, St. Paul, St. Petersburg.* (See also ¶529b.)

NOTE: It may be necessary, for reasons of space, to abbreviate city names in envelope addresses. (See ¶1390a.)

1341 a. In an address, spell out the name of the state or use a two-letter abbreviation of the state name.

Alabama	AL	Missouri	MO
Alaska	AK	Montana	MT
American Samoa	AS	Nebraska	NE
Arizona	AZ	Nevada	NV
Arkansas	AR	New Hampshire	NH
California	CA	New Jersey	NJ
Colorado	CO	New Mexico	NM
Connecticut	CT	New York	NY
Delaware	DE	North Carolina	NC
District		North Dakota	ND
of Columbia	DC	Northern Mariana	
Federated States		Islands	MP
of Micronesia	FM	Ohio	OH
Florida	FL	Oklahoma	OK
Georgia	GA	Oregon	OR
Guam	GU	Palau	PW
Hawaii	HI	Pennsylvania	PA
Idaho	ID	Puerto Rico	PR
Illinois	IL	Rhode Island	RI
Indiana	IN	South Carolina	SC
Iowa	IA	South Dakota	SD
Kansas	KS	Tennessee	TN
Kentucky	KY	Texas	TX
Louisiana	LA	Utah	UT
Maine	ME	Vermont	VT
Marshall Islands	MH	Virgin Islands	VI
Maryland	MD	Virginia	VA
Massachusetts	MA	Washington	WA
Michigan	MI	West Virginia	WV
Minnesota	MN	Wisconsin	WI
Mississippi	MS	Wyoming	WY

NOTE: The two-letter abbreviations (for example, *AL* for *Alabama*) were created by the U.S. Postal Service and should be used only with ZIP Codes in addresses. The more traditional abbreviations of state names (for example, *Ala.* for *Alabama*) should be used in other situations where abbreviations are appropriate. (See ¶¶526–527 for a list of the traditional abbreviations.)

b. When using two-letter state abbreviations, type them in capital letters, with no periods after or space between the letters.

c. When giving an address in a sentence, insert a comma after the street address and after the city. Leave 1 space between the state and the ZIP Code. Insert a comma after the ZIP Code unless a stronger mark of punctuation is required at that point.

My new address will be 501 South 71st Court, Miami, Florida 33144-2728.

13

1342 Omit the name of the county or area (such as *Long Island*) in an address. However, the name of a community, subdivision, or real estate development may be included as long as it comes before the lines containing the mail delivery address.

```
Ms. Janet G. Arnold          NOT:  Ms. Janet G. Arnold
Muir Meadows                        1039 Erica Road
1039 Erica Road                     Muir Meadows
Mill Valley, CA 94941               Mill Valley, CA 94941
```

1343 a. In international addresses, type the name of the country on a separate line in all-capital letters. Do not abbreviate the name of the country.

```
Graf-Adolf Strasse 100       4-14-11 Ginza
Dusseldorf 4000              Chuo-Ku, Tokyo 104
GERMANY                      JAPAN
```

NOTE: If you are writing from another country to someone in the United States, type *UNITED STATES OF AMERICA* as the last line of the address.

b. In a Canadian address, express the name of the province as a two-letter abbreviation, as shown below.

Alberta	AB	Nova Scotia	NS
British Columbia	BC	Ontario	ON
Manitoba	MB	Prince Edward Island	PE
New Brunswick	NB	Quebec	PQ
Newfoundland	NF	Saskatchewan	SK
Northwest Territories	NT	Yukon Territory	YT

NOTE: In an inside address or an envelope address, insert a comma and 1 space between the name of the city and the two-letter abbreviation, followed by 2 spaces and the six-character postal code.

```
21 St. Claire Avenue
Toronto, ON  M4T 1L9
CANADA
```

When giving an address in a sentence, spell out the name of the province and leave only 1 space before the postal code. Then insert a comma followed by 1 space and *Canada*.

Write to me at 21 St. Claire Avenue, Toronto, Ontario M4T 1L9, Canada.

Attention Line

1344 a. When a letter is addressed directly to a company, an attention line may be used to route the letter to a particular person (by name or title) or to a particular department. For example:

```
Shelton & Warren Industries     Carrolton Labs
6710 Squibb Road                1970 Briarwood Court
Mission, KS 66202-3223          Atlanta, GA 30329


Attention:  Mr. John Ellery     ATTENTION:   SALES MANAGER
```

NOTE: This form of address is intended to emphasize the fact that the letter deals with a business matter (rather than a personal matter) and may be handled by someone other than the person named in the attention line. However, it is simpler to type the name of the person or department above the company name and omit the attention line. When a letter without a personal or confidential notation is received by a company, it will be presumed to deal with company business and may be handled by others in the absence of the person named in the address. For this reason an attention line is not really needed.

b. If you use an attention line, type it on the second line below the inside address, starting at the left margin.

c. Type the attention line in capital and small letters or in all-capital letters.

d. Do not abbreviate the word *Attention*. Use a colon after *Attention*.

➤ *For the salutation to use with an attention line, see ¶1351.*

1345 If you are (a) using window envelopes or (b) planning to generate the envelope address by repeating the inside address as typed, you should insert the attention line in the inside address—as the first line. (See also ¶¶1389n, 1390h.)

```
Attention:  Mr. John Ellery     Attention:  Sales Manager
Shelton & Warren Industries     Carrolton Labs
6710 Squibb Road                1970 Briarwood Court
Mission, KS 66202-3223          Atlanta, GA 30329
```

NOTE: Once the attention line is placed on the first line of the address block, the argument for omitting the word *Attention* is further strengthened. (See the note in ¶1344 above.) Indeed, when the U.S. Postal Service (USPS) illustrates the use of an attention line, it typically omits the word *Attention*. In fact, the USPS uses the term *attention line* to refer to *any* information—whether a person's name (*Ms. Hilary Edwards*), a person's title (*Marketing Director*), or a departmental name (*Research Department*)—that appears on the line above the organizational name (*The E. J. Monagle Publishing Company*). If you read somewhere that the USPS wants the first line of a business address to be an "attention line," do not conclude that it is requiring the use of the word *Attention*. The USPS simply wants to have personal or departmental names or titles come above the name of the organization.

Salutation

1346 Type the salutation, beginning at the left margin, on the second line below the attention line (if used) or on the second line below the inside address. Follow the salutation with a colon unless you are using open punctuation (see ¶1309) or you are typing a social-business letter (see ¶1396b). Omit the salutation if you are using the simplified style, and replace it with a subject line. (See ¶1352.)

1347 Abbreviate only the titles *Mr., Ms., Mrs., Messrs.,* and *Dr.* Spell out all other titles, such as *Professor* and *Father.* (See Section 18 for titles used by officials, dignitaries, and military personnel.)

1348 Capitalize the first word as well as any nouns and titles in the salutation; for example, *Dear Mrs. Brand, Dear Sir.*

1349 A list of salutations begins below and continues on the next page. (See Section 18 for the salutations to be used with different forms of address.)

13

NOTE: The salutations identified as *more formal* are no longer frequently used.

To One Person (Name, Gender, and Courtesy Title Preference Known)

Dear Mr. Smith: Dear Ms. Simpson:
Dear Mrs. Gray: Dear Miss Wells:

To One Person (Name Known, Gender Unknown)

Dear Marion Parker: Dear R. V. Moore:

To One Person (Name Unknown, Gender Known)

Dear Madam: OR   Madam: (*more formal*)
Dear Sir: OR   Sir: (*more formal*)

To One Person (Name and Gender Unknown)

Dear Sir or Madam: OR   Sir or Madam: (*more formal*)
OR   Dear Madam or Sir: OR   Madam or Sir: (*more formal*)

To One Woman (Courtesy Title Preference Unknown)

Dear Ms. Malloy: OR   Dear Ruth Malloy: (see ¶1322b)

To Two or More Men

Dear Mr. Gelb and Mr. Harris: OR   Gentlemen:
OR   Dear Messrs. Gelb and Harris: (*more formal*)

To Two or More Women

Dear Mrs. Allen, Ms. Ott, and Miss Day:

Dear Mrs. Jordan and Mrs. Kent: (see ¶618)
OR Dear Mesdames Jordan and Kent: (*more formal*)

Dear Ms. Scott and Ms. Gomez: (see ¶618)
OR   Dear Mses. (OR Mss.) Scott and Gomez: (*more formal*)

Dear Miss Winger and Miss Rossi: (see ¶618)
OR   Dear Misses Winger and Rossi: (*more formal*)

(Continued on page 334.)

To a Woman and a Man

Dear Ms. Kent and Mr. Winston: Dear Mrs. Kay and Mr. Fox:

Dear Mr. Fong and Miss Landis: Dear Mr. and Mrs. Green:

To Several Persons

Dear Mr. Anderson, Mrs. Brodsky, Ms. Carmino,
Mr. Dellums, and Miss Eustace:

Dear Friends (Colleagues, Members, *or some other suitable collective term*):

To an Organization Composed Entirely of Men

Gentlemen:

To an Organization Composed Entirely of Women

Ladies: **OR** Mesdames: (*more formal*)

To an Organization Composed of Men and Women (See ¶1350).

a. Be sure that the spelling of the surname in the salutation matches the spelling in the inside address. If the person you are writing to has a hyphenated last name (for example, *Mrs. Hazel Gray-Sparks*), the salutation should include the entire last name (*Dear Mrs. Gray-Sparks*).

b. When writing to someone you know well, use a first name or nickname in place of the more formal salutations shown above. However, once you start using an informal salutation, be sure that anyone who prepares your letters for you maintains that form of address. Otherwise, a person who is used to getting *Dear Mike* letters from you may one day receive a *Dear Mr. Romano* letter and waste a good deal of time brooding over what could have caused the sudden chill in your relationship.

c. When you are preparing a letter that may be sent or shown to a number of as yet undetermined individuals, use *Dear Sir or Madam*. You may also use the simplified style and omit the salutation.

d. In salutations involving two or more people, use *and*, not *&*.

1350 For an organization composed of both men and women:

a. Use *Ladies and Gentlemen* or *Gentlemen and Ladies*. (Do not use *Gentlemen* alone.)

b. Address the letter, not to the organization as a whole, but to the head of the organization—by name and title if known, otherwise by title alone. Then the salutation would appear as shown in ¶1349.

```
Mr. James V. Quillan        President
President                   (OR Chief Executive Officer)
United Services Corporation United Services Corporation
100 Kendall Parkway         100 Kendall Parkway
Somerset, NJ 08873          Somerset, NJ 08873

Dear Mr. Quillan:           Dear Sir or Madam:
```

c. Use the name of the organization in the salutation.

```
Dear United Services Corporation:
```

NOTE: This approach is acceptable in routine or informal letters but should not be used in formal communications. (See also ¶1803c.)

d. Use the simplified letter style and omit the salutation.

1351 When an attention line is used (see ¶1344), the letter is considered to be addressed to the organization rather than to the person named in the attention line. Therefore, use one of the organizational salutations shown in ¶¶1349 and 1350. (Whenever possible, omit the attention line and address the letter directly to an individual in the organization—either by name or by title.)

The following rules (¶¶1352–1357) deal with the *body* of a letter. The body contains the text of the letter—in other words, the message (see ¶¶1354–1357). The body may also begin with a subject line (see ¶¶1352–1353), which briefly identifies the main idea in the message.

13

Subject Line

1352 In the *simplified letter style:*

    a. Use a subject line in place of the salutation.

    b. Start the subject line on the third line below the inside address. Begin at the left margin and type the subject line in all-capital letters.

    c. Do not use a term like *Subject:* to introduce the subject line. (See the illustration on page 314.)

1353 In *other letter styles:*

    a. The subject line (if used) appears between the salutation and the body of the letter, with 1 blank line above and below. (See the illustration on page 313.)

    b. Ordinarily, the subject line starts at the left margin, but it may be centered for special emphasis. In a letter with indented paragraphs, the subject line may also be indented the same number of spaces.

    c. Type the subject line either in capital and small letters or in all-capital letters.

    d. The term *Subject:* or *In re:* or *Re:* usually precedes the actual subject but may be omitted.

```
Subject:  Introductory Offer to
New Subscribers and Renewal Offer
to Present Subscribers

SUBJECT:  MORAN LEASE

In re:  Moran Lease
```

    NOTE: If the subject line is long, type it in two or more single-spaced lines of roughly equal length. (See the illustration on page 478.)

    e. When replying to a letter that carries a "refer to" notation, you may put the desired reference number or filing code in a subject line or below the date line. (See ¶1316.)

```
Refer to:  Policy 668485
```

Message

1354 Begin the text of the letter—the message—on the second line below the subject line, if used, or on the second line below the salutation.

NOTE: If you are using word processing software, you can create macros to capture the keystrokes that represent frequently used names, phrases, sentences, or paragraphs. Whenever you need to type any of these frequently used elements, you simply use a few keystrokes to *play* (call up and print) the copy contained in the macro.

1355 Use single spacing and leave 1 blank line between paragraphs.

1356 a. Align each line of the message at the left margin. However, if you are using the modified-block letter style with indented paragraphs, indent the first line of each paragraph 0.5 inch (5 spaces on a typewriter). (See the illustration on page 312.)

b. If you are using word processing software, you can *justify* the right margin—that is, have each full line of text end at the same point. If you choose this format, the computer will automatically insert extra space between words to make each line the same length. (See page 314 for an illustration of a letter with a justified right margin.)

NOTE: While full justification (aligning the lines of text at both the left and the right margins) looks attractive, the insertion of extra space between words can sometimes produce unintended "rivers" of white space running vertically down through the text. More important, studies have demonstrated that text with a *ragged* (unjustified) right margin is easier to read. Moreover, some recipients of a fully justified letter tend to regard it as a form letter and not take it seriously.

c. If you decide on a ragged right margin, try to avoid great variations in the length of adjacent lines. (See Section 9 for guidelines on dividing words in order to keep the lines of text roughly equal in length.)

d. If a letter takes two or more pages, do not divide a short paragraph (with only two or three lines) at the bottom of a page. Always leave at least two lines of the paragraph at the foot of one page and carry over at least two lines to the top of the next page. (See ¶¶1382–1387.)

NOTE: Many word processing programs have a protection feature that prevents the creation of *orphans* (printing the first line of a new paragraph as the last line on a page) and *widows* (printing the last line of a paragraph as the first line of a new page).

1357 a. Quoted Material. If a quotation will make four or more lines, type it as a single-spaced extract, and leave 1 blank line above and below the extract. (See the illustration on page 313.) If you are using word processing software, use the *double indent* feature, which will indent the extract equally from each side margin. If you are using a typewriter, indent the extract 5 spaces from each side margin. If the quoted material represents the start of a paragraph in the original, indent the first word an additional 0.5 inch (5 spaces on a typewriter).

➢ *For different ways of handling a long quotation, see ¶265.*

b. Tables. When a table occurs in the text of a letter, center it between the left and right margins. Try to indent the table at least 0.5 inch (5 spaces on a typewriter) from each side margin. (If the table is very wide, reduce the space between columns to prevent the table from extending beyond the width of the text.) Leave 1 to 3 blank lines above and below the table to set it off from the rest of the text. (See Section 16 for a full discussion on how to plan and execute tables.)

c. **Items in a List.** Type the list single-spaced with 1 blank line above and below the list as a whole. Either type the list on the full width of the letter (see the second illustration below), or indent the list equally from each side margin (as described in ¶1357a and shown in the first illustration below). If any item in the list requires more than one line, leave a blank line after each item in the list. Moreover, align any turnovers with the first word in the line above.

NOTE: If you are using word processing software, use the *indent* feature to align any turnovers with the first word in the line above.

13

---

1 inch (min.) When you are ready to distribute your analysis for the first round of comments, I suggest you send it to the following people inside the company: ↓2

    Angela Lawless, director of information systems
    Thomas Podgorski, manager of corporate planning ↓2

In addition, you may want to get reactions from two trustworthy consultants: ↓2

0.5 inch   Dr. Harriet E. Fenster, professor of computer science at Michigan State University ↓2   0.5 inch

    Wilson G. Witherspoon, president of Witherspoon Associates in Princeton, New Jersey ↓2

I can give you mailing addresses for these consultants if you decide to get in touch with them.

1 inch (min.)

---

d. **Enumerated Items in a List.** If the items each begin with a number or letter, insert a period after the number or letter and leave 2 or 3 spaces before starting the text that follows. Align the numbers or letters on the period. If an item requires more than one line, indent any turnover so that it aligns with the first word in the line above. (See the note in *c* above.)

When I review the situation as you described it in your letter of June 24, it seems to me that you have only two alternatives: ↓2

1. Agree to pay the additional amount that Henning now demands before he will start construction. ↓2

2. Drop Henning and start the search all over again to find a firm qualified to handle a project of this size and this complexity. ↓2

(Continued on page 338.)

NOTE: An enumerated list may be typed to the full width of the letter or indented 0.5 inch (5 spaces on a typewriter) from each side margin. However, if the first line of each text paragraph is indented, then for better appearance indent the enumerated list as well.

Preferred Style

> When I review the situation as y
> seems to me that you have only two alte
>
> 1. Agree to pay the additional an will start construction.
>
> 2. Drop Henning and start the se to handle a project of this size
>
> As painful as it may be, you may
> contractor than to have to deal with new
> quarter of the way through the job.

Avoid

> When I review the situation as y
> seems to me that you have only two alte
>
> 1. Agree to pay the additional amount will start construction.
>
> 2. Drop Henning and start the search a to handle a project of this size and th
>
> As painful as it may be, you may
> contractor than to have to deal with new
> quarter of the way through the job.

e. **Bulleted Items in a List.** Instead of numbers or letters, you can use *bullets* before the items in a list.

(1) If you are using word processing software, you can choose from a variety of styles to create bullets. For example:

    CIRCLES: ○ ●   **TRIANGLES:** ▷ ▶

    SQUARES: ☐ ■   **OTHER ASCII CHARACTERS:** > → *

If you use the automatic bullet insert feature, the default position of the bullet is at the left margin. Set a tab wherever you want the first line of text (and any turnover lines) to begin after each bullet. (See the note in ¶1357c.)

> When I review the situation as you described it in your letter of June 24, it seems to me that you have only two alternatives:
> ↓ 2
>
> ● Agree to pay the additional amount that Henning now demands before he will start construction.
> ↓ 2
> ● Drop Henning and start the search all over again to find a firm qualified to handle a project of this size and this complexity.
> ↓ 2
> As painful as it may be, you may find it easier to start looking for a new contractor than to have to deal with new demands from Henning once he is a quarter of the way through the job.

(2) If you are using a typewriter, the simplest way to construct a bullet is to use the small letter *o.* If you want to convert a period into a centered dot, type the period one-half space above the line.

The following rules (¶¶1358–1381) deal with the *closing* of a letter. The closing typically includes a complimentary-closing phrase (¶¶1358–1360), the writer's name and title (¶¶1362–1369), and reference initials (¶¶1370–1371). It may also include a company signature line (¶1361), a file name notation (¶1372), an enclosure notation (¶¶1373–1374), a delivery notation (¶1375), a copy notation (¶¶1376–1380), and a postscript (¶1381).

Complimentary Closing

1358 Type the complimentary closing on the second line below the last line of the body of the letter. Ordinarily, start the closing at center. In a block-style letter, start the closing at the left margin. In a simplified letter, omit the closing. (See the illustrations on pages 310–314.)

13

> **NOTE:** If you are using word processing software, you can create a macro that represents the complimentary closing and other elements that are frequently used in the closing of a letter.

1359 a. Capitalize only the first word of a complimentary closing.

b. Place a comma at the end of the line (except when open punctuation is used).

1360 a. The following complimentary closings are commonly used:

Sincerely,

Cordially,

Sincerely yours,

Cordially yours,

> **NOTE:** More formal closings—such as *Very truly yours* and *Respectfully yours*—are infrequently used these days.

b. An informal closing phrase may be inserted in place of one of the more conventional closings shown above. If the wording is an adverbial phrase (one that tells *how* or *in what manner*—for example, *With all best wishes* or *With warmest regards*), follow the closing with a comma. If the wording is a complete sentence (for example, *See you in Boston*), follow the closing with a period. In each case the comma or the period may be replaced with stronger punctuation as appropriate—that is, a question mark, an exclamation point, or a dash.

> **NOTE:** If you are using open punctuation, see ¶1309b.

c. If both a complimentary closing and an informal closing phrase are used, type the complimentary closing in its regular position, and (1) type the informal phrase at the end of the last paragraph or (2) treat the informal phrase as the final paragraph with the appropriate terminal punctuation.

d. Once a pattern of personal or informal closings is begun, it should not be discontinued without good reason. Otherwise, if a later letter returns to a more formal closing, the person who receives the letter may wonder what has happened to the established relationship. (See also ¶1349b.)

Company Signature

1361 A company signature may be used to emphasize the fact that a letter represents the views of the company as a whole (and not merely the individual who has written it). If included, the company signature should be typed in all-capital letters on the second line below the complimentary closing. Begin the company signature at the same point as the complimentary closing. (See the illustration on page 310.)

```
Very truly yours,  ↓ 2

HASKINS & COHEN INC.
```

➤ *For the use of macros, see ¶1354, note.*

13 Writer's Name and Title

1362 a. Ordinarily, type the writer's name on the fourth line below the company signature, if used, or on the fourth line below the complimentary closing. (See the illustrations on pages 310–314.)

    NOTE: If the letter is running short, you can leave up to 6 blank lines for the signature. If the letter is running long, you can reduce the signature space to 2 blank lines. (See also ¶¶1307–1308.)

b. Start typing at the same point as the company signature or the complimentary closing.

    NOTE: In the simplified letter style, type the writer's name and title on the *fifth* line below the body, in all-capital letters starting at the left margin. (See ¶1363.)

c. Although some writers prefer to give only their title and department name in the signature block, a typewritten signature should also be included so that the unsigned copies will clearly show who sent the letter. If the writer prefers to omit his or her name from the signature block, then it should be spelled out in the reference initials. (See ¶1370d.)

d. Top-level executives usually have special stationery with their name and title imprinted along with other elements of the letterhead. When using this type of stationery, supply a typewritten signature but omit the title. (For an illustration, see page 313.)

➤ *For the use of macros, see ¶1354, note.*

1363 Arrange the writer's name, title, and department on two or more lines to achieve good visual balance. If a title takes more than one line, align all turnovers at the left.

```
Janice Mahoney, Manager      Ernest L. Welhoelter
Data Processing Division     Head, Sales Department

Charles Saunders             Franklin Browning
Assistant Manager            Vice President and
Credit Department            General Manager
```

    SIMPLIFIED STYLE: MARY WELLER, MANAGER, SALES DEPARTMENT

➤ *For guidance on capitalizing in signature blocks, see ¶1325a.*

1364 A person who has a special title should observe the following guidelines in the signature block.

a. A person who wants to be addressed as *Dr.* should use an appropriate academic degree after his or her name (not *Dr.* before it).

Jane Bishop, M.D.	Nancy Buckwalter, Ph.D.
Charles Burgos, D.D.S.	Morris Finley, D.D.
Lee Toniolo, D.O.	Henry Krawitz, D.H.L.

b. A person who wishes to be addressed by a title of academic or military rank *(Dean, Professor, Major)* should type this title *after* the name or on the next line, not before it.

Helene C. Powell	Joseph F. Corey
Dean of Students	Major, USAF
(**NOT:** Dean Helene C. Powell)	(**NOT:** Major Joseph F. Corey)

c. When a title of address cannot be placed after a surname or cannot be inferred from the initials of an academic degree, then it may precede the name.

Rev. Joseph W. Dowd   Mother Ellen Marie O'Brien

13

1365 Ordinarily, a man should not include *Mr.* in his signature. However, if he has a name that could also be a woman's name *(Kay, Adrian, Beverly, Lynn)* or if he uses initials in place of a first and middle name *(J. G. Eberle)*, he should use *Mr.* in either his handwritten or his typed signature when writing to people who do not know him. If given in the handwritten signature, *Mr.* should be enclosed in parentheses. If given in the typed signature, *Mr.* should appear without parentheses.

Sincerely,   Sincerely,

(Mr.) Lynn Treadway   *Lynn Treadway*

Lynn Treadway   Mr. Lynn Treadway

1366 A woman should include a courtesy title *(Ms., Miss, or Mrs.)* in either her handwritten or her typed signature unless she is called by a special title (see ¶1364). If she gives her name without any title at all, the reader of the letter has to decide which title to use in a letter of reply. (See ¶1349 for salutations to use in such situations.)

NOTE: Enclose the courtesy title in parentheses if it appears in the handwritten signature. No parentheses are needed if the title appears in the typed signature.

a. A woman who feels that indicating her marital status in her signature is irrelevant should use *Ms.* in either her handwritten or her typed signature (but not both).

Sincerely yours,   Sincerely yours,

(Ms.) Constance G. Booth   *Constance G. Booth*

Constance G. Booth   Ms. Constance G. Booth

(Continued on page 342.)

b. A single woman who wants to indicate that she is a single woman should include *Miss* in her handwritten or her typed signature (but not both).

Cordially,	Cordially,
(Miss) Margaret L. Galloway	*Margaret L. Galloway*
Margaret L. Galloway	Miss Margaret L. Galloway

c. A married woman who retains her original name for career purposes or who does not change her surname at all may use either *Ms.* or *Miss*, as illustrated in ¶1366a–b.

d. A married woman or a widow who prefers to be addressed as *Mrs.* has many variations to choose from. The following examples show the possible styles for a woman whose maiden name was Nancy O. Ross and whose husband's name is (or was) John A. Wells.

Sincerely,	Sincerely,
(Mrs.) Nancy O. Wells	*Nancy O. Wells*
Nancy O. Wells	Mrs. Nancy O. Wells

Sincerely,	Sincerely,
(Mrs.) Nancy R. Wells	*Nancy R. Wells*
Nancy R. Wells	Mrs. Nancy R. Wells

Sincerely,	Sincerely,
(Mrs.) Nancy Ross Wells	*Nancy Ross Wells*
Nancy Ross Wells	Mrs. Nancy Ross Wells

Sincerely,	Sincerely,
(Mrs.) Nancy O. Ross-Wells	*Nancy O. Ross-Wells*
Nancy O. Ross-Wells	Mrs. Nancy O. Ross-Wells

NOTE: Giving the husband's full name in the typed signature (as in the example below) is a style often used for social purposes. It should not be used in business, and it should not be used when a married woman becomes a widow unless she indicates that that is her preference.

Sincerely,

Nancy O. Wells

Mrs. John A. Wells

e. A divorced woman who has resumed her maiden name may use *Ms.* or *Miss* in any of the styles shown in ¶1366a–b. If she retains her ex-husband's surname, she may use *Ms.* or *Mrs.* in any of the styles shown in ¶1366a and d. (**EXCEPTION:** The style that uses the husband's full name in the typed signature is not appropriate for a divorced woman.)

1367 An administrative assistant who signs a letter at the boss's request customarily signs the boss's name and adds his or her own initials. However, if the boss prefers, the administrative assistant may sign the letter in his or her own name.

Sincerely yours,

Robert H. Benedict
DK

Robert H. Benedict
Production Manager

Sincerely yours,

Dorothy Kozinski

Ms. Dorothy Kozinski
Administrative Assistant
to Mr. Benedict

1368 If the person who signs for another is not the administrative assistant, either of the following forms may be used:

Sincerely yours,

(Miss) *Alice R. Brentano*

For Robert H. Benedict
Production Manager

Sincerely yours,

Robert H. Benedict
ARB

Robert H. Benedict
Production Manager

1369 When two people have to sign a letter, arrange the two signature blocks side by side or one beneath the other.

a. If they are placed side by side, start the first signature block at the left margin and the second block at center. If this arrangement is used, the complimentary closing should also begin at the left margin. (This arrangement is appropriate for all letter styles.)

b. If the signature blocks are positioned one beneath the other, start typing the second block on the fourth line below the end of the first block, aligned at the left. Ordinarily, begin typing at center; however, in a block-style or simplified letter, begin typing at the left margin.

Reference Initials

1370 a. When the writer's name is given in the signature block, the simplest and most unobtrusive way to provide the necessary information is to give the typist's initials alone in small letters. (See the illustrations on pages 310, 313, and 314.)

NOTE: Do not include reference initials in a personal-business letter (see ¶1313 and the illustration on page 312) or a social-business letter (see ¶¶1395–1396 and the illustration on page 366). Moreover, omit reference initials on letters you type yourself unless you need to distinguish them from letters prepared for you by someone else.

b. Type the initials of the typist at the left margin, on the second line below the writer's name and title. If the writer wants his or her initials used, they should precede the initials of the typist.

c. Type the initials either in small letters or in capital letters. When giving two sets of initials, type them both the same way for speed and simplicity. If you are using word processing software, you can avoid shifting up and down by putting both sets of initials in small letters and using a diagonal to separate them. If you are using a typewriter, you can avoid shifting by using a diagonal to separate two sets of small-letter initials or a colon to separate two sets of all-capital initials.

| TYPIST ONLY: | `gdl` | OR | `GDL` |
| WRITER AND TYPIST: | `dmd/mhs` | OR | `DMD:MHS` |

➤ *For the use of macros, see ¶ 1354, note; for initials based on names like* McFarland *and* O'Leary, *see ¶516c.*

d. If the writer's name is not given in the signature block, type the writer's initials and surname before the initials of the typist; for example, *BSDixon/rp.*

1371 When the letter is written by someone other than the person who signs it, this fact may be indicated by showing the writer's and the typist's initials (not the signer's and the typist's).

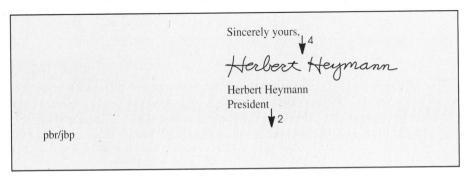

```
                                    Sincerely yours,
                                                   ↓4

                                    Herbert Heymann

                                    Herbert Heymann
                                    President
                                                  ↓2

pbr/jbp
```

File Name Notation

1372 When you create documents using word processing software, each document needs a unique file name so that it can be readily retrieved from storage. The following guidelines show how to create a file name and where to position it in a letter.

a. A file name has three components: a name consisting of 1 to 8 characters, a period (called a dot) used as a separator, and an extension consisting of 1 to 3 characters.

NOTE: Some word processing programs now permit users to create much longer file names. Therefore, follow these guidelines only if your software imposes the restrictions described in *a* above.

b. In creating a file name, try to make it as meaningful as possible. You can use the letters *a* to *z*, the figures *0* to *9*, and a small number of symbols (as indicated in your software user's manual). Do not leave any spaces in a file name, and do not use a period except as a separator between the name and the extension.

c. In selecting the name of a person, an organization, or a subject to serve as the first component in a file name, do not exceed 8 characters. If a name runs longer, abbreviate it in a way that suggests the full name. For example, a long name like *Yvonne Christopher* could be transformed into *chrstphr*—or better yet, *chrstphy* (to distinguish it from a file name created for *Henry Christopher—chrstphh*). An organizational name like *BankAmerica Corp.* could be abbreviated as *bankamer.* A subject name like *Direct Marketing Plans for 1997* could be shortened to *dmplns97.*

d. The 3-character extension that serves as the last component in a file name can be used to show (in abbreviated form) the date assigned to the document.

   (1) To express the months from January to September, use the figures *1* to *9.* For October, November, and December, use the letters *o, n,* and *d.*

   (2) To express days of the month, use the figures *1* to *31.* However, if you are planning to show the year as well, all figures over *9* will have to be expressed as a single character. Here is one possible code for the numbers 10 to 31:

10	11	12	13	14	15	16	17	18	19	20
a	b	c	d	e	f	g	h	i	j	k

21	22	23	24	25	26	27	28	29	30	31
l	m	n	o	p	q	r	s	t	u	v

   (3) To express the year, use the last digit of the year (for example, *8* for *1998*).

   NOTE: On the basis of the code shown above, an extension such as *8d7* would signify *August 13, 1997; nn7* would stand for *November 23, 1997.*

e. The 3-character extension may also be used:

   (1) To show the initials of the writer.

   (2) To indicate where a document falls in chronological order. (For example, *stewartj.12* would signify that a particular document is the twelfth sent to J. Stewart.

   (3) To identify a document in different stages of revision. (For example, *d1* could signify the first draft, *d3* the third draft, and *df* the final version of the document.

f. If you want to insert a file name notation in a letter, type it on the line below the reference initials (see ¶¶1370–1371). Some writers prefer to treat the file name notation as a reference notation and insert it after the phrase *When replying, refer to:.* (See ¶1316.)

Enclosure Notation

1373 a. If one or more items are to be included in the envelope with the letter, indicate that fact by typing the word *Enclosure* (or an appropriate alternative) at the left margin, on the line below the reference initials or the file name notation, whichever comes last.

   NOTE: Before sending the letter, make sure that the number of enclosures shown in the enclosure notation agrees with (1) the number cited in the body of the letter and (2) the number of items actually enclosed.

(Continued on page 346.)

b. The following styles are commonly used:

```
Enclosure          2 Enclosures        Enclosures:
Enc.               2 Enc.              1.  Check for $500
1 Enc.             Enclosures 2        2.  Invoice A37512
1 Enclosure        Enclosures (2)
Check enclosed     Enc. 2  (see ¶503)
```

c. Some writers use the term *Attachment* or *Att.* when the material is actually attached to the cover letter rather than simply enclosed.

➤ *For the use of macros, see ¶1354, note; for the use of enclosure notations with copy notations, see ¶1379.*

1374 If material is to be sent separately instead of being enclosed with the letter, indicate this fact by typing *Separate cover* or *Under separate cover* on the line below the enclosure notation (if any) or on the line directly below the reference initials or the file name notation, whichever comes last. The following styles may be used:

```
Separate cover 1       Under separate cover:
                       1.  Annual report
                       2.  Product catalog
                       3.  Price list
```

Delivery Notation

1375 a. If a letter is to be delivered in a special way (other than ordinary first-class mail), type an appropriate notation on the line below the enclosure notation, the reference initials, or the file name notation, whichever comes last. Among the notations that could be used are *By certified mail, By Express Mail, By fax, By Federal Express* (**OR** *FedEx*), *By messenger, By registered mail,* and *By special delivery.*

```
crj                HWM:FH                 tpg/wwc
Enc. 2             By Federal Express     Enclosures 4
By certified mail  cc Mr. Fry             By fax
```

b. When a letter is first faxed to the addressee and then sent through the mail as a confirmation copy, it is helpful to provide a "confirmation" notation on the letter being mailed so that the addressee will realize at once that the document now in hand is not a new letter but simply a duplicate of the fax. Type the confirmation notation on the second line below the date line or on the second line below any notation that follows the date (see ¶¶1315–1316). Starting at the left margin, type *Confirmation of fax sent on* and then supply the date on which the fax was transmitted.

➤ *For the use of macros, see ¶1354, note.*

Copy Notation

1376 a. A copy notation lets the addressee know that one or more persons will also be sent a copy of the letter. The initials *cc* are still the most commonly used device for introducing this notation. Although the abbreviation originally stood for *carbon copies, cc* also means *copies* (in the same way that *pp.* means *pages* and *ll.* means *lines*). Some writers object to using *cc,* especially now that the widespread use of photocopying has made the use of carbons virtually obsolete when it comes to preparing duplicates of letters and memos. However, *cc* and its related form *bcc* (see ¶1378) continue to be widely used (regardless of how the copies are made), in much the same way that a *dial tone* continues to be heard on telephone instruments that use buttons rather than a rotary dial.

NOTE: The abbreviation *cc* is used in the heading of many memo templates provided by word processing software. (For illustrations see pages 358–359.)

b. Writers looking for an alternative to *cc* may use a single *c* or the phrase *Copies to:* (**OR** *Copy to:*).

c. Type *cc* or *c* at the left margin, on the line below the mailing notation, the enclosure notation, the reference initials, or the file name notation, whichever comes last. If several persons are to receive copies, list the names according to the rank of the persons or in alphabetic order.

```
AMH:HT           mfn                   lbw/ncy
Enclosure        Enc. 4                cc:   Contract File
Registered       c:  Mrs. A.  Case           Houston Office
cc:  Ms. Wu          Mr. R.  Flynn            Sales Department
```

d. Type the initials *cc* or *c* with or without a colon following. When there are two or more names to be listed, type *cc* or *c* only with the first name. Align all the other names with the start of the first name.

```
c:  Ms. Abernathy  OR  cc Ms. Abernathy
    Mrs. Bernardo         Mrs. Bernardo
    Mr. Cohen             Mr. Cohen
```

NOTE: Whether you are using word processing software or a typewriter, set a tab 2 spaces after the *cc* or *c* for the alignment of all names.

```
cc:  Mr. Drinan      cc:  Mr. Drinan
  → Ms. Elias          → Ms. Elias
  ↑ Mrs. Fong          ↑ Mrs. Fong
  2 spaces             2 spaces
```

1377 When first names or initials are given along with last names, personal titles *(Mr., Miss, Mrs.,* and *Ms.)* may be omitted except in formal letters. Moreover, do not use personal titles if nicknames are given with last names.

```
c:  James Diaz       cc:  J. Diaz      cc Jim Diaz
    Kenneth Eustis        K. Eustis       Ken Eustis
    Margaret Foster       M. Foster       Peggy Foster
    Katherine Gabor       K. Gabor        Kay Gabor
```

1378 If you do not want the addressee to know that one or more persons are also being sent a copy of the letter, use a *blind copy notation.*

a. If you are using a computer:

(1) Print the original letter plus any copies on which the regular copy notation is to appear.

(2) Print the blind copies one at a time, with a blind copy notation showing the name of the designated recipient.

(Continued on page 348.)

b. If you are using a typewriter:

  (1) Set aside the original letter and any copies on which the blind copy notation is not to appear.

  (2) On each of the remaining copies, type a blind copy notation showing the name of the designated recipient.

c. Under certain circumstances, you may wish to let all recipients of blind copies know who the others are.

d. Place the blind copy notation in the upper left corner at the left margin on the first line below the top margin of 1 inch (6 lines on a typewriter). As an alternative, type the blind copy notation on the second line below the last item in the letter (whether reference initials, an enclosure notation, or any other notation).

e. The form of a blind copy notation should follow the form of the copy notation. If you have used *cc* or *c*, then use *bcc* or *bc* accordingly. If you have used *Copies to:*, use *Blind copies to:*.

f. The file copy should show all the blind copy notations, even though the individual copies do not. Whether the file copy is stored in computer memory or in hard-copy form, you may need to use the file copy later on to make additional copies for distribution. In such cases make sure that no prior blind copy notation appears on these new copies unless you want it to.

1379 When a letter carries both an enclosure notation and a copy notation, it is assumed that the enclosures accompany only the original letter. If a copy of the enclosures is also to accompany a copy of the letter, this fact may be indicated as follows:

```
cc:       Mr. D. R. Wellak    (will receive only the letter)
          Ms. N. A. Warren    (will receive only the letter)
cc/enc:   Mr. J. Baldwin      (will receive the letter and the enclosures)
          Mrs. G. Conger      (will receive the letter and the enclosures)
```

1380 A copy is not usually signed unless the letter is addressed to several people and the copy is intended for one of the people named in the salutation. However, a check mark is usually made on each copy next to the name of the person or department for whom that copy is intended. As an alternative, you may use a highlighting marker to identify the recipient of each copy.

```
c:  Ms. M. Starr ✓   c:  Ms. M. Starr      c:  Ms. M. Starr
    Mr. W. Fried          Mr. W. Fried ✓        Mr. W. Fried
    Mrs. C. Bell          Mrs. C. Bell          Mrs. C. Bell ✓
```

NOTE: When an unsigned copy is likely to strike the recipient as cold and impersonal, it is appropriate for the writer to add a brief handwritten note at the bottom of the copy and sign or initial it.

➤ *For the use of macros, see ¶1354, note.*

Postscript

1381 a. A postscript can be effectively used to express an idea that has been deliberately withheld from the body of a letter; stating this idea at the very end gives it strong emphasis. A postscript may also be used to express an afterthought; however, if the afterthought contains something central to the meaning of the letter, the reader may conclude that the letter was badly organized.

b. When a postscript is used:

(1) Start the postscript on the second line below the copy notation (or whatever was typed last). If the paragraphs are indented, indent the first line of the postscript (see page 312); otherwise, begin it at the left margin.

(2) Type *PS:* or *PS.* before the first word of the postscript, or omit the abbreviation altogether. (If *PS* is used, leave 2 spaces between the colon or period and the first word.)

(3) Use *PPS:* or *PPS.* (or no abbreviation at all) at the beginning of an additional postscript, and treat this postscript as a separate paragraph.

13

```
PS:   Instead of dashing for the airport as soon as the
meeting is over, why don't you have dinner and spend the
night with us and then go back on Saturday morning?

PPS:   Better yet, why don't you bring Joyce with you and
plan to stay for the whole weekend?
```

Continuation Pages

1382 Use plain paper of the same quality as the letterhead (but never a letterhead) for all but the first page of a long letter.

1383 Use the same left and right margins that you used on the first page.

1384 On the first line below the top margin of 1 inch (6 lines on a typewriter), type a continuation-page heading consisting of the following: the name of the addressee, the page number, and the date. Either of the following styles is acceptable:

```
↓ 1 inch
Mrs. Laura R. Austin     2     September 30, 1996
                                                  ↓ 3
```

```
        ↓ 1 inch
OR   Mrs. Laura R. Austin
     Page 2
     September 30, 1996
                         ↓ 3
```

NOTE: If you are using a letter template provided by your word processing software, the program may automatically insert a continuation-page heading and correctly number each continuation page.

1385 a. Leave 2 blank lines below the last line of the continuation-page heading and resume typing the letter. (If you are using the header feature of word processing software, only 1 blank line will be left between the continuation-page heading and the text of the letter, but you can adjust this space.)

(Continued on page 350.)

b. Do not divide a short paragraph (one that contains only two or three lines) at the bottom of a page. For a paragraph of four or more lines, always leave at least two lines of the paragraph at the bottom of the previous page. Carry over at least two lines to the continuation page. (See also ¶1356d.)

c. Never use a continuation page just for the closing section of a business letter. (The complimentary closing should always be preceded by at least two lines of the message.)

1386 Leave a bottom margin of 1 inch (6 lines on a typewriter). The last page may run short.

13

1387 Do not divide the last word on a page.

ENVELOPES

1388 Addressing Envelopes

a. The following chart indicates which envelopes may be used, depending on the size of the stationery and the way in which the stationery is folded (see ¶1391).

Stationery	Fold	Envelope
Standard (8½″ × 11″)	In thirds	No. 10 (9½″ × 4⅛″)
	In half, then in thirds	No. 6¾ (6½″ × 3⅝″)
Monarch (7¼″ × 10½″)	In thirds	No. 7 (7½″ × 3⅞″)
Baronial (5½″ × 8½″)	In thirds	No. 6¾ (6½″ × 3⅝″)
	In half	No. 5⅜ (5¹⁵⁄₁₆″ × 4⅝″)

NOTE: If you are using stationery and envelopes other than those shown above, keep in mind the standards established by the U.S. Postal Service for envelope size and thickness in order to qualify for automated processing:

Minimum size: 3½″ × 5″   Minimum thickness: $7/1000″$
Maximum size: 6⅛″ × 11½″   Maximum thickness: ¼″

b. If you are using the envelope feature of a word processing program, you can select the envelope size you plan to use from a preestablished menu. With regard to the placement of the return address and the mailing address, you can accept the default placement specifications provided for the envelope size you have selected, or you can modify them to suit your needs. You can also use a custom-size envelope (assuming your printer will support it) and establish appropriate placement specifications for that size.

➤ *For an illustration of an envelope prepared by WordPerfect 6 for Windows (using the envelope feature and all the default specifications), see page 352.*

1389 Typing an Address

When typing an address on an envelope:

a. Always use single spacing and block each line at the left.

➤ *See the examples on page 353. For specific details on the handling of elements within the address block, see ¶¶1317–1343.*

b. Capitalize the first letter of every word in an address except (1) prepositions under four letters (like *of* and *for*), (2) conjunctions under four letters (like *and*), and (3) the articles *the, a,* and *an* when they are used *within* a name or title. (Under certain circumstances even some of these short words are capitalized. See ¶¶1325a, 1329e.)

NOTE: The U.S. Postal Service has issued many brochures indicating that the use of all-capital letters is preferred but not required and that punctuation (such as periods with abbreviations and the comma between city and state) is not needed. Keep in mind that the all-cap style was devised primarily for the benefit of high-volume mailers, who must contend with space limitations for the address blocks they generate by computer or other automated equipment. (See ¶1390.) The traditional style (which uses capital and small letters plus punctuation as appropriate) is the style most commonly seen on envelopes. Moreover, the Postal Service's OCRs (optical character readers) are programmed to read the traditional style of address as well as the all-cap style.

c. Type the city, state, and ZIP Code on the last line. If space limitations make it impossible for the ZIP Code to fit on the same line, the ZIP Code may be typed on the line directly below, blocked at the left.

d. Leave 1 space between the state name and the ZIP Code. (The U.S. Postal Service recommends either 1 or 2 spaces.)

e. The state name may be spelled out or given as a two-letter abbreviation. The OCRs can read both forms. (See ¶1341.)

f. The next-to-last line in the address block should contain a street address or post office box number. (See ¶1338c.)

➤ *For the placement of a mailstop code, see ¶1338d.*

```
Elvera Agresta, M.D.            Mr. Peter Schreiber
218 Oregon Pioneer's Building   Director of Research
320 Southwest Stark Street      Colby Electronics Inc.
Portland, Oregon 97204-2628     P.O. Box 6524
                                Raleigh, NC 27628
```

g. If you are using the envelope feature of a word processing program to prepare an envelope, use the default positions for the mailing address and the return address. If you are using a laser printer, your software may permit you to insert the U.S. Postal Service's POSTNET bar code above or below the address block. (See ¶1390b.) For an illustration of a No. 10 envelope that reflects the default specifications of WordPerfect 6 for Windows, see page 352.

(Continued on page 352.)

¶1389

Envelope created by WordPerfect 6 for Windows, using all the default specifications.

Arlene M. Myers
1900 Sunnyslope Drive
Tampa, FL 33615

CONFIDENTIAL

Leslie J. Donovan, Ph.D.
Apartment 520
One North 88th Avenue
Miami, FL 33172

13

    h. If you are formatting the envelope yourself, here are some guidelines:

        (1) When using a large envelope (No. 10), start the address 2 inches from the top edge and 4 inches from the left edge.

        (2) When using a small envelope (No. 7, 6¾, or 5⅜), start the address 2 inches from the top edge and 2½ inches from the left edge.

        (3) OCR processing requires a minimum margin of ½ inch at the left and right of the mailing address block. Therefore, if you are dealing with an extremely wide address block, the left margins given above (4 inches for large envelopes, 2½ inches for small) should be decreased to keep the address block from intruding into the ½-inch right margin.

    i. When using a window envelope, adjust the placement of the inside address on the material to be inserted so that there will be a minimum clearance of ⅛ inch (and preferably ¼ inch) between the edges of the window and all four sides of the address block, no matter how much the inserted material shifts around inside the envelope. (See also ¶1391d.)

    j. To facilitate OCR processing under any circumstances, make sure that the mailing address starts no higher than 2¾ inches from the bottom edge, falls no lower than ⅝ inch from the bottom edge, and comes no closer to the left or the right edge than ½ inch. Do not allow any notations or graphics to fall alongside or below the area established for the mailing address. Moreover, make sure that the lines in the address block are parallel to the bottom edge of the envelope and that there is good contrast between the typed address and the color of the envelope. In addition, do not use a script or italic typeface, and avoid dot matrix print, especially if the dots that make up each character do not touch. The type should be clear and sharp, and adjacent characters should not touch or overlap.

    k. When the envelope contains a printed return address for a company or an organization, type the name of the writer on the line above the return address. If all the lines in the printed return address are blocked at the left, align the writer's name at the left (as in the second

No. 6¾ envelope with mailing notation.

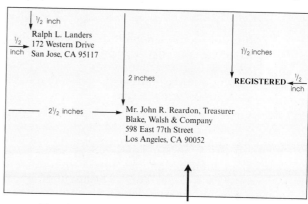

For OCR processing, start the mailing address no higher than 2¾ inches from the bottom edge. Leave a minimum bottom margin of ⅝ inch and minimum side margins of ½ inch. (See ¶1389j.)

No. 10 envelope with confidential notation.

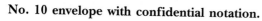
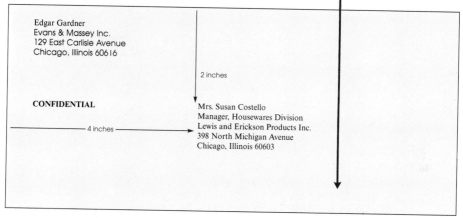

illustration on page 353). However, if all the lines in the printed return address are centered on the longest line, center the writer's name accordingly.

NOTE: With some types of printers, it may not be feasible to insert the writer's name over the printed address. In such cases you may have to resort to using a typewriter or writing the name in by hand.

l. If you have to create a return address, it should contain the following information, arranged on single-spaced lines, aligned at the left: (1) the name of the writer, (2) the name of the company (if appropriate), (3) a street address or post office box number, and (4) the city, state, and ZIP Code. If you are using the envelope feature of a word processing program, accept the default position for the return address. If you are formatting the envelope yourself, start the first line ½ inch down from the top edge and in from the left edge.

(Continued on page 354.)

m. If a notation such as *Personal, Confidential, Please Forward,* or *Hold for Arrival* is to be used, type it on the third line below the return address or on the same line as the start of the mailing address (2 inches from the top edge). Align the notation at the left with the return address. Begin each main word with a capital letter, and use boldface, italics, or underlining. For special emphasis type *Confidential* and *Personal* in all-capital letters.

NOTE: Do not allow any notations or graphics to fall alongside or below the area established for the mailing address (see ¶1389j). Copy placed in these locations will interfere with OCR processing.

n. If an attention line was used within the letter itself, it should appear on the envelope as well. The attention line may be treated exactly like a personal or confidential notation, as described in ¶1389m, or it may be typed as the first line of the address block.

➤ *See ¶1344a, note, on avoiding the use of attention lines.*

o. If a special mailing procedure is used, type the appropriate notation (such as *SPECIAL DELIVERY* or *REGISTERED*) in all-capital letters in the upper right corner of the envelope. Type the notation 1½ inches from the top edge or on the third line below the bottom edge of the stamp, whichever is lower. Position the notation so that it ends ½ inch from the right margin.

➤ *See the illustration at the top of page 353.*

p. Make sure that the spelling of the name and address on the envelope agrees with the spelling shown in the inside address (and with the spelling shown on your records or the incoming document).

➤ *For letters being sent to two or more people at the same address, see ¶1320b.*

1390 Preparing an Address for Imprinting

When preparing an address for imprinting (for example, on labels to be used in a mass mailing):

a. Keep in mind the maximum number of keystrokes you can get in any one line. If necessary, use abbreviations freely and omit all punctuation except the hyphen in the ZIP+4 Code.

NOTE: To keep the line length down to 28 keystrokes, the U.S. Postal Service has provided three special sets of abbreviations: one for state names; another for long names of cities, towns, and places; a third for names of streets and roads and general terms like *University* or *Institute*. By means of these abbreviations (see the ZIP Code directory), it is possible to limit the last line of any domestic address to 28 keystrokes.

```
Pass-a-Grille Beach, Florida 33741-9999    (39 keystrokes)
123456789012345678901234567890123456789
PAS-A-GRL BCH FL 33741-9999                (27 keystrokes)
```

Abbreviations such as those shown above serve to facilitate OCR processing, but they also serve in some cases to make the address incomprehensible to all except devoted students of USPS manuals. (See also ¶1389b, note, and ¶1390b, note.)

b. Type the lines in all-capital letters, single-spaced and blocked at the left. Try to hold the address block to 5 lines. If possible, insert the USPS's POSTNET bar code *above* or *below* the address block. (See the illustration below and the one on page 352.) In either position the bar code should fall within 4¾ inches from the bottom and come no closer than ½ inch to the left or right edge of the envelope.

No. 10 envelope showing a mailing label and the all-cap address style.

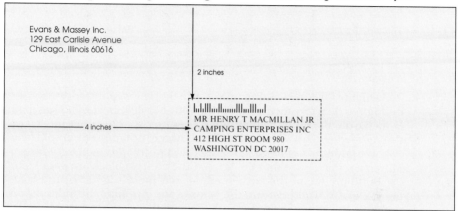

NOTE: If your organization maintains its mailing lists on tapes or disks and uses these to generate inside addresses in business letters (as well as address blocks on envelopes), the all-cap, no-punctuation style designed for the envelope will look inappropriate inside the letter. In such cases use the traditional style described in ¶1389. You will then have a format that looks attractive as an inside address and that is also OCR-readable when used on an envelope. This approach is quite acceptable to the U.S. Postal Service.

c. Type the city, state, and ZIP Code on the last line. If space limitations make it impossible for the ZIP Code to fit on the same line, the ZIP Code may be typed on the line directly below, blocked at the left.

d. Leave 1 space between the state name and the ZIP Code. (The U.S. Postal Service recommends either 1 or 2 spaces.)

e. Express the state name as a two-letter abbreviation.

f. The next-to-last line in the address block should contain a street address or post office box number. (See ¶1338c.)

➤ *For the placement of a mailstop code, see ¶1338d.*

g. If a room number, a suite number, or an apartment number is part of the address, insert it immediately after the street address on the same line. (See examples in ¶1390b and h.) When this information will not fit on the same line as the street address, place it on the line above but never on the line below. (See examples in ¶¶1317b, 1318b.)

NOTE: Do not use the pound sign (#) if a term such as *Room, Suite,* or *Apartment* is available. If you use the pound sign, the U.S. Postal Service asks that 1 space be left between the symbol and the number that follows; for example, *616 Ohio Avenue #203.*

(Continued on page 356.)

13

h. If an attention line is to be included in the address, insert it on the line directly above the organizational name or (in the absence of an organizational name) on the line directly above the street address or post office box number. If a serial number of some kind (for example, an account number or a file reference number) is required, insert it as the first line of the address block.

```
H 048369 1078 AT5
ATTN MRS M R TURKEVICH
BROCK & WILSON CORP
79 WALL ST SUITE 1212
NEW YORK NY 10005-4101
```

➤ *For the placement of a bar code in relation to the address block, see ¶1390b; for the placement of a mailstop code, see ¶1338d.*

i. To facilitate OCR processing, make sure that the mailing address starts no higher than 2¾ inches from the bottom edge, falls no lower than ⅝ inch from the bottom edge, and comes no closer to either the left or the right edge than ½ inch. Do not allow any notations or graphics to fall alongside or below the area established for the mailing address. Moreover, make sure that the lines in the address block are parallel to the bottom edge of the envelope and that there is good contrast between the typed address and the color of the envelope. In addition, do not use a script or italic typeface, and avoid dot matrix print, especially if the dots that make up each character do not touch. The type should be clear and sharp. Adjacent characters should not touch or overlap.

➤ *For the use of the all-cap style on mailing labels, see ¶1397.*

Folding and Inserting Letters

1391 The following paragraphs describe several methods for folding letters and inserting them into envelopes. See the chart in ¶1388 to determine which method is appropriate for the stationery and envelope you are using.

a. To fold a letter in thirds:

 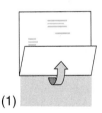 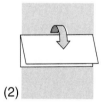 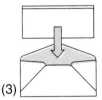

(1)   (2)   (3)

(1) Bring the bottom third of the letter up and make a crease.

(2) Fold the top of the letter down to within ⅜ inch of the crease you made in step 1. Then make the second crease.

(3) The creased edge made in step 2 goes into the envelope first.

NOTE: Use this method for 8½″ × 11″ stationery with a No. 10 envelope; 7¼″ × 10½″ stationery with a No. 7 envelope; 5½″ × 8½″ stationery with a No. 6¾ envelope. (See also ¶1388.)

b. To fold a letter in half and then in thirds:

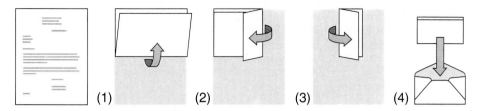

(1) Bring the bottom edge to within ⅜ inch of the top edge and make a crease.

(2) Fold from the right edge, making the fold a little less than one-third the width of the sheet before you crease it.

(3) Fold from the left edge, bringing it to within ⅜ inch of the crease you made in step 2 before you crease the sheet again.

(4) Insert the left creased edge into the envelope first. This will leave the crease you made in step 2 near the flap of the envelope.

NOTE: Use this method for 8½″ × 11″ stationery with a No. 6¾ envelope. (See also ¶1388.)

c. To fold a letter in half:

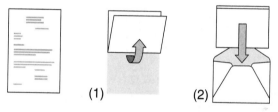

(1) Bring the bottom edge to within ⅜ inch of the top edge and make a crease.

(2) Insert the creased edge into the envelope first.

NOTE: Use this method for 5½″ × 8½″ stationery with a No. 5⅜ envelope. (See also ¶1388.)

d. To fold a letter for insertion into a window envelope:

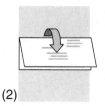
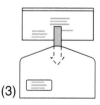

(1) Place the letter *face down* with the letterhead at the top, and fold the bottom third of the letter up.

(2) Fold the top third down so that the address shows.

(Continued on page 358.)

(3) Insert the letter with the inside address toward the *front* of the envelope. The inside address should now be fully readable through the window of the envelope. Moreover, there should be at least ⅛ inch (and preferably ¼ inch) between all four sides of the address and the edges of the window, no matter how much the letter slides around in the envelope.

MEMOS

13

1392 An interoffice memo (or memorandum) is intended to expedite the flow of written communication within an organization. For that reason many organizations provide computerized formats (and less frequently, printed forms) in order to simplify and standardize the treatment of key information.

Depending on the circumstances, a memo may be as terse as a telegram, as impersonal as a formal announcement, or as warm and casual as a personal note. Those circumstances will help you determine whether a particular memo should contain or omit such features as a salutation or a signature line.

If your organization has not established a standard format, your word processing software may provide memo templates that you can use as is or modify to suit your preferences. Here are two sample templates:

Memo template provided by WordPerfect 6 for Windows.

INTEROFFICE MEMORANDUM

To: [Name of Recipient]

CC: [CC]

From: <Name>

Date: [Date]

Subject: [Subject]

FROM THE DESK OF ...
<NAME>
<TITLE>
<COMPANY>
<ADDRESS>
<CITY, STATE ZIP>
<TELEPHONE>

Memo template provided by Microsoft Word 6 for Windows.

M E M O R A N D U M

DATE: [August 3, 1995]

TO: [Names]

FROM: [Names]

RE: [Subject]

CC: [Names]

[Type your memo text here]

13

You can always modify a memo template or create your own format. The following rules (¶¶1393–1394) provide guidelines for formatting memos. The illustration on page 360 shows how a memo would look if executed according to these guidelines.

Please remember: There is no one correct format for a memo. Design the format to meet your needs and those of the organization you work for.

NOTE: Because many memos are now distributed as e-mail, see ¶¶1708–1711 for special guidelines on preparing e-mail messages.

1393 When preparing a memo on plain paper or letterhead stationery, observe the following guidelines. (Also see the illustrations on pages 360–361.)

a. Use 1-inch side margins.

b. Leave a top margin of 2 inches. If you are using word processing software, begin typing on the first line below the top margin of 2 inches. If you are using a typewriter, begin typing on line 13. If you are using stationery with a deep letterhead, begin typing on the third line below the letterhead.

NOTE: You can reduce the top margin to 1 inch if doing so will make a continuation page unnecessary.

c. The heading of the memo should include the following guide words— *MEMO TO:, FROM:, DATE:,* and *SUBJECT:,* plus any others you wish to add. For example, below the guide words *MEMO TO:* you could insert *COPIES TO:.* If you work in a large organization and are sending memos to people who do not know you, then below the guide word *FROM:* you might want to insert such guide words as *DEPART-MENT:, FLOOR:, PHONE NO.:,* or *FAX NO.:.* Start typing the guide words at the left margin and use double spacing. Type the guide words in all-capital letters (in boldface if you have that option), and follow each with a colon.

(Continued on page 360.)

13

2 inches

MEMO TO: Joanne Malik, Forrest Talbot, Lee Wriston ↓2

FROM: Sally Klein ↓2

DATE: February 9, 1998 ↓2

SUBJECT: Convention Invitation ↓3

We have just been invited to make a one-hour presentation on catalog marketing at the annual convention of the International Marketing Institute. The convention will be held on November 12–15 at the Camelback Inn in Scottsdale, Arizona. I don't have all the details we need in order to start planning the presentation, but I would like you to block out these dates on your calendar now so as to avoid any schedule conflicts later on. ↓2

This invitation represents an excellent opportunity for us to show the profession some of the exciting things we have done in the past few years, and it could bring us a number of new clients next year. Let's give it our best shot. ↓2

As soon as I receive more information from the program coordinator, I'll set up a luncheon at which we can decide how best to proceed. ↓4

Sally

SK ↓2

job
imiconvn.298

NOTE: If you wish, you can create a heading such as *MEMORANDUM* (see the illustrations on pages 358 and 359). In that case use the guide word *TO:* rather than *MEMO TO:* (as illustrated on page 361).

d. Set a tab so that the entries following the guide words will all block at the left and will clear the longest guide word by a minimum of 2 spaces.

e. After the guide words *Memo to:* (or *To:*) and *From:*, the names of the addressee and the writer are usually given without personal titles (*Mr., Miss, Mrs., Ms.*). Indeed, when you are doing a memo to someone within your immediate unit, the use of initials or simply a first name may suffice. In short, the way you treat these names will depend on the relative formality or informality of the occasion.

John A. Mancuso OR JAM OR Jack

MEMORANDUM

TO: Bernard O'Kelly ↓ 2

COPIES TO: Steve Kubat, Pat Rosario

FROM: Janet R. Wiley *JRW*

DATE: April 7, 1997

SUBJECT: Test Marketing Arrangements ↓ 3

Dear Bernie: ↓ 2

Let me try to summarize the outcome of our excellent meeting last Friday, in which we discussed how your group might sell our product lines to the markets you serve. ↓ 2

1. Steve Kubat, chief product manager for my group, will provide you with product descriptions, catalog sheets, ad mats, and current price lists. If you need additional information, just call Steve (or me in his absence) and we'll be glad to help in any way that we can. ↓ 2

2. We will pay you an 18 percent commission on all orders you generate for our products. Please forward a copy of these orders to Steve, who will arrange to have the commission credited to your account. ↓ 2

3. We very much appreciate your offer to give us three hours at your weeklong sales meeting next month to present our products to your field staff. We'll be there. ↓ 2

4. We have agreed to give this new arrangement a six-month test to see (a) how much additional sales revenue you and your people can produce with our products and (b) what effect, if any, this special marketing effort will have on your sales of other products. At the end of the test period, we will analyze the results and decide whether to continue the arrangement, modify it in some way, or abandon it altogether. ↓ 2

I don't think we'll be abandoning it, Bernie. In fact, I feel quite confident that this new arrangement is going to produce significant gains in sales and profits for both of us. I look forward to working with you to make it all happen. ↓ 2

imm
okellyb.477

f. If you want to provide additional information (such as a department name or title, a phone number, or a fax number), you can add the appropriate guide words to the heading of the memo, or you can insert the relevant information after the person's name. For example:

Cynthia Chen, Accounting Manager

OR Cynthia Chen (Ext. 4782)

(Continued on page 362.)

g. If the memo is being addressed to two or three people, try to fit all the names on the same line.

MEMO TO: Hal Parker, Meryl Crawford, Mike Monagle

If there are too many names to fit on the same line, then list the names in one or more single-spaced columns alongside *MEMO TO:*. Leave 1 blank line before the next guide word and fill-in entry.

13

MEMO TO: Louise Landes
Fred Mendoza
Jim Norton
Ruth O'Hare

FROM: Neil Sundstrom

---

h. If listing all the addressees in the heading of a memo looks unattractive, then after the guide words *MEMO TO:*, type *See Distribution Below* or something similar (see the illustration on page 363). Then on the third line below the reference initials, the file name notation, or the enclosure notation (whichever comes last), type *Distribution:*. Use capital and small letters, followed by a colon, and italicize or underline the word for emphasis. (If you use italics, italicize the colon as well. If you use underline, do not underline the colon.) Leave 1 blank line, and then list the names of the individuals who are to receive a copy of the memo. Arrange the names either by rank or in alphabetic order, and type them blocked at the left margin. (If space is tight, arrange the names in two or more columns.)

NOTE: For purposes of actual distribution, simply place a check mark next to one of the listed names to indicate who is to receive that particular copy. As an alternative, use a highlighting marker to identify the recipient of each copy.

i. If the fill-in after the guide word *Subject:* is long, type it in two or more single-spaced lines of roughly equal length. Align all turnover lines with the start of the first line of the fill-in. (For an illustration, see page 478.)

j. Begin typing the body of the memo on the third line below the last fill-in line in the heading.

NOTE: An interoffice memo ordinarily does not require a salutation, especially if the memo is an impersonal announcement being sent to a number of people or the staff at large. (See, for example, the illustration on page 363). However, when a memo is directed to one person (like the illustration on page 361), many writers use a salutation—such as *Dear Andy:* or *Andy:* alone—to keep the memo from seeming cold or impersonal. (If a salutation is used, begin typing the body of the memo on the second line below.)

2 inches

MEMO TO: See Distribution Below ↓ 2

FROM: Stanley W. Venner (Ext. 3835)

DATE: May 10, 1998

SUBJECT: Car Rentals ↓ 3

13

We have just been informed that car rental rates will be increased by $1 to $2 a day, effective July 1. ↓ 2

This daily rate increase can be more than offset if you refill the gasoline tank before returning your rental car to the local agency. According to our latest information, the car rental companies are charging an average of 32 percent more per gallon than gas stations in the same area. Therefore, you can help us achieve substantial savings and keep expenses down by remembering to fill up the gas tank before turning your rental car in. ↓ 2

SWV ↓ 2

jmb
venners.5a8 ↓ 3

Distribution: ↓ 2

G. Bonardi
D. Catlin
S. Folger
✓ V. Jellinek
E. Kasendorf
P. Legrande
T. Pacheco
F. Sullivan
J. Trotter
W. Zysk

k.   Use single spacing and either block the paragraphs or indent them 0.5 inch (5 spaces on a typewriter). Leave 1 blank line between paragraphs.

l.   Although memos do not require a signature line, some writers prefer to end their memos in this way. In that case type the writer's name or initials on the *second* line below the last line of the message (as shown above). If the writer plans to insert a handwritten signature or initials above the signature line, type the signature line on the *fourth* line below (as shown on page 360) to allow room for the handwriting. If

(Continued on page 364.)

the writer simply inserts handwritten initials next to the typed name in the heading (as in the illustration on page 361), omit the signature line altogether.

NOTE: The position of the signature line may vary. If all the lines in the memo heading begin at the left margin (see, for example, the illustration on page 360), type the signature line at the left margin as well. If the memo uses a two-column heading format (as in the illustration on page 365), start the signature line at the same point as the fill-ins for the second column in the heading.

m. Type the reference initials (see ¶¶1370–1371) at the left margin, on the second line below the end of the message or the writer's typed name or initials, whichever comes last. (See the illustrations on pages 360–361.)

n. Type a file name notation (if needed) on the line below the reference initials. (See ¶1372 and the illustrations on pages 360–361.)

o. Type an enclosure notation, if needed, on the line below the reference initials or the file name notation, whichever comes last. Begin at the left margin. (See ¶1373.)

p. Type a copy notation, if needed, on the line below the enclosure notation, the reference initials, or the file name notation, whichever comes last. Use the same style for the copy notation as in a letter. (See ¶¶1376–1380.) If the addressee of the memo is not intended to know that a copy of the memo is being sent to one or more other persons, use a blind copy notation. (See ¶1378.)

NOTE: As an alternative, place the copy notation in the heading. (See the illustration on page 361.) On the second line below *MEMO TO:* (or *TO:*), insert the guide words *COPIES TO:* (followed by a colon) and then insert the appropriate names at the right, starting at the same point as the other fill-ins in the heading.

q. If the memo is of a confidential nature, type the word *CONFIDEN-TIAL* in all-capital letters (using boldface if you have that option). Center the confidential notation on the third line below the heading, and begin typing the body of the memo on the third line below this notation.

CONFIDENTIAL↓₃ OR C O N F I D E N T I A L ↓₃

r. If the memo continues beyond the first page, type a continuation heading on a fresh sheet of paper. (Use the same style as shown in ¶1384 for a letter.) Then continue typing the message on the third line below the last line of the continuation-page heading. (See ¶1385 for additional details on continuing the message from one page to another.)

➤ *For the use of macros, see ¶1354, note.*

1394 When typing a memo on a *printed form:*

a. Set the left margin 2 or 3 spaces after the longest guide word in the left half of the printed heading—for example, after *Subject:* in the illustration on page 365.

Interoffice Memorandum

To:	Bernard O'Kelly	From:	Janet R. Wiley
Dept.:	Special Sales	Dept.:	Software Products
Floor:	4	Floor and Ext.:	7/3825
Subject:	Test Marketing Arrangements	Date:	April 7, 1997

Dear Bernie:

Let me try to summarize the outcome of our excellent meeting last Friday, in which we discussed how your group might sell our product lines to the markets you serve.

13

NOTE: Some writers prefer to set the left margin at the point where the printed guide words begin. In this case it is necessary to set a tab 2 or 3 spaces after the longest guide word in the left half of the printed heading.

b. Set a tab 2 or 3 spaces after the longest guide word in the right half of the printed heading—for example, after *Floor and Ext.:* (floor number and telephone extension) in the illustration above.

NOTE: The guide words used in the heading of a printed memo will vary, depending on the preferences of an organization.

c. Make the right margin approximately equal to the left margin.

d. Insert the appropriate information after each printed guide word, using capital and small letters. The fill-ins should block at the left and align at the bottom with the printed guide words.

NOTE: If you are sending the memo to someone within your own department (or to someone elsewhere in the company with whom you have a close working relationship), you can omit the fill-ins after the guide words *Dept.:* and *Floor and Ext.:*.

➤ *For other guidelines to observe when typing a memo, see ¶1393d–r; for the use of macros, see ¶1354, note.*

SOCIAL-BUSINESS CORRESPONDENCE

1395 The term *social-business correspondence* applies to the following types of letters:

a. Executive correspondence addressed to high-level executives, officials, and dignitaries. (Unlike ordinary business correspondence—which deals with sales, production, finance, advertising, and other routine commercial matters—these letters deal with such topics as corporate policy and issues of social responsibility, and they are written in a more formal style.)

(Continued on page 366.)

¶1395

AVON ADVISORY COUNCIL

192 WEST MAIN STREET   AVON, CONNECTICUT 06001
PHONE 860-555-4954   FAX 860-555-4960

September 26, 19–

↓6

Dear Annie,
↓2

You and I have worked together on the Advisory Council for nearly six years, and in that time we have gotten to know each other pretty well. So you'll understand why I was deeply pained to hear that you and your husband have sold your house and are planning to move to the Northwest next month.
↓2

We have not always seen eye to eye (I still think you were dead wrong to vote against the parking lot expansion), but there is no one who has given as much thought and imagination and caring service to this town as you have.
↓2

All of us on the Advisory Council are going to miss you very much, both as a forceful participant and as a rare and generous friend, but we wish you and George the best of luck as you make new lives for yourselves. We envy your new neighbors, for they will be the beneficiaries of what we in Avon have so long enjoyed—your vital presence.
↓2

We won't forget you, Annie.
↓2

Sincerely,
↓4

Harlan

Harlan W. Estabrook
Chairman

↓6

Mrs. Anne G. Wheatley
14 Tower Lane
Avon, Connecticut 06001

b. Letters expressing praise, concern, or condolence to someone within or outside the organization. (The occasion that prompts the letter could be exceptional performance on the job or in the community, an employment anniversary, the death or serious illness of a family member, or an upcoming retirement. Such letters may be formal or informal, depending on the relationship between the writer and the person addressed.)

c. Letters to business associates within or outside the company on purely social matters.

1396 Social-business correspondence differs from ordinary business correspondence in several ways:

a. The inside address is typed at the bottom of the letter, aligned at the left margin and starting on the sixth line below the writer's signature or title (whichever comes last).

b. The salutation is followed by a comma rather than a colon.

c. Reference initials and notations pertaining to enclosures, copies, and mailing are typically omitted. (It would make good sense, however, to put such notations on the file copy in case this information is needed later on.)

d. If the letter requires a *Personal* or *Confidential* notation, place the notation only on the envelope, not on the letter itself. (For the appropriate placement of the notation on an envelope, see ¶1389m and the second illustration on page 353.)

NOTE: Include the *Personal* or *Confidential* notation on the file copy.

e. Social-business correspondence also differs by being *more* formal or *less* formal than ordinary business correspondence. For example, correspondence to high-level officials and dignitaries is customarily more formal. In such cases use the word style for numbers (see ¶¶404–406) and one of the special salutations listed in Section 18. However, in letters to business associates who are also close friends, the salutation and the complimentary closing may be very informal, and the writer's typed signature and title—and even the inside address—may be omitted. Moreover, when such letters are purely personal in nature, the writer may use plain stationery and omit the return address.

LABELS

1397 If you are using the label feature of a word processing program, you can quickly prepare a wide variety of labels (for example, mailing labels, file folder labels, and cassette labels) by following these guidelines:

a. Use commercially prepared labels (packaged in rolls and sheets) that have been specifically designed for the purpose you have in mind and that are compatible with your printer.

b. Many software programs provide a menu of label types and sizes. When you select the type and size you want to use, the program automatically sets up the label windows. All you need to do is type the necessary information in each window (as illustrated on page 368).

NOTE: You can also create your own specifications for a special type of label. See your software user's manual for the procedures to follow.

c. Before you begin to type text in each label window, consider the maximum number of characters you can fit on one line and the number of lines you can fit on one label. For example, if you are preparing mailing labels, you may very well find that some mailing addresses as you would style them in an inside address are too wide to fit on the labels you are planning to use. In such cases use the all-cap style designed by

(Continued on page 368.)

the U.S. Postal Service. The all-cap style, with its heavy reliance on abbreviations, was specifically created to take such limitations into account. (See ¶1390 and the illustration below.)

d. When applying a label to a No. 10 envelope or a smaller envelope, follow the placement guidelines provided in ¶1389h. (For an illustration showing the correct placement of a mailing label on a No. 10 envelope, see page 355.) On envelopes larger than No. 10, position the label so that it appears visually centered horizontally and vertically.

Screen dump showing label feature of WordPerfect 6 for Windows.

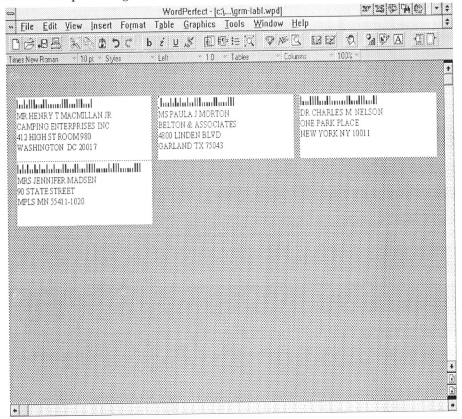

SECTION 14

REPORTS AND MANUSCRIPTS

Preparing Manuscript for an Article (¶¶1431–1432)
Preparing Manuscript for a Book (¶¶1433–1434)
Precautions for All Manuscripts (¶¶1435–1436)

REPORTS

Reports serve all kinds of purposes. Some simply communicate information—such as monthly sales figures or survey results—without any attempt to analyze or interpret the data. Others offer extensive analyses and make detailed recommendations for further action. As a result, reports come in all sizes and shapes. Some are done informally as memos or letters (depending on whether they are

14

Report Template Provided by WordPerfect 6 for Windows

Report Header Here

Heading

Logical organization is prerequisite to any good report. The points you make in body text (like here) have to be appropriately highlighted and grouped. Some of the tools you can use to properly organize this report are the predefined styles included with this template:

- _Bullet
- _Subheading
- _Heading

Subheading I

Use subheadings to help the reader distinguish between the subjects or topics of your report.

Subheading 2

Remember that this ExpressDoc template is simply a suggested layout. Feel free to modify the styles as you desire.

This is a Heading

This template is designed with a two-column layout. To switch between headings and body text, simply press the "Hard Col" button or type Ctrl + Enter.

Page 1

to be distributed inside or outside the organization). Some consist simply of fill-ins on printed or computer-generated forms. Many, however, are done in a more formal style. As you might expect, there is a wide variation to be found in what is considered acceptable—from one authority to another and from one organization to another. Regardless of which guidelines you follow, be prepared to modify them to fit a specific situation.

NOTE: If you are using word processing software, your software may provide templates that you can use as is or modify to suit your preferences. Two report templates available to users of WordPerfect 6 for Windows are illustrated on pages 370 and 371.

The first template is attractive, but because of the wide column at the left where headings are displayed, there is not much space for the text alongside—a serious consideration when you are planning to distribute many copies of a long report. The second template provides a much longer text line, but the heading structure—with the main headings aligned at the right margin and the subheadings aligned at the left margin—could prove hard for the reader to follow.

Report Template Provided by WordPerfect 6 for Windows

14

Chapter Title

_____

Heading

Subheading

Logical organization is prerequisite to any good report. The points you make in body text (like here) have to be appropriately highlighted and grouped. Some of the tools you can use to properly organize this report are the predefined styles included with this template:

- _Bullet

- _Subheading

- _Heading

- _Chapter

Subheading

Use subheadings to help the reader distinguish between the subjects or topics of your report.

Subheading

Remember that this ExpressDoc template is simply a suggested layout. Feel free to modify the styles as you desire. This report includes a filename and page number at the bottom of each page.

PAGE 1

¶1401

If you do not wish to use one of the report templates provided by your software, you can always create your own format. This section provides format guidelines for formal and informal reports. The model below shows how the first page of an informal report would appear if executed according to these guidelines.

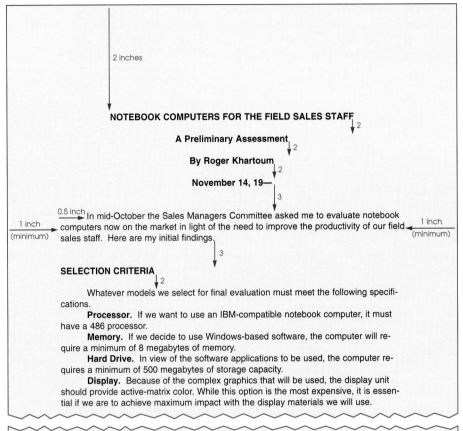

Choosing a Format

1401 If you are preparing a report at the request of someone else, always try to get some guidelines from that person on such matters as format, length, amount of detail desired, and distribution. Check the files for copies of similar reports done in the past. If guidelines or models are not provided or if you are preparing the report on your own initiative, consider the following factors in choosing a format.

a. *For whom are you writing the report?* If intended for your boss or a colleague on staff, the report could be done simply as a memo. If intended for top management or the board of directors, the report will often require a more formal approach. By the same token, an academic term paper will require a simpler format than a thesis for an advanced degree.

b. *What outcome do you hope to achieve?* If you are merely providing information without attempting to win someone over to your point of view, the simplest and clearest presentation of the information will suffice. If you are trying to persuade the reader to adopt your viewpoint and accept your recommendations, you may need to make a detailed argument and devise a more complex structure for your report.

c. *What is the existing mind-set of your reader?* If you will have to argue long and hard to win your reader over, you may need to develop a number of chapters, grouped by part. If you need to demonstrate that your argument is supported by much detailed research, you may have to quote from published sources and provide an elaborate set of data in the form of tables and charts. If you know that your intended reader already supports your argument or simply wants your judgment on a certain matter, a shorter and simpler document will usually suffice.

Parts of a Formal Report

1402 A *formal* report typically has three parts: front matter, body, and back matter. Each of these parts, in turn, typically contains some (if not all) of the following elements in the sequence indicated.

a. Front Matter

TITLE PAGE	*In a business report:* gives the full title, the subtitle (if any), the writer's name, title, and department, and the date of submission; may also indicate for whom the report was written. *In an academic report:* gives the name of the writer, the instructor, and the course, along with the date of submission. (See ¶1414.)
LETTER OR MEMO OF TRANSMITTAL	May be done as a letter (for distribution outside the company) or as a memo (for inside distribution); may be clipped to the front of the report (or to the binder in which the report is inserted); may be inserted in the report itself as the page preceding the title page. (See ¶1415.)
TABLE OF CONTENTS	A list of all chapters (by number and title), along with the opening page number of each chapter. If chapters are grouped by part, the titles of the parts also appear in the table of contents. Sometimes main headings within the chapters are also given under each chapter title. (See ¶1416.)
LISTS OF TABLES AND ILLUSTRATIONS	Separate lists of tables and illustrations are included if they are numerous and likely to be frequently referred to by the reader. (See ¶1417.)

(Continued on page 374.)

FOREWORD	Written by someone other than the author of the report. May explain who commissioned the report, the reasons for doing so, and the qualifications of the writer to prepare the report. May also offer an evaluation of the report, and may ask those who receive copies of the report to give their assessment or take some other action after they have read the report. (See ¶1418.)
PREFACE	Written by the author of the report. Indicates for whom the report is written, the objectives and the scope of the report, and the methods used to assemble the material in the report. Acknowledgments of help received on the report are usually included here (placed at the end), but to give this material special emphasis, you can treat the acknowledgments as a separate element of the front matter, immediately following the preface. (See ¶1418.)
SUMMARY	Preferably a one-page document (two pages at most) designed to save the reader's time by presenting conclusions and recommendations right at the outset of the report. If a preface is not provided, the summary also includes some of the material that would have gone there. (See ¶1419.)

b. Body

INTRODUCTION	Sets forth (in greater detail than the preface) the objectives, the scope, and the methods, along with any other relevant background information. In a report with several chapters, the introduction may precede the first chapter of the text or it may be labeled as Chapter 1. (See ¶1421.)
MAIN DISCUSSION	Sets forth all the pertinent data, evidence, analyses, and interpretations needed to fulfill the purpose of the report. May consist of one long chapter that opens with an introduction and closes with conclusions and recommendations. May consist of several chapters; these may be grouped into *parts*, with a part-title page inserted to introduce each sequence of chapters. May use different levels of headings throughout the text to indicate what the discussion covers and how it is organized. (See ¶¶1422–1426.)
CONCLUSION	Summarizes the key points and presents the recommendations that the writer hopes the reader will be persuaded to accept. In a report with several chapters, this material represents the final chapter or the final part.

c. Back Matter

APPENDIXES	A collection of tables, charts, or other data too specific or too lengthy to be included in the body of the report but provided here as supporting detail for the interested reader. (See ¶1428.)

ENDNOTES	A collection—all in one place at the end of the report—of what would otherwise appear as footnotes at the bottom of various pages in the report. This format simplifies the preparation of the report. (See ¶¶1501–1502, 1504–1505.)
BIBLIOGRAPHY	A list of all sources (1) that were consulted in the preparation of the report and (2) from which material was derived or directly quoted. (See ¶¶1532–1536.)
GLOSSARY	A list of terms (with definitions) that may not be readily understood when encountered in the body of the report. (See ¶1430.) May be treated as an appendix.

Parts of an Informal Report

1403 a. An *informal* report has no front matter. The information that would go on a separate title page appears at the top of the first page and is immediately followed by the body of the report. (See ¶¶1411–1413 for format guidelines.)

b. An informal report typically contains no back matter except possibly a list of *endnotes* (in place of separate footnotes throughout the body of the report) and a *bibliography*. (See ¶1505 for an illustration of endnotes and ¶1535 for an illustration of a bibliography.) Tables that cannot be easily incorporated in the body of the informal report may also be placed in an appendix in the back matter.

Margins

1404 Side Margins

a. Unbound Reports. If a report is to remain unbound or will simply be stapled in the upper left corner, use a 6.5-inch line with 1-inch side margins. (If the overall length of the report is not a problem, you can increase the side margins equally to give the report a more open look. See ¶1305b for guidelines on increasing margins.)

b. Bound Reports. Use a 6-inch line with a 1.5-inch left margin and a 1-inch right margin. (The extra half inch at the left will provide space for the binding.)

1405 Top and Bottom Margins of Opening Pages

The following guidelines apply to (1) the first page of each chapter, (2) the first page of each distinct element in the front matter and back matter, and (3) the first page of an informal report that consists of only one chapter (without any separate title page or other front matter). (See the illustration on page 376.)

a. On these opening pages, leave a top margin of 2 inches (12 lines on a typewriter) and a bottom margin of 1 inch (6 lines on a typewriter). On the title page and on part-title pages, where the copy is centered as a whole on the page, leave a top and bottom margin of at least 1 inch (6 lines on a typewriter).

(Continued on page 376.)

b. If you are using word processing software, begin typing on the first line *below* the 2-inch top margin. You can select the page numbering format that automatically ends an opening page with a page number centered on the last line before the 1-inch bottom margin.

c. If you are using a typewriter, leave a top margin of 12 blank lines and begin typing on line 13. On a full page of copy, the last line of text typically falls on line 57 and the page number is centered on line 60. (See ¶¶1408 and 1410 for exceptions to this standard.)

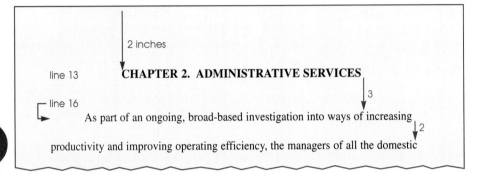

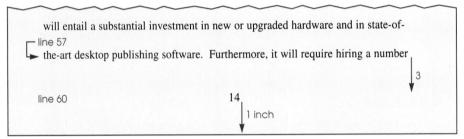

d. Ordinarily, nothing is typed in the space that represents the top margin. However, in informal academic reports, certain information is often typed in the upper right corner. (See ¶1413.)

➤ *For the numbering of opening pages, see ¶1420.*

1406 Top and Bottom Margins of Other Pages

a. If you are using word processing software (see the illustration at the top of page 377):

(1) Set the top and bottom margins at 1 inch.

(2) For pages in the *body* and *back matter* of a report, position the page number on the first line below the 1-inch top margin. Type the number at the right margin and leave 2 blank lines before continuing the text. If you want to provide additional information along with the page number (for example, the title of the report or a chapter within the report), use the header feature of your word processing software.

NOTE: If you use the page numbering feature or the header feature of your software, only 1 blank line will be left between the page number and the text, but you can adjust this space.

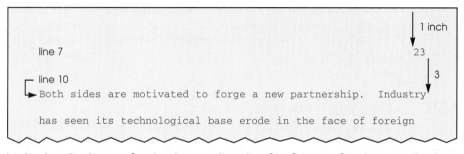

(**3**) For pages in the *front matter* of a report, center the page number on the last line before the 1-inch bottom margin and leave a minimum of 2 blank lines between the last line of text and the page number. If you want to provide additional information along with the page number, use the footer feature of your software.

NOTE: If you use the page numbering feature or the footer feature of your software, only 1 blank line will be left above the page number, but you can adjust this space.

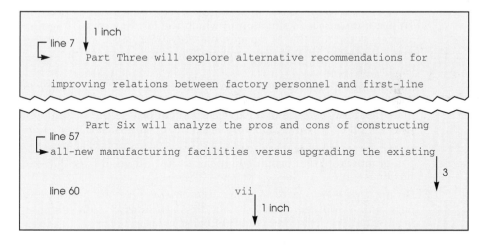

b. If you are using a typewriter (see the illustration at the top of this page):

(**1**) Leave 6 blank lines (1 inch) at the top and bottom of the page.

(**2**) For pages in the *body* and *back matter* of a report, type the page number on line 7 at the right margin and continue the text on line 10. The last line of copy on a full page of text should fall on line 60.

(Continued on page 378.)

(3) For pages in the *front matter* of a report, type the first line of text on line 7, type the last line of text on line 57, and center the page number on line 60. (See the illustration at the bottom of page 377.)

➤ *For exceptions to the standard of ending a page on line 60, see ¶¶1408 and 1410d; for the numbering of opening pages, see ¶1420.*

1407 Handling Page Breaks on a Computer

If you are using word processing software, you can avoid most page-ending problems as outlined in *a–e*. There are, however, page-ending situations in which you must use your own judgment as outlined in *f–j*.

a. The *page numbering feature* ensures that the bottom margin will always be 1 inch (or whatever margin you have selected). The computer will insert a *soft page break* when the bottom margin is reached, but because that break is "soft," you can easily adjust it if you do not like what the computer has done.

NOTE: The *preview* feature permits you to see an entire page on the screen prior to printing so that you can tell whether adjustments will be necessary. See ¶1407f–j below for page-ending situations that may require adjustments.

b. A *hard page break* permits you to end a page wherever you want and to ensure that any copy that follows will appear at the top of the next page.

c. The *block protect* feature ensures that a designated block of copy (such as a table, an enumerated list, or selected lines of text) will not be divided at the bottom of a page but will, if necessary, be carried over intact to the top of the next page.

d. To prevent widows (a situation in which the last line of a paragraph appears as the first line of a page), the *widow protection* feature ensures that at least two lines of that paragraph are carried over to the top of the next page.

e. To prevent orphans (a situation in which the first line of a paragraph appears as the last line of a page), the *orphan protection* feature ensures that at least two lines of that paragraph will appear at the bottom of a page or that the paragraph will begin at the top of the next page.

NOTE: Paragraph h below illustrates the proper handling of a four-line paragraph. Note that two lines appear at the bottom of page 378 and two lines appear at the top of page 379.

f. Do not type a *centered heading* or a *side heading* near the bottom of a page unless you can fit at least the first two lines of copy after the heading. (For illustrations, see ¶1425d–f.)

NOTE: A *run-in heading* (in the first line of a paragraph) can fall near the bottom of a page if one additional line of the paragraph will also fit there. (For an illustration, see ¶1425f.)

➤ *For a discussion of centered, side, and run-in headings, see ¶1425c–g.*

g. Do not divide a quoted extract (see ¶1424d) unless you can leave at least two lines at the bottom of one page and carry over at least two lines to the top of the next.

h. If a list of items (see ¶1424e–g) has to be divided at the bottom of a page, try to divide *between* items (not within an item). Moreover, try to leave at least two items at the bottom of one page and carry over at least two items to the top of the next.

NOTE: If you need to divide *within* an item, leave at least two lines at the bottom of one page and carry over at least two lines to the next.

i. If it is not possible to start typing a table at the desired point of reference and have it all fit on the same page, then insert a parenthetical note at the appropriate point in the text (referring the reader to the next page) and continue with the text to the bottom of the page. Then at the top of the next page, type the complete table, leave 1 to 3 blank lines, and resume typing the text. (See Section 16 for guidelines on the typing of tables.)

   NOTE: If a table is so long that it will not fit on one page even when typed single-spaced, then look for a sensible division point in the body of the table and end the first page there. At the top of the next page, repeat the complete title of the table (with *Continued* or *Cont.* inserted in parentheses at the end); also repeat any column heads before continuing with the rest of the table. If there is any possibility that a reader could mistake the first part of the divided table as the complete table, then type a continuation line (in parentheses or brackets) at the point where the table breaks off. (See ¶1638 for details.)

j. If a footnote cannot all fit on the page where the text reference occurs, continue it at the bottom of the following page. (See ¶1503f.)

➤ *For a formal definition of terms such as* pagination, block protect, orphan protection, *and* widow protection, *see Appendix B.*

14

1408 Handling Page Breaks on a Typewriter

As indicated in ¶¶1405–1406, if you want to maintain a consistent bottom margin of 6 blank lines in a typed report, then strictly speaking, the last typing on a page should appear on line 60. In most cases this should be easy to achieve. However, in a few situations you may have to end the page one line long or several lines short.

a. On full pages of text where the page number must be typed at the bottom (see ¶¶1405 and 1406), your goal is to type the last line of text on line 57 and the page number on line 60.

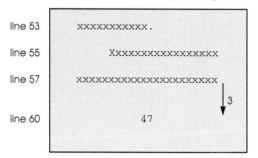

Standard Page-Ending Arrangement

line 53	xxxxxxxxxxx.
line 55	Xxxxxxxxxxxxxxxxxx
line 57	xxxxxxxxxxxxxxxxxxxxxxxx
	↓ 3
line 60	47

However, if you are typing double-spaced text on even-numbered lines, it will be impossible for you to end the text on line 57. In such a case try to end the text on line 56 and keep the page number on line 60. In order to avoid a bad page break, you can end the text on line 58 and center the page number on line 61.

Preferable Variation **Acceptable Variation**

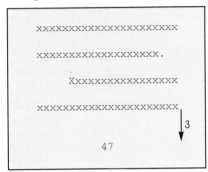

line 52
line 54
line 56
line 58
line 60
line 61

➤ *For examples of bad page breaks, see ¶1407f–j.*

b. On full pages of text where the page number goes in the upper right corner on line 7, try to type the last line of text on line 60.

Standard Page-Ending Arrangement

line 56
line 58
line 60

However, if you are typing double-spaced copy on odd-numbered lines, aim for line 59 but continue the text on line 61 if necessary to avoid a bad break.

Preferable Variation **Acceptable Variation**

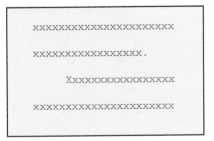

line 55
line 57
line 59
line 61

c. In dividing a paragraph at the bottom of a page, always leave at least two lines at the bottom of the page and carry at least two lines to the top of the next. Three-line paragraphs pose a special problem: you must either fit all three lines at the bottom of one page or carry all three lines over to the top of the next page.

14

1409 Controlling Bottom Margins

a. If you are using word processing software, the pagination feature will end each page so as to maintain a bottom margin of 1 inch (or whatever margin you have selected).

b. If you are using a typewriter, draw two short pencil marks (later to be erased) at the left edge of the paper. Place the first mark 1.5 inches (9 lines on a typewriter) and the second mark 1 inch (6 lines on a typewriter) above the bottom edge of the paper. Use the marks to guide you in positioning the last line of text (or the page number on pages where the number falls at the bottom).

1410 Shortening a Long Report

When the cost of photocopying and distributing a large number of copies of a long report becomes prohibitively expensive, consider the following devices for reducing the number of pages without having to cut the copy. (Note that these devices will also reduce the readability and the attractiveness of the report, so use them only in extreme circumstances.)

a. If you are using word processing software, you can reduce the type size and, if necessary, the space between words and letters. You can also choose a different typeface that yields more characters to an inch.

b. Reduce the standard top margin for all opening pages from 2 inches (12 lines on a typewriter) to 1.5 inches (9 lines on a typewriter). (See ¶1405.)

c. Reduce the top margin for all other pages from 1 inch (6 lines on a typewriter) to 0.5 inch (3 lines on a typewriter). (See ¶1406.)

d. As an alternative to *c*, maintain the standard top margin and reduce the bottom margin from 1 inch (6 lines on a typewriter) to 0.5 inch (3 lines on a typewriter). (See ¶1406.)

e. Single-space the report and leave 1 blank line between paragraphs.

f. If the report has only one level of heading, use run-in heads rather than side heads. (See ¶1425.)

g. Wherever the guidelines call for 2 blank lines between elements, use only 1 blank line. Wherever 1 blank line is called for, reduce it to half a line (if your equipment offers this option).

Informal Business Reports

These guidelines apply to business reports that consist of only one chapter and have no separate title page or other front matter.

1411 If the first page is typed on a *blank sheet of paper* (as in the illustration on page 382):

a. Leave a top margin of 2 inches (12 lines on a typewriter). Begin typing on the first line below the 2-inch top margin (line 13 on a typewriter).

NOTE: Use single spacing while executing the title, the subtitle, the writer's name, and the date. (See ¶1411b–e.)

(Continued on page 382.)

b. On the first line below the top margin, type the title of the report centered in all-capital letters. If a subtitle is used, type it centered in capital and small letters on the second line below the main title. (If the title or subtitle is long, divide it into sensible phrases and arrange them on two or more single-spaced lines.)

NOTE: Use boldface for the title and subtitle (and for the writer's name and the date as well) if you have that option.

c. Type *By* and the writer's name centered in capital and small letters on the second line below the title or subtitle.

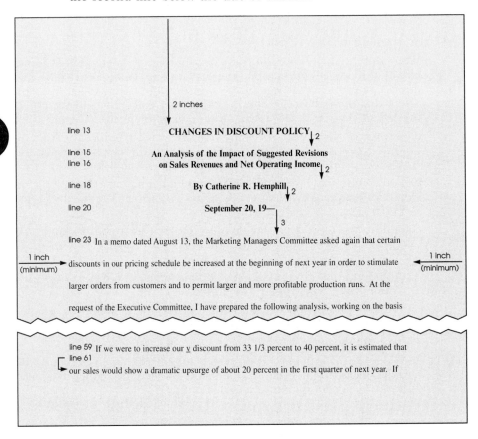

d. Type the date on which the report is to be submitted on the second line, centered, below the writer's name.

NOTE: Additional details that appear on a title page (such as the writer's title and affiliation or the name and affiliation of the person or group for whom the report has been prepared) are omitted when the title starts on the same page as the body. If these elements need to be provided, you will have to prepare a separate title page. (See ¶1414.)

e. On the third line below the date, start the body of the report. (See ¶¶1424–1426.) At this point switch to double spacing.

NOTE: On the first page of an informal business report, do not type a page number. However, count this page as page 1.

f. If the report requires more than one page, then on each continuation page type the page number at the right margin on the first line below the top margin of 1 inch (6 lines on a typewriter). Leave 2 blank lines and resume the text on the following line.

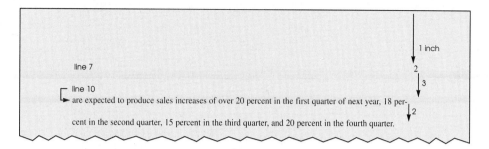

> **NOTE:** If you use the page numbering or header feature of word processing software, only 1 blank line will be left, but you can adjust this space.

g. If the report requires one or more elements of back matter—for example, endnotes or a bibliography—follow the style established for a formal report. (See ¶¶1501–1502, 1504–1505, 1532–1536.)

1412 If the first page of a report is prepared in *memo form:*

a. Give the report title (and subtitle, if any) as the *subject* of the memo. Supply all the other elements called for in the heading of the memo in the usual way. (See ¶¶1392–1393.)

b. Then begin typing the body of the report on the third line below the last fill-in line in the heading. (See ¶¶1424–1426.)

MEMORANDUM

TO: Executive Committee ↓ 2

FROM: Catherine R. Hemphill ↓ 2

DATE: September 20, 19— ↓ 2

SUBJECT: Changes in Discount Policy—An Analysis
            of the Impact of Suggested Revisions on
            Sales Revenues and Net Operating Income ↓ 3

In a memo dated August 13, the Marketing Managers Committee asked again that certain discounts in our pricing schedule be increased at the beginning of next year in order to

c. If the report requires more than one page, then type each continuation page on a blank sheet of paper. Leave a top margin of 1 inch (6 lines on a typewriter), and use the same kind of continuation heading called for in any long memo (see also ¶1393r). Leave 2 blank lines and resume the text on the following line. (If you are using the page numbering feature of word processing software, only 1 blank line will be left, but you can adjust this space.)

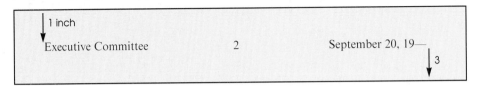

OR:

14

Informal Academic Reports

1413 An academic report that consists of only one chapter and has no separate title page or other front matter is typed exactly like an informal business report (see ¶¶1411–1412) except for the opening of the first page.

   a. Leave a top margin of 1 inch (6 lines on a typewriter). Then type the following information on four separate lines, single-spaced, in the upper right corner of the first page: the writer's name, the instructor's name, the course title, and the date. Align these four lines at the left, with the longest line ending at the right margin.

   b. On the third line below the date, type the title and subtitle (if any) just as in an informal business report. (See ¶1411b.)

   c. Start typing the body of the report on the third line below the preceding copy (the title or subtitle). At this point switch to double spacing.

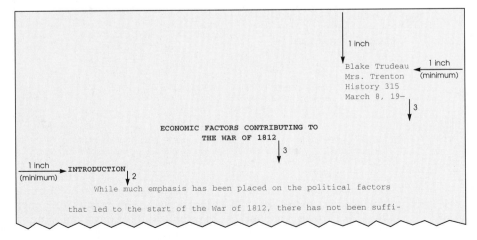

The Front Matter of Formal Reports

The following guidelines deal with the preparation of a title page, a letter or memo of transmittal, a table of contents, a list of tables, a list of illustrations, a preface or foreword, and a summary. For a formal report, only a separate title page is essential; all the other elements are optional.

1414 Title Page

There is no one correct arrangement for the elements on a title page. Here are two acceptable formats.

a. Three-Block Arrangement. Group the material into three blocks of type, and leave equal space (at least 3 blank lines) above and below the middle block. Position the material as a whole so that it appears centered horizontally and vertically on the page. (See the illustrations below and at the top of page 386.)

Business Report

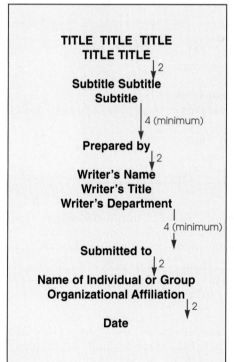

Academic Report

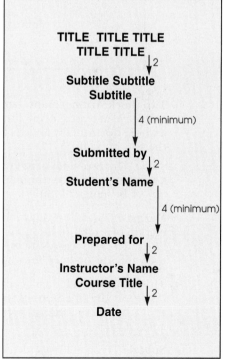

(Continued on page 386.)

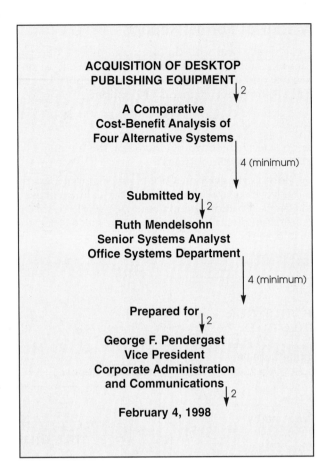

14

b. **Two-Block Arrangement.** Group the material into two blocks of type, and leave at least 5 blank lines between blocks. Center the material as a whole horizontally and vertically on the page. (See the illustration at the top of page 387.)

NOTE: The two-block arrangement works well when the title page does not attempt to show the name of the person or group to whom the report is being submitted.

c. **Margins.** Regardless of which arrangement you use, leave a minimum margin of 1 inch (6 lines on a typewriter) at the top and bottom of the title page. Also leave side margins that are at least equivalent to those used for the body of the report. (See ¶1404.)

d. **Title.** Type the title in all-capital letters, using boldface if you have that option. If the title is long, type it on two or more lines, single-spaced; try to divide the title into meaningful phrases. (See the illustration above.)

e. **Subtitle.** Type the subtitle, if any, in capital and small letters, using boldface if you have that option. If the subtitle requires more than one line, type it single-spaced. Leave 1 blank line between the main title and the subtitle. (See the illustration above.)

f. Writer's Identification. Leave a minimum of 3 blank lines before typing the writer's identification block. The writer's name may be preceded by the word *By* on the same line or by a phrase such as *Prepared by* or *Submitted by* (or simply *By*) typed 2 lines above. If appropriate, the writer's name may be followed by a title on the next line and by an organizational affiliation on the following line.

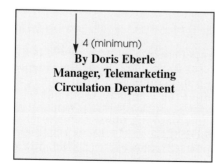

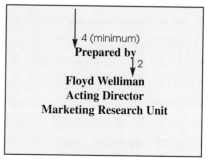

g. Reader's Identification. It is customary (but not essential) to identify the individual or group for whom the report has been prepared. Leave a minimum of 3 blank lines before typing *Submitted to* or *Prepared for* or a similar phrase. Then on the second line below, type the name of the individual or the group. On succeeding lines, supply a title, an organizational affiliation, or both.

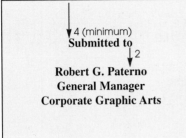

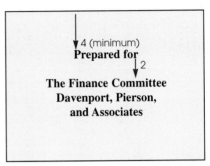

14

NOTE: As an alternative, provide the reader's identification in the form of a subtitle.

AN ANALYSIS OF COMPUTERIZED GRAPHICS EQUIPMENT ↓2

A Report to Robert G. Paterno
General Manager, Corporate Graphic Arts

---

h. **Date.** Supply the date (month, day, and year) on which the report is being submitted. Type it on the second line below the reader's identification block (or, if none is given, on the second line below the writer's identification). (See the illustrations on pages 385–386 and at the top of page 387.)

i. **Graphic Elements.** If you are using a computer with the appropriate graphics software, you can use special display type and add an organizational logo or some other graphic element to enhance the appearance of a title page.

NOTE: If you are using word processing software, your program may provide a template for a title page.

1415 Letter or Memo of Transmittal

a. A formal report is often accompanied by a letter or memo of transmittal. If you are sending the report to people outside the company, use the letter format (see the illustration on page 389); if you are sending the report only to people within the company, use a memo.

b. The message typically covers the following points: (1) a brief description of what is being transmitted; (2) a brief reference to the circumstances that prompted the report; (3) if necessary, a brief indication of why the report is being sent to the addressee; and (4) a statement about what action the addressee is expected to take. (See the illustration on page 389.)

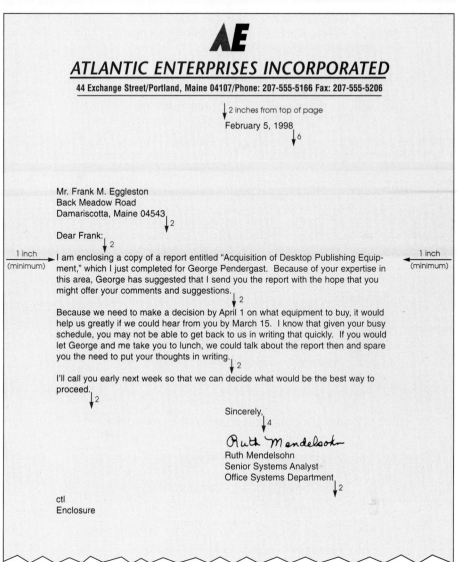

AE

ATLANTIC ENTERPRISES INCORPORATED

44 Exchange Street/Portland, Maine 04107/Phone: 207-555-5166 Fax: 207-555-5206

↓ 2 inches from top of page

February 5, 1998

↓ 6

Mr. Frank M. Eggleston
Back Meadow Road
Damariscotta, Maine 04543

↓ 2

Dear Frank:

↓ 2

1 inch (minimum) → I am enclosing a copy of a report entitled "Acquisition of Desktop Publishing Equipment," which I just completed for George Pendergast. Because of your expertise in this area, George has suggested that I send you the report with the hope that you might offer your comments and suggestions. *1 inch (minimum)*

↓ 2

Because we need to make a decision by April 1 on what equipment to buy, it would help us greatly if we could hear from you by March 15. I know that given your busy schedule, you may not be able to get back to us in writing that quickly. If you would let George and me take you to lunch, we could talk about the report then and spare you the need to put your thoughts in writing.

↓ 2

I'll call you early next week so that we can decide what would be the best way to proceed.

↓ 2

Sincerely,

↓ 4

Ruth Mendelsohn

Ruth Mendelsohn
Senior Systems Analyst
Office Systems Department

↓ 2

ctl
Enclosure

14

---

c. The letter or memo of transmittal is typically clipped to the front of the report. If the report is in a binder, the transmittal document may be clipped to the front of the binder or inserted in the binder preceding the title page.

1416 Table of Contents

a. Type the table of contents on a fresh page. (See the illustration on page 390.) Leave a top margin of 2 inches (12 lines on a typewriter). Begin typing on the first line below the 2-inch top margin (line 13 on a typewriter).

(Continued on page 390.)

b. Type *CONTENTS* (or *TABLE OF CONTENTS*) in all-capital letters (using boldface if you have that option). Center this title on the first line below the top margin.

c. On the third line below, begin typing the table of contents double-spaced. Use the same side and bottom margins as for the text pages in the body of the report. (See ¶¶1404–1409.)

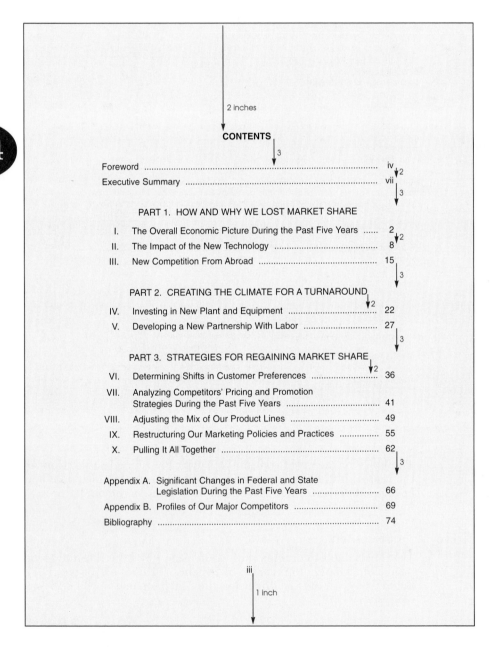

2 inches

CONTENTS

3

iii

1 inch

d. In typing the body of the table of contents, list every separate element that *follows* the table of contents in sequence—whether in the front matter, the body of the report, or the back matter. In the illustration on page 390, note the following aspects of the format:

(1) Individual entries pertaining to *chapters* begin with a chapter number (roman or arabic), followed by a period, 2 spaces, and then the chapter title typed in capital and small letters or in all-capital letters. Align the chapter numbers at the right, with the longest number positioned flush with the left margin. After each chapter title leave 1 space and type a row of solid or spaced leaders to guide the eye to the column of page numbers at the right. Leave 1 space between the final leader and the widest page number; align all other page numbers at the right. (See the illustration below and on page 390.)

NOTE: If you are using the leader feature of your word processing software, it may provide only solid leaders and leave more than 1 space before and after each row of leaders. Accept the results that your software provides. (See also ¶1631.)

(2) If any chapter title should require more than one line, type the turnover line single-spaced and align it with the first letter of the chapter title in the line above.

(3) Type individual entries pertaining to *front matter* and *back matter* at the left margin, with the title in capital and small letters or in all-capital letters, followed by a row of solid or spaced leaders and a page number (roman for front matter and arabic for back matter). Leave 2 blank lines *after* the front matter entries and 2 blank lines *before* the back matter entries.

(4) Center individual entries pertaining to *part titles* in all-capital letters. The part numbers that precede the titles may be in arabic or roman numerals or (for formality) may be spelled out. Leave 2 blank lines before each part title and 1 blank line after.

e. The *main headings* within each chapter may be included in the table of contents. One acceptable arrangement is to indent each heading 2 or 3 spaces from the start of the chapter title and type it in capital and small letters. Type the list of headings for each chapter as a single-spaced block, with 1 blank line above and below it. Page numbers may be provided with the headings if desired.

(Continued on page 392.)

f. If you are using word processing software with the appropriate features, you can create a table of contents by scrolling through the text and coding (according to level of subordination) every part title, chapter title, main heading, and subheading that you wish to appear in the table of contents. The document generated by the computer will not look like the illustration on page 390. Among other things, the roman or arabic chapter numbers may be aligned at the left. For example:

VIII.	**OR**	8.
IX.		9.
X.		10.

However, you can adjust the computer-generated format to achieve the look you want.

NOTE: If you subsequently add, delete, or change any titles or headings in the report, you can readily update your table of contents to reflect these changes by using the process described in *f* above.

1417 List of Tables or Illustrations

a. Type each list on a fresh page. Leave a top margin of 2 inches (12 lines on a typewriter). Begin typing on the first line below the 2-inch top margin (line 13 on a typewriter).

b. Type the heading—*TABLES* (or *LIST OF TABLES*) or *ILLUSTRA-TIONS* (or *LIST OF ILLUSTRATIONS*)—in all-capital letters (using boldface if you have that option). Center this title on the first line of typing. (See the illustration below.)

c. On the third line below the heading, type the first entry in the list. Use the same format as for chapter titles in a table of contents. (See ¶1416.) The tables or the illustrations may be numbered consecutively throughout the report or consecutively within each chapter. The latter technique uses the chapter number as a prefix in the numbering scheme. (See the illustration below.)

d. If you are using word processing software with the appropriate features, you can automatically number tables and illustrations throughout the report. You can also generate separate lists of the tables and the illustrations. The process is similar to using software to generate a table of contents (see ¶1416f).

NOTE: If you subsequently add or delete tables or illustrations, you can update this list by using the process described in ¶1416f.

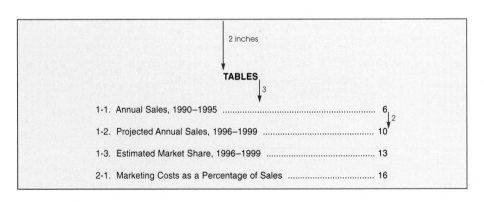

1418 Preface or Foreword

a. If a preface (written by the author) or a foreword (written by someone else) is to be provided, then on a fresh page type the appropriate title in all-capital letters (using boldface if you have that option), and center the heading on the first line below the 2-inch top margin. Note that the correct spelling is *FOREWORD* (not *FORWARD*).

NOTE: If both a preface and a foreword are to appear in the front matter, the foreword should precede the preface.

b. On the third line below the heading, begin typing the actual text. Use the same side and bottom margins as for the text pages in the body of the report (see ¶¶1404–1409). Also follow the same guidelines for spacing, indentions, and headings as in the body of the report (see ¶¶1424–1425).

c. The preface should cover the following points: (1) for whom the report is written, (2) what prompted the writing of the report, (3) what the report aims to accomplish, (4) what the report covers and what it does not try to deal with, (5) how the data and the conclusions were arrived at, and (6) acknowledgments of those individuals and organizations who helped the writer of the report.

NOTE: The acknowledgments may be treated as a separate element in the front matter, following the foreword and the preface (if both are given) and using the same format.

d. The foreword typically deals with these topics: (1) who commissioned the report, (2) the reasons for doing so, (3) the writer's qualifications for undertaking the assignment, (4) an assessment of the job that the writer has done, and (5) a call for some follow-up action on the part of those who receive copies of the report.

1419 Summary

a. If a summary (frequently called an *executive summary*) is to be provided, follow the format guidelines provided for a preface in ¶1418a–b.

b. Since this element is intended to be a time-saver, keep it short—ideally one page, at most two pages. The summary may be handled as a series of ordinary text paragraphs or as a series of paragraphs typed as items in a list (see ¶1424e–g).

1420 Numbering Front Matter Pages

a. On all pages of front matter except the title page, type a page number on the last line before the 1-inch bottom margin.

b. Type the page number in small roman numerals (*ii, iii, iv,* and so on).

c. Consider the title page as page i, even though no number is typed on that page.

d. Leave 2 blank lines above the page number, more if the text above runs short. (See ¶1406.)

NOTE: If you are using word processing software, you can direct the page numbering feature to (1) suppress the page number on the first page of the front matter and (2) insert a sequence of small roman numerals at the bottom of all the other pages in the front matter.

¶1421

The Body of Formal Reports

1421 Introduction

a. If the body of a report contains several chapters and begins with a formal introduction, treat the introduction either as Chapter 1 or as a distinct element preceding Chapter 1.

    (1) If you decide to treat it as Chapter 1, then consider *INTRODUCTION* to be the title of this chapter and handle it as you would any other title on a chapter-opening page. (See ¶1423.)

    (2) If you decide to have the introduction precede Chapter 1, then on a fresh page type *INTRODUCTION* in all-capital letters (and boldface if available), and center the heading on the first line after the 2-inch top margin. On the third line below, begin typing the actual text.

    (3) In either case treat the first page of the introduction as page 1 of the report. (See ¶1426.)

➤ *For guidelines on margins, see ¶¶1404–1409; for guidelines on spacing, indentions, and headings, see ¶¶1424–1425.*

b. If a report contains only one chapter and begins with an introductory section, treat the title *INTRODUCTION* as a first-level head (see ¶1425) and type it on the third line below the block of copy (title, etc.) at the top of the page.

1422 Part-Title Pages

a. If the report contains several chapters organized in parts, insert a separate part-title page directly in front of the chapter that begins each part.

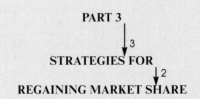

NOTE: If the body of the report begins with a formal introduction (see ¶1421a), then the part-title page for Part 1 should *follow* the introduction. (**REASON:** The introduction embraces the whole work and not simply Part 1.)

b. Type the word *PART* and the part number on one line. Underneath type the part title on one or more lines as appropriate. Use all-capital letters (and boldface if available) for emphasis, and arrange the copy for maximum display effect. Center the copy as a whole horizontally and vertically.

1423 Chapter-Opening Pages

a. Type the opening page of each chapter on a fresh page. Leave a top margin of 2 inches (12 lines on a typewriter). Begin typing on the first line below the 2-inch top margin (line 13 on a typewriter).

b. On the first line below the 2-inch top margin, center the chapter number and title in all-capital letters (and boldface if available).

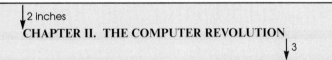

c. If the title is long, divide it into sensible phrases and arrange them on two or more single-spaced lines. Put the chapter number on a line by itself, and leave 1 blank line before starting the chapter title.

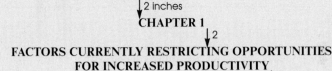

d. Begin typing the first line of copy (whether text matter or a heading) on the third line below the title.

1424 Text Spacing and Indentions

a. Text. Ordinarily, double-space all text matter. However, use single spacing or 1.5-line spacing in business reports when the costs of paper, photocopying, file space, and mailing are important considerations. (See ¶1410 for a number of ways to shorten a long report.)

➤ *For guidelines on dividing words and word groups at the ends of lines and between one page and the next, see ¶¶901–920; for guidelines on the use of footnotes, endnotes, or textnotes, see Section 15; for guidance on whether or not to justify the right margin, see ¶1356b–c.*

b. Drafts. Always double-space drafts that are to be submitted for editing or evaluation.

c. Paragraphs. Indent text paragraphs 0.5 inch (5 spaces on a typewriter). Leave 1 blank line between paragraphs, whether the text is typed with single, double, or 1.5-line spacing.

➤ *For guidelines on dividing short paragraphs at the bottom of a page, see ¶¶1407d–e and 1408c.*

d. Quoted Material. If a quotation will make four or more lines, treat it as a single-spaced extract, and leave 1 blank line above and below the extract. If you are using word processing software, use the *double indent* feature, which will indent the extract equally from each side margin. If you are using a typewriter, indent the extract 5 spaces from each side margin. If the quoted matter represents the start of a paragraph in the original, indent the first word an additional 0.5 inch (5 spaces on a typewriter).

---

1 inch (min.) →need to consider a new phenomenon in the software market. Here is an observation from Hal Pryor in a memo dated March 14: ← 1 inch (min.)
↓2

0.5 inch →We're competing in an economy where the cost of raw technology is plummeting toward zero. This plunge will 0.5 inch →drive down prices on software products as well. The only way to survive in this economy is to establish a long-term relationship with a customer, even if that means giving the first generation of a product away. ← 0.5 inch
↓2

This is a startling idea and needs to be discussed at some length in our upcoming session on pricing strategy.

14

➤ *For another illustration, see page 313.*

e. **Items in a List.** Type the list single-spaced with 1 blank line above and below the list as a whole. Either type the list on the full width of the text (as illustrated at the bottom of page 397), or indent the list equally from each side margin (as described in *d* above and illustrated below). If any item in the list requires more than one line, leave a blank line after each item in the list. If an item requires more than one line, align any turnover with the first word in the line above.

---

1 inch (min.) → The market analysis conducted by Witherspoon Associates has yielded some surprising results. For example, over 50 percent of our sales are made in low-growth markets. On that basis we need to ask: ← 1 inch (min.)
↓2

0.5 inch → Will this heavy investment in low-growth markets permit us to meet our long-range profit goals? 0.5 inch
↓2

How can we most effectively increase our sales in high-growth markets?
↓2

To what extent will domestic and international competition stymie our attempt to penetrate high-growth markets?
↓2

NOTE: Sometimes a list of one-line items (with no turnovers) is typed double-spaced to enhance the readability.

➤ *For an example, see the illustration on page 476.*

f. **Enumerated Items in a List.** If the items each begin with a number or letter, type a period after the number or letter and leave 2 spaces before typing the text that follows. Align the numbers or letters on the period. If an item requires more than one line, align any turnover with the first word in the line above.

NOTE: Either type the list on the full width of the text, or indent the list equally from each side margin. When the first line of each text paragraph is indented (as is typically done in reports), an enumerated list that falls within the text looks best indented from each margin.

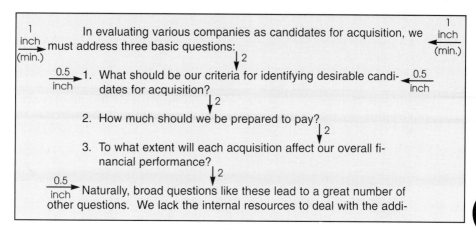

> *See ¶1357d, note, on the formatting of enumerated items in a list.*

  g. Bulleted Items in a List. Instead of numbers or letters, you can use *bullets* before the items in a list.

    (1) If you use the bullet feature of a word processing program, you can choose from a variety of styles to create bullets. For example:

      Circles: ○ ●   Triangles: ▷ ▶

      Squares: □ ■   Other characters: > → *

    The default position of the bullet is at the left margin. Set a tab wherever you want the first line of text (and any turnover lines) to begin. As a rule, leave 2 spaces between the bullet and the start of the text.

    (2) If you are using a typewriter, the simplest way to construct a bullet is to use a small letter *o.* If you want to convert a period into a centered dot, type the period one-half space above the line.

(Continued on page 398.)

h. Tables. Tables may be typed with single, double, or 1.5-line spacing. However, establish one style of spacing for all tables within a given report.

➤ *See Section 16 for a full discussion on how to plan and execute tables and for numerous illustrations.*

1425 Text Headings

Headings (or heads) are the key technique for letting readers see at a glance the scope of the writer's discussion and the way in which it is organized. Therefore, make sure that the heads used throughout the report properly reflect the coverage and the structure of the material. It is also essential that you type the heads in a way that clearly indicates different levels of importance or subordination.

Here are several techniques for achieving these objectives:

a. Try to limit yourself to three levels of text heads (not counting the chapter title). If you use more than three levels of text heads, it will be difficult for the reader to grasp the typographical distinction between one level and another. Moreover, the use of more than three levels of text heads suggests that you may be trying to cram too much into one chapter. Consider a different organization of the material to solve this problem.

NOTE: If you are using word processing software, carefully select appropriate typefaces, type sizes, attributes (such as boldface, italics, underlining, and so on), and heading style (centered head, side head, or run-in head) that clearly distinguish one level of text heading from another and the headings from the text.

b. Before preparing the final version of the report, make an outline of the heading structure as it then stands and analyze it for:

(1) *Comprehensiveness.* When the heads are viewed as a whole, do they cover all aspects of the discussion, or are some topics not properly represented?

(2) *Balance.* Is one part of a chapter loaded with heads while a comparable part has only one or two?

(3) *Parallel structure.* Are the heads all worded in a similar way, or are some complete sentences and others simply phrases? (See ¶1081.)

On the basis of this analysis, revise the heads as necessary.

NOTE: Using the outline feature of a word processing program will greatly simplify the process of reviewing and improving the wording of the heads. You can use the outline feature to generate a complete list of the heads as they currently appear in the report. Any changes in wording that you make on this list will automatically be reflected in the headings in the full text.

c. Headings come in three styles:

(1) A *centered head* is one centered on a line by itself, with 2 blank lines above (see ¶1425g for an exception) and 1 blank line below. Type it in all-capital letters, using boldface if you have that option. If the head is too long to fit on one line, center the turnover on the following line. (See ¶1425e–g for illustrations.)

(2) A *side head* starts flush with the left margin, on a line by itself. Ordinarily, it should have 2 blank lines above (see ¶1425g for an exception) and 1 blank line below. (See the illustrations in ¶1425d–g.) However, if a side head comes directly below a centered head (without any intervening text), leave only 1 blank line above the side head. (See the second row of illustrations in ¶1425e.) If you are using word processing software, type every side head in boldface, using all-capital letters or capital and small letters. If you are using a typewriter, type the side head in all-capital letters or in capital and small letters that are underlined. If the head is too long to fit on one line, type the turnover flush left on the following line.

(3) A *run-in head* (also called a *paragraph heading*) is one that begins a paragraph and is immediately followed by text matter on the same line. Like all new paragraphs, a paragraph that begins with a run-in head should be preceded by 1 blank line (whether the text is typed with single, double, or 1.5-line spacing). Indent a run-in head 0.5 inch (5 spaces on a typewriter) from the left margin. Type it in capital and small letters, using boldface, italics, or underlining. The run-in head should be followed by a period (unless some other mark of punctuation, such as a question mark, is required). The text then begins 2 spaces after the mark of punctuation. (See the illustrations in ¶1425f.)

➤ *For capitalization in headings, see ¶¶360–361, 363.*

d. In a report that calls for only *one* level of heading, choose a side heading and type it in one of the styles shown below. (See also ¶1425g.)

Computer Style   **Typewriter Style**

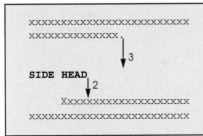

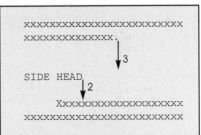

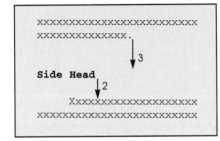

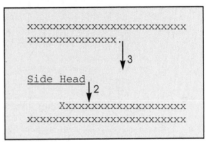

(Continued on page 400.)

e. In a report that calls for *two* levels of headings, choose one of the styles shown below. (See also ¶1425g.)

Computer Style   **Typewriter Style**

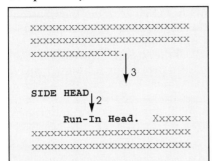
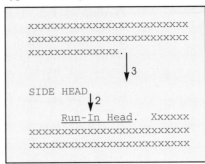

14

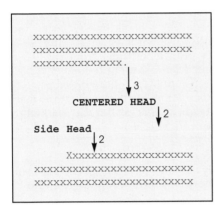
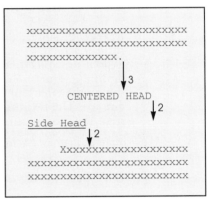

f. In a report with *three* levels of headings, choose one of the following styles. (See also ¶1425g.)

Computer Style   **Typewriter Style**

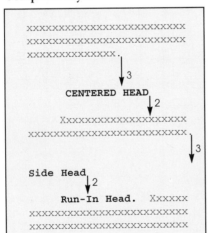
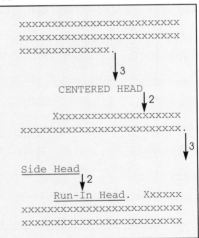

g. If the equipment you are using makes it difficult or awkward to leave 2 blank lines above centered heads and side heads, choose one of the following styles.

Computer Style

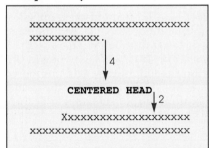

Typewriter Style

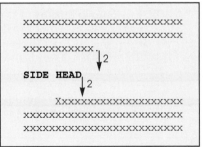

1426 Numbering Text Pages

a. If you are using the page numbering feature of word processing software, the appropriate page number will be properly positioned on each page in the correct sequence. If you later add or delete copy in a way that changes the overall length of the report, the page numbering will be automatically adjusted.

NOTE: The page numbering feature will leave only 1 blank line after a page number at the top of a page or before a page number at the bottom. However, for a better appearance you can increase this space to 2 blank lines.

b. When the first page contains the title of the report and the body starts on the same page, count this as page 1 but do not type the number on the page.

NOTE: With the page numbering feature you can easily prevent a page number from being printed, yet still have the page counted in the overall numerical sequence.

c. When the report begins with a formal title page and one or more additional pages of front matter, give these pages a separate numbering sequence, using small *roman* numerals. (See ¶1420.)

d. In a formal report, consider the first page *following* the front matter as page 1 in the *arabic* numbering sequence.

e. If part-title pages are included in the report (see ¶1422), consider them in the numbering sequence for the body of the report but do not type a number on these pages. (Thus if the first page following the front matter is the part-title page for Part I, it will count as page 1 but no number will appear.)

f. On the first page of each new element in the body or back matter of the report, center the page number on the last line before the bottom margin of 1 inch (6 lines on a typewriter). Leave 2 blank lines above the page number.

➤ *For alternative ways to end a page, see ¶¶1407–1408.*

(Continued on page 402.)

g. On all other pages in the body or back matter of the report, place the page number on the first line below the top margin of 1 inch (6 lines on a typewriter); the page number should appear at the right margin. After typing the page number, begin the first line of text on the third line below. (See ¶1406.)

h. If the final version of a report is to be printed on both sides of the paper (as in a book), the odd-numbered pages will appear on the front side of each sheet and the even-numbered pages on the back. If the report is bound, then on a spread of two facing pages, the even-numbered pages will appear on the left and the odd-numbered pages on the right. In such cases it is more convenient for the reader if the page numbers at the top or bottom of the page appear at the outside corners, as in the following illustration.

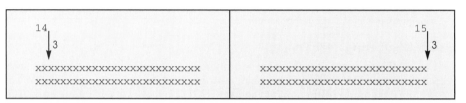

NOTE: You can direct the page numbering feature of a word processing program to alternate the placement of these page numbers in the outside corners, depending on whether the page has an odd or even number.

i. In a long report with several chapters written by different authors under a tight deadline, it may be necessary to prepare the final version of the chapters out of order. In such cases, you may use a separate sequence of page numbers for each chapter, with the chapter number serving as a prefix. Thus, for example, the pages in Chapter 1 would be numbered 1-1, 1-2, 1-3, . . .; those in Chapter 2 would be numbered 2-1, 2-2, 2-3, . . .; and so on.

NOTE: If the authors submit their material on disk, it is easy to renumber the entire report at the last minute, using one continuous sequence of numbers throughout.

The Back Matter of Formal Reports

1427 Following the last page of the body of the report are those elements of back matter that may be needed: appendixes, endnotes, bibliography, and glossary. Begin each of these elements on a fresh page. Use the same margins as for other pages in the report (see ¶¶1404–1409), and treat the numbering of these pages as discussed in ¶1426f–i.

1428 Appendixes

a. If you plan to include more than one appendix, number or letter each one in sequence. (For an example of the treatment of two appendixes, see the illustration of the table of contents on page 390.)

b. Type the word *APPENDIX* (plus a number or letter, if appropriate) and the appendix title in all-capital letters (and boldface if available), and center this element on the first line after the top margin of 2 inches (12 lines on a typewriter).

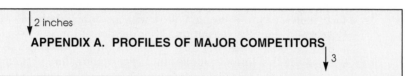

↓2 inches

APPENDIX A. PROFILES OF MAJOR COMPETITORS

↓3

NOTE: If the title is long, type it in two or more centered lines, single-spaced. Leave 1 blank line before starting the appendix title.

↓2 inches

APPENDIX A

↓2

SIGNIFICANT CHANGES IN
FEDERAL AND STATE LEGISLATION
DURING THE PAST FIVE YEARS

↓3

14

c. Leave 2 blank lines before typing the body of the appendix. Since this material may be a table, a chart, a list, or regular text, choose the format that displays this copy to best effect.

1429 Endnotes and Bibliography

For detailed guidelines on endnotes and the bibliography, see ¶¶1501–1502, 1504–1505, 1532–1536.

1430 Glossary

If you plan to provide a glossary, then on a fresh sheet type *GLOSSARY* or some other heading in all-capital letters (and boldface if available). Center this heading on the first line after the top margin of 2 inches (12 lines on a typewriter), and begin the text on the third line below. There are a variety of ways to set up a glossary.

a. Two Columns. In the left column type the terms in alphabetic order, using boldface, italics, or underlining. In the right column put the

Elliptical expression A condensed expression from which key words are omitted.

↓2

Essential elements Words, phrases, or clauses that are necessary to the completeness of the structure or the meaning of a sentence.

(Continued on page 404.)

corresponding definitions alongside. Begin the right column at least 2 spaces to the right of the longest term in the left column. Single-space each definition, and align turnover lines flush with the left margin of this column. Leave 1 blank line between entries.

b. **Hanging Indention.** Begin each term at the left margin, using boldface, italics, or underlining. Follow with a colon, a dash, or some other device and then the definition. Type the definition single-spaced, and indent turnover lines 0.5 inch (5 spaces on a typewriter) so that the term in the first line will stand out. Leave 1 blank line between entries.

---

elliptical expression: a condensed expression from which key words are
0.5 inch omitted.
↓2

essential elements: words, phrases, or clauses that are necessary to the completeness of the structure or the meaning of a sentence.

14

c. **Paragraph Style.** Indent each term 0.5 inch (5 spaces on a typewriter) from the left margin, using boldface, italics, or underlining. Follow with a colon, a dash, or some other device and then the definition. Type the definition single-spaced, with turnover lines flush with the left margin. Leave 1 blank line between entries.

0.5 inch Elliptical expression—a condensed expression from which
key words are omitted.
↓2

  Essential elements—words, phrases, or clauses that are
necessary to the completeness of the structure or the meaning
of a sentence.

NOTE: Regardless of the format selected, the terms may be typed with initial caps or all in small letters (except for proper nouns and adjectives). The definitions may also be styled either way; however, if they are written in sentence form, it is best to use initial caps for both the term and the definition. The use of periods at the end of definitions is optional unless, of course, the definitions are written as complete sentences. (See the illustration in ¶1430a for an example of the use of initial caps for both the term and the definition.)

MANUSCRIPTS

The preparation of manuscripts is subject to virtually the same considerations that apply to the preparation of reports (¶¶1401–1430). However, manuscripts differ from reports in one fundamental way: they are written with the idea of publication in mind—whether as a self-contained book, as an article in a magazine or some other printed periodical, or as an item to be included in a bulletin or newsletter. As a result, manuscripts require some special considerations concerning format.

NOTE: Some publishers now require authors to submit their manuscripts on disk as well as in the form of hard copy. Whenever possible, try to determine a publisher's manuscript submission requirements and preferences in advance.

Preparing Manuscript for an Article

1431 If you have been invited to write an article for a specific publication, ask the editor for concrete guidelines on matters of format—line length, spacing, paragraph indention, heading style, preferences in capitalization and punctuation, overall length of the article, and so on. You may also want to ask for guidance on content.

1432 If you are writing an article only with the hope that it may be accepted by a certain publication, you will enhance your chances of favorable consideration by imitating all aspects of the publication's format and style.

a. In particular, try to type your manuscript on a line length that equals an average line of copy in the finished publication. A manuscript prepared in this way will make it easy for the editor to determine how much space your article will fill in the publication. To determine the appropriate line length, copy 10 to 20 lines—on a line-for-line basis—from a representative article. Observe at what point most lines end, and set your margins accordingly.

14

b. Even if the publication puts two or more columns on a page, type only one column on a manuscript page. The wider margins will provide space for editing.

c. Type your manuscript double-spaced to allow room for editing.

d. Consistently type 25 lines of copy on a manuscript page (counting blank space above and below freestanding heads as lines of copy). In this way you and the editor can quickly calculate the total number of lines of copy.

NOTE: Be sure to keep the overall length of your manuscript within the range of the materials typically used by the intended publication. There is little point in submitting a 2000-line manuscript to a publication that carries articles of no more than 500 lines.

e. In trying to simulate the character count of a printed line on your computer or typewriter, you may have to adjust some of the normal standards for spacing and indentions. For example, leave only 1 space after periods, question marks, exclamation points, and colons (instead of the customary 2 spaces), and use only 2 or 3 spaces for paragraph indentions (instead of the usual 0.5 inch or 5 spaces).

Preparing Manuscript for a Book

If you are writing a book or assisting someone who is, consider the following guidelines in the absence of specific guidance from a publisher.

1433 If the manuscript will consist essentially of regular text matter (with perhaps a few tables and illustrations), then in establishing a format for your manuscript, you can follow the standard guidelines for a formal report with respect to spacing, headings, page numbering, and other aspects involved in typing the front matter, the body, and the back matter. Use a 6-inch line, with a left margin of 1.5 inches and a right margin of 1 inch.

(Continued on page 406.)

These margins are the same as those shown for a *bound* report in ¶1404b. A book manuscript, however, should not be bound. The 1.5-inch left margin provides extra space for editing.

1434 If you think your manuscript, when set in type, will require a special format—for example, a larger-than-usual page size to accommodate extremely wide tables or to permit notes and small illustrations to run alongside the text or to allow for a two-column arrangement of the printed text—then the easiest way to establish a format for your manuscript page is to select a published work that has the kind of format and type size you have in mind. Then, on your computer or typewriter, copy a full page of representative printed text—on a line-for-line basis, if possible—to determine the manuscript equivalent of a printed page. (If a printed line is too long to fit on one manuscript line and still leave a margin of 1.5 inches on the left side and 1 inch on the right side, choose some other typewritten format that you can readily execute.) The important thing is to determine how many pages of manuscript equal a page of printed text. Then, as you develop the manuscript, you can exercise some real control over the length of your material.

14

Precautions for All Manuscripts

1435 When sending material to a publisher, always retain a duplicate copy in case the material goes astray in the mail or the publisher calls to discuss the manuscript.

NOTE: If you have prepared your manuscript on a computer, be sure to save the file on disk. If you are subsequently asked to make changes in the manuscript, you can readily do so and then print a corrected manuscript.

1436 Your unpublished manuscript is automatically protected by the copyright law as soon as it is written, without your putting a copyright notice on it or registering it with the U.S. Copyright Office. If you are concerned that someone may copy your material without giving you appropriate credit or compensation, you may place a copyright notice on the first page *(Copyright © [current year] by [your name])* to call attention to your ownership of the material. Since the copyright law protects only the written expression of your ideas and not the ideas themselves, you should obtain the help of a lawyer if you have an original publishing idea that you are afraid may be misappropriated.

SECTION 15

Notes and Bibliographies

FOOTNOTES, ENDNOTES, AND TEXTNOTES

Functions of Notes

1501 a. In a report or manuscript, *notes* serve two functions: (1) they provide *comments* on the main text, conveying subordinate ideas that the writer feels might be distracting if incorporated within the main text; and (2) they serve as *source references,* identifying the origin of a statement quoted or cited in the text.

Comment

1. The actual date on which Governor Galloway made this statement is uncertain, but there is no doubt that the statement is his.

Source Reference

2. Bennett Harrison, *Lean and Mean: The Changing Landscape of Corporate Power in the Age of Flexibility,* Basic Books, New York, 1994, p. 39.

➤ *For a discussion of whether to type the note number on the line (as shown above) or raised slightly above the line, see ¶1523b.*

b. When notes appear at the foot of a page, they are called *footnotes.* (See ¶¶1503–1504.)

an incredible range of bloopers to be found in classified ads. One anthology

contains these gems: "Dog for sale: eats anything and is fond of children."

"Illiterate? Write today for free help." "Auto Repair Service. . . . Try us

once, you'll never go anywhere again."¹

    ↓1

——————————————

    ↓2

1. Richard Lederer, *Anguished English,* Wyrick, Charleston, S.C., 1987, p. 38.

c. When notes appear all together at the end of a complete report or manuscript (or sometimes at the end of each chapter), they are called *endnotes.* (See ¶¶1505–1506.)

2 inches

NOTES

↓3

1. Richard Lederer, *Anguished English,* Wyrick, Charleston, S.C., 1987, p. 38.

↓2

2. Ibid., pp. 39–40.

d. When source references appear parenthetically within the main text, they are called *textnotes*. (See ¶1507.)

---

but the proper use of punctuation can sometimes have serious financial consequences. Consider the following predicament.

↓ 2

0.5 inch

0.5 inch

We came upon a writer at his work . . . . Quite casually he mentioned that he was getting fifty cents a word. A moment or two later his face became contorted with signs of an internal distress. With his hand poised above the machine, he seemed to be fighting something out with himself. . . . "Listen," he said, grimly, "do you hyphenate 'willy-nilly'?" We nodded, and saw him wince as he inserted the little mark, at the cost of half a dollar. (E. B. White, "The Cost of Hyphens," *Writings From The New Yorker: 1925–1976*, Harper-Collins, New York, 1990, p. 17.)

---

e. Footnotes or endnotes are ordinarily keyed by number to a word, phrase, or sentence in the text. Textnotes (which appear parenthetically at the desired point of reference right in the text itself) do not have to be keyed this way.

f. Endnotes are growing in popularity because (1) they are easier to type and (2) they leave the text pages looking less cluttered and less complicated. They do present one drawback, however: the reader does not know in each instance whether the endnote will contain a comment of substance (which is typically worth reading) or simply a source reference (which is usually of interest only in special cases).

15

g. Textnotes are also growing in popularity for the same reasons: ease of execution and lack of clutter. While it is possible to provide in a textnote all the information that a source reference typically contains, writers more often use the textnote to provide an abbreviated reference in the text, with the understanding that the reader who wants complete information will be able to consult a bibliography at the back of the report or manuscript. (See ¶1507 for examples of these abbreviated references.)

h. If you are using the footnote feature of a word processing program, you can avoid much of the difficulty associated with the typing of footnotes. For example, the footnote feature will automatically position a footnote on the same page where the related text reference occurs. If subsequent additions or deletions in the text cause the text reference to shift to another page, the related footnote will automatically shift as well. If the footnotes are numbered in sequence, then in the event that a footnote is subsequently inserted or deleted, all the footnotes (and their related text references) will be automatically renumbered from that point on. (See the note following *i* below.)

i. If you are using the endnote feature of a word processing program, it will automatically position all endnotes at the end of the document. If you add or delete endnotes, all the endnotes (and their related text references) will be automatically renumbered from that point on.

NOTE: Some word processing programs will even format the footnotes or endnotes for the user. The program asks the user to supply the appropriate information (for example, author's name, title of publication, name of publisher, date and place of publication). The user then selects (1) one of the standard formats built into the software or (2) a format that the user has modified or created. The program then executes all the footnotes or endnotes in the chosen format. If a user is preparing a report or manuscript for different publications (each with its own style preferences for footnotes or endnotes), the user can print the document in different formats without retyping any of the material. (See also ¶1532.)

j. To take advantage of the benefits and avoid the drawbacks of these three types of notes, some writers use a hybrid system: they treat *comments* as footnotes and *source references* as endnotes or textnotes. In this way comments of substance are conveniently at hand, whereas all or most of the information about sources is tucked out of sight but accessible when needed. (See ¶1502g.)

Text References to Footnotes or Endnotes

1502 a. To indicate the presence of a comment or a source reference at the bottom of the page or in a special section at the end of the report or manuscript, insert a *superscript* (raised) figure following the appropriate word, phrase, or sentence in the text. (See ¶1502b for examples.)

NOTE: If you are using the footnote or endnote feature of a word processing program, you can easily execute superscript figures. If you are using a typewriter, you can create a superscript figure by typing the figure a half space above the line. If your equipment will not execute superscript figures easily, you can use the on-the-line style shown in ¶1502h.

b. Do not leave any space between the superscript figure and the preceding word. If a punctuation mark follows the word, place the superscript figure immediately after the punctuation mark. (There is one exception: the superscript figure should precede, not follow, a dash.)

A research study published last month by a leading relocation consulting firm[2] provides the basis for the recommendations offered in Chapter 5.

The alternative approaches discussed in this report have been taken largely from an article entitled "Getting a Handle on Health Care Costs."[1]

An article entitled "Getting a Handle on Health Care Costs"[1]—written by an eminent authority in the field—was the source of the alternative approaches discussed in this report.

c. While the superscript figure should come as close as possible to the appropriate word or phrase, it is often better to place the superscript figure at the end of the sentence (if this will cause no misunderstanding) so as to avoid distracting the reader in the midst of the sentence.

ACCEPTABLE: Her latest article, "Automating the Small Legal Office,"[1] was published about three months ago. I urge you to read it.

PREFERABLE: Her latest article, "Automating the Small Legal Office," was published about three months ago.[1] I urge you to read it.

NOTE: Leave 2 spaces after a superscript figure that follows the punctuation at the end of a sentence.

d. When a paragraph calls for two or more footnotes or endnotes, try to combine all the necessary information within one note if this can be done without any risk of confusing the reader. This approach will reduce the sense of irritation that a large number of footnotes or endnotes tend to produce.

NOTE: When this approach is used, the superscript figure is typically placed after the last word in the sentence or paragraph, depending on how the text references are dispersed.

AVOID: The following analysis draws heavily on recent studies undertaken by Andrew Bowen,[1] Frances Kaplan,[2] and Minetta Coleman.[3]

---

    1.   Andrew Bowen, . . .

    2.   Frances Kaplan, . . .

    3.   Minetta Coleman, . . .

PREFERABLE: The following analysis draws heavily on recent studies undertaken by Andrew Bowen, Frances Kaplan, and Minetta Coleman.[1]

---

1.   Andrew Bowen, . . .; Frances Kaplan, . . .; and Minetta Coleman, ...

e. The numbering of footnotes or endnotes may run consecutively throughout or begin again with each new chapter.

f. Footnotes and endnotes are sometimes keyed by symbol rather than by number. This often occurs in tables with figures and in technical material with many formulas, where a raised figure—though intended to refer to a footnote or endnote—could be mistaken for part of the table text or the formula. When the use of symbols is appropriate, choose one of the following sequences: *, **, ***, etc.; *, †, ‡, §, ¶; or *a, b, c, d, e*, etc. (in italics if you have that option).

These tests confirmed that there was a reduction over time of the flexural strength of the marble unit from 1400 to 1200 lb/in^2.**

(**NOT:** These tests confirmed that there was a reduction over time of the flexural strength of the marble unit from 1400 to 1200 lb/in^2.^{2})

NOTE: If you are using software with special character sets, you may access such symbols as †, ‡, §, and ¶. Otherwise, you will have to insert them by hand.

g. If you wish to treat *comments* as footnotes and *source references* as endnotes (as suggested in ¶1501j), use *symbols* for the notes containing comments and use *figures* for the notes containing source references.

h. While the use of *superscript* figures in the text is the style most commonly seen in business and academic reports, manuscripts, and published materials, use an on-the-line style if your equipment cannot readily execute superscript figures. Follow these guidelines:

(1) Enclose the figure in brackets (preferred style) or in parentheses.

(2) Try to position the figure so that it *follows* the end of a sentence or, better yet, the end of a paragraph. Leave 1 space before the opening bracket or parenthesis; leave 2 spaces after the closing bracket or parenthesis if a new sentence begins on the same line.

   . . . is "the age of instability." [1]   He goes on . . .

(Continued on page 412.)

(3) If the figure has to go *within* a sentence, leave 1 space before the opening bracket or parenthesis and 1 space after the closing bracket or parenthesis. Try to place the enclosed figure so that it is not next to any other mark of sentence punctuation; otherwise, a cluttered and possibly confusing situation could result. Do not use a figure enclosed in parentheses within a sentence where it could be mistaken for part of an enumeration.

Footnotes

1503 When you execute footnotes using the footnote feature of a word processing program, the software will automatically position your footnotes at the bottom of the page where the footnote reference appears in the text. The software will also (1) insert a horizontal line to separate the footnotes from the text above, (2) continue a footnote on the following page if it is too long to fit as a whole on the page where it started, and (3) automatically number your footnotes (and even renumber them if you should add or delete footnotes later on). Here is how a footnote would be executed if you use the footnote feature of WordPerfect 6 for Windows:

15

into the new century.[1] According to one source: ↓ 2

The *Internet*—also known as the Net—is the world's largest computer *network*, or *net*. "So what?" you're probably saying. "I once saw the world's largest turnip on TV, and it didn't look very interesting—and I bet it didn't taste so great, either." Well, with networks, unlike vegetables, size counts for a lot, because the larger a network is, the more stuff it has to offer.[2]

0.5 inch   0.5 inch

[1]For a detailed analysis of these technological developments, see Chapter 2, pp. 29–38.

[2]John R. Levine and Carol Baroudi, *The Internet for Dummies*, IDG Books, San Mateo, Calif., 1993, p. 7.

NOTE: You can easily change the default specifications to satisfy your own preferences. (See ¶1504.)

1504 To create your own format for footnotes, consider the following guidelines. (See the illustration on page 413.)

a. Insert an underline 2 inches long to separate footnote material from the main text above. Position the underline 1 line below the last line of text, starting at the left margin.

NOTE: If the text runs short on a page (say, the last page of a chapter), any footnotes related to that text must still be positioned at the *foot* of the page. In that case estimate the number of lines the footnote will occupy, and determine on which line the footnote material should begin in order to end at the foot of the page. Then insert the underline on the second line above the line on which the footnote material should begin.

---

into the next century.[1] According to one source:

↓ 2

    The *Internet*—also known as the Net—is the world's largest
computer *network*, or *net*. "So what?" you're probably saying.
"I once saw the world's largest turnip on TV, and it didn't look
very interesting—and I bet it didn't taste so great, either."
Well, with networks, unlike vegetables, size counts for a lot,
because the larger a network is, the more stuff it has to offer.[2]

0.5 inch

0.5 inch

↓ 1

↓ 2

    1. For a more detailed analysis of these technological developments, see Chapter 2, pp. 29–38.

↓ 2

    2. John R. Levine and Carol Baroudi, *The Internet for Dummies*, IDG Books, San Mateo, Calif., 1993, p. 7.

---

b. Start the first footnote on the second line below the underline.

➤ *For guidelines on how to construct source reference footnotes, see ¶¶1508–1531.*

c. Ordinarily, single-space each footnote, but in material that is to be edited, use double spacing to allow room for the editing. In either case leave 1 blank line between footnotes.

d. Indent the first line of each footnote 0.5 inch (5 spaces on a typewriter). Type the footnote number on the line or as a superscript figure. (See ¶1523b for details on spacing and punctuation.) If you are using the on-the-line style, align all footnote numbers on the period. Start any turnover lines within the same footnote at the left margin.

e. As a rule, allow three to four lines for each source reference footnote; this estimate allows for space above and below each footnote. Footnotes that contain comments may run longer. Remember that on pages with a page number in the upper right corner, the last line of copy (whether text or footnote) should be positioned so as to leave a minimum bottom margin of 1 inch. On pages where the page number falls at the bottom of the page, the last line of text or footnote should be positioned so as to leave at least 2 blank lines above the page number.

➤ *For additional details on ending pages, see ¶¶1407–1408.*

f. Ideally, the *complete* footnote should appear on the same page as the superscript figure or symbol that refers to it. Occasionally, however, a footnote may be so long that it will not all fit on the page, even if it begins immediately following the line of text in which the superscript figure or symbol occurs. In such a case follow the procedure described on page 414.

(Continued on page 414.)

15

(1) Once you have completed the line of text in which the footnote reference occurs, type a 2-inch underline on the following line (see ¶1504a).

(2) If the long footnote is the only footnote on the page, start it on the second line below the underline (as directed in ¶1504b–e). If other footnotes come before this long one on the page, begin the long one on the second line below the preceding footnote.

Starting a Long Footnote

a problem for businesswomen who continue to work after they marry.[2]

    ↓ 2

    1. Letitia Baldrige, *Letitia Baldrige's Complete Guide to the New Manners for the '90s*, Rawson, New York, 1990, p. 591.

    ↓ 2

    2. Judith Martin (in *Miss Manners' Guide for the Turn-of-the-Millennium*, Simon & Schuster, 1990, pp. 57–59) offers this advice to the "conservative" businesswoman who is wondering whether or not to adopt her husband's surname for business purposes: "At work, she is known by her original surname, or the one under which she happened to make her professional reputation (which might be the name of a previous husband—conservativeness does not guarantee prudence), and

15

(3) Type as much of the footnote on the page as possible. Try to end at a point that is obviously incomplete so that the reader will realize the footnote runs on to the next page. If that is not possible, you may need to insert a continuation line—for example, *Footnote continued on next page*—typed within parentheses or brackets and positioned at the right margin on the line directly below the last line of the footnote.

(4) At the top of the next page, resume typing the text (along with any needed text references to further footnotes), but plan to end the text at a point that leaves enough space to (a) finish the footnote carried over from the preceding page and (b) insert any new footnotes called for in the text above.

Continuing a Long Footnote on the Next Page

on which there still is a considerable difference of opinion.[3]

    ↓ 2

is addressed as 'Ms.' This form meets Miss Manners' standard of old-fashioned propriety for married, single, or divorced ladies."

    ↓ 2

    3. Baldrige, p. 593.

NOTE: If you expect to encounter a number of long notes that may not easily fit on the page where they are first referred to, you have an excellent reason for abandoning the footnote format and using endnotes instead. (See ¶¶1505–1506.)

➤ *For the treatment of footnotes that pertain to a table, see ¶¶1634–1636.*

Endnotes

1505 Some word processing programs may provide a default format for endnotes. Here is how endnotes would be executed if you use the endnote feature of WordPerfect 6 for Windows:

---

at KPMG Peat Marwick in Washington. To avoid gains from interest on bank deposits, consider investing that cash in Treasury bills or in short-term certificates of deposit that don't mature until next year.[2]
1."Planning Now Can Make April Less Taxing," *Business Week*, December 5, 1994, p. 112.

2.Ibid.

15

a. If you want your endnotes to start on a new page, be sure to insert a hard page break after the last line of text in the report or manuscript. (Otherwise, the endnotes may begin on the same page, on the line following the end of the text, as shown above.)

b. If you want your endnotes to be preceded by a head, type *NOTES* in all-capital boldface letters, centered on the first line below the 2-inch top margin.

c. If you do not want each entry to start at the left margin (as shown above), indent the first line 0.5 inch.

d. Leave 2 spaces after the period that follows each endnote number. Align all numbers on the period.

NOTE: You can easily modify the default format for endnotes to suit your preferences. (See ¶1506.)

1506 To create your own format for endnotes, consider the following guidelines. (See the illustration on page 416.)

a. On a fresh page type *NOTES* in all-capital letters (and boldface if available). Center this title on the first line after the top margin of 2 inches (12 lines on a typewriter), and begin the text on the third line below.

b. Ordinarily, single-space each endnote, but in material that is to be edited, use double spacing to allow room for the editing. In either case leave 1 blank line between endnotes.

(Continued on page 416.)

c. Indent the first line of each endnote 0.5 inch (5 spaces on a type-writer), and start any additional lines within the same endnote at the left margin.

d. Type the identifying number for each endnote on the line, not in a raised position. (See also ¶1523b.) Leave 2 spaces after the period that follows the number.

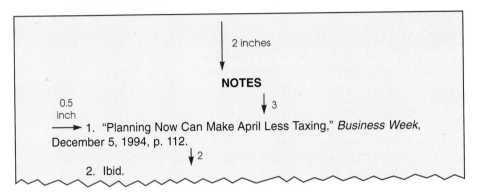

e. Use the same margins as for other pages in the body of the report or manuscript (see ¶¶1404–1408), and treat the numbering of these pages as shown in ¶1426f–g.

➤ *For guidelines on how to construct source reference endnotes, see ¶¶ 1508–1531.*

f. If the numbering of endnotes starts again with each new chapter or on each new page, insert an appropriate heading—*Chapter 1, Chapter 2,* etc., or *Page 1, Page 2,* etc.—over each sequence of endnotes in this section. Type the heading at the left margin in capital and small letters (using boldface, italics, or underlining), and leave 2 blank lines above and 1 blank line below.

NOTE: If the numbering of endnotes is consecutive throughout, no headings are needed.

g. Insert this special section of endnotes in the back matter following any appendixes. If no appendix is given, the endnotes begin the back matter. (See also ¶1427.)

NOTE: When individual chapters of a report or a manuscript are prepared by different writers, it may be advantageous to have the endnotes that each author prepares inserted at the end of the respective chapter instead of redoing all the endnotes as one continuous section in the back matter. If this approach is used, expand the heading *NOTES* in each case to read *NOTES TO CHAPTER 1, NOTES TO CHAPTER 2,* and so on. The disadvantage of this approach is that the reader will have a bit more difficulty locating the notes for each chapter than is true when all the endnotes are presented in one section at the very end.

Textnotes

1507 a. In a report or manuscript with only a few source references and no bibliography at the end, the complete source data may be inserted within the text in the form of parenthetical textnotes. (See the illustration at the top of the next page.)

recommended by the U.S. Postal Service. As for the abbreviations devised to hold down the length of place names in addresses, here is what one authority had to say:

> And all you people with beautiful words in your addresses: Cut 'em down. There's a bright golden haze on the MDWS; a fairy dancing in your GDNS; and a safe HBR past the happy LNDG at the XING, where no hope SPGS. Environmentalists are now GRN, as in how GRN was my VLY. . . . Is the language not lessened when words like *meadow, gardens, harbor, landing, crossing, green, valley*—even *islands (ISS)*—are disemvoweled? (William Safire, *In Love With Norma Loquendi*, Random House, New York, 1994, p. 166.)

➤ *For guidelines on how to construct source reference textnotes, see ¶¶1508–1531.*

NOTE: If some of the data called for in a source reference is already provided in the main text, there is no need to repeat it in the textnote.

recommended by the U.S. Postal Service. As for the abbreviations devised to hold down the length of place names in addresses, here is what William Safire had to say:

> And all you people with beautiful words in your addresses: Cut 'em down. There's a bright golden haze on the MDWS; a fairy dancing in your GDNS; and a safe HBR past the happy LNDG at the XING, where no hope SPGS. Environmentalists are now GRN, as in how GRN was my VLY. . . . Is the language not lessened when words like *meadow, gardens, harbor, landing, crossing, green, valley*—even *islands (ISS)*—are disemvoweled? (*In Love With Norma Loquendi*, Random House, New York, 1994, p. 166.)

15

b. In a report or manuscript that contains a number of source references *and* a complete bibliography, textnotes may be used as follows:

(1) At the appropriate point in the main text, supply the author's last name and the appropriate page number in parentheses. The reader who wants more complete information can consult the full entry in the bibliography.

According to a fine book on time management (Bittel, p. 27), your ability to manage time depends in part on the way you experience the passage of time.

NOTE: Some authorities omit *p.* and *pp.* as well as the comma between the name and the page number. For example:

. . . book on time management (Bittel 27) . . .

(2) If the author's name already appears in the main text, give only the page number in parentheses.

Lester R. Bittel, in his fine book *Right on Time!* (p. 27), says that . . .

(Continued on page 418.)

(3) If the bibliography lists more than one publication by the same author, then in the textnote use an abbreviated title or the year of publication to indicate which publication is being referred to.

> According to a fine book on time management (Bittel, *Time*, p. 27), . . .
>
> **OR:** . . . a fine book on time management (Bittel, 1991, p. 27), . . .

(4) If the bibliography lists publications by two or more authors with the same surname, use each author's first name or initial along with the surname.

> According to a fine book on time management (L. Bittel, p. 27), . . .

(5) If the entries in the bibliography are numbered in sequence (see ¶1534c), then the textnote can simply list the appropriate "entry number" along with the page reference. Italicize or underline the entry number to distinguish it from the page number, especially if the abbreviation *p.* or *pp.* is omitted.

> According to a fine book . . . (*18*, p. 27), . . . **OR** (18, p. 27), . . .

Constructing Source Reference Notes

The following guidelines for constructing source reference notes deal with the situations that most commonly occur—whether in the form of footnotes, endnotes, or the type of textnote discussed in ¶1507. There is no clear-cut agreement among authorities on how these notes should be constructed; rather, there are several schools of thought on the subject, and within each school there are variations between one reference manual and another.

Of all the well-established conventions and variations, the style best suited for business use—and the one presented here—is a style that employs the simplest punctuation and the most straightforward presentation of the necessary data without any sacrifice in clarity or completeness. However, certain professional organizations—for example, the American Psychological Association, the American Medical Association, and the American Chemical Society—have each established a distinctive style, the use of which sometimes shows up in other fields. Moreover, slightly different patterns are often used in academic materials, such as those featured in *The MLA [Modern Language Association] Style Manual.* If you are one of the many full-time business workers who are simultaneously taking one or more academic courses or one of the many full-time academic students who are concurrently holding down part- or full-time office jobs, you may need to familiarize yourself with more than one style. Note that along with the basic pattern for citing book titles (see ¶1508), you will find an "academic" variation that you may need to use from time to time. However, unless you are specifically directed to follow a particular style, the following "all-purpose" patterns—based on well-established conventions—should meet your needs in virtually every type of situation you encounter.

NOTE: For detailed information about specific elements within these patterns, see the following paragraphs:

> ➤ *Note number: see ¶1523.*   *Place of publication: see ¶1527.*
> *Names of authors: see ¶1524.*   *Date of publication: see ¶1528.*
> *Title of the work: see ¶1525.*   *Page numbers: see ¶1529.*
> *Publisher's name: see ¶1526.*   *Subsequent references: see ¶¶1530–1531.*

1508 Book Title: Basic Pattern

a. Business Style

1. Author, *book title*, publisher, place of publication, year of publication, page number [if reference is being made to a specific page].

1. Michael Heim, *The Metaphysics of Virtual Reality*, Oxford Univ. Press, New York, 1993, p. 43.

OR

1. Michael Heim, The Metaphysics of Virtual Reality, Oxford Univ. Press, New York, 1993, p. 43.
(If your equipment cannot print italic type, underline any element that is shown in italics in these patterns.)

NOTE: If any of these elements have already been identified in the text (for example, the author's name and the book title), they need not be repeated in the note. Moreover, if reference is made to the book as a whole rather than to a particular page, omit the page number. In the following illustration, observe that the quoted material requires more than three lines. For that reason, it is indented 0.5 inch (5 spaces on a typewriter) from each side margin. (See ¶1424d.)

in the recent revolution. According to Michael Heim, in his provocative book *The Metaphysics of Virtual Reality:*

0.5 inch

One aspect of the new reality is a powerful feedback mechanism that now undergirds our culture. The media today draw on worldwide computer links, speeding up communications by radio, newspapers, and television. Computer networks have sprung up to form a giant web for human exchange. Ideas fly back and forth, circling the globe at the speed of electricity. This new electric language forms an instant feedback loop, the likes of which have never before existed.[1]

0.5 inch   0.5 inch

1. Oxford Univ. Press, New York, 1993, p. x.

15

b. Academic Style

1. Author, *book title* (place of publication: publisher, year of publication), page number [if reference is being made to a specific page].

1. Michael Heim, *The Metaphysics of Virtual Reality* (New York: Oxford Univ. Press, 1993), p. 43.
(In endnotes, the note number is typed on the line; in academic-style footnotes, the note number is typically typed above the line. See ¶1523b.)

(Continued on page 420.)

NOTE: The key distinction between the business style and the academic style lies in a slightly different sequence of elements and a slightly different form of punctuation:

BUSINESS STYLE: ... publisher, place of publication, year of publication ...

ACADEMIC STYLE: ... (place of publication: publisher, year of publication) ...

The following patterns for books (in ¶¶1509–1516) show only the business style. However, you can readily convert them to the academic style by simply changing the treatment of these three elements.

➤ *For the academic style for entries in bibliographies, see ¶1536c.*

1509 Book Title: With Edition Number

1. Author, *book title*, edition number [if not the first edition], publisher, place, year, page number.

   1. Norma Carr-Ruffino, *The Promotional Woman: Advancing Through Leadership Skills*, 2d ed., Wadsworth, Belmont, Calif., 1993, p. 250.

NOTE: Use an edition number only when the book is not in the first edition. If included, the edition number follows the main title and any related elements, such as the subtitle or the volume number and title. (For an example, see ¶1511.) The following abbreviated forms are commonly used: *2d ed., 3d ed., 4th ed.,* and *rev. ed.* (for "revised edition").

15

1510 Book Title: With Subtitle

1. Author, *book title: subtitle*, edition number [if not the first edition], publisher, place, year, page number.

   1. Gene Marcial, *Secrets of the Streets: The Dark Side of Making Money*, McGraw-Hill, New York, 1995, p. 55.

   2. Al Ries and Jack Trout, *Positioning: The Battle for Your Mind*, 1st ed. rev., McGraw-Hill, New York, 1986, p. 46.

NOTE: Do not give the subtitle of a book unless it is significant in identifying the book or in explaining its basic nature. If a subtitle is to be shown, separate it from the main title with a colon (unless the title page shows some other mark such as a dash). If you are using italic type, italicize the main title and the subtitle. Otherwise, type an underline (without a break) from the start of the main title to the end of the subtitle. Capitalize the first word of the subtitle, even if it is a short preposition like *for*, a short conjunction like *or*, or an article like *the* or *a*. (See ¶361.)

   3. Woody Leonhard, CD-MOM: The Mother of All Windows Packages, Addison-Wesley, Reading, Mass., 1993, p. 73.

1511 Book Title: With Volume Number and Volume Title

1. Author, *book title*, volume number, *volume title*, edition number [if not the first edition], publisher, place, year, page number.

   1. E. Lipson, *The Economic History of England*, Vol. 1, *The Middle Ages*, 12th ed., Adam & Charles Black, London, 1959, pp. 511–594.

NOTE: As a rule, do not show the volume title in a note unless it is significant in identifying the book. When the volume title is included, both the volume number and the volume title follow the book title (and subtitle, if any) but precede the edition number. The volume number is usually preceded by the abbreviation *Vol.* or by the word *Book* or *Part* (depending on the actual designation). The volume number may be arabic or roman, depending on the style used in the actual book. Some writers prefer to use one style of volume number throughout the notes. (See also ¶1512.)

1512 Book Title: With Volume Number Alone

1. Author, *book title,* edition number [if not the first edition], publisher, place, year, volume number, page number.

1. Ruth Barnes Moynihan et al. (eds.), *Second to None: A Documentary History of American Women,* Univ. of Nebraska Press, Lincoln, 1994, Vol. I, p. 146.

➤ *For the use of* et al., *see* ¶*1524c; for the use of* eds., *see* ¶*1524e.*

NOTE: When the volume number is shown without the volume title, it follows the date of publication. When the volume number and page number occur one after the other, they may be styled as follows:

Style for Roman Volume Number	**Style for Arabic Volume Number**
Vol. III, p. 197 **OR** III, 197	Vol. 5, pp. 681–684 **OR** 5:681–684

1. Ruth Barnes Moynihan et al. (eds.), *Second to None: A Documentary History of American Women,* Univ. of Nebraska Press, Lincoln, 1994, I, 146.

Do not use the forms with figures alone if there is a chance your reader will not understand them.

1513 Book Title: With Chapter Reference

1. Author, *book title,* publisher, place, year, chapter number, "chapter title" [if significant], page number.

1. Will Durant and Ariel Durant, *The Age of Napoleon,* Simon & Schuster, New York, 1975, Chap. XII, "Napoleon and the Arts," pp. 278-285.

NOTE: When a note refers primarily to the title of a book, a chapter number and a chapter title are not usually included. If they are considered significant, however, these details can be inserted just before the page numbers. The word *chapter* is usually abbreviated as *Chap.,* the chapter number is arabic or roman (depending on the original), and the chapter title is enclosed in quotation marks. Some writers prefer to use one style of chapter number throughout the notes.

1514 Selection From Collected Works of One Author

1. Author, "title of selection," *book title,* publisher, place, year, page number.

1. E. Annie Proulx, "The Unclouded Day," *Heart Songs and Other Stories,* Scribner, New York, 1995, pp. 105-118.

1515 Selection in Anthology

1. Author of selection, "title of selection," **in** editor of anthology (**ed.**), *book title,* publisher, place, year, page number.

1. Wendy C. Handler, "The Family Venture," in William A. Sahlman and Howard A. Stevenson (eds.), *The Entreprenurial Venture,* Harvard Business School Press, Boston, 1992, pp. 311-321.

2. Alexandra David-Neel, "Entering the Forbidden City (1924)," in Robin Hanbury-Tehison (ed.), *The Oxford Book of Exploration,* Oxford Univ. Press, New York, 1993, p. 210.

3. E. B. White, "The Ring of Time," in Phillip Lopate (ed.), *The Art of the Personal Essay: An Anthology From the Classical Era to the Present,* Doubleday, New York, 1994, pp. 538-544.

4. Lindsy Van Gelder, "The Great Person-Hole Cover Debate: A Modest Proposal for Anyone Who Thinks the Word 'He' Is Just Plain Easier," in *75 Readings: An Anthology,* 2d ed., McGraw-Hill, New York, 1989, pp. 347-349.

15 1516 Article in Reference Work

1. Author [if known], "article title," *name of reference work,* edition number [if not the first edition], publisher [usually omitted], place [usually omitted], year, page number [may be omitted].

1. Joel Cracraft, "Animal Systematics," *McGraw-Hill Encyclopedia of Science and Technology,* 8th ed., 1997.

2. "Word Processing," *Encyclopedia Americana,* International Edition, 1994.

3. "Shange, Ntozake," *The Writers Directory,* 11th ed., St. James Press, Detroit, 1994.

4. "Computer-Aided Manufacturing (CAM)," *The Portable MBA Desk Reference,* Wiley, New York, 1994, p. 107.

NOTE: It is not necessary to give the name of the publisher or the place of publication unless there is some possibility of confusion or the reference is not well known.

5. *Merriam-Webster's Collegiate Dictionary,* 10th ed., 1993, pp. 23a-30a.

6. *The American Heritage Dictionary of the English Language,* 3d ed., 1992, pp. xxvi-xxx.

Moreover, if you are making reference to an article or an entry that appears in alphabetic order in the main portion of the work, even the page number may be omitted. If the reference work carries the name of an editor rather than an author, the editor's name is also usually omitted.

7. "Data Processing," *The Columbia Encyclopedia,* 5th ed., 1993.

1517 Article in Newspaper

> 1. Author [if known], "article title," *name of newspaper*, date, page number, column number.

> 1. Andrew Barry, "Too Late?" *Barron's*, October 31, 1994, p. 15, cols. 1-4.

> 2. Bob Donath, "Where Was I When the Page Was Blank?" *Marketing News*, October 10, 1994, p. 13, cols. 1-2.

➤ *See ¶1518, note.*

NOTE: If a particular issue of a newspaper is published in several sections and the page numbering begins anew with each section, include the section letter or number before the page number.

> 3. Deirdre Carmody, "Writers Fight for Electronic Rights," *The New York Times*, November 7, 1994, Sec. B, p. 20, cols. 4-6.

> **OR:** . . . November 7, 1994, p. B20, cols. 4-6.

1518 Article in Magazine or Journal

a. Article in Magazine

> 1. Author [if known], "article title," *name of magazine*, date, page number.

> 1. "Guilt-Free Guide to Garbage," *Consumer Reports*, February 1994, pp. 91-113.

> 2. Chris Sandlung and Liesl Lagrange, "CD-ROM in Overdrive," *PC Computing*, November 1994, pp. 138-152.

> 3. Herb Chong, "Keep Users Outta Your .INIs," *Windows Sources*, November 1994, p. 173.

> 4. Christina F. Watts, "Home Is Where the Business Is," *Black Enterprise*, November 1994, pp. 129-138.

NOTE: Omit the comma between the article title and the name of the periodical if the article title ends with a question mark or an exclamation point.

> 5. Phyllis Berman with Lisa Sanders, "Who's Bluffing?" *Forbes*, July 18, 1994, p. 44.

> 6. Mary L. Sprouse, "Investor's Tax Alert!" *Money*, December 1994, pp. 146-153.

➤ *See also the first two examples in ¶1517.*

b. Article in Professional Journal

> 1. Author, "article title," *title of journal* [frequently abbreviated], series number [if given], volume number, issue number [if given], date, page number.

> 7. Anne G. Perkins, "Women in the Workplace: The Ripple Effect," *Harvard Business Review*, Vol. 72, No. 6, November-December 1994, p. 15.

(Continued on page 424.)

NOTE: Titles of journals are often abbreviated in notes whenever these abbreviations are likely to be familiar to the intended readership or are clearly identified in a bibliography at the end.

>   7. Anne G. Perkins, "Women in the Workplace: The Ripple Effect," *HBR*, Vol. 72, No. 6, November–December 1994, p. 15.

1519 Quotation From a CD-ROM

1. Author [if known], "article title" [if appropriate], *title of work* (**CD-ROM**), publisher [may be omitted], place of publication [may be omitted], year of publication, reference to location of quotation [if available].

>   1. "Jupiter," *McGraw-Hill Multimedia Encyclopedia of Science and Technology* (CD-ROM), 1994.

>   2. *The Mayo Clinic Family Health Book, Interactive Edition* (CD-ROM), IVI Publishing, 1993.

>   3. *Mutual Funds Online* (CD-ROM), Morningstar, December 1995.

NOTE: When citing material taken from a CD-ROM, try to provide some specific guidance on how to access the quoted passage on the disk. For example, if the material is organized in numbered paragraphs or pages, give the appropriate paragraph or page number. If the quoted passage is taken from a work organized like an encyclopedia or a dictionary (that is, in the form of brief articles or entries organized in alphabetic sequence), provide the article title or key word used to identify the article or entry. Without such assistance, a person can usually input a key phrase (or character string) from the quoted material and use the search feature of a word processing program to locate the complete passage.

1520 Bulletin, Pamphlet, or Monograph

1. Author [if given], "article title" [if appropriate], *title of bulletin,* series title and series number [if appropriate], volume number and issue number [if appropriate], sponsoring organization, place [may be omitted], date, page number.

>   1. Carolena L. Lyons-Smith and Richard A. Hatch, "Selection of an Integrated Software Package for the Business Communication Course," *The Bulletin of the Association for Business Communication,* Vol. LIV, No. 2, June 1991, p. 32. (The name of the sponsoring organization has not been listed separately because it is incorporated in the title of the bulletin.)

>   2. "Appropriations Fiscal Year 1992," *ALA Washington Newsletter,* Vol. 43, No. 6, American Library Association, Washington, June 27, 1991, p. 1. (The name of the sponsoring organization can be omitted from this note if you are sure your reader will understand that *ALA* in the bulletin title refers to the American Library Association.)

NOTE: Because the pertinent data used to identify bulletins, pamphlets, and monographs may vary widely, adapt the pattern shown above as necessary to fit each particular situation.

1521 Unpublished Dissertation or Thesis

> 1. Author, "title of thesis," **doctoral dissertation OR master's thesis** [identifying phrase to be inserted], name of academic institution, place, date, page number.

> 1. David Clement Dvorak, "The Education Designed for Gainful Employment (EDGE) Program: An Analysis of Local Implementation," doctoral dissertation, Michigan State University, East Lansing, 1994, p. 169.

1522 Quotation From a Secondary Source

> 1. Author, *book title*, publisher, place, date, page number, **quoted by** author, *book title*, publisher, place, date, page number.

> 1. Mary Catherine Bateson, *Composing a Life*, Penguin, New York, 1990, p. 184, quoted by William Bridges, *Job-Shift: How to Prosper in a Workplace Without Jobs*, Addison-Wesley, Reading, Mass., 1994, p. 117.

> 2. *Business Week*, May 1, 1989, pp. 87–95, cited by George T. Milkovich and Bonnie R. Rabin, "Executive Compensation and Firm Performance," in Fred K. Foukes (ed.), *Executive Compensation: A Strategic Guide for the 1990s*, Harvard Business School Press, Boston, 1991.

NOTE: While it is always preferable to take the wording of a quotation from the original source, it is sometimes necessary to draw the wording from a secondary source. In such cases construct the note in two parts: in the first part, give as much information as possible about the *original* source (derived, of course, from the reference note in the secondary source); in the second part, give the necessary information about the *secondary* source (which is at hand). Bridge the two parts of the note with a phrase such as *quoted by* or *cited by*. The pattern shown above assumes that the quotation originally appeared in a book and that the secondary source for the quoted material was also a book. Naturally, if the original source or the secondary source is a work other than a book, use the pattern appropriate for that work.

Elements of Source Reference Notes

1523 Note Number

a. Make sure that the number at the start of a footnote or an endnote corresponds to the appropriate reference number in the text.

b. Indent the note number 0.5 inch (5 spaces on a typewriter), and type it (1) on the line (like an ordinary number), followed by a period and 2 spaces, or (2) as a superscript (raised) figure without any space following it. The on-the-line style is always used in endnotes. (See ¶¶1504–1505.)

> 1. Douglas Rushkoff, *Media Virus! Hidden Agendas in Popular Culture*, Ballantine, New York, 1994, p. 146.

OR:

> [1]Douglas Rushkoff, *Media Virus! Hidden Agendas in Popular Culture*, Ballantine, New York, 1994, p. 146.

➤ *See ¶1502e on numbering notes; ¶1502f–g on the use of symbols in place of figures.*

1524 Names of Authors

a. Type an author's name (first name first) exactly as it appears on the title page of a book or in the heading of an article. (See ¶1508a, note.)

> 1. William A. Henry III, *In Defense of Elitism,* Doubleday, New York, 1994, p. 23.

> 2. William Strunk Jr. and E. B. White, *The Elements of Style,* 3d ed., Macmillan, New York, 1979, pp. 32-33.

> 3. J. Robin Powell with Holly George-Warren, *The Working Woman's Guide to Managing Stress,* Prentice-Hall, Englewood Cliffs, N.J., 1994, p. 111.

> 4. John A. Byrne with a team of *Business Week* editors, *Business Week's Guide to the Best Business Schools,* 4th ed., McGraw-Hill, New York, 1995, p. 67.

b. When two authors have the same surname, show the surname with each author's listing.

> 5. Nancy Baker Wise and Christy Wise, *A Mouthful of Rivets: Women at Work in World War II,* Jossey-Bass, San Francisco, 1994, p. 153.

c. When there are three or more authors, list only the first author's name followed by *et al.* (meaning ''and others''). Do not italicize or underline *et al.*

> 6. Linda Witt et al., *Running as a Woman: Gender and Power in American Politics,* Macmillan, New York, 1994, pp. 100-103.

NOTE: The names of all the authors may be given, but once this style is used in a source reference note, it should be used consistently.

> 7. Linda Witt, Karen Paget, and Glenna Matthews, *Running as a Woman: Gender and Power in American Politics,* Macmillan, New York, 1994, pp. 100-103.

d. When an organization (rather than an individual) is the author of the material, show the organization's name in the author's position.

> 8. Society for Creative Anachronism, *Giants in the Earth,* Bennett & Kitchel, East Lansing, Mich., 1991, p. 54.

However, if the organization is both the author and the publisher, show the organization's name only once—as the publisher.

> 9. *Patterson's American Education, 1994,* Educational Directories, Mount Prospect, Ill., 1993, Vol. LXXXX.

> 10. ''Campaign Financing,'' *Congress A to Z: A Ready Reference Encyclopedia,* 2d ed., Congressional Quarterly, Washington, D.C., 1993, pp. 48-53.

e. When a work such as an anthology carries an editor's name rather than an author's name, list the editor's name in the author's position, followed by the abbreviation *ed.* in parentheses. (If the names of two or more editors are listed, use the abbreviation *eds.* in parentheses.)

11. Joel Krieger (ed.), *The Oxford Companion to Politics of the World,* Oxford Univ. Press, New York, 1993.

12. Claudia Ciborra and Tawfik Jelassi (eds.), *Strategic Information Systems: A European Perspective,* Wiley, New York, 1994.

NOTE: If a reference work (such as an encyclopedia, a dictionary, or a directory) carries the name of an editor rather than an author, the editor's name is usually omitted. (See ¶1516, note.)

13. *Dictionary of American Regional English,* Harvard Univ. Press, Cambridge, Mass., 1985, Vol I, p. xxxii.

RATHER THAN:

13. Frederic G. Cassidy (ed.), *Dictionary of American Regional English,* Harvard Univ. Press, Cambridge, Mass., 1985, Vol. I, p. xxxii.

f. If the author of a work is unknown, begin the note with the title of the work. Do not use *Anonymous* in place of the author's name.

1525 Title of the Work

a. In giving the title of the work, follow the title page of a book or the main heading of an article for wording, spelling, and punctuation. However, adjust the capitalization as necessary so that all titles cited in the notes conform to a standard style. For example, a book entitled *Assertiveness*, with a subtitle (*the right to be you*) shown entirely in small letters on the title page for graphic effect, would appear in a note as follows: Claire Walmsley, *Assertiveness: The Right to Be You.*

➤ *For the capitalization of titles, see ¶¶360–363.*

b. If a title and a subtitle are shown on separate lines in the original work without any intervening punctuation, use a colon to separate them in the source reference note. (See ¶1510 for an example.)

c. In general, use italics or underlining for titles of *complete* published works and quotation marks for titles that refer to *parts* of complete published works.

➤ *For the use of italics or underlining with titles, see ¶¶289, 1508a; for the use of quotation marks with titles, see ¶¶242–243.*

1526 Publisher's Name

a. List the publisher's name as it appears on the title page (for example, *John Wiley & Sons*) or in a shortened form that is clearly recognizable *(Wiley);* use one form consistently throughout. If a division of the publishing company is also listed on the title page, it is not necessary to include this information in the footnote. Publishers, however, often do so in references to their own materials.

(Continued on page 428.)

b. The following list of examples shows acceptable patterns for abbreviating publishers' names. If in doubt, do not abbreviate.

Full Name	Acceptable Short Form
Alfred A. Knopf	Knopf
John Wiley & Sons	Wiley
William Morrow and Company, Inc.	Morrow
Random House	———
The Brookings Institution	Brookings
The Free Press	Free Press
Houghton Mifflin Company	Houghton Mifflin
Addison-Wesley Publishing Co.	Addison-Wesley
HarperCollins Publisher	HarperCollins
McGraw-Hill, Inc.	McGraw-Hill
Simon & Schuster Inc.	Simon & Schuster
Merriam-Webster, Incorporated	Merriam
Little, Brown & Co.	Little, Brown
Farrar Straus Giroux	———
Yale University Press	Yale Univ. Press
University of California Press	Univ. of California Press
Penguin Books	Penguin
Basic Books	———

NOTE: The patterns of abbreviation typically depend on how the publishers are referred to in speech. Since one never hears Random House referred to as *Random*, the name is not abbreviated. By the same token, one hears Little, Brown & Co. referred to as *Little, Brown*, never simply as *Little*. Penguin Books is typically referred to as *Penguin*, whereas Basic Books is never referred to as *Basic;* hence the difference in the treatment of these names.

c. Omit the publisher's name from references to newspapers and other periodicals. The publisher's name is also usually omitted from references to dictionaries and similar works unless confusion might result or the work is not well known. (For examples, see ¶1516.)

1527 Place of Publication

a. As a rule, list only the city of publication (for example, *New York, Boston, Washington, Toronto*). If the city may not be well known to your intended audience (for example, readers from abroad) or the city is likely to be confused with another city of the same name, add the state or the country (for example, *Cambridge, Mass.; Cambridge, England*). If the title page lists several cities in which the publisher has offices, use only the first city named.

b. Omit the place of publication from references to periodicals and well-known reference works.

c. Incorporate the city name in the name of a newspaper that might otherwise be unrecognized. For example, *The Star-Ledger* (published in Newark, New Jersey) should be referred to in a note as *The Newark (N.J.) Star-Ledger.*

1528 Date of Publication

a. For books, show the year of publication. (Use the most recent year shown in the copyright notice.)

b. For monthly periodicals, show both the month and the year. (See ¶1518 for examples.)

c. For weekly or daily newspapers and other periodicals, show the month, day, and year. (See ¶¶1517–1518 for examples.)

1529 Page Numbers

a. Page references in notes occur in the following forms:

p. 3   p. v
pp. 3–4   pp. v–vi
pp. 301 f. (meaning "page 301 and the following page")
pp. 301 ff. (meaning "page 301 and the following pages")

NOTE: Whenever possible, avoid using the indefinite abbreviations *f.* and *ff.*, and supply a specific range of page numbers instead.

b. In a range of page numbers the second number is sometimes abbreviated; for example, *pp. 981–983* may be expressed as *pp. 981–83*. (See ¶460.)

c. There is a trend toward dropping *p.* and *pp.* when there is no risk of mistaking the numbers for anything but page numbers.

➤ *For the use of an en dash or a hyphen in a range of page numbers, see ¶459a.*

15

Subsequent References

1530 a. When a note refers to a work that was fully identified in the note *immediately preceding*, it may be shortened by use of the abbreviation *ibid.* (meaning "in the same place"). *Ibid.* replaces all those elements that would otherwise be carried over intact from the previous note. Do not italicize or underline *ibid.*

    1. Deborah Tannen, *Talking From 9 to 5*, Morrow, New York, 1994, pp. 61-62.

    2. Ibid., p. 94. (*Ibid.* represents all the elements in the previous note except the page number.)

    3. Ibid. (Here *ibid.* represents everything in the preceding note, including the same page number.)

b. If you plan to use *ibid.* in a *footnote*, make sure that the footnote "immediately preceding" is no more than a few pages back. Otherwise, the interested reader will have to riffle back through the pages in order to find the "immediately preceding" footnote. To spare your reader this inconvenience, use the forms suggested in ¶1531.

c. Do not use *ibid.* in a *textnote* unless the one "immediately preceding" is on the same page and easy to spot; otherwise, your reader will have to search through lines and lines of text to find it. To spare your reader, construct these "subsequent reference" textnotes along the same lines as "first reference" textnotes. (See ¶1507b.)

NOTE: With *endnotes*, the use of *ibid.* will cause no inconvenience, since it refers to the note directly above.

¶1531

1531 a. When a note refers to a work fully identified in an earlier note but *not the one immediately preceding*, it may be shortened as follows:

> 1. Author's surname, page number.

> 8. Tannen, p. 65. (Referring to the work fully identified in an earlier note; see the first example in ¶1530a.)

NOTE: When short forms are used for subsequent references, it is desirable to provide a complete bibliography as well, so that the interested reader can quickly find the complete reference for each work in an alphabetic listing.

b. When previous reference has been made to different authors with the same surname, the use of a surname alone in a subsequent reference would be confusing. Therefore, the basic pattern in ¶1531a must be modified in the following way:

> 1. Author's initial(s) plus surname, page number.

OR: 2. Author's full name, page number.

> 1. David A. Johnson, *New York City,* Wiley, New York, 1994, pp. 200-202.

> 2. Jenz Johnson, *Giga Bites: The Hacker Cookbook,* Ten Speed Press, Berkeley, 1994, p. 21.

> 3. D. Johnson, pp. 167-168.

> 4. J. Johnson, p. 16.

c. If previous reference has been made to different works by the same author, any subsequent reference should contain the title of the specific work now being referred to. This title may be shortened to a key word or phrase; the word or phrase should be sufficiently clear, however, so that the full title can be readily identified in the bibliography or in an earlier note.

> 1. Author's surname, *book title* [shortened if feasible], page number.

> 1. Peter F. Drucker, *Post Capitalist Society,* HarperCollins, New York, 1993, p. 111.

> 2. Peter F. Drucker, *Managing for Results,* Harper & Row, New York, 1986, pp. 201-2.

> 3. Peter F. Drucker, *Managing for the Future: The 1990s and Beyond,* Dutton, New York, 1992, p. 89.

> 4. Drucker, *Results,* p. 144.

> 5. Drucker, *Future,* p. 93.

If referring to an article in a periodical, use the periodical title rather than the article title.

> 2. Author's surname, *periodical title* [shortened if feasible], page number.

> 6. Les Burch, "Moving Away From 'Me Too,'" *Nation's Business,* August 1994, p. 6.

> 7. Michael Useem, . . .

> 8. Burch, *Nation's Business,* p. 64. (Referring to the work identified in note 6 above.)

d. A more formal style in subsequent references uses the abbreviations *loc. cit.* ("in the place cited") and *op. cit.* ("in the work cited").

> 1. Author's surname, **loc. cit.** (This pattern is used when reference is made to the *very same page* in the work previously identified.)

> 2. Author's surname, **op. cit.,** page number. (This pattern is used when reference is made to a *different page* in the work previously identified.)

> 1. Helen Kennerly, *Managing Anxiety,* Oxford Univ. Press, New York, 1990, p. 167.

> 2. Larry Hirschhorn, *Managing in a Team Environment,* Addison-Wesley, Reading, Mass., 1991, p. 73.

> 3. Kennerly, op. cit., p. 169. (Referring to a different page in *Managing Anxiety.*)

> 4. Hirschhorn, loc. cit. (Referring to the same page in *Managing in a Team Environment.*)

> 5. Ibid. (Referring to exactly the same page as shown in note 4. *Ibid.* may be used only to refer to the note immediately preceding. See ¶1530.)

NOTE: Do not italicize or underline *loc. cit., op. cit.,* or *ibid.*

BIBLIOGRAPHIES

15

A bibliography at the end of a report or a manuscript typically lists all the works *consulted* in the preparation of the material as well as all the works that were actually *cited* in the notes. The format of a bibliography is also used for any list of titles, such as a list of recommended readings or a list of new publications.

1532 Word processing programs do not typically provide a template for bibliographies. Some special word processing programs, however, will format not only footnotes and endnotes but bibliographies as well. These programs ask you to create a database (also referred to as a *reference library*) in which you enter the necessary data for each title you plan to cite. Then you select (1) one of the standard formats built into the software or (2) a format that you have modified or created. In effect, once you have developed the reference library, you can extract the data in the form of footnotes, endnotes, or entries in a bibliography.

NOTE: ¶¶1533–1536 provide guidelines for formatting a bibliography.

1533 Consider the following guidelines for formatting a bibliography. (See the illustration on page 432.)

a. On a fresh page type *BIBLIOGRAPHY* (or some other appropriate title) in all-capital letters (and boldface if available). Center this title on the first line after the top margin of 2 inches (12 lines on a typewriter), and begin the text on the third line below.

b. Use the same margins as for other pages in the body of the report or manuscript (see ¶¶1404–1409), and treat the numbering of these pages as indicated in ¶1426f–g.

(Continued on page 432.)

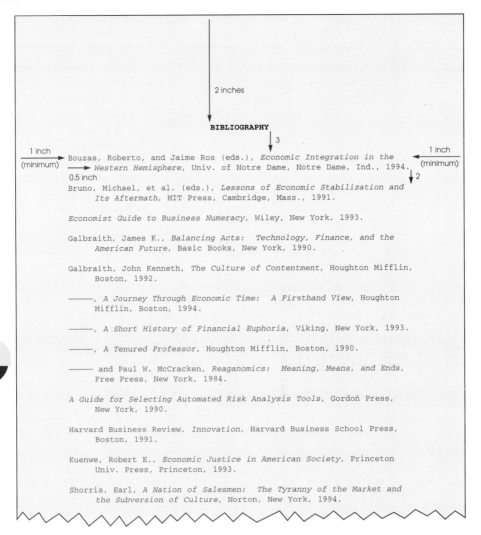

c. Begin each entry at the left margin. Ordinarily, single-space the entries, but in material that is to be edited, use double spacing to allow
room for the editing.

d. Indent turnover lines 0.5 inch (5 spaces on a typewriter) so that the
first word in each entry will stand out.

e. Leave 1 blank line between entries (whether they are single- or
double-spaced).

1534 a. List the entries alphabetically by author's last name.

b. Entries lacking an author are alphabetized by title. Disregard the word
The or *A* at the beginning of a title in determining alphabetic se-
quence. (For an example, see the tenth entry in the illustration above.
Note that this entry is alphabetized on the basis of *Guide*, following
Galbraith.)

c. There is no need to number the alphabetized entries in a bibliography unless you plan to use the style of textnotes described in ¶1507b(5). In that case begin each entry of the bibliography with a number typed at the left margin, followed by a period and 2 spaces. Then type the rest of the entry in the customary way, but indent any turnover so that it begins under the first word in the line above. (In the parenthetical textnotes, you can then make reference to different works by their bibliographic "entry number" instead of by author.)

```
 9. Bamford, Janet, et al., Complete Guide to Managing
    Your Money, Consumers Union, Mount Vernon, N.Y.,
    1989.

10. Newman, Katherine S., Declining Fortunes:  The
    Withering of the American Dream, Basic Books,
    New York, 1993.

11. Townsend, Robert, The B2 Chronicles, Pfeiffer,
    San Diego, 1994.
```

NOTE: In a bibliography with numbered entries, align the numbers on the period.

1535 When a bibliography contains more than one work by the same author, replace the author's name with a long dash (using 3 em dashes or 6 hyphens) in all the entries after the first. List the works alphabetically by title. (For examples, see the fifth, sixth, seventh, and eighth entries in the illustration on page 432. Note that these titles are alphabetized on the key words *Culture, Journey, Short,* and *Tenured.* The ninth entry involves a coauthor and therefore follows the works written by the first author alone.)

NOTE: As an alternative, multiple entries pertaining to the same author may be listed in chronological sequence according to the date of each publication.

1536 Entries in bibliographies contain the same elements and follow the same style as source reference notes except for two key differences.

a. Begin each entry with the name of the author listed in inverted order (last name first). When an entry includes two or more authors' names, invert only the first author's name. When an organization is listed as the author, do not invert the name.

```
Andrews, Kenneth R. (ed.), Ethics in Practice:  Managing
    the Moral Corporation, Harvard Business School
    Press, Boston, 1989.

Apple Computer, Inc., Demystifying Multimedia, Random
    House, New York, 1994.

Lonier, Terri, Working Solo Sourcebook:  Essential
    Resources for Independent Entrepreneurs,
    Portico, New Paltz, N.Y., 1994.

Stern, Ellen, and Emily Gwathmey, Once Upon a Telephone:
    An Illustrated Social History, Harcourt Brace, New
    York, 1994.
```

➤ *For additional examples, see the illustration on page 432.*

(Continued on page 434.)

b. Include page numbers in bibliographic entries only when the material being cited is part of a larger work. In such cases show the page number or numbers (for example, *pp. 215–232*) on which the material appears.

```
Van Blema, David, "Harrying Truman," Time, November 21,
    1994, p. 74.
```

➤ *For the use of an en dash or a hyphen in a range of page numbers, see ¶459a.*

c. In academic material, bibliographic entries typically follow a slightly different style. In the examples below, note that a period follows each of the three main parts of the entry (author's name, the title, and the publishing information). Also note that the parentheses that normally enclose the publishing information in an academic-style footnote or endnote are omitted in the bibliographic entry. (See ¶1508b.)

```
Andrews, Kenneth R. (ed.).  Ethics in Practice:  Man-
    aging the Moral Corporation.  Boston:  Harvard
    Business School Press, 1989.
```

```
Lonier, Terri.  Working Solo Sourcebook:  Essential
    Resources for Independent Entrepreneurs.  New
    Paltz, N.Y.:  Portico, 1994.
```

```
Van Blema, David.  "Harrying Truman."  Time, November 21,
    1994, p. 74. (Note that the magazine title—in this case Time—
    is considered part of the publishing information. Thus a period fol-
    lows the article title to mark the end of the title information in the
    entry.)
```

SECTION 16

TABLES

You can fit a good deal of material into a compact space when you present it in the form of a table—with items arranged in *rows* (to be read horizontally) and in *columns* (to be read vertically). However, in designing a table, you should aim for more than compactness. Your reader should be able to locate specific information faster—and detect significant patterns or trends in the data more quickly—than if the same information were presented in the regular text.

If you are using the table feature of a word processing program, you can prepare tables with little or no advance planning. Given the wide array of software programs now available, you can eliminate much (and in some cases all) of the tedious calculations entailed in planning the layout of multicolumn tables. There are software packages, for example, for financial spreadsheets and various types of statistical analyses that require you simply to input the variable data; the software will then perform all the necessary calculations and print the results in a preset format (unless you have called for specific format modifications). Moreover, you can take advantage of the centering capabilities in many programs to center copy within a table and then center the table as a whole, both horizontally and vertically, on a full sheet of paper. At any time after you begin typing, you can add or delete rows or columns, adjust the width of specific columns or of the table as a whole, and perform any other necessary procedure simply by interacting with the computer through a few dialog boxes. You can even split a very complex table into pieces, develop each piece as a separate table, and then assemble the pieces with ease and precision—with few, if any, computations necessary. (See pages 441–444 for illustrations of a table produced by using the table feature of WordPerfect 6 for Windows.)

The following paragraphs provide detailed guidelines for creating a table, whether you take full advantage of the features of your software or you plan and execute a table on a typewriter. Modify these guidelines as necessary to achieve results that are easy to understand, attractive to look at, and as simple as possible to execute.

16

Types of Tables

1601 a. **Table Text Only.** A table may simply consist of two columns of data with as few as two rows in each column.

Our analysis of the latest reports indicates that sales are up by at least 10 percent in all regions:

Eastern Region	16.2%
North Central Region	11.0%
Southern Region	18.4%
Western Region	13.9%

The primary reason for this upsurge, according to the managers of these regions, is the rebuilding of inventories, which were allowed to

NOTE: When a single-spaced table is inserted in the midst of regular single-spaced text, leave 1 blank line above and below the table (as shown above). If the table is typed with double spacing or if the table is inserted in the midst of text typed with double spacing, leave 2 blank lines above and below. With certain word processing software, it may be awkward or difficult to insert 2 blank lines when you are set up for double spacing. In such cases single-space all your tables.

b. **Open (Unruled) Table.** An open table may consist of nothing more than two columns of data, each labeled with a column head. The table is called *open* because no horizontal rules are used in the table design.

NOTE: When a table begins with unruled column heads, leave 2 blank lines above and below the table as a whole. (See also ¶1604c.)

When designing buildings for New England sites, keep in mind the typical outdoor winter temperatures. For example:

City	Temp. (°F)
Boston, Mass.	0
Burlington, Vt.	−10
Concord, N.H.	−15
Hartford, Conn.	0
Portland, Maine	−5
Providence, R.I.	0

c. **Ruled Table.** A ruled table is so called because it has three horizontal rules: one above the column heads, one below the column heads, and one below the last line of the table text.

16

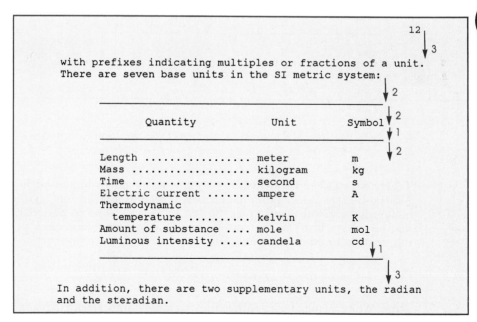

with prefixes indicating multiples or fractions of a unit. There are seven base units in the SI metric system:

Quantity	Unit	Symbol
Length	meter	m
Mass	kilogram	kg
Time	second	s
Electric current	ampere	A
Thermodynamic temperature	kelvin	K
Amount of substance	mole	mol
Luminous intensity	candela	cd

In addition, there are two supplementary units, the radian and the steradian.

NOTE: When a table begins with ruled column heads, leave 2 blank lines above and below the table as a whole. (See also ¶1604c.) If you are using the table feature of a word processing program, you can easily format a ruled table. (See ¶1601f.) If you are using a typewriter, type the first horizontal rule on the second line beneath the regular text to create the appearance of 2 blank lines.

➤ *For the use of leaders between columns, see ¶1631b–c; for the use of rules within a table, see ¶1633.*

d. **Boxed Table.** A boxed table is a ruled table to which vertical rules have been added.

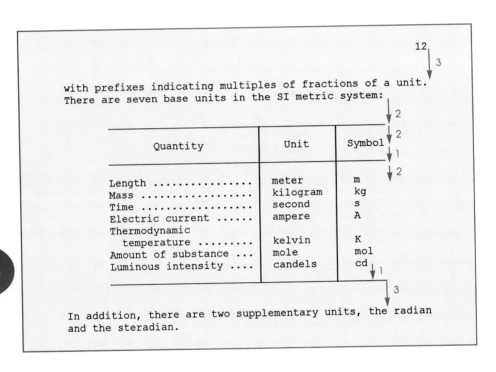

with prefixes indicating multiples of fractions of a unit. There are seven base units in the SI metric system:

Quantity	Unit	Symbol
Length	meter	m
Mass	kilogram	kg
Time	second	s
Electric current	ampere	A
Thermodynamic temperature	kelvin	K
Amount of substance ...	mole	mol
Luminous intensity	candels	cd

In addition, there are two supplementary units, the radian and the steradian.

➤ *For the use of leaders in a boxed table, see ¶1631; for the use of rules within a table, see ¶1633; for the treatment of turnovers in table text, see ¶1625c.*

e. **Tables With Other Elements.** The four types of tables identified in ¶1601a–d often carry additional elements, such as a table number, a table title, a subtitle, and notes. Moreover, *leaders* (rows of periods) may be used to lead the eye from items in one column to corresponding items in another column.

➤ *For the use of leaders between columns, see ¶1631b–c.*

NOTE: When a table begins with a title or a table number, leave 3 blank lines above and below the table as a whole. (See ¶1604c–d.)

Table With Title

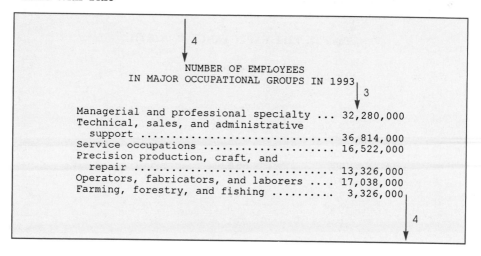

```
                         4

              NUMBER OF EMPLOYEES
      IN MAJOR OCCUPATIONAL GROUPS IN 1993
                                         3

Managerial and professional specialty ... 32,280,000
Technical, sales, and administrative
  support ............................... 36,814,000
Service occupations ..................... 16,522,000
Precision production, craft, and
  repair ................................ 13,326,000
Operators, fabricators, and laborers .... 17,038,000
Farming, forestry, and fishing .........  3,326,000

                                                    4
```

Table With Number, Title, and Subtitle

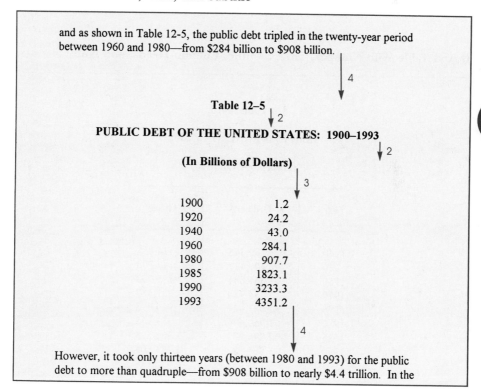

and as shown in Table 12-5, the public debt tripled in the twenty-year period between 1960 and 1980—from $284 billion to $908 billion.

                                    4

Table 12–5

2

PUBLIC DEBT OF THE UNITED STATES: 1900–1993

2

(In Billions of Dollars)

3

1900	1.2
1920	24.2
1940	43.0
1960	284.1
1980	907.7
1985	1823.1
1990	3233.3
1993	4351.2

4

However, it took only thirteen years (between 1980 and 1993) for the public debt to more than quadruple—from $908 billion to nearly $4.4 trillion. In the

(Continued on page 440.)

Open Table With Number, Title, Subtitle, Column Heads, and Notes

↓4
Table 12. LIFE EXPECTANCY AT BIRTH
↓2

From 1940 to 1993
↓3

Year	Male	Female
1940	60.8	65.2
1950	65.6	71.1
1960	66.6	73.1
1970	67.1	74.7
1980	70.0	77.5
1990	71.8	78.8
1993	72.1	78.9

↓2

Source: *The World Almanac and Book of Facts: 1995*, p. 972.
↓4

Boxed Table With Number, Title, Subtitle, Column Heads, and Note

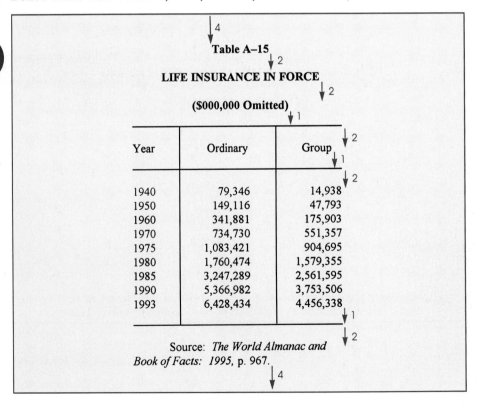

↓4
Table A–15
↓2

LIFE INSURANCE IN FORCE
↓2

($000,000 Omitted)
↓1

Year	Ordinary	Group
1940	79,346	14,938
1950	149,116	47,793
1960	341,881	175,903
1970	734,730	551,357
1975	1,083,421	904,695
1980	1,760,474	1,579,355
1985	3,247,289	2,561,595
1990	5,366,982	3,753,506
1993	6,428,434	4,456,338

Source: *The World Almanac and Book of Facts: 1995*, p. 967.
↓4

f. **Tables Created by Means of a Software Table Feature.** If you use the table feature of a word processing program to execute a table, the simplest way to proceed is to type all the copy for the table (accepting all the default settings) and then make the necessary modifications to achieve the result you want. The following sequence of illustrations shows how the table illustrated at the bottom of page 440 could be executed and then modified, using the table feature of WordPerfect 6 for Windows.

(1) One of the default settings imposes a grid of horizontal and vertical rules on the table that places each element in a box called a *cell.* Moreover, the grid boxes the table as a whole by means of rules at the top, bottom, and sides of the table. In the illustration below note that all the elements in the table—even the columns of figures—are aligned at the left.

Table A-15		
LIFE INSURANCE IN FORCE		
($000,000 Omitted)		
Year	Ordinary	Group
1940	79,346	14,938
1950	149,116	47,793
1960	341,881	175,903
1970	734,730	551,357
1975	1,083,421	904,695
1980	1,760,474	1,579,355
1985	3,247,289	2,561,595
1990	5,366,982	3,753,506
1993	6,428,434	4,456,338
Source: *The World Almanac and Book of Facts: 1995,* p. 967.		

16

NOTE: In the absence of other instructions, the table will have the same width as the regular text.

(2) You can retain the grid as is, you can change the dimensions of the cells (and the margins within the cells), or you can delete any or all of the horizontal and vertical rules. You can also change the appearance and the placement of the type. In the following illustration the cells at the top and bottom of the table have been

joined (removing the unwanted vertical rules). Then within the horizontally expanded cells, the program automatically reformats the table title and the table note each on one line. Once the cells at the top have been joined, you can center all the elements in the table heading. You can also put the table heading in boldface for greater emphasis.

	Table A–15	
	LIFE INSURANCE IN FORCE	
	($000,000 Omitted)	
Year	Ordinary	Group
1940	79,346	14,938
1950	149,116	47,793
1960	341,881	175,903
1993	6,428,434	4,456,338
Source: *The World Almanac and Book of Facts: 1995,* p. 967.		

16

NOTE: After you center the lines in the table heading, you can remove the rules that enclose the table heading (and the table note as well) to achieve a more open look as shown below.

	Table A–15	
	LIFE INSURANCE IN FORCE	
	($000,000 Omitted)	
Year	Ordinary	Group
1940	79,346	14,938
1950	149,116	47,793
1960	341,881	175,903
1993	6,428,434	4,456,338
Source: *The World Almanac and Book of Facts: 1995,* p. 967.		

(3) For better appearance, increase the space between the table heading and the start of the table text. Center the column heads and increase the space above and below them. You can also use the optional *fill* feature to shade the column heads (as shown below).

Table A-15

LIFE INSURANCE IN FORCE

($000,000 Omitted)

Year	Ordinary	Group
1940	79,346	14,938
1950	149,116	47,793
1960	341,881	175,903

NOTE: You can add shading to any cell in the table.

(4) Align whole numbers at the right, align decimals on the decimal point, and align entries consisting of words on the left. Adjust the width of each column so that the text within the column appears centered between the vertical rules.

Table A–15

LIFE INSURANCE IN FORCE

($000,000 Omitted)

Year	Ordinary	Group
1940	79,346	14,938
1950	149,116	47,793
1960	341,881	175,903
1970	734,730	551,357
1993	6,428,434	4,456,338

Source: *The World Almanac and Book of Facts:* 1995, p. 967.

(Continued on page 444.)

NOTE: Centering column text and heads between vertical rules can be a problem in some cases and does take more time. When speed and not appearance is critical, many users are content to *(a)* leave column text consisting of words (and the column heads above) aligned at the left; *(b)* align columns of figures (and the column heads above) at the right (see ¶1619); and *(c)* leave the overall table width as is (the same as the width of the regular text), as in the following illustration.

Table A–15		
LIFE INSURANCE IN FORCE		
($000,000 Omitted)		
Year	Ordinary	Group
1940	79,346	14,938
1950	149,116	47,793
1960	341,881	175,903
1970	734,730	551,357
1975	1,083,421	904,695
1980	1,760,474	1,579,355
1985	3,247,289	2,561,595
1990	5,366,982	3,753,506
1993	6,428,434	4,456,338
Source: *The World Almanac and Book of Facts: 1995*, p. 967.		

However, when a table becomes hard to read because of the excessive space between columns (as in the illustration above), you should reduce the overall width of the table.

➤ *Consult your software user's manual for specific guidance on how to use the table feature and make modifications in the table format.*

Locating Tables Within the Text

1602 a. Tables should be easy to refer to. Therefore, try to locate each table on the same page where the subject of the table is introduced in the text. In this way the reader will have ready access to the table while reading the text commentary that may precede and follow.

b. Ideally, every table should fall immediately after the point in the text where it is first mentioned. However, if placing the table within a paragraph is likely to disrupt the reader's grasp of the material, then locate the table at the end of the paragraph or at the top or bottom of the page. (See ¶1604d.)

1603 a. Avoid breaking a table at the bottom of a page. If starting a table at the ideal point means that it will not all fit in the space remaining on the page, then place the complete table at the top of the next page. (At the point in the text where the table is first mentioned, insert an appropriate cross-reference in parentheses. See ¶1608.)

NOTE: Many word processing programs have a feature called *block protect*, which prevents a page break from occurring within a block of text. (See the entry on *block protect* in Appendix B.)

b. If you have to fit a number of relatively short tables (half a page or less) in a given report, memo, or letter, consider single-spacing the table text to maximize your chances of locating each table in the ideal place. (See ¶1624 on the issue of single versus double spacing of tables.)

➤ *For other techniques to limit the length of a table to one page, see ¶1637. For guidelines on dealing with a table too long to fit on one page, see ¶1638.*

1604 If a table is to appear on a page that also carries regular text:

a. Center the table horizontally within the established margins. (See ¶1609 for guidance on centering a table within these margins.)

b. Try to indent the table at least 0.5 inch (5 spaces on a typewriter) from each side margin. In any case, the width of the table should not exceed the width of the text. (See ¶¶1640–1642 for ways to deal with an extrawide table.)

16

c. Set off the table by 1 to 3 blank lines from the text above and below, as follows:

Kind of Table	Spacing in Table Text	Blank Lines Above and Below Table	Illustration
Without column heads or table title	Single	1	¶1601a
Without column heads or table title	Double	2	
With column heads (but no table title)	Single or double	2	¶1601b, c, d
With table title	Single or double	3	¶1601e

NOTE: When you double-space a table, it may be awkward or difficult—if you are using certain word processing programs—to leave 2 blank lines above and below the table. In such cases single-space all your tables; inserting 2 blank lines will then pose no problem.

d. Placing a table in the middle of a page (with regular text above and below) requires you to leave up to 3 blank lines both above and below the table. If space is tight, place the table at the top or bottom of the page. In that way you can eliminate one set of blank lines and improve your chances of fitting the table on the desired page.

e. If you are using the table feature of a word processing program, you do not need to count the number of lines before you start to type the table. Simply insert the table copy at the desired location in the regular text, adding rows and columns as necessary. If you discover that the table will not all fit on the same page, you can move the table as a whole to the top or bottom of the page (as noted in ¶1604d), make other adjustments (as noted in ¶¶1637–1639), or place the table on a page by itself (see ¶¶1605–1608). If you use a feature called *block protect* (see ¶1603a, note), the table will not be divided at the bottom of a page; instead the table as a whole will be moved to the top of the next page.

f. If you are using a typewriter, first count the number of lines the table will require. Be sure to include in your count the blank lines within the table as well as above and below. (For a quick guide to the allowance for blank lines, see the illustrations on pages 436–444.) On the basis of this count and an evaluation of the adjacent text material and the space available, you can decide on the best location for the table.

g. Be sure you can fit at least two full lines of regular text above or below the table. If the results look unattractive, devote the full page to the table (see ¶¶1605–1608) and resume the text on the following page.

Locating Tables on Separate Pages

1605 When a table occupies more than two-thirds of a page, it can often be difficult to fit on the same page with regular text. In such cases type the table on a separate page and place it immediately after the text page on which the table is first referred to.

16

NOTE: If you are using word processing software, insert a hard page break before and after the table to ensure that the table will appear on a page by itself.

1606 If a given document contains a number of tables, most of which will each require a separate page, then all the tables (short as well as long) may be executed as an appendix at the back of a report or as an attachment to a memo or letter. This arrangement—which permits the reader to keep the full set of tables alongside the regular text (except in the case of bound reports)—can be very convenient, especially if some of the tables are repeatedly cited throughout the regular text. (This arrangement also eliminates the problem of trying to fit long tables within the text.)

1607 When a table is to appear on a page by itself, center the table horizontally and vertically within the established margins of the page. (See ¶¶1609–1610 for guidelines on centering horizontally and vertically.)

NOTE: If no margins have been established, leave a minimum margin of 1 inch on all four sides of the table.

1608 When a table is not located on the same page on which it is referred to, provide a cross-reference in parentheses to the appropriate page.

(See Table 4 on page 18.)   OR   (See Table 2-2 on page 31.)

NOTE: These parenthetical cross-references may be treated as a separate sentence (as shown on page 446) or as part of another sentence (see ¶220).

➤ *For the advisability of numbering tables to simplify the matter of cross-references, see ¶1612.*

Centering Tables Horizontally

1609 If you are using the table feature of a word processing program, the table will extend to the full width of the regular text unless you set new margins. If you decide to reduce the overall width of the table, first type the table. Then reduce the space between columns. (As a rule, leave 0.5 inch between columns; you can leave more or less space as long as the table is still easy to read.) After you have reduced the overall width of the table, center the table horizontally.

If you are using a typewriter to create a table, you must first determine the starting point for each column within the table before you can determine how to center the table horizontally. Follow this procedure.

a. Establish a *key line* as follows:

> **(1)** Select the longest item in each column, whether it occurs in the column head or the column text.

> **(2)** Determine the number of spaces to be left between columns—normally 6 spaces. You may leave any number of spaces that will produce an attractive and readable table, but do not leave less than 2 spaces.

> NOTE: In financial statements 2 spaces are customarily used between adjacent columns listing amounts of money.

> **(3)** The combination of the longest item from each column plus an allowance for the space between each pair of columns makes up the key line. Here, for example, is the key line used to plan the table at the top of page 454:

```
Year        Personal        Personal      Disposable      Personal
   123456          123456          123456            123456
```

b. Determine the centering point for the table. If the left and right margins have been established in advance, the centering point will fall halfway between these margins. If the left and right margins have not been established and are to be equal, use the exact center of the page as the centering point.

c. Clear all tab stops.

d. From the centering point, backspace once for each pair of strokes in the key line. If you have an odd stroke left over at the end, do not backspace for it.

e. At the point at which you stop backspacing, set the first tab stop. This tab stop will represent the left margin of the table and of the first column.

> NOTE: If the process of backspacing carries you beyond the left margin of the regular text, you will know that the table is too wide as it currently stands. (If a left margin has not been established and you backspace to a point that leaves a left margin of less than 1 inch, you will also know that the table is too wide.) As a first step, try reducing the

space between columns to as little as 2 spaces; repeat steps *d* and *e* to see if this approach produces an acceptable left margin. (If the table is still too wide, see ¶¶1640–1642 for other solutions.)

f. From the left margin of the table, space forward once for each keystroke in the longest item in the first column. Then space forward again for each blank space to be left between the first and second columns. At the point where you stop, set a tab stop. This will represent the start of the second column.

g. Repeat step *f* until you have set tab stops for each of the remaining columns.

Centering Tables Vertically

1610 If you are using the table feature of a word processing program and want to center a table vertically on a full 8½- by 11-inch sheet of paper, first type the table. Then center the table vertically.

If you are using a typewriter, follow this procedure:

a. Count the number of lines in the table (including the blank lines).

NOTE: There is a total of 66 lines on a standard sheet of paper. In order to maintain a minimum margin of 1 inch (6 lines) at the top and bottom of the page, the table should not exceed 54 lines. Moreover, if you are doing a report and must allow for a page number at the top or bottom of the page, your count for the table should not exceed 51 lines. If it appears that the table is running beyond these limits, consider the various alternatives for reducing the length of the table (see ¶1637). If none of these solve the problem, you will have to continue the table on a second page. (See ¶1638 for guidelines on how to execute a table on two or more pages.)

b. Find the difference between the total number of lines in the table (including blank lines) and 66, the total number of lines available on the page. (If a table will occupy a total of 39 lines, then the difference between 39 and 66 is 27.)

c. Divide the difference by 2 to find the line number on which to start the table. (Dividing 27 by 2 yields an answer of 13½.) If your answer has a fraction, ignore it. (In this case, then, you would start typing on line 13.)

Table Identification

1611 Identify tables by *title* unless they are not very numerous and the significance of the material in the table is clear without some descriptive label. (See ¶1614a.)

1612 Also identify tables by *number* unless they are quite short, not very numerous, and typically referred to only on the page on which they fall. The use of table numbers simplifies the matter of cross-references, an important consideration if you expect that a number of tables will not fit on the page where they are first mentioned or if you know that certain tables will be referred to repeatedly throughout the regular text.

NOTE: Tables may be numbered consecutively throughout a given document or consecutively within each chapter and each appendix. With the latter technique, the chapter number (or the appendix number or letter) is used as a prefix in the numbering scheme. For example, Table 3-2

16

would be the second table in Chapter 3, and Table A-5 would be the fifth table in Appendix A.

1613 The table title may be followed by a *subtitle,* which provides additional information about the significance of the table, the period of time it covers, or the manner in which the information is organized or presented. Since a subtitle should be held to one line if possible (two at the most), a lengthy comment on any of these points should be handled as a note to the table rather than as a subtitle (see ¶¶1634–1636).

1614 Type the elements of table identification as follows:

a. **Table Title.** Center the table title, using all-capital letters in boldface (if available). (See ¶1614d.)

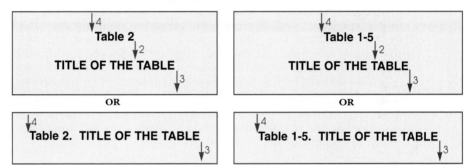

NOTE: If you are using the table feature of a word processing program, portions of the vertical grid may appear in the rows in which you plan to insert the table number, the table title, and the table subtitle. To remove the vertical rules from these rows, use the *join* feature to connect the cells across the top of the table. (See the illustrations on pages 441, 442, and 456.)

b. **Table Number.** Type the word *Table* in capital and small letters, followed by the appropriate number. To give the table number special emphasis, center it on the second line above the table title and use boldface (if available). To hold down the length of the table, type the table number on the same line with the table title; in this case insert a period after the table number and leave 2 spaces before typing the table title. (See the illustrations above and below.)

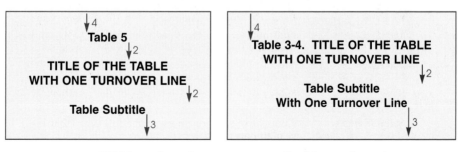

NOTE: Within a given document treat all table numbers the same way.

(Continued on page 450.)

c. Table Subtitle. Center the subtitle on the second line below the title, using capital and small letters in boldface (if available). The subtitle is usually enclosed in parentheses when it simply comments on the listing of data in some special order (for example, *In Descending Order by Sales Revenue*) or on the omission of zeros from figures given in the table (for example, *In Millions* or *000 Omitted*).

➤ *For examples of subtitles enclosed in parentheses, see the tables illustrated on pages 439–444, 454, 457, and 465.*

NOTE: If either the title or the subtitle requires more than one line, break it into sensible phrases; then single-space and center any turnover lines. If possible, try to hold the title and the subtitle to two lines each.

d. Centering each line in the table identification is easy if you are using word processing software. Simply select the *center* option. If you are using a typewriter, first determine the centering point for the table (see ¶1609b). Then from the centering point, backspace once for each pair of keystrokes in the line. (Do not backspace for an odd keystroke left over at the end.) The point at which you stop backspacing is the point at which to begin typing the line in order to center it.

e. When a table falls on a page with regular text above it, leave 3 blank lines above the first line of table identification. Leave 2 blank lines below the last line of table identification, whether the following copy consists of column heads or the table text.

Column Heads

1615 a. Unless a table is very simple and the significance of the material is clear without heads, provide a heading for each column. (A heading may be omitted over the first column, also known as the *stub*. See, for example, the table on page 465.)

b. Whenever possible, use singular forms in the column heads. Thus, for example, over a column listing a number of cities, use the heading *City* rather than *Cities*. (See the illustrations on page 437.)

c. In order to hold down the length of column heads, use abbreviations and symbols as necessary. For example:

Acct. No.	Account number
% of Total	Percent of total
FY1998 OR FY98	Fiscal year 1998 (also used to indicate that a company's fiscal year does not coincide with the *calendar* year)
1Q/1999 OR IQ/99	First quarter of 1999 (also used with 2Q, 3Q, and 4Q to signify the other three quarters of the year)
Sales ($)	Sales results expressed as a dollar amount (in other words, sales revenues)
Sales (U)	Sales results expressed in terms of the number of units sold
Sales YTD ($)	Cumulative sales revenues so far this year (that is, year to date)
% O/(U) Last Year	Percentage by which this year's results are over (or under) last year's results

16

1997A	<u>A</u>ctual results in 1997
1998B	<u>B</u>udgeted results in 1998
1998E	<u>E</u>stimated results in 1998
1999F	<u>F</u>orecast of results in 1999

NOTE: If your reader may not understand some of the abbreviations and symbols you use, explain the unfamiliar ones in a footnote to the table. For example:

```
Note:  A = actual; E = estimated; F = forecast.
```

➤ *See ¶¶1634–1636 and the illustrations on pages 456–457.*

d. Column heads should be single-spaced and may be broken into as many as five lines. Column heads are normally centered on the column width (see ¶¶1616–1618), but under certain circumstances the lines that make up the column head may all be blocked left or right on the column width (see ¶¶1616, 1619).

e. Capitalize the first letter of each word in a column head except articles (*a, an, the*), conjunctions under four letters (such as *and* and *or*), and prepositions under four letters (such as *of* and *in*). See ¶¶360–361, 363 for detailed guidance on capitalizing words in column headings.

➤ *For illustrations of different types of column heads, see pages 454–457.*

NOTE: When column heads are extremely long, consider using abbreviations in the column heads and explaining them (if necessary) in a table footnote. As an alternative, use a smaller type size if you have that option. (See ¶¶1615c, 1636.)

1616 If you are using the table feature of a word processing program, you can easily center each line in a column head. However, in some software programs (especially financial applications), if you accept the default settings, the heads over the columns of *text* are blocked *left* on the column width, whereas the heads over columns of *figures* are blocked *right* on the column width. In other cases the default alignment for all column heads is at the left. (See the illustration on page 441.)

16

1617 If you are using a typewriter, follow this procedure when centering a column head that is *narrower* than the column text below:

a. Identify the longest line in the column head and the column text; for example:

```
COLUMN HEAD:  In-Service
              12345678901234567
COLUMN TEXT:  Computer Literacy
```

b. Find the difference in the number of keystrokes between the longest line in the column head and the longest line in the column text. (In the example above, the difference is 7.)

(Continued on page 452.)

c. Divide the difference by 2 (and ignore any fraction in the answer) to find how many spaces to indent the longest line in the column head. (Dividing 7 by 2 yields an answer of 3½, so the longest line in the column head should be indented 3 spaces.)

```
###In-Service####
Computer Literacy
```

NOTE: When this method of centering is used, if a short line cannot be perfectly centered over the long line, the extra space always falls at the right.

d. To center the other lines in the column head in relation to the longest line, follow the same procedure described in *c* above. For example, if the longest line in the column head *(In-Service)* is 10 and another line *(Program)* is 7, divide the difference (3) and discard any fraction in the answer (1½). The resulting figure (1) indicates that the line in question should be indented 1 space.

```
In-Service
#Training#
#Program##
```

NOTE: The following examples provide a simple visual check on the correct alignment of lines in a column head.

```
123456#      #12345#      #1234##      ##123##      ##12###
1234567      1234567      1234567      1234567      1234567
```

1618 If you are using a typewriter, follow this procedure when centering a column head that is *wider* than the column text below:

a. Type the longest line in the column head, starting at the left margin of the column. (In this case it is the longest line in the column head that will determine the total width of the column.)

```
123456789
Household
```

b. Center any other lines in the column head in relation to the longest line. (See the examples in ¶1617d, note, as a visual check on your results.)

```
123456789
#Median##
#Income##
###per###
Household
```

c. Find the difference in the number of keystrokes between the longest line in the column head and the longest line in the column text. In this example, the longest line in the column head is 9, the longest line in the column text *($19,074)* is 7, and the difference is 2.

d. Divide the difference by 2 (and discard any fraction) to find the number of spaces to indent the longest line in the column text. In this case dividing 2 by 2 gives an answer of 1, so indent the longest text line 1 space.

```
#Median##
#Income##
###per###
Household

#$19,074#
```

e. Once you have typed the wide column head, you can reset the tab stop for this column to establish the starting point for most lines in the column text. In this example the column text will consist almost entirely of five-digit numbers; the dollar sign will appear only in the first entry and in the total line at the bottom of the column. Therefore, it makes sense to set the tab stop at the point at which the five-digit numbers will begin. (You will have to remember to space forward or back for any line that is shorter or longer.)

```
            ┌─ Tab stop for
            │  column text
            │
            ▼
   $19,074
    17,341
    15,640
    13,242
     9,903
```

NOTE: If you are using word processing software, you can easily align the figures in a column by using the decimal tab or right tab.

➤ *For guidelines on how to align items in column text, see ¶¶1625–1629. The alignment will depend on whether the items are all words, all figures (with or without decimal points), or some combination of words and figures.*

1619 In drafts and in informal reports, memos, and letters—where the occasion does not justify the time and effort that goes into centering column heads over column text—every line in the column head may align at the left or the right. For example:

```
In-Service      Source of        Average    Cumulative
Training        Revenues          Annual      Compound
Program                      Expenditures        Growth
```

NOTE: When you use left or right alignment of the lines in the column head and the column text, you may produce very odd-looking tables when a very narrow column head falls above a very wide column of text or when a very wide column head falls above a very narrow column of text. For example:

16

```
                         Applications
Name                         Received
──────────────────        ─────────────
A. Michael Ashworth              98
Dwayne Gilpatrick Jr.           182
Bradley M. Harrington           243
Gregory Jacobsen                 76
```

To avoid this result, center each line in the column head and center the column text as a block.

1620 Open (Unruled) Column Heads

a. Type column heads in capital and small letters, underlined and centered on the column width, as shown in the illustration at the top of page 454. (See ¶¶1616–1619.)

b. If the column heads in a table do not all take the same number of lines, align the column heads at the bottom.

(Continued on page 454.)

NOTE: If you are using the table feature of a word processing program, choose the *bottom alignment* option to automatically align column heads that do not take the same number of lines.

```
                                    ↓4
                           Table 14-4  ↓2
                                         ↓2
              DISTRIBUTION OF PERSONAL INCOME:  1960 TO 1993
                                                          ↓2
                        (In Billions of Dollars)
                                                   ↓3
                                            Disposable
                     Personal      Personal   #Personal#      Personal
          Year       #Income#      #Taxes##   ##Income##      Savings#
                                                                    ↓2
          1960         402.3          50.4        352.0          19.7
          1970         811.1         115.8        695.3          55.8
          1980        2165.3         336.5       1828.9         110.2
          1990        4679.8         621.0       4058.8         205.8
          1993        5375.1         686.4       4788.7         192.6

                                                                    ↓4
```

KEY LINE:

```
Year        Personal       Personal      Disposable       Personal
   123456          123456          123456             123456
```

c. Leave 2 blank lines between the final line of the title or subtitle (whichever comes last) and the first line of the tallest column head.

d. Leave 1 blank line between the column heads and the table text.

1621 Ruled Column Heads

a. If you are using word processing software, the table feature can create a grid of horizontal and vertical rules, as shown in the table below.

Table A–20

DOW JONES INDUSTRIAL AVERAGE: 1986–1993

Year	High	Low	Year	High	Low
1986	1955.57	1502.29	1990	2999.75	2365.10
1987	2722.42	1738.74	1991	3168.83	2470.30
1988	2183.50	1879.14	1992	3413.21	3136.58
1989	2791.41	2144.64	1993	3794.33	3241.95

16

In the row containing the column heads, you can (1) retain both the horizontal and vertical rules (to create *boxed* column heads), (2) retain only the horizontal rules that run the full width of the table (to create *ruled* column heads), or (3) use no rules at all (for *open* column heads). The illustration in ¶1621a retains only the horizontal rules and uses the *fill* feature to shade the column heads.

b. If you are using a typewriter, follow this procedure to create *ruled* column heads (as in the illustration below).

(1) Insert the first horizontal rule on the line directly below the final line of the title or subtitle (whichever comes last). Extend the horizontal rule the full width of the table, but do not let it over-hang the table text on either side.

(2) On the second line below the rule, start the column head with the most lines. All the column heads should align at the bottom.

(3) Type the column heads in capital and small letters, single-spaced and centered. (For guidance on centering, see ¶¶1616–1619.) Do not underline the column heads when they are ruled or boxed.

(4) On the line directly below the last line of the column heads, insert another horizontal rule the full width of the table. (When both horizontal rules are inserted, the column heads should appear to be centered between them, with 1 blank line above and below the column heads.)

(5) On the second line below the second rule, start typing the table text.

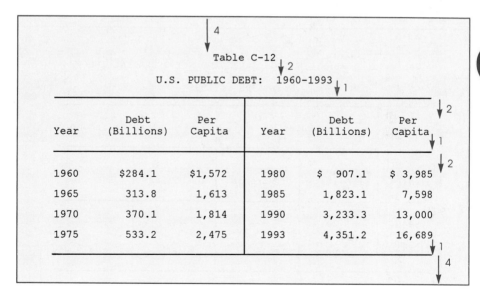

Table C-12 ↓2
U.S. PUBLIC DEBT: 1960–1993 ↓1

Year	Debt (Billions)	Per Capita	Year	Debt (Billions)	Per Capita
1960	$284.1	$1,572	1980	$ 907.1	$ 3,985
1965	313.8	1,613	1985	1,823.1	7,598
1970	370.1	1,814	1990	3,233.3	13,000
1975	533.2	2,475	1993	4,351.2	16,689

NOTE: This illustration of a table with ruled column heads also shows how to treat a table that would be long and narrow if held to its original three columns. A single vertical rule is used to separate the two halves of the table, each with the same set of column heads. If you use single vertical rules between the columns on each side, use a double vertical rule to separate the two halves of the table.

1622 Braced Column Heads

a. Some complex tables contain *braced* column heads (heads that "embrace" two or more columns). They are also called *straddle* heads because they straddle two or more columns. (See the illustration below.)

b. Type braced column heads in capital and small letters. Single-space and center any turnover lines. Align braced heads at the bottom.

c. If you use the table feature of a word processing program, you can easily center a braced heading over the appropriate columns.

d. If you are using a typewriter to center a braced heading over the columns to which it applies, follow this procedure.

    (1) First plan the arrangement of the column heads and type the ones that are to go below the braced head, centering each over its own column text. Leave room, however, for the braced head.

    (2) Count the keystrokes in the longest items in the columns to be braced, and add in the number of blank spaces between the braced columns. (See the example in the note below.)

    (3) Count the keystrokes in the longest line in the braced column head. Subtract that number from the figure calculated in step (2).

    (4) Divide your answer by 2 (and ignore any fraction) to find how many spaces to indent the longest line in the braced head.

    (5) Center any other lines in the braced head in relation to the placement of the longest line.

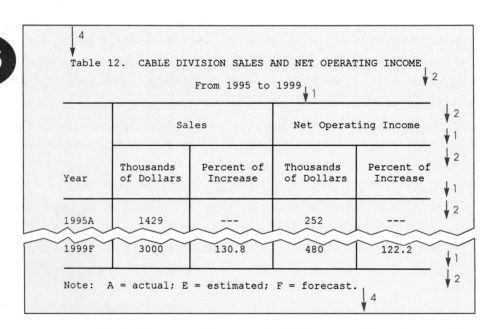

NOTE: In the illustration above a total of 26 keystrokes has to be braced in each case:

```
of Dollars      Percent of        of Dollars         Percent of
12345678901234567890123456        12345678901234567890123456
Sales                             Net Operating Income
```

To center the first braced head, subtract the keystrokes in *Sales* (5) from 26. Dividing the difference (21) by 2 yields an answer of 10½. Ignore the fraction, and indent *Sales* 10 spaces from the start of the first column to be braced. The second braced head, *Net Operating Income*, has 20 keystrokes. Subtracting 20 from 26 yields a difference of 6. Dividing 6 by 2 indicates that the braced head should be indented 3 spaces.

1623 Crossheads

a. Crossheads are used to separate the data in the body of a table into different categories. (See the illustration below.)

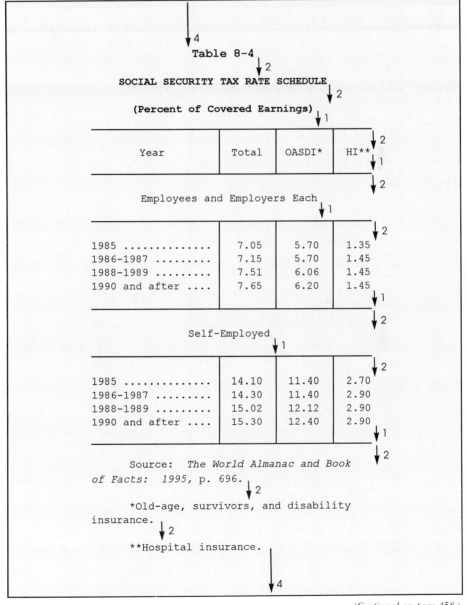

Year	Total	OASDI*	HI**
Employees and Employers Each			
1985	7.05	5.70	1.35
1986–1987	7.15	5.70	1.45
1988–1989	7.51	6.06	1.45
1990 and after	7.65	6.20	1.45
Self-Employed			
1985	14.10	11.40	2.70
1986–1987	14.30	11.40	2.90
1988–1989	15.02	12.12	2.90
1990 and after	15.30	12.40	2.90

Table 8-4

SOCIAL SECURITY TAX RATE SCHEDULE

(Percent of Covered Earnings)

Source: *The World Almanac and Book of Facts: 1995,* p. 696.

*Old-age, survivors, and disability insurance.

**Hospital insurance.

(Continued on page 458.)

b. The first crosshead falls immediately below the column heads across the top of the table; the other crossheads occur within the body of the table at appropriate intervals.

c. Type each crosshead in capital and small letters, centered on the full width of the table.

(1) If you are using the table feature of a word processing program, you can automatically center each crosshead after you join the cells in that row.

(2) If you are using a typewriter, center each crosshead on the full width of the table. Backspace from the centering point to determine where to begin typing each crosshead.

d. Each crosshead should be preceded and followed by a horizontal rule running the full width of the table. (For proper spacing above and below each crosshead, see the illustration on page 457.)

e. If there are vertical rules in a table (as in the illustration on page 457), they should not intrude into the space set aside for the crossheads. If you are using the table feature of a word processing program, you can eliminate the unwanted vertical rules by joining the cells into which they intrude.

Table Text

1624 Spacing

a. The table text may be typed with single or double spacing. However, within the same document try to treat all tables alike.

b. Double-space tables for better readability. However, if overall length is a concern and you wish to maximize your chances of locating each table on the page where it is first mentioned, use single spacing. (See also ¶1603.)

NOTE: If a single-spaced table runs quite long, you can break up the solid mass of table text by inserting a blank line or a horizontal rule at regular intervals or at points that serve to group the rows in a meaningful way.

c. As a rule, type the table text with the same spacing (or less) used for the regular text. Thus when the regular text is *single-spaced*, then all the tables should also be single-spaced. When the regular text is *double-spaced*, then all the tables may be typed with double or single spacing.

d. The following guide indicates where to begin typing the table text.

If the Table Text Is Preceded by:	Start Typing the Table Text on the:
Text with single spacing	Second line below
Text with double spacing	Third line below
Column heads—open	Second line below
Column heads—ruled or boxed	Second line below rule
Table title	Third line below
Table subtitle	Third line below

16

NOTE: When you double-space a table, it may be awkward or difficult—if you are using certain word processing programs—to leave 2 blank lines before starting to type the table text. In such cases single-space all your tables; inserting 2 blank lines will then pose no problem.

➤ *For examples of proper spacing, see the illustrations on pages 436–444.*

1625 Items Consisting of Words

If the table text consists of items expressed entirely in words:

a. Capitalize only the first word of each item in the table text plus any proper nouns and proper adjectives.

NOTE: In special cases, where it may be important to show whether terms are capitalized or written with small letters, the first word in each item need not be consistently capitalized. (See, for example, the second and third columns of the table at the bottom of page 437.)

b. Use abbreviations and symbols as necessary to hold down the length of individual items. (See ¶1615c for examples.)

c. Align each item at the left margin of the column. If any item requires more than one line, indent the turnover line 2 or 3 spaces. However, if a column contains both main entries and subentries, begin the main entry at the left margin of the column text, indent the first line of subentries 2 or 3 spaces, and indent all turnover lines 4 to 6 spaces.

NOTE: If you are using the table feature of a word processing program, turnover lines will automatically begin at the left margin of the column text. This format is acceptable if you are using horizontal rules or extra space to separate the rows. If, however, you are single-spacing the table without horizontal rules or extra space between rows, indent the turnover lines as indicated above.

16

```
Photographs, prints,         Total weekly
   and illustrations ...        broadcast
Scientific or tech-             hours ......
   nical drawings ......     General
Commercial prints .....         programs ...
Reproductions of             Instructional
   works of art ........        programs ...
```

➤ *For guidelines on the use of leaders (rows of periods), see ¶1631.*

d. If an item in the first column requires more than one line and all the other items in the same row require only one line, align all the items in that row at the bottom.

```
Chemical and allied products ... 151      201
Petroleum refining and related
   products ....................  69      73 ◄——— Aligned at
Paper and allied products ...... 391     364       the bottom
```

(Continued on page 460.)

e. If two or more items in a row each require more than one line, align all entries in that row at the top.

Aligned at the top

| Employee benefit report | Prepared quarterly | Data based on administra- tive records |

f. Do not use a period as terminal punctuation at the end of any item except in a column where all entries are in sentence form.

1626 Items Consisting of Figures

a. If a column of table text consists of items expressed entirely in figures:

(1) Align columns of whole numbers at the right.

(2) Align columns of decimal amounts on the decimal point.

(3) In a column that contains both whole numbers and decimals, add a decimal point and zeros to the whole numbers to maintain a consistent appearance.

(4) Omit commas in four-digit whole numbers unless they appear in the same column with larger numbers containing commas. Never insert commas in the decimal part of a number.

```
    325      465.2137
      1     1250.0004
152,657        1.0000
  1,489       37.9898
```

NOTE: Some writers prefer to retain the comma in four-digit numbers under all circumstances.

(5) If you are using word processing software, align the figures in a column by using a decimal tab or a right tab.

➤ *For the way to handle a total line in a column of figures, see ¶1628c.*

b. If a column of table text consists entirely of "clock" times (as in a program or schedule):

(1) Align the figures in "on the hour" expressions at the right.

```
11 a.m.
12 noon
 1 p.m.
 8 p.m.
12 midnight
```

(2) Align the figures in "hour and minute" expressions on the colon. (Add two zeros to exact times to maintain a uniform appearance.)

```
 8:15 a.m.
10:30 a.m.
12:00 noon
 1:45 p.m.
12:00 midnight
```

(3) When the items in a column each consist of a starting and an ending time, either align all the items at the left or align them on the hyphen or en dash within the items. (See the illustration at the top of page 461 and on page 477.)

```
8:30-9:30        OR      8:30-9:30
10:30-11:30              10:30-11:30
12:30-1:30               12:30-1:30
2:30-3:30                2:30-3:30
4:45-6:00               4:45-6:00
```

NOTE: In the "24-hour" system of expressing clock time (in which midnight is 0000 and 11:59 p.m. is 2359), the alignment of clock times poses no problem since all times are expressed in four digits (with no colons and no need for reference to *a.m.* or *p.m.*). However, if you are using a proportional typeface, align these expressions of clock time on the hyphen or en dash.

```
0830-0930
1030-1130
1230-1330
1430-1530
```

1627 Items Consisting of Figures and Words

If a column consists of both figures and words (as in the second column below), align the items at the left. Note, however, that a column consisting of words aligns at the left (as in the first column below) and a column consisting only of whole numbers aligns at the right (as in the third column below).

Type of Food	Average Serving	Calorie Count
Bacon	2 strips	97
Beef, roast	4 oz	300
Broccoli	1 cup	44
Tomato, raw	Medium size	30

16

1628 Amounts of Money

a. In a column containing dollar amounts, insert a dollar sign only before the first amount at the head of the column and before the total amount. The dollar signs should align in the first space to the left of the longest amount in the column.

```
$  45.50      $    165      $ 423.75
  2406.05        3,450        584.45
   783.25       98,932       1228.00
 _____      _____      _____
$3234.80      $102,547      $2236.20
```

NOTE: If you are using a proportional typeface (one in which the individual characters are not equal in width), it may be difficult to align the dollar sign at the head of the column with the dollar sign before the total amount. To avoid this problem, consider these alternatives. If the table uses column heads, try to incorporate the dollar sign in the heading—for example, ($000,000 *Omitted*); then there is no need for dollar signs alongside the figures below. Otherwise, consider using a monospace typeface such as Courier (in which all characters have the same width); then the vertical alignment of the dollar signs poses no problem.

(Continued on page 462.)

b. Do not insert commas to set off thousands in four-digit numbers unless they appear in the same column with larger numbers. (See the examples in ¶1626a and ¶1628a.) Moreover, if all the amounts in a column are whole dollar amounts, omit the decimal and zeros (as in the second example in ¶1628a). However, if any amount in a column includes cents, use a decimal and zeros with any whole dollar amount in the same column (as in the third example in ¶1628a).

c. If the table text ends with a *total* line (as in the illustration below):

   (1) In an *open* table (one with no rules between columns of figures), simply type a row of underlines directly under the last amount. Make the underline as wide as the longest entry in the column (including the dollar sign at the left). In a single-spaced table, type the total amount on the line directly below the underline (as in the first example below). To give the total amount greater emphasis, type it on the second line below the underline (as in the second example below). In a double-spaced table, type the amount on the second line below the underline (as in the third example below).

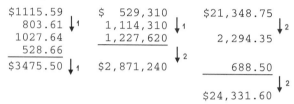

```
$1115.59         $   529,310         $21,348.75
  803.61 ↓1       1,114,310 ↓1                  ↓2
 1027.64          1,227,620            2,294.35
  528.66         _____
$3475.50 ↓1      $2,871,240 ↓2          688.50
                                     _____  ↓2
                                     $24,331.60
```

NOTE: If you are using word processing software, then before you type the last amount above the total, choose *underline* as the appearance option for the typeface you are using.

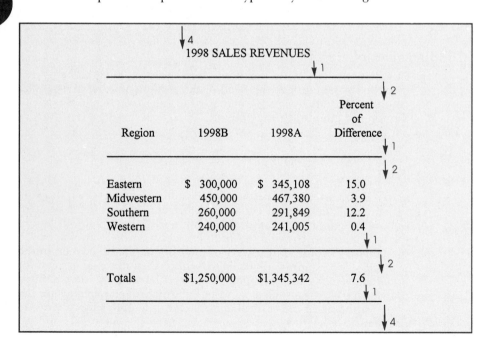

| | | 4 |
| 1998 SALES REVENUES ↓1 | | |

Region	1998B	1998A	Percent of Difference ↓2 ↓1 ↓2
Eastern	$ 300,000	$ 345,108	15.0
Midwestern	450,000	467,380	3.9
Southern	260,000	291,849	12.2
Western	240,000	241,005	0.4 ↓1 ↓2
Totals	$1,250,000	$1,345,342	7.6 ↓1 ↓4

(2) In a *ruled* table (one with horizontal rules only), either treat the underline as shown in the examples in the middle of page 462 or type a continuous underline the full width of the table (as shown in the table at the bottom of page 462) or extend it only across the full width of all the figure columns.

(3) In a *boxed* table (one with horizontal and vertical rules), either type a continuous underline the full width of the table (as shown in the table at the bottom of page 462) or type the underline the full distance between verticals in any column that contains a total.

d. If a *total* line is needed, type the word *Total* or *Totals* in the first column, depending on the number of totals to be shown in this row. Use an initial cap only or (for emphasis) all-capital letters. Start the word at the left margin of the column or indent it 0.5 inch (5 spaces on a typewriter).

1629 Percentages

a. If all the figures in a column represent percentages, type a percent sign (%) directly after each figure unless the column heading clearly indicates that these are percentages.

b. Percentages involving decimals should align on the decimal point. If necessary, add zeros after the decimal part of the number so that each figure will align at the right. If any percentage is less than 1 percent, add one zero to the left of the decimal point.

Increase	Percent of Increase	Increase (%)
55.48%	11.63	24
0.80%	4.00	37
2.09%	24.60	120
13.00%	0.40	8

1630 Special Treatment of Figures in Tables

a. Columns of long figures can be reduced in width by omitting the digits representing thousands, millions, or billions and indicating this omission in parentheses. For example:

(In Thousands)	**OR**	(000 Omitted)
(In Millions)		(000,000 Omitted)
(In Billions)		(000,000,000 Omitted)

NOTE: The word forms on the left are easier to grasp.

b. If the parenthetical comment applies to all columns of figures in the table, insert it as a subtitle to the table. However, if the comment applies only to one column of figures, insert the parenthetical comment in the column head.

NOTE: Sometimes because of space limitations a comment such as *(000 Omitted)* is reduced to *(000)*. The latter form is permissible if you are sure your reader will understand it.

(Continued on page 464.)

c. If the parenthetical comment applies to columns of dollar amounts, this fact can also be noted within parentheses and the dollar sign can then be omitted from the column text.

($000 Omitted)   OR   (In Thousands of Dollars)   OR   ($000)

d. When omitting thousands, millions, or billions from a wide column of figures, you may use rounding or a shortened decimal (or both) to reflect the portion of the number that is being omitted.

Complete Version	Shortened Versions		
Sales Revenues	Sales Revenues ($000 Omitted)	Sales Revenues (In Millions)	Sales Revenues ($000,000)
$ 5,878,044	5,878	$ 5.9	6
29,023,994	29,024	29.0	29
14,229,683	14,230	14.2	14
$49,131,721	49,132	$49.1	49

e. A negative figure in a column may be designated by enclosing the figure in parentheses or by inserting a minus sign (represented by a hyphen) directly to the left of the negative figure.

$1642.38	28.2%	Sales in 1997 ...	$264,238
−82.41	−14.5%	Sales in 1998 ...	262,305
$1559.97	6.1%	Gain/(loss)	$ (1,933)

1631 Leaders

a. If the items in the first column vary greatly in length, use leaders (rows of periods) to lead the eye across to the adjacent item in the next column. Every line of leaders should have at least three periods.

b. If you are using the *leader* feature of a word processing program, you can direct the program to insert a row of leaders where needed. The leaders will typically stop 2 or 3 spaces before the adjacent items in the next column. Accept whatever spacing the leader feature provides. (See the illustration on page 465.)

NOTE: The leader feature in some programs offers you a choice of solid leaders (...) or open leaders (. . .). In other programs the leader feature only provides solid leaders.

c. If you are using a typewriter, follow this procedure:

(1) Use solid leaders (...) because they are faster and simpler to type. Open leaders must be aligned vertically.

(2) Leave 1 blank space before the start of a row of leaders and before the start of the second column.

(3) In a table without vertical rules, you can easily determine in advance where the leaders should end. Simply backspace twice from the start of the second column, and at that point type a period to mark where the leaders are to stop.

NOTE: If you are planning to leave 6 spaces between columns, then between the longest item in the first column and the start of the adjacent item in the second column there should be 1 space followed by

16

four periods and then another space. See, for example, the table at the bottom of page 437. The key line for this table would appear thus:

```
Amount of substance .... kilogram      Symbol
          123456     '          123456
```

However, in a table with only two columns, the space between columns (and thus the number of periods) can be adjusted to create the table width you want. In the table at the top of page 439, the minimum number of periods (three) has been used. Therefore, the key line for this table would read:

```
Managerial and professional specialty ... 32,280,000
                                       12345
```

(4) If you are planning to use leaders in the first column of a boxed table (as shown in the illustration below), proceed as follows:

(a) Determine the space to be left between columns. (Assume the standard 6 spaces. Since the vertical rules will be centered between columns, allow 3 blank spaces on either side of each vertical rule.)

(b) In planning a key line, take the longest line in the first column and to it add a space, three periods, plus another space. REASON: The shortest row of leaders must have three periods (see ¶1631a), and there must be 1 blank space before and after (see ¶1631c). In short, add five keystrokes to the longest line in the first column to arrive at the first vertical rule.

(c) Then add three keystrokes to allow space between the first vertical rule and the start of the second column. (These three keystrokes will balance the 3 spaces that occur between the end of the second column and the next vertical rule; see the illustration below.)

16

Table 3.   NATIONAL INCOME BY SELECTED INDUSTRIES

(In Billions of Dollars)

	1980	1990	1993
Agriculture, forestry, and fisheries	61.4	97.1	105.3
Construction	126.6	234.4	228.0
Finance, insurance, and real estate	279.5	679.8	816.0
Government enterprises ...	321.8	657.9	765.3
Manufacturing	532.1	846.9	928.2
Services	341.0	948.3	1171.0

KEY LINE:

```
Government enterprises#...#123341.0123456948.3123456171.0
```

1632 Accounting for Omitted Items

When there is no entry to be typed in a given row, you can simply leave a blank at that point. However, if doing so may raise a question in the mind of your reader, consider these alternatives:

a. Type the abbreviation *NA* (meaning "not available" or "not applicable") centered on the column width.

b. Type a row of periods or hyphens. Use as few as three (centered on the column width), or type the row to the full width of the column.

```
23,804      23,804      23,804
16,345      16,345      16,345
......      ----          NA
38,442      38,442      38,442
```

➤ *See page 456 for another illustration.*

Table Rules

1633 If a table requires rules, use one of the following methods to insert them:

a. If you are using the table feature of a word processing program, you can print the table with a grid of horizontal and vertical rules that divides the rows and columns into boxes called *cells*. Retain the rules that you want to keep and delete the others.

b. If you are using a typewriter, you can use one of the following techniques to insert table rules.

(1) Insert all rules on the typewriter by means of underlining. Place a horizontal rule above and below the column heads and at the bottom of the table; do not underline the column heads. These rules should extend to the full width of the table. As shown in the illustrations on pages 454–457, type each rule on the line immediately following the preceding copy. This creates the appearance of a blank line above the rule. Leave 1 blank line between an internal rule and any table copy that follows; leave 2 or 3 blank lines (see ¶1604c) between the bottom rule and any running text that follows. If you plan to use vertical rules to separate the columns, insert the page sideways after you have finished typing the table text and type the vertical rules, using underlining. Do not type rules at the left and right sides of the table unless you want a fully boxed table.

(2) Insert all rules with a ballpoint pen and a ruler after you complete the typing. Be sure to leave space for these rules when typing the table.

(3) Insert all horizontal rules on the typewriter, as described in (1) above. Insert all vertical rules with a ballpoint pen.

NOTE: In a table that is to contain vertical rules, leave a minimum of 2 spaces between columns.

Table Notes

1634 a. If a table requires any explanatory notes or an identification of the source from which the table text was derived, place such material at the foot of the table. (Do not treat it as part of a sequence of notes related to the main text.)

b. Use a horizontal rule to separate the table text from the table notes. In a ruled or boxed table, the horizontal rule at the bottom of the table text will provide the necessary separation. In a table without full-width horizontal rules, provide the separation by typing a 1-inch rule. If you are using word processing software, leave 1 blank line above the horizontal rule you insert. If you are using a typewriter, type a 1-inch underline on the line directly below the last line of table text; this will create the appearance of 1 blank line.

c. Begin the first table note on the second line below the horizontal rule.

d. If all the notes occupy no more than one full line each, begin each note at the left margin of the table text (for the sake of appearance) and single-space the notes. However, if any of the notes turn over onto a second line, indent the first line of each note 0.5 inch (5 spaces on a typewriter), start all turnover lines at the left margin of the table text, and leave 1 blank line between each pair of notes. (See the illustration below.)

1635 If the material in the table has been derived from another source, indicate this fact as follows:

a. Type the word *Source* with an initial cap or in all-capital letters, followed by a colon, 2 spaces, and the identifying data. (See ¶¶1508–1522 for models to follow in presenting this bibliographic data.)

b. A source note should precede any other table note.

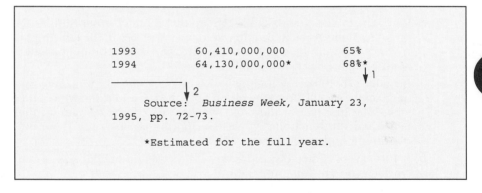

1636 a. If you use abbreviations or symbols that the reader may not understand, explain them in a note at the bottom of the table. This explanation should follow the source note (if any) and precede any other table note. If more than one abbreviation or symbol needs decoding, the explanation can be handled as a series of separate notes (each preceded by a raised symbol or letter), or it may be done all in one note. For examples of both styles, see pages 456 and 457.

b. Except for source notes (like the one illustrated above) and a single note explaining symbols and abbreviations (like the one shown on page 456), every table note should begin with a raised symbol or letter that keys the note to the appropriate word or figure in the table text (or title or subtitle) above. Type the corresponding symbol or letter immediately after the appropriate word or figure above, without any intervening space. (See ¶1636d, note.)

(Continued on page 468.)

    c. Use the following sequence of symbols: *, **, ***   **OR**   *, †, ‡, §, ¶. (See ¶1502f.)

    d. Use raised lowercase letters (ᵃ, ᵇ, ᶜ, etc.) in place of symbols when there are more than five footnotes for a given table.

       NOTE: Avoid the use of raised *figures* to identify table notes. They could be confusing if used in conjunction with figures in the table text. Moreover, if raised figures are already used for notes pertaining to the main text, it is wise to use letters or symbols so as to distinguish notes that pertain to a specific table.

    e. In assigning symbols or letters in sequence, go in order by row (horizontally), not by column (vertically).

Dealing With Long Tables

1637 To keep a table from extending beyond the page on which it starts, consider these techniques:

    a. Put the table number (if any) on the same line as the table title rather than on the second line above. (See also ¶1614b.)

    b. Use single spacing for the table text. (See also ¶1624.)

    c. Shorten the wording of the table title, subtitle, column heads, and items in the table text to reduce turnover lines. Use abbreviations and symbols toward this end. (See also ¶1615c.) If necessary, provide a brief explanation in the table notes of any abbreviations and symbols that your reader may not immediately understand. (See also ¶1636.)

    d. When the table text entails a long item that is out of proportion to all the other items (or is to be entered in several places in the table text), try to convert the item into a table note, keyed by a symbol or letter appropriately placed in the table above.

    e. If a table is both narrow and long, you can save space by repeating the same sequence of column heads on both the left and right sides of the table. The first half of the table text appears on the left side of the table, and the remaining table text appears on the right. (See the illustration and note on page 455.)

    f. If you have a choice of various type sizes, select a smaller size of the typeface you are using for the other tables.

1638 If a table requires more than one page, follow this procedure:

    a. At the bottom of the page where the table breaks, type a continuation line—for example, *Table continued on page 14*—unless it is quite obvious that the table continues on the next page. Type the continuation line in parentheses or brackets, positioned so as to end at the right margin on the line directly below the point at which the table breaks.

       NOTE: If you are breaking a table with ruled or boxed column heads, do not type a full-width horizontal rule at the bottom of the page where the table text breaks off. This horizontal rule should appear only at the very end of the table text.

    b. At the top of the page on which the table continues, repeat the table number (if any) and the table title, followed by the word *Continued* or *Cont.* in parentheses. Also repeat the column heads before resuming the table text.

   c. Ordinarily, all table notes should appear only on the page on which the table ends. However, to avoid inconveniencing a reader, place the appropriate notes at the bottom of each page, even if this means that some notes will have to be repeated on two or more pages. Insert a 1-inch horizontal rule before such notes (as described in ¶1634).

1639 Do not start a table at the bottom of one page and continue it on the top of the next page if the entire table will fit on one page (either by itself or with regular text). In such a case start the table at the top of the next page and insert a cross-reference in the text. (See ¶1608.)

   NOTE: Many word processing programs have a feature called *block protect,* which prevents a page break from occurring within a block of text. (See the entry on *block protect* in Appendix B.)

Dealing With Wide Tables

1640 To keep a wide table from extending beyond the margins established for the page, consider the following techniques. (If they do not solve the problem, see ¶¶1641–1642 for two other approaches.)

   a. Reduce the space between columns to as little as 2 spaces. (To preserve the clarity of the table, you can insert vertical rules.)

   b. Use abbreviations and symbols to hold down the length of lines in the column heads and the column text.

   c. If only a few entries are disproportionately wide or are repeated in the table and make it difficult to fit the table in the space available, consider the possibility of converting these items to table footnotes. (See also ¶1637d.)

   d. If you have a choice of various type sizes, select a smaller size of the typeface in order to make the table fit within the space available.

1641 Making a Reduced Copy

If the suggestions in ¶1640 do not keep a wide table from extending beyond the margins established for the page, consider using a photocopier that can produce copies in reduced size. Follow this procedure:

   a. Type the extrawide table across the 11-inch dimension of a separate sheet. (See ¶1642.) Reduce the space between columns to as little as 2 spaces in order to limit the overall width of the table.

   b. Make a reduced photocopy of the table that brings the table width down to the desired size. Make sure, however, that the table is still readable.

   c. Mount the reduced version of the table horizontally in the desired location, either on a page with regular text or on a separate page.

   d. Make a fresh copy of the pasted-up page so that all the material appears on the same surface.

16

1642 Turning the Table Sideways

a. Whenever possible, a table should read horizontally, just like the regular text. However, when other alternatives do not work or cannot be used, turn the table so that it runs vertically on a page by itself. In such a case the left margin of the table will fall toward the bottom of the page and the right margin toward the top.

NOTE: If you are using word processing software, you may have the option of *landscape printing*, that is, printing text on the 11-inch dimension of standard stationery. (*Portrait printing* is the term that describes the customary printing of text on the 8½-inch dimension of standard stationery.)

b. In planning the layout of a turned table, be sure that the overall dimensions of the table will fit within the established margins for the regular pages in the given document. If no margins have been established, leave a minimum margin of 1 inch on all sides of the turned table.

NOTE: If a turned table is to be part of a *bound* report, leave a minimum top margin of 1.5 inches. This top margin will represent the left margin when the turned table is bound into the report. (See also ¶1404b.)

16

SECTION 17

OTHER BUSINESS DOCUMENTS

———————

Section 17 provides models for a number of common business documents. The models reflect formats widely used, but they are not to be regarded as rigid patterns that must be followed without deviation. Feel free to modify these formats to fit the needs of the situation at hand. As always, good sense and good taste (rather than an artificial notion of "absolute correctness") should prevail.

GENERAL FORMAT CONSIDERATIONS

Paragraphs 1701–1703 deal with the issues of establishing margins, the treatment of headings, and the choice of alternative type styles if you are using a computer. These format considerations apply to all the specific types of documents discussed later in Section 17.

Margins

1701 a. Top Margin. If you are using plain standard (8½" × 11") stationery for the first page of a business document, use a top margin of 1 to 2 inches but limit it to 1 inch in order to fit more copy on the page and avoid the need for a second page. If you are using letterhead stationery or a memo form for the first page, begin typing on the third line below the letterhead or the memo heading. If the document requires more than one page, use plain paper for the continuation pages and leave a top margin of 1 inch.

b. Side Margins. If you are using standard stationery, leave 1-inch side margins. This provides a 6.5-inch line for the text of the document. Use a shorter line for the text if (1) you are using a smaller size of stationery, (2) you want to bring columns of text closer together for easier reading, or (3) you want to achieve a more open look or a more balanced arrangement on the page. (See, for example, the illustration on page 476.) In any case, consult the chart in ¶1305b for the appropriate margin settings.

c. Bottom Margin. Leave a bottom margin of at least 1 inch (6 lines on a typewriter).

17

Headings

1702 a. Main Heading. The title of the document or the name of the organization ordinarily appears centered on the first line, in all-capital letters. Additional details (such as a date or a location) appear in capital and small letters on separate lines, with 1 blank line between them. Use boldface for all elements in the heading if you have that option. Leave 2 blank lines after the last line of the main heading before starting the body of the document. (For examples, see pages 475–478, 480, and 482.)

b. Continuation Heading. If a document requires more than one page, insert a continuation heading like the one used on the second page of a letter. If you are using word processing software, use the header feature to create and automatically position the continuation heading. (See ¶1384 for further details.)

NOTE: The second page of a résumé typically uses a slightly different continuation heading. (See pages 491, 493, and 495 for examples.)

Type Styles

1703 All the illustrations in Section 17 have been generated by WordPerfect 6 for Windows, using different typefaces. These models reflect the use of boldface and italics where special emphasis is warranted. If these options are not available to you, use underlining and all-capital letters instead.

EXECUTIVE DOCUMENTS

The following paragraphs (¶¶1704–1706) present commonly used formats for agendas, minutes, and itineraries. A suggested format for a fax cover sheet (¶1707) and guidelines for formatting e-mail (¶¶1708–1711) are also provided.

Agendas

1704 An *agenda* is a list of items to be considered or acted upon. The format of an agenda varies with the circumstances. The agenda for an informal staff meeting may be done as a simple numbered list of topics in a memo addressed to the attendees. (See the illustration on page 475.) The agenda for a formal meeting (for example, of a corporate board of directors) will typically call for a more structured list of topics. (See the illustration on page 476.) The agenda for a formal program (for example, for a conference or a seminar) will be structured around a timetable, with specific time slots allotted to formal presentations by speakers and topical discussions in small groups. (See the illustration on page 477.)

There is no single "correct" way to set up an agenda. The illustrations on pages 475–477 are intended only to suggest various ways in which an agenda can be formatted. The format you decide to use should be tailored to fit the needs of the meeting or program being planned.

Minutes

1705 *Minutes* provide a record of what was discussed and decided upon at a meeting. The minutes of small committee meetings within an organization are usually done in an informal style, in much the same way that the agendas for such meetings are also prepared. (Compare the informal agenda on page 475 with the informal minutes on page 478.) When the participants at a meeting come from a number of different organizations (as they would, for example, at meetings of professional associations and societies), the minutes tend to be somewhat more formal. And when the minutes may have to serve some legal use, they are typically done in a highly formal style. According to the American Society of Corporate Secretaries, increasing government regulation and stockholder lawsuits make it critically important that the minutes of a meeting of a corporation's board of directors be complete and accurate, since they may have to serve as legal evidence of what the corporation's directors did or intended to do. The *short form* of corporate minutes (illustrated on page 480) simply describes the decisions that were made, along with some brief indication of the key facts on which those decisions were made. By contrast, the *long form* describes in some detail the arguments for and against the decisions finally arrived at.

17

¶1706

Itineraries

1706 An itinerary should clearly set forth the travel arrangements and the appointment schedule of the person making the trip. If the itinerary is intended only for the use of the person traveling, it should be possible to eliminate certain items and abbreviate details that the person is quite familiar with. However, if the itinerary will be distributed to others (who may need to contact the person who is traveling), present the information as fully and as clearly as possible. (For an example, see the illustration on page 482.)

Fax Cover Sheets

1707 Most messages sent by fax (facsimile) equipment are accompanied by a fax cover sheet that indicates (1) the name and fax number of the person receiving the fax, (2) the name and fax number of the person sending the fax, (3) the number of pages being sent, and (4) the name and the telephone number of the person to be called in case the transmission is not satisfactorily completed. There are different ways to prepare a fax cover sheet. If you are using word processing software, your software may provide a fax template that you can use as is or modify to suit your preferences. If you are designing a fax cover sheet as a form to be filled in by hand, you will need to add fill-in lines. The illustration and text shown on page 483 suggest how an existing fax template taken from WordPerfect 6 for Windows might be modified to create a fax cover sheet as a form.

NOTE: The ready availability of small stick-on labels that accommodate all the essential information in a compact form is appealing to many people, who are pleased to save time and money as a result of not having to create or transmit a separate fax cover sheet. Therefore, do not feel compelled to use a fax cover sheet if a commercially prepared stick-on label will serve your purpose.

(Text continues on page 484.)

17

Agenda—Informal (Memo) Style

MEMO TO: Marketing Managers Committee ↓2

FROM: Dorothy Innie *DI* ↓2

A

DATE: July 10, 19— ↓2

SUBJECT: Agenda for July 20 Meeting ↓3

Our July 20 meeting will begin at 9:30 a.m. in the small conference room on the second floor. (The large conference room, where we normally meet, has been reserved by Mrs. Harper for an all-day meeting.) ↓2

Please come prepared to discuss the following topics: ↓2

1.   Sales through June for each product line. ↓2

2.   Year-end sales forecast vs. budget for each product line.

B

3.   Recommendations for changes in this year's marketing plans and requests for supplemental funding.

4.   Proposed changes in next year's marketing strategies.

C

5.   Preliminary marketing budgets for next year. (Please put these in writing for me so that I can share them with Bill Carr, our friendly bean counter in the Finance Department.) ↓2

ma ↓3

Distribution: ↓2

G. Albers
R. Fagan
K. Garcia-Lorca
S. Koechlin
F. Li
C. Mandel
T. Pavlick
P. Washington

17

A   Memo Format. For the format of a memo done on plain paper (as shown here) or on letterhead stationery, see ¶1393. For the format of a memo done on a printed memo form, see ¶1394.

B   Numbered List. Note that turnovers are aligned with the first word above. Leave 1 blank line between items (even if all the items require only 1 line each) so as to make the list easier to read. For further details on the format of a numbered list, see ¶1357d.

C   End Punctuation. The items in an agenda typically require no end punctuation. However, if any item involves the use of a complete sentence (as in item 5 in this illustration), place a period at the end of every item. For details on the use or omission of periods with items in a list, see ¶107.

Agenda—Formal Style

```
                    UNDERLOCK AND KEYE INC↓2

                            Agenda↓2

                  Regular Meeting of Directors↓2

              Wednesday, September 23, 1998-10 a.m↓2

                     Boardroom, Fifth Floor↓3


D       1.  Call to order↓2

        2.  Approval of minutes

        3.  Report on August operations-G. A. Herzenberg

A       4.  Report on corporate financial matters-A. J. McGill

        5.  Report on corporate development matters-L. Soaries       C

        6.  Review of international operations-W. Burgos

        7.  Discussion of Real Estate Committee report

        8.  Overview of the performance of major competitors-T. Foy

        9.  New business
D
        10. Adjournment

B
```

17

A Margins. Note the use of wide (1.75″) side margins and a 5-inch line for the text. This agenda has a number of very short items. If it were done on a standard (6.5″) line, it would have an unbalanced look, with a relatively small left margin and a very large right margin.

B Numbered List. When a numbered list contains 10 or more items, align the single- and double-digit figures on the period. Begin the double-digit figures at the left margin.

C End Punctuation. Note that no periods are needed at the end of the items in this illustration. (See also ¶107.)

D Formal Items. In a formal agenda it is customary to include such items as *Call to order, Approval of minutes, New business,* and *Adjournment* (or similar types of expressions).

Agenda—Program for a Conference or Seminar

A   **SOFTWARE APPLICATIONS SEMINAR** ↓2

Saddle Brook Marriott ↓2

July 13-14, 19— ↓3

B   **Wednesday, July 13** ↓2

8:00–9:00	Registration and Continental Breakfast ↓2	**C**	Lobby
9:00–9:40 **D**	Software Applications: A State-of-the-Art Overview Speaker: Joyce Stocker-Olsen		Salons A and B
9:50–10:30	Word Processing and Communications Applications Speakers: Louis Serrano and Roy Pfaltz **F**		Salons A and B
10:30–10:50	Coffee Break		Lobby
10:50–11:30	Desktop Publishing and Graphics Applications Speakers: Sandra Scroggins and Ed Fox		Salons A and B
11:40–12:20	Spreadsheet and Database Management Applications Speaker: Esther W. Benoit **F**		Salons A and B
12:30–1:45	Lunch		Ballroom
1:45–3:15	<u>Concurrent Sessions</u>		
E	Session 1: WordPerfect 6.1 for Windows Speaker: Irwin Manoogian		Red Oak Suite

A **Headings.** Include the location and date(s) of the conference or seminar in the main heading unless the program is part of a larger document that features this information prominently in some other way. If the program is **B** scheduled to last more than one day, insert an appropriate side heading above each day's listing of events.

C **Columnar Format.** Ordinarily, leave 0.5 inch (6 spaces on a typewriter) between columns. However, if you plan to use leaders (a row of periods) to visually connect each item in the second column with its counterpart in the third column, leave 2 or 3 spaces between the final period in the second column and the start of the third column. (See ¶1631 for further de- **D** tails.) Align the text in each column at the left. With automatic justifica-tion you can block the text in the last column (showing room location) at the right. For the alignment of **E** "clock" times in a column, see ¶1626b.

F **Speaker Identification.** The speakers listed on the program may be further identified by title, organization, and/ or place of residence. Use commas to separate these elements of identifica-tion and, if you wish, use parentheses to enclose these elements as a whole. For example:

> Roy Pfaltz, software consultant, Newton, Massachusetts

OR: Esther W. Benoit (vice president, Programmatic Associates, Los Altos, California)

17

Minutes—Informal (Memo) Style

A   **MEMO TO:**   Marketing Managers Committee
↓ 2

      FROM: Paula Washington
↓ 2

      DATE: July 21, 19— ↓ 2

B   **SUBJECT:**   Minutes of the Marketing Managers
                   Committee Meeting of July 20, 19—
↓ 3

C   **Present:**   Dorothy Innie (presiding), Georgia Albers, Ruth Fagan, Katherine
               Garcia-Lorca, Sid Koechlin, Charles Mandel, Tim Pavlick
↓ 2

      Absent: Fay Li ↓ 2

      Guest: Bill Carr ↓ 3

                                          E

D   1. **Sales through June for each product line.** Each product line is behind budget for
        the first six months of the year. Bill Carr of the Finance Department reported that
        the company as a whole is running 11.2 percent behind budget and 6.3 percent
        behind last year's sales for the first six months.

      2. **Year-end sales forecast vs. budget for each product line.** Ruth Fagan and
        Sid Koechlin each reported that on the basis of recent reports from the sales will

F   The next meeting of the Marketing Managers Committee will be held on August 24 in
     the *large* conference room (as usual). ↓ 2

     Paula Washington ↓ 2

     nb ↓ 3

     Distribution: ↓ 2

     D. Innie
     G. Albers
     R. Fagan
     K. Garcia-Lorca
     S. Koechlin
     F. Li
     C. Mandel
     T. Pavlick

17

A Memo Format. For the format of a memo done on plain paper (as shown here) or on letterhead stationery, see ¶1393. For the format of a memo done on a memo form, see ¶1394.

B Subject Line. For better appearance, the entry following *Subject:* has been broken into two lines of roughly equal length. (See ¶1353d, note.)

C Attendance Data. This block of copy, which starts on the third line below the memo heading, indicates who was present at the meeting (the person who presided is listed first), who was absent, and who attended as a guest.

D Content Considerations. List each topic in the order in which it was discussed at the meeting. (Compare these minutes with the agenda shown on page 475.) Use boldface, italics, or underlining to highlight each topic. End with a period

E if the comments are to continue on the same line (as shown here). Omit the period if the comments are to appear below the highlighted topic; in that case leave 1 blank line before starting the comments and block each line of the comments on the first word of the topic above (not on the number at the left

F margin). Give the date and location of the next meeting in a concluding paragraph, starting at the left margin.

17

Minutes—Formal Style

A

UNDERLOCK AND KEYE INC. ↓2

Minutes ↓2

Regular Meeting of Directors ↓2

September 23, 19— ↓3

B
D   A regular meeting of the Board of Directors of Underlock and Keye Inc. was called to order at 4 Riverfront Plaza, Louisville, Kentucky, at 10 a.m. pursuant to the notice sent to all directors in accordance with the bylaws. ↓2

E   The following directors were present, constituting all the directors: Jared C. Allison II, Kenneth L. Calderone, Deborah

---

E   Also present by invitation were William Burgos, Thomas Foy, Gregory A. Herzenberg, Angela J. McGill, and Lester Soaries.

Jared G. Allison II, Chairman, presided and David K. Rust, Assistant Secretary, recorded the proceedings of the meeting.   **J**

The minutes of the last meeting were approved.

Mr. Allison introduced Gregory A. Herzenberg, Executive Vice President of Operations, who reported on August operations.   **J**

F   Henry Koyama reviewed the recommendations of the Real Estate Committee on the matter of building a new facility or renovating the existing facility to accommodate the Corporation's information processing needs over the next ten years.   **I**

After further discussion, upon motion duly made and seconded, the following resolutions were unanimously adopted: ↓2

C   RESOLVED, that the Corporation is hereby authorized to undertake construction and rehabilitation activities

---

G   The next meeting of the Board will be held on November 24 at 10 a.m.

H   There being no further business before the meeting, it was, on motion duly made and seconded, adjourned at 1:05 p.m. ↓3

_____

Assistant Secretary

17

A   **Heading.** Use all-capital letters for the name of the company in the first line. Use capital and small letters for the other lines. For the date line, use the date on which the meeting was held (not the date on which the minutes were prepared). Use boldface (if available) for all the elements in the heading.

B   **Format Considerations.** Use 1-inch side margins. Indent the first line of each paragraph 0.5 inch (5 spaces on a typewriter). Treat resolutions as extracts, indented as a block 0.5 inch (5 spaces on a typewriter) from each side margin.

C   Type *RESOLVED* in all-capital letters, followed by a comma and *that* (as illustrated). As an alternative, type *RESOLVED* followed by a colon and *That*.

D   **Content Considerations.** Use the opening paragraph to indicate the name of the company; the time and the place where the meeting was "called to order" (the first item on the agenda shown on page 476); and whether it was a regular

E   or special meeting. Use the next paragraphs to indicate which directors were present (all were in this illustration); which were absent; which company officers and invited guests were present; who presided; and who recorded the proceedings and prepared the minutes. The body of the minutes should note

F   in each paragraph what business was transacted and what actions were taken.

G   Use the next-to-last paragraph to indicate the date and time of the next meet-

H   ing. Use the final paragraph to indicate the time of adjournment.

I   **Capitalization Style.** Minutes done in a formal style use a formal style of capitalization. Note that short forms such as *Corporation* and *Board* are capitalized. Also note that in formal minutes such titles as *Chairman, Assistant Secretary,* and

J   *Executive Vice President of Operations* are capitalized when used after a person's name. (See ¶313d.)

17

Itinerary

```
                              ITINERARY
                                  ↓2
                         For Wallace F. Galloway
                                       ↓2
                         April 12–14, 19—
                                       ↓3

A     Tuesday, April 12
                       ↓2
      6:00 a.m.          B    Limo to airport:  Town Taxi (454-1040)        G
                                                                  ↓2
      7:00 a.m.               Depart Rochester, Mohawk Flight 401

C     8:15 a.m.               Arrive Westchester

                        D    Limo to meeting: Arthur's Limo (203-555-5347)  G
                             Driver will meet you at baggage carousel.

                             Destination:   Burnham & Frye Inc.
                                            225 High Ridge Road
                                            Stamford, CT
                                            203-555-1216

      9:00 a.m.–2:30 p.m.     Meet with Ed Burnham and Norbert Pell.  They will   F
                             make lunch arrangements.

      2:30 p.m.               Limo to NYC:  Call Arthur's Limo (203-555-5347)
                             if 2:30 pickup time has to be changed.

                             Hotel:   Marriott Marquis
                                      1535 Broadway
                                      212-398-1900
                                      Conf. No. 8941HWXQ; late arrival guaranteed

      6:30 p.m.               Dinner with Doris and Jack Cuneen; meet at restaurant
                             (Palio, 151 West 51st Street, 212-245-4850)
                                                                   ↓2
A     Wednesday, April 13

      9:00 a.m.–4:00 p.m.     Board meeting in headquarters building, 49th floor
                             Sam Hurley will drive you to the airport.

      5:25 p.m.               Depart Newark, Northwest Flight 1809

E     6:40 p.m.               Arrive Washington, National Airport
```

17

A **Headings.** If the itinerary is to cover more than one day, insert an appropriate side heading above each day's scheduled list of activities.

B **Columnar Format.** Leave a minimum of 0.5 inch (6 spaces on a typewriter) between columns. For the alignment
C of "clock" times in a column, see ¶1626b.

D **Spacing.** Leave 1 blank line between entries. Single-space any turnovers.

E **Content Considerations.** Provide the names of airports only when there is more than one airport serving the city (in this case, Washington, D.C.). Try
F to provide the first names (rather than simply titles or initials) for all the individuals whom the traveler is scheduled to meet. Provide phone
G numbers for all transportation services, hotels, and restaurants in case the plans have to be rescheduled or canceled.

Fax Cover Sheet

facsimile
T R A N S M I T T A L

BURNHAM & FRYE INC.
225 High Ridge Road
Stamford, CT 06905

Date: **B** _____

To: _____

_____

_____

Fax number: _____

From: _____

A   _____

Fax number: _____

Number of pages
[including this
cover sheet]:   _____

Message: _____

_____

**If any part of this fax transmission
is missing or not clearly received,
please call:**

Name: _____

Phone number: _____

A **Format Considerations.** If you are using software to create a template for a fax cover sheet that only you will use, insert any information that will not change (such as your name and fax number) as a part of the template. However, if you are creating a form to be used by a number of people, provide blank fill-in lines to accommodate this variable information.

B **Fill-in Lines.** If you are designing a fax cover sheet as a form to be filled in by hand, arrange the fill-in lines so that all entries can start at a common point.

C **Confidentiality Statement.** If you are faxing something that is confidential (and this may sometimes not be a wise thing to do), you may want to add an appropriate message to the cover sheet. For example:

CONFIDENTIAL

The contents of this fax transmission are confidential. If this transmission has been directed to the wrong office, please destroy the contents of this fax immediately and notify [*sender's name*] at [*phone number*].

To further ensure the confidentiality of the transmission, call the appropriate person in the receiving office and (1) confirm the fax number to be used and (2) confirm that the person will be standing right by the receiving equipment while the fax is being transmitted.

17

¶1708

E-Mail

The number of e-mail users grew from 5.9 million in 1991 to 38 million in 1995 and is expected to continue growing at a rapid rate for the rest of the nineties. There is good reason for the speed with which this new technology has taken hold: the use of e-mail serves to overcome the problems associated with the delivery of regular mail (referred to as *snail mail* by some e-mail users) and the frustrations that result from playing telephone tag (leaving messages but never connecting). Do keep in mind, however, that e-mail is not the best means of communication for all situations, particularly when matters need to be treated confidentially. (See ¶1709d.)

The following guidelines (¶¶1708–1711) suggest how to compose and format e-mail messages so as to make the most of what this technology offers.

1708 Before composing an e-mail message, remember that the person you are addressing may receive as many as 50 to 100 such messages a day. Many recipients report increasing frustration over the time it takes to read each day's e-mail messages, especially if many of those messages are the electronic equivalent of junk mail. To avoid frustrating the recipients of your e-mail:

a. Keep the distribution of your e-mail messages to a minimum. Given the ease of transmitting an e-mail message to everyone on an existing mailing list, you could be sending messages to people who don't need to see them and thus be adding to their e-mail overload.

b. Keep your messages short. Try to hold the overall length to 25 lines (the number of lines that will fit on one screen). Limit each line to a maximum of 80 characters.

c. Consider how much background your reader needs to have in order to understand your message. If you are responding to an issue raised in the earlier e-mail message, it is a great temptation to repeat the earlier message along with your response. Try to paraphrase the earlier message as briefly as possible so as to spare your reader unnecessary verbiage.

d. Provide a subject line for each message you compose. A subject line helps the recipient of a great many messages screen them quickly to determine which require the fastest action. (See ¶1711b.)

e. Restrict each message to one subject. It is better to send two separate messages than to cover several topics in one message.

f. Organize your sentences in short, single-spaced paragraphs to make your message easier to understand. Do not indent the opening line of each paragraph, but leave 1 blank line between paragraphs.

g. Edit and proofread each message carefully, and make the necessary corrections before sending the message. Because e-mail messages are usually composed on the computer, it is easy to make (and overlook) mistakes in grammar, usage, spelling, and style. (See ¶¶1202–1204.)

h. Do not use all-capital letters in your messages. Follow the standard rules of capitalization.

1709 When you are composing e-mail messages, keep these points in mind:

a. Watch your tone in composing the message. Before you send it, read the message from the recipient's point of view to make sure that your words and your tone are not likely to be misconstrued.

17

NOTE: Some e-mail users insert *smileys* [for example, :-)] in their messages to indicate their feelings about what they are writing. However, many people find the use of smileys overly cute and feel they are no more necessary in e-mail messages than in any other kind of written communication. (For further discussion of smileys, see Appendix B.)

b. Do not send a message composed in anger (an act known as *flaming*). Moreover, if you receive *flames* (angry messages), it is wiser to ignore them than to respond in kind.

c. Do not use e-mail to send unsolicited ads or other material that the recipient is likely to regard as junk mail. People who receive such material often take revenge by responding with flames. Some recipients may go so far as to make use of special programs referred to as *bozo filters*. These programs automatically intercept and delete all future messages from such bozos.

d. Put nothing in an e-mail message that you would not want anyone other than the intended recipient to see. For example, do not provide credit card numbers or other confidential information that could wind up in the wrong hands. Moreover, do not use e-mail if you want to criticize or reprimand someone. In all such cases use another medium of communication. Remember: The privacy of the e-mail messages you send cannot be guaranteed.

e. Respect the privacy of the messages you receive. Do not pass such messages on to others unless you are sure the sender will not object.

1710 E-mail messages can be distributed through local and wide area networks, bulletin board systems, on-line services, and the Internet. Procedures for sending and receiving e-mail messages will therefore differ, depending on the system you use. Even the construction of mailing addresses will vary as a result.

a. A mailing address has two parts separated by @ (the symbol for *at*).

b. The part that precedes @ is called the *mailbox*. It typically consists of your *username* (the name you use to log on a computer); for example, *ritajbella, rjbella, rjb, ritaj*. However, some systems assign you an arbitrary mailbox. CompuServe users, for example, receive mailboxes composed entirely of figures. (See the second illustration on page 487.)

c. The part that follows @ is called the *domain*. It represents the mail system on which you receive your mail. The domain consists of two or more elements separated by periods (referred to as *dots*). If you use America Online, the domain is *aol.com*; if you use CompuServe, the domain is *compuserve.com*. (Dots are used between the elements of the domain but not at the end.) If you are sending e-mail to someone within your own domain, you can omit the domain from the mailing address.

d. Here are a few e-mail addresses:

the President of the United States	president@whitehouse.gov
The Internet Society	isoc@isoc.org
Laboratory for Computer Science at MIT	lcs@mit.edu
NewbieNewz (an electronic newsletter for newcomers to the Internet)	newbienewz-reqest@io.com

17

(Continued on page 486.)

NOTE: The final element in the domain indicates what kind of system is being used. For example, *com* signifies "commercial," *gov* "governmental," *edu* "educational," and *org* "organizational."

1711 The format of an e-mail message is very much like that of a simplified memo. (See the illustrations on page 487.) The first illustration shows how an e-mail message looks after the sender has written it. The second illustration shows how the same message will appear to the person who receives it.

a. After the guide word *To* insert the recipient's name and mailing address. If the message is addressed to more than one person, use a comma to separate the entries showing each recipient's name and mailing address.

NOTE: Under certain circumstances you may also have to insert the name of the system you are using—for example, *Internet*. (See the illustration at the top of page 487.)

b. After *Subject* or *Re* insert an appropiate subject line. As noted in ¶1708e, try to deal with only one subject in each message. Since the recipient may look at only the subject line to decide how important your message is, be sure to choose attention-getting wording.

c. Your e-mail template may provide a guide word such as *Copies* or *Cc* so that you can insert the name and mailing address of anyone who is also intended to receive this message.

d. Your e-mail template may also provide a guide word such as *Reply to.* Make an entry here if you want the recipient to send a response to an address other than the one shown in the *From* entry.

e. You do not need to indicate whom the message is from. The software program will automatically insert your mailing address (as well as your full name) after *From*. It will also automatically display the date and time when the message was transmitted. (See the illustration at the bottom of page 487.)

NOTE: The program will automatically display additional lines of information such as routing data. You may also have the option of displaying your conventional mailing address, your phone number, your fax number, and any other information you wish. (See the illustration at the bottom of page 487.)

f. In the interest of brevity, salutations and complimentary closings are often omitted. However, follow your personal preferences in such matters. (In the illustration at the bottom of page 487 note the use of *Kate* as a salutation and *Thanks* as a closing.)

➤ *For guidelines on message length, paragraphing, spacing, and capitalization, see ¶1708.*

g. Users of e-mail sometimes rely on special abbreviations to shorten their messages. For example:

BTW	by the way	BAK	I'm back at the keyboard
IMHO	in my humble opinion	LOL	I'm laughing out loud at what I just read
GMTA	great minds think alike		
J/K	just kidding	ROTFL	I'm rolling on the floor laughing at what I just read
BRB	be right back		

17

E-Mail Message Sent

```
To:       Kate Christopher, internet: gmch89a@prodigy.com
Subject:  Misplaced Disk

Kate:

I have misplaced the floppy disk that accompanies the first edition of the computer dictionary
you publish. Is there any chance that you could send me a replacement disk? I'll be glad to pay
whatever charges are involved. Thanks.

                                    Jim
```

E-Mail Message Received

```
------------------------------------------------------------------
PRODIGY (R) Services Messages                02/03 ET  4:13 PM
------------------------------------------------------------------

    From:   James Alexander
 Subject:   Misplaced Disk
    Date:   02/03  4:13 PM

Date:       02 Feb 95 18:59:44 EST
From:       James Alexander     [75060.2477@compuserve.com]
Subject:    Misplaced Disk


Kate:

I have misplaced the floppy disk that accompanies the first
edition of the computer dictionary you publish. Is there any
chance that you could send me a replacement disk? I'll be glad
to pay whatever charges are involved. Thanks.

                            Jim

**********************************************************************

James Alexander                     75060.2477@compuserve.com
Computer Management Associates
455 West Sierra Avenue                    Phone: 707/555-9985
Cotati, CA 94931                            Fax: 707/555-6640
**********************************************************************


-------- Original Message header fol
From 75060.2477@compuserve.com Thu Feb 02 19:00:45 1995
[PIM 3.2-342.56]
Received: from arl-img-1.compuserve.com by
maily1.prodigy.com with SMTP id AA79074  (5.65c/IDA-1.4.4
For <gmch89a@prodigy.com>-; Thu, 2 Feb 1995 19:01:05 -0500
Received: by arl-img-1.compuserve.com (8.6.9/5.941228sam)
id TAA16147; Thu, 2 Feb 1995 19:01:04 -0500
Date: 02 Feb 95 18:59:44 EST
From: James Alexander <75060.2477@compuserve.com>
To: Kate Christopher <gmch89a@prodigy.com>
Subject: Misplaced Disk
Message-Id: <950202235944_75060.2477_CHK67-1@CompuServe.COM>

-------------- End of message  --------------
```

17

¶1712

RÉSUMÉS

Preparing a Résumé

1712 When you prepare a résumé, keep the following things in mind:

a. The purpose of a résumé is not to get you a job but to get you an *interview* for a job.

b. The purpose of a résumé is not to tell a prospective employer about *your* long-term goals and aspirations but to indicate *what you can do for the employer* with the experience you have acquired and the skills you have developed.

c. Do not describe your past jobs in terms of duties and responsibilities. Emphasize things that you have achieved, capabilities that you have acquired, decision-making skills you have put to good use, activities you have initiated, sales and profits that have increased (and expenses that have decreased) because of your efforts.

d. Describe your achievements and skills in a way that indicates they are readily applicable to other types of jobs and other fields.

e. Do not overstate your achievements by claiming to have done certain things single-handedly when it will be clear to the prospective employer that your achievement had to be part of a team effort. In the attempt to come across as a self-starter, don't jeopardize your reputation for honesty.

f. While you want your résumé to stand out from all the others that are submitted at the same time, think of how an employer will view your résumé. If you're applying for a job in advertising, design, or some other creative field, an original format or even an off-the-wall approach may get you the positive attention you crave. But if you're after a job in management, finance, or marketing—where an image of maturity and dependability is important—you'll gain more ground by emphasizing how you can help the employer rather than by taking a far-out approach.

g. Weigh the advantages of preparing a custom-tailored résumé for each situation (in which you organize and focus your strengths in light of a specific employer's needs) over the savings in time and money that comes from preparing an all-purpose résumé designed to fit a variety of job opportunities and a range of employers' needs. When you use a computer, the prospect of preparing custom-tailored résumés is not as overwhelming as it might be if you were preparing each document on a typewriter.

h. Keep the résumé as short as possible (no more than two pages). Some employers may ask for a one-page résumé.

i. Choose a format that yields a clean, uncluttered look. (See the models on pages 490–495.)

j. Do not mention how much you earned in previous jobs or how much you expect to earn in the future.

k. Do not refer to your age, your marital status, your height and weight, your hobbies, or other personal details unless they clearly enhance your suitability for the job in question.

17

l. Do not supply reasons for having left previous jobs or for gaps in your employment history. However, do prepare yourself for dealing with these issues if they come up in the interview.

m. Do not give references on the résumé. It is not even necessary to state that references are available upon request. Be prepared, however, to supply names, addresses, and phone numbers at the interview.

n. Use good-quality paper (of at least 20-pound weight and preferably 24), and consider having your résumé executed and reproduced professionally if you cannot create a crisp-looking document with the equipment you have at your disposal.

Choosing a Format

1713 There is a wide range of formats you can choose from. Indeed, in a number of books dealing exclusively with the topic of résumés, you will find as many as a hundred models showing all kinds of variations in layout and approach. In addition, some word processing programs provide at least one résumé template that provides a general format with suggestions concerning the contents of each section of the document.

The illustrations on pages 490–495 show three different ways to format a résumé for Alison L. Bumbry, who majored in marketing at college, has had a number of secretarial and administrative positions in the marketing field, and is now attempting to move up to a managerial job in the same field.

The first two models illustrate the *chronological* approach, in which a person's employment history is sequenced by date, starting with the most current job and working backward. This is the approach most widely used and the one many employers feel most comfortable with.

In the first model (on pages 490–491) note that the dates for each job are highlighted in the left column; the corresponding job title, the name and location of the employer, and comments about the job are grouped together at the right. Also note that all the information about job *experience* typically comes before the information about *education*. If you are just out of school and have little job experience to cite, put the educational information first.

17

The second model (on pages 492–493) also lists the jobs in reverse chronological order, but it highlights the job titles (rather than the dates) in the left column. This approach is especially effective when your employment history shows steady upward progress in a chosen field and you are applying for the next logical position in your career path.

The third model (on pages 494–495) illustrates the *functional* approach, which groups a person's achievements and skills in functional areas such as management, administration, marketing, and writing. The functional approach is the hardest to implement, but it does have the advantage of grouping your key strengths in meaningful categories (rather than leaving it to the employer to ferret out these patterns of strength from your chronological job descriptions). This approach is especially helpful (1) when you are trying to change from one field to another (since it emphasizes generic types of abilities that can be applied in various settings) and (2) when you are trying to play down gaps or frequent job changes in your employment history.

Résumé—Chronological Style (Emphasizing Dates)

A
ALISON L. BUMBRY
AB   Apartment 145
395 West Center College Street
Yellow Springs, Ohio 45387

Home: 513-555-7944
Fax: 513-555-8341
Office: 513-555-0162

B   **OBJECTIVE:**   A marketing management position in which marketing and administrative experience plus strong writing and computer skills can be used to maximize sales and profitability of one or more product lines.

C   **EXPERIENCE:**

July 1994–Present   ADMINISTRATIVE COORDINATOR FOR DIRECTOR OF   **D**
MARKETING, Zimmer & Boyle Inc., Dayton, Ohio

E   • Created and managed a database to control budgeted expenses for advertising and promotion.
F   • Participated in designing and implementing market research studies to   **G**
determine potential size of market for new product lines.
• Coordinated focus group sessions to determine customer attitudes toward our product lines and those of competitors.
• Initiated desktop publishing program to create space ads, catalogs, and mailing pieces. Saved the company over $50,000 in the first year of operation.

February 1992–   ADMINISTRATIVE ASSISTANT TO SALES MANAGER
June 1994   Zimmer & Boyle Inc., Dayton, Ohio

• Analyzed field sales reports and wrote summaries highlighting problems requiring immediate action and those suggesting need for changes in product design, order fulfillment procedures, and customer service.
• Resolved customer complaints by taking direct action whenever possible or by routing the complaint to the appropriate person. Followed up to ensure complaint was properly handled.
• Supervised a secretary who handled all correspondence and clerical tasks.

May 1990–   SECRETARY TO MARKETING MANAGER
January 1992   Crouch and Cowar Incorporated, Toledo, Ohio

• Developed detailed marketing plans, working from rough outlines provided by marketing manager.
• Created and managed a segmented database of names of customers and qualified prospects for direct marketing campaigns.
• Wrote copy for mail campaigns and catalogs.
• Established media contacts to obtain free publicity for new products and special offers.

17

A Heading. The heading should give all the key data an employer needs to get in touch with you. One possible arrangement is to present the data in two blocks: one aligned at the left margin, the other at the right.

B Objective. Use your "objective" statement to indicate the type of job you're looking for, the strengths you can bring to the job, and what you think you can accomplish for the employer's benefit.

C Experience. In this format the dates for each job are featured in the left column. At the right, each job history

D begins with the job title (in all-capital letters), followed by the employer's name and location (in capital and small letters) on the following line.

E The specific achievements in each job history are presented in a series of bulleted entries. If you are using word processing software, your program will offer you many options for bullets. If not, create bullets by means of

ALISON L. BUMBRY

September 1988– April 1990	ASSISTANT TO DIRECTOR OF PUBLIC RELATIONS The Toledo Museum of Art, Toledo, Ohio

- Wrote news releases for new exhibits and special events.
- Wrote, designed, and laid out fund-raising brochures.
- Established and maintained effective media contacts with regional news-papers and TV and radio stations.

H   EDUCATION: B.S. in marketing, 1988; minor in English
Arizona State University, Tempe, Arizona

- Wrote feature articles for *The Arizona Sundial* during sophomore and junior years.
- Created (with two partners) an on-campus birthday celebration service.   **G**
  Managed the service during junior and senior years. Tested various direct marketing techniques to solicit orders from parents of students.

I   CONTINUING   Courses in copywriting, telemarketing techniques, niche marketing, and
EDUCATION: computer graphics, Wright State University, Dayton, Ohio, 1994–1996.

J   COMPUTER   WordPerfect 6.1 for Windows, Microsoft Windows 95, PageMaker 5.0 for
SKILLS: Windows, PowerPoint 4.0 for Windows, Access 2.0 for Windows, dBase 5.0
for Windows.

K   COMMUNITY   Wrote, designed, and laid out annual fund-raising brochures (since 1994) for
SERVICE: the Dayton Homeless Shelter Coalition, using desktop publishing and com-puter graphics software.

the small letter o. Note that many en-
F tries begin with vigorous verbs (such
as *created, initiated, resolved,* and *supervised*) to create the image of a dynamic, take-charge kind of person.
G Note also that to maintain credibility,
the writer uses such terms as *participated in* and *created (with two partners)*
to acknowledge the contribution of
others whenever appropriate.

H Education. Provide information on
college and any postgraduate degrees
in that order. Provide information
about your high school education
only if that is the highest level so far
attained. If you are currently enrolled
in a degree program, note this fact
along with an estimated date of completion. For example: Pursuing a two-
year program in business administration at Glendale Community College;
will receive an A.A. degree in June
1998.

I Continuing Education. Note any job-
related courses you have taken. If you
are changing careers or fields, note
any other continuing education activity that shows you are a person com-
mitted to learning new things.

J Special Skills. Note any special skills
that could be job-related; for example, mastery of software programs,
experience with certain equipment or
machinery, mastery of spoken or written foreign languages.

K Community Service. Note any activity
that is job-related or that shows concern about the needs of others.

Optional Sections. Also provide job-
related information under such labels as these: *Professional Affiliations*
(memberships), *Professional Activities*
(speeches and published articles and
books), *Military Service,* and *Special Interests.*

17

Résumé—Chronological Style (Emphasizing Job Titles)

ALISON L. BUMBRY

AB Apartment 145
395 West Center College Street
Yellow Springs, Ohio 45387

Home: 513-555-7944
Fax: 513-555-8341
Office: 513-555-0162

OBJECTIVE: A marketing management position in which marketing and administrative experience plus strong writing and computer skills can be used to maximize sales and profitability of one or more product lines.

EXPERIENCE:

A Administrative Coordinator for Director of Marketing

ZIMMER & BOYLE INC., Dayton, Ohio, July 1994–Present **B**

C Created and managed a database to control budgeted expenses for advertising and promotion. Participated in designing and implementing market research studies to determine potential size of market for new product lines. Coordinated focus group sessions to determine customer attitudes toward our product lines and those of competitors. Initiated desktop publishing program to create space ads, catalogs, and mailing pieces; saved the company over $50,000 in the first year of operation.

Administrative Assistant to Sales Manager

ZIMMER & BOYLE INC., Dayton, Ohio, February 1992–June 1994

Analyzed field sales reports and wrote summaries highlighting problems requiring immediate action and those suggesting need for changes in product design, order fulfillment procedures, and customer service. Resolved customer complaints by taking direct action whenever possible or by routing the complaint to the appropriate person; followed up to ensure the complaint was properly handled. Supervised secretary who handled all correspondence and clerical tasks.

Secretary to Marketing Manager

CROUCH AND COWAR INCORPORATED, Toledo, Ohio, May 1990–January 1992

Developed detailed marketing plans, working from rough outlines provided by marketing manager. Created and managed a segmented database of names of customers and qualified prospects for direct marketing campaigns. Wrote copy for mail campaigns and catalogs. Established media contacts to obtain free publicity for new products and special offers.

17

A Experience. In this format the job titles (rather than the dates) are featured in the left column. At the right

B the name and location of the organization plus the employment dates are given on one or two lines. Arranging

C the specific achievements for each job in one paragraph is a common format, but it is not as readable as the bulleted format used in the résumés on pages 490–491 and pages 494–495.

ALISON L. BUMBRY

Assistant to Director of Public Relations	THE TOLEDO MUSEUM OF ART, Toledo, Ohio, September 1988–April 1990
	Wrote news releases for new exhibits and special events. Wrote, designed, and laid out fund-raising brochures. Established and maintained effective media contacts with regional newspapers and TV and radio stations.
EDUCATION:	B.S. in marketing, 1988; minor in English Arizona State University, Tempe, Arizona
	Wrote feature articles for *The Arizona Sundial* during sophomore and junior years. Created (with two partners) an on-campus birthday celebration service; managed the service during junior and senior years. Tested various direct marketing techniques to solicit orders from parents of students.
CONTINUING EDUCATION:	Courses in copywriting, telemarketing techniques, niche marketing, and computer graphics, Wright State University, Dayton, Ohio, 1994–1996.
COMPUTER SKILLS:	WordPerfect 6.1 for Windows, Microsoft Windows 95, PageMaker 5.0 for Windows, PowerPoint 4.0 for Windows, Access 2.0 for Windows, dBase 5.0 for Windows.
COMMUNITY SERVICE:	Wrote, designed, and laid out annual fund-raising brochures (since 1994) for the Dayton Homeless Shelter Coalition, using desktop publishing and computer graphics software.

17

¶1713

Résumé—Functional Style

ALISON L. BUMBRY

AB Apartment 145
395 West Center College Street
Yellow Springs, Ohio 45387

Home: 513-555-7944
Fax: 513-555-8341
Office: 513-555-0162

OBJECTIVE: A marketing management position in which marketing and administrative experience plus strong writing and computer skills can be used to maximize sales and profitability of one or more product lines. **B**

A ACHIEVEMENTS: **MARKETING EXPERIENCE** **B**

C
- Participated in designing and implementing market research studies to determine potential size of market for new product lines.
- Coordinated focus group sessions to determine customer attitudes toward our product lines and those of competitors.
- Analyzed field sales reports and wrote summaries highlighting problems requiring immediate action and those suggesting need for changes in product design, order fulfillment procedures, and customer service.
- Developed detailed marketing plans, working from rough outlines provided by marketing manager.

ADMINISTRATIVE EXPERIENCE **B**

C
- Controlled budgeted expenses for advertising and promotion.
- Resolved customer complaints by taking direct action whenever possible or by routing complaint to the appropriate person. Followed up to ensure complaint was properly handled.
- Established and maintained effective media contacts with regional newspapers and TV and radio stations to obtain free publicity for new products and special offers.
- Supervised a secretary who handled all correspondence and clerical tasks.

WRITING SKILLS **B**

C
- Wrote copy for mail campaigns and catalogs.
- Wrote summaries of field sales reports to underscore need for immediate action.
- Wrote copy for fund-raising brochures for art museum.

17

A **Sideheads.** In this illustration the customary sidehead *EXPERIENCE* in the left column has been replaced by *ACHIEVEMENTS* because the term *experience* has been used in two of the four sideheads in the right column.

B Note how the wording of the "objective" statement (in which *marketing and administrative experience plus strong writing and computer skills*) provides the springboard for the functional sideheads in the right column (*MARKETING EXPERIENCE, ADMINISTRATIVE EXPERIENCE, WRITING SKILLS,* and **C** *COMPUTER SKILLS*). Note how the entries under these sideheads in the right column have been reordered (and in some cases reworded) so as to emphasize the applicant's strengths in each functional area, independent of the job setting in which these strengths were developed.

ALISON L. BUMBRY

COMPUTER SKILLS B

C
- Initiated an in-house desktop publishing program. Saved the company over $50,000 in the first year of operation.
- Designed and laid out space ads, catalogs, mailing pieces, and fund-raising brochures.
- Created and managed a database to control budgeted expenses for advertising and promotion.
- Created and managed a segmented database of names of customers and qualified prospects for direct marketing campaigns.
- Mastered WordPerfect 6.1 for Windows, Microsoft Windows 95, PageMaker 5.0 for Windows, PowerPoint 4.0 for Windows, Access 2.0 for Windows, and dBase 5.0 for Windows.

D EMPLOYMENT HISTORY:
- Administrative coordinator for director of marketing, Zimmer & Boyle Inc., Dayton, Ohio, July 1994–Present.
- Administrative assistant to sales manager, Zimmer & Boyle Inc., Dayton, Ohio, February 1992–June 1994.
- Secretary to marketing manager, Crouch and Cowar Incorporated, Toledo, Ohio, May 1990–January 1992.
- Assistant to director of public relations, the Toledo Museum of Art, Toledo, Ohio, September 1988–April 1990.

EDUCATION:
B.S. in marketing, 1988; minor in English
Arizona State University, Tempe, Arizona

- Wrote feature articles for *The Arizona Sundial* during sophomore and junior years.
- Created (with two partners) an on-campus birthday celebration service. Managed the service during junior and senior years. Tested various direct marketing techniques to solicit orders from parents of students.

CONTINUING EDUCATION:
Courses in copywriting, telemarketing techniques, niche marketing, and computer graphics, Wright State University, Dayton, Ohio, 1994–1996.

COMMUNITY SERVICE:
Wrote, designed, and laid out annual fund-raising brochures (since 1994) for the Dayton Homeless Shelter Coalition, using desktop publishing and computer graphics software.

17

D Employment History. Although this section would not appear in a purely "functional" résumé, an employment history provides prospective employers with a brief chronological listing of previous job titles, the name and location of previous employers, and employment dates. Including this section in a functional résumé often serves to mollify employers who are more comfortable with résumés done completely in the chronological style.

OTHER EMPLOYMENT DOCUMENTS

As part of the job-seeking process you will need to write three types of letters: letters of application, follow-up letters after an interview, and (hopefully) a letter of acceptance. Specific guidelines are provided in ¶¶1715–1717, but a few general guidelines (¶1714) apply to all employment communications.

1714 General Guidelines

    a. Keep your letters short—less than one full page if possible.

    b. Resist the temptation to copy sample letters word for word. Draw on these samples for ideas, but create your own letters—letters that communicate the distinctive flavor of your personality.

    c. Edit and proofread your letters carefully. Simple typographical errors (not to mention more serious errors in grammar, style, and usage) will create a negative impression that damages your job-seeking campaign.

    d. Always try to address your letters to a specific person, using that person's full name and title. If necessary, call the specific organization to obtain this information.

    NOTE: The model letters on pages 499–501 are all written by Alison Bumbry, the fictitious person whose job qualifications are set forth in the résumés shown on pages 490–495. In these letters Ms. Bumbry is trying to move up to a marketing management position.

1715 Application Letters

Letters you write to apply for a job will vary to some extent, depending on whether you are (1) following up on an ad, (2) taking the initiative to find out whether any openings exist for a person with your skills and experience, or (3) following up on the suggestion of a mutual friend or acquaintance to explore job opportunities with a specific person within an organization. Yet all application letters have the same three objectives: to indicate what you have to offer the organization, to transmit your résumé, and to obtain an interview. Consider the following guidelines when you write an application letter.

17

    a. Before you draft your letter, try to get as much information as you can about the organization you have in mind. For example, what products or services does it offer? What special strategy or philosophy governs the way the organization operates? Such information can help you focus your letter more effectively and will let the recipient of the letter know that you have taken the initiative to learn something about the organization.

    NOTE: If you are responding to a blind ad (one that provides no organizational name and only a box number address), you will not be able to undertake this research. However, the ad will spell out the qualifications desired, something not usually available to you when you are simply exploring the possibility of job openings.

    b. Begin your letter by indicating whether you are responding to an ad, following up on the suggestion of a mutual friend or acquaintance, or simply exploring what job opportunities currently exist.

c. Indicate what you have to offer the organization. If you are responding to an ad that states the qualifications desired, clearly indicate how your skills and experience relate to each of the qualifications listed. If you are simply exploring job openings, do not focus on specific tasks that you have performed in the past. Instead, highlight the things you have accomplished as a result of the way you applied your skills and experience. This approach will make it easier for someone to gauge how well you might fit the job available, even if you have not performed those exact tasks in the past.

NOTE: The recipient of your letter will probably be receiving many other application letters at the same time. It is important, therefore, that your letter and your résumé make you stand out from the others. In your letter you should aim to achieve—in much shorter form—the same things you are trying to achieve in your résumé. (See ¶1712a–d for further details on this point.)

d. The primary short-term objective of this letter is to arrange for an interview. Rather than wait for the recipient of your letter to call you, indicate that you will call on a specific date to determine whether an interview can take place. In stating when you will call, allow enough time for your material to be delivered and looked at. Keep in mind that the recipient may be inundated with other matters or may be traveling and thus may not look at your letter and résumé as quickly as you would like.

NOTE: Keep a record of when you promised to call so that you follow through on time. Calling a day or two later could suggest that you are not a very good manager of your time.

➤ *For a model application letter written in response to an advertised opening, see page 499.*

1716 Follow-Up Letters

After an interview, follow up immediately with a letter that covers the following points:

a. Thank the interviewer for (1) taking the time to see you, (2) giving you better insight into the available job and the organization you would be working for, and (3) considering your qualifications in light of the available job.

b. Reinforce the positive impression you tried to make during the interview, and briefly restate why you think you would be an asset to the organization.

c. Offer additional information about your qualifications if they were not fully discussed during the interview. If you promised during the interview to supply additional information, do so now.

d. Address questions that arose during the interview that you were not fully prepared to answer at the time. If you know (or simply sense) that the interviewer had some doubts about your qualifications, use this opportunity to overcome such doubts if you can.

(Continued on page 498.)

NOTE: If the interviewer made it clear at the time that you were not right for the current job opening, send a follow-up letter nonetheless. Offer thanks for having been considered for this job, and express hope that you will be considered for other jobs that may open in the future. On the other hand, if *you* decide the job is not right for you, send a follow-up letter in which you thank the interviewer and ask not to be a candidate.

➤ *For an illustration of a follow-up letter, see page 500.*

1717 Acceptance Letters

Of all employment communications, this is the easiest—and the most pleasant—letter to write. Use this occasion to:

a. Formally accept the job.

b. Confirm the key details of your working arrangements (including starting date) that have been previously discussed. If any of these details are not clear, ask the person who hired you to spell them out.

c. Express your pleasure in coming to work for the organization and, more specifically, for the person who has offered you the job.

➤ *For an illustration of an acceptance letter, see page 501.*

(Text continues on page 502.)

17

A Letterhead. The attractive letterhead design that Alison Bumbry has executed on her computer will help make her application letter stand out. It is the same letterhead she used on the first page of her résumé.

B First Paragraph. Alison uses her opening paragraph to indicate how she found out about the job, what she knows about the organization, and how her qualifications stack up against the job requirements stated in the ad.

C Displayed List of Qualifications. Alison does her best to play down her lack of specific knowledge about the technical publishing market and her lack of field sales experience. In this situation a résumé formatted in the functional style (see pages 494–495) will best highlight her strengths in the areas of marketing, administration, writing, and computers.

D Final Paragraph. Alison takes the initiative in saying she will call to see whether an interview can be arranged. At the same time, she stresses her willingness to focus the interview on how she can help the organization achieve *its* goals and objectives.

Application Letter

A   **ALISON L. BUMBRY**

AB   Apartment 145
395 West Center College Street
Yellow Springs, Ohio 45387

Home: 513-555-7944
Fax: 513-555-8341
Office: 513-555-0162

March 3, 19—

Mr. Oliver Digby
Director of Human Resources
Hunt and Ketcham Inc.
1228 Euclid Avenue
Cleveland, Ohio 44115

Dear Mr. Digby:

B   I am writing about an opening for a marketing manager that you advertised in the March 2 *Plain Dealer*. I have used a number of Hunt and Ketcham texts in the computer courses I have taken in the past few years, so I know that your company publishes books of consistently high quality. As the following comparison shows, my experience and background come close to satisfying all of the requirements stated in your ad.

Your Requirements	**My Qualifications**
C College degree	B.S. in marketing plus continuing education courses in marketing and computer software applications
Knowledge of technical publishing market	Over six years' experience in sales and marketing divisions of two educational publishing companies
Field sales experience	Extensive contact with field sales reps and customers, resolving a wide range of sales support and customer service problems

The enclosed résumé will provide additional information about my marketing experience.

D   I would very much appreciate the opportunity to meet with you and discuss the ways in which I can help Hunt and Ketcham achieve its marketing objectives and its profit goals. I will call your office on March 10 to determine whether there is a convenient time for you to see me.

Sincerely,

Alison L. Bumbry

Alison L. Bumbry

Enclosure

17

Follow-Up Letter

ALISON L. BUMBRY

AB Apartment 145
395 West Center College Street
Yellow Springs, Ohio 45387

Home: 513-555-7944
Fax: 513-555-8341
Office: 513-555-0162

March 24, 19—

Mr. Oliver Digby
Director of Human Resources
Hunt and Ketcham Inc.
1228 Euclid Avenue
Cleveland, Ohio 44115

Dear Mr. Digby:

A Thank you for taking the time last Friday to explain why my lack of field sales experience in the technical publishing market would prevent me from being considered for the marketing manager's position at Hunt and Ketcham.

B Thank you also for arranging an interview that same day with your director of sales. Ms. Cantrell gave me a very detailed picture of a field rep's responsibilities. She also stated that in light of all my prior experience in educational publishing, I ought to make the transition to technical publishing very easily. I was also encouraged to learn that after a year or two of experience in the field, I would be a strong candidate for any marketing manager's position that might open at that time.

C Ms. Cantrell has promised to let me know within the next four weeks whether she is in a position to offer me a field rep's job. If she does, I very much look forward to seeing you again. In any event, thank you very much for all the help you have given me.

Sincerely,

Alison L. Bumbry

Alison L. Bumbry

17

A First Paragraph. Alison thanks the interviewer for clarifying the demands of the job and pointing out where her qualifications fell short.

B Second Paragraph. Alison thanks the interviewer for steering her to another opportunity in the organization and for setting up an interview that same day. (Alison should also send a follow-up letter to the second person who interviewed her.) Note that she reaffirms her hope for a marketing management job in a year or two.

C Third Paragraph. Alison ends on a warm note, thanking the first interviewer for all his help.

Acceptance Letter

ALISON L. BUMBRY

AB Apartment 145
395 West Center College Street
Yellow Springs, Ohio 45387

Home: 513-555-7944
Fax: 513-555-8341
Office: 513-555-0162

April 28, 19—

Ms. Jennifer Cantrell
Director of Sales
Hunt and Ketcham Inc.
1228 Euclid Avenue
Cleveland, Ohio 44115

Dear Jennifer:

A I am very pleased to accept the job of field sales representative, with the state of Ohio as my territory. What especially appeals to me is that this job not only represents an excellent opportunity in itself; it provides a springboard for higher-level marketing jobs with Hunt and Ketcham.

B The materials that Oliver Digby sent me answered all my questions about compensation arrangements and company policies. I have now completed and returned all the necessary paperwork. As I understand it, I am to start work on June 2, spending the month in Cleveland for orientation and training. I assume that someone in your department will provide me with information about my accommodations during the month of June.

C I am genuinely excited about the prospect of working with you and for you. I can tell from our conversations how supportive you are of the people who report to you. When I think of how much I will learn under your direction and supervision, I realize how lucky I am to be joining Hunt and Ketcham.

D If there is anything you think I should be reading or doing in the next month, please let me know. I would welcome the chance to get a head start on the job before I actually report for work on June 2.

Sincerely,

Alison L. Bumbry

Alison L. Bumbry

17

A First Paragraph. Alison accepts the job with pleasure, both for its immediate opportunities and for its long-term prospects.

B Second Paragraph. Alison uses this paragraph to deal with the technical details involved in starting a new job.

C Third Paragraph. Alison expresses her pleasure (perhaps a bit too effusively) at the prospect of working for the person who has offered her the job.

D Final Paragraph. Alison shows initiative in offering to undertake advance preparation for the job before she officially starts work.

OUTLINES

1718 An outline can be used to *plan* the content and organization of a document. The outline identifies (1) the topics that are to be discussed and (2) the sequence in which they are to be introduced. In some cases, an outline may consist of a simple list of points to be covered. In other cases an outline may contain several levels of subtopics under each main topic (as in the illustration on page 503).

1719 After you have finished drafting a document, you can use an outline to *review* the document in terms of content and organization. An outline of this kind typically lists the key words or phrases used as headings throughout the document to identify topics and subtopics as they are each introduced. When you use an outline for reviewing purposes, you can more easily answer questions like these:

- Have all topics been included?
- Have all topics been fully developed?
- Does the heading structure—that is, the sequence of heads—provide a balanced representation of all aspects of the discussion, or are some parts of the text loaded with heads while parts have very few?
- Are the heads all worded in a similar way, or are some complete sentences and others simply phrases?

NOTE: If you are using software with the outline feature, you can create an outline by scrolling through the text and coding (according to level of subordination) every heading in the text. If you revise the heading structure in the document, you can use the outline feature to generate a new outline to confirm that the document is now properly organized.

1720 You can use the outline feature to create a table of contents or a list of tables or illustrations (see ¶¶1416–1417). If you have already used the outline feature to generate an up-to-date outline of all the titles and heads, you can create a table of contents from this outline by selecting only those levels of heads that you want in the table of contents and suppressing all the others. For a table of contents, be sure to include any part titles and chapter titles that appear in the outline.

1721 The use of numbers and letters with the items in an outline indicates the relative importance of these items to one another. The illustration on page 503 shows six levels of heads, but many outlines do not require that many and a few may require more.

    a. In the illustration on page 503, the first level of items is identified by roman numerals, the second by capital letters, the third by arabic numerals, the fourth by small letters, the fifth by arabic numerals in parentheses; and the sixth by small letters in parentheses.

    ➤ *For another system of enumeration, see ¶1723b as well as the illustration on page 505.*

    b. At least two items are needed for each level used in an outline. If your outline shows a roman I at the first level, it must also show a roman II; if you use a capital A at the second level, you must also use a capital B; and so on.

Standard Outline Format

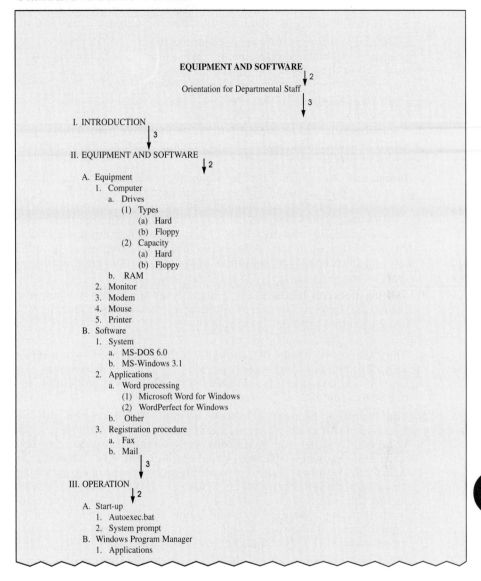

EQUIPMENT AND SOFTWARE ↓2

Orientation for Departmental Staff ↓3

I. INTRODUCTION ↓3

II. EQUIPMENT AND SOFTWARE ↓2

   A. Equipment
      1. Computer
         a. Drives
            (1) Types
               (a) Hard
               (b) Floppy
            (2) Capacity
               (a) Hard
               (b) Floppy
         b. RAM
      2. Monitor
      3. Modem
      4. Mouse
      5. Printer
   B. Software
      1. System
         a. MS-DOS 6.0
         b. MS-Windows 3.1
      2. Applications
         a. Word processing
            (1) Microsoft Word for Windows
            (2) WordPerfect for Windows
         b. Other
      3. Registration procedure
         a. Fax
         b. Mail ↓3

III. OPERATION ↓2

   A. Start-up
      1. Autoexec.bat
      2. System prompt
   B. Windows Program Manager
      1. Applications

17

1722 When you are formatting an outline, keep these guidelines in mind:

  a. Margins. Ordinarily, use side and bottom margins of 1 inch. Leave a top margin of 2 inches, but reduce it to 1 inch if doing so will prevent the outline from taking a second page.

  b. Heading. Type the title in all-capital letters. Use capital and small letters for the other lines. Use boldface for the complete heading if you have that option. Leave 1 blank line between lines in the heading, and leave 2 blank lines below the last line of the heading.

(Continued on page 504.)

c. Enumerations. The numbers or letters that identify the items at different levels in an outline should all be followed by a period and 2 spaces. At the first four levels, align the numbers or letters on the period.

NOTE: The outline feature in word processing programs typically aligns roman and arabic numerals at the left (as shown in the examples alongside). However, you can change this arrangement to align the numbers or letters on the period.

VIII.	8.	G.
IX.	9.	H.
X.	10.	I.
XI.	11.	J.
XII.	12.	K.

d. Capitalization. Use all-capital letters for first-level items (those preceded by roman numerals). Use capital and small letters for items at all lower levels.

e. Indentions. When using roman numerals to identify first-level items, start the widest numeral (III or VIII, for example) at the left margin. Align all the other roman numerals on the period. Align the second level of items (those beginning with A and B) on the first word after the roman I. Align the third level of items (those beginning with 1 and 2) on the first word after A in the second level; however, if the third level of items has more than nine items, align all of these figures on the period.

f. Spacing Between Items. Leave 2 blank lines above and 1 blank line below each first-level item. For all other levels, use single spacing with no blank lines between items.

1723 a. The illustration on page 503 shows an outline executed in accordance with all the format guidelines provided in ¶1722. For illustrations of a table of contents and a list of tables that reflect these guidelines, see pages 390 and 392.

b. The illustration on page 505 shows the same outline created with the outline feature (with all the default settings) of WordPerfect 6 for Windows. Note that the indentions are based on tabs preset 0.5 inch apart and that single spacing is used throughout. Also note that the WordPerfect outline feature uses a different system for enumerating the different levels. For example, first-level items are identified by arabic numerals (1 and 2) rather than by roman numerals; the second-level items are identified by small letters (a and b) rather than by capital letters; the third-level items are identified by small roman numerals (i and ii) rather than by arabic numerals; and so on.

c. When you are creating an outline for your own use (say, for planning or reviewing purposes), the outline produced by the outline feature is quite acceptable. However, when you are creating a table of contents or a similar element that will be part of a formal document, modify the default settings to achieve the format illustrated on page 503.

GUIDELINES FOR DESIGNING FORMS

1724 When you are designing a form with fill-in lines:

a. Lay out the fill-in lines so that most entries—and preferably all entries—can start at the same point. Reducing the number of tab stops required makes the task of filling out the form a great deal easier.

17

Outline Format Using the Outline Feature of WordPerfect 6

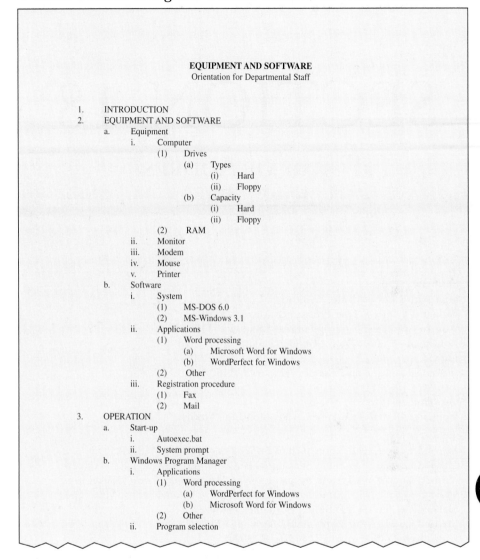

EQUIPMENT AND SOFTWARE
Orientation for Departmental Staff

1. INTRODUCTION
2. EQUIPMENT AND SOFTWARE
   a. Equipment
      i. Computer
         (1) Drives
            (a) Types
               (i) Hard
               (ii) Floppy
            (b) Capacity
               (i) Hard
               (ii) Floppy
         (2) RAM
      ii. Monitor
      iii. Modem
      iv. Mouse
      v. Printer
   b. Software
      i. System
         (1) MS-DOS 6.0
         (2) MS-Windows 3.1
      ii. Applications
         (1) Word processing
            (a) Microsoft Word for Windows
            (b) WordPerfect for Windows
         (2) Other
      iii. Registration procedure
         (1) Fax
         (2) Mail
3. OPERATION
   a. Start-up
      i. Autoexec.bat
      ii. System prompt
   b. Windows Program Manager
      i. Applications
         (1) Word processing
            (a) WordPerfect for Windows
            (b) Microsoft Word for Windows
         (2) Other
      ii. Program selection

17

    NOTE: The design of the fax cover sheet (illustrated on page 483) permits all entries to begin at the same point.

    b. Use double spacing between the fill-in lines, and make the lines long enough to accommodate handwritten as well as typed entries.

    c. In any case, use equal vertical space between the fill-in lines. In that way no adjustment in line spacing will be required when the fill-in entries are inserted.

1725 When you are designing a multicolumn form, look for ways to reduce the number of tab stops required to fill in the form. For example, arrange the top of the form so that any entries to be inserted in the heading can start at the same point as entries in one of the columns below.

SECTION 18

FORMS OF ADDRESS

Member of Board of Education (¶1805e)
Principal (¶1805f)
Teacher (¶1805g)

Government Officials (¶1806)
President of the United States (¶1806a)
Vice President of the United States (¶1806b)
Cabinet Member (¶1806c)
United States Senator (¶1806d)
United States Representative (¶1806e)
Chief Justice of the U.S. Supreme Court (¶1806f)
Associate Justice of the U.S. Supreme Court (¶1806g)
Judge of Federal, State, or Local Court (¶1806h)
Governor (¶1806i)
State Senator (¶1806j)
State Representative or Assembly Member (¶1806k)
Mayor (¶1806l)

Diplomats (¶1807)
Secretary General of the United Nations (¶1807a)
Ambassador to the United States (¶1807b)
Minister to the United States (¶1807c)
American Ambassador (¶1807d)

Members of the Armed Services (¶1808)
Army, Air Force, and Marine Corps Officers (¶1808a)
Navy and Coast Guard Officers (¶1808b)
Enlisted Personnel (¶1808c)

Roman Catholic Dignitaries (¶1809)
Pope (¶1809a)
Cardinal (¶1809b)
Archbishop and Bishop (¶1809c)
Monsignor (¶1809d)
Priest (¶1809e)
Mother Superior (¶1809f)
Sister (¶1809g)
Brother (¶1809h)

Protestant Dignitaries (¶1810)
Protestant Episcopal Bishop (¶1810a)
Protestant Episcopal Dean (¶1810b)
Methodist Bishop (¶1810c)
Minister With Doctor's Degree (¶1810d)
Minister Without Doctor's Degree (¶1810e)

Jewish Dignitaries (¶1811)
Rabbi With Doctor's Degree (¶1811a)
Rabbi Without Doctor's Degree (¶1811b)

18

¶1801

The following forms are correct for addressing letters to individuals, couples, organizations, professional people, education officials, government officials, diplomats, military personnel, and religious dignitaries.

IMPORTANT NOTE: In the salutations that follow the forms of address, the most formal one is listed first. Unless otherwise indicated, the ellipsis marks in the salutation stand for the surname alone.

Because of space limitations, only the masculine forms of address have been given in some illustrations. When an office or a position is held by a woman, make the following substitutions:

For *Sir,* use *Madam.*

For *Mr.* followed by a name (for example, *Mr. Wyatt*), use *Miss, Mrs.,* or *Ms.,* whichever is appropriate.

For *His,* use *Her.*

For *Mr.* followed by a title (for example, *Mr. President, Mr. Secretary, Mr. Mayor*), use *Madam.*

➤ *For a detailed discussion of how to construct inside addresses, see ¶¶1317–1343; for further information on salutations, see ¶¶1346–1351; for details on how to handle addresses on envelopes, see ¶¶1389–1390.*

1801 Individuals

a. Man With Courtesy Title

Mr. . . . *(full name)*
Address

Dear Mr. . . .:

b. Woman—Courtesy Title Preference Known

Ms. (OR Miss OR Mrs.) . . . *(full name)*
Address

Dear Ms. (OR Miss OR Mrs.) . . .:

NOTE: Always use the title that a woman prefers.

c. Woman—Courtesy Title Preference Unknown

Ms. . . . *(full name)*
Address

Dear Ms. . . .:

OR:

. . . *(full name with no title)*
Address

Dear . . . *(first name and surname):*

d. Individual—Name Known, Gender Unknown

. . . *(full name with no title)*
Address

Dear . . . *(first name or initials plus surname):*

e. Individual—Name Unknown, Gender Known

. . . *(title of individual)*
. . . *(name of organization)*
Address

Madam:
Dear Madam:

OR:

Sir:
Dear Sir:

f. Individual—Name and Gender Unknown

. . . *(title of individual)*
. . . *(name of organization)*
Address

Sir or Madam:
Dear Sir or Madam:

OR:

Madam or Sir:
Dear Madam or Sir:

g. Two Men

Mr. . . . *(full name)*
Mr. . . . *(full name)*
Address

Gentlemen:
Dear Messrs. . . . and . . .: (see ¶1349)
Dear Mr. . . . and Mr. . . .:

18

h. Two Women

Ms. . . . *(full name)*
Ms. . . . *(full name)*
Address

Dear Mses. (OR Mss.) . . . and . . .:
Dear Ms. . . . and Ms. . . .:

OR:

Mrs. . . . *(full name)*
Mrs. . . . *(full name)*
Address

Dear Mesdames . . . and . . .:
   (see ¶1349)
Dear Mrs. . . . and Mrs. . . .:

OR:

Miss . . . *(full name)*
Miss . . . *(full name)*
Address

Dear Misses . . . and . . .:
Dear Miss . . . and Miss . . .:

OR:

Ms. . . . *(full name)*
Mrs. . . . *(full name)*
Address

Dear Ms. . . . and Mrs. . . .:

OR:

Miss . . . *(full name)*
Ms. . . . *(full name)*
Address

Dear Miss . . and Ms. . . .:

OR:

Mrs. . . . *(full name)*
Miss . . . *(full name)*
Address

Dear Mrs. . . . and Miss . . .:

i. Woman and Man—No Personal Relationship

Ms. (OR Mrs. OR Miss) . . . *(full name)*
Mr. . . . *(full name)*
Address

Dear Ms. (OR Mrs. OR Miss) . . .
   and Mr. . . .:

OR:

Mr. . . . *(full name)*
Ms. (OR Mrs. OR Miss) . . . *(full name)*
Address

Dear Mr. . . . and Ms. (OR Mrs.
   OR Miss) . . .:

➤ *For forms of address for teenagers and younger children, see ¶1322d–e.*

1802 Couples

a. Married Couple With Same Surname—No Special Titles

Mr. and Mrs. . . . *(husband's full name)*
   (see ¶1323d)
Address

Dear Mr. and Mrs. . . . *(husband's surname):*

b. Married Couple With Same Surname—Husband Has Special Title

Dr. and Mrs. . . . *(husband's full name)*
Address

Dear Dr. and Mrs. . . . *(husband's surname):*

c. Married Couple With Same Surname—Wife Has Special Title

Senator . . . *(wife's full name)*
Mr. . . . *(husband's full name)*
Address

Dear Senator and Mr. . . . *(husband's surname):*

d. Married Couple With Same Surname—Both Have Special Titles

Dr. . . . *(wife's full name)*
Dr. . . . *(husband's full name)*
Address

Dear Drs. . . . *(husband's surname):*

Captain . . . *(husband's full name)*
Professor . . . *(wife's full name)*
Address

Dear Captain and Professor . . . *(husband's surname):*

e. Married Couple With Different Surnames

Ms. (OR Miss) . . . *(wife's full name)*
Mr. . . . *(husband's full name)*
Address

Dear Ms. (OR Miss) . . . *(wife's surname)*
   and Mr. . . . *(husband's surname):*

18

(Continued on page 510.)

OR:

Mr. . . . *(husband's full name)*
Ms. (OR Miss) . . . *(wife's full name)*
Address

Dear Mr. . . . *(husband's surname)* and Ms.
 (OR Miss) . . . *(wife's surname):*

NOTE: If either spouse has a special title
(like those shown in ¶1802b–d), use that
special title here as well.

**f. Married Couple With Hyphenated
Surname**

Mr. and Mrs. . . . *(husband's first
 name and middle initial, plus wife's
 original surname followed by hyphen
 and husband's surname)*
Address

Dear Mr. and Mrs. . . . *(wife's
 original surname followed by hyphen
 and husband's surname):*

**g. Unmarried Couple Living
Together**

Ms. (OR Miss) . . . *(full name)*
Mr. . . . *(full name)*
Address

Dear Ms. (OR Miss) . . . and Mr. . . .:

OR:

Mr. . . . *(full name)*
Ms. (OR Miss) . . . *(full name)*
Address

Dear Mr. . . . and Ms. (OR Miss) . . .:

1803 Organizations

**a. Organization of Women
and Men**

. . . *(name of organization)*
Address

Ladies and Gentlemen:
Gentlemen and Ladies:
Dear . . . *(name of organization):*
 (see ¶1350c)

OR:

Mr. . . . *(name of organization head)**
President *(or other appropriate title)*
. . . *(name of organization)*
Address

Dear Mr. . . .:*

---

*See the note at the top of page 508.

OR:

Chief Executive Officer *(or other
 appropriate title)*
. . . *(name of organization)*
Address

Sir or Madam:
Madam or Sir:
Dear Sir or Madam:
Dear Madam or Sir:

b. Organization of Women

. . . *(name of organization)*
Address

Mesdames: (see ¶1349)
Ladies:

c. Organization of Men

. . . *(name of organization)*
Address

Gentlemen:

1804 Professionals

a. Lawyers

Mr. . . . *(full name)**
Attorney-at-Law
Address

OR:

. . . *(full name)*, Esq.†
Address

Dear Mr. . . .:*

**b. Physicians and Others With
Doctoral Degrees**

Dr. . . . *(full name)*
Address

OR:

. . . *(full name)*, M.D.†
Address

Dear Dr. . . .:

1805 Education Officials

**a. President of College or
University**

. . . *(full name, followed by comma
 and highest degree)*
President, . . . *(name of college)*
Address

---

†When an abbreviation such as *Esq., M.D.,* or
Ph.D. follows a name, do not use a courtesy
title such as *Mr., Ms.,* or *Dr.* before the name.
(See also ¶¶518c, 519c.)

18

OR:

Dr. . . . *(full name)*
President, . . . *(name of college)*
Address

OR:

President . . . *full name)*
. . . *(name of college)*
Address

Dear President . . .:
Dear Dr. . . .:

b. Dean of College or University

. . . *(full name, followed by comma and highest degree)*
Dean, . . . *(name of school or division)*
. . . *(name of college)*
Address

OR:

Dr. . . . *(full name)*
Dean, . . . *(name of school or division)*
. . . *(name of college)*
Address

OR:

Dean . . . *(full name)*
. . . *(name of school or division)*
. . . *(name of college)*
Address

Dear Dean . . .:
Dear Dr. . . .:

c. Professor

Professor . . . *(full name)*
Department of . . . *(subject)*
. . . *(name of college)*
Address

OR:

. . . *(full name, followed by comma and highest degree)*
Department of (**OR** Professor of) . . . *(subject)*
. . . *(name of college)*
Address

OR:

Dr. (**OR** Mr.) . . . *(full name)**
Department of (**OR** Professor of) . . . *(subject)*
. . . *(name of college)*
Address

Dear Professor . . .:
Dear Dr. (**OR** Mr.) . . .:*

d. Superintendent of Schools

Mr. (**OR** Dr.) . . . *(full name)**
Superintendent of . . .
. . . *(name of city)* Schools
Address

Dear Mr. (**OR** Dr.) . . .:*

e. Member of Board of Education

Mr. . . . *(full name)**
Member, . . . *(name of city)* Board of Education
Address

Dear Mr. . . .:*

f. Principal

Mr. . . . *(full name)**
Dr. . . . *(full name)*
Principal, . . . *(name of school)*
Address

Dear Mr. . . .:*
Dear Dr. . . .:

g. Teacher

Mr. . . . *(full name)**
Dr. . . . *(full name)*
. . . *(name of school)*
Address

Dear Mr. . . .:*
Dear Dr. . . .:

1806 Government Officials

a. President of the United States

The President
The White House
Washington, DC 20500

Mr. President:*
Dear Mr. President:*

b. Vice President of the United States

The Vice President
United States Senate
Washington, DC 20510

OR:

The Honorable . . . *(full name)*
Vice President of the United States
Washington, DC 20510

Dear Mr. Vice President:*

18

---

*See the note at the top of page 508.

(Continued on page 512.)

c. Cabinet Member

The Honorable . . . *(full name)*
Secretary of . . . *(department)*
Washington, DC   ZIP Code

Dear Mr. Secretary:*

d. United States Senator

The Honorable . . . *(full name)*
United States Senate
Washington, DC 20510

OR:

The Honorable . . . *(full name)*
United States Senator
Local address

Dear Senator . . .:

e. United States Representative

The Honorable . . . *(full name)*
House of Representatives
Washington, DC 20515

OR:

The Honorable . . . *(full name)*
Representative in Congress
Local address

Dear Representative . . .:
Dear Mr. . . .:*

f. Chief Justice of the U.S. Supreme Court

The Chief Justice of the
   United States
Washington, DC 20543

OR:

The Chief Justice
The Supreme Court
Washington, DC 20543

Dear Mr. Chief Justice:*

g. Associate Justice of the U.S. Supreme Court

Mr. Justice . . . *(last name only)**
The Supreme Court
Washington, DC 20543

Dear Mr. Justice:*
Dear Justice . . .:

h. Judge of Federal, State, or Local Court

The Honorable . . . *(full name)*
Judge of the . . . *(name of court)*
Address

Dear Judge . . .:

i. Governor

The Honorable . . . *(full name)*
Governor of . . . *(state)*
State Capital, State   ZIP Code

Dear Governor . . .:

j. State Senator

The Honorable . . . *(full name)*
The State Senate
State Capital, State   ZIP Code

Dear Senator . . .:

k. State Representative or Assembly Member

The Honorable . . . *(full name)*
House of Representatives
   (OR The State Assembly)
State Capital, State   ZIP Code

Dear Mr. . . .:*

l. Mayor

The Honorable . . . *(full name)*
Mayor of . . . *(city)*
City, State   ZIP Code

OR:

The Mayor of the City of . . .
City, State   ZIP Code

Dear Mr. Mayor:*
Dear Mayor . . .:

1807 Diplomats

a. Secretary General of the United Nations

His Excellency . . . *(full name)**
Secretary General of the United
   Nations
United Nations Plaza
New York, NY 10017

Excellency:
Dear Mr. Secretary General:*
Dear Mr. . . .:*

---

*See the note at the top of page 508.

b. Ambassador to the United States

His Excellency . . . *(full name)**
Ambassador of . . . *(country)*
Address

Excellency:
Dear Mr. Ambassador:*

c. Minister to the United States

The Honorable . . . *(full name)*
Minister of . . . *(department)*
Address

Sir:*
Dear Mr. Minister:*

d. American Ambassador

The Honorable . . . *(full name)*
American Ambassador
(OR The Ambassador of the United
    States of America)
Foreign address of U.S. Embassy

Sir:*
Dear Mr. Ambassador:*

1808 Members of the Armed Services

The addresses of both officers and enlisted personnel in the armed services should include title or rank and full name followed by a comma and the initials USA, USN, USAF, USMC, or USCG. Below and in the next column are some specific examples with appropriate salutations.

a. Army, Air Force, and Marine Corps Officers

Lieutenant General . . . *(full name)*,
    USA (OR USAF OR USMC)
Address

Dear General . . .:†
(NOT: Dear Lieutenant General . . .:)

b. Navy and Coast Guard Officers

Rear Admiral . . . *(full name)*, USN
    (OR USCG)
Address

Dear Admiral . . .:†

c. Enlisted Personnel

Sergeant . . . *(full name)*, USA
Address
OR:
Seaman . . . *(full name)*, USN
Address

Dear Sergeant (OR Seaman) . . .:

1809 Roman Catholic Dignitaries

a. Pope

His Holiness the Pope
OR:
His Holiness Pope . . . *(given name)*
Vatican City
00187 Rome
ITALY

Your Holiness:
Most Holy Father:

b. Cardinal

His Eminence . . . *(given name)*
    Cardinal . . . *(surname)*
Archbishop of . . . *(place)*
Address

Your Eminence:
Dear Cardinal . . .:

c. Archbishop and Bishop

The Most Reverend . . . *(full name)*
Archbishop (OR Bishop) of . . . *(place)*
Address

Your Excellency:
Dear Archbishop (OR Bishop) . . .:

18

---

*See the note at the top of page 508.

(Continued on page 514.)

†Use the salutation *Dear General* . . . whether the officer is a full general or only a lieutenant general, a major general, or a brigadier general. Similarly, use *Dear Colonel* . . . for either a full colonel or a lieutenant colonel and *Dear Lieutenant* . . . for either a first or a second lieutenant. Also use *Dear Admiral* . . . for a full admiral, a vice admiral, or a rear admiral.

d. Monsignor

The Reverend Monsignor . . . *(full name)*
Address

Reverend Monsignor:
Dear Monsignor . . .:

e. Priest

The Reverend . . . *(full name, followed by comma and initials of order)*
Address

Reverend Father:
Dear Father . . .:
Dear Father:

f. Mother Superior

The Reverend Mother Superior
Address

OR:

Reverend Mother . . . *(name, followed by comma and initials of order)*
Address

Reverend Mother:
Dear Reverend Mother:
Dear Mother . . .:

g. Sister

Sister . . . *(name, followed by comma and initials of order)*
Address

Dear Sister . . .:
Dear Sister:

h. Brother

Brother . . . *(name, followed by comma and initials of order)*
Address

Dear Brother . . .:
Dear Brother:

1810 Protestant Dignitaries

a. Protestant Episcopal Bishop

The Right Reverend . . . *(full name)*
Bishop of . . . *(place)*
Address

Dear Bishop . . .:

b. Protestant Episcopal Dean

The Very Reverend . . . *(full name)*
Dean of . . . *(place)*
Address

Dear Dean . . .:

c. Methodist Bishop

The Reverend . . . *(full name)*
Bishop of . . . *(place)*
Address

OR:

Bishop . . . *(full name)*
Address

Dear Bishop . . .:

d. Minister With Doctor's Degree

The Reverend Dr. . . . *(full name)*
Address

OR:

The Reverend . . . *(full name)*, D.D.
Address

Dear Dr. . . .:

e. Minister Without Doctor's Degree

The Reverend . . . *(full name)*
Address

Dear Mr. . . .:*

1811 Jewish Dignitaries

a. Rabbi With Doctor's Degree

Rabbi . . . *(full name)*, D.D.
Address

OR:

Dr. . . . *(full name)*
Address

Dear Rabbi (OR Dr.) . . .:

b. Rabbi Without Doctor's Degree

Rabbi . . . *(full name)*
Address

Dear Rabbi . . .:

---

*See the note at the top of page 508.

PART 3

References

APPENDIX A
GLOSSARY OF GRAMMATICAL TERMS

Adjective. A word that answers the question *what kind* (*excellent* results), *how many* (*four* laptops), or *which one* (the *latest* data). An adjective may be a single word (a *wealthy* man), a phrase (a man *of great wealth*), or a clause (a man *who possesses great wealth*). An adjective modifies the meaning of a noun (*loose* cannon) or a pronoun (*unlucky* me, I was *wrong*).

Adjective, predicate. See *Complement*.

Adverb. A word that answers the question *when, where, why, in what manner,* or *to what extent*. An adverb may be a single word (speak *clearly*), a phrase (speak *in a clear voice*), or a clause (speak *as clearly as you can*). An adverb modifies the meaning of a verb, an adjective, or another adverb. (See also *Adverbial clause*.)

> We closed the deal *quickly*. (Modifies the verb *closed*.)
> Caroline seemed *genuinely* pleased. (Modifies the adjective *pleased*.)
> My presentation went *surprisingly* well. (Modifies the adverb *well*.)

Adverbial conjunctive (or **connective**). An adverb that connects the main clauses of a compound sentence; for example, *however, therefore, nevertheless, hence, moreover, otherwise, consequently*. (See also ¶178.)

Antecedent. A noun or a noun phrase to which a pronoun refers.

> She is the *person who* wrote the letter. (*Person* is the antecedent of *who*.)
> *Owning a home* has *its* advantages. (*Owning a home* is the antecedent of *its*.)

Appositive. A noun or a noun phrase that identifies another noun or pronoun that immediately precedes it. (See ¶¶148–150.)

> Mr. Mancuso, *our chief financial officer,* would like to meet you.

Article. Considered an adjective. The *definite* article is *the;* the *indefinite* articles are *a* or *an*. (See page 253 for a usage note on *a–an*.)

Case. The form of a noun or of a pronoun that indicates its relation to other words in the sentence. There are three cases: nominative, possessive, and objective. *Nouns* have the same form in the nominative and objective cases but a special ending for the possessive. The forms for *pronouns* are:

Nominative	Possessive	Objective
I	my, mine	me
you	your, yours	you
he, she, it	his, hers, its	him, her, it
we	our, ours	us
they	their, theirs	them
who	whose	whom

A

Nominative case. Used for the subject or the complement of a verb.

> *She* publishes a newsletter. (Subject.)
> The person who called you was *I*. (Complement.)

Possessive case. Used to show ownership and other relationships. (See ¶¶627–651, especially the examples in ¶627.)

> *Your* copy of the report contains a statistical analysis. *Mine* doesn't.

Objective case. Used for (1) the object of a verb, (2) the object of a preposition, (3) the subject of an infinitive, (4) the object of an infinitive, and (5) the complement of the infinitive *to be.*

> Can you help *us* this weekend? (Object of the verb *help.*)
> Brenda has not written to *me.* (Object of the preposition *to.*)
> I encouraged *her* to enter the biathlon. (Subject of the infinitive *to enter.*)
> William promised to call *me* but he didn't. (Object of the infinitive *to call.*)
> They believed me to be *her.* (Complement of the infinitive *to be.*)

Clause. A group of related words containing a subject and a predicate. An *independent* clause (also known as a *main clause* or *principal clause*) expresses a complete thought and can stand alone as a sentence. A *dependent* clause (also known as a *subordinate clause*) does not express a complete thought and cannot stand alone as a sentence.

> I will go *(independent clause)* if I am invited *(dependent clause).*

Adjective clause. A dependent clause that modifies a noun or a pronoun in the main clause. Adjective clauses are joined to the main clause by relative pronouns *(which, that, who, whose, whom).*

> Their bill, *which includes servicing,* seems reasonable. (Modifies *bill.*)

Adverbial clause. A dependent clause that functions as an adverb in its relation to the main clause. Adverbial clauses indicate time, place, manner, cause, purpose, condition, result, reason, or contrast.

> These orders can be filled *as soon as stock is received.* (Time.)
> I was advised to live *where the climate is dry.* (Place.)
> She worked *as though her life depended on it.* (Manner.)
> Please write me at once *if you have any suggestions.* (Condition.)
> *Because our plant is closed in August,* we cannot fill your order now. (Reason.)

Coordinate clauses. Clauses of the same rank—independent or dependent.

> *Carl will oversee the day-to-day operations,* and *Sheila will be responsible for the finances.* (Coordinate independent clauses.)
> *When you have read the user's manual* and *you have mastered all the basic operations,* try to deal with these special applications. (Coordinate dependent clauses.)

Elliptical clause. A clause from which key words have been omitted. (See ¶¶102, 111, 119, 130b, and 1082d.)

> *Now, for the next topic.*   *Really?*   *If possible,* arrive at one.

Essential (restrictive) clause. A dependent clause that cannot be omitted without changing the meaning of the main (independent) clause. Essential clauses are *not* set off by commas.

> The magazine *that came yesterday* contains an evaluation of new software.

Nonessential (nonrestrictive) clause. A dependent clause that adds descriptive information but could be omitted without changing the meaning of the main (independent) clause. Such clauses are separated or set off from the main clause by commas.

> She has had a lot of success with her latest book, *which deals with corporate finance.*
> Her latest book, *which deals with corporate financial analysis,* has sold quite well.

Noun clause. A dependent clause that functions as a noun in the main clause.

> *Whether the proposal will be accepted* remains to be seen. (Noun clause as subject.)
> They thought *that the plan was a failure.* (Noun clause as object.)
> Then he said, *"Who gave you that information?"* (Noun clause as object.)

A

Comparison. The forms of an adjective or adverb that indicate degrees in quality, quantity, or manner. The degrees are positive, comparative, and superlative. (See ¶1071.)

Positive. The simple form; for example, *new, efficient* (adjectives); *soon, quietly* (adverbs).

Comparative. Indicates a higher or lower degree of quality or manner than is expressed by the positive degree. The comparative is used when two things are compared and is regularly formed by adding *er* to the positive degree *(newer, sooner)*. In longer words the comparative is formed by adding *more* or *less* to the positive *(more efficient, less efficient; more quietly, less quietly)*.

Superlative. Denotes the highest or lowest degree of quality or manner. The superlative is used when more than two things are compared and is regularly formed by adding *est* to the positive degree *(newest, soonest)*. In longer words the superlative is formed by adding *most* or *least* to the positive *(most efficient, least efficient; most quietly, least quietly)*.

Complement. A word or phrase that completes the sense of the verb. It may be an object, a predicate noun, a predicate pronoun, or a predicate adjective.

Object. Follows a transitive verb. (See *Verb.)*

I have already drafted the *contract.*

Predicate noun or pronoun. Follows a linking verb (such as *is, are, was, were, will be, has been, could be*). It explains the subject and is identical with it. (Also called a *predicate complement, subject complement,* and *predicate nominative.)*

Miss Kwong is our new *accountant. (Accountant* refers to *Miss Kwong.)*

The person responsible for the decision was *I.* (The pronoun *I* refers to *person.)*

Predicate adjective. Completes the sense of a linking verb. (Also called a *predicate complement.)*

These charges are *excessive.* (The adjective *excessive* refers to *charges.)*

NOTE: In this manual, the term *complement* is used to refer only to a predicate noun, pronoun, or adjective following a linking verb. The term *object* is used to denote the complement of a transitive verb.

Compound modifier. A phrase or clause that qualifies, limits, or restricts the meaning of a word. Also referred to as a *compound adjective.* (See also ¶¶813–832.)

Conjunction. A word or phrase that connects words, phrases, or clauses.

Coordinating conjunction. Connects words, phrases, or clauses of equal rank. The coordinating conjunctions are *and, but, or,* and *nor.*

Correlative conjunctions. Conjunctions consisting of two elements used in pairs; for example, *both . . . and, not only . . . but (also), either . . . or, neither . . . nor.*

Subordinating conjunction. Used to join dependent clauses to main (independent) clauses; for example, *when, where, after, before, if.* (See ¶132.)

Connective. A word that joins words, phrases, or clauses. The chief types of connectives are conjunctions, adverbial conjunctives, prepositions, and relative pronouns.

Consonants. The letters *b, c, d, f, g, h, j, k, l, m, n, p, q, r, s, t, v, w, x, y, z.* The letters *w* and *y* sometimes serve as vowels (as in *saw* and *rhyme*). (See also *Vowels.)*

Contraction. A shortened form of a word or phrase in which an apostrophe indicates the omitted letters or words; for example, *don't* for *do not.* (See ¶505b–e.)

Dangling modifier. A modifier that is attached either to no word in a sentence or to the wrong word. (See *Modifier* and ¶¶1082–1086.)

Direct address. A construction in which a speaker or a writer addresses another person directly; for example, "What do you think, Sylvia?"

Elliptical expressions. Condensed expressions from which key words have been omitted; for example, *if necessary* (for *if it is necessary*). (See also *Clause; Sentence.*)

Essential elements. Words, phrases, or clauses needed to complete the structure or meaning of a sentence. (See also *Clause; Phrase.*)

Gender. The characteristic of nouns and pronouns that indicates whether the thing named is *masculine (man, boy, he), feminine (woman, girl, she),* or *neuter (book, concept, it).* Nouns that refer to either males or females have *common* gender *(person, child).*

Gerund. A verb form ending in *ing* and used as a *noun.*

> *Selling* requires special skills. (Subject.)
>
> I enjoy *selling.* (Direct object of *enjoy.*)
>
> She is experienced in *selling.* (Object of preposition *in.*)

> **Dangling gerund.** A prepositional-gerund phrase that is attached either to no word in a sentence or to the wrong word. (See ¶1082c.)

Imperative. See *Mood.*

Indicative. See *Mood.*

Infinitive. The form of the verb usually introduced by *to* (see ¶¶1044–1046). An infinitive may be used as a noun, an adjective, or an adverb. (See *Phrase.*)

NOUN:	*To find affordable housing these days* is not easy. (Subject.)
	She is trying *to do a hatchet job on my proposal.* (Object.)
ADJECTIVE:	I still have two more contracts *to draft.* (Modifies *contracts.*)
ADVERB:	He resigned *to take another position.* (Modifies *resigned.*)

Interjection. A word that shows emotion; usually without grammatical connection to other parts of a sentence.

> *Oh,* so that's what he meant.   *Wow!* What a weekend!

Modifier. A word, phrase, or clause that qualifies, limits, or restricts the meaning of a word. (See *Adjective; Adverb; Dangling modifier.*)

Mood (mode). The form of the verb that shows the manner of the action. There are three moods: indicative, imperative, and subjunctive.

> **Indicative.** States a fact or asks a question.
>
> Our lease has expired.   When does our lease expire?

> **Imperative.** Expresses a command or makes a request.
>
> Call me next week.   Please send me your latest catalog.

> **Subjunctive.** Used in dependent clauses following main (independent) clauses expressing necessity, demand, or wishing (see ¶¶1038–1039); also used in *if, as if,* and *as though* clauses that state conditions which are improbable, doubtful, or contrary to fact (see ¶¶1040–1043).
>
> I demand that we *be* heard.   It is imperative that he *be* notified.
> We urge that she *be* elected.   If he *were* appointed, I would quit.
> I wish I *were* going.   If she *had* known, she would have written.

Nonessential elements. Words, phrases, or clauses that are not needed to complete the structure or meaning of a sentence. (See also *Clause; Phrase.*)

A

Noun. The name of a person, place, object, idea, quality, or activity.

Abstract noun. The name of a quality or a general idea; for example, *courage, freedom.*

Collective noun. A noun that represents a group of persons, animals, or things; for example, *audience, company, flock.* (See ¶1019.)

Common noun. The name of a class of persons, places, or things; for example, *child, house.* (See ¶¶307–310.)

Predicate noun. See *Complement.*

Proper noun. The official name of a particular person, place, or thing; for example, *Ellen, San Diego, Wednesday.* Proper nouns are capitalized. (See ¶¶303–306.)

Number. The characteristic of a noun, pronoun, or verb that indicates whether one person or thing (singular) or more than one (plural) is meant.

NOUN: beeper, beepers   PRONOUN: she, they   VERB: (she) works, (they) work

Object. The person or thing that receives the action of a transitive verb. An object may be a word, a phrase, or a clause.

> I need a new laptop *computer.* (Word.)
> She prefers *to work with hard copy.* (Infinitive phrase.)
> We did not realize *that your deadline was so tight.* (Clause.)

Direct object. The person or thing that is directly affected by the action of the verb. (The object in each of the three sentences above is a *direct* object.)

Indirect object. The person or thing indirectly affected by the action of the verb. The indirect object can be made the object of the preposition *to* or *for.*

> Molly gave (to) *me* a hard time about my sales performance this quarter.

Ordinal number. The form of a number that indicates order or succession; for example, *first, second, twelfth* or *1st, 2d, 12th.* (See ¶¶424–426.)

Parenthetical elements. Words, phrases, or clauses that are not necessary to the completeness of the structure or the meaning of a sentence.

> Gina Sala, *my wife's older sister,* is my accountant.

Participle. A word that may stand alone as an adjective or may be combined with helping (auxiliary) verbs to form different tenses (see ¶¶1033–1034). There are three forms: present, past, and perfect.

Present participle. Ends in *ing;* for example, *making, advertising.*

Past participle. Regularly ends in *ed* (as in *asked* or *filed*) but may be irregularly formed (as in *lost, seen,* and *written*). (See ¶1030a–b.)

Perfect participle. Consists of *having* plus the past participle; for example, *having asked, having lost.*

When a participle functions as an *adjective,* it modifies a noun or a pronoun.

> The *coming* year poses some new challenges. (Modifies *year.*)
> *Having retired* last year, I now do volunteer work. (Modifies *I.*)

Because a participle has many of the characteristics of a verb, it may take an object and be modified by an adverb. The participle and its object and modifiers make up a *participial phrase.*

> *Seizing the opportunity,* Orzo offered to buy the business. (*Opportunity* is the object of *seizing.*)
> *Moving aggressively,* we can control the market. (*Aggressively* modifies *moving.*)

Dangling participle. A participial phrase attached either to no word in a sentence or to the wrong word. (See *Phrase* and ¶1082a.)

Parts of speech. The eight classes into which words are grouped according to their uses in a sentence: verb, noun, pronoun, adjective, adverb, conjunction, preposition, and interjection.

Person. The characteristic of a word that indicates whether a person is speaking *(first person),* is spoken to *(second person),* or is spoken about *(third person).* Only personal pronouns and verbs change their forms to show person. All nouns are considered third person.

	Singular	**Plural**
FIRST PERSON:	*I* like this book.	*We* like this book.
SECOND PERSON:	*You* like this book.	*You* like this book.
THIRD PERSON:	*She* likes this book.	*They* like this book.

Phrase. A group of two or more words that lack a subject and a predicate; used as a noun, an adjective, or an adverb. (See *Predicate.*)

Noun phrase. A phrase that functions as a noun (such as a gerund phrase, an infinitive phrase, or a prepositional phrase).

I like *running my own business.* (Gerund phrase as object.)
To provide the best possible service is our goal. (Infinitive phrase as subject.)
Before 9 a.m. is the best time to call me. (Prepositional phrase as subject.)

Adjective phrase. A phrase that functions as an adjective (such as an infinitive phrase, a participial phrase, or a prepositional phrase).

The time *to act* is now! (Infinitive phrase indicating what kind of time.)

Adverbial phrase. A phrase that functions as an adverb (such as an infinitive phrase or a prepositional phrase).

Let's plan to meet *after lunch.* (Prepositional phrase indicating when to meet.)

Gerund phrase. A gerund plus its object and modifiers; used as a noun.

Delaying payments to your suppliers will prove costly. (Gerund phrase as subject.)

Infinitive phrase. An infinitive plus its object and modifiers; may be used as a noun, an adjective, or an adverb. An infinitive phrase that is attached to either no word in a sentence or to the wrong word is called a *dangling* infinitive. (See ¶1082b.)

To get TF's okay on this purchase order took some doing. (As a noun; serves as subject of the verb *took.*)
The decision *to close the Morrisville plant* was not made easily. (As an adjective; tells what kind of decision.)
Janice resigned *to open her own business.* (As an adverb; tells why Janice resigned.)

NOTE: An infinitive phrase, unlike other phrases, may sometimes have a subject. This subject precedes the infinitive and is in the objective case.

I have asked *her to review this draft for accuracy.* (*Her* is the subject of *to review.*)

Participial phrase. A participle and its object and modifiers; used as an adjective.

The committee *considering your proposal* should come to a decision this week.
I prefer the cover sample *printed in blue and yellow.*

(Continued on page 522.)

Prepositional phrase. A preposition and its object and modifiers; may be used as a noun, an adjective, or an adverb.

From Boston to Tulsa is about 1550 miles. (As a noun; serves as subject of *is.*)

Profits *in the automobile industry* are up sharply this quarter. (As an adjective; indicates which type of profits.)

You handled Dr. Waterman's objections *with great skill.* (As an adverb; indicates the manner in which the objections were handled.)

Prepositional-gerund phrase. A phrase that begins with a preposition and has a gerund as the object. (See *Gerund* and ¶1082c.)

By rechecking the material before it is set in type, you avoid expensive corrections later on. (*By* is the preposition; *rechecking,* a gerund, is the object of *by.*)

Essential (restrictive) phrase. A phrase that limits, defines, or identifies; cannot be omitted without changing the meaning of the sentence.

The study *analyzing our competitors' promotion activities* will be finished within the next two weeks.

Nonessential (nonrestrictive) phrase. A phrase that can be omitted without changing the meaning of the sentence.

The Stanforth-Palmer Company, *one of the country's largest financial services organizations,* is expanding into satellite communications.

Verb phrase. This term is often used to indicate the individual words that make up the verb in a sentence. Sometimes the verb phrase includes an adverb. A verb phrase can function only as a verb.

You *should work together* with Nora on the report. (The verb phrase consists of the verb form *should work* plus the adverb *together.*)

Positive degree. See *Comparison.*

Predicate. That part of a sentence which tells what the subject does or what is done to the subject or what state of being the subject is in. (See also *Verb.*)

Complete predicate. The complete predicate consists of a verb and its complement along with any modifiers.

Barbara *has handled the job well.*

Simple predicate. The simple predicate is the verb alone, without regard for any complement or modifiers that may accompany it.

Barbara *has handled* the job well.

Compound predicate. A predicate consisting of two or more predicates joined by conjunctions.

Barbara *has handled the job well* and *deserves a good deal of praise.*

Predicate nominative. See *Complement.*

Prefix. A letter, syllable, or word added to the beginning of a word to change its meaning; for example, *a*float, *re*upholster, *under*nourished.

Preposition. A connective (such as *from, to, in, on, of, at, by, for, with*) that shows the relationship between a noun or pronoun and some other word in the sentence. The noun or pronoun following a preposition is in the objective case. (See ¶¶1077–1080.)

Martin's work was reviewed *by Hedley and me.*

Principal parts. The forms of a verb from which all other forms are derived: the *present,* the *past,* the *past participle,* and the *present participle.* (See ¶¶1030–1035.)

Pronoun. A word used in place of a noun. (See ¶¶1049–1064.)

DEMONSTRATIVE: *this, that, these, those*

INDEFINITE: *each, either, any, anyone, someone, everyone, few, all,* etc.

INTENSIVE: *myself, yourself, himself, herself, ourselves, themselves,* etc.

INTERROGATIVE: *who, which, what,* etc.

PERSONAL: *I, you, he, she, it, we, they,* etc.

RELATIVE: *who, whose, whom, which, that,* and compounds such as *whoever*

Punctuation. Marks used to indicate relationships between words, phrases, and clauses.

Terminal (end) punctuation. The period, the question mark, and the exclamation point—the three marks that may indicate the end of a sentence.

NOTE: When a sentence breaks off abruptly, a dash may be used to mark the end of the sentence (see ¶207). When a sentence trails off without really ending, ellipsis marks (three spaced periods) are used to mark the end of the sentence (see ¶291b).

Internal punctuation. Commas, semicolons, colons, dashes, parentheses, quotation marks, apostrophes, ellipses marks, asterisks, diagonals, and brackets are the most common marks of internal punctuation.

Question.

Direct question. A question in its original form, as spoken or written.

He then asked me, "What is your opinion?"

Indirect question. A restatement of a question without the use of the exact words of the speaker.

He then asked me what my opinion was.

Independent question. A question that represents a complete sentence but is incorporated in a larger sentence.

The main question is, Who will translate this idea into a clear plan of action?

Quotation.

Direct quotation. A quotation of words exactly as spoken or written.

I myself heard Ed say, "I will arrive in Santa Fe on Tuesday."

Indirect quotation. A restatement of a quotation without the use of the exact words of the speaker.

I myself heard Ed say that he would arrive in Santa Fe on Tuesday.

Sentence. A group of words representing a complete thought and containing a subject and a predicate (a verb along with any complements and modifiers).

Simple sentence. A sentence consisting of one independent clause.

I have no recollection of the meeting.

Compound sentence. A sentence consisting of two or more independent clauses.

Our Boston office will be closed, and our Dallas office will be relocated.

Complex sentence. A sentence consisting of one independent clause (also called the *main clause*) and one or more dependent clauses.

We will make an exception to the policy if circumstances warrant.

(Continued on page 524.)

A

Compound-complex sentence. A sentence consisting of two independent clauses and one or more dependent clauses.

> I tried to handle the monthly report alone, but when I began to analyze the data, I realized that I needed your help.

Elliptical sentence. A word or phrase treated as a complete sentence, even though the subject and verb are understood but not expressed.

> Enough on that subject.   Why not?

Declarative sentence. A sentence that makes a statement.

> Our company is continually testing cutting-edge technologies.

Interrogative sentence. A sentence that asks a question.

> When will the conference begin?

Exclamatory sentence. A sentence that expresses strong feeling.

> Don't even think of smoking here!

Imperative sentence. A sentence that expresses a command or a request. (The subject *you* is understood if it is not expressed.)

> Send a check at once.   Please let us hear from you.

Sentence fragment. A phrase or clause that is incorrectly treated as a sentence. (See ¶102b.)

Statement. A sentence that asserts a fact. (See also *Sentence.*)

Subject. A word, phrase, or clause that names the person, place, or thing about which something is said.

> *The law firm with the best reputation in town* is Barringer and Doyle.
> *Whoever applies for the job from within the department* will get special consideration.

Compound subject. Two or more subjects joined by a conjunction.

> *My wife and my three sons* are off on a white-water rafting trip.

Subjunctive. See *Mood.*

Suffix. A letter, syllable, or word added to the end of a word to modify its meaning; for example, trend*y,* friend*ly,* count*less,* receiver*ship,* lone*some.*

Superlative degree. See *Comparison.*

Syllable. One or more letters that represent one sound.

Tense. The property of a verb that expresses *time.* (See ¶¶1031–1035.) The three *primary* tenses correspond to the three time divisions:

PRESENT:	they think
PAST:	they thought
FUTURE:	they will think

There are three *perfect* tenses, corresponding to the primary tenses:

PRESENT PERFECT:	they have thought
PAST PERFECT:	they had thought
FUTURE PERFECT:	they will have thought

There are six *progressive* tenses, corresponding to each of the primary and perfect tenses:

PRESENT PROGRESSIVE:	they are thinking
PAST PROGRESSIVE:	they were thinking
FUTURE PROGRESSIVE:	they will be thinking
PRESENT PERFECT PROGRESSIVE:	they have been thinking
PAST PERFECT PROGRESSIVE:	they had been thinking
FUTURE PERFECT PROGRESSIVE:	they will have been thinking

There are two *emphatic* tenses:

PRESENT EMPHATIC:	they do think
PAST EMPHATIC:	they did think

Transitional expressions. Expressions that link independent clauses or sentences; for example, *as a result, therefore, on the other hand, nevertheless.* (See also ¶138a.)

Verb. A word or phrase used to express action or state of being. (See also *Mood.*)

Enniston *has boosted* its sales goals for the year. (Action.)

My son-in-law *was* originally a lawyer, but he *has* now *become* a computer-game designer. (State of being.)

Helping (auxiliary) verb. A verb that helps in the formation of another verb. (See ¶¶1030c, 1033–1034.) The chief helping verbs are *be, can, could, do, have, may, might, must, ought, shall, should, will, would.*

Transitive verb. A verb that requires an object to complete its meaning.

Fusilli *has rejected* all offers to purchase his business.

Intransitive verb. A verb that does not require an object to complete its meaning.

As market growth *occurs* and customer interest *builds,* our sales expectations *are rising* and top management's excitement *has increased.*

Linking verb. A verb that connects a subject with a predicate adjective, noun, or pronoun. The various forms of *to be* are the most commonly used linking verbs. *Become, look, seem, appear,* and *grow* are also used as linking verbs. (See *Complement* and ¶1067.)

Laura *seemed* willing to compromise, but Frank *became* obstinate in his demands.
Was he afraid that any concession might make him *appear* a fool?

Principal parts of verbs. See *Principal parts.*

Verbal. A word that is derived from a verb but functions in some other way. (See *Gerund; Infinitive; Participle.*)

Voice. The property of a verb that indicates whether the subject acts or is acted upon.

Active voice. A verb is in the active voice when its subject is the doer of the act.

About a dozen people *reviewed* the report in draft form.

Passive voice. A verb is in the passive voice when its subject is acted upon.

The report *was reviewed* in draft form by about a dozen people.

A

Vowels. The letters *a, e, i, o,* and *u.* The letters *w* and *y* sometimes act like vowels (as in *awl* or in *cry*). (See also *Consonants.*)

APPENDIX B
GLOSSARY OF COMPUTER TERMS

As the world of the office continues to undergo a series of rapid technological changes, a whole new vocabulary continues to evolve. The following glossary provides brief and simple definitions of the key terms and concepts that are part of this new vocabulary.*

NOTE: When boldface type is used to highlight a word or phrase within a definition, it signifies that the highlighted word or phrase is defined elsewhere in this glossary.

➤ *See ¶544 for a list of common computer abbreviations and acronyms.*

Access. To call up information out of **storage.**

> **Random access.** A technique that permits stored information to be directly retrieved, regardless of its location on the **storage medium.**

> **Sequential access.** A technique for retrieving stored information that requires a sequential search through one item after another on the **storage medium.**

Access time. The amount of time it takes a **computer** to locate stored information.

Active matrix display. A type of **monitor** typically used on **laptop** or portable **computers;** provides a brighter, more readable display than older **LCD** equipment.

Adapter card. A **circuit board** that plugs into a **computer** and gives it additional capabilities. (See *Circuit board.*)

AI. See *Artificial intelligence.*

Algorithm. A step-by-step procedure designed to solve a problem or achieve an objective.

Alphanumeric. Consisting of letters, numbers, and symbols.

Antivirus software. A **program** designed to look for and destroy a **virus** that may have infected a **computer's memory** or **files.**

Application software (also called *application* or simply *app*). A **program** designed to perform **information processing** tasks for a specific purpose or activity (for example, **desktop publishing** and **database management**). (See also *Killer app.*)

Artificial intelligence (AI). **Computer** systems that attempt to imitate human processes for analyzing and solving problems.

Ascending sort. Sorting records from A to Z or 0 to 9. (See *Descending sort.*)

ASCII (pronounced *as-kee*). An acronym derived from American Standard Code for Information Interchange. ASCII is a standard 8-**bit** code that represents 256 **characters.** The use of this standard code permits **computers** made by different manufacturers to communicate with one another.

Background printing. The ability of a **computer** to print a **document** while other work is being done on the **keyboard** and the **display screen** at the same time.

---

*A number of works were consulted in the preparation of this glossary, but two were especially helpful: *Peter Norton's Introduction to Computers,* Glencoe, Westerville, Ohio, 1995, and *Que's Computer User's Dictionary,* 5th ed., 1994.

Backup. **Storage** of duplicate **files** on **disks, diskettes,** or some other form of **magnetic medium** (such as tapes) as a safety measure in case the original medium is damaged or lost. (One word as a noun or an adjective: *backup* procedures; two words as a verb: *back up* your hard disk.)

Basic Input/Output System (BIOS). A set of **programs** stored in read-only **memory** (ROM) on IBM-compatible **computers.** These programs control the **disk drives,** the **keyboard,** and the **display screen,** and they handle start-up operations.

Baud rate. The rate of **data** transmission between two **computers** or other electronic equipment.

BBS. See *Bulletin board system.*

Binary numbering system. A numbering system in which all numbers are represented by various combinations of the digits 0 and 1.

BIOS. See *Basic Input/Output System.*

Bit. An acronym derived from binary digit. The smallest unit of information that can be recognized by a **computer.** Bits are combined to represent **characters.** (See also *Byte.*)

Bitmap. A method of storing a graphic image as a set of **bits** in a computer's **memory.** To display the image on the screen, the **computer** converts the bits into **pixels.**

Bits per second (bps). A measurement that describes the speed of **data** transmission between two pieces of equipment. (See *Baud rate.*)

Block. A segment of **text** that is selected so that it can be moved to another location or processed in some other way. (See *Block delete; Block move; Cut and paste.*)

Block delete. A **command** to delete (or erase) a segment of **text.**

Block move. A **command** to reproduce a segment of **text** in another place and at the same time erase it from its original position. (See *Cut and paste.*)

Block protect. A **command** to prevent a **page break** from occurring within a block of **text** (for example, a table). (See also *Orphan protection* and *Widow protection.*)

Boilerplate. Standard wording (for example, sentences or paragraphs in form letters or clauses in legal documents) that is held in **storage.** When needed, it can be used as is, with minor modification, or in combination with new material to produce tailor-made **documents.** (See *Macro.*)

Boot (short for *bootstrap*). To start a **computer** and load the **operating system** to prepare the computer to **execute** an **application.** (See *Application software.*)

bps. See *Bits per second.*

Buffer. A holding area in **memory** that stores information temporarily. Also called *cache.*

Bug. A defect in the **software** that causes the **computer** to malfunction or cease to operate. (See also *Debugging; Glitch.*)

Bulletin board system (BBS). An **on-line** information system, usually set up by an individual (called a *system operator,* or **SYSOP**) on a nonprofit basis for the enjoyment of other individuals with similar interests. (See also *Internet.*)

Bundled software. **Software** that is sold along with a **computer** system; several software **programs** that are packaged together (also called *software suites*).

Bus. An internal pathway along which electronic signals travel between the components of a **computer** system.

Button bar. An on-screen element that offers a user instant access to commonly used **commands.** The commands are represented by **icons** on a row of buttons shown at the top of the screen. Also called a *tool bar.*

B

Byte. The sequence of **bits** that represents a **character.** Each byte has 8 bits.

Cache. See *Buffer.*

Card. See *Circuit board; Adapter card.*

Carpal tunnel syndrome. A wrist or hand injury caused by using a **keyboard** for long periods of time. A type of repetitive strain injury (RSI). (See also *Mouse elbow.*)

Cathode-ray tube (CRT). See *Display screen.*

CD-ROM (pronounced *cee-dee-rom*). An acronym derived from compact disk—read-only memory. A form of optical **storage.** One compact **disk** can hold up to 250,000 **text** pages; it can also be used to store **graphics,** sound, and video.

Cell. A box or rectangle within a table or **spreadsheet** where a **column** and a **row** intersect; an area in which information can be entered in the form of **text** or figures.

Central processing unit (CPU). The brains of an **information processing** system; the processing component that controls the interpretation and execution of instructions. (See *Motherboard.*)

Character. A single letter, figure, punctuation mark, or symbol produced by a **keystroke** on a **computer.** Each character is represented by a **byte.**

Character set. The complete set of **characters**—alphabetic, numeric, and symbolic—displayable on a **computer.** (See *ASCII.*)

Character string. A specified sequence of typed **characters,** usually representing a word or phrase. A character string is often used to locate a particular word or phrase wherever it appears in a **document** so that it can be automatically replaced with another word or phrase. If a person's name has been consistently misspelled or a date appears incorrectly in several places, the error can be easily corrected. (See also *Search and replace.*)

Characters per inch (cpi). The number of **characters** in a **font** that will fit within 1 inch.

Characters per second (cps). The number of **characters** printed in 1 second; a measurement frequently used to describe the speed of a **printer.**

Check box. A small box that appears on screen alongside each option displayed in a **dialog box.** When an option is selected, an X or a check mark appears inside the box.

Chatline. See *Newsgroup.*

Chip. An **integrated circuit** used in **computers.**

Circuit board. A board or card that carries the necessary electronic components for a particular **computer** function (for example, **memory**). The circuit boards that come with the original equipment perform the standard functions identified with that type of equipment. Additional circuit boards expand the kinds of functions that the equipment can perform. (Also called a *board,* a *card,* or an *expansion board.*)

Clear. A **command** to erase information.

Click. To quickly press and release a **mouse** button *once* while the **cursor** (mouse pointer) is positioned over a specific item on the screen. (See also *Double-click.*)

Client/server computing. A **network** of **computers** that consists of a file server (a computer that runs a **database management system**) and individual clients (computers that request and process **data** obtained from the file server).

Clipboard. A holding area in **memory** where information that has been copied or **cut** (text, **graphics,** sound, or video) can be stored until the information is inserted elsewhere. (See *Copy; Cut; Cut and paste.*)

Column. A vertical block of **cells** in a table or **spreadsheet.** (See also *Row.*)

B

Command. An instruction that causes a **program** or **computer** to perform a function. A command may be given by means of a special **keystroke** (or series of keystrokes), or the command may be chosen from a **menu.**

Compatibility. The ability of one type of **computer** to share information or to communicate with another computer. (See also *ASCII.*)

Computer. An electronic device that is capable of (1) accepting, storing, and logically manipulating **data** or **text** that is **input** and (2) processing and producing **output** (results or decisions) on the basis of stored **programs** of instructions. Some computers are also capable of processing **graphics,** video, and voice input. Most computers include a **keyboard** for **text entry,** a **central processing unit,** one or more **disk drives,** a **display screen,** and a **printer**—components referred to as **hardware.**

Control character. A special **character** that is never printed but causes a visible result during printing. For example, spacing, tabulation, and carriage return are all achieved by means of control characters.

Control menu. An on-screen **Windows** element that appears in a box in the upper left corner of a window. The control menu allows the user the option of adjusting the size of the window, closing or reopening the window, or switching to another window.

Copy. To reproduce information elsewhere. The original information remains in place. (See *Cut.*)

cpi. See *Characters per inch.*

cps. See *Characters per second.*

CPU. See *Central processing unit.*

Crash. A malfunction in **hardware** or **software** that keeps a **computer** from functioning. (See also *Bug; Glitch*)

CRT. Cathode-ray tube. (See *Display screen.*)

Cursor. A special **character** (usually a blinking underline, dot, or vertical line) that indicates where the next typed character will appear on the **display screen.** Also refers to the **mouse** pointer (arrow) or **I-beam pointer.** (See also *Prompt.*)

Cursor positioning. The movement of the **cursor** on the **display screen.** Most **computers** have four keys to control up, down, left, and right movement. Many computers also permit the use of a **mouse** to position the cursor.

Cut. To remove **text** from its original location and place it on a **clipboard.** (See *Paste; Copy*).

Cut and paste. To move a **block** of **text** from one place to another.

Cyberspace. A realistic simulation of a three-dimensional world created by a **computer** system. Also referred to as *virtual reality.*

Data. Information consisting of letters, numbers, symbols, sounds, or images—in a form that can be processed by a **computer.**

Data compression. A procedure for reducing the volume of **data** so as to shorten the time needed to transfer the data.

Data processing. The mathematical or other logical manipulation of numbers or symbols, based on a stored **program** of instructions. Also known as *electronic data processing (EDP).* (See also *Information processing.*)

Database. A stored collection of information.

Database management system (DBMS). The **software** needed to establish and maintain a **database** and manage the stored information.

B

DDE. See *Dynamic data exchange.*

Debugging. Locating and eliminating defects in a **program.** (See also *Bug.*)

Decimal tab. A type of tab that aligns **columns** of figures on the decimal point.

Default settings. The preestablished settings (for margins, typeface, type size, tab stops, and so on) that a **program** will follow unless the user changes them.

Delete. A **command** to erase information in **storage.**

Descending sort. Sorting records from Z to A or 9 to 0. (See *Ascending sort.*)

Desktop. The electronic work area on a **display screen.**

Desktop computer. A **microcomputer.**

Desktop publishing (DTP). A system that processes **text** and **graphics** and, by means of page layout **software** and a **laser printer,** produces high-quality pages suitable for printing or in-house reproduction.

Dialog box. A message box on the screen that supplies information to—or requests information from—the user.

Dictionary. A **program** used to check the spelling of each word entered in the **computer.**

Directory. A list of the **files** stored on a **disk.**

Disk. A random-**access,** magnetically coated **storage medium** used to store and **retrieve** information. (See also *Diskette; CD-ROM.*)

Disk drive. The component of a **computer** into which a **disk** is inserted so that it can be read or written on.

Disk operating system. See *DOS.*

Diskette. A small, nonrigid **disk** with limited **storage** capacity (normally 30 to 200 pages). Also known as a *floppy disk.*

Display screen. A device similar to a television screen and used on a **computer** to display **text** and **graphics.** Also called a *cathode-ray tube (CRT),* a *video display terminal (VDT),* or a *monitor.*

Distributed processing system. A form of a **local area network** in which each user has a fully functional **computer** but all users can share **data** and **application software.** The data and **software** are distributed among the linked computers and not stored in one central computer.

Document. Any printed business communication—for example, a letter, memo, report, table, or form. (See *File.*)

DOS. An acronym derived from disk operating system. A **program** that allows the **computer** to manage the **storage** of information on **disks** and controls other aspects of a computer's operation.

Dot matrix printer. A **printer** that uses pins to produce **characters** made up of small dots. (See also *Laser printer.*)

Double-click. To quickly press and release a **mouse** button *twice* while the **cursor** is positioned over a specific item on the screen. (See *Click.*)

Download. To transfer information to the user's **computer** from another computer.

Drag-and-drop editing. A **software** feature that allows the user to (1) highlight **text** to be moved and (2) use a **mouse** to drag the text to a new location.

B

DTP. See *Desktop publishing.*

Duplexing. A procedure that permits two **computers** to transmit **data** to each other simultaneously.

Dynamic data exchange (DDE). A technology that permits the user to transfer or **paste data** from one **application** (for example, a **spreadsheet**) to another (for example, a report). Because of the dynamic link created by this technology, any change in the data in the original application will be automatically reflected in the data copied in the second application. (See also *Object linking and embedding.*)

Easter egg. An unexpected image or message that pops up on the **display screen** when the user innocently enters a secret combination of **keystrokes.** Programmers playfully code Easter eggs into **software** and **operating systems** as a way of surprising and amusing users engaged in more serious tasks.

Editing. The process of changing information by inserting, deleting, replacing, rearranging, and reformatting. Also known as *changing* or *customizing.*

EDP. See *Data processing.*

Electronic mail (e-mail). The transfer of messages or **documents** between users connected by an electronic **network.**

Elite type. Any **monospace font** that prints 12 **characters per inch.** (See *Pica type.*)

Ellipsis marks. Three dots (. . .) that appear as part of a **menu** option. Ellipsis marks indicate that a **dialog box** will appear if that option is selected.

E-mail. See *Electronic mail.*

Encryption. Coding confidential **data** so that only a user with the necessary **password** can read the data.

Enter. To **input data** into **memory.** (See *Type.*)

Escape key. A key that permits the user to leave one segment of a **program** and move to another.

Execute. To perform an action specified by the user or the **program.**

Expert system. See *Artificial intelligence.*

Export. To save information in a **format** that another **program** can read.

Fax (n.). A shortened form of the word *facsimile.* A copy of a **document** transmitted electronically from one machine to another.

Fax (v.). To transmit a copy of a **document** electronically.

Fax modem. A device built into or attached to a **computer** that serves as a facsimile machine and a **modem.**

Field. A group of related **characters** treated as a unit (such as a name); also the area reserved for the entry of a specified piece of information.

File. Stored information on a **disk** or tape identified by a **file name.**

File name. The name assigned to a **file** stored on a **disk.** Every file must have its own distinctive name.

File transfer protocol (FTP). A set of guidelines or standards that establish the **format** in which **files** can be transmitted from one **computer** to another.

Floppy disk. See *Diskette.*

Folder. A **storage** area on a **disk** used to organize **files.**

Font. A **typeface** of a certain size and style. Includes all letters of the alphabet, figures, symbols, and punctuation marks. (See *Monospace font; Proportional font.*)

B

Footer. Repetitive information that appears at the bottom (the foot) of every page of a **document.** A page number is a common footer. (See also *Header.*)

Footnote feature. The ability of a **program** to automatically position footnotes on the same page as the **text** they refer to. If the text is moved to another page, any related footnotes will also be transferred to that page.

Footprint. The amount of space a **computer** occupies on a flat surface.

Format. The physical specifications that affect the appearance and arrangement of a **document**—for example, margins, spacing, and **font.**

Forms mode. The ability of a **program** to store the **format** of a blank **document** or form so that it can later be viewed on the **display screen** and completed by the user. Once a fill-in has been entered, the **cursor** automatically advances to the beginning of the next area to be filled in. (See also *Style sheet; Template.*)

Forum. See *Newsgroup.*

Freeware. Copyrighted **software** that is available for use without charge.

FTP. See *File transfer protocol.*

Function keys. Keys on a **keyboard** (for example, F1) that give special **commands** to the **computer**—for example, to set margins or tabs. (See also *Control character.*)

Glitch. A **hardware** problem that causes a **computer** to malfunction or **crash.** (See *Bug.*)

Global. Describing any function that can be performed on an entire **document** without requiring individual **commands** for each use. For example, a global **search-and-replace** command will instruct the **computer** to locate a particular word or phrase and replace it with a different word or phrase wherever the original form occurs in the document.

Graphical user interface (GUI). A **software** feature that permits the user to **click** on **icons** or select options from a **menu.**

Graphics. Pictures or images presented or stored using a **computer.**

GUI (pronounced *goo-ee*). See *Graphical user interface.*

Hard copy. **Text** or **graphics** printed on paper; also called a **printout.** (See also *Soft copy.*)

Hard disk. A rigid type of **magnetic medium** that can store large amounts of information.

Hard hyphen. A hyphen that is a permanent **character** in a word. A word that contains a hard hyphen will not be divided at this point if the word comes at the end of a line. (See also *Soft hyphen.*)

Hard page break. A page-ending code or **command** inserted by the user that cannot be changed by the **program.** A hard page break is often used (1) to prevent a table from being divided between two pages and (2) to signify that a particular section of a document has ended and the following **text** should start on a new page.

Hard return. A **command** used to end a paragraph, end a short line of **text,** or insert a blank line in the text. (See also *Soft return.*)

Hard space. A space inserted between words in a phrase that should remain together (for example, the word *page* and the number, month and day, number and unit of measure). The hard space ensures that the phrase will not be broken at the end of a line.

Hardware. The physical components of a **computer:** the **central processing unit,** the **display screen,** the **keyboard,** the **disk drive,** and the **printer.** (See also *Software.*)

Header. Repetitive information that appears at the top (the head) of every page of a **document.** A page number is a common header. (See also *Footer.*)

Home. The upper left corner of the **display screen;** the starting position of a page or **document.**

Hot key. A **keyboard** shortcut that allows quick access to a **command** or **menu** option.

Hot zone. The area before the right margin, usually seven to ten **characters** wide; the user can adjust the width. Words that cross this area may have to be divided or moved to the next line.

Hypertext. A technology that links **text** in one part of a **document** with related text in another part of the document or in other documents. A user can quickly find the related text by clicking on the appropriate keyword, key phrase, **icon,** or button.

Hyphenation. The ability of a **program** to automatically hyphenate and divide words that do not fit at the end of a line. If the **text** is later revised so that the divided word no longer begins at the right margin, the hyphen is automatically removed and the word prints solid. (See also *Soft hyphen.*)

I-beam pointer. A **mouse**-controlled **cursor** that looks like a capital I.

Icon. A symbol (such as a picture of a trash can or a file folder) that represents a certain function. When the user **clicks** on the icon, the appropriate function is **executed.**

Import. To **retrieve** any **text** or other information created by one **program** (for example, images created by a **graphics** program) and transfer it to another program (for example, a **spreadsheet** program).

Indexing. The ability of a **program** to accumulate a list of words or phrases that appear in a **document** (along with their corresponding page numbers) and to print or display the list in alphabetic order.

Information processing. The coordination of people, equipment, and procedures to handle information, including the **storage, retrieval,** distribution, and communication of information. The term *information processing* embraces the entire field of processing words, figures, **graphics,** video, and voice **input** by electronic means.

Ink-jet printer. A nonimpact printer that forms **characters** by spraying tiny, electrically charged ink droplets on paper.

Input (n.). Information entered into the **computer** for processing.

Input (v.). To **enter** information into the **computer.** (See also *Type; Key.*)

Insert. To add information to a **file.**

Integrated circuit. Multiple electronic components combined on a tiny silicon **chip.** (See *Microprocessor.*)

Integrated software. Software that combines in one **program** a number of functions normally performed by separate programs.

Interface. The electrical connection that links two pieces of equipment so that they can communicate with each other. Also, the **software** that controls the interaction between the **hardware** and the user.

Internet (or **Net).** A system that links existing **computer networks** into a worldwide network. The Internet may be accessed by means of commercial information services (such as America Online, CompuServe, and Prodigy) as well as some nonprofit **bulletin board systems.**

I/O. An abbreviation for *input/output.*

Justification. Aligning lines of **text** at the left margin, the right margin, both margins, or the center. Text aligned at both margins is considered *fully justified.* Text aligned only at the left margin is said to have a *ragged right margin.*

K or **KB.** See *Kilobyte.*

Kern. To make fine adjustments in the space between any two **characters.**

B

Key. To **enter characters** into the **memory** of a **computer.** (*Key* is being replaced by the word *type.* See *Type.*)

Keyboard. The device used to **enter** information into a **computer.**

Keystroke. The depression of one key on a **keyboard.**

Killer app (short for *application*). **Software** that is considered "so great it will blow you away." (Mosaic, a program that facilitates information retrieval for **Internet** users, was considered a killer app when it was introduced.)

Kilobyte. A measurement of the **storage** capacity of a **computer.** A single kilobyte represents 1024 **bytes.** *Kilobyte* may be abbreviated *K* or *KB*; however, *KB* is the clearer abbreviation since *K* also stands for the metric prefix *kilo* (meaning 1000).

LAN. See *Network.*

Landscape orientation. The positioning of a page so that information is printed across the long dimension of the paper. (See *Portrait orientation.*)

Language. The **characters** and procedures used to write **programs** that a **computer** is designed to understand.

Laptop computer. A portable **microcomputer,** normally battery-powered.

Laser printer. A nonimpact **printer** that produces sharper **text** and **graphics** than any other type of printer. (See also *Dot matrix printer; Ink-jet printer.*)

LCD. See *Liquid crystal display.*

Line or **paragraph numbering.** The ability of a **program** to automatically number each line or paragraph sequentially in a **document.** The line or paragraph numbers can be deleted before the preparation of the final **printout.**

Line spacing. The ability of a **program** to automatically change vertical line spacing (for example, from double to single to double again).

Liquid crystal display (LCD). A type of **monitor** typically used on **laptop computers** or portable **computers.** (See also *Active matrix display.*)

Load. To transfer information or **program** instructions into a **computer's memory.**

Log off. To exit or leave a **computer** system. (Two words as a verb; hyphenated as a noun or an adjective. See ¶803f.)

Log on. To **access** a **computer** system. (Two words as a verb; hyphenated as a noun or an adjective. See ¶¶802, 803e.)

M or **MB.** See *Megabyte.*

Macro. A time-saving feature (like telephone speed dialing) that allows the user to store in **memory** a set of **keystrokes** (such as the name of a person or an organization, a frequently used phrase or sentence, or the complimentary closing and writer's identification in a letter). By means of only a few keystrokes or a **menu** command, the user can **retrieve** the complete set of keystrokes and **insert** it into other **documents.**

Magnetic medium. Any device coated with a magnetic material that can be used to store information entered in a **computer**—for example, magnetic tapes, **disks,** and **diskettes.**

Mail merge. The process of taking information from a **database** and inserting it into a form letter or other **document** in order to customize the document for an individual recipient. For example, mail merge can be used to create the inside address and the salutation for a form letter. (See also *Forms mode.*)

Mainframe. A large **computer** system.

Megabyte. A measurement of the **storage** capacity of a **computer.** One megabyte represents more than 1 million **bytes.** *Megabyte* may be abbreviated *M* or *MB*; however, *MB* is clearer since *M* also stands for the metric prefix *mega* (meaning 1 million).

Megahertz. A measurement used to identify the speed of the **central processing unit.** One megahertz is equal to 1 million cycles per second.

Memory. The part of a **computer** that stores information. (See also *Storage.*)

> **Random-access memory (RAM).** The temporary memory that allows information to be stored randomly and accessed quickly and directly (without the need to go through intervening **data**).

> **Read-only memory (ROM).** The permanent **memory** of a **computer;** a set of instructions that has been built into the computer by the manufacturer and cannot be accessed or changed by the user.

Menu. A list of choices shown on the **display screen.** For example, a **format** menu would include such options as the type style and the type size to be selected. A menu is often referred to as a *pull-down menu* or a *pop-up menu* because it appears on screen after the user **clicks** on the **menu bar** or on some other item on the screen.

Menu bar. The bar across the top of the screen or window that displays the names of available **menus.**

Merge. A **command** to create one **file** by combining information that is stored in two different locations. For example, a **computer** can merge the **text** in a form letter with a mailing list to produce a batch of letters with a different name, address, and salutation on each letter. (See also *Mail merge.*)

Microcomputer. A small and relatively inexpensive **computer,** commonly consisting of a **display screen,** a **keyboard,** a **central processing unit,** one or more **disk drives,** and a **printer,** with limited **storage** based upon a **microprocessor.** Also referred to as a *desktop computer* or a *laptop computer.*

Microprocessor. An **integrated circuit** on a silicon **chip** that serves as the **central processing unit** of a **computer.**

MIPS. An acronym derived from millions of instructions per second. Used to measure the speed of a **computer.**

Modem. An acronym derived from modulator/demodulator. A device that (1) converts digital signals into tones for transmission over telephone lines and (2) converts the tones back into digital signals at the receiving end.

Monitor. The **display screen** of a **computer.**

Monospace font. A **typeface** such as Courier in which each **character** has exactly the same width (`like this`).

Motherboard. The **computer's** main **circuit board,** which contains the **central processing unit,** the **memory,** and expansion slots for additional circuit boards (called *adapters* or *cards*). See *Adapter card.*

Mouse. A hand-operated electronic device used to move a **cursor** or pointer on the **display screen.** Mostly used with **microcomputers.**

Mouse elbow. A repetitive strain injury (similar to tennis elbow) that is caused by repeatedly using a **mouse.** (See also *Carpal tunnel syndrome.*)

MS-DOS (pronounced *em-ess-doss*). Derived from Microsoft disk operating system. An operating system used on IBM-compatible **microcomputers.**

Multimedia. The use of several types of media (such as **text, graphics,** animation, sound, and video) in a **document** or an **application.**

B

Multitasking. The ability of a **computer** to **execute** more than one **program** at a time.

Net. See *Internet.*

Netiquette. A set of guidelines for formatting and composing **e-mail** messages.

Network. A system of interconnected **computers.** (See *Notwork; Sneakernet.*)

> **Local area networks (LANs)** use cable to connect a number of computers within the same location or at most a 2-mile radius.

> **Wide area networks (WANs)** use telephone lines or other **telecommunications** devices to link computers in widely separated locations.

> **Internet** is a system that links existing networks into a worldwide network.

Newbie. A newcomer to a **bulletin board system** or some other **network** facility.

Newsgroup (also called a *chat line* or a *forum*). An electronic discussion group tied into a **bulletin board system.** Each newsgroup is typically organized around a specific interest or matter of concern.

Notebook computer. A lightweight portable **computer** that can fit into a briefcase.

Notwork. A **network** that does not live up to its advance billing.

Number crunching. Processing large amounts of numerical **data.**

Object linking and embedding (OLE). A process that permits the user to take material (referred to as an *object*) from one source and **insert** (*embed*) it in another **document.** If the user subsequently makes changes in the original material, those changes will be automatically transferred to the second document as a result of the OLE linking process. (See also *Dynamic data exchange.*)

OCR. See *Optical character reader.*

Off-line. Describing the state of an electronic device (for example, a **printer**) not ready to receive **data.**

OLE. See *Object linking and embedding.*

On-line. Describing the state of an electronic device ready to receive data.

Open. To transfer a **file** from a **disk** into a **computer's memory.**

Operating system (OS). Software that manages the internal functions and controls the operations of a **computer.**

Optical character reader (OCR). A device that can scan **text** from **hard copy** and **enter** it automatically into a **computer** for **storage** or **editing.** Also called an *optical scanner.*

Orphan protection. The ability of a **program** to prevent the first line of a paragraph from printing as the last line on a page. When the first line of a paragraph does appear as the last line on a page, it is referred to as an *orphan.* (See also *Widow protection.*)

OS. See *Operating system.*

Outlining. The ability of a **program** to automatically number and letter items typed in an indented **format.**

Output. The results of a **computer** operation.

Overwriting. Recording and storing information in a specific location on a **storage medium** that destroys whatever had been stored there previously.

Page break. A **command** that tells the **printer** where to end one page and begin the next. (See *Hard page break; Soft page break.*)

B

Page numbering. The ability of a **program** to automatically print page numbers on the pages that make up an entire **document.** If the document is revised, with a gain or loss in the total number of pages, the page numbering is automatically adjusted.

Pagination. The ability of a **program** to take information and automatically divide it into pages with a specified number of lines per page. If the information is changed because of the addition, deletion, or rearrangement of copy, the material will be automatically repaged to maintain the proper page length. (See also *Soft page break.*)

Password. A user's secret identification code, required to access stored material. A procedure intended to prevent information from being accessed by unauthorized persons.

Paste. A **command** that transfers information from a **clipboard** and inserts it in another location. (See *Cut and paste.*)

PC. See *Personal computer.*

PDA. See *Personal digital assistant.*

Peripheral. A device that extends the capabilities of a **computer** (for example, a **printer**).

Personal computer (PC). A **microcomputer** for personal and office use.

Personal digital assistant (PDA). A palm-sized, handheld **computer.**

Personal information manager (PIM). A **database management system** that permits a user to store and **retrieve** a wide range of personal information (for example, names, addresses, phone numbers, appointments, and lists of people to call and things to do).

Pica. A measurement used for a **font;** equal to 1/6 inch or 12 **points.**

Pica type. Any **monospace font** that prints 10 **characters per inch.** (See *Elite type.*)

Pitch. The number of **monospace characters** printed in a 1-inch line of **text.**

Pixel. An acronym derived from picture element. The smallest element (a dot) on a **display screen.** Pixels are used to construct images on the screen.

Point. A measurement used to indicate the size of a **font;** 72 **points** equals 1 inch. (See also *Pica.*)

Pop-up menu. A menu that appears in a **dialog box.**

Port. A socket on a **computer** into which an external device (such as a printer cable) can be plugged.

Portrait orientation. Positioning paper so that information is printed across the short dimension of the paper. (See *Landscape orientation.*)

Print preview. A **software** feature that reduces the pages of a **document** so that a full page (or two facing pages) can be seen on the screen before being printed. This feature permits the user to spot and correct problems in **format** and **page breaks.**

Printers. Output devices of various types that produce copy on paper. (See *Dot matrix printer; Ink-jet printer; Laser printer.*)

Printout. The paper copy of information produced on a **printer.**

Program. An established sequence of instructions that tells a **computer** what to do. The term *program* means the same as **software.**

Prompt. An on-screen symbol (for example, a **cursor**) that indicates where to **type** a **command;** a message that indicates what action is to be taken.

Proportional font. A **typeface** in which the width of each **character** varies (as in this sentence), so that the letter I takes much less space than the letter M. (See *Font.*)

Protocol. A set of standards for exchanging information between **computers.**

B

Radio button. An on-screen element that allows a user to select one option from a group of items. An empty circle precedes each option not selected. A dot appears in a circle to signify that the user has selected that option.

RAM. See *Memory, random-access.*

Read. To transfer information from an external **storage medium** into internal storage. (See also *Storage, external* and *internal.*)

Record (n.). A collection of all the information pertaining to a particular subject.

Redline. A **word processing** feature that shows deleted material by displaying it in a shaded panel, by printing a line through the **text,** or by using some other method. Redlining allows a user to see what has been deleted. Any redlined text may be easily removed from a **document** to produce the final copy.

For example, this portion of text is shown using the redline feature.

Response time. The time a **computer** takes to **execute** a **command.**

Retrieve. To call up information from **memory** so that it can be processed in some way.

ROM. See *Memory, read-only.*

Row. A horizontal block of **cells** in a table or **spreadsheet.** (See also *Column.*)

RSI. Repetitive strain injury. (See also *Carpal tunnel syndrome; Mouse elbow.*)

Ruler. A bar (displayed on the screen) that shows the width of the page, the margin settings, the paragraph indentions, and the tab stops.

Save. To store a **program** or **data** on a **storage** device such as a **disk.**

Scanner. An **input** device that can copy a printed page into a **computer's memory,** thus doing away with the need to **type** the copy. A scanner can also convert artwork and photographs into a digital format and store these in memory.

Screen dump. A **printout** of what is displayed on the screen. (For an example, see the illustration in ¶1397.)

Screen saver. A **program** that changes the screen display while the user is away from the **computer.** Without the use of a screen saver, a screen image that remains on display for any length of time can damage the screen.

Scroll. To move information horizontally or vertically on a **display screen** so that one can see parts of a **document** that is too wide or too deep to fit entirely on one screen.

Scroll bar. An on-screen element that allows a user to **scroll** by using a **mouse.**

SCSI. See *Small computer system interface.*

Search and replace. A **command** that directs the **program** to locate a **character string** or information (**text,** numbers, or symbols) wherever it occurs in a **document** and replace this material with new information. (See *Global.*)

Small computer system interface (SCSI, pronounced *scuzzy*). A type of **hardware** and **software interface** for connecting **peripherals** such as a **disk drive** or a **CD-ROM.**

Smiley. In **e-mail** messages, a facial expression constructed sideways (for the "lateral-minded") with standard **characters.** For example:

:-)	I'm smiling.	>:-(	I'm angry.	:-J	I'm being tongue-in-cheek.
:-D	I'm laughing.	:-@	I'm screaming.	:-+	I'm exhausted—my tongue
:-(	I'm sad.	:-&	I'm tongue-tied.		is hanging out.
:-<	I'm very sad.	:-x	My lips are sealed.	%-)	I've been staring at the
:'-(	I'm crying.	#-)	I'm feeling no pain.		screen too long.

B

Although some smileys are quite witty, many people find them excessively cute. Therefore, don't use smileys unless you are sure the recipient will appreciate them.

Snail mail. A term employed by **e-mail** users to refer to regular mail service.

Sneakernet. The procedure for transferring **files** from one **computer** to another when the computers are not connected by an electronic **network**. (Users remove **diskettes** from one computer and carry them on foot to another.)

Soft copy. Information shown on the **display screen**. (See also *Hard copy.*)

Soft hyphen. A hyphen that divides a word at the end of a line; considered soft (nonpermanent) because the hyphen will automatically be deleted if the word moves to another position as a result of a change in the **text**. (See *Hard hyphen; Hyphenation.*)

Soft page break. A line inserted by the **program** to show where a page will end. If copy is added or deleted, the original **page break** will be replaced with a new soft page break at the appropriate place. (By contrast, a **hard page break** will remain fixed, no matter what changes are made in the copy.) (See also *Pagination.*)

Soft return. A **software** feature that automatically breaks **text** between words at the right margin. The line ending is considered soft (nonpermanent) because the line ending will change if the user adds or deletes **text**. (See *Hard return; Word wrap.*)

Software. The instructions that a **computer** needs to perform various functions. The term *software* means the same as **program**. (See also *Hardware.*)

Sort. To arrange **fields, records,** or **files** in a predetermined sequence.

Split screen. The ability of some **programs** to display information in two or more different areas on the screen at the same time.

Spreadsheet. A **program** that provides a worksheet with **rows** and **columns** to be used for calculations and the preparation of reports.

Storage. The **memory** of a **computer**.

> **External storage.** A **magnetic medium** such as a **disk, diskette,** or tape used to store information; can be removed from the **computer**.

> **Internal storage.** An integral component of a **computer;** cannot be removed.

Storage medium. See *Magnetic medium.*

Store. To place information in **memory** for later use.

Style sheet. A collection of the user's formatting decisions regarding **typeface,** type size, margins, **justification,** paragraph indentions, and the like.

SYSOP (pronounced "siss-op"). An acronym derived from system operator. A person who operates a **bulletin board system.**

Tab grid. A series of preset indentions (usually a half inch apart). If the tabs are reset by the user, the grid will change to show the new location of the tabs.

Telecommunications. The process of sending and receiving information by means of telephones, satellites, and other devices.

Teleconferencing. Conducting a conference by using **computers,** video, and **telecommunications** to share sound and images with others at remote sites.

Template. A preestablished **format** for a **document,** stored in a **computer.** The template determines the margins, the type style and size to be used for the **text,** placement instructions for various elements (such as the date line), and design specifications for certain items (such as a letterhead). A user can simply call up the appropriate template, **insert** text where needed, and then print a final document. The user can modify the original template or create a new template to satisfy personal preferences. (See also *Forms mode.*)

B

Terminal. Any device that can transmit or receive electronic information.

Text. The information displayed on a screen or printed on paper.

Text entry. The initial act of typing that places **text** in **storage.** (See *Type.*)

Tool bar. See *Button bar.*

Type. To enter **characters** into the **memory** of a **computer.** For a number of years the verb *type* began to be replaced by the verb *key* as a way of emphasizing the difference between a **computer** and a typewriter. However, the simpler verb *type* has made a comeback in computer terminology and is now the word commonly seen in users' manuals and on **display screens.**

Typeface. All the **characters** of a single type design. (See *Font;* ¶1305d for samples.)

Typeover. See *Overwriting.*

User-friendly. Describing equipment or **application software** that is easy to use.

Vaporware. **Software** that is being widely advertised, even though it is still in the developmental stage and has serious problems which may doom its eventual release.

Video display terminal (VDT). See *Display screen.*

Virtual reality. See *Cyberspace.*

Virus. A **program** designed as a prank or as a malicious act. When a virus invades another program, it can cause serious damage to **memory** or **disks.** (See *Antivirus software.*)

Widow protection. The ability of a **program** to avoid printing the last line of a paragraph as the first line on a page. When the last line of a paragraph does appear as the first line on a page, it is referred to as a *widow.* (See also *Orphan protection.*)

Windowing. The ability of a **program** to split its **display screen** into two or more segments so that the user can view several different **documents** or perform several different functions simultaneously. (See also *Split screen.*)

Word processing. The electronic process of creating, formatting, **editing,** proofreading, and printing **documents.** (See *Information processing.*)

Word wrap. A **software** feature that detects when a word will extend beyond the right margin and automatically transfers it to the beginning of the next line. (See also *Hot zone.*)

Workstation. A **desktop computer** that runs **application software** and serves as an access point in a **local area network.**

WYSIWYG (pronounced *wizzy-wig*). An acronym derived from what you see is what you get. A **computer** design standard that permits the user to see on the screen how the information will look when it is printed.

B

INDEX

This index contains many entries for individual words. If you are looking for a specific word that is not listed, refer to ¶719, which contains a 12-page guide to words that are frequently confused because they sound alike or look alike (for example, *capital—capitol—Capitol* or *stationary—stationery*).

NOTE: The **boldface** numbers in this index refer to paragraph numbers; the lightface numbers refer to page numbers.

Boldface numbers refer to paragraphs; lightface numbers refer to pages.

    Boldface numbers refer to paragraphs; lightface numbers refer to pages.

Boldface numbers refer to paragraphs; lightface numbers refer to pages.

Boldface numbers refer to paragraphs; lightface numbers refer to pages.

Quotation marks (*cont.*)
 in lists, **284a**
 with long quotations, **264–265**
 with poetry, **267–268, 284b**
 punctuation with, **247–265**
 single
  punctuation with, **245–249**
  for quotations within
   quotations, **245–246, 265b**
 spacing with, **299**
 as symbol for inches, **432**
 with titles of literary and artistic
  works, **242–244**
 for translated expressions, **241**
 with well-known sayings, **234**
 with *yes* and *no*, **233**
Quotations, **523**
 abbreviations in, **247, 253, 257,
  258**
 at beginning of sentence, **253–
  255**
 bracketed insertions, **281–283,
  296**
 capitalization in, **199b, 263,
  272–273, 277–278, 301c**
 dialogues and conversations,
  269–270
 direct, **227–234, 523**
 displayed extract, **265a, 268,
  271;** *illus.,* 419
 at end of sentence, **256–258**
 indirect, **228, 523**
 with interrupting expressions,
  262–263
 in letters, **1357a**
 of letters, **266**
 long, **264–265**
 omissions in, **274–280**
 paragraphs in, **265b**
 of poetry, **267–268, 284b**
 punctuation with, **247–265**
 within quotations, **245–246**
 in reports, **1424d**
 within sentence, **259–261**
 standing alone, **252**
 style in, **271**
 of words in series, **232**

Radio stations, **523**
raise–rise, 270–271
rather than, **1007**
Ratio, **193, 299, 450**
re- as prefix, **835, 837**
real–really, 271
reason is because, 271
Reference library of word
  processing program, **1532**
Reference notations, **1316,
  1393m, 1396c;** *illus.,* 312
References, parentheses with, **220**
Religious dignitaries, forms of
  address, **1809–1811**
Religious orders, **157, 519,
  1324c–d**
Religious references, **349–350**
Religious titles, **517c–d, 1324c–d**
Reports, **1401–1430**
 academic, **1401a, 1405d, 1413,
  1414;** *illus.,* 384, 385

Reports (*cont.*)
 appendixes, **1402c, 1428;** *illus.,*
  403
 back matter, **1402c, 1427–1430**
 bibliography, **1402c, 1532–
  1536;** *illus.,* 433
 body, **1402b, 1421–1426**
 bulleted items in, **1424g;** *illus.,*
  397
 chapter-opening pages, **1423;**
  illus., 376, 395
 conclusion, **1402b**
 drafts, **1424b**
 endnotes, **1402c, 1501–1502,
  1505–1506, 1508–1531**
 enumerated items in, **1424f;**
  illus., 390–392, 396–397
 footnotes, **1501–1504, 1508–
  1531**
 foreword, **1402a, 1418**
 formal, parts of, **1402**
 format, guidelines for choosing,
  1401, 370–372; *illus.,* 372
 front matter, **1402a, 1414–1420**
 glossary, **1402c, 1430;** *illus.,* 403–
  404
 headings, **108, 1402b, 1425;**
  illus., 399–401
 indentions in, **1424**
 informal
  academic, **1413;** *illus.,* 384–
   385
  business, **1411–1412;** *illus.,*
   382–384
  parts of, **1403**
 introduction, **1402b, 1421**
 letter or memo of transmittal,
  1402a, 1415; *illus.,* 389
 list of tables or illustrations,
  1402a, 1417; *illus.,* 392
 lists in, **1424e–g;** *illus.,* 396, 397
 main discussion, **1402b**
 margins, **1404–1409, 1427;**
  illus., 376, 377
 memo format for, **1412**
 numbering pages, **1420, 1426,
  1427**
 page-ending considerations
  on a computer, **1407**
  on a typewriter, **1408;** *illus.,*
   379–380
 paragraphs in, **1424c**
 part-title pages, **1402b, 1422;**
  illus., 394
 preface, **1402a, 1418**
 quotations in, **1424d;** *illus.,* 396
 shortening, **1410**
 spacing in, **1424**
 summary, **1402a, 1419**
 table of contents, **1402a, 1416;**
  illus., 389, 390
 tables in, **1424h** (*see also*
  Tables)
 templates, **1414 (note),** 370–
  371 (*illus.*)
 textnotes, **1501, 1507, 1508–
  1531**
 title page, **1402a, 1414;** *illus.,*
  385, 388
  template, **1414, note**

Request, punctuation of, **103**
Residence, comma in, **153, 161**
Restrictive clauses and phrases
  (*see* Essential elements)
Résumés, **1712–1713;** *illus.,* 490–
  495
 templates, **1713**
retroactive to (not *from*), **1077,** 271
Return address, **1313, 1314e**
Reverend, the, **517d, 519c,
  1324c–d, 1809–1810**
rise–raise (see *raise,* 270–271)
Roman Catholic dignitaries, forms
  of address, **1809**
Roman numerals, **468–469**
 after names, **122f, 156, 518d,
  1324a**
 possessives of, **639**
 filing rules for, **1213, 1218**
 period not used with, **109d**
Run-on sentences, **128**

said, 271
Saint, **518e, 529b, 1340c**
 filing rules for, **1210c, 1213b,
  1215d**
Salutations
 in business letters, **1346–1351,
  1801–1811**
 in memos, **1392, 1393j;** *illus.,*
  365
 punctuation after, **194, 1309,
  1346, 1393j, 1396b**
 in social-business letters, **1396**
same, 271
scarcely, 271
Scores, **401a, 451**
second (*2d* or *2nd*), **122f, 156, 425–
  426, 503, 518d, 1213d**
Second pages, **1304b, 1382–1387,
  1393r**
self, **836, 1060**
semiannual (see *biannual,* 258)
Semicolons, **176–186**
 in compound-complex
  sentences, **133**
 dash and, **213, 215c**
 dash in place of, **204**
 with dependent clauses, **186**
 with *for example, namely, that is,*
  etc., **181–183**
 with independent clauses, **128,
  142, 176–177, 181, 187**
 parentheses and, **224a**
 quotation marks and, **248**
 in series, **184–185**
 spacing with, **299**
 with transitional expressions,
  178–182
Senior, Sr., **122f, 156, 158, 518,
  615d, 639, 1213d, 1324a**
Sentence structure, **1081–1086**
Sentences, **523–524**
 capitalization, **196–199, 301**
 complex, **130–132, 523**
 compound, **123a, 126–129, 523**
 compound-complex, **133–134,
  524**
 dash at end of, **208, 216**

Boldface numbers refer to paragraphs; lightface numbers refer to pages.

Boldface numbers refer to paragraphs; lightface numbers refer to pages.

Boldface numbers refer to paragraphs; lightface numbers refer to pages.

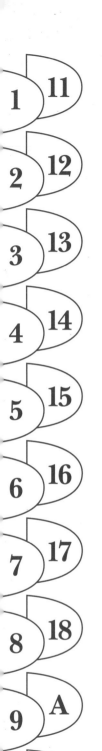

PART 1.   GRAMMAR, USAGE, AND STYLE

PART 2.   TECHNIQUES AND FORMATS

PART 3.   REFERENCES